MAURITIUS ILLUSTRATED

MAURITIUS ILLUSTRATED

HISTORICAL AND DESCRIPTIVE COMMERCIAL AND INDUSTRIAL FACTS, FIGURES, AND RESOURCES

COMPILED AND EDITED BY
ALLISTER MACMILLAN

GYAN

Published by

Gyan Publishing House
5, Ansari Road
Daryaganj, New Delhi-110002
Phone: 011-47034999, 9811692060
E-mail: books@gyanbooks.com

Distribution Network
gyanbooks.com
India, USA, Canada, UK, Australia, France

ISBN : 978-81-212-3767-3 (PB)
First Published, London, 1900

2nd Impression 2020

Printed at: Gyan Press, Delhi.

Mauritius Illustrated
Edited by: Allister Macmillan

MAURITIUS ILLUSTRATED

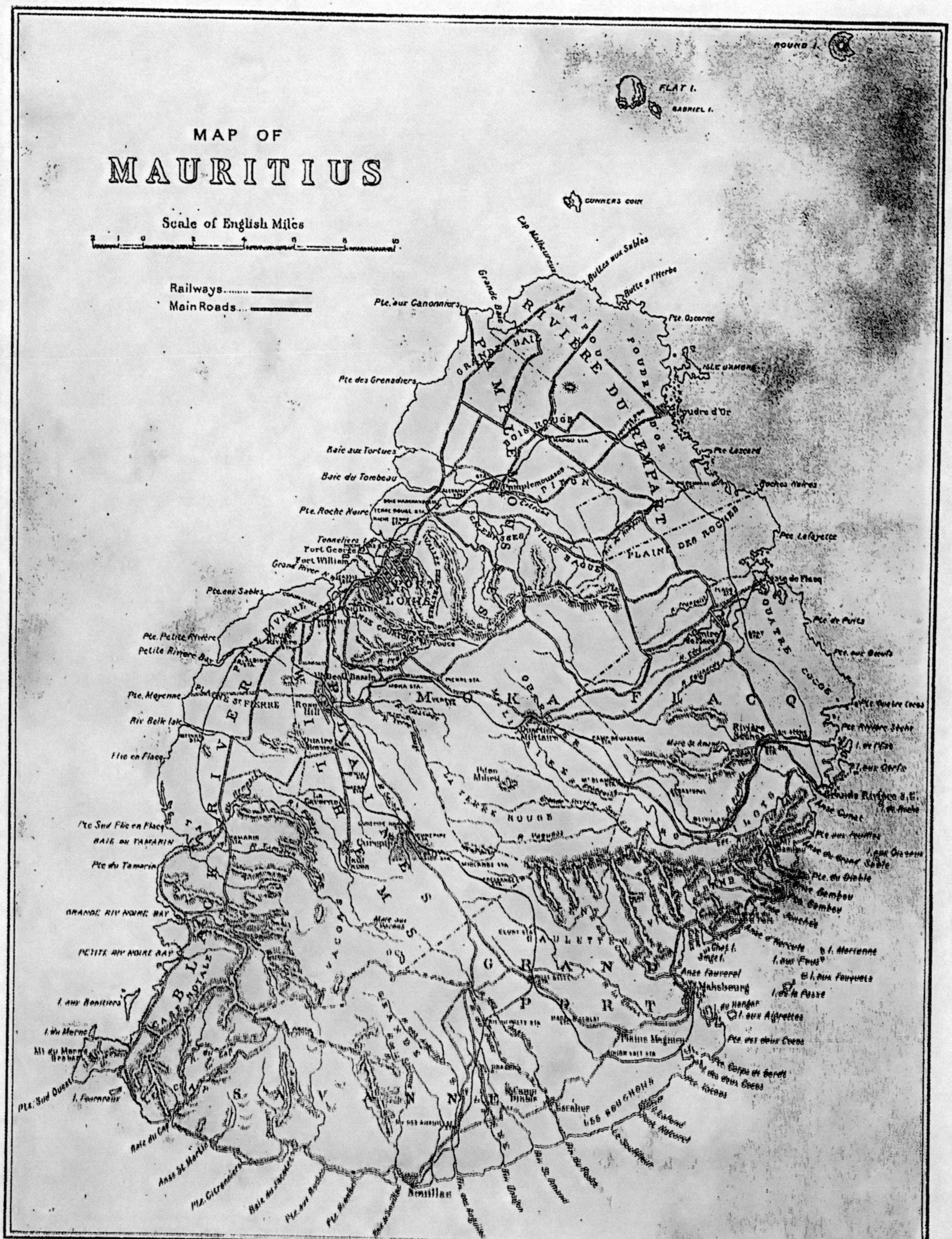
MAP OF
MAURITIUS
Scale of English Miles
Railways
Main Roads
ROUND I.
FLAT I.
GABRIEL I.
GUNNERS COIN
Cap Malheureux
Butte aux Sables
Butte à l'Herbe
Grande Baie
Pte. aux Canonniers
Pte. Oscorne
Pte des Grenadiers
PAMPLEMOUSSES
RIVIÈRE DU REMPART
POUDRE D'OR
Poudre d'Or
BOIS ROUGE
Pte Lascard
Baie aux Tortues
Baie du Tombeau
Pamplemousses
PITON
Roches Noires
Pte. Roche Noire
Pte Lafayette
PLAINE DES ROCHERS
Tonneliers I.
Fort George
Fort William
Pte. aux Sables
PORT LOUIS
Poste de Flacq
Pte de Puits
Pte. Petite Rivière
Petite Rivière Bay
Pte. aux Boeufs
Pte. Moyenne
MOKA
FLACQ
QUATRE COCOS
Riv. Belle Isle
Pte Quatre Cocos
Pte Rivière Sèche
Flic en Flacq
Piton Milieu
LA TERRE ROUGE
Pte. aux Cerfs
Grande Rivière S.E.
Anse Cunat
Pte Sud Flic en Flacq
BAIE DU TAMARIN
Pte du Tamarin
Pte. aux Feuilles
Pte. du Diable
GRANDE RIV NOIRE BAY
PETITE RIV NOIRE BAY
SAVANNE
GRAND PORT
Anse Jonchée
I. Marianne
I. aux Fouquets
I. de la Passe
Mahebourg
I. aux Aigrettes
Pte. des deux Cocos
Plaine Magnien
I. aux Benitiers
I. du Morne
Mt du Morne Brabant
Pte. Sud Ouest
I. Fourneaux
LES SOUCHONS
Baie du Cap
Anse St Martin
Pte. Citronniers
Baie du Jacotet
Pte aux Roches
Pte. Marmite
Souillac
Riv. des Anguilles
Riv. Dragon
Riv. St Amand
Riv. du Poste

MAURITIUS.

ILLUSTRATED.

TROIS MAMELLES AND RÉUNION SUGAR FACTORY.

HISTORICAL AND DESCRIPTIVE
COMMERCIAL AND INDUSTRIAL
FACTS, FIGURES, & RESOURCES.

Compiled and Edited by ALLISTER MACMILLAN.

PREFACE

IF you have never been to Mauritius, or have no interests acquainting you with the island, it is not unlikely that you cannot, without hesitation, locate its position on the map of the world; and, indeed, it may be that you cannot tell in which hemisphere it lies. Geography is not a subject in which the average person is very proficient, and Mauritius is synonymous with some vague far-distant place in the minds of many whose knowledge in other directions is both extensive and profound. Ignorance of the whereabouts of this flourishing little outpost of the British Empire is well exemplified by the letters received in the island addressed "Mauritius, West Indies," "Mauritius, South Africa," and in other curious and amusing ways that are as remarkable as the ignorance regarding its nationality.

About 300 miles east of the African coast, and separated by the Mozambique Channel, is Madagascar, with an area of 230,000 square miles, the third largest island in the world, and belonging to France. At a distance of 550 miles east of Madagascar is Réunion, or Bourbon, another French island, with an area of 750 square miles. North-east of Reunion, 115 miles away, is Mauritius, between latitude 19° 50′ and 20° 31′ south and longitude 57° 18′ and 57° 48′ east of Greenwich. From London *via* the Cape of Good Hope it is distant 9,000 miles, and *via* the Suez Canal 7,500 miles. From Bombay it is distant 2,500 miles; from Melbourne, 4,570 miles; from Colombo, 2,200 miles; and from Natal, 1,570 miles.

The total length of Mauritius, from Cap Malheureux in the north to Souillac in the south, is nearly thirty-nine miles, and its breadth, from Flic en Flacq on the west coast to Quatre Cocos on the east, is twenty-nine miles. The area of the island is about 716 square miles, thirty per cent. of which is under cane cultivation; and the area of the small islets around the coast is four square miles, making in all 720 square miles (or 460,800 acres—441,801 arpents). The circumference of the island is about 104 miles, and the coast line with indentations about 154 miles.

At a distance of about 350 miles to the north-east of Mauritius lies its dependency of Rodrigues, with an area of forty-two square miles. Réunion, Mauritius, and Rodrigues are called the Mascarene Islands; and the great Indian Ocean in which they lie stretches unbrokenly on the east to Australia, on the south to the Antarctic Ocean, and on the north to India and the southern seaboard of Asia.

Previous to the opening of the Suez Canal in 1869 Mauritius, lying on the route to India, was of much strategical importance to the British; and although the busy desert waterway, in which England is the chief shareholder, has lessened very considerably the activity of the island as a place of call for the repairing of ships and the replenishing of stores, it is still of great political value in view of the possible blocking of the Canal in time of war.

The harbour of Port Louis, the capital of the island, is one of the finest and safest in the world. It is about a mile long, almost as broad, and affords excellent anchorage. From it, in the stirring times of the French occupation, between 1715 and 1810, went forth vessels that wrought havoc and destruction on the English merchantmen; and the Ile de France (Isle of France), the name by which it was then known, was one of dread to the owners of ships and merchandise running under the English flag in the neighbouring seas.

The scenery of Mauritius is of remarkable variety and beauty, and upon the great plains covered with the sugar-cane, with the mountains, blue and magnificent, hiding the sapphire sea, one can easily imagine oneself upon some continent instead of on an island about the size of the county of Surrey. Probably in no other place in the world is there greater diversity of landscape and seascape—of mountain, forest, river and waterfall loveliness—within so small a compass as in Mauritius.

Before the advent of the steamer it was not unusual to see in the harbour of Port Louis as many as two hundred sailing ships, and the forest of masts was a picturesque demonstration of the great trade of the island. But what took many sailing ships to carry can now be accommodated in one steamer; and it would be interesting to know how many of the old sailing vessels would be equivalent to the numerous steamers necessary for the vastly increased trade of the island.

Till 1866 Mauritius was as healthy a place as could be found anywhere. In that year an epidemic of malaria, supposed to have been brought from India, carried off in Port Louis upwards of 18,000 people—more than one-third of its inhabitants—and led to the creation of the charming and bracing upland townships where the better classes of the community now live. Port Louis is, therefore, inhabited chiefly by coloured people, Mahommedans, and Hindoos; although during the cool months of July and August, when Curepipe, the principal centre of white population, is drenched with rain, many of the families who do not decamp to the beautiful seaside resorts of the island spend the season in Port Louis, which is then quite healthy, and regains some of its pristine social animation.

Although many of the fine old mansions, where the rich Mauritians of former days lived, have been demolished, there are still in Pope Hennessy Street, Rempart Street, and other residential thoroughfares of Port Louis, some splendid houses eloquent of the past. Streets once filled with homes of wealth, beauty, and gladness are now streets of silence and dreams, where worn-out dogs sleep in the shade, and fowls snuggle undisturbedly on the ground warm in the sunshine.

Different indeed, however, are the streets in the commercial section, choked, as many of them often are, with produce-laden carts drawn by great-horned oxen, and driven by scantily-clad Indians. Cross-legged on mats and cushions on the window ledges of their stores sit Mahommedan merchants, who close their establishments at mid-day on Fridays to worship Allah in the mosque, situated in the heart of the Asiatic quarter that pulsates with all the characteristics of the mysterious East:—Indian women, clanking with jewellery on their arms and ankles and toes, and in their noses and ears, the vivid hues of the clothing of both them and their men folk giving to the streets a kaleidoscope of colour; sombrely-clad Chinese, minus pig-tails now; itinerant vendors of cakes, drinks and concoctions "wonderfully and fearfully made"; beggars in all stages of decrepitude; fowls and pigeons fattening on the droppings of grain from the carts and around the doors of the warehouses; and everywhere in the city are ownerless dogs of all kinds, suffering from the most loathsome forms of canine disease. Previous to my arrival in Mauritius, the police had endeavoured to destroy these poor creatures; but during the five months I was in the island there appeared to be no diminution in the appalling number of horribly diseased specimens of canine misery that foraged starvingly about the markets and streets. Surely an intelligent and thorough campaign could be conducted that would rid the city of an evil to which the authorities have apparently become so much accustomed that they fail to realise its shame and hygienic danger.

Lying at the foot of the magnificent Moka range of mountains, and occupying an area of 2.1 square miles, Port Louis has an individuality entirely its own. It is a meeting-place of the old and the new. In it progress ever battles with antiquated conservatism born of centuries of isolation and misrepresentation. With a resident population of about 42,000 people of many different races and religions, it, like the entire island, is full of political strife. Orthodox tenets of political economy cannot be applied here as in other countries. Nature has set up lines of demarcation that cannot be overstepped without disaster and chaos. In this remote little sea-girt world are conditions and problems that cannot be understood or solved except by long residence in it, and careful study and experience of the diversity of its interests and the peculiarity of its circumstances.

As has been said, the better classes live in the upland towns and villages; consequently, the bustle and animation of Port Louis during the day is in striking contrast to its desertion and stillness at night. From their handsome homes, surrounded by beautiful gardens, the business men come in large numbers daily to the hot, busy city. The first trains are chiefly filled with artisans, clerks, shop assistants, and the general rank and file. By the later trains arrive the heads of Government departments and commercial concerns, brokers, and professional men. Every morning they wait at their respective railway stations, and long years of habit have so accustomed some of them to their own particular seats in their own particular carriages, that the worthy and estimable gentlemen would feel out of place by any change in their daily routine of travel. The journey from Curepipe, 1,800 feet above the level of the sea, to Port Louis, a distance of sixteen miles and occupying about an hour, is a descent from the temperate to the tropic zone; and Vacoas, Phœnix, Quatre Bornes, Rose Hill and Beau Bassin, the intervening centres of population along the railway, exemplify the marvellous varieties of climate in the island.

The Central Station, Port Louis, as each incoming train is emptied of its throng of passengers, never fails to impress the stranger; and for some time the streets leading to the centre of the city are black with men on their way to their daily avocations. The adjective black is justified by the fact that most of the French Mauritians attire themselves in dark clothing; and now and again a silk hat and frock coat denote that professional dignity, in the opinion of their wearers, must not be sacrificed, even although the thermometer registers 90° Fahr. in the shade. It must, however, be said that many change, when they reach their business places, into lighter garments, and when about to depart for home wisely resume their heavier apparel, because of the great climatic difference between Port Louis and the upland districts, especially Curepipe.

Ladies of the upper classes are not often seen in Port Louis. Many of them do not visit the capital from one year's end to the other; so that it is essentially a city of men, a bustling emporium of trade, dominated by sugar and its potentialities. In the great warehouses of the dock companies are stored many thousand tons of the island's sweet produce, upon which the entire life of the community depends. The stock of sugar in these warehouses is probably greater than any collection of it elsewhere in the world; and ever about them are innumerable swarms of wasps and bees seeking the delectable crystals.

Of all the many communities of which I have had intimate experience during fifteen years' travel throughout the world, that of Mauritius is the one I will ever remember with the greatest pleasure and appreciation. With the exception of about 600 natives of the United Kingdom and the military, the white inhabitants of Mauritius, numbering about 10,000 out of a population of nearly 400,000, are of French blood. Well-bred and well-educated, of charming manners, unfailing courtesy, and generous hospitality, the French Mauritians manifest characteristics that are a blending of the best qualities of both the French and the English. They are a people by themselves, and their origin and their environment in their lovely little country, with its teeming coloured population, have given them a mentality reminiscent of the times when birth and blood were of more significance than now. Descendants, in many cases, of some of the noblest and proudest families that upheld the glory of old France, it is not surprising that this spirited, punctilious people, so tenacious of custom and precedent, so cognizant of honour and rights, individual and collective, and of an exclusiveness engendered by difference of language and religion, should not have fused very readily with the race that had been for centuries the bitterest foe of France—a race that has not always had in the government of the island the worthiest and the wisest of representatives. But, happily, the racial prejudices and misunderstandings have disappeared, and from the grave of the ancient antipathy has arisen patriotism and loyalty to England equal to any within her great dominions.

No people are more devoted to their homes than the Mauritians, and, probably, nowhere in the world are families so large and so united as in this fertile island, where home life is exemplified in its most pleasant and most commendable aspects. No wonder, therefore, that the great majority of the young Mauritians, who win distinction in the schools and colleges of England and France, return to their native country to follow their respective professions, and that there are in all departments of activity in Mauritius men of remarkable ability, which finds, unfortunately, too often but little scope for its manifestation in so small a place.

Writing of the Mauritians in the *Empire Review* of May, 1901, Sir Hubert E. H. Jerningham, K.C.M.G., Governor of the island from 1893 to 1896, said :—

"The better classes spoke French admirably, and constituted a feature of that delightful land. Remnants for a great part of the exodus from France in the reigns of Louis XIV., Louis XV., and Louis XVI., when the luxury of the Court left little to younger sons of families to live upon unless they emigrated to French colonies, they had not lost their sense of noble bearing, high-born generosity of feeling, and well-bred courtesy and kindness, though they had dropped the empty titles which their ancestors had borne ; nor is there, perhaps, except in some parts of Canada, and, may be, in New Orleans, a land where there is, outside of Paris, London, Berlin, Vienna, and Rome, a more aristocratic small circle in its highest sense than in Mauritius."

Sir George H. Bowen, G.C.M.G., Governor of the island in 1879-1880, in his volume *Thirty Years of Colonial Government*, says :—

"The society in Mauritius is more lively than in many other colonies on account of the strong admixture in it of French grace, ease, and vivacity. The aristocracy of the island consists of the French planters, many of whom are descended from Royalist families of the *noblesse* that emigrated during the first French Revolution, and these retain much of the courtly manners of the ancient *régime*."

Mr. E. F. Knight, in his work *In a Tropical Land*, adds another testimony to the high character of the Mauritians, as follows :—

"It is true that the French society here and the small English society, which is chiefly official and military, mix little. The difference of tongue and religion—the French community being strictly Roman Catholic—with different ways of living, too, and the fact that English and French so rarely understand each other in any country where they come in contact, account for this mutual exclusiveness. It is a pity that this is the case, for the Mauritians of that upper class compose as charming and highly cultured a society as will be found in any part of the Empire. In this island the Englishman, unless he conducts himself badly, will meet with nothing but extreme courtesy from people of every class—a courtesy that is rather of the old-world France than of the modern, and a genuine kindliness. Those Englishmen who, like myself, have lived with French Mauritians, enjoyed their graceful hospitality, and gathered from their sentiments as regards England and the English, know that it would be well for the Empire were every community within its limits as loyal as this one."

It is difficult for me to adequately express here my high appreciation of the great kindness I received from all classes of the people in Mauritius. My sojourn in the island was happy indeed, and I much regretted that the work in connection with this volume rendered it impossible for me to avail myself of all the many invitations to indoor and out-door enjoyments that were showered upon me.

To His Excellency Major Sir John Robert Chancellor, R.E., C.M.G., D.S.O., the present able and popular Governor, and to Mrs. Chancellor, who, as President of the Ladies' Fine Needlework Association and in other directions, is demonstrating her solicitude for the welfare of the people, I tender my heartiest thanks for their kind hospitality and the helpful interest which they evinced in my labours.

I also wish to record here my thanks to the gentlemen who assisted me so willingly and so ably, and in whose literary contributions lie the chief merit of this volume. They represent the best available talent in the island for the various subjects dealt with, and their names are a guarantee of their capacity and accuracy of knowledge in the directions indicated.

I am specially indebted to Mr. A. Walter, F.R.A.S., Director of the Royal Alfred Observatory, not only for his masterly writings in the following pages, but also for the kind permission he granted me to cull from his excellent annual publication, *The Mauritius Almanac*, statistics and other information that enhance considerably the completeness and utility of *Mauritius Illustrated*.

My thanks are likewise due to the various photographers who rendered me great assistance. Having had to operate in the rainy season, many of the pictures were only secured at no small expenditure of time and trouble. Most of the portraits are from photos taken specially by Mr. J. A. Gentil in his studio at Port Louis. The greater number of the views of the island are from photos, also taken specially, by Mr. G. Réhaut, of Port Louis, and from those supplied by Mr. A. Rambert and others. Nearly all the illustrations of the sugar factories, business places, and private residences are reproductions of Mr. Réhaut's work. Photos and particulars of a few of the local prominent men have been unobtainable.

Finally, whatever may be the merits or demerits of this book, it is the first of the kind ever published concerning the island, and is a conscientious effort to present, in as interesting and useful a form as possible, all that relates to the colony and its people. That it may be of benefit to Mauritius is the earnest hope of

ALLISTER MACMILLAN.

The Royal Botanic Gardens Pamplemousses.

Musings By *Allister Macmillan.*

GARDENS of abiding shadows, haunted by the souls of things
All among the leafy branches there are eerie whisperings
Of the present resurrected from the fateful long-ago,
Only dimly recollected by the measure of its woe.

Indefinable responses to the pregnant mystery,
Evidencing past existence, in the mists of memory,
When alternate good and evil, proving ever loss or gain,
By eternal laws were fashioned in the crucibles of pain.

Odours of departed summers, echoes of the sounds that thrilled.
When there were no disillusions and the wells of life were filled;
When the days were full of gladness for the harvest that would be—
Ah! the unexpected harvests that are reaped in misery!

Hopes for ever dissipated, agony too great for tears;
Sacrifices unavailing through the long and weary years;
Phantoms of oespair unending, visions of the might-have-been
Conjured up amongst the shadows in the magical demesne.

Flashing insects scintillating—gleams of blue and green and gold
Flowers of every kind and colour shedding perfumes manifold;
Sighing of caressing zephyrs, mystic voices of the wood,
And the murmur of the streamlet meandering in the solitude.

Sobbing, past decaying herbage underneath entangled trees,
For neglected time and talents and lost opportunities;
Not commission, but omission, shall within the balance weigh—
So the streamlet, sadly sobbing, in the silence seems to say.

Every grove has greater dramas than the shallow mind can know
There are secrets of the ages where the living juices go;
Unexpected revelations of Divinity await
That will demonstrate the meaning of the tragedies of fate.

Every blossom tells a story, every thorn has meaning too;
That which was in former ages lives in other forms anew;
Many are the threads and colours of the ultimate design
Forming in the fabric growing in the weaving loom of time.

There is not a single substance dead and rotten in the sod
That has not a wondrous service in the purposes of God;
There is not the slightest effort, whatsoever it may be,
That is not a certain portend of evolving destiny.

Farther than the mind can travel, closer than the eye can see,
There are countless worlds of wonder, great and small infinitely
And the vivifying sunbeams, where the tiny atoms dance,
Are the essences of being and the keys of circumstance.

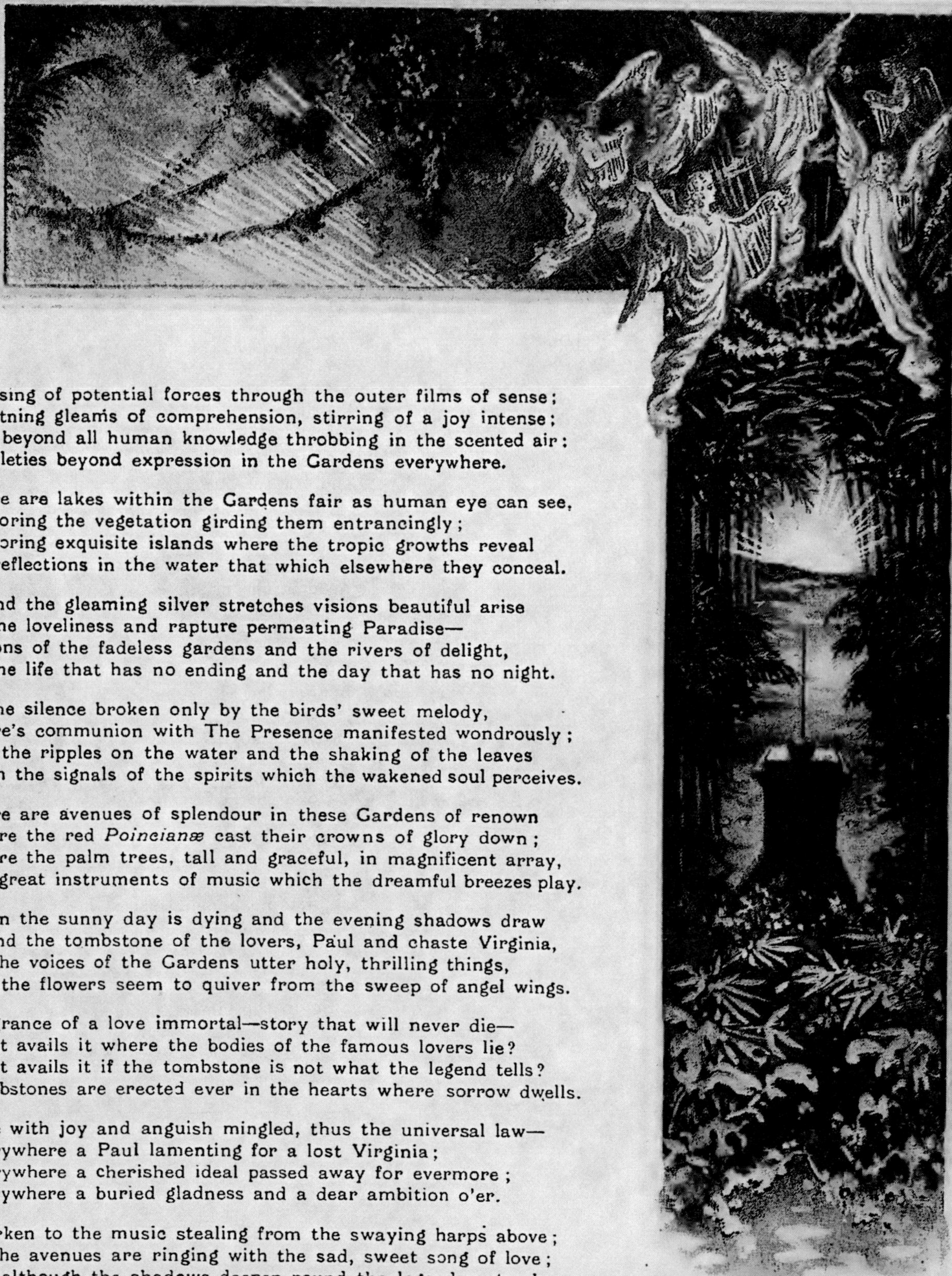

Pressing of potential forces through the outer films of sense;
Lightning gleams of comprehension, stirring of a joy intense;
Life beyond all human knowledge throbbing in the scented air:
Subtleties beyond expression in the Gardens everywhere.

There are lakes within the Gardens fair as human eye can see,
Mirroring the vegetation girding them entrancingly;
Mirroring exquisite islands where the tropic growths reveal
By reflections in the water that which elsewhere they conceal.

Round the gleaming silver stretches visions beautiful arise
Of the loveliness and rapture permeating Paradise—
Visions of the fadeless gardens and the rivers of delight,
Of the life that has no ending and the day that has no night.

In the silence broken only by the birds' sweet melody,
There's communion with The Presence manifested wondrously;
And the ripples on the water and the shaking of the leaves
Seem the signals of the spirits which the wakened soul perceives.

There are avenues of splendour in these Gardens of renown
Where the red *Poincianæ* cast their crowns of glory down;
Where the palm trees, tall and graceful, in magnificent array,
Are great instruments of music which the dreamful breezes play.

When the sunny day is dying and the evening shadows draw
Round the tombstone of the lovers, Paul and chaste Virginia,
All the voices of the Gardens utter holy, thrilling things,
And the flowers seem to quiver from the sweep of angel wings.

Fragrance of a love immortal—story that will never die—
What avails it where the bodies of the famous lovers lie?
What avails it if the tombstone is not what the legend tells?
Tombstones are erected ever in the hearts where sorrow dwells.

Love with joy and anguish mingled, thus the universal law—
Everywhere a Paul lamenting for a lost Virginia;
Everywhere a cherished ideal passed away for evermore;
Everywhere a buried gladness and a dear ambition o'er.

Hearken to the music stealing from the swaying harps above;
All the avenues are ringing with the sad, sweet song of love;
And although the shadows deepen round the legendary tomb,
Stands it in its whiteness guiding like a beacon in the gloom.

Farewell, Gardens of Enchantment! the long trail is calling me—
Calling through the night of sadness to the promised ecstasy
Of the bright, eternal morning reigning in the realm I saw
Visioned by the lakes of silence, dreaming of Virginia.

WRECK OF THE "ST. GERAN" AND DEATH OF VIRGINIA.
(From an old engraving in the Museum, Port Louis.)

MAURITIUS ILLUSTRATED

Historical and Descriptive, Commercial and Industrial, Facts, Figures, and Resources.

HISTORY.

By ALBERT PITOT,

Advocate, Edinburgh ; Licencie en Droit, Paris. Author of "T'Eylandt Mauritius Esquisses Historiques, 1598-1710."

MAURITIUS forms, with the neighbouring Islands of Réunion (or Bourbon) and Rodrigues, the Mascarene Archipelago, lying east of Madagascar, in the Indian Ocean. Long before Europeans visited this group it was certainly known to Arabian navigators, as early charts of the sixteenth century, drawn up from those found on board Moorish vessels captured by the Portuguese in the Indian seas, represent these islands under various Arabian appellations, the most frequent being *Dina Moraze*, or *Noraze*, *Dina Margabin*, and *Dina Arobi*.

According to modern scholars, *dina* is supposed to be the corruption of the Sanscrit *dvipâ*, an island; *Moraze*, an incorrect transcription of *Moluce*, turtle, applying to Rodrigues; *Margabin* would signify "western" and imply Réunion; *Arobi*, a sort of venomous fish, and may indicate Mauritius. It is strange enough that, about a century later, in 1601, when a Dutch vessel happened to lie at anchor near Morne Brabant, the south-western extremity of this island, the men who partook of a certain fish, which they had caught in abundance, showed undoubted signs of poisoning.

Very little is known of the discovery of the Mascarene Archipelago by a European nation. It is taken for granted, however, that it was encountered by the Portuguese in the first years of the sixteenth century, although the date of that event and the name of the navigator are impossible to ascertain with accuracy. The only documents available are very old and imperfect maps, often representing more islands than actually exist. The reason for this abnormal excess of indications is that geographers, being in those days unable to control whatever information they came across, thought it simpler to preserve old names, whilst marking down the more recent as they came to hand; so that, in some of the old charts, the Mascarene group may be seen noted twice, even thrice, and in very different situations.

The custom which generally held good with Portuguese navigators was to consult the almanac and name any new land they met on their voyage, first after the saint inscribed at that date, next after their flagship, and lastly after their commander. One of the islands is given on the early maps as Sa. Apollonia; as that saint was honoured on the 9th February, the natural inference is that Mauritius was discovered on the 9th February, and the others a few days later. This being admitted, there only remained to make sure of the year when a Portuguese squadron—for Portuguese ships always travelled in company—could have passed in this neighbourhood in the first fortnight of February. Among several theories, the following has met with approval:—In November, 1506, fourteen Portuguese vessels, commanded by Tristan Da Cunha and Alfonso Albuquerque, anchored at Mozambique. With the object of visiting the shores of Madagascar, which had been recently discovered, Da Cunha abandoned his flagship and embarked on a small craft better suited for a coasting cruise. Albuquerque may have accompanied him, leaving his ship, the *Cirne*, to the care of his lieutenant, Diego Fernandez Pereira. During the absence of his chief, why should not this officer, apprised by the Arabian maps of the existence of adjoining islands, have attempted to ascertain the fact? Reaching Réunion on the 9th February he may have called it Sa. Apollonia; meeting Mauritius next, he may have named it Cirne; and, finally, designated Rodrigues as Diego Fernandez, which, abbreviated as *Dgo Frz*, was probably rendered afterwards as *Domigo Friz*.

SEA VIEW FROM BEL AIR ESTATE, SAVANNE.

This inference is, however, open to several criticisms. To begin with, it is contrary to the tradition that Pedro Mascarenhas was the discoverer of Mauritius and called it *Cirne*, changed afterwards into *Cerne* without any good reason. Yet tradition must not be followed too blindly. One thing is certain: Mascarenhas, leaving Lisbon in 1511, appeared for the first time in the Indian Ocean in 1512. But then it is doubtful whether he could have got in the vicinity of Mauritius at the commencement of February. On the other hand, it is fairly certain that he did land there in 1528 on his homeward voyage, although this group was already discovered at that date. Again, those maps, imperfect though they be, seem to designate Mauritius rather than Réunion under the name of Sa. Apollonia. Lastly, the name *Cirne* appears thereon much later—in fact, not before 1595.

As for Cirne, attempts have been made to identify it with the Cerne known to the ancients; but it is now admitted beyond doubt that the true Cerne is the island of Arguin, in the Gulf of Guinea, on the west coast of Africa. Some writers have suggested that this might have been the name of a Portuguese family, although they are at a loss to say what connection those Cirnes might have had with Mauritius.

Others claim that the Portuguese, finding on that island huge birds bearing some resemblance to swans, called it the Isle of Swans (Do Cirne). This would be a clever theory if the birds alluded to were not the ugly and clumsy Dodos, which the Portuguese could not possibly have mistaken for swans, the most graceful of all birds. In this respect the fault lies entirely with the translators of Dutch records of the end of that century. Those who wrote them, however, made no such error. They compared Dodos to swans for their size: "as large as swans," "larger than swans," were their actual words.

The name of the ship *Cirne* would prove a more acceptable explanation. This was the name of Albuquerque's flagship in 1507. Nevertheless, how is it that this denomination does not appear on maps till some seventy years posterior to that of Sa. Apollonia? Be it what it may, according to those very maps Mauritius was then called either *Sa. Apollonia* or *Cirne;* Bourbon *Mascarenhas;* and Rodrigues *Domigo Friz* or *Diego Rodrigues.*

The Portuguese never settled in Mauritius; they were content at different times to let loose here a number of pigs, goats, deer and monkeys, the latter, according to Abbé de La Caille, being regarded by them as a great delicacy. Their visits were so irregular that towards the close of the same century they seem to have forgotten the existence of the island altogether.

SEA VIEW FROM BEL AIR ESTATE, SAVANNE.

THE DUTCH PERIOD.

In August, 1598, a squadron of eight Dutch ships, under Admirals Van Neck and Van Warwyk, on their way to the East Indies, was dispersed by a storm shortly after having passed the Cape of Good Hope. Van Warwyk held an eastward course with five vessels and fell in with the Island Do Cierne (*sic*) in the afternoon of the 17th September. On the next day he sent boats in several directions in search of a landing place, which he found on the south-eastern coast, and there he anchored on the morning of the 19th.

After having made sure that the island was uninhabited, he took possession of it in the name of the States and called it Mauritius, after the Statholder Maurice of Nassau. The harbour he was in received the name of Port Warwyk. A board was nailed to the trunk of a lofty tree, close to the beach, bearing the arms of Holland, Zeeland, and Amsterdam. A parcel of land was cleared and planted with orange and lime trees, peas, beans, and other vegetables, and some domestic fowls were set at liberty. The squadron remained there for about a fortnight, and then proceeded to Batavia.

The favourable report Van Warwyk gave of the abundance of refreshment to be obtained in Mauritius and the excellence of its climate, tempted other travellers to repair there. In 1601 and 1602 the island was visited by Harmansen, in 1606 by Matelief, and in 1607 by Van der Hagen, some landing at the south-eastern port, some at the north-western, but never was there the slightest attempt made by them at colonisation.

In 1610 Pieter Both, of Amersfoort, proceeding to his governor-generalship at Batavia, took refuge at Mauritius to get his vessel overhauled after it had been badly damaged by rough weather. Five years later, his time of office being over, he desired to visit Mauritius again on his way home; but in the month of February he was caught by a terrific storm, and perished on the reefs of Tombeau Bay. Three men only escaped destruction and were picked up later by a stray ship. After this disaster it would appear that the Dutch carefully avoided the shores which they had formerly been glad to frequent, and their records make no mention of Mauritius for a long time. But the island was visited in 1628 by an Englishman, Sir Thomas Herbert, who has left a most grandiloquent and exaggerated description of its beauties. After him Frenchmen from Dieppe took to landing there for cargoes of ebony, which was then considered of great value.

Ambergris was occasionally met with on the sands, and a small fragment of it was then worth a fortune. In order to put a stop to the depredations of foreigners, the Dutch East India Company determined upon occupying Mauritius. As they had forestalled so many monopolies it was not surprising that they started that of ebony as well.

Cornelius Simonsz Gooyer (1638-39).

Cornelius Simonsz Gooyer accordingly arrived on the 7th May with a detachment of twenty-four men, who took up quarters at Port South-East and built a fort there. Their main occupation consisted in preparing shipments of ebony, which now and then a ship would take to Batavia. Gooyer did not remain long in office; he was replaced the next year by Adriaan Van der Stel, who disposed of eighty-six men, a number which in no case was to be exceeded, although three-fourths of them were invalids from the Sunda Islands, whom the Governor-General sent to recuperate their health in the then bracing climate of Mauritius. With such an impotent set of men the ebony business could not be very profitable. The authorities at Batavia, therefore, deemed it less expensive to people the island with convicts, whose daily diet consisted of one biscuit, half a farthing's worth of salt fish per man, and as much water as they could drink.

Adriaan Van der Stel (1639-45).

Jacob Van der Meersch (1645-48).

In 1645 Van der Stel was recalled, and was succeeded by Jacob Van der Meersch. The French and English had now settled in Madagascar, the former at Fort Dauphin and Ste. Luce, the latter at the Bay of St. Augustine. Van der Meersch was directed to keep his eyes on their doings and to have a post of soldiers at the Bay of Antongil, where he could also procure slaves, most of whom were shipped to the more flourishing Dutch colonies. Those three settlements having been ruined, the Dutch were recalled from Madagascar, and Van der Meersch tendered his resignation.

Reynier Por (1648-53).

Reynier Por took his place with a garrison reduced to fifty men. Soon after, ebony proved so abundant on the home market that the prices went down. Por was, therefore, commanded to reduce its export considerably, and, for the occupation of his men, to take to planting sugar-canes, which the rats ate up as soon as they were ripe. After four years' residence, Por asked to be recalled. As was customary, he had recommended his second, Joost Van der Woutbeek; but the Batavia Government sent instead Maximiliaan de Jongh, although the commander was allowed to make his choice between the two candidates. He died, however, before having done so.

De Jongh and Van der Woutbeek (1653).

De Jongh and Van der Woutbeek thought it simpler to share the authority between them, which continued for a few months till, at Batavia, this system was deemed contrary to the rules of the Company, and Woutbeek was asked to resign.

Maximiliaan de Jongh (1653-54).

With the view of preserving their own situation, the commanders of Mauritius were naturally prone to extol the merits of the colony, whilst from Batavia a very different account was given by officials worried by the extra work entailed by the wants of a colony which did not produce a single article of consumption. The Court of Directors at Amsterdam, who had carefully abstained from giving an opinion, were now feeling more disposed to listen to the Batavia version, more especially because in April, 1652, the Dutch had taken possession of the Cape of Good Hope, the situation of which at the extremity of the African Continent, made it a shipping resort far superior to Mauritius. For the present they simply made the smaller colony a dependency of the larger; the garrison was reduced to twenty men, and the commander's salary retrenched in proportion. De Jongh declined remaining in office and was replaced by Abraham Evertsz.

Abraham Evertsz (1656-58).

The next year the Directors went a step further and agreed upon abandoning Mauritius altogether, unless good reasons should be forthcoming for the preservation of the settlement. As there were apparently no such good reasons at Batavia, the Governor-General lost no time in sending a vessel to remove the inhabitants. The abandonment took place on the 16th July, 1658. Everything was destroyed by fire, and His Excellency, reporting thereon, felt confident that for twenty years to come it would be impossible to find in Mauritius a single ebony tree worth cutting down, so that foreigners would probably be loth to settle there.

Scarcely a year had elapsed, however, when the Directors changed their minds again; no ebony was to be procured at the Cape, whilst, on the other hand, agriculture, pursued there under practical conditions, met with fair success. They enquired accordingly whether the same system could not be carried out in Mauritius. From Batavia the matter was referred to the Cape authorities, who reported thereon; after having taken cognizance of the documents, the Batavia officials addressed them to Amsterdam, and the conclusion oscillated between yea and nay. On the 24th August, 1663, orders came at last to the Cape for the re-occupation of Mauritius, but nearly a year elapsed again before this was effected.

Jacobus Nieuwland (1664).

Jacobus Nieuwland landed at Port South-East with twelve men, who, instead of taking to their work, consumed whatever eatables and drinkables were in the stores, and then retired to the woods, leaving the Governor, who was very ill, to look after himself, so that he soon died. A few days later his corpse was discovered by the captain of a ship newly arrived, and from the dead Governor's diary information was learned of what had occurred. The deserters were brought back to the Cape and seven of them were sentenced to various punishments.

Dirk Jansz Smient (1664-69).

Dirk Jansz Smient was then despatched to the island with thirty-two men, in order to resume the ebony trade. The forests in the northern and western districts had been cleared to a great extent; but Smient, discovering a plain not far from the eastern coast, where ebony grew in plenty, called it Noortwyk Vlaakte (Northerly Plains, now Flacq), and opened a road thence to a small haven, the present Trou d'Eau Douce, where the ebony was shipped in barges coastwise to the Fort.

George Frederik Wreeden (1669-72).

Everything was getting on fairly enough, but, owing to the false accusations of the spies employed by the Company, Smient was recalled and replaced by George Frederik Wreeden, an inveterate drunkard and a disreputable character, who personally derived considerable profit from amber smuggling, and, to avoid being suspected, made the Cape authorities believe that ambergris was nothing but the sap secreted by the submarine roots of a particular tree which grew in abundance in the island. He accordingly alleged that large forests of this could be planted and that the Company would amass untold wealth thereby. While sailing round the island in a large pinnace, Wreeden, being more under the influence of liquor than usual, was drowned with five of his companions.

Swen Felleson (1672).

He should have been replaced by his secretary, Wabrandt, but the colonists assembled and unanimously elected the head cooper, Swen Felleson, a good man, no doubt, but certainly unfit for the position. If the men of his class consented to obey his commands, those of higher rank refused to do so.

Philip Col (1672-73).

A few weeks later a sloop cast anchor before the Fort. It had been detached from a squadron commanded by Hubert Hugo, recently appointed to the government of Mauritius by the Cape authorities. Hugo, who was still ignorant of Wreeden's death, had been commissioned to fetch a batch of slaves at Mozambique first, and as the sloop could not keep pace with the rest, she was sent direct to Mauritius. On board was an officer named Col, with instructions to enquire into the state of affairs and take the supreme command in case of need. Under the prevailing circumstances Col did not hesitate to do so, and exerted himself to restore order. He did it in a strange way, at all events. With him had come several families of colonists who had intended to start farming. They did not seem at all anxious to begin work, and, strange to say, instead of remonstrating, Col induced them to draw up a petition, which he would recommend to the Governor of the Cape, explaining how farming could not succeed in Mauritius because the soil was too rocky, the climate too hot, the crops constantly devoured by caterpillars, locusts, and rats. Cattle breeding was alleged to be useless, as nothing was easier than to procure game for consumption, and wild animals would multiply more readily than the tame. Col assembled a Council of his own officials and the officers of the sloop, at which the petition was approved, and the *would not be* farmers sent back.

Hubert Hugo (1673-77).

Hubert Hugo had returned to the Cape by this time, and was not a little surprised at his lieutenant's behaviour. He lectured those who had returned, and persuaded them to follow him to Mauritius, where he arrived on the 13th February. It would have been better if he had dispensed with those people altogether. Wholly disinclined for work, they, however, took to fishing, shooting, and turtle-hunting with such assiduity that they would have soon exhausted the entire resources of the island in these directions. Hugo was a man of fairly sound judgment, but vain and fond of boasting of his capacities. What he could really have accomplished is no easy matter to guess; yet it is doubtful whether he could have performed the grand things he had in his mind. At all events, he had no chance of showing off his abilities, as he was never supported in the least by the Cape Government. His efforts to redress the laziness of his people created, of course, much discontent. Considering the sort of men employed secretly by the Company to spy upon him, continual complaints were made about him. Disgusted with this state of things, he gladly hailed his transfer, and Isaac Lamotius was given charge of the settlement.

Isaac Lamotius (1677-92).

This man was of education and a good draughtsman, who drew up a fair map of the island, the first which gave an idea of its configuration. He was also versed in botany, zoology, and quack medicine. He followed the directions he had received to be cautious and remain on friendly terms with his subordinates, but erred in hobnobbing too much with people far below his standing, which was enough to ruin his authority. When he realised this he adopted an opposite course, and soon became harsh, despotic, unjust, and overbearing. He committed such excesses that the Governor of the Cape sent a Commissioner, Roelof Deodati, to enquire into his misdeeds. Lamotius, convicted of concussion and malversation, was sent to Batavia, and there sentenced to six years' penal servitude.

Roelof Deodati (1692-1703).

Roelof Deodati, who then took command of the island, was an Italian by birth, clever, shrewd, but crafty, bragging and inconstant. His government was, perhaps, the most sensational of this Dutch period. He was notorious for the cruel treatment he inflicted upon Leguat and his companions, the unwilling Rodrigues colonists, who had sailed from there in a small craft of their own making, and reached Mauritius on the 29th May, 1693. For nearly three years Deodati kept them in close confinement at Isle Marianne, a barren rock opposite Grand Port, so as to prevent them from complaining at Batavia of his appropriation of a piece of amber, which they had picked up at Rodrigues without being aware of its intrinsic value.

In 1695 Mauritius was laid waste by a most terrific hurricane. A few months later the Fort was burnt to ashes by a gang of maroon slaves, who were arrested, sentenced to death, and executed on the spot with such barbarity that Deodati was ordered to send offenders to the Cape in future, instead of taking the law into his own hands.

The Peace of Ryswyck having brought about the suppression of the Letters of Marque granted to buccaneers by the Governors of the English West Indies, those desperate men transferred the scene of their depredations to the Indian Ocean, and settled in the Isle of St. Mary, off Madagascar, at the entrance to the Bay of Antongil, where they soon became the terror of the neighbourhood. In 1697 Mauritius received the first visit of one of those pirates, who showed himself most arrogant in speech, although he committed no offence. In January, 1702, another brig, commanded by Captain Bowen, was wrecked at Rock Island, at the mouth of Grand River, S.E. The crew, 170 in number, reached the mainland on a raft, asked for refreshments, which they liberally paid for, and offered to purchase a sloop on which they might go away. This was granted, as Deodati did not feel in a position to resist, and they departed two months later.

RIVER SECHE, VACOAS.

But this was not all; the colonists still suffered occasionally from the attacks of maroon slaves. A plague destroyed their chief articles of consumption—wild oxen and deer, which lay dead in heaps in the woods. In 1702 another storm was attended by a tremendous inundation, which washed off to sea a number of animals, both wild and tame. These repeated calamities led Deodati to relinquish his government. On the 27th September, 1703, he was allowed to retire, and the administration passed to his assistant, Abraham Momber Van de Velde, a hard-working man, thoroughly honest and disinterested, but not particularly clever.

Abraham Momber Van de Velde (1703-10).

In 1704 Captain Bowen made another appearance in a new ship, anchoring near Ile aux Tonneliers, in front of the north-western harbour, where he stayed two months and behaved sensibly enough. During the next year the island experienced another cyclone and another epizooty. In 1706 a terrible drought changed the rivers into pools of stagnant water, the dead fish in which created a fearful stench. Scarcely any water was left for drinking purposes; pastures were parched, cows had no longer any milk for their calves, and oxen were turned into skeletons. The commander had to disperse his men afar, in small groups, in search of their daily food; maroon slaves became more and more audacious, and set fire to the buildings at Noortwyk.

Since the hurricane in 1695, and the first appearance of pirates, the Court of Directors had lost all confidence in the prospects of Mauritius. In July, 1706, they sent instructions to the Cape and Batavia for the removal of the whole population. It was not, however, till the 23rd September, 1707, that a vessel came to bring back to the Cape those who chose to settle there. The inhabitants were so disheartened that they felt glad to get away, but most of them preferred proceeding to Batavia, so that the ship took only 54 passengers. On the eve of their departure, Van de Velde thought fit to commemorate this first exodus by a banquet, at which he made a fine speech, punctuated by several rounds of cannon. The wadding set fire, by mishap, to the thatched roofs of the buildings, and the whole fort was soon ablaze. Van de Velde was severely blamed for his negligence; he had no business, it was said, to make such a waste of the Company's ammunition.

He had been instructed, before he left, to gather all the dogs in the island and let them loose to devour the game, so that other nations might be deterred from settling there. Luckily enough a sort of plague set in and annihilated the dogs before they accomplished much mischief.

Thirteen months after, two ships arrived—one bound for Batavia and the other for the Cape. There still remained 320 people in the island, and the captain of the former vessel, having no provisions for so many passengers, refused to accommodate more than 78. Van de Velde got together what he could find of sweet potatoes and other eatables, but did not succeed in providing for more than 114 persons; the Cape ship took 35 more. For the remaining 93 a ship was requested as soon as possible, since scarcely any food was left in the whole island, but another year elapsed before she could be got ready.

Meanwhile further difficulties had arisen. France was then at war with Holland; two French vessels came to the island, and, in spite of protestations, left there 81 Dutch prisoners, thus nearly doubling the number of people to be transported. Fortunately enough, the ship which anchored at Port North-West ten days later was of sufficient capacity and fairly well victualled. As the stormy season had set in, the captain objected to proceeding to Port South-East, and, accordingly, the inhabitants had to take to small crafts round the coast in order to get on board. On the 25th January, 1710, a hurricane damaged the vessel at Port North-West, and she sank with all the available boats, compelling the people to travel on foot through thickly-wooded forests where no roads existed, some of them getting drowned while crossing swollen streams.

At last, on the 13th February, the colonists having embarked on the other vessel, proceeded on their voyage. The whole establishment had been destroyed as usual, houses burnt down, plantations laid waste; but eight persons were left behind—two maroon slaves, four deserters from the ship, and two Malays, who declared themselves too ill to attempt the voyage.

The travellers arrived at Batavia on the 4th May, and Van de Velde died soon after. On taking possession of his books, the Government of Batavia was not a little perturbed to see that the Cape authorities had forfeited his salary as a compensation for 5,406 florins—the amount of the estimated loss sustained by the Company by the fire at the Fort. As Momber had been in receipt of 40 florins a month he would have needed more than eleven years to liquidate the debt!

THE FRENCH OCCUPATION.

THE EAST INDIA COMPANY.

Mauritius remained uninhabited for five years and was frequented only by pirates, who terrified to such an extent the neighbouring colony of Bourbon, which the French East India Company had founded since 1694, that the officer in charge there—Mr. Parat—complained to the Home Government. As the Company was fast declining, the Minister induced the rival body of the Associated Shipowners of St. Malo to take possession of Mauritius in the name of the King, should it still be unoccupied. Captain Guillaume Dufresne, who was at that time in the Red Sea with the *Chasseur*, was commissioned for this purpose and landed in the island on the 20th September, 1715. Having satisfied himself that the place was deserted, he solemnly took possession of it for the King and called it Isle of France. His orders not extending to any attempt at colonisation, he left a few days later, and although the Governor of Bourbon occasionally sent there colonists from his own island, they all declined to remain and had to be taken back.

After the death of Louis XIV. the Isle of France was given to the new Eastern Company, established in 1719. Mr. de Fougeray Garnier was despatched on the *Triton*, and took over the island on the 23rd September, 1721. Mr. de Nyon had been appointed Commander, but, pending his arrival, the Bourbon authorities sent an officer, Mr. Durongoüet le Toullec, with about fifteen persons, to occupy the new colony.

de Nyon (1722-25).

Mr. de Nyon took his post early in 1722 and settled at Port South-East, which received the appellation of Port Bourbon. The population of the island then amounted to 160 persons in all—soldiers, colonists and slaves. Port North-West was called Port Louis, and was given in charge to a small detachment, protected by earthen works of defence. Mr. de Nyon was replaced by Mr. Brousse from the Government of

Brousse (1725-29).

Bourbon, assisted by a Provincial Council possessed of executive and judicial capacities; its decisions could be appealed against before the Superior Council of the neighbouring island. But things did not go on smoothly, and it was decided that the Isle of France should in future have an independent Commander. The first to act as such was Mr. de

de Maupin (1729-35).

Maupin, who completed the fort commenced by Mr. de Nyon, and sent a favourable account of the strategical importance of the island. On account of the ruling trade winds, he recommended the transfer of the headquarters to Port Louis. Several engineers were sent to execute his plan, but as time was lost in insignificant enterprises, one of the engineers—Mr. de Cossigny—resigned and returned home, where he submitted such an encouraging report of the situation of the Isle of France, that the Government insisted upon the adoption of his views. It was, however, no easy matter to create everything out of nothing; it was necessary to entrust the operation to an active, intelligent, honest, cool-headed man, who could take advantage of all circumstances, even unfavourable, assert his authority, put a stop to petty rivalries, and steadily prosecute his aim in spite of recriminations. Such a character was not readily procurable, yet it happened that the Company had the very man in its service.

MAHE DE LA BOURDONNAIS.
(From an old Engraving in the possession of Mr. Edouard Rouillard.)

Mahé de La Bourdonnais (1735-47).

He was Mahé de La Bourdonnais, who possessed a thorough knowledge of both colonies, having sailed a long time in the surrounding seas as second officer. He had several interviews with the Minister, Mr. Orry, who was surprised at his good sense, the vastness of his practical ideas, and the assurance of a man who knew what he was about and was ready to accomplish it. He was appointed Governor of both colonies, and it is only fair to state that he was the founder of the Isle of France's prosperity.

A Superior Council was established in the island instead of the previous jurisdiction of the first degree. La Bourdonnais created a city and a good harbour at Port Louis, which had been nothing but a desert, built docks, defences, batteries, forts, stores, a hospital, a Government House, and an aqueduct bringing pure water from Grand River North-West. He encouraged agriculture, planted cotton, indigo, grains, manioc, fruit trees, vegetables, sugar-cane; opened the first sugar factory at Ville Bague, and was a pioneer of the silk industry. Such activity, of course, gave rise to numerous complaints, but he heeded them not. His ambition was to make Port Louis a free harbour, an emporium of the East, and to keep there a number of armed vessels, some entirely of colonial build, ready, at the first tidings of war with England, to pounce upon British merchant ships before sufficient forces could be gathered to oppose him. This was highly approved by both the Court and Company; but they never gave him the slightest chance to realise the latter project. In 1741 La Bourdonnais proceeded to India with five of the Company's vessels, to the assistance of Pondicherry, which was threatened by the Mahrattas. He found everything quiet there, but Mahé, on the Malabar Coast, was besieged, and his timely appearance saved that place from destruction. He then returned to the Isle of France and put his squadron in order, as he daily expected to hear that war had broken out. Whilst he was thus engaged, he received orders to disarm and send back his ships. Reluctant as he was, he was bound to obey, and after their departure a private letter came from the Minister expressing the hope that he *had not* punctually executed the commands he had received.

BEGINNING OF THE CONSTRUCTION OF PORT LOUIS, IN 1738, UNDER THE DIRECTION OF MAHÉ DE LA BOURDONNAIS.

(From an old Engraving in the Town Hall, Port Louis.)

This was in the year 1744, and, sending in his resignation, he devoted all his time to the internal welfare of the colonies which had been entrusted to his care. It was then that took place, off Amber Island, the wreck of the *St. Géran*, immortalised by Bernardin de St. Pierre's story *Paul and Virginia*.

Suddenly the report arrived that war had been declared and that his services could not be dispensed with. He also received the extraordinary injunction not to open hostilities, although he might defend himself if attacked. The reason given for this absurdity was that, should both Companies be careful in keeping a strict neutrality, the English Navy would continue to respect French merchant vessels!

Nevertheless, in April following, Dupleix, Governor of Pondicherry, called him to his aid, advising him of what was taking place at sea. It was, of course, what La Bourdonnais had expected. The English squadron, four vessels strong, was capturing every French vessel of commerce, and Admiral

Peyton declared that he was actually serving them as La Bourdonnais had proposed to serve the English.

La Bourdonnais had with him four vessels of the Company and one fast sailing brig. He equipped this force with black sailors and raised a corps of volunteers. Soon after, a ship arrived from France with the intelligence that five others would follow, which he would have to arm as well. The latter did not make an appearance till the beginning of 1746, when everything had to be provided for them. On the 24th March his squadron was ready and he despatched it, appointing Foulpointe as meeting place, which was reached in a storm. One vessel was destroyed, and the others, more or less damaged, were repaired in a desert country. After forty-eight days La Bourdonnais proceeded to India with ten vessels. Off the Coromandel Coast he had an engagement with the English, and moored before Pondicherry, where it was agreed, between him and Dupleix, that he would besiege Madras. The capture of that city was the principal cause of the antagonism between the two commanders, Dupleix insisting upon its being preserved and its defences increased, La Bourdonnais being of opinion that it should pay a considerable ransom, as he felt certain that, in the event of peace, the English would insist upon its restoration to them. Matters soon got worse and worse; La Bourdonnais was accused by Dupleix of high treason, and soon after left for the Isle of France, where he found already in office Mr. David, his successor, who had orders to arrest him and send him to France as a prisoner. After having considered the merits of his case, this officer did not find himself justified in inflicting such harsh treatment upon a man of the standing of La Bourdonnais; so he simply sent him away, giving him the command of one of the vessels. On the voyage La Bourdonnais was captured by the English and brought to London, where he was instantly set at liberty with the highest consideration. He thence proceeded to Paris, and on his arrival there, in February, 1748, he was immediately arrested and sent to the Bastille, where he remained for three years. His innocence was at last proclaimed, but his health was so seriously impaired by physical and moral sufferings that he died on the 9th September, 1753, at the age of fifty-four years.

Barthélemy David (1747-53).

Barthélemy David was instructed to renounce the warlike policy of his predecessor and bestow all his care on agriculture. This was a strange decision in time of war, and the Isle of France might have suffered dearly for it in the following year, when a British fleet, under Admiral Boscawen, cruised for five days on the western coast. Fortunately enough this officer's belief was that the Isle of France was impregnable, and he was deceived by some clever show of resistance well calculated to make him dread a hot reception. As Pondicherry was his main object, he accordingly sailed away. Mr. David then built Le Réduit, which he made a stronghold where the female population might take refuge in case of an invasion. Soon after this he retired, and was replaced by the Commander of Bourbon, Mr. de Lozier Bouvet.

de Lozier Bouvet (1753-56).

During his peaceful administration the Isle of France was visited by Mr. d'Après de Mannevillette and Abbé de la Caille, who drew up the first exact map of the colony and determined the height of its mountains. It was then that the Company, adopting Pierre Poivre's views, endeavoured to introduce cloves and nutmegs into the colony, in spite of the Draconian precautions of the Dutch in the Malay Islands to prevent their exportation. Mr. de Lozier Bouvet gave Poivre a small brig of 160 tons for this dangerous expedition, which met with some success; the precious plants thus obtained being entrusted to the care of several respectable inhabitants.

Rene Magon (1756-59).

René Magon, who was appointed next, strove to develop plantations, those of grains especially, and introduced large herds of cattle from Madagascar; he also gave his support to a saltpan created at Caudan, and to the foundry establishment of Messrs. Hermans and de Rostaing at Montagne Longue, where iron ore had been discovered in La Bourdonnais' time. He also sent an expedition to occupy the Seychelles group.

War having broken out again, in December, 1757, Mr. Magon had to give assistance to an expedition, under Count d'Aché and General Lally, on its way to India. On its return, after several fruitless attempts, that squadron was partially destroyed by a hurricane in Port Louis Harbour. Mr. Magon soon after this retired to live at his residence at Ville Bague.

Desforges Boucher (1759-67).

Mr. Desforges Boucher was appointed in his stead. The Company's affairs were now in such a disorderly state that this Governor's best intentions were paralysed. The Directors were constantly altering their plans, and, as the Indian establishments had been ruined by the English, nothing could be received therefrom at the Isle of France, whereas goods from Europe were locked up in the Company's stores, to be retailed at enormous prices for the benefit of some dishonest officials. On the inhabitants complaining of this, Mr. Desforges Boucher authorised them to send two delegates to France to explain the unbearable state of things. When they arrived at Lorient, however, they were informed that the Company had sold the Isles of France and Bourbon to the Government for twelve and a half millions of livres. But before the Royal authority could be established there, the Company had to liquidate its affairs : this took three years' time, so it was not till 1767 that the administration of these colonies was given over to the Royal Government.

THE GOVERNMENT FOR THE KING.

Jean Daniel Dumas (1767-69).

Mr. Jean Daniel Dumas held the title of Governor-General of the Isles of France and Bourbon, and Mr. Poivre that of Intendant and President of the Superior Council. The latter's authority was mostly restricted to matters of finance, in which, however, it was supreme. The Superior Council was now bereft of its administrative functions, preserving only those of a Supreme Court of Justice. Although the attributions of both chiefs had been carefully laid down, misunderstandings were bound to occur between two men who instinctively disliked each other. Mr. Dumas, warned by the Cabinet, held in suspicion the former officers of the Company, some of whom were still sitting in the Superior Council. Mr. Poivre felt an aversion towards a superior who had unwittingly hurt his susceptibility and was certainly not his equal in intellectual abilities. He made the great mistake of openly disclosing his feelings upon his arrival, the result being that the malcontents had no great difficulty in gaining him over to their side.

PIERRE POIVRE.
(From an old Engraving in the possession of Mr. Edouard Rouillard.)

Shortly after, a number of respectable inhabitants presented to the Governor an address, in which they denounced several exactions of a heinous nature committed by the Company's agents. The Council, which was in fact a judge in its own cause, did not hesitate to bring an action for libel against the persons mentioned, and had three of them arrested and imprisoned in the fort at Ile aux Tonneliers. Mr. Dumas released them instantly, and warmly rated the Procureur-General, Mr. Desribes. The Council soon found an opportunity of revenge in confirming some antiquated administrative regulations, although it was perfectly aware that it had no longer anything to do with that part of the service. Mr. Dumas retorted by proclaiming martial law, which the Council refused to allow being registered in its records. The Governor then entered the Council room at the head of a detachment of soldiers, and had the document written down in the Council's books in spite of the unanimous protestation of the members, who retired, Poivre leading the way. The Procureur-General was ordered to be kept under arrest in his own house, and Mr. Rivalz de St. Antoine, one of the Councillors, was banished to Rodrigues. In so doing, Mr. Dumas had evidently exceeded his powers and was accordingly recalled; but Mr. Poivre was severely rebuked by the Cabinet for having encouraged this idle opposition. On the departure of Mr. Dumas the government was temporarily administered by Mr. de Steinauer, who did not remain more than four or five months in office.

de Steinauer (1769).

Desroches (1769-72). Mr. Desroches then assumed the command, and did all in his power, though fruitlessly, to keep on good terms with the Intendant. The liquidation of the Company being at last ended, that body was declared bankrupt and its privileges abolished. Free trade was accordingly granted to all French citizens in these islands.

Mr. Desroches did much to improve the general appearance of Port Louis; new streets were opened, cutting each other at right angles; the Line Barracks were erected; and the old cemetery, which till then had occupied the site of the present "Company's Gardens," was closed and a new one begun outside the town, near the seashore at Cassis. Mr. Desroches directed Chevalier de Tromelin to dredge the harbour, in order to preserve its depth; a causeway was laid between the mainland and Ile aux Tonneliers, altering the course of the rivulets which formerly discharged into the harbour; and a channel was dug, allowing the largest vessels to moor in Trou Fanfaron. He had also the slopes of the adjoining mountains planted with trees.

Poivre, now disposing of the colonial finances, reverted to his long-cherished scheme respecting the most valuable spice trees, in which he was supported by the Governor. Poivre had purchased the old residence of the Company's Governors at Mon Plaisir, where he planted many varieties of spice and other trees. This domain, after his departure, was purchased by the Government and entrusted to Poivre's bosom friend, Nicolas Céré, under whose able direction it soon became famous under the name of King's Garden. It is now the beautiful Royal Botanic Gardens, Pamplemousses.

THE MARKET PORT LOUIS, IN FORMER TIMES.
(From an old Engraving in the possession of Mr. Edouard Rouillard.)

de Ternay (1772-76). Mr. de Ternay replaced Mr. Desroches, and Mr. Maillart Dumesle Mr. Poivre. Those two officers strove their utmost to advance the welfare of the colony, and, owing to peace and the freedom of commerce, it soon was brought to a highly flourishing state.

de La Brillane (1776-79). Mr. de La Brillane was next appointed Governor. Soon after his arrival, the first cloves and nutmegs were gathered in great pomp, and solemnly sent to the King as a token of the future prosperity of the Isle of France.

In 1778, war having broken out once more, the Government granted Letters of Marque to corsairs, and many were they who availed themselves of the privilege in the Indian Ocean.

In spite of his efforts, Mr. de La Brillane had not managed to gain the sympathy of the colonists. His health being impaired, he insisted upon his recall, but died before his request was granted, and was buried in the parochial church of Port Louis.

Vicomte de Souillac (1779-87). Vicomte de Souillac, then Commander at Bourbon, was appointed in his stead. Three years' residence among the colonists had made him fully cognizant of their requirements, and he was beloved by them all. He took great pains for the embellishment of Port Louis, and to him is due the fountain in front of the Cathedral. He had to provide troops, ammunition and provisions for the expedition sent to India under Bussy, and for the squadrons of Messrs. d'Orves and de Suffren. At the death of Bussy, Vicomte de Souillac was made Governor-General of the French establishments in India, and had to remove to Pondicherry, his new capital.

d'Entrecasteaux (1787-89).

His successor was Mr. d'Entrecasteaux, who made himself equally appreciated during his short tenure of office. The French influence in India was then at an end. Of France's former power Pondicherry alone remained, with sundry insignificant settlements. It was decided to remove the headquarters of the Governor-General to the Isle of France, and accordingly the Governor of Pondicherry, now Comte de Conway, was ordered to take Mr. d'Entrecasteaux's place.

Comte de Conway (1789-90).

Comte de Conway was, by a natural impulse, averse to the liberal ideas which were now gaining ground in the colony. He disbanded the popular corps of volunteers through fear, it is said, that they might join the population in some hypothetical insurrection.

In presence of financial catastrophes which had of late befallen the colony, it had been deemed of the utmost necessity to issue a fiduciary currency, and on the 1st January, 1790, all the Government expenses were to be settled in paper. When the time came, the garrison loudly objected to this mode of payment, and as no specie was available, an arrangement was resorted to in favour of the garrison.

THE COLONIAL ASSEMBLIES.

Comte de Conway (1790).

The discontent which had been pervading some classes of the population now broke out in an unexpected manner. On the 31st January a sloop, commanded by Mr. Gabriel de Coriolis, an officer of the Royal Navy, anchored in the harbour. The crew disembarked wearing three-coloured cockades, which they profusely distributed amongst the population, giving news at the same time of the latest events, and advising them to elect committees, as had been done in Paris. Having received no official information of all this, the Governor scarcely knew what line of conduct to adopt, but thought the best policy was to make a show of energy. Bills had been posted up inviting the inhabitants to assemble. The Governor ordered them to be torn down, which increased the tumult. Several ringleaders were arrested, but were soon released by the excited multitude. As the soldiers were amongst the noisiest, Comte de Conway decided upon entering into composition and agreed to wear the cockade. He then sent for Mr. de Coriolis, reproached him with the disorder he had provoked, and told him he must now put a stop to it. Coriolis promised to do his best, but invited de Conway to grant permission to hold an assembly all the same. This assembly was held a few days later, when Coriolis kept his word and exhorted the inhabitants to obey the existing authorities until later news arrived. But this advice was unheeded, and a motion was carried proclaiming the French Revolution and appointing a committee of seven persons who would convoke a General Assembly of the colony, in which two deputies would be chosen to sit in the National Assembly in France, draw up the electoral status of each citizen, and hold permanent sittings until instructions were received from the Home authorities. It was agreed, on the other hand, that public peace should not be troubled and that every citizen should be bound to give assistance to the authorities whenever needed. In the course of an interview they had with the Governor, the Commissaries admitted the nullity of the attributions so conferred upon them, but were of opinion that a General Assembly should be instantly convoked, so as to prevent further disorders; meanwhile they offered their support to the authorities, who were reluctantly compelled to accept it.

GOVERNMENT BUILDINGS, PORT LOUIS, IN FORMER TIMES.
(From an old Sketch in the possession of Mr. Edouard Rouillard.)

On the 30th April, 1790, the General Assembly held its first sitting in the parochial church, declared itself permanent and inviolable, and delegated its powers to rural municipalities.

On the 25th May the naval squadron came from India, under Comte Macnemara, who warned his men against the disorder caused by "thoughtless agitation and criminal ambition." This, of course, the Assembly took as an insult. In June following news from France arrived to the effect that the National Assembly prescribed exactly the same measures as had been already adopted. Clubs were opened everywhere and the General Assembly of the Colony, assuming the designation of Colonial Assembly, now pretended to prosecute several superior officers from India who had been denounced as lukewarm, but was opposed in this by Comte de Conway. Under pretence of his keeping a secret correspondence with the Cabinet, a search was made in his papers. This he could not brook either; and, resigning his office to Mr. de Chermont, commander of the garrison, until the arrival of the Lieutenant-Governor of Bourbon, Mr. de Cossigny, he took up his quarters on board a frigate which left one month later.

de Cossigny (1790-92).

The two delegates to the National Assembly named by the Isle of France were about to leave for Europe, when it was rumoured that Comte Macnemara intended to overtake them on the voyage and suppress their written instructions. As a token of his not intending to leave the colony at all, the Assembly requested Macnemara to hand over the rudder of his frigate, with which he complied. A few days after he was denounced as having libelled the same body in a private letter, which had been seized at the post office through the advice of his own private secretary. A number of soldiers of the Regiment of Pondicherry took to boats in a high state of excitement, boarded the ship and summoned Macnemara to follow them to the Assembly. To this he again agreed, placing himself under the safeguard of their honour as soldiers.

Some members there insisted upon his being immediately condemned to death; but the great majority suffered him to explain his conduct. He denied having made use of any insulting language and bitterly complained of the breach of trust practised against him. His coolness made a favourable impression, and the Assembly discharged him. As he had asked to be sent to the barracks, four members were named to accompany him. Mr. de Cossigny was also going there, but by some fatal chance he proceeded along Government Street while Comte Macnemara went down by Church Street. On his way the latter was hooted, threatened, struck with sticks, and his escort could hardly prevent his being actually mobbed.

At the corner of Royal Street he saw the ominous post which had been raised in front of Government House. Easily guessing what was to happen next he made a rush for a shop, ran up the stairs with the idea of climbing on to the roof and thence escaping into Government House Gardens. He was, however, stopped by a bolted door, and, on turning round, saw a soldier close at his heels with a drawn sword, at whom he pointed his pistol, but the arm missed fire. He was immediately brought down, thrown over the stairs and dragged by his feet into the street, where his head was severed from his body, stuck on a pole and promenaded through the town. Late at night, one of his sailors found his corpse lying near Pont Bourgeois, and secretly buried it in the cemetery. An inquiry was ordered, which did not disclose any evidence permitting the arrest of his murderers, mostly soldiers. His crew was wildly excited and had to be kept on board till the frigate departed. After this mournful event the popular effervescence immediately subsided.

The Assembly then drew up the draft of a Charter which was adopted on the 2nd April, 1791, and sanctioned by the Executive on the 21st as the Colonial Constitution of the Isle of France.

Comte de Malartic (1792-1800).

Comte de Malartic arrived on the 18th June as Governor, together with four Civil Commissioners sent expressly to effect changes in the administration of the eastern colonies; two of these, Messrs. Le Boucher and Lescalier, were to act at the Isle of France. Malartic was an aged, good and religious man, and his appointment was the very last act of King Louis XVI. Wonderful to say, his chivalrous and patriarchal ways made him dear to all political parties in those unbelieving times.

In 1793, as some merchant ships were about to sail for Europe under the escort of a frigate, the shipowners insisted upon a second man-of-war joining them, to which the Commander of the station, Admiral de St. Félix, objected, in view of the strict orders from the Cabinet and the weakness of his own forces. He was then accused of intending to betray the merchant ships to the English and summoned to resign. His answer was that he could not desert his post in time of war, but, in order to restore peace, he agreed that another frigate should accompany the convoy to the Cape of Good Hope, and no farther. Being ill, he proceeded to Bourbon to restore his health, when, of a sudden, the omnipotent Clubs denounced him for having left his post, and insisted upon his dismissal. The Assembly was compelled to approve this and the Governor to give his sanction. St. Félix protested against that body meddling in questions which concerned the Executive alone. This was enough to make them demand his arrest. To this Malartic again assented, with the object of gaining time; but he was soon obliged to have the order carried out. St. Félix and five others were arrested at Bourbon, brought to Port Louis, and imprisoned in a tower which then stood at the entrance to Place d'Armes. There they remained in confinement for fifteen months, when a reaction, created by the downfall of Robespierre in France, allowed their being set at liberty after a sham trial, in which their innocence was proclaimed. (1794.)

France, being then at war with enemies on all sides, could not possibly send to the Isle of France sufficient naval forces to protect its commerce, and it became necessary to have recourse to Letters of Marque. Corsairs were armed in great number and soon did such havoc to the English trade that the East India Company decided upon capturing the island, and considered the feasibility of an expedition being concentrated at Rodrigues under the command of General Meadows. Meanwhile, two men-of-war — the *Centurion* and the *Diomed*— were sent out for blockading both islands. This might have proved a serious affair, as the colony did not produce sufficient articles of consumption.

FORMER METHOD OF TRAVEL IN MAURITIUS.

The above palanquin was borrowed by the Editor from the Port Louis Museum, and the lady who kindly consented to sit in it for the photograph is a well-known English actress who was on a visit to the colony.

"These conveyances are now almost entirely superseded by the very general use of European carriages; but from the state of the roads when the island was first captured the palanquin was the common means of transport for all, both in town and country. It is indeed a luxurious mode of conveyance. Preserving a reclining posture, seldom otherwise than agreeable in such a climate, the traveller, extended on a soft cushion, is carried along at a tolerably rapid pace; and whilst he is effectually protected from the ardent rays of the sun, he is refreshed by the breeze which gently plays upon him through the medium of Venetian blinds.

"Before the English occupation not a street in Port Louis was possible for a carriage and scarcely for a cart; in fact, at the capture of the island in 1810 there was but one single European carriage in the colony. This was an English curricle, the owner of which, when he desired to take a drive, had his vehicle led up to the Champ de Mars, then the only level piece of ground, whither he followed on foot or in a palanquin. When his airing was concluded he sent away his carriage—the state of the streets not allowing him to drive it home."—From *Views in the Mauritius, or Isle of France*, by T. Bradshaw, published in London in 1832.

The colonial forces at that time amounted to two small frigates carrying fifteen guns each, the *Cybèle* and the *Prudente*, under the orders of Captain Renaud, who had replaced Admiral St. Félix. Two little brigs, the *Coureur* and the *Jean Bart*, each being armed with six pieces of cannon, were then in the harbour. Renaud joined them to his squadron, thus opposing forty-two guns in all to the ninety-four displayed by the English vessels, and reinforced their crews with fifty soldiers and a number of volunteers. He set sail on the 19th October, rounded the island by the north and descended along the coast of Flacq. On the 22nd, off Bambou Mountain, he sighted the English and made straight for them. The action was desperate; although badly damaged, the French inflicted such severe injuries on their opponents that the latter had to withdraw to get their vessels thoroughly repaired. Renaud had succeeded in his object, in spite of a loss of 136 men.

In June, 1795, there arrived two Agents of the French Directory, Baco and Burnel, with special orders for proclaiming the immediate emancipation of slaves without any compensation to their owners.

They came with four frigates under Rear-Admiral de Sercey, and were escorted by 2,000 troops under General Magallon. As soon as they had moored the Assembly determined upon opposing their landing, by force if necessary; but this measure was baffled at the last moment by the garrison, which threatened to side with the envoys from the Directory. Incensed at the treatment they received the two Agents now proceeded to the Assembly, menacing it with suppression and the incorporation of the rebels in the Indian troops. The Assembly protested, and retorted that if the Agents meant to ruin the colony every one would rise against them and that they themselves would be the first victims of their rash attempt. It was very strange, it was observed, that pretending to be the bearers of important orders, they had not yet made them public. A committee was appointed to discuss with them the terms of an agreement. The conference lasted three days, when the Agents were compelled to disclose part, at least, of their dictatorial powers. Outside Government House, where this was going on, the crowd got exasperated on hearing that the Agents would listen to no arrangement, and, breaking into the hall, they threatened Baco and Burnel—a pistol being fired at the former, but without effect. Their immediate departure was insisted upon, and, seeing that resistance was impossible, the Agents consented to embark on a corvette, Malartic being pressed to sign orders to that effect. They were to have been transported to the Philippine Islands, but intimidated the captain on the way and prevailed upon him to take them back to France.

At the end of 1799 the frigate *Preneuse*, Captain Lhermitte, returning from a successful cruise along the coast of Africa, came in view of Grand Port and followed the shore closely as far as Cape Malheureux, when two English vessels of seventy-four guns, the *Tremendous* and *Adamant*, came down upon him from the north. Lhermitte, endeavouring to out-distance them, manœuvred to pass between Gunner's Quoin and the mainland, whilst the enemy, not daring to venture in such shallow waters, had to sail all round that rock. Lhermitte had made considerable progress and was proceeding on fairly to gain his anchorage, when, in front of Tombeau Bay, he was suddenly becalmed and his ship driven on the shoals by a strong current. The wind now set in in an opposite direction, causing the frigate to stick firmly on a reef, whilst the English vessels were fast approaching. At 3 p.m. the action began, but soon after, as the tide was running low, the frigate, already shaken by the rounds of artillery, stooped more and more and came down on her side, her deck facing the open sea. All resistance being vain, Lhermitte sent his crew on shore, set fire to his ship and brought down his colours. He was taken on board the *Tremendous*, and, as he handed his sword to Commodore Hotham, that officer gave him his own in exchange, releasing him on parole two days after. A few weeks later a disturbance took place at Réunion through a group of Royalists, who, believing in an imminent restoration of the Bourbon dynasty, sought to proclaim the independence of both colonies. After having vainly endeavoured to dissipate their futile hopes, Malartic was compelled to proceed to Réunion with a few members of the Assembly, and, at the ensuing conference, the Royalists were made to see the uselessness of their intentions and agreed to refrain from any further efforts in that direction. (February, 1800.)

Six months later, on the 28th July, the Governor died of apoplexy, at the age of seventy years, his death being lamented by all classes. His funeral took place with great pomp on the 30th, and his body, after lying in state in the chapel of the Hospital until the 16th August, was buried in the Champ de Mars. Commodore Hotham, who commanded the British cruisers, asked as a favour to be present at the interment; this being readily granted, his squadron drew up before the harbour under flag of truce, and the English officers were cordially received, re-embarking when the solemnity was over.

Malartic's corpse was placed in a provisional tomb until a monument could be erected to his memory a little farther up the plain. The final resting place was ready in time to permit the corpse being transferred there exactly one year after; but the monument itself was not completed until forty-six years had elapsed. Although not entirely similar to the original plan, it might never have been erected but for the generosity of Lady Gomm. Curiously enough, forty-six years later again, on the 29th April, 1892, this obelisk was upset by a terrific cyclone, but was speedily rebuilt by the care of the Committee of Historical Researches.

General Magallon (1800-03).

General Magallon took charge of the government at the time when Lord Mornington, Governor-General of Bengal, was planning an important expedition against the island under the command of his younger brother, Lieutenant-Colonel Arthur Wellesley, afterwards Duke of Wellington; but as the brothers did not agree, their project was set aside for some time.

News soon came of the 18th Brumaire, of the Consulate, and in January, 1802, of the Peace of Amiens. In the following year it was rumoured that General Decaen would be sent to take possession of the Establishments in India, which had been restored to France by that treaty. He accordingly left Brest with a squadron, under Admiral Linois, and proceeded direct to Pondicherry, where he was not a little surprised at meeting ten English vessels riding at anchor. Decaen sent one of his frigates, the *Belle Poule*, to Madras to inform the British authorities of his arrival, and began disembarking troops and the officers of the civil service. Still the English did not seem very willing to deliver up the settlement, and, as rumours were afloat that war had broken out again, Decaen felt anxious and dreaded some treachery. The next day a French corvette arrived, confirming the outbreak of war and bringing instructions for him to repair to the Isle of France without loss of time. Taking advantage of the night, Decaen slipped out of the harbour, abandoning 200 soldiers, the officials, and the frigate he had sent to Madras. Although chased by the English he was not overtaken.

On the 17th August, the *Belle Poule* anchored at Port Louis. No longer finding Decaen's squadron before Pondicherry, she also had left for the Isle of France, and the captain declared that he had recently fallen in with several men-of-war who had pursued him. This news created considerable excitement, and whilst an attack was expected the squadron in question came in view, but it proved to be Linois' division.

General Decaen landed in full uniform at the head of his troops and abstained from communicating with anyone. On the 25th September, the *Berceau* brought confirmation of the war and the appointment of Decaen as Captain-General of the French Establishments at the west of the Cape of Good Hope.

GENERAL DECAEN'S ADMINISTRATION.

General Decaen (1803-10)

General Decaen assumed his office on the 27th September. Mr. Léger was invested with the functions of Colonial Prefect, almost similar to those of the Intendant, and Mr. Crespin with those of Commissary of Justice. The Courts of Law were replaced on the same footing as they had stood in 1792. In virtue of a decree of the Consuls appointing the new Government, the Colonial Assembly was suppressed and the Constitution of the Isle of France suspended for ten years. The Governor's behaviour caused much discontent at first, but it was all through a misunderstanding. He had been greatly prejudiced against the inhabitants, and was in the firm belief that the Assembly had constantly exceeded its powers and thrown the colony into a state of most lamentable anarchy. Anxious to put a stop thereto, he kept aloof until he had completed the reorganisation of the administration, after which he sought to ascertain exactly what had taken place and found how much he had been misled. Frankly acknowledging his error, he soon won the goodwill and affection of the colonists.

On the 15th December of the same year, an English schooner of twenty-nine tons took shelter from rough weather in Baie du Cap, at the most southerly extremity of the island. She was commanded by Captain Matthew Flinders, of the Royal Navy, who came from Australia, where he had mapped out the coasts of that country. Having lost two vessels entrusted to his care during an exploration on the coasts of Queensland, he had secured this small craft for the purpose of returning to England.

As his casting anchor in such an out-of-the-way place seemed rather suspicious, a pilot was sent to bring his boat to Port Louis. Flinders held a safe-conduct for the *Investigator*, his first vessel, but had not renewed it for his little *Cumberland*. This thoughtlessness was deemed extraordinary in an officer of his standing, and his declaration that he was ignorant of the resumption of hostilities was inconsistent with the flag of truce which he had hoisted upon nearing the shore. As a captain of the Royal Navy, it was claimed that he must certainly have been aware of the position of the principal port, and, as he assumed a very arrogant attitude upon being questioned, the Governor's suspicions increased. A conversation carried on on both sides with equal prejudice resulted in his being looked upon as a spy. Upon being officially informed of this, Flinders' indignation made him write to Decaen in such abusive terms that the Governor thought it below himself to send him a reply. Flinders then renewed his complaints, even accusing Decaen of having premeditated his arrest only for the sake of handing over his papers to a rival traveller, the French

Captain Baudin. Decaen then put a stop to all correspondence with him on the plea of his ungentlemanly behaviour.

Suffering from scurvy, weary of his solitude—for he was confined all by himself in a hotel room—Flinders was eventually allowed to keep company with other prisoners of war. Then was the English officer visited by some kind-hearted colonists, who did all in their power to alleviate his misfortune, and even prevailed upon the Governor to allow his residing in the country on parole.

On the 12th March, 1806, the Council of State in France approved Decaen's decision in this affair, but, considering the circumstances of the case, ordered the release of Flinders. The situation of the colony having then become worse, Decaen took upon himself to disobey, and stated his reasons for so doing in a lengthy report. Flinders, accordingly, remained at the Isle of France till the 8th May, 1810, when he was embarked on a cartel ship which did not leave till a month later.

The Treasury was empty, and there being no remedy except to fill it at the enemy's expense, it was agreed between Decaen and Admiral Linois that the latter should attempt the capture of the British Chinese convoy as it passed the Straits of Sunda. Linois failed in his object and returned after having seized only one vessel in the Bay of Bengal. Decaen could not forbear manifesting his displeasure in such harsh language that Linois took offence and, after several cruises, without returning to the Isle of France, set sail for Europe, but was captured by the English off the Canary Islands.

CAPTAIN MATTHEW FLINDERS.
(From a Painting in Mr. Andre de Chazal's office, Port Louis.)

In order to induce neutral ships to visit the Isle of France and Réunion, Decaen opened Port Louis and St. Denis to their commerce. In order to perform in detail what Linois had failed to accomplish by one effort, he granted the greatest facilities for the equipment of corsairs, whose captures provided for most of the colony's expenses; but still the Government could do no more than make both ends meet.

In 1806 Decaen made a tour of the island for the purpose of organising its defence, and was satisfied that the post at Old Grand Port would be more advantageously situated on the opposite side of the bay, where he built retrenchments, with stores and barracks, and created a small town which he called Mahébourg, after La Bourdonnais. He also put the battery at Isle de la Passe in good repair. As Port Louis was filling up again, he did for Caudan what Tromelin had done for Trou Fanfaron in Port Louis Harbour, by altering the course of the rivulets which had emptied their waters there. He added a second story to Government House and built an Exchange Room at the corner of Place d'Armes and National (now Royal) Street. As the Powder Magazine above the Company's Gardens was a permanent source of danger to the town, it was converted into a place of confinement for prisoners of war. The Courts of Justice were erected on the site they now occupy, although they have been considerably enlarged; the Colonial College, or Lycée, was built at Champ de Lort and opened on the 2nd December, 1806. Decaen constructed a suspension bridge over Grand River North-West, a little above the one now existing, but it was destroyed some fifteen years after by a flood.

On the 16th August, 1806, being the Emperor's birthday, Decaen changed the names of Port Louis and Port South-East into Port Napoleon and Port Imperial, Bourbon becoming Ile Bonaparte. This flattery was rewarded by the grant of two small squadrons, one under Hamelin in 1808, and the other under Duperré in 1809; but it would have been still better if the Home authorities had honoured the Governor's signature by a discretionary power for drawing bills on the Imperial Treasury.

The immense damage which the privateers were doing to the British interests induced the Viceroy of India, Lord Minto, to revert to his predecessor's scheme, which had been abandoned chiefly through the belief that an attack could not succeed against such strong and well-defended islands. Lord Minto informed the British Cabinet that action had become extremely urgent, and proposed to open stores at Rodrigues for the use of the blockading squadrons. In May, 1809, a garrison of 250 European and 200 Sepoys, left there under Colonel Keating, was from time to time considerably augmented in view of a future action.

In September following, after several fruitless demonstrations at St. Rose and St. Pierre, the English made a first regular attack on St. Paul, where they captured a frigate and a quantity of stores, remaining in possession of the town for four days. This made them realise the possibility of performing a feat which, until then, they had deemed impracticable. They also kept reconnoitring the coasts of the Isle of France, at Jacotet, Baie du Cap, Bras de Mer, St. Martin, and Mapou, and although they were driven back they obtained thereby fairly accurate information as to the sort of opposition they would be likely to encounter.

After this things went on rapidly. In the night of 14th August, 1810, taking advantage of misty weather, a detachment of the English frigates—the *Sirius* and the *Nereid*—seized by surprise the battery of Ile de la Passe, defended by thirty-five men, where the English obtained a strong position. They then made several descents on the coast from Pointe du Diable to Old Grand Port, a tract of country where they could scarcely expect to meet with any resistance or even with any inhabitants. Accordingly, on the 17th August, and without suffering any loss, 170 men, supported by three strongly-armed gunboats, captured the battery at Pointe du Diable defended by a handful of men, spiked the guns, slew the commander and three men, and took three prisoners. Proceeding thence to Old Grand Port, some twelve miles off, on the same day they beat back a company of National Guards sent to oppose them.

But, on the 18th, as the English Captain Willoughby was proceeding to the mouth of Grand River South-East, he descried from 600 to 800 French soldiers and militia occupying the batteries opposite, and abstained from giving them battle. For it must be understood that his object was not to effect the conquest of that part of the island, or even to reconnoitre its defences, which were almost nil, but to spread along the coast by means of stray slaves—whose co-operation was not always easy to obtain—bundles of a proclamation drawn up by Mr. Farquhar, the Governor of the neighbouring island, inviting the inhabitants to waive allegiance to a despotic Government which was doomed to perish, and to place themselves under the protection of Great Britain, whereby great happiness would accrue to them. This childish attempt at corruption, as Colonel Malleson termed it some three-quarters of a century later, was not, however, attended with much success. Under those circumstances, Decaen understood that in order to dislodge the invaders from Ile de la Passe, it would be necessary to attack them by sea. He accordingly ordered Hamelin to get his squadron ready for that purpose, as Duperré was then absent on a cruise.

THE BATTLE OF GRAND PORT.

We now come to the historic battle of Grand Port, and may be excused for giving a translation, nearly at full length, of the excellent description of it in Mr Léon Huet de Froberville's interesting volume, *Le Combat du Grand Port et la fin de l'Occupation Française,* which was published in Mauritius in 1910 to commemorate the centenary of that celebrated struggle.

On the 20th August, 1810, a French division of five ships, returning from a cruise in the Mozambique Channel, came in sight of Grand Port. They were the *Bellone*, Captain Duperré, Commander-in-Chief; the *Minerve*, Captain Bouvet; and the *Victor*, a corvette commanded by Lieutenant Morice.

The last was no other than Robert Surcouf's famed *Revenant,* incorporated in the Imperial Navy by Decaen under the title of *Iéna*, afterwards captured by the English who named her the *Victor;* but, retaken by the French ship, the *Bellone,* still preserved the name of *Victor.* The two other large ships were the *Wyndham* and the *Ceylon,* of the English East India Company, captured by the squadron off Mayotte on the 5th July. They were both proceeding at that time from the Cape to Madras, were armed with thirty guns each, and carried 400 men of the 24th Infantry. On board were General Weatherhall with his staff, his daughter and sons, and some other distinguished passengers. After having hastily equipped them as vessels of war, Duperré had entrusted the *Ceylon* to Lieutenant Moulac, of the *Minerve*, and the *Wyndham* to Ensign Darod, of his own frigate.

Warned as early as the 18th, by signals from the *Iphigenia*, which was cruising outside Grand Port, that the naval forces at Port Napoleon were ready to set sail, Willoughby at once understood that, should the two French squadrons unite, Captain Pym's three remaining frigates would be overwhelmed by a far superior foe; so he determined to entice into the bay, by a stratagem which proved a complete success, the five vessels which were being sighted. He ordered the fort and the *Nereid* to fly the French colours and the signal, "The enemy is cruising off Gunner's Quoin." To this the French replied by hoisting their respective numbers, so as to make themselves known.

Having consulted with Bouvet, Duperré decided upon obtaining news from his supposed countrymen on the Ile de la Passe. The *Victor* was accordingly instructed to lead the way, whilst the other ships would follow in a line, the *Minerve* first and the *Bellone* last. Duperré and all his officers were then in the belief that the vessel at anchor close to the islet was the old frigate *Sémillante*, which, having been sold to a commercial firm, had her name altered into the *Charles*, and was expected to arrive at the Isle of France about that time. Bouvet alone had suspicions from her appearance that she might be English. The squadron now made for Ile de la Passe, when, at 11.30 a.m., a midshipman from the *Bellone*, Henri Maurat, fell overboard. Duperré signalled this incident and advised that his manœuvre would become independent accordingly. Fruitless attempts were made to save the young man, and they considerably altered the order of sail, the *Wyndham* leaving her post and the *Minerve* and the *Ceylon* laying to with the object of awaiting Duperré, and also preparing for action, owing to Bouvet's persistence in suspecting the nationality of the frigate at anchor. These doubts he had once more signalled to his superior, who neverthless reiterated orders to gain the harbour.

At 1 o'clock, as the *Victor* was about to reach the anchorage, the *Nereid* and fort suddenly replaced the French flag with the Union Jack and fired their broadside at pistol range upon the corvette, ordering her to strike her flag. Dumbfounded at this unexpected attack, Morice obeyed the command, and Willoughby prepared to send two of his lieutenants to take possession of his ship.

Duperré, fearing lest all that part of the island had fallen into the hands of the English, signalled his vessels to come back. But it was too late; unable to turn either to larboard or starboard from fear of perishing on the shoals of Point Laverdi or the rocks of Ile de la Passe, Bouvet determined to force his way inward. The *Minerve* and *Ceylon*, steering within a few yards of the fort and the *Nereid*, had to bear the brunt of their combined artillery, twenty-three men being disabled on board the first and eight on the *Ceylon*; the *Minerve's* hull was also pierced by several shots at water line. While passing along, Bouvet commanded the *Victor* to cut her cable and follow instantly. This was at once obeyed, and the three vessels cast anchor at the junction of two passes, out of reach of the fort's guns.

The *Bellone* now came up and entered the pass, signalling the *Wyndham* to do the same; but this vessel continued her route, putting on more sail to gain the wind, as she had got too near the shoals and could neither enter the channel, nor stop, nor even turn round on account of the rough sea. As Duperré was passing the battery he noticed that its fire was ineffective, but this was not the case with the *Nereid*. So he tacked as if he intended to board her, and, passing astern, he shattered her with a terrible volley and joined his squadron, signalling at the same time to the *Wyndham* to gain the nearest harbour. The latter continuing, however, in a southerly direction, was captured the next morning in Black River Bay and sent to Bourbon.

The English, who had already sustained some severe loss and damage, were in great perplexity. At the moment when the fort had struck down the French colours, this flag got ignited by some means, and fell upon a heap of cartridges, causing an explosion which killed three men and severely burnt twelve others. Five guns from the battery and one placed near the *Nereid's* anchorage had been disabled. That very morning Willoughby had sent 160 men on shore at Old Grand Port, and was now expecting their capture. They returned, however, about 2.30 p.m., shortly before the *Bellone* came up, the men having actually crossed the *Minerve* and *Ceylon* in the narrow channel. At one time they got so near the *Minerve* that the oars of one of the boats had to be lifted up and the other boat collided with the frigate. But by a most extraordinary circumstance, which was never explained, the officers and crew on the French vessels saw all those men pass by, without attempting to sink them or even to ask them a single question! The *Nereid* had also suffered from the volleys of the *Bellone* and had three killed and several wounded.

Duperré now ordered his ships to take up a position at the end of the bay, in front of Monkey Island, for he had very soon observed, from the French colours displayed on the shore, that the island

CAPTAIN-GENERAL DECAEN.

CAPTAIN WILLOUGHBY.

CAPTAIN DUPERRÉ.

CAPTAIN BOUVET.

HEROES OF THE BATTLE OF GRAND PORT.

[The blocks for the above illustrations were kindly lent by Mr. Leon Huet de Froberville, author of *Le Combat du Grand Port et la fin de l'Occupation Française*.]

had not been captured. In the apprehension of other English vessels turning up, which would have made the odds too unequal, he assembled a Council of War of the four captains, and proposed to disembark, to place his forces under Decaen's command for an action on land, and to set fire to his vessels, rather than allow them to fall into the enemy's hands. Bouvet indignantly opposed this plan, and insisted upon engaging in action, whatever might be the result. His firmness gained Moulac over to his side; so it was agreed to leave the arrangement entirely to the Captain-General's decision. Meanwhile, as Decaen was still at Port Napoleon, Duperré wrote to him a letter by Morice, who took to horse, but met with an accident on his way and was badly hurt. Pending Decaen's arrival, the squadron prepared for the fight.

On the other hand, Willoughby, being convinced that the French would attack him, was striving to give them a hot reception. He could not, of course, be aware that they sorely lacked provisions and ammunition, that they had had to arm two prizes, and that they had now on board from 700 to 800 prisoners of war, whom it was urgently necessary to get rid of first. He drew up a parapet close to the landing place at Ile de la Passe, to prevent landing there, and despatched Lieutenant Deacon to bring news to Captain Pym, of the *Sirius*, of his determination to make an onslaught on the French, if seconded by another frigate.

On the 21st August, at 9 a.m., Willoughby sent two officers under flag of truce, under pretence of claiming the *Victor* which had surrendered the day before, but more especially to observe carefully the position of the enemy. Duperré replied that his request would be placed before Decaen himself.

The whole day was employed by the French in sending the prisoners on shore and getting the frigates ready for action. It was not till the 22nd that Decaen, who had left Port Napoleon the evening before, could reach Mahébourg. Previous to this he had sent to Duperré a company of marines and a supply of ammunition. The greatest activity was prevailing at Mahébourg to get accommodation ready for the sick, wounded, and prisoners, to send the necessaries to the squadron, and to assist Duperré. The inhabitants most eagerly gave their support to the authorities.

Decaen, being now informed of what had occurred, entirely approved Bouvet's idea and peremptorily refused to consider Willoughby's claim concerning the *Victor*. He decided upon taking prompt measures to oppose the attack of an enemy "master of the pass and twice as strong." This he entrusted to Bouvet, on account of that officer's thorough knowledge of the harbour. Bouvet accordingly moved off the buoys indicating the channels leading to the anchorage and brought the frigates to bear, as an action at anchor was certainly to take place.

The *Bellone*, being the pivot of the defence, took its position in a line with Monkey Island, close to the shoals extending south of the channel, so that the English could not get round her. The *Ceylon* lay to windward, and a little farther away in the same direction was the *Minerve*, these three vessels being separated by an interval of a frigate's length. Between the *Bellone* and the *Ceylon*, leeward of the frigate, the *Victor* took her post. The whole squadron was broadside on towards Mahébourg, on the larboard side being the open sea. The marines detached by Decaen from Hamelin's division were distributed amongst the vessels.

Bouvet was still busy with these arrangements when, at noon, the *Sirius* was sighted in the south-east. Willoughby signalled: "Ready for action, the enemy being inferior in force," a questionable assertion for which he was blamed later. He sent to the *Sirius*, as a pilot, the mate, Robert Lesly, who had no knowledge whatever of the coast. Captain Pym approved his idea of attacking the French, and the *Sirius* and *Nereid* made their advance. The former, which had taken the lead, came upon a shoal, about a league off from the French, and did not get afloat again till the morning of the 23rd with Willoughby's assistance and after considerable effort. At noon, on the same day, two more English ships came up, the *Iphigenia*, Captain Lambert, and the *Magicienne*, Captain Curtis, which the French at first mistook for Hamelin's squadron. At 2 p.m. they moored beside the *Sirius* and *Nereid*.

Now Pym resolved upon an immediate action. Confident in the belief that there was no further danger, the English frigates came down straight upon their opponents to occupy their respective positions—the *Sirius* (thirty-six guns) against the *Bellone* (forty), the *Nereid* (thirty-six) against the *Bellone* and *Victor* (twenty), the *Iphigenia* (thirty-six) against the *Minerve* (forty-eight), the *Magicienne* (twenty-eight) between the *Minerve* and *Ceylon* (thirty). The *Nereid* led the way, piloted by a black mate. It was now 4.30 p.m. On board the French vessels everything had been got ready, and Duperré, who had made an inspection, declared himself satisfied.

The English frigates were progressing under no other sails but their small jibs. On the shore Decaen, his officers, and a great number of colonists, were contemplating this with undisguised anxiety. At about 5.30 p.m., as dusk was setting in, and while the frigates were still at long range, Bouvet, in the hope of causing some fatal nervousness to the English steersmen, opened fire with the *Minerve*, an example which was immediately followed by the others. Meanwhile, the *Nereid*, drawing less water, succeeded in getting right over the shoal behind which the *Bellone* was posted, and cast anchor within pistol range of that vessel. The *Sirius*, coming next, threw herself on to a coral reef and stuck there with her prow towards the enemy. The *Magicienne* and *Iphigenia* then altered their course to avoid the same mishap; but this did not prevent the former, whilst proceeding to her station, running upon a reef quite close to the *Minerve*, where her entire beam was exposed to the volleys of both that frigate and the *Ceylon*. The *Iphigenia* escaped accident by casting anchor in good time in the very pass which the *Minerve* was defending, within a cannon shot of the French. Such was the position of the adversaries when the battle began: The *Bellone* was exposed to the direct broadside of the *Nereid* and the forward volleys of the *Sirius*; the *Minerve* to the direct fire of the *Iphigenia*, forward shots of the *Magicienne* and oblique fire of the *Sirius*; the *Ceylon* to the direct fire of the *Iphigenia* and oblique shots of both the *Magicienne* and *Sirius*. The noise was deafening, over two hundred guns going off at once.

MONUMENT AT MAHEBOURG COMMEMORATING THE BATTLE OF GRAND PORT.

On taking up her position, the *Nereid* opened fire on the *Victor* with such terrible effect that that small corvette was shattered, deprived of nearly all her officers, and driven adrift on the mudbanks at the mouth of the River des Créoles, altogether out of range of the cannon. Then did Willoughby turn upon the *Bellone*, and a terrible engagement took place between them. But some serious complications soon changed the order of battle. As the *Magicienne* was endeavouring to get afloat again, the men employed at the capstan were one after another shot down and the capstan itself smashed. Still, as the tide set in, she could slightly alter her position and direct her guns against the *Minerve's* side. This frigate now manœuvred to avoid her deck being swept by the guns of both the *Magicienne* and *Iphigenia*. In so doing, and whilst she was slipping her front cable, her stern ropes were severed by a shot, with the result that the south-eastern breeze drove her right behind the *Ceylon*, against a shoal on which she touched. The *Ceylon*, unequal to the combined volleys of two frigates, cut her cables and hoisted top sails to follow the *Minerve*, came in contact with the poop of that vessel and gently pushed her forward. Duperré now finding his situation precarious, proceeded to join the two other French vessels, placing Willoughby in a most dangerous predicament and compelling him to move as well.

The three French vessels now got jammed together, Duperré's frigate alone offering her larboard at full length to the English ships, but concealing most of the *Minerve's* battery, where four guns only could be of any service; whilst the latter masked all but nine port holes of the *Ceylon*. Still the French were no longer exposed to the *Iphigenia's* fire, as she was altogether concealed by the *Nereid*. As for the *Sirius*, nothing was changed in spite of Captain Pym's unceasing efforts to lift her up. The *Magicienne*, on the other hand, found herself in the most advantageous position of being able to command at full length the decks of the *Minerve* and *Ceylon*, whereby she caused much havoc to their hulls and rigging, and had to dread nothing save from the *Minerve's* four guns. The French squadron was decidedly in a critical situation.

At 7 p.m. the fight was raging at its height, the terrific cannonade being intermixed with continuous discharges of musketry. At 8 o'clock, Duperré, while standing on the quarter-deck of the *Bellone*, was wounded in his face by some grapeshot and fell senseless in the battery. Believing he had been killed, his officers wrapped him up in a flag and took him down to the surgery. Bouvet, being apprized of this, took command of the *Bellone*, leaving his own frigate to Lieutenant (afterwards Admiral) Roussin. Bouvet's fire proved most deadly. Flying bridges were hurriedly constructed between the three vessels, in order to provide the *Bellone* with a constant supply of ammunition. An improvised battery was established on the larboard gangway of the *Minerve*, giving her command over the *Magicienne's* fire. All this was, of course, performed under the English volleys and while the decks were encumbered with wounded and slain, as well as at imminent risk of conflagration, or explosion, through the blazing wadding which kept pouring upon the French vessels.

In the meantime, Decaen was directing the action on shore, as well as he could, with one

[Photo by permission, Ladies' Fine Needlework Association.

LION MOUNTAIN, MAHÉBOURG.

18-pounder, and Vandermaësen with another field-piece. On the other side of the bay, some colonists attempted to make use of the antiquated guns at Battery de la Reine, four in number, but without any carriages; however, after firing two or three shots at random, they had to give up the attempt, as it certainly proved more dangerous for themselves than for the enemy.

At 11 p.m. there was a lull, and the French took advantage of it by resting. At 12 o'clock the cannonade ceased altogether. Bouvet now went down to have a conference with Duperré, but found him asleep and felt loth to disturb him; so he consulted his fellow officers, who all agreed to rely entirely upon whatever he might decide.

At 4 a.m. Decaen sent him word that the *Nereid* had surrendered. He had been informed of this by one of the prisoners from Ile de la Passe, one Sance, who, being with nineteen others on board the *Nereid*, had attempted to swim up to the *Bellone* to give this intelligence, but finding the sea too rough had been obliged to gain the shore. This seemed so extraordinary that Bouvet determined to wait till daylight to make sure. According to Sance, the *Nereid* was in a most piteous state, her deck covered with *débris* of yards and rigging, her masts, hanging down along her sides; but the Union Jack was still displayed at the top of what remained of her mizen-mast.

Now, this is what had occurred on that vessel. At about 10.30 p.m., Willoughby, being badly hurt in his head, his eye wrenched out of its socket by a splinter of wood, with nearly all his officers and men disabled or killed, his guns dismounted, and his vessel terribly battered, stopped firing after five hours' fighting, and sent Lieutenant Weiss to inform Captain Pym of his desperate situation, as well as to inquire whether it was possible to tow the *Nereid* out of reach, or at least to abandon her with what was left of his men, and, by setting fire to her, get a chance of destroying the three French ships. Pym's answer was that Willoughby should leave his vessel to its fate and personally take refuge on board the *Sirius*. This, of course, Willoughby refused to do, being unwilling to forsake his companions. He therefore sent a lieutenant to the *Bellone* to declare that he had surrendered; but the boat in which this officer attempted to sail was pierced right through by a cannon shot and had to be taken back at once. At midnight the main-mast came down and the rigging caught fire. At 2 a.m. the French prisoners from Ile de la Passe shouted to the *Bellone* that the *Nereid* had surrendered, but the noise prevented their being heard. It was then that Sance swam to the shore.

At day-break, however, Bouvet, seeing the English colours still flying on the frigate, opened fire on her again. Her men were obliged to cut down the stump that remained of their mast to make him stop, for as neither ropes nor rigging were left, there was no possibility of climbing to the flag. However, the French had to postpone the attempt of taking possession of the *Nereid*, for the volleys of the *Magicienne* kept sweeping the sea all round and baffled their efforts in that direction. It was, therefore, necessary to silence that vessel first.

OLD SLAVE PRISON, BEL MARE ESTATE, FLACQ.

On the other hand, Captain Lambert formed another plan which might have brought the fight to an early conclusion. He proposed to board the *Bellone* with the *Iphigenia* and have a hand to hand engagement. He sent word of this to Captain Pym by Lieutenant Chase, and, pending his senior's answer, he proceeded near to the *Nereid*, when the French concentrated their fire upon him so terribly that he had to relinquish the effort, especially as Captain Pym, still cherishing the hope of getting his fine frigate afloat, opposed his rash venture and ordered him to tow the *Iphigenia* out of reach of the enemy, which he did accordingly by 10 a.m.

The French squadron's victory was now almost a certainty. Bouvet at once announced this to Decaen, but the English frigates still continued firing. At 3 p.m. the fire of the *Magicienne* stopped, and Bouvet seized this opportunity of sending Roussin with some men to take possession of the *Nereid*. With him went a midshipman, young Wantzloeben, a native of the Isle of France, fourteen years old, who gave an account of what he witnessed there. The frigate's deck was covered with wounded and dead men and severed limbs. On a chest on the quarter deck something was rolled up in a Union Jack, which Roussin uncovered with deep emotion. This was Willoughby himself, who lay senseless, unable to answer the French officer's sympathetic inquiries. Down in the batteries gun carriages were broken to pieces, guns turned over, port holes smashed. On the lower deck a number of wounded were being attended to by surgeons. At the foot of the mizen-mast a group of men lay prostrate, in deep despair, their heads reclining on their arms, evidently awaiting their fate, whatever it might be. During the night, they said, they had vainly tried to place a light on the vessel's poop to show they had surrendered; but every one who had attempted this had been shot down by the fire from the *Bellone*.

The *Nereid* went into action with 281 men—officers, sailors and soldiers—and 230 of them were either killed or wounded! About fifteen others had gone in the boat dispatched to Captain Pym and had been taken on board the *Sirius*.

According to Admiral Bertie, Willoughby had not struck his flag till "after a glorious resistance, almost unparalleled in the brilliant annals of the British Navy"; whilst Admiral Jurien de la Gravière, who was acquainted with most of the heroes of Grand Port, declared that the British Navy could not, on that eventful day, have made choice of a braver champion.

The dead were thrown into the sea and the wounded sent on board the *Victor*. Willoughby was carried in a hammock to the *Bellone* and laid near Duperré, Head-Surgeon Scott being allowed to look after him. The French flag was now hoisted on the *Nereid*, her guns spiked, and Roussin left with the nineteen French prisoners who were still on board.

The cannonade still continued. At 5 p.m. the *Magicienne* gave up the fight, water being nine feet deep in her hold. At 7.30 p.m. she was abandoned, the crew passing on board the *Iphigenia*, and Captain Curtis set fire to his frigate. Then had the French to take precautions against an explosion. Between 10 and 11 p.m., the *Magicienne's* guns, being loaded and pointed against the French, went off one after another, carrying destruction all around. A moment after, the frigate was blown up with appalling noise. Although her crew was fully as strong as that of the *Nereid*, she had only eight killed and twenty wounded. The French employed the remainder of the night in observing the *Sirius* and *Iphigenia*, and attempting to float their own vessels again.

[Photo by permission, Ladies' Fine Needlework Association.

BAIE DU CAP.

On the 25th, at daybreak, the *Iphigenia* recommenced her efforts to get away, and the assistance she attempted towards the *Sirius*, which could in no way alter its position, was fruitless.

Bouvet, for his part, was busy in a similar manner He gave up for the moment the idea of floating the frigates, finding it easier to begin with the *Victor*. Soon after, Pym relinquished his efforts to save his splendid vessel, which had not lost a single man. He sent his crew on board the *Iphigenia*, and at 9 a.m. he set fire to the *Sirius*, which exploded two hours later, just as the *Victor*, having got into deep water, was advancing towards her.

In the afternoon, Decaen and his staff proceeded to the *Bellone* to congratulate Bouvet, and insisted upon Duperré consenting to be taken to Mahébourg, where he and Willoughby were accommodated in the house of a colonist, Mr. de Robillard, and most kindly nursed and looked after. The wounded were also sent on shore.

At 8 p.m., before the *Iphigenia* had reached the anchorage at Ile de la Passe, Captain Lambert sent Lieutenant Watling to Bourbon in a pinnace, with letters to Commodore Rowley, advising him of the melancholy circumstances. This boat was seen at a distance by the *Entreprenant*, a corvette belonging to Hamelin's squadron, and chased but not overtaken.

On the 26th, in the morning, the *Minerve* was at last floated, and she and the *Victor* made for the *Iphigenia*, whilst the *Bellone*, being also lifted up, moored close to the *Nereid*. The *Ceylon* was still in the same position; but, although contrary winds prevented the seizure of this desired prize, the *Iphigenia's* escape was opposed.

At 11 a.m., on the 27th, appeared at last Hamelin's squadron, composed of the *Venus*, commanded by himself, the *Manche*, Captain Dornal de Guy, and the *Astrée*, Captain Lemarant. The *Entreprenant* now rallied her squadron. Hamelin had left Port Napoleon on the 21st August, and, with the view of reaching Mahébourg sooner, had taken a southward course. Meeting with tremendous seas, he was compelled to alter his direction and proceeded north and east, being constantly delayed by adverse winds, and especially by the lack of men; for about a third of the crews had been detached to defend the batteries ashore, and some of those had afterwards been sent to the aid of Duperré.

Until then the *Iphigenia* had stoutly prepared for action, keeping only 500 men on board and sending the remainder to occupy the battery at Ile de la Passe so as to make an energetic defence. About 3 p.m. Hamelin had come close to the island; Pym then realized the impossibility of opposing those combined forces; the more so as provisions and water were sorely needed, both on the frigate and in the fort.

Being well assured that the English could not escape, Decaen signalled to Hamelin to keep aloof and abstain from communicating with the shore. This, however, Hamelin did not rightly understand; so he took upon himself to offer a capitulation to Captain Lambert, requesting the immediate surrender of the frigate and fort, and promising that the prisoners should be sent to Bourbon within a month, to which Lambert agreed after some discussion.

BAIE DU CAP.

Early on the 28th, Decaen, being ignorant of these arrangements, now sent an ultimatum to Captain Lambert, who informed him of the agreement to which he had just assented. The Captain-General, wroth as he was at Hamelin's interference, liberally granted the conditions stipulated, and at 11 a.m. the French flag floated on the *Iphigenia* and the fort of Ile de la Passe.

The French losses had been extremely heavy; out of the 600 men composing Duperré's division the *Bellone* had 13 killed and 35 wounded; the *Minerve*, 15 killed and 42 wounded; the *Victor*, 4 killed and 1 wounded; the *Ceylon*, 4 killed and 19 wounded; and the detachment of marines, 15 wounded; making in all 36 killed and 112 wounded, some most severely.

Such was this memorable fight, in which the most splendid courage was displayed on both sides. "The noble behaviour of the *Nereid's* officers and crew," says James, "threw such a halo of glory around the defeat at Grand Port that, in public opinion at least, the loss of the four frigates was scarcely considered a misfortune!"

Years after, Colonel G. B. Malleson wrote: "Thus ended the first attempt of the English on the Isle of France. If we are bound to admire the pluck, the daring, the determination displayed by our countrymen, we cannot, in candour, refuse an equally appreciative acknowledgment of the combined skill and courage by which Duperré converted an apparently certain defeat into a most decisive victory."

Commenting on the battle, *The Planters' and Commercial Gazette*, of Mauritius, in its issue of December 7th, 1912, said:

"Mauritians, and most Englishmen in Mauritius, know the unpretentious monument on Regatta Point at Mahébourg that commemorates the officers and men, British and French alike, who fell in the battle; and old residents will not have forgotten the fine historic château, just outside the town, with its brass plaque recording that Willoughby, Captain of the *Nereid*, and Duperré, the French Commodore, were tended, side by side, within its walls.

"That old house not long since passed into the hands of a disciple of the Utilitarian School, who has shown his sound common-sense by promptly extracting from the estate the largest possible return for his money. In accordance with this business-like policy, its orchards and gardens have been cleared away and canes planted up to its venerable walls, its avenue of fruit trees has been felled, and its very brass plaque sold perhaps ere now for what it would fetch as old metal.

"Such methods are admittedly strenuous, practical, and up-to-date; but that 'We are not cotton-spinners all' is as true to-day as when Tennyson wrote it sixty years ago. Those of us who do not reckon all values in terms of rupees and cents, and still retain a certain veneration for the past, were weak enough to feel some regret when the old house changed hands.

"But no voice was raised in protest, no campaign was started in the local press, no public subscription opened, no wealthy and patriotic Mauritian came forward eager to purchase the famous building and present it to his grateful countrymen; and even our usually paternal Government omitted on this occasion to appear as *deus ex machina* and do for the Mauritians what they ought to have done for themselves.

"Thus was lost the opportunity of acquiring for a moderate sum a historic mansion, admirably fitted to serve as a museum for relics of the French occupation and similar objects of local interest; and such a chance is, alas! unlikely to recur.

"We English can perhaps afford to forget our defeat at Grand Port, since it left the main issue unaffected and offered merely a local and temporary check to our naval supremacy won at Trafalgar in 1805. But Frenchmen and Mauritians of French descent may surely be permitted to dwell with pride on the completeness of the victory won in Mahébourg Bay by French frigates over a British squadron of practically equal strength."

It was not till the 2nd October that Duperré. squadron, having been put in tolerable order, could leave Mahébourg for Port Napoleon, which it entered two days later.

This was for the French a complete success; they gained thereby two splendid frigates, whilst the English were left with one only, the *Boadicea*, and two corvettes, the *Otter* and *Staunch*. But fate had decided that the colony would derive no advantage from this temporary superiority. For some time to come Duperré's squadron was not expected to be fit for action. Only three frigates were immediately available, the *Venus*, *Iphigenia* and *Astrée*, and two corvettes, the *Victor* and *Entreprenant*. Had they at once pounced upon the English, they might have annihilated them and regained possession of Bourbon (Réunion); but quick action was indispensable and circumstances were unfavourable.

Duperré being wounded, Decaen would have by choice given the supreme command to Bouvet had he not feared to hurt the feelings of Hamelin, that officer being Bouvet's senior. His first mistake was in making two squadrons of one, and his next was his belief that the headquarters of the British forces were at St. Paul and not at Rodrigues. His plan was then to keep a strict blockade against Bourbon and to bring about its capitulation before reinforcements could arrive. He chose Bouvet for this object, and gave him command of the *Iphigenia*. Bouvet left Mahébourg on the 3rd September, accompanied by the *Astrée*, *Entreprenant* and *Victor*. The latter he sent to Port Napoleon to procure ammunition, and gave her an appointment off St. Rose. As she had not appeared on the 9th, Bouvet left the *Entreprenant* behind to wait for her and proceeded up the coast with the *Astrée*. On the 12th, in the morning, he descried three English men-of-war sailing out of St. Paul, and, meeting before St. Denis the *Africaine*, which had arrived from the Cape during the night, Bouvet withdrew in order to join his corvette, with the English in chase. As the *Africaine* was a fast sailer, she soon got ahead of the others and came into range at 3 a.m. This was just what Bouvet had expected, and, stopping immediately, he engaged in action with the result that at 4.30 the English frigate surrendered. At the break of day Commodore Rowley appeared with the three other vessels; but as his two frigates had badly suffered during the night, Bouvet did not await him. The *Boadicea*, therefore, took the *Africaine* in tow and led her back to Bourbon.

On the 17th, the English frigate *Ceylon* passed in front of Port Napoleon, coming from Madras with troops, the army chest, and the staff of the expedition under General Abercombie. Hamelin set off after her with the *Venus* and *Victor*, and closed on her at 1.30 a.m. about two leagues from St. Denis. During the terrific cannonade which ensued, the *Venus* lost one mast, the *Ceylon* her three top masts, and, as the *Victor* was coming up, the *Ceylon* surrendered at 5 a.m. Hamelin then ordered the corvette to tow her and make back for the Isle of France; but, steering under lower sails, they proceeded very slowly owing to the rough sea. The *Victor*, delayed by the heavy weight she was dragging, remained behind and was sighted by Rowley rapidly approaching with three ships; more sails were at once put on the *Victor*, but her cable broke, and the *Ceylon* was left a derelict. Hamelin, seeing he had no chance of escaping, determined to save the corvette at least, and commanded her to gain Port Napoleon, whilst he wheeled round to engage in unequal fight. After a desperate resistance he was obliged to surrender, and was taken a prisoner to St. Paul.

Meanwhile reinforcements were coming up to the British. On the 3rd November the Bombay squadron reached Rodrigues; on the 6th the Madras detachment; on the 12th all the forces available at Bourbon. Two more squadrons were expected, one from Bengal and the other from the Cape. It was decided to set out on the 22nd, and, on that very day, the Bengal contingent made an appearance and joined the fleet already under sail. The armament now consisted of 21 vessels, 46 transports, 11,300 European soldiers, 2,000 marines, and 2,700 Sepoys—16,000 men in all—while Decaen could only bring 2,000 effective men together.

The British fleet, delayed by strong currents, came in sight of the Isle of France on the 26th November, first twenty in number, then thirty-four on the 27th, sixty-five on the 28th, and seventy-four on the 29th; all anchoring along the Mapou coast. As the troops disembarked the small garrison at Grand Baie blew up Battery Malartic and retired. The English made their way towards the capital and were stopped for a time by the National Guards of Rivière du Rempart. After a most trying march they reached Powder Mills at 1 a.m. thoroughly exhausted. At break of day Colonel Macleod captured the small batteries of Baie aux Tortues and Tombeau Bay.

Decaen directed General Vandermaësen, with 1,300 men and the African battalion, to take a position in the plain at the foot of Montagne Longue; the Pamplemousses militia was ordered to occupy the heights, but failed to do so. Decaen then set out with twenty-five horsemen to reconnoitre within 100 yards of the enemy, when he was briskly pursued and retired. Three hundred men were detached to destroy the bridge on River du Tombeau; but this, also, was carelessly done.

On the 1st December, at sunrise, General Abercombie passed River du Tombeau on the cross-pieces of the bridge which had been left in place; but the artillery, of course, had to ford the stream and suffered some loss in so doing. Then the English assembled in the open country and marched forward. Vandermaësen suffered them to come to close quarters, when he assailed them with such a volley of musketry that they were thrown back in confusion. Still, reinforcements kept pouring on. A body of Sepoys now climbed to the top of Montagne Longue, which the French had neglected to occupy, and thence commanded the whole battlefield. Fearing he might be cut off, Vandermaësen retired slowly, in good order, whilst the Battery Dumas broke the impetus of the pursuers, forcing them to camp out of reach for the night.

Decaen was anxious to attempt still another effort. On the 2nd December, as he was about to march forward, he was told that the English, turning round Montagne Longue, had penetrated into Moka and were advancing on the capital through the Crève-Cœur Pass. Delaying his attack until he had obtained a supplement of information, he found he had received a false alarm, occasioned by a detachment of French seamen who, suffering from the heat, had taken off their vests and were displaying their red flannel shirts.

At the same time the Cape squadron had anchored and was setting down troops at Petite Rivière. Decaen, realizing that all was lost, and to avoid more bloodshed, asked for a truce in order to discuss the terms of a capitulation. At 11 p.m. Vandermaësen and Duperré were commissioned for this object, whilst the English commander appointed General Warde and Commodore Rowley. The conference lasted till 1 a.m. and was more than once on the verge of proving fruitless, the English willingly consenting to some demands but refusing to consider others. It was necessary to refer to the Captain-General, who finally gave in. At 3 a.m., every article being agreed upon, the draft was signed by the four Commissioners and sent to Generals Decaen and Abercrombie for their ratification.

The terms of the capitulation were that the troops were to retire with arms and luggage. They were not to be considered as prisoners of war, and were to be sent back to France at the cost of the Britis

Government. The inhabitants were to preserve their properties, religion, laws, and customs, and to be at liberty, during two years, to leave the colony with all their belongings.

This capitulation, in the opinion of Napoleon himself, was one of the most honourable that was ever granted.

THE BRITISH OCCUPATION.

R. T. Farquhar (1810-17).

The first English Governor, Mr. (afterwards Sir) Robert T. Farquhar, wa possessed of remarkable sharpness; he soon found out that the colonists, who had been depicted to him as a set of pirates and demagogues, were, on the contrary, most peaceful, good-natured and hospitable; particularly nice, however, on the point of honour, quick-tempered and resentful of unfair treatment; but as ready to cool down at the first manifestation of kindness. He strove to gain their hearts by coaxing both their sentiments and prejudices; and, in spite of the objections of some of the Government officials, he persisted in the dexterous policy which won for him, before long, the esteem and gratitude of the colony.

BEAU SEJOUR RIVER DAM, ROSE HILL.

On the other hand, a good many officers of the army could not brook the idea of being subordinated to a civilian; one or two even imagined that they had more right than Mr. Farquhar to the post he occupied, and complained to the Government at home. Their protestation at first met with some success, for on the 8th April, 1811, Mr. Farquhar was sent back to Bourbon and ordered to give up the management of the Isle of France to General Warde. He had expected that much, for the plot had been so secretly concocted that he only got information of it after the documents had been forwarded. He instantly parried the attack, and was confident that upon the arrival of his despatch things would be put in order; with the result that three months after, on the 11th July, he was reinstated.

General Warde's short tenure of office was signalled, in his very first public act, by the change of name of the colony, which hitherto had continued being called Isle of France, and now officially became Mauritius.

Next, on the 8th May, three French frigates appeared in sight of Grand Port. These were the long-promised assistance expected from France, and arrived, of course, too late. As soon as their commander realized that the colony had yielded to the English he retired, but was pursued, and, after an engagement at Tamatave, two of his frigates were captured.

In the month of January, 1813, the Act of Parliament for the Repression of the Slave Trade came into force. Mr. Farquhar perfectly understood the injustice of strictly enforcing this measure upon a newly-occupied colony, whose situation was particularly delicate, as slavery had ever been recognised by its laws, which were guaranteed by the capitulation. He thought it wiser to keep his eyes shut for a time, until he could obtain by persuasion what he could scarcely expect to gain by sheer force, and this was one of the motives brought forward by his enemies as a pretence that he had actually patronized the commerce of slaves.

During the same year, the island was visited by Lord Moira, Governor-General of Bengal, who was greeted with a show of regard and sympathy for his wonted kind treatment of the French prisoners of war in India.

It was not until the 15th October, 1814, that official information was conveyed of the Treaty of Peace by which Mauritius was ceded to Great Britain, whilst Bourbon was restored to France. This, of course, was a sore disappointment for many; but one good result of peace was the opening of Port Louis to foreign trade, and the colony immediately profited by it, although eighteen months later the Home Government inaugurated a system of troublesome restrictions.

On the 9th July, 1815, when the return of Napoleon from Elba was known, a sort of frenzy got the better of a few hair-brained persons, who sought the overthrow of the British authority in the belief that the neighbouring island of Bourbon would join in the rising. But in this they were deceived. The conspirators, a ridiculously small number, were to assemble at Plaine Magnan, march upon Mahébourg, and thence upon the capital. Their plan was, however, disclosed by the idle babbling of some of their number. General Butler, being informed of everything on the night preceding the appointed day, set out from Mahébourg, and, on reaching the place of assembly, saw about four hundred men, who scattered and fled in every direction at the first blast of the bugle. Two of the ringleaders were arrested and deported; one escaped and was never heard of again. At all events, the hopes of the Bonapartist party were soon ended when, a few days later, the news came of Napoleon's defeat at Waterloo.

BUNGALOW AT CHOISY, FLACQ.

The Act of Abolition was a fair pretext for Mr. Farquhar to cast his eyes upon Madagascar, a country which had long occupied his thoughts. He soon satisfied himself that, of all the petty chieftains reigning there, Radama was the man to be courted, as he would before long be the sole master of that immense territory. He sent him an envoy, flattered his pride by a display of amity and admiration, and made him agree to a treaty forbidding the exportation of slaves from his country, while, on the other hand, he would receive from the British Government a yearly subsidy of £2,000.

On the 25th September, 1816, about the fourth part of Port Louis was destroyed by a terrible conflagration, which could not be mastered until £35,000 worth of goods and property had been annihilated. In this emergency Mr. Farquhar's behaviour was worthy of all praise. He strove to assist the victims of the calamity, sheltering the houseless in the Government stores and in tents pitched at Champ de Mars, ordered distributions of victuals, stopped judicial proceedings in commercial matters, and sent ships abroad in search of assistance. He assembled a committee of notabilities, to whom he submitted what he had already achieved and what he intended doing next, and entrusted them with the care of rebuilding the destroyed part of the town. As the port had been closed some time before in virtue of instructions from the Home Government, he took upon himself to re-open it pending the approbation of the Prince Regent. He thought also of a permanent distribution of water in the section of Port Louis which had hitherto been deprived of it, and, for this object, and for many others of Municipal administration, he appointed Councils of Commune in Port Louis and the districts (8th September, 1817).

Mr. Farquhar then proceeded on leave to England, and, on the day of his departure, was rewarded by a most enthusiastic demonstration.

Major-General Hall (1817-18).

Major-General Hall, his temporary successor, was far from admiring his abilities; he even disliked him thoroughly and did all in his power to ruin what he had done. Major-General Hall was, however, a man of sound judgment on the whole, save in one particular subject. He was haunted by the ghost of the slave trade, which he saw everywhere, and, with the purpose of disclosing contraventions, he made use of every means, encouraging informers, even among the slaves, to whom he promised their liberty in payment of their good offices.

At that period several neutral ships happened to be in the harbour, laden with contraband goods, which their commanders had no intention of discharging. Major-General Hall insisted upon their being seized and prosecuted before the Admiralty Court. As the Commissary of Justice refused to acknowledge the competency of that tribunal, on the ground that breaches of the Customs laws were to be examined by Civil Courts, he was suspended, as well as the Collector of Customs, Colonel Draper, who, as a witness, had cleared the captains and agents of the ships of all fraudulent intent.

On the night of 28th February, 1818, Mauritius was visited by a most violent hurricane, which caused immense destruction to property. As soon as it was over, the Commune of Port Louis pointed out to Major-General Hall the dearth which was likely to befall the colony. He retorted that losses had been exaggerated on purpose, that nothing would be needed if monopolists would only retail articles of consumption at reasonable prices. Instead of constantly begging the Government's assistance, he suggested that the rich should start subscriptions, and that it would be far better for everybody if they assisted the authorities in eradicating the slave trade, which, he alleged, was still going on, a perpetual shame to the whole country. Moreover, he stated that he knew what he was about and could do very well without the Commune's advice.

Of course the Commune replied sharply, and Hall's astounding answer was that in former times everything went on smoothly without a Commune, and as he could not see the use of such an assembly, he asked it to have the goodness to disperse.

On the 4th June, being the anniversary of the birth of King George III., Major-General Hall held a levee, which proved a failure. On the very same day the suspended Commissary of Justice gave a dinner to Mr. de Freycinet, the French navigator, at which a good many notabilities were present, especially the Procureur-General, Mr. Virieux. This was enough for the irate soldier to dismiss the latter instantly.

Major-General Hall could not possibly back Mr. Farquhar's ideas about Madagascar; accordingly he recalled Mr. Hastie, the plenipotentiary at the Court of Radama, and cut off all intercourse with the Hova King.

On the 9th November, however, he received a severe rebuke from the Secretary of State, was ordered to reinstate immediately all those whose services he had dispensed with, and, that being done, to leave the colony after having transmitted his powers to the first officer in command of the garrison, pending the arrival of his successor, Major-General Ralph Darling. The President of the Council of Commune, thinking the moment had come to obtain the restoration of that body, applied to Major-General Hall, who would listen to nothing of the kind, as his orders contained no special mention of the Commune. He was replaced for about two months by Colonel Dalrymple, who recalled Mr. Virieux to his post and assented to the Council of Commune's request.

Major-General Darling (1819-20).

Major-General Darling was animated by the best possible motives, but totally lacked decision, and was too prone to accept everybody's advice, which, of course, only increased his constitutional perplexity. He was bound to become a puppet in the hands of the first man of strong mind who could influence him, and, unfortunately, that strong mind belonged to a man unscrupulous, ambitious, despotic and thoroughly hostile to the Mauritians, whose friendship he had of late pretended to court, but only as a means of revenge against Major-General Hall. This person was Mr. George Smith, the Commissary of Justice.

Major-General Darling honestly believed that the great majority of the population did not support the slave trade; but this comforting assurance was shaken by his ordinary adviser, through the occurrence of some fresh contraventions. Nevertheless, he never debased himself in imitating the shameful violence of his predecessor.

All went well enough till the 29th October, 1819, when H.M.'s frigate *Topaze*, Captain Lumley, arrived from Ceylon in a most lamentable sanitary condition. She was immediately granted access to the harbour for the mere sake of pleasing officers of the Royal Navy. The sick were sent to the public hospital and the convalescent landed at Ile aux Tonneliers. The Major-General was greatly surprised at the remonstrance of the Council of Commune regarding this breach of the quarantine laws, for he candidly declared his ignorance of the existence of such regulations; but he, nevertheless, refused permission for the re-embarkation of the sick and the removal of the frigate to some distance to leeward. He merely consented to take the advice of the chief Medical Officer, who was of opinion that there was not a shadow of danger.

On the 18th November a first casualty was reported of a strange disease, which was followed day by day by several others of an identical nature, all resembling *cholera morbus*. The doctors were assembled and could not agree as to the contagion of the malady, which increased in malignity; deaths became daily more numerous; the citizens fled to the country, Port Louis was deserted, and it became difficult even to bury the dead. During that very crisis Captain Lumley declared that, as the stormy season was setting in, he must take refuge in the inner harbour, at which the public got indignant and demanded the frigate's immediate departure for Seychelles, where she could spend the stormy season, as had always been done before. To this Captain Lumley finally assented (January, 1820).

Just then, the introduction of some slaves was denounced, and Major-General Darling, already exasperated at having been publicly reproached for allowing the outbreak of the epidemic through his lack of firmness, addressed an infuriated letter to the Commune, accusing the Mauritians of having, "in defiance of Divine laws," presented their request for the departure of the *Topaze* under pretence of "a hypothetical contagion," in order to give themselves up more freely to a heinous traffic. His insinuations were refuted by the Commune with more acrimony than was perhaps becoming, which resulted in its being once more dissolved.

In April following the *Topaze* was back, and although the cholera was then over, she had now to undergo an unwonted display of precautions. Captain Lumley insisting once more upon entering Trou Fanfaron, as his ship was in need of repairs, the chief Medical Officer, who had hitherto been a confirmed anti-contagionist, but had apparently changed his mind, now declared that, as the frigate had been put in quarantine, the law must be obeyed, and she would have to proceed to Flat Island, where she could be conveniently repaired and thoroughly disinfected as well.

Sir Robert T. Farquhar (1820-23).

Mr. Farquhar was knighted soon after his return to the island and the resumption of government on 5th July, 1820. He had failed to fulfil most of the promises he had made to the inhabitants at his departure, but this was not his fault, as he had been very acrimoniously impeached before the Cabinet, and all his ability was needed to clear himself. In this he succeeded, but his influence with the Government had waned, and he was distinctly made to understand that he had exposed his own interest in courting popular favour in a newly-conquered colony. Nevertheless, he had obtained the great boon of the opening of Port Louis Harbour to foreign nations on terms of reciprocity; but the good effect of this was then partly hindered by a financial crisis which lasted a considerable time.

With respect to the slave trade, Sir Robert Farquhar, far from persisting in the same errors as Major-Generals Hall and Darling, thought it more efficacious and more to the point to make an appeal to the honour of the inhabitants, suggesting also—and this was calculated to stimulate the energies of the more indolent—that, cholera having spread in Madagascar, a fresh introduction of blacks from that island would very likely be accompanied by a new introduction of the disease. He succeeded in his object, and, in spite of the assertions of prejudiced persons, it is a noteworthy fact that from that time the obnoxious trade was entirely suppressed in Mauritius, with the exception of one or two fruitless attempts a few months later.

Sir Robert's first care was to renew negotiations with Radama, and to invite that monarch to send him ambassadors. When these sailed for Mauritius they were accompanied by a prisoner of war, a chieftain named Ratsitatane, whose presence was dreaded by the Hova King among his people. This person was kept in custody without the public having any knowledge of his presence; but his confinement was not so strict as to forbid his having intercourse with the outside world. A Government apprentice (this was the term for blacks seized by the naval authorities on board slave ships), one Laïzaf, a Malagassy and a great rogue to boot, persuaded Ratsitatane that the slaves and the coloured population in Mauritius were dissatisfied and longed for independence, and that they would immediately start an insurrection if they found a leader whom they could openly acknowledge, for free men would in no case obey the commands of a slave, however clever he might be. The very man wanted, said Laïzaf, was, of course, Ratsitatane; and that simple-minded creature agreed to every proposal, contrived to escape in broad daylight, and took refuge on the Pouce Mountain, where his confederates were to join him. Having so far conducted the whole scheme, Laïzaf now went and denounced the plot to the police, who immediately apprised the Governor, at Réduit.

Meanwhile, at 4 p.m., on the 20th February, 1822, the citizens were not a little surprised at hearing the report of a musket, and at seeing a group of armed blacks promenading on the top of Champ de Lort Mountain. Assembling in alarm, they became aware, for the first time, of the presence of Ratsitatane in the colony, and of his evident intentions. They took to arms without loss of time and blamed the authorities' inaction. Then came Sir Robert, who, after a few words with Major-General Darling, directed twenty-five soldiers to climb up the mountain, while another detachment proceeded round Anse Courtois, to cut off the rebels, who, as soon as they saw the military coming up, fired a volley at random and took to their heels.

This happening whilst the Hova ambassadors were residing in Mauritius, led to the belief that they were the instigators of the plot, and the error was difficult to eradicate. Ratsitatane was captured the next day, and he and twenty-five of his followers sent to jail. Six of them were sentenced to hard labour, and Laizaf, one Latulipe, and Ratsitatane sentenced to death. The two latter were executed, and their heads exposed at the very place of the intended rising. Laïzaf was no doubt the most guilty, nay, the only guilty party; but, as he had turned informer under promise of escaping capital punishment, his sentence was commuted to penal servitude for life.

REGATTA DAY AT SALINE, NEAR PORT LOUIS.

This was the last important act of Sir Robert Farquhar while Governor of Mauritius, and as his successor, Sir Lowry Cole, was already appointed, he handed over the administration of the colony *pro tem.* to Major General Darling. His departure, on the 20th April, 1823, was by no means attended by the same demonstration of good will as he had been given five years previously. Major-General Darling remained quietly in office till the 13th June, when the new Governor replaced him.

Sir Lowry Cole (1823-28).

Sir Lowry Cole was a loyal and generous soldier, an active and amiable man, who soon won the esteem of the Mauritians in spite of his being rather strict about etiquette.

Sir Robert Farquhar had done much for agriculture; he had understood that cotton, coffee, indigo, cloves and nutmegs were particularly exposed to devastations from cyclones, and had the intuition that sugar-cane, more resistant and admirably adapted to the Mauritian soil, would before long take the lead of all those plantations and enrich the colony. The inhabitants shared in his belief and planted canes on a large scale; but they had to wrestle with a difficulty, the more discouraging because it was provoked by the Home Government itself, with the view of protecting the West Indian interests, which at all times were most actively represented in the House of Commons. Mauritius sugars were then liable in the United Kingdom to an extra import duty of 10/- per cwt. This, although not amounting to absolute prohibition, was most unfair treatment. During his previous stay in England, Sir Robert Farquhar had complained to the Government, but had had to give way to secret and very powerful influences; notwithstanding, he was so actuated by the justice of the cause that he publicly declared it would inevitably triumph before long. Still, as time passed without this result being obtained, Sir Robert, when he left the island with the intention of canvassing for a seat in Parliament, promised the Mauritians never to relinquish his efforts until he had attained his aim. He had in Sir Lowry Cole an enthusiastic supporter, and at last, in 1825, the colony was freed from its sugar handicap.

Cane plantations immediately developed enormously as new lands were cleared, roads opened, and steam power applied to mills. From 18,000,000 lbs., the colony's output rose in 1827 to 41,000,000 lbs., and increased from year to year. This sudden dawn of prosperity provoked the resentment of the Anti-Slavery Society, who, through a most stubborn antagonism of race and narrow-mindedness, held the Mauritians in deep aversion, and strove by all means, especially by perfidious and false insinuations, to ruin them in the eyes of the English people. Sad to say, the Society's influence was so great with the Cabinet that the colony was subsequently traduced in Parliament, and both Sir Robert Farquhar and Sir Lowry Cole had no easy task in refuting the calumnies that were spread.

A Commission of Inquiry had been appointed some years before to report upon the administration of the Cape, Mauritius, and Ceylon; it was composed of Mr. Bigge, Major Colebrooke, and Mr. Blair, and reached Mauritius in 1826. These gentlemen remained in the island for more than two years, and their report, which came out some twenty-four months later, merely repeated, with the exception of a few reasonable recommendations as to retrenchment in the Civil Service, the false accusations got up by the Anti-Slavery Society.

THE POUCE, FROM MOKA.

The British Plenipotentiary at the Court of Radama having died, that monarch began to display petty signs of independence and to refuse being dictated to by the Mauritius Government. He set up a commercial tariff increasing the Customs dues to such an extent that the Mauritian trade, consisting chiefly of oxen and salt meat, would be well-nigh ruined. Sir Lowry Cole remonstrated with him, and pointed out that Radama himself would be the loser by it. As Radama did not concur therein, the Governor sent his own nephew, Lieut. H. Cole, and another officer, Lieut. Campbell, to try and persuade him *viva voce*. The wily potentate managed to avoid having an interview with them. As they were on their way from the coast, and had nearly reached the capital, he sent word to them to turn back, as he himself was proceeding to Tamatave, and would see them there. They returned accordingly, but Lieut. Cole, who had lately been suffering from malaria, so terrible in those parts, died of the disease.

Radama now saw that he had gone too far, and tried to accommodate matters by a most strange proceeding. His secretary managed to get possession, for a few hours, of the letter addressed to the officers on their way, to which a *post-scriptum* was dexterously added, mentioning that if they preferred continuing their journey to Antananarivo, they would be welcomed there. Lieut. Campbell stoutly denied that this option had existed in the letter when it first reached them; Radama's secretary was positive that it had; and as there remained then only two witnesses, one for and one against, the King deeply deplored the young officer's demise and abstained from giving an opinion. An inquiry was made thereon by a new envoy, Doctor Robert Lyall, specially chosen by the Home Government on account of his diplomatic abilities, but he never succeeded in getting at the truth. He may have been instructed not to press Radama too hard, and so the matter ended.

The last part of Sir Lowry Cole's administration was signalled by a casualty which nearly brought an end to the cordiality of his intercourse with the inhabitants. A ship arrived from Ceylon with Sir Hudson Lowe as a passenger. This officer stayed for three days in the colony and went about without attracting any notice. At the time of his departure, however, just as he was proceeding to the quay in company with the Governor's aide-de-camp, a group of young men, notorious for their Napoleonic sympathies, hooted and pelted him with stones. Sir Lowry deeply resented this offence to a guest and a fellow soldier, his equal in rank, and, wrongly believing that the insult had been directed against the British Army, held the whole population responsible for the misbehaviour of some twenty foolish individuals. The more sensible of the inhabitants energetically protested and pointed out that Sir Hudson Lowe, as an individual and not as a British officer, had been the victim of this ungenerous attack, and that the great majority of the population had had no share in it. His Excellency replied that he never had the slightest doubt about it, and that his words had apparently been misconstrued.

On the 18th June, 1823, Sir Lowry Cole, who had been appointed Governor of the Cape of Good Hope, handed over the administration of Mauritius to Sir Charles Colville and remained two months more in the island as a private individual, until he embarked upon a vessel of war for the seat of his new government.

"COMPANY'S GARDENS," PORT LOUIS, showing Offices of the Medical Health Department.

Sir Charles Colville (1828-33).

Sir Charles Colville, K.C.B., was placed in a very awkward situation. Although of a most polite and sympathetic nature, he had assumed a terrible responsibility to which he was certainly not equal. The Cabinet, compelled to fulfil engagements taken with the Abolitionists, began to adopt a series of harsh, vexatious, and even ridiculous measures, under pretence of ameliorating the condition of slaves. The first of these was the creation of a Protector of Slaves, armed with almost unlimited powers. The population objected to this novelty because those very functions were already vested in the Procureur-General, and especially because the newcomer, knowing nothing of the colony, would too surely be animated by prejudice and ill-will. But the Protector was, nevertheless, appointed, and proved to be the very sort of man that had been dreaded.

After this, year after year, and oftener still, further so-called ameliorations were enforced, and the Protector's intervention became more and more unbearable.

In 1830 the report of the Commissioners of Inquiry was published, as well as an essay in the *Anti-Slavery Reporter*, the latter accusing the colony at large, and even the Courts of Justice and authorities, of the most atrocious barbarity towards the slaves. It was now suddenly announced, by two Members of Parliament to several commercial firms in Mauritius, that the Abolitionists had obtained from the Cabinet an order for the immediate emancipation of the slaves who had been introduced since 1814. This was one of the Commission's recommendations. Although the local Government had not been officially advised of this measure, the population took alarm and decided upon sending Mr. Adrien d'Epinay as a delegate to remonstrate with the Colonial Office on the danger of such a decision, and to present, at the same time, a project of emancipation of their own, together with a series of revindications, the chief of which were the maintenance of the colonial laws as guaranteed by the capitulation; the resumption of the Colonial Constitution of 1791, which had never been abrogated, but simply suspended for ten years in 1803; the creation of a representative body to share in the internal administration; and the admission of Mauritians to all offices in the Civil Service, etc. "The Mauritians are British subjects," they said, "and, as such, demand nothing more than being treated as all other British citizens are."

Mr. Adrien d'Epinay left the island on 10th October, 1830, and was received in London by Lord Goderich, Secretary of State for the Colonies, who, after some discussion, granted him the annulment of the measure concerning slaves introduced since 1814. As for a representative assembly, his Lordship would only consent to a Legislative Council composed of half of official and half of unofficial members. He promised many things more ; but as soon as the colonial envoy had departed, the Anti-Slavery Society more than ever recovered its influence over Lord Goderich. Mr. Adrien d'Epinay arrived back in Mauritius on 25th October, 1831.

Early in 1832 Mr. John Irving, M.P., agent of the colony in London *vice* Sir Robert Farquhar, deceased, communicated to his constituents the draft of an Order in Council, dated 2nd November, 1831, and presented to the House of Commons for discussion, by which the power of the Protector of Slaves was brought to such an extent that he became, as it were, the supreme legal authority in the colony, the law conferring upon him capacities which were denied to regular Courts of Justice. Slaves were thereby allowed at any time and in any number to absent themselves in order to complain to the Protector, and in all cases the burden of proof lay on their masters. A general outburst of indignation arose, and once again protestations were presented to Sir Charles Colville, who could only answer that he had not been officially advised of the existence of such a measure. This was true enough for the time being, but still, the inhabitants knew too well now what they could expect from the Cabinet, and did not place any confidence in this equivocal assertion. That they were so far right was proved by the fact that, on the 23rd March following, the Order in Council in question reached the local Government, although it was not intended that it should be put into force immediately. At the same time it was announced that the Minister had chosen Mr. John Jeremie, lately Chief Justice at St. Lucia, to fill the post of Procureur-General. This man, whom the colony's friends in London depicted as a "firebrand of discord" and as an instrument of the Anti-Slavery party, had already reached the Cape, and could be expected before very long.

PLAINE VERTE, SUBURB OF PORT LOUIS.

In the well-meant but thoughtless intention of making himself better known to the colony he was about to upset, Jeremie had had himself preceded by a series of Essays which he had published the year before, and in which, although he stoutly denied it later, he made no secret of his prejudices against the Mauritians, and, what was worse, during his stay at the Cape, he caused to be printed in a newspaper a few lines in which his animosity was clearly established. Of course, the general belief after all this was that he was sent on purpose to proclaim the immediate emancipation of slaves, without any compensation to their masters. Excited as they were, the Mauritians could certainly not realize that their fears were exaggerated. It must also be borne in mind that the chief cause of this particular feeling was due to the perusal of Mr. James McQueen's *Letters to the Duke of Wellington*, which had reached the colony some time before. So they determined to oppose, by all constitutional means, the entering of Mr. Jeremie upon his duties. It was not so much the man himself they dreaded, as the effect which his

GOVERNMENT HOUSE, RÉDUIT.

coming would produce on the slave population. Mr. Jeremie's appointment, as Mr. A. d'Epinay so rightly declared afterwards, was nothing but a particular grievance in a whole series of grievances.

The slaves had very soon been informed of these matters, which could not leave them indifferent; and as some ominous signs of insubordination had been noticed among them, the inhabitants requested Sir Charles Colville to allow the creation of a militia for the purpose of keeping watch over the slaves and preventing mischief, which was readily granted.

Mr. Jeremie arrived in the evening of 3rd June, 1832. Report of his coming had immediately been spread in the districts, and the country people had forthwith set out for town, walking all night. On the following morning, an enormous crowd anxiously assembled in front of Government House. The Port Louis militia was present and assisted the troops in keeping order. All shops, offices, and even the bazaar, were closed, and it had been decided that they should continue so as long as Mr Jeremie would remain in the colony. This sort of negative protestation had received the name of "Inertia." In the afternoon, Sir Charles Colville, who had been impatiently expected all day, at last drove down from Réduit; he was instantly approached by a group of persons who presented him with an address expressing the wish that the Procureur-General would not be allowed to disembark. Sir Charles could not grant this, of course, but he promised that Mr. Jeremie would not disembark till the next day. On the 5th June, between 6 and 7 a.m., Mr. Jeremie landed, escorted by a strong body of troops. As he proceeded along Place d'Armes to Government House he was hooted and hissed. On the same afternoon he was sworn in and took his seat in the Council, although his installation at the Supreme Court was postponed to the 22nd, owing to the usual holiday at the Courts of Justice.

On this eventful morning, at 10 o'clock, just as a large crowd was awaiting him on Place d'Armes, Mr. Jeremie slipped out of Government House by the back door, accompanied by Sir Charles's private secretary. Choosing the moment when a detachment of mounted police was going up Government Street, he dodged between the horses to escape notice. Close behind him, as if to cover his rear, went the carts of the scavengering and night-soil service. Nobody ever dreaming that he would proceed in such company, he managed to reach the Court House unobserved. But the Vice-President, Mr. Virieux, was not to be found there and refused to appear, because, in his opinion, the Court was not regularly constituted, and all proceedings would therefore be null. The ceremony was accordingly adjourned in spite

of Mr. Jeremie's exasperation. He retired to his office, but when he attempted to leave it the crowd had thronged in front of the door to such an extent that it was necessary to request the troops to give assistance to the police. The soldiers soon made way for him; but, as he ventured outside, he met with such a hot reception —his hat being knocked down with a stick—that he lost his temper and commanded the troops to charge the mob. In so doing they made use of their bayonets and several persons, mostly belonging to the coloured population, were slightly wounded.

VERANDAH OF GOVERNMENT HOUSE, RÉDUIT.

As Government Street was full of onlookers the police, in order to avoid further bloodshed, ingeniously resorted once more to the malodorous carts, which came rattling down the street at full speed, easily dispersing the people who had nothing but umbrellas with which to defend themselves—a unique method of quelling a riot.

On the next day the Governor was requested to authorize a public meeting, where the real desire of the people regarding Mr. Jeremie could be made known. This was granted for the 27th June; and the unanimous desire expressed there was that Mr. Jeremie should not remain in Mauritius. Sir Charles, however, declined giving his sanction until a sitting of the Legislature, on the 7th July, to which he invited fifty-seven persons of distinction. There a motion was presented by Mr. A. d'Epinay to the effect that, instead of being dismissed, Mr. Jeremie should be directed by the Government to proceed to England with all despatch, in order to give an account of the lamentable state of things in the colony. This was seconded by Colonel Draper and carried by an immense majority. Still, Sir Charles hesitated again and put off his final decision until the day after, when a regular meeting of the Council could examine the question. The result was identical, in spite of Mr. Jeremie's attempt to intimidate both Governor and officials as to the responsibility they might assume. A few public functionaries backed him up; some abstained from giving an opinion; two of them, Chief Justice Blackburn and Colonel Draper, were independent enough to vote according to their conscience, and sided with the unofficial members who unanimously insisted upon Mr. Jeremie's departure. Sir Charles at last consented, but stipulated that Mr. Jeremie's commission would have to be registered first. As soon as the news became public shops and offices were opened as usual, after having been closed for forty days.

DRAWING ROOM OF GOVERNMENT HOUSE, RÉDUIT.

At 4 o'clock in the morning of July 28th, before daybreak, Mr. Jeremie left surreptitiously the Line Barracks, where he had lately taken up his abode, and, escorted by a detachment of troops, embarked near the Artillery Bridge, promising that he would soon return, when the Mauritians would have to pay dearly for his humiliation. It was evident that the colony had everything to dread from a man who, in that state of mind, would be at liberty to relate the events after his own fashion. A memorial was, therefore, addressed to the Home Government, explaining all that had occurred. But before this could reach London Mr. Jeremie had already given his own version to Lord Goderich, and insisted upon the impudence of the "rebels" who had taken up arms with no other end than to oppose by force the execution of His Majesty's commands. Mr. Jeremie was accordingly directed to return to his post; but, before he could set out, it was decided, as Sir Charles Colville had sent in his resignation and his successor was already appointed, to hasten the new Governor's departure.

Sir William Nicolay (1833-40).

Sir William Nicolay, C.B., was accordingly despatched in a flurry, bearer of a series of thundering Orders in Council, which he was instructed to make known upon landing. He reached Port Louis on the 30th January, 1833, in a high state of apprehension, believing he would find the island in open rebellion. No such condition prevailed, however. He peacefully took possession of his post, and began by informing Messrs. Virieux, Draper, and Adrien d'Epinay that His Majesty dispensed with their respective services of Vice-President of the Court of Appeal, Collector of Customs, and Member of the Legislature. Next he published the Orders in Council of which he was the bearer, and which commanded, under pain of death, the immediate disbandment of the armed corps of Volunteers, which, be it said, had already been dispersed immediately after Mr. Jeremie's departure some six months previously.

In this emergency the inhabitants decided to send Mr. d'Epinay once more to England to put matters right and explain how far the Minister had been deceived by one-sided reports. He set out with Sir Charles Colville on the 26th February.

Now Sir William Nicolay could not help feeling a little ashamed of the part he was called upon to play. His first minute to Lord Goderich expressed his surprise at finding everything so quiet in the island, and his conclusion that what had been reported had certainly been much exaggerated. Nevertheless, Mr. Jeremie had also his supporters in Mauritius, and these exerted themselves to the utmost to prevent Sir William Nicolay's cooling down until the Procureur-General's return.

Mr. Jeremie was back on the 29th April, escorted by 500 soldiers. Thus had the Minister willed in spite of the remonstrances of many of the principal London merchants who had interests in the island. The reason for it was not, it appears, so much from a natural aversion towards acknowledging his own errors, or a charitable desire of healing Mr. Jeremie's wounded feelings, as from the necessity of courting the favour of the Abolitionists, in view of the forthcoming elections. Mr. Jeremie, however, assumed his office without meeting the slightest opposition, and, at the same time, the seat of Judge in the Inferior Court was bestowed upon one Mr. John Reddie, a very young Scotch advocate, who had been sent out a few months before in order to back his patron in case of need, which he did!

Mr. Jeremie hated Chief Justice Blackburn, and did all in his power to ruin him, whilst Mr. Reddie's impudence towards his superior passed all conception. After sundry incidents which disclosed the new Procureur-General's nervousness, that officer prevailed upon the Governor to order the late body of Volunteers to surrender their arms and ammunition. But they had never been equipped with anything but sporting guns, which it was perfectly lawful to possess; neither muskets, nor stores of gunpowder—cannons were even mentioned in the proclamation!—had ever been at their disposal. Consequently none of these were forthcoming, in spite of reiterated searches.

Having failed in this first object, Mr. Jeremie now gathered information of an alleged plot at Grand Port for the attack of one of the line regiments on its way from Mahébourg to Port Louis, and the overthrow of the Government. This was supposed to have taken place the year before, a few days after his arrival. Five gentlemen of Grand Port were consequently arrested, arraigned for high treason on the 29th August, 1833, and detained for 210 days before being brought to trial. Mr. Jeremie's aim for such a lengthened procedure was to upset the Supreme Court and get a magistracy appointed after his own heart. He now lodged in the hands of the Governor a recusation of the judges of that tribunal, couched in such insulting terms that the Executive appointed to decide upon the merits of the case rejected his recusation with some very pointed criticisms.

The Grand Rebellion case was opened on the 10th March, 1834, and occupied eighteen sittings, during which Mr. Jeremie showed himself as he really was: an able debater, no doubt, but a man of vindictive disposition, highly prejudiced against the accused, and absolutely incapable of mastering his temper. The verdict returned was an acquittal on all charges. Soon after, even before he had been advised of the result, the Minister ordered Mr. Jeremie's dismissal, chiefly on account of his outrageous behaviour towards the Supreme Court, and the extraordinary delays he had allowed to elapse before the case of the accused was disposed of. A few days later Mr. Reddie was also dismissed, and the colony freed from both of them They did not patiently bear their punishment, however; when they arrived in London they did all they could to have the decision repealed, and abused Messrs. Blackburn, Draper and d'Epinay, Sir William Nicolay himself, and even three Ministers who had in succession been at the head of the Colonial Office—Lord Goderich, Mr. Stanley and Mr. Spring Rice. According to their own view of the case everybody had blundered except Messrs. Jeremie and Reddie.

Mr. d'Epinay now came back from England. He had met with the greatest difficulty this time before he could obtain an interview with the Minister. Of course, prejudice was rife against him; yet he managed to force his own account of the recent events, and as at that very moment the Cabinet had to oppose some extravagant pretensions of the Abolitionists with regard to emancipation, Mr. d'Epinay's advice was more than once solicited and proved most valuable. In short, if he did not obtain any direct advantage for the colony, his presence greatly advanced its interests. After his return to Mauritius, Sir William Nicolay, who could never brook his independent ways, kept on showing Mr. d'Epinay signs of his antipathy, until the departure of the latter in 1837 to settle in France.

Things then went on quietly enough. The principle of compensation had been adopted by Parliament, but the Abolitionists at home endeavoured by all means to deprive the colony of the portion of indemnity to which it was entitled, and they succeeded in some measure. When the emancipation of slaves took place on the 1st April, 1835, not the slightest disorder occurred. Of course, the new class of free men refused categorically to employ themselves as labourers any longer, and planters were obliged to resort to Indian immigration, which was alternately authorised and forbidden. Years elapsed before the question could be settled.

The close of Sir William Nicolay's government was signalled by an extraordinary incident which nearly created a conflagration between England and France. The Mauritians had nothing whatever to do with it; and, but for the indignation they may have felt in presence of such arbitrary proceedings, their behaviour was correct and such as might have been expected.

In August, 1839, two French corvettes, the *Lancier* and the *Isère* entered Trou Fanfaron to be thoroughly repaired. A few days after, the British merchant ship *Greenlaw*, Captain Driver, cast anchor in the harbour. The French officers had been invited to a dance on shore, and had lent their flags to decorate the hall. On the 7th September the flags were returned in the absence of the two commanders, Messrs. de Chanfray and de Tinant, who were on a visit to some friends in Grand Port. Before packing up the ensigns, the men on board tied them one after another, just as they came, and hoisted them to get dry. It happened that some British flags unintentionally occupied the lowest position. This highly displeased Captain Driver, who determined to take revenge of what he considered an insult to his country. On the next day he ordered the French colours to be attached under his vessel's bowsprit, so that they trailed in the sea. The position of the corvettes prevented a view of what was going on at the *Greenlaw's* bowsprit; but as one of the *Isère's* boats came back from the shore, the officer in charge of the ship was warned by his men of the dishonoured flag, and, instantly proceeding on board the *Greenlaw*, requested Captain Driver to remove it at once. He refused under pretence that he was doing nothing more than retaliating for the insult to the Union Jack on the previous day. The French officer replied that no insult had been meant, and assured him that the arrangement of the flags had been quite fortuitous. In spite of this explanation, Captain Driver would not give in unless so ordered by the Governor.

When the French commanders came back, they lodged a complaint with Sir William Nicolay, who readily admitted their explanations and, with some reluctance, directed Captain Driver to write a letter of apology and to hoist the French flag as a reparation, at the top of his main-mast on the Sunday following, as the offence had taken place on a Sunday.

Everything seemed quite settled, but, unfortunately, His Excellency was prevailed upon to change his mind, and ordered the French commanders to display the Union Jack at the time the *Greenlaw* would hoist the French colours. This the officers refused to do, saying bygones were bygones, and pointed out that compliance with the Governor's order would be tantamount to admitting that they had committed an outrage of which they had not been guilty. Sir William made no reply, but on the Sunday following a number of troops and artillery were sent to occupy the banks of Trou Fanfaron, threatening with destruction the two corvettes, one of which was bereft of her rudder, and the other lay on her side, with her flank wide open. When the appointed time came, and no British flag was hoisted by the French, it was expected that something dreadful would happen. Two hours elapsed, however, and then the troops and artillery were withdrawn.

The Governor's explanation, in an order he addressed to the garrison, was that he had felt reluctant to make a show of violence against two disabled vessels. He, however, prohibited the French crews from having any communication with the main-land except those of a strictly businesslike nature. Unaware of this prohibition, Mr. de Tinant went the next day as usual to look after his ship's affairs, was kept at dinner by a friend, and in the evening proceeded to the quay to return on board the *Isère*, when he was arrested, taken to the guard-house, and, in spite of his protestation, brought to the Governor by the officer in charge. Sir William Nicolay, who had retired to bed, would not trouble to set him free till next morning.

In the following afternoon the corvettes left for Bourbon as well as they could, and the Governor there, Mr. de Hell, sent his Mauritian colleague a sharply-worded official letter, which was soon heard of in Europe and made a great commotion for some time.

In the following year a British corvette, the *Lily*, anchored in Port Louis harbour with smallpox on board. The sanitary authorities decided this time upon strictly enforcing the quarantine laws; but, in spite of their exertions, the disease crept in, and a few months later an epidemic broke out, which fortunately did not prove of a very malignant nature.

Sir William Nicolay's administration having come to an end, he left Mauritius on the 20th February, 1840, and was certainly regretted by nobody; for if he, personally, did no harm, he at all events never attempted to do any good to the colony.

Before his successor arrived the Government was provisionally entrusted to Colonel Power, the Officer in Command of the Forces. During his rule of four months and a half the only event worth recording is the announcement of Adrien d'Epinay's death, which took place in Paris on the 9th December, 1839. In accordance with his request, his body was brought back to his native land, and arrived on board the *Amphitrite* on the 26th May, 1840. His funeral took place on the 1st June and was attended by an immense crowd of people. On leaving the Cathedral the procession drove to Pamplemousses Cemetery, where his body was laid in the grave, after some appropriate speeches from his bosom friends, retracing the distinguished Mauritian's career.

Sir Lionel Smith (1840-42).

Sir Lionel Smith, K.C.B., became Governor of Mauritius on the 6th July, 1840. He was a man of polite manners, broad views, and energetic temper, altogether devoid of passion and prejudice, and had no other aim but the advancement of the colony by the removal of the hindrances which had, ever since the emancipation, been encountered by the planters in carrying on their industry. To attain this end he refuted the unfounded assertions, unceasingly circulated in England by the Mauritians' stubborn and narrow-minded opponents, as to their cruelty to coolies. He then strove to obtain for them the resumption of Indian immigration; but his tenure of office was too short for their welfare. He died at Réduit on the 2nd January, 1842, of pneumonia, by which he had been attacked while attending his sick wife, who also died three days later.

Sir William Gomm (1842-49).

Colonel Staveley then administered the colony till the arrival of the new Governor, Sir William Gomm, K.C.B., on the 21st November following. He brought the gratifying news that Indian immigration was at last authorized, under the supervision of an agent residing in India, and this was, of course, followed by a series of local regulations on the matter. On the other hand several measures, which transpired a little later, were not so thankfully received by the population. Ever since 1841 it had been decided by the Home Government that, in future, the English text of local laws would be the only official version. Formerly both French and English texts were held as such. In 1846 a further step was taken in that direction, and it was declared that from the 15th July, 1847, all proceedings before the Superior Courts, comprising the Court of Appeal, the Assize Court, the Tribunal of First Instance, and the Vice-Admiralty Court, should be carried on exclusively in English. This produced a feeling, not exactly of discontent, but of sadness, inasmuch as it was the disappearance of another cherished custom of old times.

In the hope of counterbalancing such melancholy thoughts, Lady Gomm started the idea of completing Malartic's monument in the Champ de Mars, by means of a Fancy Fair, whereby the necessary funds were secured, and the work finished in the following year. She also gave a series of dancing parties; one of which was held on the 14th July, a most injudicious date. The population deeply resented it as a premeditated contempt of the general feelings, and crowded round the Lodge La Triple Espérance, where the ball was taking place. Several Mauritian families, who had not cared to respect the prevailing sentiment, were loudly vociferated as they entered the hall.

At the same time, the Court of Appeal was still sitting in a house at the corner of Government and La Bourdonnais Streets, and a young barrister, Mr. C. Antelme, who was to make himself a name by and by, was intentionally procrastinating the debates in order to gain time; so that, when the clock struck twelve, he was still speaking in his mother-tongue. In a few pathetic words he alluded to the Order in Council and sat down. When he left the Court he was frantically cheered and accompanied as far as Church Square, where another large crowd had assembled and was contemplating the removal of several wounded persons, as well as commenting bitterly on what had taken place.

GOVERNOR MALARTIC'S MONUMENT, CHAMP DE MARS.

As the police were unable to put a stop to the demonstration before the Lodge, the stewards of the ball called for military assistance. A detachment of troops then came up and made an onslaught on the onlookers, injuring a certain number of them. Not content with this the ball committee, composed mostly of officials, strove to give a mere row the importance of a long-prepared rebellion. A number of the noisiest demonstrators were sent to the assizes under a charge of that nature, against which they protested with the utmost vigour. It took a whole year before the matter was settled by its being transferred, as a simple charge of disturbance, to the police court, where the case was dismissed. During that time the local Press was rife with excited comments on the proceedings; and Sir William Gomm well nigh lost the scanty popularity he had managed to gain for himself.

Sir George Anderson (1849-50).

Sir James M. Higginson (1851-57).

Being appointed to a superior command in India, he left Mauritius on the 5th May, 1849, and was replaced first by Colonel T. Blanchard, and, a fortnight after, by Colonel H. L. Sweeting, till the arrival, on the 8th June, of the next Governor, Sir George Anderson, C.B., whose time of service did not exceed sixteen months, during which the Municipality of Port Louis was created. On his demise the colony was given in charge to Major-General Sutherland until the arrival, on the 8th January, 1851, of Mr. James M. Higginson, the new Governor. The first care of this gentleman, who was knighted a year or two afterwards, when he was on leave in England doing his best to obtain important advantages for the colony, was to follow the example set by Sir Lowry Cole, and so often neglected by his successors. He visited the rural districts in order to make himself acquainted with the inhabitants and their wants.

After having enjoyed the benefits of Indian immigration, which of late had been extended to the Bombay Presidency, Mauritius now began to experience one of the most trying drawbacks of the system. On the 15th May, 1854, cholera, probably introduced by a coolie ship, broke out in the Civil Prisons, and, in the space of six weeks, caused 207 deaths in Port Louis. The epidemic then seemed to subside, but, two years later, in March, 1856, it suddenly made its reappearance in the most virulent manner, this time attacking all classes of the population. Four months it raged, in spite of all efforts for its suppression, the total number of deaths which it occasioned being upwards of 3,500. It again recommenced successively in 1859, 1860, 1861, and disappeared altogether in 1862.

On the 10th September, 1857, Sir James Higginson left Mauritius in charge of Major-General Hay, who performed the duties of Officer Administering the Government till the 20th November, when Sir William Stevenson, K.C.B., was installed as Governor.

Sir William Stevenson (1857-63).

This gentleman soon learnt to appreciate the population, and became for the Mauritians as warm and generous a friend as Sir Robert Farquhar and Sir Lowry Cole had been of old.

The next year one of the boons demanded by Sir James Higginson was granted by the appointment of an engineer, Mr. Longridge, to make a survey of the island with the view of constructing railway lines. The report was adopted in Council in February, 1859, and the work immediately began.

Six months after there was unveiled on the quay, facing Government House, the statue of La Bourdonnais, a tardy tribute of public gratitude to the man of genius who had been the father of the colony's prosperity and even of its existence.

Thirteen years' experience of the difficulties brought about by the suppression of the French language in the Courts of Justice of a colony where it was the mother-tongue of the people, led the Mauritians to petition Queen Victoria for equal recognition and sanction of both the French and English languages, but the petition was refused.

Sir William Stevenson, who had been for some time in indifferent health, died at Réduit on the 9th January, 1863, was buried on the 12th at Moka, and was succeeded, *pro tem.*, by Major-General Johnstone.

Sir William Stevenson was assuredly one of the best Governors that ever ruled over the colony, and this was so well admitted that, at a meeting held at the Town Hall and presided over by the Mayor of Port Louis, it was decided to raise a statue to his memory. Some time previously the execution of a monument of a similar nature, in honour of Adrien d'Epinay, had been entrusted to that distinguished patriot's youngest son, Prosper, the now celebrated artist, who was also commissioned for one of Sir William Stevenson. Both statues were completed during the next Governor's administration, and did much credit to the talented, but then unknown, young man.

Sir Henry Barkly (1863-70).

Sir Henry Barkly, K.C.B., arrived on the 26th November following. His government is important in the annals of Mauritius, inasmuch as during it many useful measures which had been planned by his predecessors came into effect.

On the 1st March, 1864, the lighthouse at Ile aux Fouquets, off Mahébourg, was built; the one at Pointe-aux-Canonniers was constructed during the latter period of Sir William Nicolay's rule. In January, 1867, the old beacon ship near the Bell Buoy in Port Louis Harbour was lighted for the first time; it was superseded in 1911 by the lighthouse at Petite Rivière.

About the beginning of 1867 three financial institutions were started; two of them—the Crédit Foncier de l'Ile Maurice and the Mauritius Land Credit and Agency Co., Ltd.—have disappeared, but the third, the Crédit Foncier of Mauritius, Ltd., is still in existence.

In August of the same year the North Line of Railways was opened to traffic, and the Midland Line was ready in the year following.

On the 9th November, 1865, Port Louis was for the first time lighted by gas, this having been effected by a London firm, who had secured the contract from the Municipality.

If Sir Henry Barkly had hitherto been fortunate in reaping what others had sown, he was now called upon to witness some dreadful calamities which befel the colony in succession. The first of these was on the 12th February, 1865, when, through torrential rains which had been falling for several days, the rivers were swollen to such an extent that Port Louis and the adjoining parts of Pamplemousses and Plaines Wilhems districts suffered from an unprecedented inundation. Twenty-one lives were lost, and the damage caused to property was considerable.

In December, 1866, malaria broke out with fearful and increasing malignity. At the outset of the epidemic the medical profession was doubtful as to the nature of a malady hitherto unknown in the island, and which, on the whole, appeared quite distinct from malaria. All the remedies commonly prescribed by the Pharmacopœia were of no avail, and it was not till experiments were made with quinine sulphate, that it proved to be the only efficacious agent to allay the terrible attacks of the prevailing fever. The drug was, however, so seldom employed at the time that chemists kept but a very limited stock of it. Quinine accordingly soon commanded fantastical prices, and the supply of it was quickly exhausted. Three or four months elapsed before the medicine could be obtained from Ceylon, and then from Europe, and this contributed in some measure to increase the high rate of mortality.

The epidemic raged, at that period, mostly along the leeward coast of the island and in the low northern plains of Pamplemousses and Mapou. In Port Louis, from February to July, 1867, casualties were simply appalling. Of a population of 60,000 souls, the number of deaths from fever read as follows: February, 994; March, 2,801; April, 4,130; May, 3,491; June, 2,664; July, 2,382. The poorer classes, of course, suffered most dreadfully. The total deaths in the island, due to malaria alone, amounted to 31,920, or one-ninth of the general population, whilst in Port Louis they rose to 18,469, nearly one-third of its inhabitants!

One could hardly venture in the streets of the town without meeting funeral processions everywhere. Corpses often had to be left in a line at the doors of churches for their turn of admission. Similar dismal scenes took place, on a still larger scale, at the Western Cemetery, which had soon to be enlarged, and, as it proved insufficient, another was started at Bois Marchand.

Eleven hospitals were opened in the colony, the Civil Hospital at Port Louis being crowded so early as February, 1867, and the Immigration Buildings were turned into supplementary wards. In March a Government hospital was established at Grand River; in the following month the police station of Abercrombie was fitted to receive the members of the police force.

In presence of such a calamity the well-to-do citizens began to desert Port Louis for the higher and healthier districts of Plaines Wilhems and Moka, and this was the origin of the populous centres which now exist in these localities.

Meetings were held to collect funds to be distributed to the sufferers, and large contributions were also received from England. An inquiry was established, which resulted in the conclusion that the epidemic had originated from several causes, chiefly through the excavations necessitated by the laying of the railway line. That belief has, however, been abandoned, as it is beyond doubt that the fever made its first appearance at Petite Rivière, where no such excavations had been performed but where a marsh had been dug up. According to the now prevailing theory, it must have been introduced by coolies from some indeterminate part of India where it raged. With them probably came the dreaded *anopheles*; or these mosquitos, perhaps already acclimatized, but hitherto harmless through lack of infected blood, finding at last a contaminated medium, soon disseminated the malady. At all events, this scourge has never been eradicated up to the present date.

In March, 1868, a violent hurricane, which lasted nearly three days, caused immense havoc to buildings and plantations. It carried off two spans of the Grand River railway viaduct, each measuring 126 feet in length and weighing fully as many tons. Fortunately enough, five engines happened to be on the other side of the ravine, so that passenger traffic was resumed in a few days by means of changing trains and crossing the river below on a narrow swinging bridge admitting only foot passengers. Goods traffic was resumed five months after, on the completion of a temporary wooden bridge, which proved of good service until the viaduct was rebuilt some years later.

Among the numerous improvements contemplated by the preceding Governors—some of which have now been realized—was the drainage of Port Louis. A Commission was appointed on the 23rd June, 1868, to consider the ways and means of its achievement, and a specialist, Mr. Bazalgette, was sent from England to report thereon; but the people, believing in the telluric germ theory and not yet recovered from the alarm occasioned by the recent malaria epidemic, were terrified at the prospect of every street in Port Louis being cut open and turned over. A meeting was held to protest against this being done and, in consideration

TROU FANFARON. LINE BARRACKS. THE CITY OF PORT LOUIS.

of the recent melancholy events, the idea was abandoned and not put forward again until another quarter of a century.

Sir Henry Barkly had just been appointed to the governorship of the Cape of Good Hope, when he was informed of the impending visit of H.R.H. The Duke of Edinburgh, who was on a tour to the chief British colonies. He accordingly postponed his departure, and was fortunate enough to entertain his Royal guest, who arrived at Mauritius at the end of May, 1870. Shortly after, Sir Henry Barkly left the government of Mauritius in charge of Major-General E. Selby Smith, until the arrival of Sir Arthur Hamilton Gordon, K.C.M.G. As a member of the Aborigines Society, this Governor felt naturally inclined to sympathize with the lower classes, and as soon as he arrived he made no secret of this commendable attitude.

Sir Arthur Hamilton Gordon (1871-74).

His zealous efforts in this direction were, however, keenly resented by the planters, who asserted that the Indian labourers, finding in him a Governor after their own heart, had become more discontented and less amenable to discipline.

At that very moment there happened to be an alien residing in the colony, one Adolph de Plévitz, a Prussian of low rank and morality, who made himself the willing, though unsought for, auxiliary of His Excellency's philanthropic schemes. Dwelling in an out-of-the-way place, he easily managed, without being

CAPITAL OF MAURITIUS. CHAMP DE MARS.

suspected for a long time, to solicit the complaints of the unsophisticated Indians, to school them properly and to direct them straight to Réduit, where their exaggerated, if not altogether imaginary, wrongs would doubtless be set right. Consequently, whole gangs of coolies would, under the slightest pretence, leave their work to call on the Governor, who listened but too complacently to their stories and sent them back comforted. Still more, the Governor himself, incognito, took to making surreptitious visits to the planters' estates and District Courts, where he carried on a sort of investigation of his own, which greatly increased the resentment of the planters

Plévitz, assisted by two or three other persons of similar character, now published a pamphlet in which the planters were accused of grievous injustice towards their employees. On the other hand, the Governor having confidentially pointed out to the Secretary of State the urgency of thoroughly modifying the Immigration system, was ordered by him to give publicity to this despatch. In presence of a document emanating from the highest authority in the colony, appearing to back most of the charges which had recently been made against the planters, the Chamber of Agriculture, as their representative, considered that the matter needed a public redress, and a petition, signed by hundreds of notabilities, was sent to Her Majesty, praying that a regular inquiry be made on the subject. Sir Arthur Gordon very sensibly observed that Inquiry Commissions had never done any good. It was impossible, he said, that among the honest and law-abiding planters of Mauritius some black sheep might not be found. Such being the case the Commissioners would easily get prejudiced and would become too prone to allocate to the colony at large the misconduct of an insignificant minority. The planters, however, felt so confident in their innocence that they rejected this good advice—seeing from whom it came, they perhaps did not think it perfectly disinterested—and insisted upon having a Commission.

In 1872 the Commissioners, Messrs. W. E. Frere and V. A. Williamson, arrived and heard a great number of witnesses, including one or two who had decidedly broken the law, especially as regards the payment of wages and hospital treatment. The planters were represented by their counsels, the Hon. V. Naz, Messrs. W. Newton and G. Guibert. Mr. Naz showed great ability, and his defence of the colony was so remarkable as to attract the attention of the Home Government. Some years after, the post of Procureur - General, being vacant, was offered to this gentleman, who was later made a Companion, and then a Knight, of the Order of St. Michael and St. George.

VIEW FROM BARON D'UNIENVILLE'S RESIDENCE, LA LUCIE ESTATE, FLACQ.

In spite of their efforts, the report published the next year was just what Sir Arthur Gordon had anticipated; every individual failing of a ridiculous minority was represented as the constant criminal habit of the whole body of planters, and a series of stringent measures were recommended. Sir Arthur Gordon did not remain in Mauritius long enough to see them put into effect; he left in October, 1874, and his departure was naturally not regretted except by those on whose behalf he had exerted himself so actively.

Sir Arthur P. Phayre (1874–79).

The administration was in charge of the Hon. E. Newton, Colonial Secretary, for about a month, until the advent of Sir Arthur P. Phayre, K.C.M.G., K.C.S.I., C.B., a thoroughly straightforward man, who soon made the people understand that he was compelled to execute orders of a harsher nature than he would have desired. In 1878 a new Labour Law was accordingly framed which, more or less modified, has been in force till quite recently, when some still less acceptable conditions were imposed at the request of the Indian Government.

In the year 1877 the island was visited by a hurricane more severe than the one which had occurred nine years previously, though of less duration, and much damage was done both to crops and buildings. About the same time the Savanne Branch Railway was inaugurated; the Moka branch was opened later, under Sir George Bowen's government.

Sir George F. Bowen (1879–83).

After Sir Arthur Phayre's correct tenure of office came the indifferent administration of Sir George Bowen, K.C.M.G., a distinguished humanist assuredly, but by no means an ideal Governor. He spent most of his time on leave; and the people would not have found fault with this, had he not been seconded by the Colonial Secretary, Mr. F. N. Broome, who, through some all-powerful influence, had been gratified with a perfect novelty for the time—a commission of Lieutenant-Governor.

Whilst Mr. Broome was presiding over the destinies of Mauritius, an Ordinance was submitted to the legislature on the reafforestation of the island, drawn up from the recommendations of a specialist, Mr. Thompson, who had been sent for this object some years previously. One of the clauses of the new law directed that mountain and river reserves, hitherto composed of strips of land 50 feet wide, would in future be extended to 150 feet, without any compensation to landowners. The unofficial members of the Council protested very strongly against this autocratic method of dealing with private property, which, together with some other not very commendable doings of the Lieutenant-Governor's entourage, provoked a movement in which all classes joined; and resulted in a petition being sent to Her Majesty for a modification f the Government Council by the introduction of elected members who should have a larger share of inf ience in questions of local interest. As can well be imagined, Mr. Broome, in transmitting the petition to the Secretary of State, stoutly recommended its rejection; and so the matter dropped for some time.

Sir John Pope Hennessy (1883-89).

Sir John Pope Hennessy, K.C.M.G., who took command of Mauritius in June, 1883, soon asserted himself as the true friend of the colonists, and expressed his surprise at their being deliberately shut out from some of the higher posts in the Civil Service, which should be theirs by right. After having ascertained that the reform question was still one of the constant wishes of the people, he took up the matter himself, recommending it to the new Secretary of State, Lord Derby, of whose liberal views he was well aware. The Mauritians' request, so warmly supported, was granted contrary to all expectations; but, of course, this had created much discontent amongst the English section of the community, who, apart from prejudice against a Governor who was both a Roman Catholic and an Irishman, whose prior conduct in the different colonies he had administered had been compared to "an angry boil on the body of the Empire," could not tolerate the idea of being deprived of a monopoly so long established that they had come to regard it as their undoubted patrimony. They strove, therefore, to have the measure revoked, in which they succeeded through a further change in the Colonial Office. Nevertheless, the principle itself, the election of members, was left untouched, but most of the privileges accorded were now encroached upon, or turned from their original intent. With this the Mauritians had to acquiesce, and the result was the present Constitution, promulgated on the 25th October, 1885.

VIEW FROM BARON D'UNIENVILLE'S RESIDENCE. LA LUCIE ESTATE, FLACQ.

The first elections took place in January, 1886, and gave rise to acute party feeling. The reformists, being at variance on certain points, separated into two groups, the Conservatives and the so-called Democrats. The members belonging to the latter party, four in all, were gained over by the anti-reformists to oppose the Governor, against whom were lodged accusations which proved perfectly groundless. It was seriously alleged, among other grievances, that the *Fenian,* as they politely termed him, actually sought to make the question of Home Rule in Mauritius auxiliary to that of Home Rule in Ireland, in view of *an eventual separation ! ! !*

The political strife went steadily on, the opposition being avowedly headed by the Colonial Secretary himself, Mr. Clifford Lloyd, who managed at last to secure an inquiry into Sir John's administration, under the astounding pretence that *his mind was hopelessly deranged ! ! !*

Sir Hercules Robinson, Commissioner-General of the Cape of Good Hope, was chosen for that unpleasant purpose, and, after a sham investigation which lasted but a few days, availed himself of his commission, and suddenly suspended Sir John Pope Hennessy. He himself then assumed the governorship (14th December, 1886), which two days later he handed over to Major-General Hawley, and returned to South Africa.

Sir John Pope Hennessy left Mauritius in the following March, thoroughly determined to clear himself before the Secretary of State of the aspersion made upon his character. He had, however, been preceded by the Hon. (later Sir) William Newton (to whom reference has already been made on page 58), a Mauritian barrister of note and one of his firmest admirers, whom the people had entrusted with a petition to Her Majesty demanding the reinstation of Sir John, and with the care of defending him before the Privy Council. Even those who had not entirely approved Sir John's policy now forgot their grievances and gave vent to their indignation at such a scandalous excess of power!

Sir John Pope Hennessy was reinstated, and his return to Mauritius was the occasion of an unprecedented popular manifestation. The latter part of his government was peaceful; he devoted all his care to the development of agriculture and industry; he did much to encourage all kinds of secondary plantations, the importance of which he had fully realized. Tea growing in this island is due to him, and, had time permitted, he would have started the india-rubber industry. Another boon, and not the least, was the damming up of Mare aux Vacoas, thereby permitting the distribution of pure water in some of the most populous districts of the island. Apart from these achievements and his unbounded charity towards the poor, his constant and reliable friendship towards the people of Mauritius would have been sufficient for the great popularity in which he was held by all classes in the island.

Twenty years later, on the 22nd December, 1908, a statue was erected in front of the Port Louis Theatre, at the lower end of Government Street which now bears his name, to the memory of a man who, barring a few errors, had been one of the best Governors this colony ever possessed.

Sir Charles C. Lees (1889-92).

The administration of his successor, Sir Charles C. Lees, K.C.M.G., was uneventful; his temper was well suited to the circumstances of a people who now longed after quiet; for though a man of honour he was by no means a man of action.

In 1890 the Gas Company's contract came to an end. The Company declined renewing it, and entered into liquidation, for circumstances were altered now. Port Louis was almost deserted at night, and heavy losses had consequently attended the Company's operations. Ever since the appearance of malaria, the population of the capital had been considerably reduced by the permanent abandonment of it, first by the upper classes, and then by the middle classes, for the healthier parts of Plaines Wilhems district, where populous centres were created, soon taking the name of towns. The capital, therefore, instead of progressing, had to fall back for years on the antiquated system of oil-lamps, although it was petroleum this time, and no longer cocoa-nut; whilst its more advanced rivals of the heights, Curepipe, Quatre Bornes, Rose Hill, and Beau Bassin, already appreciated the benefit of electricity, which was not introduced into Port Louis until 1909. It must be mentioned, however, that the Municipality, desirous of outshining the other towns, had decided upon the city having a plant of its own, which occasioned the delay. But the possession of it does not appear to substantiate the ambitions with which it was first mooted.

Towards the end of Sir Charles Lees' government he was, while absent on leave, replaced by the Colonial Secretary, Mr. (later Sir) H. E. H. Jerningham, who also held a commission of Lieutenant-Governor. It was during the latter's interim government that Mauritius was visited, on the 29th April, 1892, by perhaps the most dreadful cyclone ever recorded in its annals. Although it raged but for a few hours, it turned a third of Port Louis into a melancholy heap of ruins. The Champ de Lort region suffered most of all, and the Royal College and General Malartic's obelisk in Champ de Mars were devastated, In the rural districts immense damage and destruction were done to buildings both public and private. sugar factories with their costly machinery, and plantations; 1,100 people lost their lives, more than 2,000 were wounded, and 50,000 became altogether houseless; the sugar crop was reduced by fully fifty per cent.

CYCLONE OF APRIL 29th, 1892.

To convey an idea of that awful calamity, we certainly cannot do better than give an account written on the spot by the Lieutenant-Governor, Mr. H. E. H. Jerningham himself, which appeared in *Blackwood's Magazine*, in September, 1892 :—

"On the 28th April, 1892, Mauritius, the old *Ile de France*, still vied with the island of Ceylon for pride of place as the most beautiful and the most fertile Colony of the British Crown in the Eastern Hemisphere. The cane crop had weathered the summer gales, which on February 12th, and again a fortnight after, had assumed very sinister aspects; and planters, who for some years past had valiantly fought against low prices and beetroot competition, were silently revelling in the prospect that, the hurricane season being over, the year 1892 was likely to mark a new era of prosperity. The garden of Pamplemousses, which Mauritians were wont to consider, and with justice, the third botanical garden in the world, was resplendent with tropical vegetation; while that of Réduit, which had been nursed with love and pride by every successive Governor for upwards of a hundred years, was looking its best in its luxuriant display of palms and flowers and gorgeously-coloured foliage.

"At 9 p.m. on the 29th all this was no more; the island had lost its beauty, the cane its promise, the planter his hopes, and the gardens their charms. A short twenty-four hours had sufficed to perpetrate this end, and fortunate had it been could the mischief have stopped there, for the soil's fertility cannot be affected by a storm, and the soil of Mauritius is pre-eminently fertile and recuperative; but 1,100 people had been killed, 2,000 had been wounded; one-third of the capital had been levelled to the ground; thirty out of fifty churches and chapels had been demolished or rendered useless; sugar-mills had been wrecked, crushing mercilessly men, women, and children who had sought refuge under their solid walls; every Indian hut had been blown away, whole villages swept from the places where they stood, and some 50,000 homeless people were left to seek for shelter and food, which a few hours before they were quietly enjoying, through their own exertions and labour.

"Nothing could withstand in places the terrible force of the wind on the fatal day of the 29th of April. It will be for scientific men to explain how trees planted more than a century back, and of eight and twelve feet diameter, were felled to the ground; how the iron-like teakwood branches were snapped and cut and broken as mere brushwood; how girders of iron eighteen inches thick were indented and twisted so as to become useless, as in the case of the great pulley-ladders of a sea-dredger; how, in fine, a column of stones, each weighing more than a ton and fast rivetted with iron clamps and cement, was thrown down like a pack of cards: and it will be for meteorologists to explain how an island of 33 by 31 miles in extent, through which the centre of the cyclone is passing, can escape at all from a wind so violent as the above denotes.

"In the tables of observations the velocity of the wind is set down at 120 miles at its maximum, which corresponds to a pressure of 67 lbs. to the square foot. It does seem as if this pressure, moved at double the rate of an express train, must render house-habitation useless as a place of refuge in a storm; yet in my inspection of the island I have seen a house destroyed, the walls surrounding its yard crushed to atoms; and a pigeon-house on four miserable posts saved! Why? Everything was unexpected, singular, and unprecedented, in this calamitous stroke dealt by Nature with a viciousness that savoured of a woman's vengeance. The barometer fell to the lowest reading on record, viz, 27.961 inches at 2.30 p.m.; while it had stood at 29.660 at 6 a.m. on the morning of the storm, and got back to 29.719 at 9 p.m. after its passage; and the record dates since the year 1759.

"The wind blew at N.E. by E. at the rate of twenty-two miles at 6 a.m., viz., in a direction which has ever indicated that the disturbance, when there is one—and there are many in each year—has passed to the southward of the island. At noon it was N.E. by half E at a rate which had increased to sixty-eight miles an hour, which showed that the storm was on us, but its centre likely to avoid the island; and at 1 p.m., being still in the same direction, the wind flew at a rate of ninety-six miles indicating hurricane fury. At 2 p.m., the barometer still falling, the wind lulled to fifty-six miles an hour at the Observatory, where the centre did not pass, and to two miles in the centre, a mere whisper of impending danger. Those who realised the fact were able to save themselves. It is greatly to be feared that the majority did not, and that the greater part of the deaths which have been recorded, and the ruin that was produced, are due to this fact; for all of a sudden, at 4 p.m., with a violence appreciable even to ears accustomed to the roar of the first part of the storm, the wind blew at the rate of 121 miles an hour, and carried all before it. Noble trees that had stood the first blast went down, and in a short two hours upwards of 200,000 trees had been overthrown, and all the rest bereft of their bark, their leaves, and their branches, throughout the island. Such velocity had been unknown. The storm had come from the N.E., and there are only two other instances of a cyclone having approached the island from that quarter—in January, 1863, and in January, 1869—when little damage was done. Gales in Mauritius have been known in May, and even in June, notably in 1785, when the storm lasted twenty-four hours, but no hurricane; and though there have been three hurricanes in April since 1773, none were later than the 10th of that month, so that, even as to date, the hurricane of 1892 was exceptional, and will probably on those accounts modify many accepted principles of the students of the laws of storms; unless, indeed, the new interest in the spots on the sun's disc can explain, by their number and their degree of magnitude, the exceptional variations in the air-currents which revolve about the earth in its whirlwind course around the sun.

"From the above enough is gathered to understand that the disturbance of 1892 was probably exceptional, and therefore that it was excusable on the part of the meteorologists of the island to telegraph on the evening of the 28th, in reply to an anxious query of my own, that the wind, having reached N.E. by E., and the barometer being higher than at the same hour on the 27th, there was nothing to be apprehended.

LIGHTERS STRANDED AT PORT LOUIS, AFTER THE CYCLONE OF APRIL, 1892.

"Notwithstanding this consoling message it brought no comfort, and the sense of impending evil kept gnawing at my heart, knowing and appreciating the dangers of even a full gale at a time when the cane crop would suffer severely from a violent shaking.

"At 8 a.m. on the 29th April another anxious telegram brought no response, and, surmising that communications between Le Réduit and the town, and thence to the Observatory had been interrupted, though not yet anticipating what was to come, it became necessary to give up all intention of going to Port Louis in order to secure this old residence of the Governors of Mauritius, which an English Governor once called a barn between two ditches, in total disrespect of its natural beauties.

"But as these had to fight Nature as best they could, the barn, with its 240 doors, windows, and shutters, had to be preserved, and the work of closing ports to the N. and E. commenced at 8.30 a.m.

"Towards 10 a.m. broken branches were flying in the air like dust, and the merciless blasts, whenever they came, like guns pointed at the target they were to hit, remorselessly levelled the tallest and proudest trees. At eleven the summer benches, which, on the verandahs around the house, had been rapidly secured against any ordinary storm, became the toys of furious gusts, and were lifted into the air and dashed to pieces some sixteen yards away over a hedge of rose trees on the gravel path beyond.

"Till then, between the gusts, there had ever been those silent moments, more terrible than the gusts themselves, which characterise the cyclonic storm, as if the wind gathered its strength in earnest to strike each blow more deadly than the last, but at noon the intervals of quiet were filled in by a roar and a seething noise, such as the sea alone produces when lashed to fury, and an ominous thud, but of scarcely perceptible sound, announced that a portion of the roof had been carried away. All efforts were then directed inside, and the lights were lighted, while the remaining hurricane shutters were being closed to the south and the west. The clanking of doors that would not close or were burst open, the hissing of the tempest through every chink, the cracking of glass panes, and crashing of glass upon the floor, and the sea of waters that flooded the rooms beneath the roof-shorn wing of the house, the still falling barometer, and the booming of the blast against the building, as if enraged at its withstanding any pressure at all, constitute a recollection not to be forgotten by the two occupants of Le Réduit and their three servants on that day.

"Suddenly the roar ceased, the hissing sank to a whisper, a calm succeeded the storm, and a haze like a November fog filled the air. Cautiously a door was opened; we issued with difficulty into the open, looked round, and one exclaimed, 'This is the centre!' and the other, 'Mind what follows!'

"At four, as the last hurricane shutter was with difficulty nailed and secured, a boom like that of a ball from a hundred-ton gun resounded, and we knew that the battle raged anew though the centre had passed. Should we pass with it? Could the house resist this tremendous force? What should our next step be? Already two-thirds of the big barn was *hors de combat*, and our only refuge was the ball-room, which was still intact. For an hour the noise was stupendous, deafening, sickening, but the glass was going up; and our lives were still what they were worth. Would it be the same elsewhere in the island? The course of the hurricane must have saved some parts of it, probably Port Louis, which lay some thousand feet below, behind the Signal Mountain and the Pouce, which hide it from this elevation. Let us hope. Presently the great guns in the horrible fight ceased their roar, and we were proof against the arms of smaller calibre. They, too, were silenced soon, and at 8 p.m., done mentally and physically, we sat down for the first time that day 'by Babylon's water,' to weep or to sleep, but to wake at daybreak with expectations of the worst.

PORT LOUIS AFTER THE CYCLONE OF APRIL, 1892.

"Never did a more glorious day shine upon Mauritius than on the morrow of the 29th of April. It was awe-striking; it was magnificent; it was horrible. Winter, cold snowy winter, from the northern hemisphere, had come upon the tropics, upon this emerald sunny isle. Forests had been fighting, and were white with peeled-off bark; stumps of trees, mere broomsticks, were everywhere lording over fallen giants; the alleys, avenues, and roads were littered with rubbish and broken branches; gaping wounds in the house where a rivet had proved untrue and allowed the onslaught of the wind upon the roof. With difficulty could way be made to the camps, and servants' houses, and stables. Everywhere the roofs had been similarly lifted bodily, tiles and all, and deposited yards away, upon the prongs of what had once been trees.

"No means of riding or driving, yet to town one must. Was the town safe? Three hours' journey there on foot, the greater part of the way revealed everywhere the same horrible spectacle of devastation; but it increased in horror as it was proceeded with, with an inward fever haste to know the worst and be about and doing after the forced inaction of black Friday last. The canes that on the Thursday had looked so fine, so promising of wealth, and so consoling, lay flat upon the soil where they had not been broken in two, and their gone leaves revealed how full of sugar were the sticks. Would they be lost for the time of cutting? The canes looked like so many bodies shorn of their clothing and lying dead in life

"Presently Rose Hill came in view, houses down, crushed, fallen, ruined. Were there human beings beneath? Yes; a report came that at the mill of *Bassin* a hundred people were buried under its wrecked remains. Impossible! Onwards to town. Railway gauges obstructed by fallen carriages; general manager working like a navvy to hurry the clearance of the line. When would it be cleared? Impossible to tell; it was being scoured by an engine, but the line was littered with fallen trees and telegraph posts; he could not say. Again on; right and left wide gaping houses; roofs sunk through the floor, destroying at one fell swoop furniture, clothing, the resources of a whole family, if not the family itself; tenements shorn of a whole side; verandahs on the roofs, and the roofs in neighbouring gardens; not a single Indian hut to be seen—all blown away—but an Indian woman at work seeking a piece of linen out of the soaked rubbish and drying it in the cold sun, for the little mites by her side in the open field. Is this the case throughout? What about the food, and the shops, and the rice-magazines?

"Farther onwards: a church down, literally smashed to matchwood; benches crushed and altar gone, only a plaster statue stands up in the ruins; no one about. Is everybody dead? At last! The outskirt of Port Louis; nothing much in the outlying western suburb; but the noise increases. What is it? It sounds like a demoniac medley of wrangling, and moaning, and screaming, but it is pleasant in its dolefulness; it is human; it is a group of people imploring an Indian policeman to hurry and save a whole family of ten who are under a crumbled house. He hurries at a word, and as the western part of the town is reached, the town of the dead is reached; long convoys of litters wherein mangled bodies and the dying, the living who are wounded, and orphans who were not orphans yesterday, are being carried to the hospitals. But the Civil Hospital cannot contain them all? No, but the Protestant Cathedral of St. James has been converted into a hospital since last night, and there, too, they are being conveyed. What has happened? Wind, flood, and fire, four hundred dead, as many wounded, more under the ruins. How fire? It broke out during the last hour of the storm and slowly made its way through the whole of a quarter, burning and destroying property and life: women burnt beside dead corpses of relatives they would not leave, preferring to be charred than desert their own; others stunned, paralysed by fear, and rivetted to their burning homes. Still onwards, to the Municipality, a refuge for hundreds of wounded, houseless, dazed, and horror-stricken people, whom a legion of doctors, attendants, and charitable souls are powerless to succour in the measure of their wants. Farther to the great thoroughfares; but where are they? Whole houses litter the roads, houses bodily removed and deposited with one long crash on the streets, in front and over which are now travelling the little army of gallant soldiers in fatigue-party detachments, bringing to their distressing task of recovering bodies all the gentleness of woman with the rough energy of men of will and purpose.

CHAUSSÉE DISTRICT, PORT LOUIS, BEFORE THE FIRE OF 1893.

"The air is foul with human decomposition. The streets resound with moans and half-whispered tones. A black pall hangs over the city. Government House has escaped the fury of the storm, but is invaded by a crowd of inquirers. How are the bodies to be buried? How are the people to be fed? How are we to escape famine or pestilence, or both? Almost all in authority are away. How so? Unable to go to their homes on the previous night, they slept as best they could in the train which was to start at 1 p.m. on Friday and could only be despatched at 7 a.m. this morning on a portion of its course. Nearly 600 people were at the station during the storm—the most noted and important persons of the colony, planters, merchants, men of business—clamouring to get away, anxious about their people and their possessions, and preserved from death by the iron will of the manager of railways. Onward again to the principal hospital. It is crowded, besieged, and presents a ghastly sight of old and young, men and women and children, the victims of the relentless storm that drove into their sides and bodies the very walls, and stones, and rafters on which they relied for protection. It is a charnel house, where admittance is asked in order to die, and where human charity, greater even than the disaster, is almost powerless in its efforts to save life.

"Farther, and the docks have been turned into ambulances and sheltering houses, where further marks of devotion, heroism, and suffering come to the fore.

"How is this gigantic misery to be ever relieved? How can so much harm have come in such short few hours? It is heart-rending, desperate.

"In the harbour tall ships right and left silently ask pity and help in their stranded condition. Others have been jammed together in a frightful fraternal embrace which has pierced their sides. Even the ponderous ladders of the sea-dredger have been twisted and curved as if their weight of iron was of no account to the destroying wind.

"Is nothing saved? The streets near the harbour are littered with clumsy, heavy lighters full of damaged rice, which the sea would not swallow, but carried into the town upon the rising surf. The Arab quarter seems safe. It is the granary of the island, and one shudders at the thought of famine, which must have followed upon its destruction. It is safe, and hope rises as the Mussulman merchants, grateful to Allah in this hour of distress, assure their Christian brother man that the price of rice will not be raised.

"Back to the western portion of the town, on to the Royal College. Foundered, crushed, ruined; no one dead, and yet how near his end was its sole occupant at the time of its collapse! Walls swaying to and fro, columns jerking out of their foundation; mad with fear and powerless, the wind that blew the building down enabled him to save himself through the very opening it had rammed. On again to the Convent of Bon Secours, a mass of rubbish, where heroic deeds were done last night. Children and nuns and old invalids were the buried inmates. The storm spared neither, but at the call for help the young scions of old Mauritian stock, who, with their elders, were waiting at the railway station for the signal to leave the town, rushed to the spot and worked all night to recover the dead; but they could not give life to the eleven children and the one poor nun who were killed, pulverised under the heap of stones.

"Enough for the day. If thus in town, what will it be in the districts? They must be visited, for when the heart is full of sorrow even the realisation of the worst dispels the apprehension of a further evil, and the means must be at once devised how to help this generous and kindly people in their great hour of distress.

"The dead must be decently buried, the wounded properly attended; the people must be fed, clothed, housed, and Government must not stint its help at this time, for this is an industrious people and a trustful one, the possessors of a soil so rich, so recuperative that Nature will return to it with interest what it has taken, and at no distant time; a people, indeed, who have weathered many storms and many reverses, and who may still live to find that He who ruled this frightful visitation will turn it in all likelihood into a merciful dispensation.

"Till then help is necessary; they must be helped, and they shall."

In this emergency Mr. Jerningham showed himself a kind-hearted man and an intelligent administrator, doing all in his power to alleviate the direful calamity. In response to his eloquent appeal to the Government at home, a loan was granted, to be refunded in twenty years, which permitted planters to evade imminent ruin, and by degrees to retrieve their losses. Besides this, the colony received liberal assistance from private sources in Great Britain as well as from various parts of the Empire, from the neighbouring French colony of Réunion, and, in proportion with their means, from the Seychelles Islands, which were then a dependency of Mauritius.

Mr. Jerningham was rewarded for his praiseworthy behaviour by being confirmed in the post he provisionally occupied, and was soon after knighted and made a K.C.M.G. He was, however, doomed to witness further catastrophes. In July of the very next year (1893), a conflagration

Sir Hubert E. H. Jerningham (1892-97).

destroyed one of the most commercial parts of central Port Louis, especially the Chaussée, wherein were situated the principal shops. Six months after, in February, 1894, the weather being cyclonic, although the wind was not strong enough to prevent railway circulation, a train passing over St. Louis Bridge, near Pailles Station, was caught by a terrific squall and several cars were hurled down into the stream, some forty or fifty feet below. Fortunately, as only a small number of passengers were in the cars, few persons were injured and no death had to be deplored.

At the end of 1893 the cable laid by the Eastern Telegraph Company was opened, thereby placing Mauritius within a few hours' communication with all parts of the world.

About the same time the drainage question was revived, and, after a vigorous opposition from the supporters of the quondam malarian theory, it was adopted by the Council owing to the anti-telluric arguments of the Hon. Sir Virgil Naz and the Hon. Henri Leclézio in favour of the scheme, which, on the whole, has not brought about any of the calamities predicted by the local Jeremiahs.

RAILWAY CARRIAGES BLOWN FROM ST. LOUIS BRIDGE, PAILLES STATION, FEBRUARY, 1894.

Sir Hubert Jerningham's time was over in 1897, when he was replaced by Sir Charles Bruce, K.C.M.G., who was not a stranger to the colony, having been Rector of the Royal College in 1868 and Colonial Secretary in 1883, under the Governments of Mr. F. N. Broome and Sir John Pope Hennessy, although, from personal motives, he did not stay long in the last-mentioned office. His appointment was hailed with gladness by the Mauritians, who knew they would find in him a ready protector.

Sir Charles Bruce (1897-1903).

His government was signalled by some more of the series of misfortunes with which the island has been so often visited.

In January, 1899, bubonic plague made its first appearance here, and, although more than thirteen years have elapsed, it still continues to rage every year, coinciding generally with the sugar crop, as the cutting of the canes and the burning of the thrash drive rats from the fields into the estate camps and villages. The mortality from this cause was never exceedingly high, nothing equal to what it was for cholera or malaria at the outset; but the authorities seem powerless in their efforts to get rid of it. On the other hand, this very disease, which broke out at about the same time at Tamatave, Madagascar, was eradicated in that place in a few weeks, and has never since reappeared there.

Three years after, just as the sugar crop was beginning, surra broke out, and quickly carried off all the mules and horses used for transporting canes to the mills. Oxen proved more resistant at first, but they also soon died. On most estates, in order to finish the crop, it was necessary to resort to the primitive contrivance of carts drawn by six or eight men, who, of course, obtained an extra remuneration. This was a serious disaster to agriculture, already heavily handicapped by low prices of sugar. The planters had to look to mechanical traction, and the Home Government now consented to a fresh loan for that object. Accordingly, since the year 1903, a considerable amount of tramway material and many traction engines have been introduced, and at present there is no estate of any importance where this new mode of transport has not superseded the ancient system.

In August, 1901, Mauritius was visited by two distinguished guests—Their Majesties King George V. and Queen Mary, then Duke and Duchess of Cornwall and York—when a statue of the late Queen Victoria was unveiled by her grand-daughter in front of Government House, Port Louis. During their short stay the Royal couple readily gained the hearts of the Mauritians by their simplicity of manners and affability.

Sir Charles Bruce did much good during his tenure of office; if all the measures he adopted were not equally unimpeachable, the reason is that human nature is liable to error, and chiefly because he had to obey strict orders from the potentates of Downing Street. Although he no longer preserves any official ties binding him to the island, he has never grudged, in several trying circumstances, to take the defence of the Mauritians; and it is a comfort for them, at least, to see their former Governor, full of mettle and energy in spite of old age, ever ready, of his own accord, to stand for their interests.

Sir Cavendish Boyle (1903-11).

Sir Cavendish Boyle, K.C.M.G., was appointed to the government of the island in no easy circumstances. The price of sugar had continued low, and a succession of reduced crops had thoroughly embarrassed the public finances; for Mauritius the sugar industry is the chief, if not the sole, factor of public wealth. An important reserve fund, which had been wisely set aside in years of plenty to meet the necessities of less favourable times, was now well nigh exhausted. Year after year expenditure had exceeded revenue, and the retrenchment ordered by the Colonial Office had proved insufficient.

SECTION OF THE CHAUSSÉE, PORT LOUIS, AFTER THE FIRE OF 1893.

In this emergency the planters, represented by the Chamber of Agriculture, petitioned for a further loan of £400,000 with a view to adopt up-to-date improvements and place the local industry in a position to compete with its less-handicapped rivals. Not only should mills be fitted up with better machinery, but a Department of Agriculture should be established to point out to the planters the best and most economical methods of cultivation and manipulation; irrigation should be resorted to wherever possible; agricultural banks opened to assist small planters especially, at a low rate of interest; and a complete renewal of the railway material was also asked for, as that department was no longer equal to public requirements.

This petition was refused by the Secretary of State on the grounds that the Home Government would not be justified in making a *gratuity* to a Crown Colony. Yet it must be borne in mind that the planters had never thought of soliciting a gratuity, but a simple advance of funds, which would doubtless have been as regularly paid up as the Hurricane and Mechanical Transport Loans, both of which have proved of advantage to the local Government. Remonstrance, however, was of no avail against red tape, and the only item allowed was an inquiry into the disorganization brought about long before on the Government Railways by the shortsightedness of previous managers, supported, of course, by the local authorities, who never cared to provide for the renovation of the rolling stock, and preferred to show in their yearly accounts an excess of revenue.

The Railway Inquiry was carried out by Sir David Hunter, of the Natal Government Railways, who commented on the inefficient manner in which the department had been operated, and recommended that immediate steps should be taken to remedy the same.

By the by, inquiries are apparently becoming quite a hobby in the Colonial Office, and it seems that nothing can be done without them. About the time of the Railway Inquiry Sir Ronald Ross came to report on malaria, and made very comprehensive and very wise suggestions, which have not yet been executed although five years have elapsed! Another specialist, Sir William Taylor, was sent at the end of 1912 to try and improve things in the Customs Department, which never went on properly since it was reorganized some time previously according to the views of a Royal Commission; but his report has not been made public. Other experts are expected, one to deal with the Irrigation Scheme and one with Agricultural Banks; more still will surely follow.

A most unfortunate habit among persons who happen to visit this island is to abuse the Mauritians at large in papers and in magazines, without having taken the trouble to ascertain the truth of all the idle talk to which they may have listened. This is most disagreeable indeed for the people, although it does not matter much so long as the canards emanate from private individuals; but it is quite a different affair when they come from persons acting in a public capacity, and still more when they get inserted in an official document. This is exactly what occurred a few years ago, when one, Mr. Gleadow, sent in a lengthy report on reafforestation, wherein he indulged in some most offensive and unjustifiable comments on the Mauritians, which caused such indignation that a part of the peevish gentleman's tirade was suppressed, it is said, by Government order.

But this is not all. Even at the Council table, in 1907, the Acting Colonial Secretary, Mr. D. Cameron, a very intelligent man notwithstanding, was guilty of a flagrant breach of good manners. He was sharply rebuked by one of the unofficial members, and, as he declined withdrawing his criticisms, the public immediately and energetically protested, and asked for redress from the Governor. In order to sooth down the excitement, Mr. Cameron was transferred to some other colony.

Soon after, as Sir Cavendish Boyle was proceeding to Europe on leave, he was asked to patronise the scheme proposed by the Chamber of Agriculture, and promised to do his best to convince the Home Government of its necessity.

After his departure, matters got more and more entangled; Sir Graham Bower, K.C.M.G., the Colonial Secretary, a former officer of the Royal Navy, who now provisionally held the helm of the administrative bark, as he himself expressed it, soon found himself at a loss to provide for the current expenses, and went the length of uttering the word *bankruptcy* in speaking of Government finances! Being brought to book, he solicited the advice of the unofficial element of the Council as to the policy to be adopted. Further taxation and retrenchment were, of course, contemplated; the former proved, on the whole, a material impossibility; as for the latter, the economy realised was scarcely worth mentioning. In this predicament, some members observed that the only chance of getting out of the scrape would be to revert to the Chamber of Agriculture's plan.

The Home Government being once more approached on the subject, now replied that the only possibility of its considering this proposal must be subordinate to the colony applying for a Royal Commission to investigate the matter. The Chamber of Agriculture, which very likely had not altogether forgotten what had taken place in 1872, declined the offer, alleging that it was not when the island was on the verge of ruin that it could be expected to bear an additional charge of paying the expenses of an Inquiry Commission. To this the Secretary of State agreed and pointed out that the burden would lie chiefly upon the Imperial Government, although the Commission must be demanded by the colony itself. In the Council of Government this proposal met with the favour of the younger members, who deemed it the only means of doing away with a most intolerable state of things; whilst, on the other hand, it was but reluctantly accepted by those who were old enough to remember Sir Arthur Gordon's wise saying that Inquiry Commissions never did any good.

Accordingly, on the 18th June, 1909, arrived Sir Frank Swettenham, Sir Edward O'Malley and Mr. Woodcock, K.C. Their inquiry lasted for about six weeks, during which they heard, publicly and privately, a great number of witnesses of all standing. As they seemed to insist more particularly upon the urgency of fresh taxes, the member for Moka, the Hon. H. Leclézio, C.M.G., pointed out that further taxation was impossible, as the colony was already overburdened. Upon their asking him what remedy he would propose instead, he replied that he would suggest nothing, but that things would amend by and by as they had done more than once. The sugar industry being the principal source of revenue in Mauritius, it had long been observed, said Mr. Leclézio, that the combination of large crops and high prices always brought an afflux in the Treasury. When only one of these factors existed, Government generally managed to make both ends meet; but when both were absent, there was always a deficit. That being so, it was evident that more perfect methods of working would increase the quantity of produce and diminish expenses in such a way as to counterbalance low prices, and result in an excellent general average, which would benefit both the Government and the planters.

Although the Commissioners made light of Mr. Leclézio's theory, it was thoroughly substantiated in the very next year, when a fair crop with tolerable prices changed the deficit in the budget into an excess of revenue.

The completion of the Commissioners' Report occupied more than a year, and when it was made public it caused a general disappointment among those who still believed in the efficacy of Inquiry Commissions. Some points were, however, conceded. Assistance was recommended for the island's chief industry, but with such a stinginess as made it altogether useless. A Department of Agriculture was granted, which, after four years, is just beginning its existence and has not yet had time to make its influence felt. As for Agricultural Banks and Irrigation, their possibilities were adjourned till the advice of experts could be obtained.

Meanwhile, the Legislature, appointed for five years, had to be renewed. In January, 1911, fresh elections took place and were contested with intense party feeling. During the night of the 18th, some false rumour having reached town regarding a pretended assault committed upon one of the members for Port Louis, at his residence at Curepipe, a mob, composed mostly of uneducated Creole blacks, among whom were a number of urchins not more than fifteen years of age, who probably had been catechised in view of possible events, invaded the streets of the capital at daybreak, and, assembling in front of the railway station, attacked, at 7 a.m., peaceful passengers as they came down from the rural districts to attend to their business. After this, the lawless crowd took to sacking the offices and private houses, still unoccupied for the most part, of persons well-known for their opposition views. The printing plant of six newspapers was severely damaged, and a few days elapsed before they could appear again, whilst those in accord with the contrary politics were, of course, left untouched. The rooms of the Chamber of Agriculture were also terribly damaged.

HIS EXCELLENCY SIR JOHN ROBERT CHANCELLOR, R.E., C.M.G., D.S.O.,
Governor of Mauritius.

The police proved altogether incapable of restoring order, and had the troops not come down from Vacoas Camp, though their arrival was unfortunately delayed, the disorder would have been still greater. As was to be expected, the appearance of soldiers led to the immediate dispersion of the rioters without any attempt at resistance. For a short time the streets of Port Louis were patrolled day and night, but no further trouble occurred.

During the subsequent inquiry, presided over by Major-General Sir H. McDonald, and composed of several officers of the army, assisted by the Substitute-Procureur-General, a number of individuals were deferred to the Police Court and sentenced to various periods of imprisonment; but it was clearly demonstrated that they had only been instruments in the hands of ringleaders, who cunningly managed to get themselves out of trouble.

Sir John Robert Chancellor (1911).

Sir John Robert Chancellor, R.E., C.M.G., D.S.O., began his duties as Governor in November following, ten months after these disorders, which are not likely to occur again under his administration. As Sir Lowry Cole and Sir James Higginson had done on their arrival, he visited the districts of the island and soon gained the esteem of the Mauritians by his impartiality, his frankness of manners and kindness, and his energetic exertions on their behalf.

It may be held as a good omen that one of the first ceremonies he was called upon to attend should have been the unveiling, in Champ de Mars, of the statue of King Edward VII, The Peacemaker, another fine example of the work of the great Mauritian artist, Prosper d'Epinay.

Sir John Robert Chancellor has, of course, been instructed to bring into effect most of the recommendations of the Commissioners of Inquiry, but he is proceeding slowly and wisely, and we may say he has already gained for the colony some important modifications, such as the nomination of two distinguished Mauritians to the posts of Chief Justice and Procureur-General. The sugar industry is also indebted to him for obtaining the resumption of Indian Immigration, bluntly suppressed some time ago in accordance with the views of the Sanderson Committee.

As some of the Commissioners' ideas have already proved utter failures, it is not at all improbable that a good many others will have to be discarded. May this serve as a lesson for the Mauritians, and make them ponder in future over the wisdom of the saying, *Timeo Danaos et dona ferentes*, which one of their Governors translated for them in these plain words: "Inquiry Commissions never did any good."

SECTION OF PORT LOUIS, SHOWING THE HARBOUR.

GEOLOGY AND TOPOGRAPHY.

By ALBERT PITOT.

ALBERT PITOT.

LIKE most of the neighbouring islands, Mauritius is decidedly of volcanic origin, although it may appear difficult, at first sight, to reconcile this assertion with several circumstances which seem most conclusive in favour of an opposite theory; as, for instance, the absence of very lofty mountains—the highest, Piton de la Rivière Noire, or Black River Mountain, having an altitude of only 2,711 feet—the lack of a regular primary crater, of scoria, or of volcanic vitrifications, and, in short, of any of those traces which subterraneous fires commonly leave behind them. An erroneous belief in the non-volcanic origin of Mauritius might also rest on the exceptionally remote period of the island's formation, the degradations brought about by the constant flow and infiltrations of rain-water, the decomposition of rocks through the agency of untold centuries, and the falling in of part of the mountains. Such are the principal, but not the only, causes which have given a definite shape to the island's peaks, lowered their summits, and impressed their sides.

But, on proceeding to examine carefully the constituents of those very rocks, it must be admitted, without the slightest hesitation, that none but volcanic eruptions could have produced them; for the rocks exemplify more or less inclined strata which, in many parts of the island, point towards one common centre, and are composed of porous lavas, often mixed with others of a compact, granitic and porphyrous nature.

The general appearance of Mauritius is a mass rising from the sea, now gently, now suddenly and even abruptly, and forming in its centre an elevated table-land. On the verge of this table-land stand three principal chains of peaks, the most conspicuous being Pieterboth (2,685 feet), the Pouce (2,650 feet), Signal Mountain (1,061 feet), the Corps de Garde (2,359 feet), Rempart (2,532 feet), Trois Mamelles (2,187 feet), Black River (2,711 feet), Bambou (2,059 feet), and Morne Brabant (1,809 feet) Mountains, all of them being covered with vegetation to their very summits.

The sea-board declivity of these mountains descends, as a rule, in a gentle slope; whereas their opposite side, facing the central highland, is precipitous and almost perpendicular, showing the disposition of the several beds of rocks of which they are composed. These layers, which are certainly of volcanic formation, are so inclined as to point from the centre of the table-land downwards to the sea, a feature common to most of the Mauritius mountains; so that they may reasonably be looked upon as the remnants of a gigantic volcano, which, after having hollowed out an enormous cavity in its middle, could no longer stand on its base, and accordingly, toppling over, disappeared in the abyss whence it had come, this having been produced either by an unprecedented eruption, or by a tremendous earthquake. Meanwhile, the other mountains, located at that period at the foot of the giant, and consequently less exposed than the parts nearer the centre, escaped total destruction.

Colonel Pike (*Subtropical Rambles in the Land of the Aphanapteryx*) suggests that this terrible convulsion may have upheaved at the same time the adjacent islands of Rodrigues and Réunion, and perhaps Madagascar as well. Then, when the lava had cooled and decomposed into a mould over what had remained of the crater, there sprung up palms and other trees in thick forests, where, with the exception of a few land-shells, no animal life existed. New convulsions thereafter spread a further bed of burning lava over that luxuriant vegetation, of which a proof is to be found on the northern side of Mauritius, at Flacq and Rivière du Rempart, in fossilised remains of the primeval trees, without any admixture of marine deposits, for they contain neither shells nor corals.

In the southern districts it would appear that the volcanic action assumed a different character. The ground being probably less elevated, the subsidence of the forests was so gradual as to allow the trees to become embedded in a compact mass of Neptunian sediments, where indelible impressions of their forms were left in the then soft substance, as neatly as casts taken in plaster of Paris. These impressions are to be seen especially at Mahébourg, Ile aux Aigrettes, and Petite Savanne. Colonel Pike submitted several samples of the mould in question to severe chemical tests by acids, but failed to discover in them any fibrous tissue.

The soil in the centre of the island is not merely constituted of the débris of the once huge bluff, but of lava as well, superposed in regular layers—a proof that their origin must have been posterior to that of the surrounding chain, for this could not have occurred had the extinction of volcanoes coincided with the catastrophe which destroyed the central peak. It must then be inferred that subterraneous fires outlived that great event, and, at some subsequent period, made their way through the ruins, which they covered, and spread their lava over the whole surface of the desolate track.

PIETERBOTH.

Evidences of those ancient disturbances may be noticed here and there on the central plateau, in the shape of mounds of moderate altitude, the most striking of them being the Piton du Milieu, 1,931 feet in height. These mounds possess a complete system of organisation of their own, being composed of the lava which issued from their summits, where in many cases cavities exist, as at Trou aux Cerfs, Grand Trou, Kanaka, Grand Bassin, and Bassin Blanc; the two latter being now filled with water. In some instances the former cavities have been obliterated, but they must all have been craters from which lava flowed, and were probably eruptions after the main volcano had become extinguished. Situated, as they are, outside the chain of mountains already referred to, their conical shape, resembling more or less a sugar loaf, supports that opinion, although it is now almost impossible to ascertain the truth concerning them, owing to the decomposition of the elements of which they are formed.

The best preserved crater is undoubtedly the Trou aux Cerfs, at Plaines Wilhems, on the eastern slope of which is built part of the town of Curepipe. It consists of a hill partly covered with shrubs, in which, at first sight, an extinct volcano could scarcely be recognised. On reaching its summit, however, the central depression, about 800 feet in diameter, and 50 feet in depth, suddenly comes to view. A winding path gives access to the bottom, which measures about a fourth of an acre in area. The lavas there are mostly decomposed, so that but few traces of them can be seen nowadays.

Another secondary volcano is Grand Bassin, in the district of Savanne, about 1,800 feet in altitude. Its circumference is irregular and forms a lake 1,200 by 500 feet, with a small islet in it, which must have once been a lava-producing crater. Basalts and lavas of all descriptions form its banks. Besides springs rising inside the lake itself, the mountains lying south-west, west-south-west, and north-west, and being sixty, eighty, and even one hundred and fifty feet higher, provide it with a constant supply of water, so that the level of the lake is almost always the same. On the left of the path leading to Grand Bassin there still remains part of the crater's lofty walls, covered all over with trees. It was once supposed that the depth of Grand Bassin was unfathomable, but soundings have proved that it scarcely exceeds fifty-five or sixty feet.

Bassin Blanc, a little farther to the south, in the mountains, is another supposed extinct volcano, with a small lake in a sort of circular funnel half a mile in circumference, the banks of which are densely covered with trees to the water's edge.

There can be no doubt, either, that Morne Brabant, Black River, Tamarin, and Bambou Mountains, and others on the circumference of the island, were once secondary craters, the activity of which was posterior to, or contemporaneous with, the great central volcano. Port Louis itself is built close to the centre of such a crater, Champ de Mars, the plain adjoining the town and extending to the foot of the mountains which enclose it, except where the town begins. This plain is composed of a ferruginous clay originating in lava decomposition, where are found lamellous, half-transparent, crystals of sulphated lime. The Pouce, the most conspicuous mountain of the chain overlooking Port Louis, presents at its top an extensive plain sloping gently in a northern and southern direction, at the back of which rises a basaltic peak, 2,650 feet above the sea level, in the shape of a gigantic thumb. Vallée des Prêtres is also an adventitious crater, towered over by the bold summit of Pieterboth Mountain, which is 2,685 feet high, and the second in elevation in the island. Of a basaltic formation, Pieterboth is reared almost perpendicularly and culminates in a sharp cone, on the apex of which is balanced a rock 35½ feet high, and 27 feet in diameter at its summit; the appearance of this huge rock having a fantastical resemblance to a well-known toy, the cup and ball.

We must go so far back as the close of the eighteenth century to find the first trustworthy report of a successful ascension of that uncommonly-shaped mountain. The feat was accomplished on the 8th September, 1790, by one Claude Peuthé, all by himself. His narrative was certified by the well-known Mauritian engineer, Lislet Geoffroy, who watched his progress with a spy-glass, from the roof of the long-demolished "Hôtel du Génie Militaire," in Rempart Street, close to the Barracks, Port Louis. On reaching the summit of the cone, Peuthé, throwing himself backwards as far as he could without losing his balance, made use of a bow to shoot, right over the overhanging rock, an arrow to which a string had been tied. When, after some fruitless attempts, he had succeeded in doing this, he managed, by means of a long bamboo switch, to get hold of the extremity of the string hanging on the other side, to which he attached a strong rope and pulled it back till it had passed over the top, when he firmly secured both ends of the rope to the rock. Finally he proceeded to climb along that rope, which proved no easy matter, in one part at all events, for it was clinging fast to the surface of the protruding rock at its widest diameter.

The same performance was renewed exactly forty years later, on the 7th September, 1830, by Captain Lloyd, Civil Engineer and Inspector-General, and Lieutenants Philpots, Keppel, and Taylor, accompanied by twenty-five blacks and sepoys, using ladders to get over the more difficult parts. Captain Lloyd had his rifle with him, instead of a bow and arrow, to shoot string and rope over the summit. Some thirty years after iron cramps and regular metallic stairs were fixed to the rock here and there for the benefit of would-be climbers; but if the feat is thereby made easier, it still requires no small amount of pluck and nerve to be accomplished.

A third secondary crater, several miles wide, lies between Rempart Mountain, on the north-east, and Tamarin Mountain, on the south-west, part of which is called the Cabinet. This is a deep ravine through which Tamarin River descends from Mare aux Vacoas by a series of seven consecutive waterfalls—the Seven Cascades—which present a magnificent sight. At a place named La Fenêtre (The Window) the cliff terminates abruptly on the north side in a precipitous chasm, disclosing the district of Black River some hundreds of feet below. A little farther in the same direction tower the threefold basaltic summits of the Trois Mamelles, 2,187 feet in altitude, looking like the ruins of some Titanic stronghold.

Colonel Pike suggests that, as the boiling mass of lava cooled down and contraction ensued, a first fissure was produced, which separated those three peaks, and was progressively widened by new eruptions, when streams of lava forced their way through the apertures to the sea. "Little by little, every succeeding hurricane hurled down masses of disintegrated rocks and piled them in the fantastic heaps where they now lie. Then light, air and water, silently at work through countless centuries, gradually wore out the rough edges of the peaks, and made them what they now are."

Rempart Mountain, 2,532 feet high, is another precipitous summit presenting a similar character. This considerable adventitious crater comprised within its circumference a further lava outlet, which stood right at the back of Tamarin Bay.

Morne Brabant and Ile aux Fourneaux may be considered as the last remains of a crater which was

COLOURED EARTHS, CHAMAREL.

swallowed up by the sea. Morne Brabant is a bold eminence, rising directly from the ocean to an altitude of 1,809 feet, and is separated from the main-land by an isthmus.

At Baie du Cap may still be traced the walls of another volcano, Cassin Mountain, rising several hundred feet, and terminating in a perpendicular bluff 300 feet high. This mountain is formed of tabular basalt, large columns of which now and then drop into the sea, owing to disintegration by the action of the waves at their base. Here also are met superposed layers of stalactites, which seem to hold but very slightly to the rock.

A few miles up Baie du Cap, in the mountains separating Savanne from Black River district, is the splendid cascade of Chamarel, 850 feet above the sea, where River du Cap, working its way through an amphitheatre of abrupt rocks, falls perpendicularly, some 300 feet, on to the edge of a grotto, sending up a spray of white vapour which rises about half the height of the cascade. The water tumbles into an oval pond, whence it flows through a deep ravine, to form a second waterfall a little above Baie du Cap.

On the top of the ravine, about a mile downwards from the fall, on the Black River side, is a barren plain measuring seven or eight acres, covered with rank and parched grass and other scanty vegetation; it presents a continuous series of parallel furrows, somewhat resembling a long-abandoned graveyard. This is the spot where coloured earths are displayed in horizontal ridges, known in the country as "Les Côtes de Melon" (The Melon's Slices). There is, of course, no external sign of their existence, and the ground must be carefully examined to realise this curious phenomenon. Their different hues, varying from yellow and yellowish brown to bright red, purple and coal-black, are said to be some forty in number. A chemical analysis was made of them at the request of Mr. A. J. Broad, manager of the Mauritius Estates and Assets Co., Ltd., proprietors of Chamarel, by Messrs. Augustus Voelcher and Sons, of London, establishing that they were very tenacious ferruginous clays almost devoid of organic matter and deficient in most of the principal elements of soil fertility. They contain scarcely any nitrogen, and have some traces of lime, still less of potash and phosphoric acid, but, *per contra*, an enormous proportion of iron and alumina.

CHAMAREL WATERFALL.

Under the sea, in the bay of Grand Port, is another crater, the walls of which are still visible from a boat on a clear day; it is about 900 feet in diameter and of great depth, as may be inferred from the dark colour of the water just above its centre.

Ile de la Passe and adjoining islets form one of the walls of this crater. They all are the result of an upheaval, but their formation is more recent than that of the main-land. Ile de la Passe is composed of friable greyish sandstone lying in strata at an angle of 30 deg. east and west, which was thrown up by a sudden convulsion. This group of islands was probably upheaved by the volcano in the bay; they seem to have been at one time more elevated than they now are, and covered with palm and cocoa-nut trees, casts of which are met with at Ile aux Fouquets. They were probably submerged, and underwent a fresh upheaval; they may even have been once united to the main-land, for the sea, in some places around them, is so shallow that even a light pirogue gets occasionally grounded there.

A few more secondary craters are to be found in the southern part of Flacq. On the banks of Grand River South-East, about 600 feet from the sea shore, is Mare aux Lubines, a basin perfectly circular with a depth of about fifty feet, and surrounded by a sort of causeway of black lava. It contains fresh water and is used as a fish pond. During strong tides the sea works its way into it through subterraneous channels, and this basin may have played some part in the upheavals of certain portions of the island.

Another is Mare de Cherval, on the right of the Chemin des Hollandais, going to Quatre Cocos.

Puits des Hollandais (Dutch Well), which also contains water, is regarded by Quoy, the French naturalist, as an extinct volcano. So are Trou Bourrignon, Trou Figue, and Trou Glacis, similar in all respects. Trou d'Eau Douce is a pond of fresh water, filled by an abundant spring quite close to the sea, at the end of a spacious bay formed by Point des Quatre Cocos; its area is half an acre. When the tide rises, the sea is forced into it and makes the water brackish; but when it again recedes, the water rapidly regains its freshness and clearness. The great fissures formed in the sides of the mountains we have mentioned, and those forming the deep ravines in which rivers wind their way, are evidently the result of disruption. Between Mount Ory, in Moka, and Corps de Garde Mountain, in Plaines Wilhems, a stream of burning lava, extending over several miles, once flowed to the sea, hollowing out the precipitous beds of Grand River North-West and River Profonde. So, also, between Corps de Garde and Rempart Mountains, exists another cut in the general wall, through which a current of molten matter discharged itself at one time, giving rise to the Seven Cascades. An analogous phenômenon is again and again repeated in most parts of Mauritius.

Corps de Garde Mountain, 2,359 feet in elevation, descends in an easy slope on its seaboard side, but is very precipitous facing the interior. Its flat summit is said to be more extensive than that of Table Mountain, near Cape Town, although it is about 175 feet less in height.

Camisard Mountain (1,592 feet), between Grand Port and Flacq, in the neighbourhood of Piton du Bambou (2,059 feet) and Trois Ilots, consists of twin conical peaks, rising perpendicularly and presenting a magnificent example of columnar basaltic rock, in hexagonal and pentagonal prisms, from two to six feet long, very regular in structure and of a bluish-grey hue. They must have formed part of an immense mass of molten matter, which, on cooling, resulted in the fissures observed in them. One section appears to have toppled over before it had perfectly solidified, the columns lying there in an irregular confused heap, inclined west and east, and their transverse section is very neatly shown wherever they have been broken sharply. There are also found layers of calcareous tufa, which can easily be cut with an axe, but hardens soon afterwards through the action of the atmosphere.

At Flacq the flow of lava, which is distinctly apparent, may be traced to one great crater in the centre of that district The mounds and débris of basaltic prisms found extensively around the Poste de Flacq are of paramount interest to geologists.

Near Turtle Bay, in Pamplemousses, Colonel Pike observed many large boulders, 20 feet above the sea-level, of ancient formation and much water-worn, appearing to have been submerged for a considerable period. Their cavities are filled with corals, which are covered over with a thick encrustation of lava somewhat embedded in them. On the other hand, in Black River district, at a place called Vacoua, near Tamarin Point, on the right of the road to Battery la Preneuse, are two masses of madrepores, about 20 feet high, in which are inserted some large basaltic stones and corals. Small shrubs have grown in their cavities.

In various parts of Mauritius there are caverns, or subterraneous cavities, at a moderate depth below the ground, which sometimes extend a long way. One called Trou Fanchon may be seen at Plaine Magnan, Grand Port, on the right of the high road from Port Louis to Mahébourg. The entrance to it measures 20 feet by 40 feet wide. At 100 feet in the interior, among fallen stones, which occasionally drop from the vault, some water filters through its sides.

Bailly, the French geologist, visited, in 1802, two of these caves at Flacq, and one at Petite Rivière. The inlet to all of them is on a sloping ground surrounded with vegetation; the opening being certainly due to the sinking in of part of the vault, which is not more than four or five feet thick. At Petite Rivière, on Chébel Estate, close to the railway station, this falling-in must have blocked up a portion of the cave, which probably continued in an opposite direction, towards the summit of a neighbouring hill called Petite Malabar. The shape of the cave is a semi-circle, the diameter of which would be represented by the floor of the cavern, and its sides are of compact blackish lava, presenting small irregular cavities, as well as crystals of peridot. A perfectly symmetrical cornice runs right and left over the sides, three or four feet above the floor. Its structure differs altogether from the rock to which it adheres; its colour is grey, its grain friable, resembling dry mud, and must have been deposited there by a flow of lava passing through the cave, which consolidated the parts in contact with the rock as it cooled down, and formed the walls of the cavern. The floor is very muddy, and rises more and more on proceeding in a seaward direction. It is composed of the earth carried in by rain and constantly diluted by infiltrations from the vault. It is said that this cave has its exit on the sea-shore, several miles distant, at Pointe aux Caves; but it is too narrow, in some parts, to allow a man to accomplish the journey through it, even if he crept along on his knees.

Bailly visited at Flacq, or rather at Rivière du Rempart, two other caves which he found almost similar, except that the floor there was full of water filtrating through the rocks. The people in the neighbourhood used it for drinking purposes, he said, as there was no river at hand.

In that same part of Mauritius a flow of compact lava made its way through a forest, as is indicated by cylindrical holes found here and there, on the sides of which is moulded the easily recognizable impress of bark; in others are encrusted fragments of charcoal and débris of vegetable matter. That flow of lava must have been very slow in its progress, and partially cooled; otherwise it would have burnt and destroyed all organic matter it came across, and left no trace at all of what had existed there previously. This place, called Plaine des Roches, borders the districts of Flacq and Rivière du Rempart, and extends to the sea at Poudre d'Or. The ground, strewn all over with flagstones of lava forming a regular pavement, appears to have been thoroughly undermined and to cover some extensive caves, for, as it is traversed by the railway line, a hollow resounding sound is produced whenever a train rolls over it.

Ile d'Ambre, off the coast, opposite Poudre d'Or, is also formed of volcanic rocks, and was very likely produced by an immense flow of lava running in the same direction, from the interior of Mauritius, as well as from a large volcano now submerged, in the north-east, having its centre somewhere between Gunners' Quoin and Flat Island. This is plainly seen on the eastern coast of Ile d'Ambre, where lava has cooled in regular waves. The greatest length of that islet is one mile and a half from east to west; but its width varies considerably on account of the deep indentations of the shore. Its area is about 600 acres, and its culminating point is only fifty feet above the sea-level. It presents the same configuration as the neighbouring part of Rivière du Rempart, where, however, the flows of argillo-ferruginous lava are more scarce and more decomposed, and there exist, also, less scoriated rocks than in Plaine des Roches.

What mostly proves, contrary to Le Gentil's assertion, that Ile d'Ambre is due to volcanic causes, and is not madreporous, and what, at the same time, is one of the most striking features of that islet, is the so-called crater—a hole in the central part, elliptic in shape, but very nearly circular, being 150 to 200 feet in both directions, thirty feet deep, ten of which are full of brackish water. The sides and walls of the depression are basaltic, the bottom somewhat wider than the opening. Its banks are not at all raised, as is the case in ordinary craters; but this must have been produced more recently by some accidental disintegration.

Although the lavas in Mauritius are in a high state of degradation, it is easy to realize that they are commonly composed of a kind of clayey ferruginous porphyry containing also various substances of which the most common is peridot. This porphyry is somewhat compact, but more generally porous, with small holes of a black or iron grey colour, possessing a pungent clayey smell when moistened, a strong magnetic action on the loadstone, producing a sonorous sound and letting off sparks when struck with a steel hammer. Such are the characteristics of lavas of that kind, although they may sometimes be modified as to colour, consistency, or other properties. Besides peridot, it is not infrequent to find in them feldspar and pyroxen.

The porous lavas are of two kinds: first, those with large cavities; secondly, those with small pores. The latter are filled with calcareous infiltrations. In the others foreign substances are but seldom found; they are darker in shade, lighter in weight, more bloated, and bear a great resemblance to scoria from iron-works.

Apart from the substances mentioned, and which are generally found, there are others, such as a primitive chabosia and crystallized phosphated iron, the latter frequently covering the sides of the cavities, in porous lavas, with a bluish dust. There is also a sort of red or purple lava, almost entirely decomposed, and presenting the appearance of a puzzolana which would have been altered by length of time.

Lavas are, as a rule, exposed to decomposition through the combined action of air and rain-water, which transforms them into an earthy mould by oxidizing the iron they contain, and thereby giving them a more or less reddish hue. Rain-water, in flowing over such decomposed lavas, carries off this earthy matter and deposits it over the low lands on the sea board, in horizontal layers, so perfectly regular that they look as if they had been actually formed in the places where they are now seen. Some of these, however, have retained the position where Nature first formed them, and this is a very curious phenomenon. In various parts of Mauritius are strata of hard lavas, separated from each other by layers of the mould originating in the decomposition of the rock on which they rest. That decomposition seems to have stopped whenever a flow

"LA FENÊTRE" (THE WINDOW), NEAR TAMARIN FALLS.

of lava covered the already fairly altered stratum ; and the new lava underwent a similar process in its turn, till a fresh eruption stopped its disorganization.

We shall now proceed to examine the formation of some small islands adjoining the northern coast of Mauritius. Proceeding from west to east, the first we meet is Gunners' Quoin, off Cape Malheureux. It is 518 feet high, composed of crumbling volcanic sandstone disposed in strata lying south-east, at an angle of 30 deg. with the horizon ; the strata being distinctly visible from the level of the sea to the rock's summit. Part of this island, at its eastern base, is covered with volcanic stones and lavas that once flowed over it from a neighbouring disappeared volcano—the same, probably, which upheaved Flat and Amber Islands.

Flat Island opposite the Mapou Coast comes next. On its northern shore coral blocks are found forty or fifty feet above the level of the sea, and masses of coral rise everywhere above the prevailing vegetation.

According to Dr. Ayres (*Geology of Flat and Gabriel Islands*) : "In the part facing Round Island are found fossilized remains of an extensive forest, consisting of stumps of trees closely planted, about two feet in diameter. The greater part of these are endogenous, presenting the appearance of the enlarged bases of palms, though many of the roots appear to possess an exogenous character. The outer crust is hard, lined on the inner and hollowed surface by a loose intertwined network of coarse fibres, such as are seen in the interior of cocoa and other palms, and screw-pines. On some parts of the denuded surface of the volcanic rocks roots are thickly interlaced, and the still finer fibres of the roots appear to form the chief parts of the formation, which is about fifteen feet deep, hard, and resembles a muddy substance recently callified. Here and there a perfect stem is visible, intermixed with masses of loose corals and shells of existing species. On the ground above the lava, covered with grass and herbage, trunks of trees are visible, broken or lying on the surface; one of them, four or five feet long, presenting the appearance of the trunk of a palm. No sea-shells are found in this stratum occupied by the roots of trees, though abundant in the coral strata below."

Colonel Pike adds: "Between those different strata, volcanic stones and pebbles lie in great regularity, indicating the various periods of activity of the neighbouring volcano."

Close to Flat Island is a curious steep rock, the Pigeonnier (Pigeon House), where a lighthouse has been erected. It is probable that this rock formed part of the wall of the already-mentioned volcano, the rest of which was swallowed up by the sea. On its eastern declivity is a sort of amphitheatre of pure basaltic rocks, heaped up in confusion by some volcanic agency at a more recent date.

Still farther east, Round Island, 1,054 feet in altitude, also owes its origin to an upheaval from the sea. As its names indicates, it is a semi-spherical mass of rock rising from the ocean in the shape of a haystack. On several Dutch maps of the sixteenth century it is, in fact, designated as the "Haystack." There is no actual landing place there; the only part where it can be approached is in the south-west, where a sort of narrow causeway, scarcely two or three feet wide, runs over the perpendicular wall. One has to jump from the boat when the waves lift it up to the level of this scanty projection. Close by, a few slippery basalts of unequal height, forming a sort of rudimentary stair, give access to a cavern, produced, says Colonel Pike, "by an immense mass of detached rock having tumbled into the sea, leaving a cliff which overhangs it and forms a very good shelter. It rises from the sea at an angle of 45 deg. for about 100 feet. . . . When the opening is reached, one must descend about twelve feet to come to the floor of the cave. The passage from the basis upwards, through a gulch about 700 feet, is rough and difficult. The different strata lying on each other are perfectly visible, and define well the different periods of this formation. The peculiar form of these rocks is also very remarkable; some parts resemble the ruins of old Gothic structures, others a series of elegant pulpits carved out of red sandstone; many represent baptismal fonts. The top of the mountain is 1,000 feet above the sea level, where stands a huge block of basalt ten to fifteen feet high, which is the culminating point, from which is seen in the distance, north-eastwards, Serpent Island, 531 feet high, about half a mile off, white all over with guano, as if with snow. . . .

"Round Island is a crater formed of strata of friable brownish volcanic sandstone and tufa, all round the axis of the cave, rising more and more from its base to the summit. In one of the fissures, in the north-east, are found a great number of stratified lavas, indicating the different periods of their formation. Not a fossil or water mark is to be seen in those strata below the surface, but above it is a white rock, similar to the variegated marble in which fossil shells are found, mostly microscopic. These were evidently a compact mass of limestone, probably having undergone a partial metamorphic process.

"The general geological features of Round Island stand as a key to open out the immensity of the period in which volcanic action was going on here and at Mauritius, and are a proof that since those isolated rocks were upheaved, an immensurable interval of time must have elapsed. Near and round the top and centre of the island are groups of volcanic rocks, many tons in weight, but there is no appearance of any flow of lava. They may have been thrown up from some neighbouring volcano, and deposited there before the upheaval of the island. There is not the slightest sign of depression or indication of a crater on the summit. Long after the upheaval of Round Island volcanic action was apparently still vigorous at Mauritius and its vicinity. Very active were submarine volcanoes which rose above the sea and were again depressed. The Diamond Rock and others, appearing so near the surface that the waves break over them in the calmest weather, are evidently the tops of very high submerged mountains which were once, in all probability, united to the main-land. At Table Rock, where the landing place is situated, is a flow of lâva from the south-west, which is filled with detached pieces of scoria, similar to that at Mauritius, but differing from that in the structure of the island."

MORNE BRABANT.

POINTE NATUREL.

TROU AUX CERFS.

[Photos by permission, Ladies' Fine Needlework Association.

Returning to Mauritius, and following up the shore, may be noticed almost everywhere the agency of polypous animals and madrepores. They have raised from the bottom of the ocean a wall which encircles the whole island as a protecting belt from the incursion of the waves, whilst rendering access to its shores dangerous. The work performed by these minute creatures continues with unceasing energy, and had its beginning in the remotest times. They have already built up the exterior reefs which surround the main-land, and have even constructed perfect islets, such as Ile aux Tonneliers, and a few more which we shall mention presently

On the coast of Petite Savanne, at Ste. Marie, at the mouth of River des Galets, close to the shore and a few feet under water, are seen huge blocks of the porous madrepores, variously coloured, some snow-white, others pink, light green or mauve, of the most beautiful effect.

Not only are such petrifications to be found in the sea, or on the coast, but they may even be observed in the interior of Mauritius, especially at Pamplemousses, alternating with beds of lava; a proof that that part of the island was formerly under the sea, and that burning lava, flowing under the billows before it had solidified, covered over the strata of madrepores. As soon as that layer had solidified and its temperature was lowered, the tiny creatures resumed work and continued until a new eruption interfered once more with their operations. One would suppose that the level of the sea had not always been constant, as strata of calcareous rocks have been discovered in very elevated localities. Cossigny mentions strata dug up at 500 feet above the level of the sea, where fragments of petrified turtles were found. In the vicinity of Chamarel, Colonel Pike also came across "corals in a perfect state of preservation, buried in débris of cretaceous formation; but none of the species now exist in the warm tropical seas where they once lived." He also identified beds more than fifteen feet in thickness, between Port Louis and Grand River North-West, the Customs House at Port Louis being built entirely over one of these formations. Near River du Poste, between Grand Port and Savanne, at an altitude of about 1,000 feet, he discovered a stratum of plastic clay twelve feet deep, underlying a thick bed of gravel.

LE CAP, SAVANNE.

It is a fact that such deposits could only be formed under water; so that two explanations are possible: "Either the water was elevated above these points for a sufficiently long time to form thick beds of them, or these beds were raised up from the bottom of the sea to the height where we now find them." As there is no proof to warrant that the sea ever altered its level to such an extent within the time of history, Colonel Pike concludes very rightly in favour of an upheaval, an opinion supported by positive events which have taken place on the earth's surface within the memory of man.

The most remarkable instance of islets of madrepore formation along the coast of Mauritius is assuredly Ile aux Aigrettes, at the entrance to the Bay of Grand Port, close to Mahébourg. Ile aux Aigrettes is calcareous all over, rising thirty feet above the sea and covered with dense vegetation, mostly shrubs, with some actual trees here and there. The clay composing it presents some very curious characteristics; it is extremely hard, although small fragments of it may be broken with a hammer; its colour is ashy-grey externally and yellowish-white inside; it is formed of a madrepore sand similar to that found at the bottom of the sea, inside the reefs. The surface of Ile aux Aigrettes presents a strongly variegated aspect, crevices, cones, fissures, excavations, perpendicular cylindric holes, others smaller and horizontal, and finally, cornices, projecting right over the sea. The whole island seems to be undermined at its base, so as to form, at a height of four, five, and six feet, an irregular vault, which reaches sometimes ten or twelve feet.

Very often embedded in these holes is seen another variety of clay, reddish and ferruginous, which is very porous and assumes the shape of cylinders rising like the trunks of trees above the grey limestone. As it is more subject to decomposition by sea water, it has altogether disappeared in some places, leaving round holes in its stead, which have occasionally been filled up by other materials.

Monkey Island, within the bay, opposite Treize Cantons, is of an analogous formation; but the sea has so constantly kept hewing out its base, that it has taken the form of a huge mushroom.

There are two islets of an identical nature off Black River, at the west of Ilot du Morne. They are the Bénitiers rocks, one eighteen and the other ten feet in diameter. Their foundations have also been eaten up by the sea, whereby they have the appearance of two parasols. But the base of the smaller, lying southward of the other, having been entirely worn away, it was upset by a hurricane in 1824, and now lies on its side. In concluding this essay, we cannot do better than mention two other curiosities of Nature which may be observed on the south coast of Grand Port, not far from Virginia Estate. The first is called Pointe Naturel (Natural Bridge); it is a long narrow rocky causeway protruding into the sea, and has been hollowed out by the waves in two different places, so as to form two very regular arches separated by a pile.

BAIE DU CAP.

The other is the Souffleur, of which the following description was given by Lieutenant Taylor about 1830:—

"A huge mass of rocky matter runs out into the sea from the main-land, to which it is joined by a neck of rock not two feet broad. The constant beating of the tremendous swell that rolls in has undermined it in every direction, till it has exactly the appearance of a Gothic building with a number of arches in the centre of the rock, which is about thirty-five or forty feet above the sea. The water has forced two passages vertically upwards, which are worn as smooth and cylindrical as if cut by a chisel. When a heavy sea rolls in, it of course fills in an instant the hollow caves underneath, and finding no other egress, and being borne in with tremendous violence, it rushes up those chimneys and flies, roaring furiously, to a height of fully sixty feet. The moment the wave recedes, the vacuum beneath causes the wind to rush into the two apertures with a loud humming noise which is heard at a considerable distance. . . . The waves roll on long and unbroken, fully twenty-five feet high, till, meeting the head-land, they break clear over it, sending the spray flying over to the mainland, while, from the centre of this mass of foam, the Souffleur shoots up with a noise which may be distinctly heard two or three miles off."

EXTINCT BIRDS OF THE MASCARENE ISLANDS.

By ALBERT PITOT.

I.—THE DODO.

THE object of this essay is to briefly summarize all that relates to the Dodo, and to say how after its very existence had been scornfully denied by some, careful inquiries and clever deductions succeeded in establishing the fact that the preposterous, winged creature was not a mythical and fantastic product of imagination.

The reconstitution of an almost complete skeleton, by means of fossil bones of the bird, brought to light by excavations, has at last shown the truth of assertions which, although supported by unimpeachable documents, were still open both to criticism and scepticism. About half a century ago the question was finally settled. Not only had the Dodo existed, but it had existed in Mauritius exclusively; it was one of the few indigenous specimens peculiar to this island's fauna.

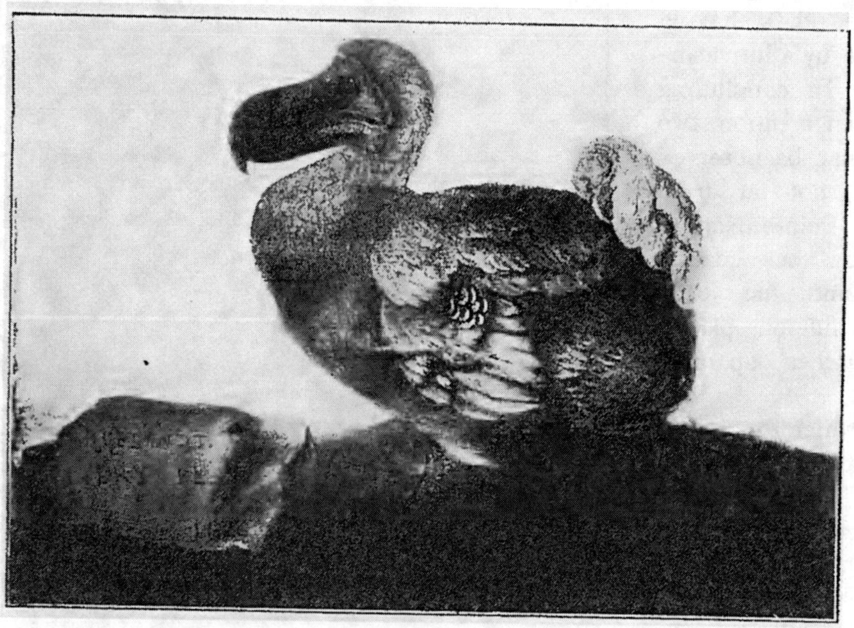

THE DODO.

(From the Copy in the Museum, Port Louis, from the Painting by Roelandt Savery, dated 1626.)

The Dodo has been described by those who saw it as a clumsy and ungainly bird, of a slow and indolent gait, a little larger than a swan or a full-grown turkey, weighing fifty pounds at least; its body being massive, altogether devoid of elegance, heavily built, and covered over with a blackish sort of down. Its head was protuberant and strongly characterized, totally bald and of a parchment-like appearance, of a whitish colour from the eyes downwards to the beak, which was stout, long, bent in the shape of a petrel's, of a pale greenish-yellow hue, and of such a powerful structure that the Dodo could easily grind the seeds of wild trees; and snatch off the extremely tough pericarp of the Pandanus (*Vacoa*), its ordinary food. It also used its beak with equal facility as a defensive weapon in case of need; and this can be readily believed, for according to Pieter Willem Verhuffen, or Verhoeven, who visited Mauritius in 1611, his men, while capturing Dodos, had to take great care to avoid the strokes of their bills, which inflicted severe wounds.

The Dodo's wings were perfectly rudimental, not even capable of raising the bird off the ground, and, as Sir Thomas Herbert (*A Relation of One Year's Travels in Africa and Asia, 1677*) had it, "seemed only destined to place the Dodo among the bird tribe," being composed of not more than three or four black, thick and curved plumes. The Dodo's hind part was rounded and deprived of a tail, save for a tuft of scanty ash-coloured and frizzled feathers, "as many in number," François Cauche claimed, "as the bird counted years of existence," and not unlike, according to Sir Thomas Herbert, "a Chinaman's beard." Its eyes were small and ugly, its legs short, thick, stumpy, protected all over by darkish scales. "Its stomach was fiery," said Herbert, "and could even digest stones!"

The presence in the Dodo's stomach of pebbles, "nearly as large as a man's fist," if credit is to be given to some narrators, was ascertained by most travellers. It is likely enough that, after the habit of the ostrich and Molucca pigeon, the Dodo actually used such stones to triturate the more or less tough eatables upon which it lived.

The bird's appearance was sad and gloomy, "as if," according to Herbert, "it were conscious of the injustice with which Nature had treated it." Its cry, asserted Cauche, was similar to that of a goose.

The female bird laid only one egg at a time, white and about the size of "a halfpenny loaf," which it deposited on a heap of dry grass arranged in the shape of a nest, and near which it was careful to place a white pebble of the size of a hen's egg. Cauche is the only one to mention that peculiarity, although he does not explain the reason for such an arrangement.

The Dodo generally dwelt in plains on the skirts of a forest, and very seldom ventured on broken ground. According to some, its flesh was detestable, hard, tough, oily and indigestible; so that the first Dutch travellers who tasted it called it *Walgvogel* (nauseous bird); whilst others, later, gladly partook of its breast, which was for them a great delicacy. Four, three, and even two of the birds were enough to satisfy the crew's appetite at a time.

The Dodo has been designated under various appellations, and it is no easy matter to determine with precision their etymology, nor the time when they were first given; *Walgvogel*, however, is an exception, but the surname was not preserved very long. *Dodaer*, *doder*, *dodo* and *dronte* (*Didus Ineptus* of Linnæus), were the names it simultaneously received; another form, *Totersten*, is either a corruption of the plural *Dodaersen* or of *Todaerses*, the name given by Jean Chrétien Hoffmann to the *Aphanapteryx*, an altogether different bird.

Strickland and Melville, in their most excellent book, *The Dodo and its Kindred*, derive *Dodaer* from the Dutch *Doodoor* (stupid, lazy), and are of opinion that this must have been a slang term used by sailors. Mr. Alfred Newton, of Cambridge (*A Dictionary of Birds*), thinks it was simply the popular word for the *Dabchick*, or small Grebe, a bird whose tail consists of a tuft of feathers like the Dodo's. Another explanation was offered by Mr. Léon Doyen, Professor in the Mauritius Royal College some forty years ago, a man of vast intellectual powers, who assembled an enormous quantity of authentic documents relating to the history of this island, and began writing a masterly work, which unfortunately was never ended nor published. In an unfinished manuscript essay on the Birds of Mauritius, he suggests that *Dodaers* might come from two Dutch vulgar words, *dod*, dirty, and *aarse*, which need not be translated.

Sir Thomas Herbert was the first to call it Dodo, as derived from the Portuguese *doudo*, stupid. This English gentleman landed in Mauritius on the 10th June, 1628, when coming back from Persia, where he had followed an embassy sent by King Charles I. to the Padishah. His description of this island is as erroneous as it is fantastically enthusiastic. But a fortnight before, on the 28th May, one Emmanuel Altham, embarked on another ship of the same squadron, landed here and wrote to his brother, in Essex, the following letters, wherein he refers to the Dodo as a rarity.

The first letter runs thus:—

"Right wor and lovinge brother,

. . . . . . We were ordered by ye said councell to go to an island, called ye Mauritius, lying in 20d. of south latt.; where we arrived ye 28th of May; this island havinge many goates, hogs and cowes upon it, and very strange fowles, called by ye portingalls *Dodo*, which for the rareness of the same, the like beinge not in ye world but here, I have sent you one by Mr. Perce, who did arrive with ye ship *William* at this island ye 10th of June.—Your most lovinge brother,—Emmanuel Altham,—June ye 18th 1628, ffro ye Mauritius."

In the margin is written:—

"Of Mr. Perce you shall receve a jarr of ginger for my sister, some beades for my cosins your daughters, and a bird called a *Dodo*, if it live."

The following is the address:—

"To ye right woor my most lovinge brother Sr Edward Altham, at Marke Hall, in Essex. Deliver."

The second letter reads:—

"You shall receve a jarr of India ginger for my sister your wife, as also some beades for my cosins your daughters, and with all a strange fowle which I had at the island Mauritius, called by ye portingalls a Dodo, which for the rareness thereof I hope will be welcome to you. Mauritius ye 18th June 1628. Your most lovinge brother, Emmanuel Altham."

Some forty years ago, these letters got into the hands of Dr. John Bramston Wilmot, of Tunbridge Wells, who lent them to Mr. Alfred Newton, the famed naturalist, to be placed before the London Zoological Society, which was accordingly done on the 19th May, 1874. At the death of Dr. Wilmot, the interesting documents which, had they been his property, he would have offered to a public library, were burnt along with waste papers. But Mr. Newton had fortunately made a literal transcription of both of them while they were in his possession.

Supporting his opinion by Herbert's and Altham's testimonies, Mr. Newton seems quite prepared to accept Herbert's theory, although he declares that, had the loquacious baronet been alone in his assertion, he would by no means have felt disposed to endorse the views of such an amateur etymologist.

Strickland, who was not aware of the existence of the letters in question when he wrote his book, accuses the pedantic Sir Thomas Herbert of having knowingly altered the form *Dodar*, so as to make it agree with his philologic theory.

As for the term *Dronte*, nobody ever gave any explanation of it.

Cauche saw the bird later than Herbert, in 1638, and without taking the trouble to ascertain the name by which it was called, he believed that the Dodo came from an adjoining island designated Nazareth, and termed it Bird of Nazareth, supporting that name by a map of the sixteenth century on which Rodrigues figures as the Island of Nazareth, or Island of Nazari. Mr. L. Doyen, in the essay to which we have already alluded, thinks that Cauche, having first landed at Rodrigues, may have seen there a kindred of the Dodo, and that this led him to mistake one bird for another. Strickland brings forward the rather risky opinion that Cauche mistook *Bird of Nausea* with *Bird of Nazareth.*

It is probable that, after the first visit of the Dutch to Mauritius, some specimens of the Dodo were introduced into Europe as rarities; but no proof of this is forthcoming till about forty years later; whilst sketches made by travellers were numerous, many of which have been engraved. In course of time paintings were produced, actual portraits having most likely been executed from living models.

De Bry, in his *India Orientalis*, has an interesting etching showing for the first time the *Walgvogel*, as he terms it, and the footnote mentions that the travellers brought a live specimen to Holland.

From a sketch made by Van de Venne, Clusius, in his *Exotica*, gave some time afterwards a drawing of the bird.

The manuscript of Harmansen's travels, dated 1601–1603, and preserved in the Archives at The Hague, contains five pen-and-ink sketches of the *Dodor*, some of which possess an extraordinary lifelike appearance.

Bonteköe, who did not land in Mauritius, but in Mascarenhas (Bourbon), in 1619, presents a fair enough outline of a bird, which may be the Solitaire peculiar to that island, although it bears a strong resemblance to the Dodo.

Strickland mentions several paintings signed by Roelandt Savery, who was born at Courtrai, in Flanders, in 1556, and died in 1639. A picture preserved at Berlin represents the animals in Eden; and in a corner stands the clumsy Dodo, beside which, on a stone, can be read the author's signature: *Roelandt Savery fe. 1626*. In another painting by the same artist, bearing the date 1628, and now in the Belvedere Collection, Vienna, the Dodo forms part of a group of birds, and its appearance is so natural that the painter must have certainly painted it from life.

A portrait, dated 1627, and signed Griemare, is to be seen at Sion House, in the Duke of Northumberland's Gallery. A drawing of the Dodo, attributed to the Dutch painter, Hoefnage, born about 1545, formerly existed in the Library of the Austrian Emperor Francis I. According to Van Frammerfeld, this had been executed, prior to 1626, from the original bird which was kept in Emperor Rudolph's aviary. This bird's head, or rather, part of its head, was accidentally found, in 1850, at the Museum at Prague.

There still exist other paintings by Roelandt Savery; one is in The Hague Museum, showing Orpheus charming the whole creation and even the Dodo; another is in the Broderip Collection, belonging to the London Zoological Society; a third is at Pommersfeld, near Bamberg, in the Schönbrun Gallery; a fourth, formerly belonging to Dr. Sayffery, is at Stuttgart. All of them are signed, although they bear no date; but they all were probably executed between 1626 and 1628.

The large Sloane Picture, in the British Museum, has no date either; another, still larger, dated 1651, and attributed to John Savery, junior, the nephew of Roelandt, is preserved at Oxford. At Haarlem, in the hands of Dr. Van der Willege, about 1840, was a picture without date, attributed to Pieter Holsteyn. Sir Thomas Herbert gives a rough outline of the *Doodor*, which, nevertheless, is tolerably recognizable. Most of these illustrations are produced in Strickland's work; but Mr. Alfred Newton is the only person who gives one of the pen-and-ink sketches in Harmansen's manuscript.

So much for illustrations of the bird; let us now consider it as it lived.

The first positive assertion we come across of the despatch of a Dodo to Europe is to be found in the two letters addressed by Emmanuel Altham to his brother, on the 18th June, 1628, describing the bird he was sending as a most extraordinary creature. But there is no proof that the specimen ever reached its destination. Altham himself does not seem at all confident that it would, for he adds in a postscript these three words: "*if it live.*"

On the other hand, in 1634, Thomas Crossfield, of Queen's College, Oxford, makes an entry in his diary, to the effect that one Mr. Gossling had offered "a *Dodor* (a black bird from India) to the School of Anatomy."

Four years later Sir Hannon Lestrange stopped, in the streets of London, in front of a huge painted sign-board depicting a fantastic fowl. On entering the establishment, he was brought before a big bird, larger than a turkey, with legs and claws fairly similar to that fowl's, though somewhat shorter and stronger. The keeper called it a Dodo, and invited the onlookers to feed it with pebbles about the size of a nutmeg.

THE DODO.

These curious but imperfect figures of the Dodo are facsimiles, reduced about one-fifth of the original size, of pen-and-ink sketches, dated Mauritius, 1602, in the manuscript of Harmansen's Voyage, 1601-03, preserved in the Record Office at The Hague. The reference to them in the manuscript is as follows:—

"These birds are found in great numbers in Mauritius. They cannot fly, are very good to eat, and form a most valuable article of consumption for vessels' crews. In their stomachs are occasionally found pebbles of the size of an egg, more or less. They were called Griffins, or Kermesse Geese, because the vessels anchored at Mauritius at the time of the Amsterdam Annual Fair, Kermesse (September, 1602)."

The third from the top was reproduced by Messrs. Alfred Newton and Hans Gadow in their *Dictionary of Birds*. The others were never published until 1906, when they were copied by Mr. Albert Pitot, the writer of the present article, in his book *T'Eylandt Mauritius, Esquisses Historiques, 1592-1710*. Mr. Pitot obtained them from traces made between 1860 and 1870, on thin oiled paper, from the original, for Mr. Leon Doyen, Professor at the Royal College, Mauritius, by Mr. Leopold Estourgies, in the Record Office at The Hague. When Mr. Doyen died his valuable collection of documents, composed of French translations of the Dutch official papers preserved at The Hague and literal certified copies from the Paris and Versailles Archives, passed into the possession of the late Mr. Eugene Leclezio, from whose son, the Hon. Henri Leclezio, C.M.G., they were obtained by Mr. Pitot.

These are the only live specimens of which positive mention has ever been made; to them may also be added Emperor Rudolph's bird. Meanwhile the Dodo was getting scarce in Mauritius; travellers no longer seem to have seen it; the Dutch established in the island a few years later make no mention of it. Governor Hubert Hugo alone, in 1674, writes that a maroon slave, who had been at large for eleven years and was then captured, asserted that only twice had he noticed some of the birds in very secluded places.

Seven years afterwards, Benjamin Harris, who visited Mauritius on board the *Berkeley Castle*, speaks of the Dodo as if he had actually seen it, which, we think, is most improbable. At all events, it is easy to understand that such a slow-moving creature should have readily been destroyed, not so much by men as by domestic animals, pigs especially, which the Dutch were in the habit of setting at liberty in Mauritius, and which, being left to themselves in the then unoccupied island, must have made great destruction of the Dodo's eggs and young, to say nothing of full-grown birds, whenever hunger pressed them. Consequently, in 1693 at the latest, the Dodo had certainly disappeared altogether; otherwise Leguat, who was such an attentive observer and very exact in his descriptions, would assuredly have spoken of it.

Now for naturalized specimens:—

In the catalogue drawn up by Tradescant, in 1651, of the rarities exhibited at South Lambeth, mention is made, among *whole birds*, of a *Dodar* from Mauritius, "which cannot fly on account of its corpulence."

Strickland hints that this might have been, *sic transit gloria mundi*, the stuffed body of the very bird Lestrange had seen thirteen years before, unless it was given to the exhibitor by Sir Thomas Herbert, who, in a letter to Sir Elias Ashmole, mentions having presented Mr. Tredeson (*sic*), of South Lambeth, with several curious objects gathered in his travels. Yet the author adds that, should Sir Thomas Herbert have really killed, stuffed and brought a Dodo to London, it is not likely that he would have failed in boasting about it, with which we quite agree.

Be that as it may, this naturalized specimen, whilst it formed part of Tradescant's collection, was mentioned by Willoughby in his *Ornithology*, in 1676. Towards 1684 it figured in the Ashmolean Collection at Oxford, and was catalogued by Llhwyd. Hyde spoke of it in 1700 in his *History of the Religion of the Persians*. It remained in the Ashmolean Collection for half a century, and must have become somewhat deteriorated, for in 1755 the Directors of the Museum gave orders for its destruction. In conformity with the founder's instructions, however, the head and right foot of the bird were preserved and are still extant there.

Clusius, in his *Exotica*, published in 1605, affirms having seen the foot of a Dodo.

In a Catalogue of Natural Curiosities, shown in 1665, by one Hubert, *alias* Forbes, near the western extremity of St. Paul's, London, in the building formerly known as the Music Hall, is noted the leg of a Dodo, "a large bird from Mauritius which cannot fly." This leg became some time afterwards the property of the Royal Society, and figured in 1681 in a list prepared by Gaw. It was then transferred to the British Museum, where it may still be seen. It is a left leg, but it differs so much in size from the Oxford specimen that both cannot possibly be attributed to the same bird.

In 1666 Olearius, in his catalogue of the Gottorf Museum, at Copenhagen, describes the bird's skull, a specimen which had been mislaid, and found again there sixty years later.

Finally, in 1775, took place the destruction of Ashmole's stuffed Dodo at Oxford, its right foot, however, being preserved.

The rapid extinction of the Dodo, which only the first Dutch travellers probably had ever seen, the abandonment of Mauritius by colonists of that nation, and the subsequent occupation of the island by the French, all formed circumstances which combined to root out tradition itself respecting the bird. Baron Grant, who sojourned at the Isle of France from 1740 to 1760, is positive that the Dodo did not exist in his time.

Linnæus had classed it among gallinaceous birds; Buffon very rightly placed it apart altogether. In 1778, Mr. Morel, Secretary to the Port Louis Hospital, having his curiosity aroused by the observations of the illustrious zoologist, made an inquiry amongst the oldest inhabitants, none of whom, however, had the slightest knowledge of the existence of the Dodo. Thirty-eight years later, on the 20th September, 1816, a banquet was held at Port Louis, Mr. Farquhar occupying the chair, to commemorate the centenary of Dufresne's taking possession of the Isle of France. Among the guests were nineteen of the oldest inhabitants, aged from seventy-eight to ninety-two years, and when the Dodo was discussed, none of those old people had ever heard of it before.

The great paucity of information regarding the Dodo led to general scepticism and denial that such a preposterous bird could ever have existed; but this unbelief was ably combated by Duncan, manager of the Ashmolean Museum, who published in 1828 a masterly essay on the subject. Ten years later, about 1838, Broderip substantiated whatever he could procure of proofs in a remarkably clear article. Then came H. E. Strickland and A. G. Melville with a complete monography of the Dodo and its kindred, comprising an analysis of everything that had been written about the bird till 1848, quoting Linnæus and Buffon, and the erroneous opinion of Blainville, who claimed that the Dodo was a bird of prey akin to the vulture. Cuvier, although such a genius, wrote with almost incredible inaccuracy on the matter, and Lesson's composition on the same subject is just as erroneous. Brandt, of the Imperial Academy of St. Petersburg, placed the Dodo among the graillies, closely allied to the plover; Reinhardt, of Copenhagen, classified it among the pigeon tribe (*Columbidæ*); and his conclusion was adopted by Strickland and Melville. They were soon followed by Owen, who accorded the Dodo a place in the order *Rasores*.

The question remained in that state for seventeen years, when an unexpected occurrence created a great sensation in the scientific world. A Government schoolmaster at Grand Port, Mauritius, Mr. George Clark, a man of quiet manners, occupying an inferior situation, but thoroughly versed in natural sciences, read Strickland's book with interest, and made several inquiries in Mauritius concerning the Dodo, without meeting with the slightest success. Some years later, a distinguished scholar, Dr. Ayres, happening to visit Mahébourg, met Clark and questioned him as to the likelihood of discovering fossil remains of animals, if excavations were made around the old Dutch settlement. Clark thought this was most improbable, as the whole surface of the soil there was constantly washed over by torrents coming down from the mountains, which closely lined the shore. But his firm belief was that a good many bones could be collected in some neighbouring marshes and alluvial lands. This had been his constant opinion, although he had never been able to test it through lack of time and money.

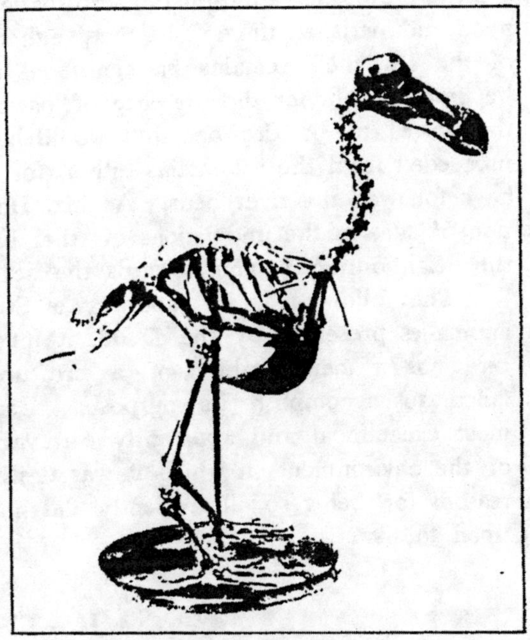

SKELETON OF THE DODO, IN THE MUSEUM, PORT LOUIS.

Very soon after, about 1864, as the railway line was being constructed, Clark expected that the trenches opened up might disclose some fossils, and made inquiries accordingly, but with fruitless result.

In September, 1865, Mr. Gaston de Bissy, a planter of the district, directed his employees to dig up the marsh, Mare aux Songes, on his estate for the purpose of using the mould as a fertilizer. At a depth of two or three feet below the surface, the men discovered a mass of bones, mostly of turtle and deer. Clark being informed of this, asked Mr. de Bissy to set aside such bones as could be found, explaining at the same time his quest. Clark himself visited the estate and was personally present at the excavations, and although nothing unusual was forthcoming, he was by no means discouraged. Obtaining from Mr. de Bissy two labourers, he got them to penetrate into the blackish water, over three feet deep, where with their feet they searched the mud carefully. After several futile attempts, three bones of a large bird were brought up—a whole tibia, part of another, and a broken tarsus. This most valuable discovery led Clark to persevere, and, in a comparatively short time, he had assembled all the bones, with the exception of the digits and some vertebræ, to form a complete skeleton. Sir Robert Owen offered to prepare this skeleton himself, after Clark had sent the bones to the British Museum.

The skeleton was accordingly constructed, and all zoologists were compelled to accept unreservedly the opinion of Reinhardt, supported by Strickland, Melville, and Owen himself, that the Dodo was nothing but a gigantic, brevipennate, and frugivorous pigeon.

Later still, in 1889, Mr. Théodore Sauzier, a Mauritian residing in Paris, visited his native island

and obtained assistance from the Colonial Government to make further researches in Mare aux Songes, which resulted in the discovery of a considerable number of bones of Dodos, parrots, deer, turtles, and the aphanapteryx. A few specimens were sent by Mr. Sauzier to Sir Edward Newton, formerly Colonial Secretary of this island (brother of the distinguished zoologist), who had taken much interest in Mr. Clark's investigations. An entire skeleton constructed by Mr. A. Milne Edwards, of Paris, was presented to the Mauritius Museum by Mr. Sauzier, who accompanied it with a copy of Savery's Berlin picture of the Dodo, as shown by the photographic reproduction on page 82.

Searches are still being privately continued throughout Mauritius. We have had occasion to examine a collection of fossils got together by an amateur, Mr. Thirioux, who, besides numerous remains of turtles, parrots, lizards and aphanapteryx, has succeeded in setting up his own complete skeleton of a Dodo, after exploring the environs of Pouce Mountain, Anse Courtois, Vallée des Prêtres and Corps de Garde Mountain, whilst following his taste for natural history.

Mr. Clark's discovery cannot possibly be attributed to mere chance; it was, on the contrary, the result of patient deductions and searches in the very places where fossils were likely to be found. The first explanation of the considerable layer of bones found in Mare aux Songes was that during some hurricane or other atmospheric perturbation, the animals had taken refuge together in the neighbourhood and perished there; and that, either through the action of rains, or a flood, or even an invasion of the sea, their remains had gathered together in that marsh, at a very remote period. This would be probable but for the presence of parrot bones, for it is evident that parrots would not have suffered themselves to be drowned, but would have taken refuge in the forests. The bones could not have proceeded from the mountains either, for being washed from there by the rains, they must, of a surety, have followed the river beds. As Mr. Doyen says, the deposit was decidedly the result of the accumulation of ages in the undulations of the basaltic plain which proceeds thence, by a gentle slope, from the neighbouring heights towards the sea.

The following is a summary of Strickland's conclusions on the subject: In spite of apparent anomalies presented by the Dodo, it must not be believed, as Bory St. Vincent suggested, that this bird was a mere embryo of a creature, a ridiculous and shocking attempt in which Nature had failed to accomplish its purpose. Each type of animal possesses its own structure, even in the most exceptional and apparently extravagant forms, which corresponds to the conditions and necessities of the environment in which it was destined to live. The Dodo, clumsy and ugly as it was, had its reasons for being so; it evidently did not require more for the circumstances in which it was called upon to live.

II.-THE APHANAPTERYX.

According to Mr. Alph. Milne Edwards, the distinguished French zoologist, this indigenous bird of Mauritius was the same as the "*Red hen with a snipe's beak,*" mentioned by François Cauche in 1620, and the *Todaerses* referred to by Jean Chrétien Hoffmann, in 1673-75. It had, however, been roughly sketched, in 1617, as an illustration to the narrative of Pieter Van den Broeck, a traveller after whom the Aphanapteryx — *i.e.*, a bird without any apparent wings — has been surnamed *Aphanapteryx Broeckii, Schlegel.* Earlier still, in 1610, a portrait from a live model had been painted on vellum; it was discovered, during the last century, by Von Frauenfeld, in the Library of the Austrian Emperor, and a copy of that portrait, of which the illustration on the next page is a reproduction, was presented, some twenty years ago, to the Port Louis Museum by Mr. Théodore Sauzier. Posterior to Hoffmann, no mention is made of the Aphanapteryx, so that it is difficult to establish the time when it became extinct. But as mention is made of it in 1675, it is probable that it outlived by a few years its contemporary the Dodo. No allusion is made to it in the manuscripts of Commerson, or Julien Desjardins; and if it had existed when the former arrived at the Isle of France, in 1768, it could not possibly have escaped detection by such a careful and eminent zoologist.

The Aphanapteryx, a brevipennate bird, with light, fawn-coloured, hair-like plumes, and a long, thin and slightly curved bill, bore some resemblance to the *Kiwis* of New Zealand, and also to the Madagascar *Ibis*, called by the natives *Tsi-akouakou* (a hen which is not a hen), of which two naturalized specimens are to be seen in the Port Louis Museum. Yet it appears that the Mauritius Aphanapteryx was somewhat smaller in size. Like the Kiwis and Ibis, it mostly dwelt in forests, living on insects which it could procure there easily.

THE APHANAPTERYX.
(From the Copy in the Museum, Port Louis, from a Painting on Vellum in the Library of the Austrian Emperor.)

Subsequent to Mr. Sauzier's discoveries in Mare aux Songes, in 1889, Mr. Milne Edwards wrote a learned essay on the Aphanapteryx, and described some of its bones, principally the lower mandible, tibia and metatarsian tarsus. Messrs. Alfred Newton and Hans Gadow gave a monography of the same bird, which unfortunately is erroneous in some essential parts, and should be re-written, owing to a few bones of a different species, the *Fulica Newtonii*, of which we shall speak presently, having been included by mistake amongst those submitted to their examination. Newton and Gadow have, however, figured and described a pelvis, femur, humerus and upper mandible. New discoveries have since been made of a great number of fossil bones in a perfect state of preservation, which leave no possible doubt regarding the error to which we have alluded.

From the collection of fossil bones gathered by Mr. E. Thirioux, photographs of which accompanied a report submitted in 1903 to the Royal Society of Arts and Sciences of Mauritius by Mr. Donald d'Emmerez de Charmoy, Curator of the Museum, a complete and perfect skeleton of the Aphanapteryx has been constructed, and is also on exhibition in the Museum.

The Aphanapteryx is reproduced on the cover and title page of Colonel Pike's book on Mauritius, *Subtropical Rambles in the Land of the Aphanapteryx*, although no mention is made therein of the bird, except in the preface, where the author promised the publication, which was never effected, of a further volume on the fauna and flora of the island.

PIGEON HOLLANDAIS.
(This specimen of another extinct bird of Mauritius is the only one of the kind in the world, and is in the Museum, Port Louis.)

III.—THE FULICA NEWTONII.

This extinct water-fowl was described by Messrs. H. Gadow and Alf. Newton, in 1892, from bones discovered in 1889 in the Mare aux Songes by Mr. Théodore Sauzier. It appears to have been a species peculiar to Mauritius, where it was to be found in the seventeenth century, although Leguat makes no mention of it. According to Mr. Milne Edwards, it was of the size of the Chili water-hen. It may have had some analogy with the Bourbon *Porphyrio Notornis*, or *Blue Bird*, spoken of by Dubois.

Fossil bones of the *Fulica Newtonii*, the property of Mr. Paul Carié, of Mauritius, show at all events that it was a Ralline bird, not widely different from the Sultana Fowl of Madagascar, except that its tarsi and metatarsi were considerably shorter, and its tarsian phalanxes and humerus more developed. The latter peculiarity demonstrates that the *Fulica* could easily fly, although it was rather clumsy in appearance. This distinguishes it from the Bourbon Blue Bird, which Dubois asserts could not fly at all; so that both birds could not have been identical.

IV.—THE RODRIGUES SOLITAIRE.

In a line with the Dronte or Dodo is naturally placed the wingless bird from Rodrigues, the Solitaire, which Leguat has so excellently described. The Solitaire was so called because it was seldom seen in groups. The male was of a greyish-brown hue, with feet like a turkey's. The beak of the Solitaire was somewhat more bent than a turkey's. It had no tail; its neck was long, its eyes quick and shining, its head crestless, its very short wings were only used by it for fighting purposes, or to twirl about "whenever those birds wished to call each other, turning round with great velocity, with a kestrel noise." Its pinions were curiously developed, each having at its extremity, under the feathers, a small round bony mass, not unlike a musket ball; this and its beak were the bird's chief defences. Though difficult to capture in the woods, they were easily overtaken in open ground, as they did not run very fast. Being fat from March to September, their flesh, especially of the young, was then excellent. Some males weighed over forty-five pounds.

The female was brown and more or less dark in hue; Leguat suggests that there were among them *blondes* and *brunettes*. They had over their beaks a sort of pad composed of more brightly-coloured feathers, not unlike a "widow's hood"; their plumes were exceedingly glossy—those on the thighs were rounded like shells; on their crops were two protuberances of a whiter tinge than the rest, "not at all unlike a beautiful woman's breast"; their gait was most graceful.

The Solitaire was not shy, but could not be tamed. When kept in confinement, it would obstinately allow itself to perish of hunger and thirst, and even, according to Leguat, "would actually shed tears."

Its gizzard always contained a brown pebble, about the size of a hen's egg, "slightly rugged, flattened on one side and rounded on the other, very hard and heavy. This stone was found even in the young, and very likely they were born with it, as their throat was half too narrow to allow of their swallowing it." Leguat's companions used it to whet their knives. From what we know of the Dodo, it may be supposed that the Solitaire also swallowed those pebbles for an identical purpose.

The Solitaires made their nests of palm leaves heaped up one foot and a half deep, in a particularly clean place. The female laid only one egg, larger than that of a goose, which was alternately incubated by both male and female, during seven weeks, when it was hatched. Throughout that entire period, as well as during the development of their young, they rigorously opposed kindred birds from coming within two hundred paces of the nest, the male driving off the males and the female the females. Even when the young was able to look after itself, the male and female did not separate, but constantly remained together. A few days after the young had left the nest, some forty other Solitaires would come leading another young one of about the same age, and the whole company would proceed to a secluded place, where the young couple were left alone. This was called by Leguat "a bird's wedding"; and the description, somewhat exaggerated doubtless, brought upon him some sarcastic criticisms from Cuvier and Lesson, who refused to believe his statements, and wondered how the Solitaire could have disappeared without leaving any trace. Leguat gives a very rough sketch of the bird, which suffices to form an idea of what it must have been like.

In 1789 bones, supposed to be of the Dodo, crusted over with calcareous deposits, were discovered at Rodrigues, in a cave near the sea, not very far from Port Mathurin, by an inhabitant, Mr. Labistour, whose son-in-law, Mr. Roquefeuille, presented them afterwards to Julien Desjardins, the founder of the Mauritius Museum. Desjardins sent them to Cuvier, who mislaid them. Later, Mr. Charles Telfair, having procured other specimens, sent them in 1833 to the London Zoological Society. Those were also lost, but others sent by Mr. Telfair to the Andersonian Museum, at Glasgow, may still be seen there.

In 1867 Sir Edward Newton, then Colonial Secretary at Mauritius, ordered fresh searches to be made at Rodrigues by Mr. George Jenner, Civil Commissioner. A great number of bones were thereby discovered, proving the absolute truth of Leguat's narrative; at the extremities of the Solitaire's pinions were even noticed the bony protuberances in the shape of a musket ball.

Later still, in 1874, other discoveries were made by Mr. H. H. Slater.

V.—THE GIANT.

The Giant was for the first time mentioned in Marquis Duquesne's instructions relative to the Isle of Eden (Bourbon), written in 1690, with the view of recruiting colonists for that island; it is therein described as "a bird mounted on stilts," and was soon after roughly and inexactly represented by François Leguat, who gives the following account of Giants:—

"Their head rises about six feet high; they are extremely elevated on their legs, and their neck is exceedingly long; their body is scarcely larger than that of a goose. They are white all over, excepting a spot under their wings which is of a reddish hue. Their beak is similar to that of a goose, although slightly more pointed, and their toes are wide apart and very long. They live in marshes, and dogs often succeed in seizing them, as they require some time to rise on the wing. We saw one at Rodrigues once and caught it with our own hands, so fat was it. This was the only bird of that species we met in that island, which led us to believe it had been carried there by some wind too strong for it to resist. Its flesh is tolerably good to eat."

Dr. Schlegel, of The Hague Museum, after a careful examination of Leguat's plate, conjectured that the Giant must have been a water-fowl of unusual size, a struthious bird, which, like the Solitaire, had become extinct for a number of years.

This may serve as an example of how insufficient, superficial, and faulty information on a subject is liable to give rise to most persistent misrepresentations. Such a fallacy might certainly be excused in old Leguat, who did not boast of being either an expert zoologist or a clever artist; but it is surprising that such modern scholars as Dr. Schlegel and Mr. Oustalet, of the Paris Museum, should have deliberately shared in his error, without any other appearance of good reason than a badly-drawn sketch. For, on the whole, as Strickland says so pertinently, Leguat's text, as compared with what Buffon wrote of flamingoes, does not establish such discrepancies between the Giant and the ordinary graillies as to justify the erroneous conclusion in question.

FLAMINGOES CAPTURED IN MAURITIUS.
(Now in the Museum, Port Louis.)

No fossil bones of the alleged extinct Giant bird having ever been found, the belief generally adopted is that it was nothing but the common flamingo. This assuredly was the bird seen by Admiral Van Warwyk on his first voyage to Mauritius, in 1598, and alluded to in his narrative as follows:—

"We found *herons* there, not shyer than the other birds, but far more nimble, which, owing to their long legs, managed to escape and keep out of reach; not without having left, however, some of their plumes in the hunters' hands."

But it does not at all follow that the early Dutch settlers were guilty of the same mistake we have just exposed, for on the map of Mauritius drawn up by Lamotius, about 1680, may be seen, on the north-east coast, a spot indicated as *Vlaminks Hoek* (Flamingoes' Corner), which does not, however, coincide exactly with the actual Mare aux Flamants.

That flamingoes existed in Mauritius at that time cannot be denied; but it is not sure whether they were indigenous, or fortuitously carried thither from the eastern coast of Africa, where their presence had already been noted, by some strong and persistent gales, as occurred about the year 1873, when a number of these birds were noticed, especially on the shores of Black River. Unfortunately, they were wantonly destroyed on landing—the more easily as they were well-nigh exhausted—by ignorant fishermen and huntsmen who, attracted by their beautiful pink plumage and uncouth gait, expected to derive profit from the sale of their spoils. The Port Louis Museum then occupied, in Monsieur Street, the western wing of the Royal College Buildings, which were destroyed by the cyclone of 29th April, 1892, rebuilt on a somewhat different plan, and, a few years later, transformed into the Civil Hospital.

Schoolboys of those days must surely remember having seen the dead bodies of the magnificent flamingoes frequently brought to the old Museum for naturalizing purposes. The illustration on the preceding page is a photographic reproduction of two of them in the Museum.

At all events, one of Leguat's remarks is perfectly correct—flamingoes must have been extremely scarce in Rodrigues, considering the situation of that island, lying about 350 miles to the east of Mauritius.

VI.—THE BOURBON SOLITAIRE AND BLUE BIRD.

If Mauritius and Rodrigues had each its own particular apterous birds, Bourbon also possessed two of them, and very unlike each other. John Tatton, quartermaster of the *Pearl*, Samuel Castleton's ship, mentions a white bird as large as a turkey. Bontekōe calls it a Dodo and has left a sketch of it, not unlike the *Walgvogel*. He writes as follows :—

" There are also in that island (Mascarenhas) *Dod-eersen*, having such short wings that they cannot fly, and being so fat that they can scarcely walk ; when they attempt to run, they are compelled to drag their hind parts on the ground."

After this description it might be believed that the Dodo did exist at Bourbon; but, on the other hand, it is not supported by any testimony. The account of Bontekōe, who had never visited Mauritius, was written down from memory a long time afterwards. On leaving Bourbon, his ship was wrecked, and he alone succeeded in making his escape. It is more probable that he simply remembered having seen a wingless bird at Bourbon, and had mistaken it for the Dodo, of which so many travellers had already spoken.

Carré, a French traveller, has it thus :—

" I have seen there a sort of bird I never met anywhere else; it is the one the inhabitants call the Solitary Bird, because it really loves solitude and always stays in the most secluded places; nobody has ever seen two or more assemble together. It keeps constantly by itself. It would well enough resemble a turkey, were not its legs longer. The beauty of its feathers is most pleasant to

SECTION OF PORT LOUIS NEAR SIGNAL MOUNTAIN.

contemplate; these are of an unstable yellowish hue. Its flesh is delicious; it forms one of the ordinary dainties of the country, and could certainly figure on our tables. We endeavoured to keep two of these birds, as a present to His Majesty in France, but as soon as they were on board the vessel they suffered themselves to die of grief, refusing either to eat or drink."

Tatton says the Solitaire is white, Carré claims it is yellowish, from which it may be inferred that it was probably cream-coloured.

Dubois, another traveller, mentions two sorts of birds, the Solitaire and the Blue Bird. "The Solitaire," he says, "keeps always by itself; it is about the size of a large goose, and white, with the ends of its wings and tail black; its tail is like an ostrich's, its neck long, its beak resembles a snipe's, but is stouter; its legs and claws are similar to a turkey's; it flies but very little."

On the other hand, Tatton and Bontekoe assert that it cannot fly at all, and are probably correct.

From all those descriptions, Strickland comes to the conclusion that the Bourbon Solitaire was altogether different in form, in the shape of its beak and in its colour, from the Mauritius Dodo and the Rodrigues Solitaire.

The Blue Bird was of the same size, its feathers being blue all over, its beak and legs red, its claws like a hen's; it did not fly, but ran so fast that it easily escaped capture.

Dr. Schlegel, of The Hague Museum, has classed, as follows, the Bourbon Blue Bird amongst gigantic water-fowls, together with the Giant which Leguat had described at Rodrigues:

"1o. The Giant, *Gallinula* (*Leguatiana*) *Gigantea*,"—a mistake, as we have already said.

"2o. The Blue Bird, *Porphyrio* (*Notornis*) *Cœrulescens*." This is the *Cyanornis Erythroryncha* of Bonaparte.

Mr. Billard, who resided at Bourbon from 1817 to 1820, found in the archives of that colony, at St. Denis, traces of one at least of those wingless birds, which he, however, wrongly calls Dodo, or, and more rightly, Solitaire. They were still extant in the time of La Bourdonnais, that is from 1735 till 1746, as he sent one as a rarity to the Directors of the East India Company. Baron Grant, in his *History of Mauritius*, mentions some notes on Bourbon taken by an officer of the British Navy, according to which there existed about 1713, at Plaines des Cafres, a sort of bird which never went down to the shore, and was so little shy that it could easily be killed with a stick. This might have been the Solitaire; but when Bory St. Vincent visited Bourbon in 1801 that kind of bird had certainly disappeared entirely from there.

Unfortunately for what concerns the brevipennate birds of Bourbon, nothing is certain; for, apart from the descriptions we have quoted, there exist no authentic documents to support them, no indication of the appearance of those two birds, no drawing, no etching which might assist in setting up their skeletons; nothing of that nature has as yet been discovered.

SECTION OF PORT LOUIS.

FAUNA.

DOWN through the ages, while man elsewhere was slowly evolving from savagery to civilisation, and later still, while civilisation saw the birth and death of great Empires, this little remote island in the vast lonely sea stretching from Asia to the south polar regions, was an Eden of primeval life that knew not the fierce beasts of prey which terrorised the rest of the world. When discovered by the Portuguese at the beginning of the sixteenth century, Mauritius, although uninhabited by man, was full of different kinds of birds and reptiles, some of which, long extinct, have been of unbounded interest and zealous research to the most eminent naturalists of modern times. Knowledge of those vanished indigenous creatures has been derived from the writings and sketches of early visitors to the island, like Cauche and Leguat, whose descriptions have been substantiated by local discoveries of bones that have never been duplicated in any other part of the globe.

Original Fauna.

The island, with its mild and salubrious climate, afforded to worn-out crews a delightful sanatorium, where they could recuperate their health and strength and replenish their larders for the continuation of their long voyages. Its various pigeons of brilliant colouring, utterly devoid of fear because unaccustomed to molestation, were easily captured by hand; enormous ground parrots, scarcely able to fly, the clumsy Dodo, the equally flightless Aphanapteryx, and giant tortoises and turtles, whose flesh was more appreciated than that of the birds, were killed with the greatest ease in thousands or captured alive and taken on board the ships. The large lizards, too, shared in the destruction by man of the original fauna of the island; but two of their descendants are still living, in captivity, in Round Island.

GIANT TORTOISE IN THE LINE BARRACKS, PORT LOUIS.
(Said to have been in the city since 1766.)

This constant wholesale slaughter, which was aided by the depredations of pigs—tame when imported but turned wild when set at liberty—and the destruction of the forests consequent on the French occupation of the island, when the land was required for cultivation, soon led to the complete disappearance of certain species; whilst those which survived had to struggle desperately in competition with the various imported animals, which, set at liberty indiscriminately, thoroughly adapted themselves to the conditions of the island.

Birds.

It has been established that at the time of its discovery the island had only four mammiferous species, but twenty-four ornithological species and twelve species of reptiles. Of the twenty-four original species of birds only eight now survive. The greater number of these are localised in the forest preserves in the south of the island, and are threatened with extinction in spite of the severity of the measures taken for their protection. Export of the birds of Mauritius to other countries decimated their numbers so greatly, that a law was passed some time ago prohibiting the capture or sale of any species of native origin, these being found in greatest number in the forests of Savanne. Amongst the rarest is the ringed parrot, which is very similar to the Indian species, but larger. Even rarer still is the Cuisinier thrush, the male being of an ashen grey and the female of a reddish colour. This bird is a lover of dark thickets, and there is no mistaking its deep hurried notes.

The phaeton birds are of two sorts, those with black stripes and those with red stripes. The former is the smaller, and is of a pure white with a large black stripe on the upper part of the wings, and with a yellow beak. It nests in the hollow parts of trees in the forests, and on the rocks in the mountains. The second is much handsomer, and is of a pinkish white all over, with a dark red beak and stripes on its tail. The young birds are beautifully spotted with black on the upper part of the body. These birds are very common, notwithstanding the decimation to which they were subjected previous to their protection by Government.

The bold and handsome Meyer's dove utters its sad and monotonous note, like a dirge for its approaching extinction. It is a splendid bird, which will not breed in captivity, and is gradually becoming rarer.

The "Chicken Eater" is less rare than the preceding ones, and is a very pretty species of falcon, brownish-yellow above and white underneath, mottled with black. The woodcock and the banana bird (the latter so named on account of its feeding on the insects found in the banana blossoms) are very seldom seen now flying through the brushwood and along the water-courses. The white bird and the manioc bird are caterpillar eaters of the first rank, appearing at dawn to free the trees from parasites. They flew in large flocks, and heralded the day by their chirping, but are now rare.

The small heron frequents the mouths of rivers and marshes, where it finds in abundance the small crabs on which it lives. Its dull plumage and its disagreeably flavoured flesh make it neglected by sportsmen; otherwise it would soon have been exterminated, for it flies slowly and is not timid.

The partridges, introduced from India and China, were very abundant before the advent of the mongoose, but are now becoming scarce; and so, also, are the Indian and Chinese quails, which were formerly also exceedingly plentiful.

The Cardinal bird was introduced from Madagascar, and has spread over the whole island. In summer the male has a brilliant red plumage, of which he seems very vain, and perches on the tops of branches as if seeking admiration.

The Bengal finch proclaims by its name the source of its origin. It lives in immense flocks in the plains. Its plumage is dull, but is enlivened by a bright red patch on the breast, and its beak is coral red.

The nightingale, introduced in 1892, has become a great pest owing to its destructive habits. The martin, brought from India to free the island from its swarms of grasshoppers, is well protected by law. The Republican bird—although introduced about twenty years ago—is only found in the north of the island. At nesting time the Republican birds assemble in great numbers, and build in palm trees, from which they remove the leaves and hang their oval nests on the branches.

The native canary and the Cape canary are both very sweet singers; the former is still quite common, and frequents the warm places on the shore; but the latter has completely disappeared from Mauritius since the cyclone of 1892.

The pingo is a native of the Malay Peninsula, and resembles the other *fringillidæ* in its habits; as it is not very common, its depredations in grain fields are not much noticed. The sparrow was introduced, according to Hartlaub, about sixty years ago, and is much less numerous to-day than it was formerly. The raven was imported about 1750 from the east coast of Africa to destroy the rats and mice. There is a small colony of ravens in the courtyard of the old Civil Hospital.

The wood-pigeon was probably introduced from Madagascar, but it exists in all the surrounding islands. Although it is very prolific, it has grown extremely scarce in the forests. At Mon Désert Carié, however, it is protected to a great extent, and is consequently in some number there.

The large turtle dove, from Ceylon, is very common, and does considerable harm to growing grain. The small turtle dove, a native of Tenasserim, was imported from the Malacca Peninsula, and is common along the shore, where it lives in the plantations.

Amongst other birds from Madagascar which have very often been captured and killed in Mauritius are the wood-pigeon, the Peregrine falcon, the cuckoo, and others of smaller size.

The shore birds are fairly numerous, but only in summer, and include the curlew, *La Barge* variety, the turnstone, several kinds of plovers and terns, and during the cyclones frigate-birds and petrels.

There are also in the marshes many teal and wild duck, formerly imported from Madagascar or coming over here of themselves, as well as larks.

The destruction of birds which lived in very great numbers in the sugar canes is indeed regrettable, for they were admirable helps to agriculture by reducing field pests.

The following is a list of the birds of Mauritius in the Museum, Port Louis, as shown in the illustration on the opposite page:—

BIRDS OF MAURITIUS IN THE MUSEUM, PORT LOUIS.

(Names as given at the Museum.)

LEFT SECTION, reading from left to right.

FIRST ROW.

1. *Foudia Erytrocephala* (Female) (Banana Bird).
2. 8 *Zosterops Chlorophea* (Manioc Bird).
3. 8 *Zosterops Mauritiana* (White Bird).
4. *Foudia Madagascariensis* (Cardinal Bird).
5. 8 *Loxia Orizivora.*
6. *Foudia Madagascariensis* (Female).
7. *Critagra Chrysopyga.*

SECOND ROW.

8. *Estrelda Astrild* (Bengal Finch).
9. *Foudia Erytrocephala* (Banana Bird).
10. *Synœcus Sinensis* (Chinese Quail).
11. *Muscipeta Borbonica* (Woodcock).
12. *Synœcus Sinensis* (Female).
13. *Munia Punctularia* (Pingo).
14. *Hirundo Borbonica.*

THIRD ROW.

15. *Acridotheres Tristis* (Martin).
16. *Stepsilas Interpres.*
17. *Oxynotus Ferrugineus* (Cuisinier Thrush).
18. *Slug-Slug.*
19. *Turnix Nigricollis* (Madagascar Quail).
20. *Pynonotus Jocosus* (Boule-Boule).
21. *Charadrius Geoffroyi.*

FOURTH ROW.

22. *Larus.*
23. *Hypsipetes Olivacea* (Merle).
24. *Phæton Candidus.*
25. *Butoride Atricapilla.*

LEFT SECTION, reading from left to right—*continued.*

FIFTH ROW.

26. *Palæornis Eques* (Ringed Parrot).
27. *Francolinus Ponticerianus* (Indian Partridge).
28. *Charadrius Varius.*
29. *Numenius Phacopus.*
30. *Columba Meyeri* (Dove).

RIGHT SECTION, reading from left to right.

FIRST ROW.

31. *Anas Melleri.*
32. *Oxynotus Ferrugineus.*
33. *Dendrocygna Viduata* (Sarcelle).
34. *Phæton Rubricauda* (Female).

SECOND ROW.

35. *Tringa Subarquata.*
36. *Phæton Rubricauda.*
37. *Geopelia Striata* (Wood Pigeon).
38. *Coturnix Argoondah* (Indian Quail).
39. *Phæton Rubricauda* (Young).

THIRD ROW.

40. *Porphyrio Madagascariensis.*
41. *Ardea Bubulcus* (Small Heron).
42. *Francolinus Perlatus* (Chinese Partridge).
43. *Numida Mitrata* (Guinea Fowl).

FOURTH ROW.

44. *Tinnunculus Punctatus* ("Chicken Eater").
45. *Agapornis Cana.*
46. *Passer Domesticus* (Sparrow).
47. *Collocalia Francica.*

Reptiles.

The exotic reptiles are of three sorts—an iguana from Réunion, and two small snakes from India—the *Thyphlops Brahminus* and the *Lycodon Aulicum.* These latter do not attack human beings, and their bite is said to be non-poisonous. They are regarded as being useful because they devour mice and insects.

The skink and the gecko of Round Island are interesting native species. The small species of the Grand Terre are skinks, which frequent the bare rocks of the coast, and the hemidactyls. One of the latter is of a bluish-green colour, beautifully spotted with red, and is very common on the palm and banana trees.

Giant Tortoises.

Only a few of the giant tortoises remain, and all of them are in captivity. One or two are owned privately; others are in the Royal Botanic Gardens, Pamplemousses; and one is in the Line Barracks, Port Louis. The latter is said to have been imported from the Seychelles in 1766, and found in the city in 1810, when the island was taken by the British.

As already mentioned, Mauritius, like the other neighbouring islands, was, at the time of its discovery, full of these remarkable creatures. Curiously enough, each of the islands was the home of several distinct species, all of which were peculiar to their respective habitats. Leguat, writing near the close of the seventeenth century, states that herds of tortoises, comprising as many as 3,000, might be counted in Rodrigues; and Darwin, when he visited the Galapagos group during his famous voyage in the *Beagle* in the early part of the nineteenth century, relates that the tortoises were exceedingly

BIRDS OF MAURITIUS, IN THE MUSEUM, PORT LOUIS.

(Names on the opposite page.)

numerous there, and travelled at certain seasons to and from the mountains, along regular beaten tracks, for the purpose of obtaining food and water. Frequently, when in the forest, the traveller would be startled by the loud roar of the males in the breeding season, and, if he was tired of tramping, a sure, if somewhat unstable, mount could be secured by bestriding one of the huge reptiles, which, after a short pause, would resume its journey as if nothing had happened.

The one shown in our illustration was probably by no means young at the time of its alleged capture 150 years ago, and, as it is impossible to ascertain the age to which these gigantic land chelonians attain, it is not improbable that the island's oldest inhabitant, which is about four feet long and weighs about five hundredweight, is the oldest living creature in the world.

Bats and Frogs. There are four kinds of bats in Mauritius, including two fine fruit-eating specimens, the *Pteropus Edwards* and the *Pteropus Rubricollis*, which live in the forests during the day and come out at night to feed on the fruit in the orchards. There are also bats of a small kind—*Nycticeius Borbonicus*—which live on insects.

There is only one species of frog—*Rana Mascareniensis*—which is very abundant in all the stagnant pools.

RARE WHITE MONKEY.

COMMON MONKEY.

Deer and Pigs. The deer which roam in the forests and mountains of Mauritius were introduced from Sumatra. The stags attain considerable size, and when full grown have very fine antlers. It often happens during the deer drives that the dogs put up wild pigs, which are fairly numerous in some parts of the island, especially in the marshes. They are the progeny of the domestic pigs originally set free in the island by the early colonists. A furious full-grown boar, with long tusks, is a dangerous animal to face at close quarters, but, as a rule, they try to get away, and only attack if badly wounded. The flesh is dark coloured, and when young is very good eating.

Monkeys. Monkeys are very plentiful in the island, and appear to have been introduced from Ceylon. They abound in the sugar-cane plantations near the forests, where they commit considerable ravages, and they also pillage the nests of the forest birds. It is very difficult to exterminate these destructive creatures, for they always have their sentinels to give warning of the approach of any danger; and they disappear with remarkable rapidity, jumping great distances from precipice to precipice, or swinging from bough to bough through the forest. They are of considerable size and their fur is of a greenish-brown hue. One or two curious specimens have been found with white coats and pink eyes, and the accompanying illustration is from a photograph of one of them at the Museum in Port Louis. Many of the Creoles consider the flesh of the monkey a great delicacy, and from the fat they make oil which they deem an effective remedy for rheumatism.

Mongoose and Hare. The mongoose was introduced from India to kill the rats with which the island is overrun; and although it lessened considerably the number of these rodents, which are descendants of those that escaped from the ships of the early colonists, it has multiplied greatly and is causing immense damage amongst the feathered tribes and the hares that abound everywhere, especially on the coast.

Tandrac. The tandrac was imported from Madagascar, and has spread throughout the island. It was extremely plentiful before the arrival of the mongoose, which feeds on it, and which soon rendered it scarce, in spite of its great fecundity. This is very unfortunate, as the tandrac was valuable to agriculture by destroying a large number of insects; and it also formed a great part of the food of the poorer people.

Insects. Even the original insects of the island did not escape destruction after the arrival of human beings. The native plants on which those insects lived grew scarcer in proportion to the rapid development of the cultivation of the sugar-cane, and caused the disappearance of numerous beetles and butterflies, including, amongst many others, the beautiful *Leptocères* and *Vanessa*. It was estimated by the late Julien Desjardins, the eminent Mauritian naturalist, that the different varieties of insects in the island numbered one thousand. The most common are of foreign origin and are very destructive. Amongst the large ephemeral species, the *Papilio*

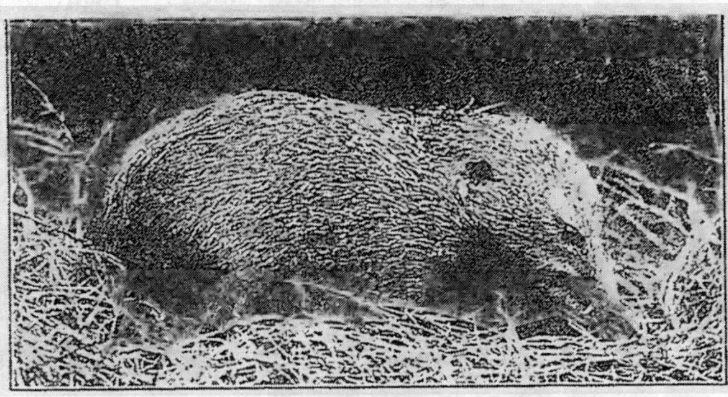

TANDRAC.

MONGOOSE.

Demodecus, the *Vanessa Radama*, the *Atellanta Phalanta*, and the *Danaïs Chrysippus* come from Madagascar and the coasts of Africa.

The Borer. Perhaps the most destructive insect is the *borer*, so called because it eats its way into the heart of the young canes. It was introduced into the island about 1850 among new species of canes which were brought in a ship called the *Elizabeth* from Ceylon. So great was the havoc caused by this insect some years ago that it was feared the entire sugar crop would be ruined; but fortunately the energetic measures taken for its extermination have greatly lessened its activities. The worst depredations of the *borer* are in the young plantations, where it feeds upon the heart of the infant plant and destroys it. Gangs of boys, armed with sharp knives, are employed to examine the young canes, and where the presence of the *borer* is discovered, the shoot is cut and the insect killed. This continual watch for the *borer* forms no small item in the planter's annual budget of expenditure.

Phytalus Smithii. The colonists were very considerably alarmed and puzzled in 1911 by the sudden and mysterious appearance of an insect of inordinately destructive capabilities in a plantation of canes at Mon Rocher Estate, in the Pamplemousses District. It was noticed that the young canes there were dying with alarming rapidity, for which there was no apparent reason; but it was soon discovered that a new enemy to the cane plant had made its appearance, and was threatening incalculable damage. On digging up the affected plants a species of grub, or "moutouc" as it is called locally, was discovered in immense quantities. It was the larva of a beetle that had never been seen in the colony before. It propagated with most alarming rapidity, so much so that at one

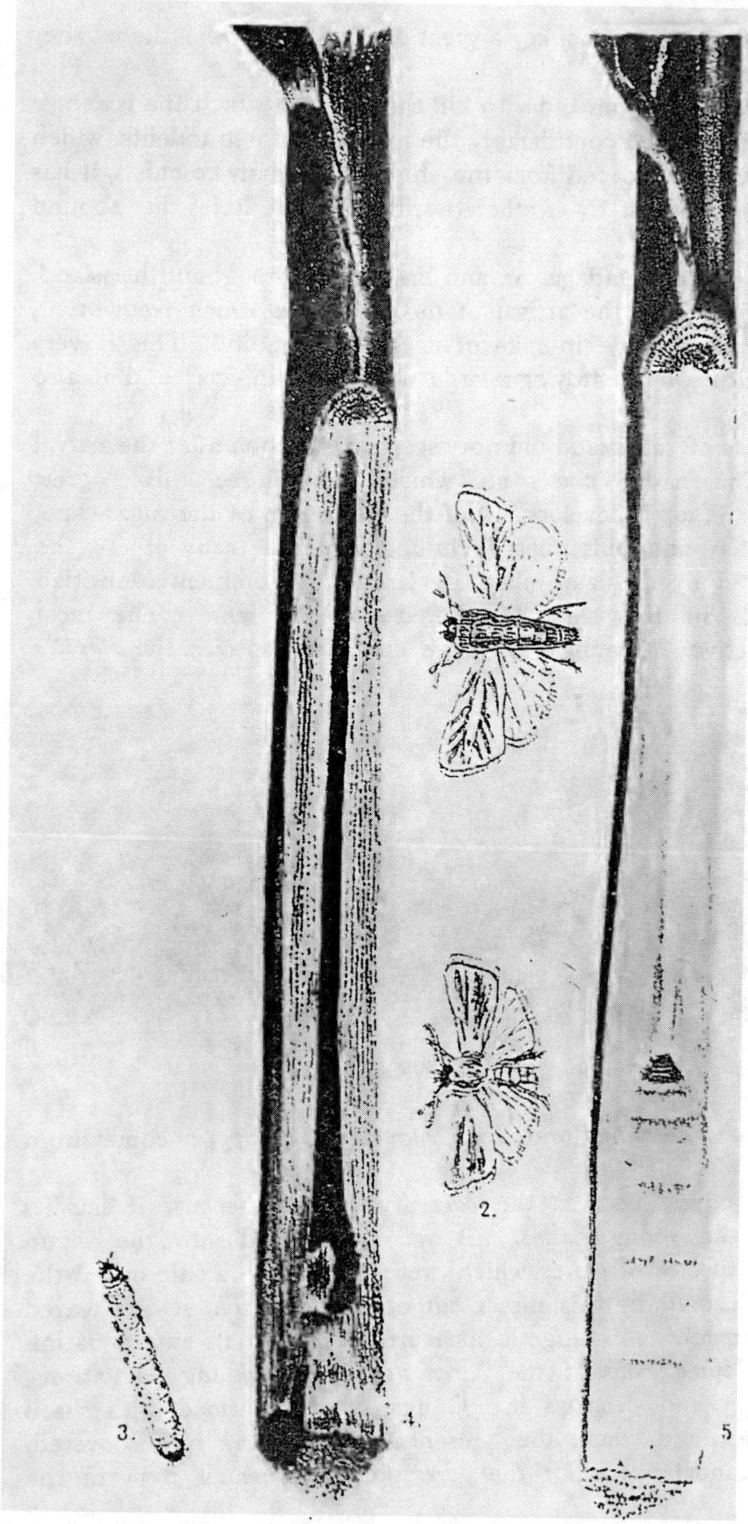

EFFECT OF THE "BORER" ON YOUNG CANES.

1. Female moth. 2. Male moth. 3. "Borer." 4. Virgin cane of six months' growth attacked by borer (½). 5. Healthy virgin cane of six months' growth (½).

(Reproduced by permission from *The Sugar Industry of Mauritius*, by A. Walter, F.R.A.S.).

time fear was experienced that it would spread all over the island and completely destroy the standing crop. The colonists were in a state of anxiety on account of the ravages caused by this insect, against which it seemed almost impossible to make headway. The fields first attacked were ploughed up, and millions of the larvæ were found and destroyed, whilst at night fires were lighted to decoy the matured beetles in their flight. So serious was the danger that the Colonial Secretary, the Hon. George Smith, C.M.G. (after whom the insect was named, and who was then administering the government in the absence of Sir Cavendish Boyle, K.C.M.G.), visited the scene of danger and inspected the affected plantations; whilst the Chamber of Agriculture and the local Press urged upon Government to take immediate steps to combat the extraordinary progress made by this hitherto unknown pest.

A well-organised and practical plan of campaign was set on foot and carried out by Mr. D. D'Emmerez de Charmoy, Curator of the Museum and Government Entomologist, and Mr. P. Koenig, Director of the Department of Forests and Gardens. A large number of men and boys were employed to capture the matured beetles at night, with the result that in one night 16,000 were secured; and by the end of December fifteen tons, or about 26,000,000, of the insects had been destroyed.

In view of these extraordinary figures the planters became more and more alarmed; but the stringent measures taken by the Government at the outset had the most salutary effect; the danger was fortunately met in time; the affected area was to a certain extent isolated, and the "moutouc" scare eventually died away.

Other Pests. Besides the *borer*, the insects most dangerous to plants include the *Oryctes Tarandus*, which attacks the sugar-cane; the *Adoretus Versutus*, which attacks all trees, and especially the vines and rose trees; the Cut-Worm, *Prodenia Littoralis*, which ravages the young plantations; the cucurbitaceous fly, *Dacus Ferruginea*, which causes the falling off of pumpkins and other vegetables of the same nature; the orange fly, *Ceratitis Capitata*, many kinds of *plusides*, and a great number of cochineal insects, which infest fruit and other trees and plants.

The coasts and low-lying districts of the island are dangerous to health because of the prevalence of the dreaded *Anopheles Costalis* mosquito, the spreader of malaria. In the marshes and ponds caused by the summer rains abound the *Culex Fatigans*, which appears by night, and the *Stegonia Fascista*, which appears by day, both being common all over the island.

METHOD OF COUNTING THE CAPTURED "PHYTALUS SMITHII" BEETLES.
16,000 caught in one night.
(Reproduced by permission from Mr. D. D'Emmerez de Charmoy's Report.

The gorgeous ichneumon fly is also to be seen, constantly waging war upon cockroaches and other insects, in the bodies of which, when it has overcome them, it lays its eggs.

The butterflies are not very numerous, but among them are some magnificent varieties, one with yellow and black wings, and another with wings like black velvet splashed with sky-blue; while of moths the most noteworthy is probably the "Death's Head," which is fairly common in the warmer localities.

The beautiful aeroplane of the insect world, the swift-speeding dragon fly, known locally as the "lascar," is also represented in several varieties, with bright blue, green, or red bodies and delicate gossamer wings.

Ants of several varieties abound in Mauritius, the worst kind being the *Caria*, or white ant, which does much damage to wooden buildings, furniture, books, documents, etc.

The *myriapoda* are not numerous as to species. There is only one kind of scorpion and two or three centipedes, an *iulus* and a *scutigerus*.

Spiders.

On the other hand the spider tribes are very numerous and varied. The *Olios Leucosius* lives in houses in the company of other species, which spin their nets in the dark corners of cellars and store-rooms. The fly-catchers, *Salticus*, are very common and very pretty. The finest spiders are found among the *Epoires*; two species were exterminated by the nightingales, and a third was only saved by its nocturnal habits.

D. D'EMMEREZ DE CHARMOY,
Curator of Museum and Government Entomologist.

Amongst the insects allied to the spiders are a number of parasites of cosmopolitan habits, inclusive of the *carapates*. There is a very curious little species of these, the *Holothyrus Coccinelus*, which is strongly poisonous. It is commonly called the "duck-killer," as it causes the death of the poultry which swallow it. It lives in moss and in damp places.

Land Shells.

The land shells have mostly disappeared: the fine species of *cyclostomes helix* snail only exist in a sub-fossil state, and have been replaced by the *Couroupa Achatina Panthera* snail, which does much damage to agriculture.

The river species are very few; amongst the most common are the *Melanies*, which abound in all the rivers and streams, the *Lyanees*, and a very fine species of a pale green streaked with brown.

Finally, the zoology of Mauritius is exceedingly interesting, not only because of the individual characteristics of each living thing, but also because of the disappearance of former species and their replacement by new species thoroughly adapted to the altered conditions of the island.

ECONOMIC FLORA.

By PAUL KOENIG, Director of Forests and Gardens.

PAUL KOENIG.

THE original flora of Mauritius has been considerably altered by the direct agency of man and the intervention of plants from other countries. We shall deal here only with the more important factors and results of these changes. The primeval vegetation of the island has often been recorded as being of great beauty and grandeur.

Indigenous Forests.

During the Dutch and French occupations the land was covered with an unbroken evergreen forest, extending from near the sea-shore up to the summit of the mountains, and only crossed by a few paths which still exist or were gradually improved into roads. Those virgin forests retained their special character till the middle of the nineteenth century.

Major Mackenzie Fraser drew a map in 1835, testifying that two-thirds of the total area of the island was still under wood. The picture of such tropical forests has been traced by many writers :—" It conjures up a vision of sombre vistas, like the nave of a cathedral, the pillars formed by enormous boles of trees soaring up into the dim and religious half-light caused by the interlacing branches forming the vault of the fane."

The trees constituting the remains of the virgin forests do not, however, exceed eighty to one hundred feet in height, on account of the shallowness of the soil; but their diameter is from three to four feet. The leaves are as thick as leather; the growth is very slow indeed, and the timber very heavy. Below the upper canopy of the forest secondary trees, varying in species according to the different degrees of moisture in the air and in the soil, form an underwood; climbers and lianas unite the higher and lower canopies of the forest, and graceful tree-ferns and epiphytes complete this unique mass of vegetation. It is recorded that in 1816 it comprised 125,500 acres without interruption.

The ruling species of trees are Natte, Makak, Tambalacoque, Colophane, Tatamaka, Sandal, Olive, Cannelle, Pomme, etc., in the moist localities; Puant, Benjoin, Ebony, etc., in drier places. The auxiliary species in the lower canopy are Clou, Bigaignon, Sagaye, Ronde, Manahe, Lousteau, Fer, Rivière, Canne, Balais, etc., etc., all very useful for building purposes.

Destruction of Forests.

Under the pressure of agriculture large areas of woodlands began to be felled. The creation of railways in 1864 marked an era of heavy devastation, which reached its maximum in 1871-72, in spite of the enactment of laws that remained so many dead letters till 1875, when the work of destruction was made to stop—at least on slopes of mountains and the banks of rivers.

In 1880 a Forest Officer from India, Mr. R. Thompson, was called to repair the damage done, and he drew up a statement of the lands which it was necessary for the Government to purchase in view of the protection of the water supply of the colony. There only remained at that time in possession of the Crown 3,568 acres of heavily dilapidated forests.

The reconstitution of State forests was started, and, after an expenditure of Rs.3,000,000, there were added 30,200 acres. A Department was also formed to preserve these woodlands, and was entrusted with the necessary legal powers. At the same time, the systematic re-stocking of the gathering grounds of a few water-courses was begun.

The changes brought about by the widespread destruction of forests in Mauritius have often been referred to in other countries. They were carefully analysed here by Mr. A. Walter, Director of the Observatory

THE ROYAL BOTANIC GARDENS, PAMPLEMOUSSES.

Changes due to Destruction of Forests.

whose conclusions showed that the increase of the mean daily temperature of the air in the uplands amounted to at least 0·7° Centigrade during summer, and that, although the total rainfall had not actually diminished, the number of rainy days had decreased in the south-eastern, inland, and southern districts, where the operations of deboisement had been most actively carried on.

Another result of the disappearance of the original forests was the gradual extinction of certain species of trees which could no longer reproduce by seeds or otherwise: Tambalacoque, Cannelle, Puant, etc., among the ruling species now scarcely bear any fertile seeds.

Natural Invaders.

Again, as the indigenous flora of the island was giving way under the axe of the lumberman, the introduced species of trees and shrubs were taking possession of the available ground, having, as a rule, more powerful means of reproduction and being quick growers. A few of the invaders, however, were somewhat useful trees, namely the Jamrosa, Goyavier de Chine, Yatis, etc., in moister localities, and the Logwood, Bois Noir, Bois d'Oiseaux, Acacia, Tamarind, etc., at the lower altitudes.

RAILWAY IN THE KANAKA FOREST.

But tracts much wider by far were soon covered with thorny scrub (like the Framboise marronne, Vieille fille, Raquette, etc., etc.), that filled up all blanks and constitute a heavy item in the clearing of land previous to any cultivation.

Baker's Flora.

The flora of Mauritius and the Seychelles was described in 1877 by Mr. Baker, of Kew Gardens, from specimens of plants sent there from the collections of local botanists—Commerson, Bojer, Bouton, etc. The work in question is a standard reference for the classification of most of the plants then growing in the colony. Further information has been added on the same subject by the contributions of Dr. Johnstone and Mr. Bewsher, and by the assistance afforded in classification by Professor Martelli, Mr. Lloyd, and others.

The present area under forests controlled by the State is as follows:—

Crown Lands, about	68,296 acres.
Mountain Reserves	10,330 „
River Reserves	6,000 „
Vacant Estates	240 „
Total	84,866 „

The Crown Lands include: (*a*) About 7,500 acres of "Pas Geometriques" along the coast, three-quarters of which are leased under tree-planting conditions to adjoining owners, and bear chiefly pure filao (*Casuarina equisetifolia*) forests, managed under short rotation for firewood; (*b*) About 5,000 acres of open forests, containing large numbers of dead and dying trees, which the Government have recently realized the necessity of utilizing, and which, it is hoped, will bring in some revenue, before the valuable timber is ruined by the combined effects of wind, insects, and fungi; (*c*) About 35,500 acres of young crops of indigenous trees, more or less invaded by introduced species, and which are progressing under protection; (*d*) 4,600 acres of pines, eucalypti, and mixed plantations of exotic trees.

VANILLA CULTIVATION.

The Mountain Reserves are private forests situated, as a rule, above 1,200 feet altitude, the protection and management of which rest with the Government.

River Reserves are wooded belts along water-courses, and their width depends on the volume of the streams, *i.e.*, feeders with less than 10 cubic feet of water per minute have 10 feet reserves, rivulets of 10 to 50 cubic feet per minute bear 25 feet reserves, and rivers of more than 50 cubic feet have 50 feet reserves. These are private properties, like Mountain Reserves, and their management has lately been improved with the view of guarding against malaria.

Botanic Stations.

In the colony exist three botanic stations which have exercised a certain influence on its economic development. The Royal Botanic Gardens, Pamplemousses, at an altitude of 200 feet above the level of the sea, extend over 92 acres, and have an annual rainfall of 73 inches. They include the house and lands of Mon Plaisir, where resided Governor La Bourdonnais and his successors for some years.

Intendant Pierre Poivre founded the Gardens of Pamplemousses in 1769, near the Governor's country residence, in view of experimental cultivation of spices (cloves, nutmegs, which he introduced in 1770 from the Moluccas, Cacao, etc.), sugar, indigo, mulberry, etc. A great festival was held when the first nutmeg ripened in the colony.

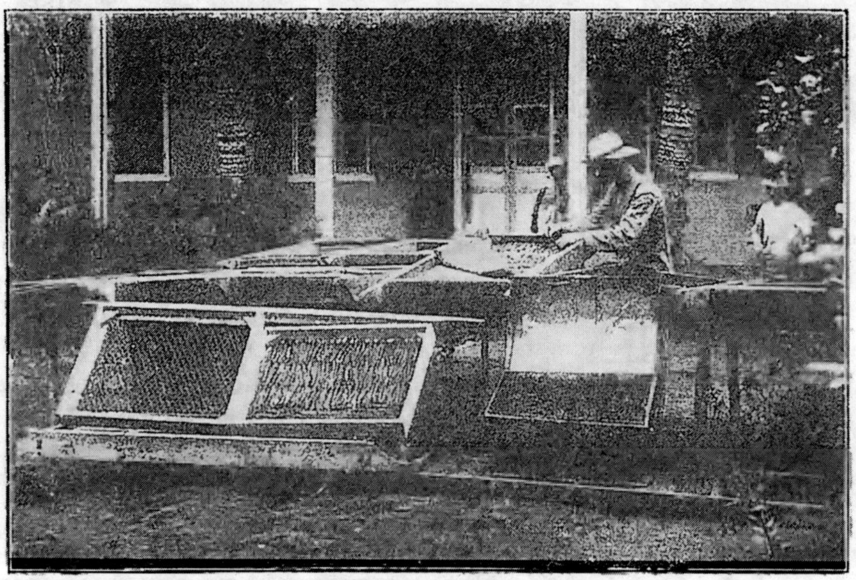

SORTING VANILLA.

Jean Nicolas Céré succeeded Poivre in 1775, and he urged on the cultivation of coffee, cotton and sugar-cane. Céré's son was curator of the Gardens from 1810 to 1820, and White and Newman succeeded him. In 1836 Mon Plaisir House was sold, and the greater part of the Gardens was alienated. Falling into a deplorable condition, they would have been abolished had it not been for Sir Joseph Hooker, Director of Kew Gardens, and Earl Grey, Secretary of State for the Colonies. In 1848 Governor Sir William Stevenson voted the necessary funds for the restoration of the Gardens, which were gradually brought back under

Mr. James Duncan to their former state. In 1868 Dr. C. Meller, Director of the Gardens, was instructed to proceed to Australia and New Caledonia, for the purpose of getting new varieties of sugar-canes, as those existing in the colony had been much impaired by disease. He sent the Port-Mackay and other canes to Mauritius, and died in New South Wales in 1869. Mr. S. Caldwell went in his place, sending the Chicago and other canes, which were raised at the Gardens. In the paintings made of these canes, the Tanna from New Hebrides was represented much like the now renowned cane called Big-Tanna. Mr. John Horne was commissioned to Fiji, in 1877, for new sugar-canes, and from those he sent there were distributed several useful ones amongst planters. From 1901 several selections of seedling canes from the West Indies were received, and among those that gave best results were D/130, B/208 and D/74.

FRENCH GARDEN, REDUIT.

Pamplemousses Gardens are full of magnificent trees and plants, both ornamental and economic. Palms—those princes of vegetable nature, in the words of Linnæus—are particularly abundant, and gracefully lined in avenues of indigenous and exotic species, numbering over a hundred. There are also junipers, araucarias, mahoganies, etc., which produce seedlings for the reafforestation of the island. Eucalypti, filaos, etc., are raised on a large scale and sold at low rates to the public in view of fostering arboriculture by private enterprise; so also are improved varieties of cassava, tobacco, coffee, etc., imported from other countries.

The Curepipe Gardens.

The Botanic Gardens at Curepipe cover 56½ acres, at an altitude of 1,800 feet, and have an annual rainfall of 104 inches. They consist of large forest nurseries, where are grown exotic conifers for reafforestation of Crown Lands, an Arboretum where the growth of exotic trees is observed previous to their adoption on a larger scale, and flower gardens, lawns, etc., for the benefit of the public.

The Réduit Grounds.

The Governor's country residence, situated in a domain of 370 acres, was erected in 1749, with the approval of the Compagnie des Indes, by Mr. David, Governor-General of the Isles of France and Bourbon, and extended by Mr. Desforges-Boucher. On the desire of the Company, a garden was created there in 1755, as the first Jardin des Plantes of the colony, under the care of Aublet, whose successor, Joconde, under General Decaen, grew tea as an experimental crop.

The "French Garden" at Le Réduit, at an altitude of 900 feet, contains several gigantic trees, which have withstood cyclones. Governor Sir George Bowen introduced the eucalyptus in 1880, and six or eight varieties are now useful seed-bearers. Sir John Pope Hennessy, in 1886, imported the Chinese Pine from Hong-Kong, and this is now the principal tree for reafforestation in windy localities. Camphor, toon and other trees also bear seeds in this Botanic Station, part of which was set aside, in 1893, for the creation of the Station Agronomique.

Orchards and Fruits.

A rapid review of the principal fruit trees of the colony will show the various resources in that direction. Mango is perhaps the best of tropical fruits. Among the grafted varieties grown are Aristide, Rosat, José, Auguste, Goa L'Etang, etc. Again, Figette, Maison Rouge, Baissac, Gelée, Torse, etc., reproduce true by seed, the retail price from November to February being 50 cents to one rupee per dozen fruits.

The grafting of mango trees was done on a large scale in 1851 by Mr. Payet, who fixed the good varieties in several private orchards that are still in possession of the best fruits, and a limited number of these find their way to the market. By selection and grafting considerable extension can be given to this tree, both for local consumption and for export.

Litchis are also very good in Mauritius, fetching about 40 cents per 100 from November to January. The tree is produced by layers, and is pretty widely distributed at lower altitudes.

The Sweet Sop (*Atte*) grows wild and is not the object of any care. The fruit ripens in March. Attempts at grafting have often failed, and the propagation otherwise than by seed is not apparently easy.

FOREST REST HOUSE, POUCE VALLEY.

The Bullock's Heart of the same family is not so good. The Longan, Avocado Pear, Loquat, etc., are other tropical fruits eaten raw. The Banana gives rise to a certain amount of local trade in the hands of Indian gardeners, who sell it at a half to one cent each. The best varieties are Gingely, Naine and Mignonne, which are eaten raw; Siméroé, Malgache, Ollier, etc., are often cooked. The Bread-fruit, also cooked, bears in summer and is reproduced by root-suckers. Guavas are plentiful and are made into jellies.

Of European fruits, Peaches of good kinds are rarely grown. Grafted Oranges are rare. Lemons, Limes and other citrus fruits are fairly abundant, but suffer from Scale insects, which there is scarcely any attempt to keep in check by the usual methods. The Vine Grape has succeeded in some cases, but is often a failure through insect and fungus diseases. Strawberries are cultivated, and Raspberries are gathered wild.

Pineapples are grown extensively in certain localities, being generally of medium or small size, but sweet; they are sold at five cents each in summer. Better Pineapples are occasionally raised under the names of Victoria, Miel, etc., by persons who take the trouble of hoeing up the soil deep and manuring, but this is not frequent.

Fruit culture is susceptible of great improvement in Mauritius, by systematic action, both in view of the local market and of export to South Africa and other centres of consumption.

Medicinal Plants. The scientific study of the local medicinal plants was first taken up in 1857 by Louis Bouton, who, on the invitation of Governor Higginson, published in the *Transactions of the Royal Society of Arts and Sciences of Mauritius* an elaborate statement, written in English and French, with botanic and vernacular names, of the drugs used with success by Creoles, and of their respective merits, as testified to by reliable persons. The work was resumed in 1886 by Dr. Clement Daruty, who added the result of further experience and researches, and published in French a pamphlet, which has lately gone through a second edition, where mention is frequently made of the "active principle" of plants. It would not be possible here to detail these plants, but it must be stated that several of them have been accepted by medical practitioners, and are productive, in certain ailments, of well-defined results. The recent presidential address of Sir Edward Evans, at the British Pharmaceutical Conference at Edinburgh, bore on the importance of the cultivation of drugs in British Dominions, and was followed by interesting response in India and elsewhere. The system of medicine depending upon the herbs and plants of Mauritius is worthy of attention.

CAYENNE PALMS, ROYAL BOTANIC GARDENS, PAMPLEMOUSSES.

MINOR INDUSTRIES.

Aloe Fibre. The *furcræa gigantea* grows wild in Mauritius on waste lands of low altitudes. In 1879 the fibre came suddenly into great demand on the European markets, and in that year the exportation rose from four or five tons to 863 tons. The annual output of the fifty fibre factories of the colony is now over 2,137 tons, worth about Rs.605,000, the cost of production being Rs.175 to Rs.250 per ton, according to the motive power applied, hydraulic force being of course the cheapest. The leaf contains 4 per cent. fibre, and the scraping machine used extracts 2½ per cent. The chief obstacle in the way of progress of this industry is the heavy rate for conveyance of the leaves, and this can be remedied by regular plantations and the use of mechanical transport. Already 4,000 acres have been regularly planted.

Vanilla. Vanilla was grown on a pretty large scale from 1878 to 1892, the largest quantity of produce exported being 26½ tons in 1885, worth about Rs.309,000. Towards 1887 a fungus disease, attacking stem and leaves, proved destructive to the plant, and the cyclone of 1892 completed its ruin. With more careful treatment, the cultivation has been taken up again, and since a few years two or three tons are exported annually.

Tea. The tea shrub is cultivated on about 400 acres, the hybrid Assam variety being generally raised on the uplands. The yield is 400 to 500 lbs. per acre. There are two factories, the whole output of which—Pekoe and Fannings teas—is consumed locally; the retail price is about 90 cents per pound, and the demand is on the increase. The produce has been favourably reported on by the Imperial Institute, and the Government encourages the extension of the cultivation by allowing certain Crown Lands for lease.

Coffee.

Coffee used to be an important asset of the colony. In 1816 there were 2,500 acres under this plant. The repeated losses through cyclones, the leaf disease, and the extension of the sugar-cane are reasons put forward for its being now quite limited in cultivation. The Liberian and Moka varieties are both equally represented in the existing plantations.

Tobacco.

Tobacco is produced on a small scale, the tax on the unit of area cultivated being Rs.160. The samples referred to European experts were not found satisfactory, the soil being apparently too rich in sulphates for growing the plant without the correction of chemical fertilizers. But in presence of the large quantity of imported tobacco (worth half a million rupees), there is reason to believe that the Department of Agriculture will reconsider the question and suggest a suitable method of cultivation and of curing.

Cotton.

Cotton is recorded as having been grown on 4,600 acres in 1816. But it was given up for the sugar-cane. In 1905 and 1911, careful experiments were made with Sea Island cotton in different soils and climates; the results were negative, the causes of failure being snails and insect pests, and also the destructive action of weather on the young plant and on the ball when opening.

Food-stuffs.

Manioc or cassava is cultivated both for animal food and for human consumption. Two or three varieties are known locally, yielding per acre ten tons or more of roots which fetch Rs.20 or Rs.25 a ton. A trial of manufacture of tapioca, made a few years ago, was a failure, probably through want of sufficient manioc for the factory to be a paying concern.

Maize can be sown twice a year, and is sold at Rs.5 per 100 lbs. It does not keep long, being generally moist, and there is no drying apparatus in the colony.

Sweet potatoes are grown on a certain scale by Indian gardeners, and a yellow variety for the table is very good.

Aroids, principally the Cambare Violette, and the Cambare Betty, are raised in moist localities, and eaten by the poor.

The Chouchou (*Sechium edule*) is a climbing plant, the fruits of which yield abundantly, and are a regular boon for the poor, who cook them as curry.

Prædial larceny is the serious drawback to the development of these auxiliary-products of the farm in the Mauritius, and the action of the Police has often been inefficient for repression thereof.

PICKING TEA, CUREPIPE.

CREOLE PATOIS AND FOLK-LORE.

By ALBERT PITOT.

It is by no means necessary to go very far back in the past to discover the period when Mauritian folk-lore, or Creole patois, had its birth. When the French settled here for the first time, in 1722, the island had been altogether abandoned twelve years before by its former occupants, the Dutch. Not a soul was left in it who could set up a claim to the paternity of an indigenous folk-lore. Those early colonists came originally from various French provinces, from Brittany and Normandy for the most part, and brought with them a few slaves from Bourbon. As the work of colonization proceeded, however, it was found of paramount importance to procure a fresh supply of servile labour. The greater number of the blacks first introduced were from the neighbouring island of Madagascar; some also came from Mozambique, and as time passed others were obtained from the Guinea Coast, in West Africa.

INDIAN HOME.

But a difficulty soon arose; as the masters were generally ignorant of the dialects spoken by the blacks, and as the blacks themselves could not always understand each other, daily transactions were paralyzed until a common idiom was created between them to facilitate their intercourse. Thus was the Creole patois formed. What it was exactly, at its outset, it is impossible to say with surety, since no records were ever kept on the subject. Nevertheless, it is most likely that it contained at first a prominent proportion of Malagassy and African terms, which eventually gave way as the synonymous French words prevailed. At present a few names of plants, animals and primitive utensils are the only traces left of the Malagassy vocabulary in the Mauritian Creole patois.

Creole patois in its pure form—that is to say, such as it was spoken from the second half of the eighteenth century till about 1850 or 1860, when the colonists began to be aware of the drawbacks of profuse Indian immigration—Creole patois, we say, was nothing but a corruption, or rather, a thorough simplification, of the French, doing away altogether with that which was deemed superfluous.

Taking parts of speech as an illustration, the article is either done away with, or, when it is preserved, ceases being an independent word, and becomes, as a prefix, an integral part of some nouns, as *licien* (*le* chien, dog), *lérat* (*le* rat, rat), *lacase* (*la* case, hut), *lamisique* (*la* musique, music). But in other substantives the initial syllable is dropped, as *gouïe* (aiguille, needle); in some monosyllabic nouns the syllable is doubled, *lilit* (lit, bed).

The substantive knows neither gender nor number, but in case of the article being used as a prefix to two homonymous words which are not of the same gender in French, the Creole patois will always use the feminine: *lamance robe*, *lamance pioce* (a gown's sleeve, a hoe's handle). The Creole patois can also, at any moment, make a substantive of a verb—*coute so causé* (listen to his tale).

For degrees of comparison, the Creole patois has adopted the French *meilleur* and *pire*, but in enforcing their meaning by placing before them the adverb *plis* (plus, more): *plis meillère*, *plis mié*, *plis pire* (literally, more better, more worse).

Distributive numeral adjectives are always reduplicated: *ène ène, dé dé*, etc. *Nous va donne cinque piasses ène ène doumounde* (we shall give five dollars to each man).

The nominative case of personal pronouns is obsolete, the objective being always preferred, perhaps on account of its easier pronunciation: *mo* (moi, me), *to* (toi, thee), *li* (lui, him, her), *nous* (nous, us), *vous* or rather *ous* without the initial letter (vous, you), *zautes* (les autres, others), this being a derogation from the above rule.

Auxiliary verbs are also rejected as useless; the verb *to have* does not exist properly, and is replaced by *gagné* (to get), or *éna* (*il y ena*, there is some). The verb *to be* is still more ignored, so that Creole blacks would be at a loss to express in their idiom its rendering in Hamlet's monologue. Yet, when the idea of existence must be conveyed, the Creole patois ingeniously gets over the difficulty by construing the sentence without any verb at all: *Mo malade* (I am sick); *li en bas lilit* (it is under the bed).

Verbs do very well without inflexions or declension. In order to express tenses, the Creole has recourse to certain auxiliaries of his own making. For the past, *ti* or *té* (*été*, been), or *fine* or *fini* (finished, achieved): *mo ti allé, mo fine tombé* (I went, I fell down). For a recent past, *fec*; *li fecallé* (*il ne fait que s'en aller*—he has just gone). For the future: *pour* (for) is used: *mo pour allé* (I shall go—literally, I for go), etc., etc.

INDIAN FAMILY.

The French form of pronominal verbs is never used in Creole, the possessive pronoun being transformed into an equivalent—nay, into a more forcible epithet: *so lécorps* (his body), *so nénez* (his nose), *so latête* (his head), *li va touye so lécorps* (he will kill himself), *li mouce so nénez* (he blows his nose), *li après peigne so latête* (she is busy combing her hair). It is strange to note that the Creole patois has adopted, unawares of course, a construction identical with the English.

When a frequent recurrence is to be expressed, the verb is reduplicated, thus: *causé*, to speak, becomes *causecausé*, to chatter, to babble. The two French prepositions *à* and *de*, *to* and *of*, which are so frequently used in that language, are entirely set aside in the Creole patois, the construction adopted being the very same as for the verb *to be*: *lacase so papa* (his father's house). So are the French conjunctions *ot*, and; *ni*, neither; *ou*, or. As for interjections, they are numerous, picturesque, and by no means devoid of energy; the following are a few examples, in regard to which we insert in brackets the sentiments they express: *Houn!* (affirmation); *Hounwhoun!* (negation); *Couh!* (admiration); *Ahiah!* (doubt); *Ahouah!* (defiance); *Ayoh!* (pain); *Papa! Maman! Mayoc! Manami!* (admiration, the latter being a corruption of the French *mon ami*); *Vouti!* (menace, from the French *veux-tu*, will you?); *Kskss!* (provocation).

Onomatopœia has been the principal factor when the Creole has created new words; the blacks have always shown an enthusiastic relish for representing in speech inarticulate sounds and noises. A few examples will suffice to illustrate this propensity: *fére guidiguidi* is to tickle, and by extension, the armpit is commonly called *guidiguidi* or *digdig*; *gnangnan* is used for a lazy and effeminate person; *éne catacata* means a coquette, a flirt; *balalame* designs a tall awkward fellow with long hanging arms; *quémequéme* is a puzzled individual; *fére sapsap* is to flirt, etc.

A few prostheses are particularly worth mentioning. Having heard the French say *le bon Dieu, de bon matin, bonne année*, the blacks have thus translated the words, *Dieu, matin* and *année*: *bondié, bomatin, bananée*; and accordingly they frequently make use of such strange constructions: *Bondié napas bon pour moi* (literally, good God is not good for me); *bomatin mo lève tard* (literally, early in the morning I rise late); *éne mauves bananée* (a bad good year).

In a great number of sentences, the meaning of which, if written, would prove equivocal, is rendered perfectly explicit by the accentuation of the words as they are spoken, which sets down the speaker's intent without the slightest shadow of doubt; a Creole will never have any uncertainty in such a case as to what is really meant.

Most words are more or less corrupted through defective pronunciation, some races of blacks being altogether incapable of uttering properly certain consonants or certain syllables; so we have *tourou* for trou (a hole), *coulou* (clou, a nail).

When a noun begins with a vowel or mute *h*, it is in general, for euphony's sake probably, preceded by an *n* or *z*, as *nhabit* (habit, a coat), *zhistoire* (histoire, a story). When a substantive is too long for utility, the Creole does not hesitate to cut off the first syllable, thus *bitation* for habitation, an estate; *tranzé* for étranger, a stranger. The French classical plural *aux* of nouns in *al* is never used; the Creole prefers saying *dé çouvals* (deux chevaux, two horses); *quate fanals* (quatre fanaux, four lanterns). But, on the other hand, he will call an animal *ène zanimau*; an eye is *ène liziés, li* or better, *ène coté liziés*. This is of little importance to the black so long as he makes himself understood.

Of course, the Creole patois is meant to express only a limited number of ideas, referring especially to facts of daily recurrence in the social life of the parties interested. No abstractions are possibly entertained. As we have already said, the verb *to be* is ignored in Creole; the black Creole knows for certain that he exists, and does not bother arguing over it, and such words as *virtue, honour* and the like express qualities which he has evidently no occasion to consider. Some words expressing abstract ideas have nevertheless crept in, but they are turned from their proper meaning to signify something very different. For instance, *ambition* for the Creole does not represent anything but greed, love of money: *zot trop lambition* means in good Creole "they are too eager after money." *Instinct* is used for irony, chaffing: *napas faire to linstinct av moi*—do not chaff me.

It must be borne in mind that their masters were mostly natives of French maritime provinces, and this explains the number of nautical terms which have passed into Creole: *largué* (lâché, let loose), *souqué* (saisir, to catch), *lofé* (to steer windward, to stroll), etc.

The Creole delights in images, some of which are most happy conceptions, appropriate also and by no means lacking in energy, but not always fit to be printed. If they have to invite somebody to run away, according as circumstances are more or less pressing, they will reject the prosaic word *galoupé* (galoper, to run), which carries no particular idea of swiftness, but say *bourré* (to stuff, to cram), *vanné* (to winnow), *taillé* (to cut). If the narrator has to mention that he himself had to fly for his dear life, he will make use of one of those phrases embodying a superlative expression of rapidity: *lézailes av moi* (wings have grown on me), *houn! àcote moi?* (hey! where am I?). Ever since the abolition of slavery, in 1835, the black Creole population of Mauritius has been slowly but surely undergoing a change. Scarcely more than a century and a half old, devoid of sufficient resistant ethnical characteristics to keep its own, it has been constantly modified, first by European intercourse, and next, and in a far greater measure, by intermixing with Indian races, so plentifully introduced in this colony by seventy-five years of increasing sugar production. The original standard type of the black Creole is fast disappearing, and the day is not far distant when he will be a perfect rarity, not unlike the extinct *Didus ineptus*.

The same process has been undergone in the meantime by the Creole patois. Although by no means likely to disappear altogether, it has proved unable to preserve its purity of olden times. Being by its extreme simplicity the natural medium between foreigners and the population, it has received from strangers every neologism which they have been pleased to impose. It has become hopelessly corrupted, and is getting more and more so every day, owing to its being disfigured by English, Indian and Chinese constructions; so that, were it possible for P'pâ Lindor, the black Nestor of old days, to come amongst his great-grandchildren now, he would very often be at a loss to understand their speech, and be perfectly justified in reproaching them with not having preserved the very essence of the Creole patois, *so qualité même*, as he had it.

But it does not follow at all that the Creole should feel any sympathy for copper-coloured aliens; far from it, the black Creole, especially of the lowest class, despises thoroughly the Indian coolie. A coolie is not a man in his eyes; he is scarcely a thing, *ène nation tripe* (this, we think, requires no translation). An example will show it; An Indian gets run over by a cart, and somebody asks if the man has been badly hurt; *napas ène doumounde, ène malabar,* will answer a Creole (it is not a man, only a malabar); *malabar* is the Creole equivalent for all Indians, whatever part of Hindustan they come from.

As the Creole black has been altered physically, so he has changed morally; new wants have given him a new mental outlook. It is only the early nucleus of that section of the population which can lay a claim to a sort of literature of its own, if such a term is not preposterous when applied to such crudities. Struggle for life concomitant with the expansion of the Creole's intellectual powers (?) has given rise to very different qualities.

LEGENDS AND TALES.

Legends cannot possibly be written out in the original text, for tradition has preserved nothing but their essence, without giving them a regular form. They are assuredly the earliest manifestations of popular imagination, yet they are so very old that nobody remembers anything but the ideas they embody.

INDIAN CONJURERS AND SNAKE CHARMERS.

As a rule, all the earliest legends incidentally refer to La Bourdonnais, who was immensely popular with the blacks. Had they to mention some extraordinary animal, some fantastic brown-bearded deer, for instance, with tremendous antlers far larger than those of a royal stag, some of those wild creatures that no bullet could ever bring down, the blacks, as a tribute of their well-deserved admiration of the founder of the colony, would even in our time call it *La Bourdonnais.* So far as we have been able to trace it, this characteristic originated as follows. Shortly after his arrival, La Bourdonnais was busy building up Port Louis, supervising the workmen just like an ordinary overseer, and devising plans with his engineers. When the sun was high, and the heat was excessive, he would repair to a shady spot not very far off, beside a brook of crystal water, where a cascade tumbled into a most inviting pond. This was no other than the Butte à Tonniers Rivulet, and the waterfall's site coincides exactly with the corner of Hazard and Poudrière Streets. *Quantum mutatus!* There did the great man, after having thrown his garments over some *framboises maronnes,* indulge in an invigorating swim. It happened one day that a thirsty stag came down to the water's edge. Frightened at the sight of a human being in such a secluded nook, it started away with the gubernatorial breeches unwittingly entangled in its antlers. When La Bourdonnais came out of his bath, he found himself in a very awkward position, but as his presence was urgently needed on the quay, he bravely put on his shirt, vest, riding coat, stockings and red-heeled shoes, not forgetting his wig and three-cornered hat, nor his *grand cordon de St. Louis,* and proceeded as solemnly as usual to the dockyard. So polite were his people, and so respectful of discipline, that none of them, it is said, manifested any surprise at seeing the Governor so wonderfully and indecorously attired.

Another legend tells of a monstrous eel, which, for those credulous people, represented evidently some fabulous dragon and went also by the name of La Bourdonnais. Its circumference was as large as a wine cask and it was fully forty feet in length. Some blacks swore they had seen it a number of times, without, of course, ever attempting to catch it. This wonderful water serpent's abode was Grand Bassin, a small lake on the confines of Savanne district, the depth of which nobody had ever succeeded in ascertaining until about the year 1830, when Captain Lloyd, the Colonial Engineer, discovered that it was not more than sixty feet deep; but of course things may have altered since those primitive times!

Having noticed that the water there constantly kept the same level, the natural inference among slaves was that Grand Bassin was in direct communication, by means of a subterraneous canal, with some lake in Madagascar; and this belief was all the more firmly established because some declared having positive knowledge of maroons having occasionally escaped to their own country by diving through this secret channel. The only difficulty was that they must then have remained a week or two under water, but men in those times were apparently amphibians, and possessed of far greater endurance than the present degenerated specimens of dark humanity!

A detachment of slave-hunters once happened to be on the track of a gang of maroons, and came to the banks of Grand Bassin. The blacks readily jumped into the water, and so did their pursuers; the blacks dived, and they dived after them; the blacks found the entrance to the tunnel, and so did the slave-hunters; but at that critical moment up came the La Bourdonnais eel with wide open jaws, and so frightened the latter that they gave up the chase altogether.

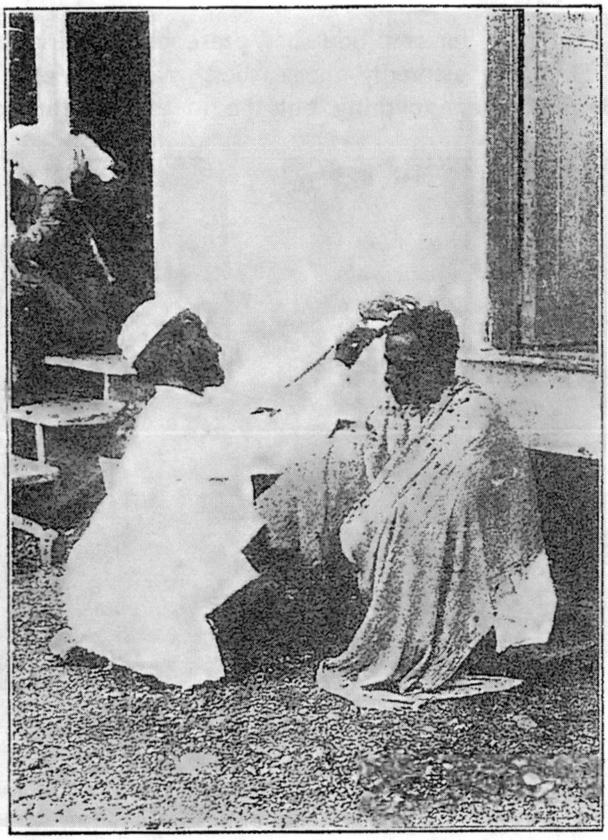

INDIAN BARBER.

Other legends relate to treasures buried by corsairs. The classical way of performing in those circumstances was of extreme simplicity. A slave was made to dig a hole at night in some secluded spot, and when it was large enough, and the gold, jewels and other *et cetera* had been carefully deposited therein, the wily corsair would kill the poor fellow so as to leave no witness, and bury his body along with the valuables.

Amongst those tales is that of Pointe aux Sables, off Grand River North West, the hero of which was the celebrated Malroux. If he really committed the foul crime attributed to him, he, however, derived no profit from it, for, on his very next expedition, on board the *Amphitrite*, he met with a most horrible death.

He was successful beyond all expectations at first, when he captured the *Pearl*, one of the Moorish vessels which were loaded yearly with the contributions sent to Mecca by the Mussulman devotees from the Persian Gulf and Bombay Coast, consisting of gold and silver coins and ingots, jewels, precious stones of every description, and stallions of the purest breed. But the *Amphitrite* came across the British corvette *Trincomalee*, which attacked her with fury. After an hour's desperate fighting, Malroux boarded the man-of-war and was almost certain of his prize when the English blew up their vessel. This was so rapidly effected that the *Amphitrite* had no time to remove to a safe distance; the *Trincomalee* was, of course, reduced to atoms, and the *Amphitrite* was so badly shattered that she had to be abandoned, the whole crew taking refuge on the *Pearl*. Malroux was the last to leave his ship, but as he was departing, he suddenly remembered having left in his chest some papers of importance, and, maybe, some casket brimful of diamonds and rubies. Accordingly, he ordered the boat to wheel round, and reached the *Amphitrite* as she was about to sink. In great haste he rushed downstairs to his room, which was already flooded, and securing the precious documents, ran up to the deck, which was now on a level with the sea. As he jumped into the boat, his head got entangled in the net which had been stretched over the quarter-deck as a protection from the enemy's missiles. In spite of his efforts and those of his men, he found it impossible to get off, and he sank with his ship and all its treasure.

Although treasure stories have given rise to much exaggeration, the potentialities of discovery in that direction cannot be altogether denied. Although not supported by any documentary evidence, there was once a rumour of treasure found in the eighteenth century by one Mr. Le Normand, who resided at Baie du Cap, and whom Bernardin de St. Pierre mentions in his *Voyage à l'Ile de France*; but the discovery was posterior to the author's visit. Another treasure was found some sixty years ago at Grand Port, on Anse Jonchée estate, by the owner himself; all the documents concerning this being still preserved, it is said, in the French Consulate at Port Louis. Such instances of good luck, however, being of a strictly private nature, they are delicate questions to deal with, and consequently it is as difficult to estimate their value as to get at the truth concerning them.

A good many treasure tales were still told about sixty or seventy years ago; and the belief in hidden treasures is not altogether extinct, as may be gathered from the energy displayed, not very long since, by a society of treasure-seekers at Flic en Flacq, on the Black River coast. Some there are, it is said, who are carrying out identical researches at Rodrigues, but it is needless to anticipate.

It has been reported, unofficially of course, that about 1864, at Grand Sable, in Old Grand Port, an Indian, having just purchased a quarter of an acre of land, was one day busy planting some sweet potatoes and *pommes d'amour* (tomatoes), when his hoe struck the lid of an iron box. Nobody was ever told how much wealth he thus secured, for the coolie was clever enough to refrain from giving notice to the police, being well aware that the Government would claim its share of the treasure trove. Soon afterwards he returned to his native land, wealthy beyond his wildest dreams. The whole story was disclosed by his Medea, whom the fickle Jason had left behind after having got hold of the golden fleece.

INDIAN CAKE SELLERS.

Creole tales amongst the blacks no longer multiply as of yore, and these individuals even feel little disposed, should they perchance remember any, to narrate for the mere gratification of simple curiosity, one of the stories their fathers used to relate so willingly and so profusely.

We may feel thankful that some twenty-five years ago, though it was very late indeed, a Mauritian of great merit, Mr. Charles Baissac, professor of French Literature in the Royal College and a *littérateur di primo cartello*, should have had the patience to write down a number of the tales in question in the original Creole idiom, as he heard them from the lips of carefully selected old people; for, as time passes, the task is getting more and more difficult.

The first colonists, coming from different parts of France, brought from their own country a stock of tales, which they would narrate, at resting time, for the benefit of their offspring. The slaves listened to them with great interest, and, of course, endeavoured to translate them in the prevailing idiom to their friends and children. Their memory not being always very good, it often happened that two or three stories got muddled up together in the most extraordinary manner. When mnemonic powers failed them entirely, the story was simply cut short, or, in case of an extra clever narrator, the catastrophe was replaced by something of his own composition; and it is easy to guess what the result must have been.

As a rule, most of the Creole stories have either a French or an Indian origin; very few are entirely of Creole source, but the details and characters are evidently Creole, and are wonderfully adapted to local circumstances and environment, with the piquancy and individuality peculiarly their own.

We shall now give the reader a specimen of that narrative power, followed, of course, by an English word-for-word translation. This example, as well as those we give of songs, *sirandanes* and proverbs, and in fact, nearly the whole substance of this essay, has been borrowed from Mr. Baissac's most interesting volumes, *Le Patois Créole de l'Ile Maurice* and *Le Folk-lore de l'Ile Maurice*.

ZISTOIRE IÉVE AV TOURTIE DANS BORD BASSIN LÉROI.

Longtemps longtemps dans payi Maurice, ti éna éne léroi qui ti gagne éne grand bassin. Làdans même li té baingne so lécorps tous lé bomatins, à cause docteir ti commande li. Avlà éne zour li arrive dans bord bassin; dileau sale, napas capave baigné. Léroi appelle gardien, bourre li. Lendimain, dileau sale. Troisième zour, dileau sale. Léroi pèse gardien dans licou, li sacouyé, li dire li:

"Eh! toi, to vlé mo trape lagale dans ça dileau lè. Quand dimain bassin napas prope, to va guété sipas mo ronflé toi!"

Gardien peir. Asoir li prend fisil, li cacié dans feilles sonses bord bassin; lanouite noir noir, napas laline. Lheire canon tiré, li tende doumounde vini; li couté: tac, tac, tac; ça ti éne iéve! Avant gardien gagne létemps lève fisi, iéve vine drette av li, li dire li:

"Bonzour, bonzour, gardien! Coment mo content trouve vous! longtemps ça même mo rôdé; à cause mo iéna bon bon quiqueçose pour donne vous. Goûte ça dimiel mo famille fine envôye noi Trois Zilots! vous va dire moi sipas zamais vous ti trouve dimiel coment ça."

INDIAN "GOON" FESTIVAL AT BON AIR SUGAR ESTATE.

Gardien prend calebasse, li avale éne gorzée:

"Sifait va! li goût même."

Gardien tacé sembe calebasse là, li-vidé li. Mais sipas qui zespèce féyaze iéve fine mété dans dimiel là: gardien nèque létemps allonze so lécorps dans bord bassin; sôméye pèse li, li ronflé. Iéverié, li tire so linze, li pique dans bassin.

Iéve là malice; lhére li assez, li sourti dans bassin, li brouille laboue, li faire éne dileau çocolat dans bassin là; li allé.

Grand bômatin léroi vini. Li nèque guette so dileau: napas appelle en colère ça! Gardien encore dourmi dans bord bassin; léroi touque ça bâton là même qui iéve té brouille dileau, li tombe làhaut gardien, beirré, ronflé, manman! Gardien napas longtemps pour lévé; lézailes av li! li vanné même, li sauve dans bois, zamais li fine tourne encore.

Leroi faire sonne trompette: "Bisoiné ne gardien pour veille bassin: houite piasses par mois, dimi balle douriz, vivres magazin. Mais quand gardien là laisse doumounde brouille dileau dans bassin, va coupe so licou." Zanimaux tende ça crié là, zaute tout peir, personne napas dimande pour prend place: coq peir, licien peir, lazoie peir.

Trois zours passé. Iéve baigné, brouille dileau; léroi napas conné qui li va faire, so lécorps commence gratté même dipis septe zours qui li napas capave baingné.

Quatrième zour, zofficier léroi vine dire li qui iéna doumounde qui dimande gardien bassin. Léroi dire: Faire rentré! ça ti éne faye tourtie. Léroi guette li, li commence en colère:

"Toi ça qui va fouti empèce doumounde sale mo dileau?"—

"Oui, mo roi! moi-même ça!"

"To conne condition: quand dileau brouillé, mo va saute to licou?"—

"Oui, mo roi! mo conne condition; et coment laviande tourtie bon pour manzé, vous va capabe faire cari av moi. Mais mo crois pas qui vous pour goûte moi ça voyaze là! vaut mié vous dire vous cousinier plime éne manman poule."

"Bon, mo commère! dimain bomatin nous va guété. Rente dans to louvraze àsoir?"—

"Tourtie allé. Li alle lacase so camrade; li faire li frotte so lacoque partout partout av goudron. Lheire soleye coucé, li arrive bord bassin, li pelote dans ptit cimin à cote iéve pour passé, li aspéré.

Tac, tac, tac, iéve vini. Iéve trouve ça quiqueçose noir noir là dans milié cimin, li arrêté, li guété. Latête tourtie fine ramasse en bas lacoque: narien bouzé. Tac, tac, tac, iéve approce doucement doucement, narien bouzé. Iéve maziné; li vireviré, li guété, li guété: narien bouzé. Bon moment li reste tranquille, tranquille; tourtie coment roce même. Ça coup là; lékeir iéve arrête batté, li naplis gagne peir, li dire:

"Roce même ça donc! mo conné astheire! Eh vous zaute! léroi là éne bon doumounde oui! bien sir ça éne ptit banc qui li fine comande so domestique amène dans bord bassin pour mo capabe assisé, lhére mo bisoin tire quilotte pour alle baingne mo lécorps dans so dileau!"

Iéve rié; li assise làhaut roce. Coment dire roce là bouzebouzé morceau. Iéve senti ça, li nèque dire:

"Comme ça même domestique travaille dans paye Maurice! zaute fine blié cale mo fauteil."

Ene coup là li vlé dicendé pour cale so ptit banc; napas môyen bouzé, li fine tacé av goudron. Tourtie sourti so latête en bas lacoque:

"Qui to croire, compère? Moi, mo croire qui çá voyaze là to maillé même."

Iéve sec. Mais li bisoin sayé pour çappe so lavie; li dire tourtie!

"Hé toi! hé toi, commère: to voulé badine av moi, hein? Avlà mo cause doucement: largue moi, largue moi, mo dire toi! napas faire mo colère lévé!"

Tourtie té commence marcé pour amène li lacase léroi; li nèque dire li:

"Quand to content, causé pour soulaze to lécorps. Ene fois! dé fois! to napas voulé largue moi?"

Bam! iéve flanque li éne coup lapatte derrière: lapatte côlé! Bam! laute lapatte oussi tacé. Tourtie napas oquipe ça, li marcé, li sive so cimin. Iéve dire li:

NEGRO CHILDREN CARRYING BANANAS FROM THE TAMARIN FALLS.

"Eh toi! mo plis fort dans mo lapatte divant, oui! Coute moi! largue moi bon keir!"

Tourtie marcé, napas réponde. Boum! éne coup lapatte gauce. Boum! éne coup lapatte droite: collé! collé! Iéve so quate lapattes amarre coment coçon qui camilas amène bazar. Mais pauve malhéré là bisoin saye encore. Li faire vantard av tourtie, li dire li:

"Acoute bien: mo cause éne dernière fois. Tout mo laforce dans mo latête, éne marteau fer ça! Quand mo tape éne coup lhaut toi, mo crase toi coment éne papaye mir. Largue moi, mo dire toi, largue moi!"

Tourtie marcé, napas réponde narien. Iéve lève lève latête, ramasse tout so laforce, tape éne coup. Bôm! latête collé.

Avlà zaute fine arrive lacase léroi: tourtie rié, iéve ploré.

Quand léroi trouve ça iéve là colle collé làhaut tourtie, quand même li en colère li blizé rié." Tourtie dire li:

"Avlà li là, mon roi! napas tourtie qui vous pour manze dans vous diné, mais iéve qui vous va manzé; quand couit li av divin blanc li bien bon."

Léroi tire so sabe, li saute latête iéve, li envoye lacousine. Après ça li appelle so domestique: " Eh toi! Mo alle baingné; vine frotte moi dans dileau; mo lécorps sale oui!"

Literal Translation:—

THE STORY OF A HARE AND A TURTLE ON THE BRIM OF THE KING'S POND.

Very long ago there lived in Mauritius a king who owned a large pond. There he was wont to take a bath every morning, for his physician had so ordered. Once, he comes to the pond's edge; the water is dirty; he cannot take his bath. He sends for the guardian and chides him. The next day the water is dirty; the third day the water is dirty. The king catches his guardian by his neck, shakes him about and says:

"Eh! you son of a dog, do you want me to get the itch in that water? If to-morrow my pond is not clean, you will see whether I do not give you a thrashing."

MAHOMMEDAN WOMAN.

The guardian is afraid. At night he takes his gun and hides behind some calladiums on the bank of the pond. The night is perfectly dark; there is no moon. When the gun is fired (the eight o'clock recess gun) he hears somebody coming; he listens: tac, tac, tac—it is a hare. Before the guardian has time to raise his gun, that hare comes straight at him and says:—

"Good day, good day, guardian! I am so glad to see you. I have been awaiting this opportunity for a long time, because I have something very nice to give you. Taste that honey my people have sent me from Trois Ilots; you will tell me whether you have ever eaten such honey."

The guardian takes the proffered calabash and swallows a mouthful.

"Most decidedly, it is excellent!"

The guardian sticks to the calabash and empties it. But I don't know what sort of drug (literally "foliage") the hare had mixed with the honey. The guardian has only time to stretch himself on the bank when sleep catches him; the hare laughs, undresses and dives into the pond. That hare was a perfect rogue. When he has enough, he gets out, picks up a long stick, stirs the mud, makes a chocolate water in the pond and goes off.

Early in the morning the king arrives. He just looks at the water; it is not a rage he gets in. The guardian is still asleep on the bank. The king seizes the very stick of which the hare had made use to stir the water. He falls upon the guardian, gives it to him with all his might—oh, mother! The guardian does not take long to rise; wings have grown on him; he flies away to the woods and has never come back since.

The king orders the trumpet to sound: "A guardian is requested to watch a pond, eight dollars a month, half a bale of rice and store's rations. But if the guardian allows people to stir the water, he will get his head cut off."

When the animals listen to that proclamation they are in such a fright that nobody presents himself to take the post; the cock is afraid, the dog is afraid, the goose is afraid.

Three days elapse. The hare takes his bath and stirs up the mud. The king does not know what to do; his body begins to itch; for seven days he has been unable to take his bath.

On the fourth day one of his officers tells him there is somebody applying for the post of guardian. The king answers: "Let him come in!"

It was a miserable-looking turtle. The king glances at her and begins to get angry.

"Is it you who pretend to prevent people from dirtying my bath?"

"Yes, my king, it is I."

"You know what the agreement is; if the water is stirred, I will cut your head off?"

"Yes, my king, I know the agreement, and as turtle flesh is good eating, you will be able to make a first-rate curry of me. But I don't think you will taste of me this time; you had better tell your cook to pluck a mother hen."

"All right, old woman, we shall see to-morrow morning. Begin your work to-night."

The turtle departs; she goes to visit a friend and has her shell well rubbed over with tar. When the sun has set, she comes to the pond and conceals herself in the footpath where the hare is bound to pass; she waits. Tac, tac, tac, here comes the hare. But he sees something darkish in the path; he stops, he looks. The turtle has withdrawn her head under her shell; nothing moves. Tac, tac, tac, the hare gets near, softly, softly; nothing moves. The hare considers, he turns about, looks about: nothing moves. For a pretty long time he stands still, still; the turtle is like a perfect stone. Then the hare's heart ceases beating; he is no longer afraid, he says:

"A stone it is and nothing else; I know it now! Eh! you, that king is a good chap! Surely this is a small bench he has ordered his servant to place near the pond, that I may sit down upon when I take off my breeches to bathe in his pond!"

The hare laughs; he sits down upon that stone. One should say that stone is moving about a little. The hare feels it and just observes:

"This is the way servants work in Mauritius; they have forgotten to put a wedge under my chair."

Then he wishes to go down and wedge up his little bench. There is no possibility of moving; he has stuck with the tar. The turtle pops her head from beneath the shell:

CHINESE WOMEN.

"What do you think, old fellow? I, for my part, think you are well caught this time!"

The hare is dumbfounded; still he is obliged to try and save his life. He says to the turtle:

"Eh! you, old girl! you want to joke with me, hey? Now I am talking gently: let me go, let me go, I tell you! Do not raise my anger!"

The turtle was already moving off to bring him to the king's house. She only replies:

"If it pleases you, you may talk away to ease your mind."

"Once, twice, you refuse to let me go?"

Bam! the hare strikes at her with his hind leg: the leg gets stuck! Bam! the other leg gets stuck also. The turtle does not mind it; she walks on, she keeps following her road. The hare says:

"Eh! you, I am stronger in my forelegs, I warn you! Listen to me! let me go of your own accord!"

The turtle goes on without answering. Boum! a stroke with the left paw. Boum! a stroke with the right paw: stuck! stuck! The hare's four legs are fettered just as those of the pig which Chinamen bring to the bazaar. But the poor fellow must try again. He brags to the turtle; he says:

"Now, listen well! I am speaking for the last time. All my strength resides in my head: it is a very iron hammer! Should I strike a blow at you, I would crush you like a ripe *papaye*. Let me go, I tell you, let me go!"

The turtle walks on without answering. The hare raises his head several times, he gathers all his strength, strikes a blow. Bôm! his head gets stuck.

Now they have come to the king's house; the turtle laughs, the hare weeps.

When the king sees that hare stuck on the turtle's back, although he is in a rage, he cannot help laughing. The turtle says:

"There he is, my king! It is not turtle you will eat for your dinner, but hare you will eat; when it is cooked with white wine it is very nice."

The king draws his sword, cuts off the hare's head and sends him to the kitchen. After that he calls his servant:

"Eh! you, I am off to take my bath. Come and scrub me over in the water; my body is dirty, I can tell you!"

Now, as Mr. Baissac very rightly observes, what do you think of that king whose bath is such a constant care? Is it not a thorough Creole conception of royalty?

SONGS AND SEGAS.

What is true of Creole tales is still more so of Creole songs. Yet, in this respect, it is no great pity indeed; for those in no case gave a very bright idea of the Creole's power of prosody. Some were simple mutilations of French sentimental *romances*; or, when their authors wanted to be original, they became generally obscene, if not thoroughly cynical, or incomprehensible altogether. Here are a few most carefully selected illustrations.

The first may bear the following title:

Perversion.

Mo famme, dans to maladie,
To napas manze narien!
—Mo mari, cé qui mo oule manzé,
Dans lépays napas iéna!
Mo mari, si ous content moi,
Mo mari, vine donne-moi lamain,
Laisse-moi défonce poulailler.

("My wife, in your illness you eat nothing!" "My husband, what I wish to eat is not to be found in this country. My husband, if you love me, my husband, come and help me! Let me break in a hen coop!")

Seduction.

Ptit fille, vine dans mo lacase!
Mo napas manque narien:
To a prend par pongnées douriz,
To va fane av to ptit poules.

(Young girl, come to my hut; nothing is wanting there; you will take handfuls of rice, and throw them to your chickens.)

Warning.

To cause moi lamour
Derrière lacousine;
Si mo papa va trouve toi,
Li va casse to léreins.
Aïoh! mo ptit coco, aïoh! mo ptit coco,
Coment li goût, coment li goût!

("You are talking love to me behind the kitchen; if my papa sees you, he will break your backbone. Aïoh! darling, aïoh! darling, how sweet it is! how sweet it is!")

Old, old story!

"Marie Louise av Zosselin
Zaute dicende en bas bosqué.
Qui to faire là Marie Louise,
—Mo après veille dizèfs martin.
—Napas la magnère, Marie Louise,
Pour to veille dizèfs martin;
Guette lasécheresse à présent.
Tout martins tine làhaut lamare."

(Marie Louise and Josselin have gone down to a thicket. "What are you doing there, Marie Louise?" "I am looking for martins' eggs." "This is not the way, Marie Louise, to look for martins' eggs; see the drought which prevails just now—all the martins keep beside pools.")

NEGRO GIRL.

(N.B.—The *martin* is a very common insectivorous bird.)

Very different indeed from the Creole songs are the picturesque ségas, which have disappeared entirely, and so, alas! have the words and music which once kept time to them.

Séga tunes are numerous and immensely varied, although identical in rhythm; they are pleasant to hear, being composed in a minor mood, on a *quatre temps* measure exceedingly brisk and lively, not unlike the galop, the chief feature of which is that the first beat of each bar is energetically accentuated. This was effected in practice by a peculiar stroke of the fingers on the *marouvané*, a Malagassy sort of tomtom, forming the blacks' orchestra along with the African *bobre*, an instrument exactly in the shape of a bow the string of which would be a wire fastened in the middle to a dry calabash resting against the player's chest, the performance being accomplished by striking that chord with a small stick, a foot in length. Both those instruments and a rhythmic clapping of hands supported the obligatory voices of the singers, who possessed a wonderful sense of measure, and kept time with remarkable uniformity.

A couple of dancers, a man and a woman as a rule, or two men, one of whom was dressed as a woman, would enter the ring and begin the séga with a heavy thumping of their feet on the ground, a peculiar and lascivious twisting of their loins, and an upward and downward balancing of their arms. The woman kept almost at the same place all the time, simply wheeling round, first to the right, then to the left, whilst the man followed her motion, closely turning round her in a semicircle, so that they constantly faced each other. Their action was at first moderate, but increased in velocity by degrees, till it became a regular twirl; when, after a lapse of time, the couple, being out of breath, giddy, and thoroughly exhausted, had to make room for others.

We have chosen, from amongst the most popular ségas, three once favourite tunes with the blacks, which have been noted for us by our friends, Messrs. Octave Thévenau and Marcel Chastellier, two clever musicians. We now insert them with the Creole words, followed by a literal translation, so as to give to the English reader a fair idea of what was a séga of olden times. It is, of course, not to be expected to find in them either scientific music or harmonious poetry.

Translation.—"Lalo curry! Mulatto girl, you indulge in heavy drinking (bis). You drink pure water, Mulatto girl, and pretend it is liqueur; you eat bambaras, Mulatto girl, and pretend they are camarons."

(N.B.—The *lalo* is a colonial vegetable, not unlike the Arabian *nafe*. *Sousouna* is a Malagassy term for drunkenness; *pique sousouna* means accordingly "to have a relish for strong liquor." *Bambaras* is a glutinous, viscous, disgusting snake-like sort of octopus found in shallow sea-water and highly appreciated by the Chinese. *Camaron* is the name of the Mauritian fresh-water crayfish.)

The pointedness, if we may venture to say so, of the song, which is composed of any number of *extempore* verses, consists in the antithesis between what the girl does and what she pretends to be doing; the stronger the opposition the better it is appreciated, as showing off the girl's conceit more completely.

Here is another:

Translation.—"I am so fond of Isabella, that my eyes keep sticking to her!"

Now for the last example:

Translation:—"Ramsamy Courtin (a servant), go you to the bazaar; a goat's head, six sous (a penny-worth) of mouroungue sticks; with the remaining cash take one sou of salt (a farthing's worth). Here is 25 sous (4d.), Ramsamy, do not forget massala!"

(N.B.—*Mouroungue* is an Indian tree, the ligneous pods of which, containing a strawy fibre, are highly appreciated by the blacks in a curry. *Massala* is an Indian curry paste.)

The genesis of this song is probably the following, according to Mr. Baissac: A well-to-do individual wishes to get his daughter married, and invites a young man to dinner, which is the probable reason for such a prodigal display of luxuries as those Ramsamy Courtin is ordered to secure. In verses that may follow, he will take his intended son-in-law over his house and property, proudly making a review of all his belongings without any exception whatever, which gives rise to some Creole witticisms. Of course, every singer is welcome to insert any humorous details he may imagine; so the number of possible verses is unlimited, and the song may continue *usque ad nauseam*, or to speak good Creole, *zisqu'à napas bon*.

But such happy times are nò more! Nowadays, the twentieth century black would consider it an insult if he were asked to indulge in one of those epileptic ségas in which his forefathers formerly delighted. He goes in now for fashionable quadrilles, lancers and waltzes. His dancing parties are worth seeing; everything passes as in the most select company, with one exception, however—in engaging a partner, a well-educated young man will never fail to ask a young beauty to *faire la partie* with him; literally "to play the game"; but the English translation can scarcely convey the meaning of such a polite invitation.

SIRANDANES.

Sirandanes have perhaps escaped the common fate, and are not irremediably lost. Sirandanes, says Mr. Baissac, are short enigmas, the sense of which is hidden behind an allegory, sometimes very far-fetched, but often calling forth a most happy image. This was the favourite pastime of the blacks in the remote times called by them *temps margoze*. (N.B.—As the *margoze* is one of the most bitter vegetables, the expression speaks for itself.)

When work was over and supper ended, they used to sit in front of their huts, around some glib-tongued old individual, and listen to stories, always the same, of which they never got tired. When the narrator had given his share, and he at least was showing signs of fatigue, he suddenly would cry out, *Sirandane! Sampèque!* was the ready answer, and the game opened with a series of problems, first the better known, which called forth immediate and correct replies even from the smallest urchins. After some rounds of these came the more difficult queries, which would stretch their intellectual powers to the utmost. He who was clever enough to find out the proper explanation was cheered and looked upon as a bright scholar indeed. And so the time passed, till they indulged in a séga before retiring for the night.

INDIAN DANCING GIRL.

Sirandanes have outlived Creole lore; they are not entirely forgotten, by reason, perhaps, of their brevity and pointedness. But still, no fresh masterpiece of the kind is nowadays produced; the mould is getting rusty; nobody now dreams of composing sirandanes either!

A few examples will surely be welcome:—

Dileau diboute?—Canne. (Standing water?—A sugar cane.)

Dileau enpendant?—Coco. (Hanging water?—A cocoanut.)

Pitit batte manman?—Lacloce. (A child who beats his mother?—A bell.)

Pitit bonhome grand çapeau?—Çampion. (A small man with a big hat?—A mushroom.)

Qui ti boui prémier marmite dileau dans pêye Maurice?—Difé. (Who boiled the first kettle in Mauritius—Fire.)

Mo éna ène bane ptit bonhomes, zour zaute fête zautes tout habille en rouze?—Piments. (I have a lot of small people; on their holiday they are all dressed in red?—Chillies.)

Lacorde marcé, béf dourmi?—Ziraumon. (The rope walks, the ox lies down?—A pumpkin.)

Qui ça moussié qui amène so lacase làhaut so lédos?— Couroupas. (Who is the gentleman who carries his house on his back?—A snail.)

Nhabit, napas quilotte?—Cancarlat. (He has a coat, but no breeches?—A cockroach.)

Ménace doumounde, napas causé?—Lédoigt. (I threaten, but I do not speak?—A finger.)

Qui lalangue qui zamés té menti?—Lalangue zanimaux. (Whose tongue is it which never told a lie?—An animal's tongue.)

Attrape li, mo alle çace l'aute?—Ça même qui lamain dire av labouce l'hére après manzé. (Catch it, I'll go and fetch some more?—It is what the hand says to the mouth, when a man is eating.)

PROVERBS.

Let us now mention a few Creole proverbs:—

Zaffères mouton napas zaffères cabris. (Sheep's business is not goats' business; *i.e.*, do not trouble about what does not concern you).

Çaquène senti so doulère. (Each of us feels his own pain).

Li fine vende so coçon. (He has sold his pig; *i.e.*, he spends his money as he never did before.)

Malade vine làhaut iève, li alle làhaut tourtie. (Sickness comes on a hare; it goes away on a turtle.)

Temps Francés zourmons té plis gros qui temps Anglés. (Under the French rule pumpkins were bigger than under the English.) Lindor being an old man, is an enthusiastic admirer of days gone by.

We will conclude with three specimens of the up-to-date epistolary efforts of the present Creole generation. It must be observed that these letters are not written in Creole—oh! no, but are meant to be the best French the writers could display.

The first is a love affair:—

"MADEMOISELLE,—J'ai un grand amour sur le coeur pour vous aussi Mademoiselle quand je vous voit je pet tombé en faience tellement je suis troublé par votre jolie petite figure mignone, mon coeur sé sotte comme un boule lastic il tape tellement fort qu'il y a des moments que je crois avoir mes intestins en lambo, ... et tout ça ma bonne chéri c'est vous, oui c'est vous qui me rend la vie dire comme ça, ma tête s'entourne quand je vois votre jolie petite mizo rire et me laisser voir de jolies petites défenses, ainsi mon ami c'est pas tout ça dites moi m'aimez vous oui ou non parce que je sens que je vais tombé en siccope bientôt, is vous me dites non ainsi vous me dites oui.

". . . . Hier à soir j'ai pas fermé les yeux tellement j'étais tourmenté avec les pices et les pinaises vers les deux heures du matin j'ai pensé à votre douce visage voilà que je n'ai fait que pléré tout ça la passe qui vous n'avez pas un amour virginal à la flère d'orangé sur votre coeur pour moi.

". . . . Adieu, mon coeur chéri d'amour je vous aime pour la vie."

Translation:—

"MADEMOISELLE,—I have a great love in my heart for you, so, Mademoiselle, when I see you, I am exposed to faint (the literal translation would be *to fall into crockery*, *faïence* being mistaken for *défaillance*), so much am I disturbed by your pretty and delicate little face; my heart jumps like an indiarubber ball, and beats so hard that at times I think my bowels are in tatters, and all that, my good darling, it is you—yes, it is you—who makes my life so miserable; my head gets giddy when I see your pretty little snout laughing and showing off your pretty little tusks; so, my friend, let us speak to the point. Tell me, do you love me, yes or no? because I feel I shall have a swoon before long if you say no; so you say yes.

"Yesternight I could not close my eyes so much was I tormented by fleas and bugs; about two in the morning I thought of your sweet face and kept crying all the while, all that because you have not a virginal orange-blossomed love in your heart for me.

"Good-bye, my dear heart of love; I love you for my life."

The second is an offer of marriage:—

"MA CÈRE MADAME,—Ayant entendi parler des la botés de vot fille et moimême j'ai vis de mes desieux de la splendére de son caracter je vous écris o ma cére madame pour que jai le consentement de vous affin que z'épouse Sofi apres paques ma cére madame repondé moi parce que je balotte de fraieur en esperan vot réponse. Je rest madame vot future et madame vot grand camrade pour tout ma vie.

"Vive Sofi, madame!

Translation :—

"MY DEAR MADAM,—Having heard people speak of your daughter's beauties *(sic)*, and having myself witnessed with my own eyes the splendour of her temper, I write, oh! my dear madam, to obtain your approval, so that I may marry Sophy after Easter; my dear madam, answer me because I shake with fear whilst awaiting your reply. I remain, madam, your future (son-in-law probably) and, madam, your great comrade for all my life.

"Long live Sophy, madam!"

Next, so hard times incite practical men, an application for a situation:—

"MONSIEUR,—Votre très humble serviteur ayant perdu les resources de continuer son travail, s'avance devant vous pour vous demander votre inaltérable protection, non pour lui, mais pour l'amour d'un Dieu puissant. Et le Souverain Omniscient vous rendra au centuple d'avoir compté sur votre généreuse égide."

Translation :—

"SIR,—Your most humble servant having lost the resources of continuing his work, presents himself before you to crave your unalterable protection, not for himself, but for the love of a Powerful God. And the All-knowing Sovereign will pay you back a hundredfold for having relied on your generous shield!"

We cannot surely do better than address the final example to the reader:—

"MONSIEUR,—Ne croyant pas abuser de votre affabilité que vous avez toujours témoignée à mon égard et dont vous êtes si fier, je demeure. Monsieur, un de vos fidèles et réciproques serviteurs."

Translation :—

"SIR,—Not believing I have trespassed upon your affability which you have always shown me and of which you are so proud, I remain, dear Sir, one of your faithful and reciprocal servants."

PLACE D'ARMES AND LA BOURDONNAIS STATUE, FORT LOUIS.

THREE HEROINES OF THE ISLE OF FRANCE.

By ALBERT PITOT.

I.—VIRGINIA.

DID Virginia really live? Such is the problem which, at one time, deeply excited public curiosity. Countless attempts have been made in all directions to elucidate the mystery, and, of course, have led to the most contradictory hypotheses. In spite of the subtlest deductions the question still lies open, and it is doubtful whether it will ever be finally settled, for the reason that such a solution is a material impossibility.

If we endeavour to discover, among the old families once residing at the Isle of France, a person who entirely led the life of Virginia, that is to say, who performed with accuracy and in their minutest details all the acts attributed to the heroine of the tale, then we must come to the discouraging conclusion that Virginia never existed and was but a production of the author's fancy.

Without going the length of setting down, with Sainte Beuve the celebrated French critic in his *Causeries du Lundi*, that "such lifelike beings as Paul and Virginia were entirely the result of the poet's imagination," it must be acknowledged, on the other hand, that such an exclusive way of considering the question would be most unfair; for from what has transpired from the efforts of seekers after truth, it may be admitted, with all appearance of probability, that most of the incidents described in the narrative have been, in fact, acted, although they cannot possibly be attributed to only one person, but to two or three, and even a greater number of Virginias, and that Bernardin de St. Pierre, availing himself of the well-known privilege belonging to imaginative writers, ingeniously assembled them so as to form one ideal heroine.

The best proof we can give in support of this explanation is that the author actually made use of an identical method in relating the only event it is possible for us to control by means of authentic documents—viz., the wreck of the *St. Géran*.

From the testimonies of the survivors, still preserved in the colony's records, the catastrophe did not occur in the month of December nor during a violent storm, but, in fact (through the ignorance and presumption of both captain and officers), in a splendid moonlight night on the 17th August, 1744, the sea being even fairly smooth, although strong currents prevailed, as is almost always the case in the neighbourhood of a particularly indented shore strewn with a number of islets.

The following is the correct version:—The *St. Géran* had left Lorient on the 24th March, 1744, with several passengers bound for the Isles of France and Bourbon; among them were Mr. de Villarmois, Mr. Guinée, a Bourbon planter, and two Creole young ladies, who were returning home to the Isle of France, after having been educated in Paris. These ladies, Mesdemoiselles de Mallet and Caillou, were engaged to two of the vessel's officers, Messrs. de Peyramon and Longchamp de Montendre. About the 15th June, the ship had embarked a number of blacks at Gorée. Hitherto the exceptionally prosperous voyage had only been marred by the illness of a number of the crew.

At 4 p.m. on the 17th August, the *St. Géran* came in sight of Round Island, not six leagues off the northern shore of the Isle of France. As night was coming on, the weather being glorious and the moon about to rise, Captain Delamarre, who was on his first visit to these latitudes, thought of proceeding at once with the voyage and mooring in Tombeau Bay, to which the second officer, Mr. Malès, and the lieutenant, Mr. l'Air, objected, claiming that with a disabled crew it would not be possible to man the anchors. On the other hand, pretending to be well acquainted with the coast, they declared that there was no danger at all in keeping under main-sail till daylight. A boatswain named Ambroise, overhearing them, observed that from his long personal experience of the island, he could assure them that, as soon as the vessel would be moored, the firing of a gun would suffice to bring the harbour boats up with more men than would be necessary. Malès, thereupon, ordered him to hold his tongue and boxed his ears for his impudence.

The *St. Géran* accordingly continued running alternately on the starboard and on the larboard tack. At midnight two sailors, on warning the officer on duty that the ship was dangerously nearing the shore, were answered by him that it did not signify. Suddenly, between 2 and 3 a.m., somebody gave the

Paul and Virginia, having lost their way on their return from Black River, are found by Domingue and his Dog.

The Slave Beater.

The Visit of Governor La Bourdonnais.

Departure of Virginia for France.

SCENES FROM THE TALE OF PAUL AND VIRGINIA.

(From old Engravings in the Museum, Port Louis.)

warning of breakers ahead; and before the ship's course could be altered, she came upon a reef, whilst a strong surge dashed her on to the shoals off Amber Island. The bell was rung and every soul on board hastened in confusion to the deck. The boats were unfastened, but the main-mast came down with a crash. In order to ease the vessel, the captain ordered the mizen-mast to be cut; it fell to leeward, dragging the foremast along with it, so that the boats were smashed by the timber with which the waves kept beating the ship's sides. Simultaneously the vessel's keel broke in two, the deck gave way, and the stem and stern stood almost erect, towering over the débris. All being now lost, prayers were said and hymns sung. A raft was then hastily constructed. At about 6 o'clock some sixty people made a rush for it, but it disappeared, and they were swallowed up by the billows. Captain Delamarre and a sailor named Edme Caret clung to a plank on which they managed to get seated. Caret advised his captain to take his clothes off, so as to be able to swim easier. Delamarre, however, declined to do so, alleging the dignity of his rank and the existence in his pocket of important papers with which he could not part. They had already succeeded in getting off the shoals, when another raft passed by, mounted by seven or eight men, who entreated Delamarre to join them, saying he would be safer there than on his plank. The captain complied with their request, but a terrible surf seized the raft and carried it and all upon it to the high sea. Caret, who had meanwhile lost his plank, dived and clung to the rocks at the bottom till the flood of surf had passed; and when he came up to the surface again his companions had disappeared. He swam with all his might, and at last reached the shore on Ile d'Ambre in a state of utter exhaustion.

Only ten men and one negress escaped drowning; but the woman and a pilot who had saved her died shortly after their landing. The remaining nine, eight sailors and a passenger, Mr. Dromart, stayed on that deserted place for three days, when, feeling a little stronger, three of them ventured to swim across to the mainland and were picked up, near Mare aux Flamants, by a party of huntsmen, who hurriedly proceeded to rescue the other six survivors.

Such is the only trustworthy account of the wreck, from which one is bound to acknowledge that Bernardin de St. Pierre has altogether modified the episode relative to Virginia being entreated to divest herself of her garments. In reality, this happened to Captain Delamarre, who unwittingly played the part of the heroine; so that we have thus, at all events, a most unforeseen Virginia. This, of course, has not prevented legends springing up. Magon St. Elier, in his *Tableaux Pittoresques de l'Ile Maurice*, asserts, on what authority he does not even say, that Mr. de Montendre so supplicated Mlle. Caillou, and upon her refusal, he took from his breast a lock of hair, which she had presented to him, kissed it and stoically awaited death by her side.

The following similar account differs, however, in the persons concerned. One Mr. de Mallet, an officer in the Regiment of Pondicherry, who died at a very advanced age, in 1819, used to relate—so wrote an anonymous author in the *Archives de l'Ile Maurice*, a newspaper which was published about that time—that his sister, Virginia, was on board the *St. Géran* when the wreck took place in December, 1743 or 1744, during a violent gale (this being altogether incorrect, does not speak much for the trustworthiness of what follows). She was engaged to one Mr. de Peyramon, who also insisted upon her removing her clothes, and as she refused to do so he threw himself into the sea, swam to the shore, and returned holding a green bough he had plucked from a tree, thus proving that it was possible to escape; but as she persisted in her determination he stayed beside her, and both were washed off by the waves.

Whilst this was taking place, Madame de Mallet, the young lady's mother, who resided in the island at a considerable distance from the spot, had a prophetic dream, in which she actually saw her daughter on the disabled ship, and prevailed upon her husband to send a few blacks—one of them was called Domingue—to Poudre d'Or, where they met Mr. de La Bourdonnais and his staff, who told them Virginia had perished.

Here we note that what was attributed to Mlle. Caillou in the first version is now placed to the credit of Mlle. de Mallet, and, of course, one of these accounts, if not both, which is more likely, must be untrue. For it is perfectly certain that the wreck was not heard of till two days after, from the mouths of three of the survivors, and that neither La Bourdonnais nor anybody else was present at the scene. As for the green bough, it bears such a strong resemblance to the one Noah's dove brought to the Ark, that one cannot help feeling diffident about it.

The reference to the name given to the heroine, Sainte Beuve, in the essay we have mentioned, suggests the following explanation, which seems very reasonable indeed:—In his youth, Bernardin de St. Pierre, while residing at St. Petersburg, had been engaged to a niece of General de Bosquet, Mlle. de la Tour, who died before they were married. Several years afterwards, at Berlin, he was on the point of wedding Mlle. Virginie Taubenheim, who also met with a premature death; so that "a pleasant remembrance led the author to unite both these names in that of one of his most graceful creations."

In an essay published by the *Cernén*, in its issues of 15th and 25th January, 24th February and 4th April, 1900, Mr. Alfred Harel, a Mauritian residing in Paris, gave the following interesting information, which he had obtained from his grandmother, Madame Victoire Harel, who had long dwelt in the vicinity of Montagne Longue. She had the facts related to her by her own father, Mr. François Couacaud, of Rochefort, in France, who practised the medical profession in the district of Pamplemousses from 1774 to 1805, and personally knew Madame de la Tour and Bernardin de St. Pierre, when the latter visited the Isle of France. Mr. Harel's theory does not, however, elucidate the question at issue.

According to Mr. Harel, one Jacques Joseph de la Tour married, in 1735, at Vannes, in Brittany, Catherine Millard, of that city, then aged seventeen. The couple left Lorient on the *Lys* shortly after and proceeded to the Isle of France, where they settled at Montagne Longue, at the foot of Pieterboth Mountain. From this marriage five children were born—Jean Baptiste, Michelle Gilonne, Baptiste François, Charles, and Paul. Mr. de la Tour died on the 4th August, 1765, that is to say before Bernardin de St. Pierre had visited the island. During his residence there the author got acquainted with the widow, and frequently called upon her. Although she could not write and was scarcely able to read, she was of a superior intellect, an accomplished model of a faithful wife and a devoted mother. Bernardin de St. Pierre being particularly struck with young Gilonne's charming qualities, was naturally reminded of both mother and daughter when he made such a touching description of Virginia's home and its inmates.

PAUL PRAYING ON VIRGINIA'S GRAVE.
(From an old Engraving in the Museum, Port Louis.)

So far nobody seemed to have cared about Paul, except Mr. Harel, who informs us that Paul also did exist, and that he was Gilonne's *fiancé*, his real name being Jacques Gaspard Bernard. Those two interesting young people, "who had learnt to love each other in the humble cottage at Pieterboth, were married in St. François Church, at Pamplemousses, on the 7th October, 1760."

The total of the preceding accounts gives no less than five possible, and even impossible, Virginias:—1st, Mlle. de la Tour, of St. Petersburg; 2nd, Mlle. Taubenheim; 3rd, Captain Delamarre himself; 4th, either Mlle. Caillou or Mlle. de Mallet; 5th, Gilonne de la Tour.

Our countryman, Mr. Léoville l'Homme, a littérateur and a poet, wrote a series of very judicious comments, which appeared in the *Planters' Gazette* between the 8th and 30th April, 1900, wherein he readily admitted the probable accuracy of Mr. Harel's claims, but acknowledged his having been sorely disappointed, as from the title of the narrative, *The Truth about Virginia*, he expected to be offered a complete elucidation of the mystery, whereas things continued to remain in the dark. His opinion was that Bernardin de St. Pierre, whilst writing his novel, may have recollected some legend of two lovers who, after having been brought up together, were ultimately separated from motives of social difference. This, with sundry other remembrances, the author made use of in his narrative, applying them to one person alone;

from which the inference may be drawn that "Paul and Virginia have possibly existed, but certainly not such as Bernardin de St. Pierre depicted them."

We shall continue to quote Mr. l'Homme's interesting deductions for what concerns the pretended tomb of the two lovers. Cemeteries were scarce in those days; people were buried wherever it was convenient, mostly on their own lands. Tombs were, and are still occasionally thus met with, either in groups or isolated, without bearing any inscription; so that it is not to be wondered at if, after half a century had elapsed, it became almost impossible to recognise with certainty the exact spot where a person had been buried. It may have been so as regards the two lovers in the romance. Mauritius has, nevertheless, possessed a tomb of Paul and Virginia, and even two, for some time at least. The first is situated in the Royal Botanic Gardens, Pamplemousses, and the other was on a spot in the vicinity of the present railway station; both places being considerably remote from St. François Church, where the author placed their grave.

In the *Revue Pittoresque de l'Ile Maurice*, a periodical which appeared about 1843, is a lithograph showing the monuments, for they are two in number, overshadowed by a thicket of bamboo trees, and consisting of two similar urns resting on two pedestals, with a pool of water right and left. Those urns probably no longer existed eighteen years later; for Mr. L. Simonin, in a volume published in 1861, *L'Ile Maurice et la Société Mauricienne*, whilst giving an identical description of the spot, says that he was shown "two small cubes of masonry, formed of red bricks, in the shape of supports commonly used for columns. They appeared to have been erected some sixty years previously, and already showed signs of decay, mostly on account of tourists constantly breaking off fragments of them as souvenirs, after having covered every available space with their signatures, dates of their visits, and sundry appropriate sentimental remarks." He closes his narrative, however, with this questionable assertion: "The Creoles are pleased to consider them as authentic."

LEGENDARY TOMB OF PAUL AND VIRGINIA IN THE ROYAL BOTANIC GARDENS, PAMPLEMOUSSES.

Nixon, the author of the *Sketches on Mauritius*, 1848, does not share in that venturous belief, at all events, although he does not deny the attraction of the cenotaphs :—

"Although not genuine, the people who flock to the spot will not suffer themselves to be diverted of the romantic illusion which is attached to the grave. If the voyager returns to Europe without this local knowledge, he is supposed to have seen nothing and is branded as little less than a savage."

The reason for two distinct graves has been rather pointedly given by a Scotch lady who stayed in Mauritius about 1820—*A Recollection of Seven Years' Residence in Mauritius, by a Lady*; although, be it said, her documentary evidence is not unimpeachable. She asserts there was only one tomb at first, but as some of those enthusiastic foreigners who then visited Pamplemousses Gardens, and never failed to pay a tribute of emotion to Virginia's grave, enquired what had been done with poor Paul, the owner of the ground, in order to meet such a reasonable claim, gave orders for another tomb to be built close by, in all points similar to the first.

According to Mr. Albert Rae, a Mauritian, and one of the most competent searchers of documents concerning the past of his native island, those tombs, if tombs they really are, were constructed on the lands of a Mr. Noble, behind the present railway station; the spot is now planted in canes, and, sad to say, no trace of the structures has been preserved.

Mr. Rae hints that the original one was possibly the remains of a monument raised, about 1775, by the grateful colonists to the memory of King Louis XV., for what reason we really do not know. The cenotaph may then have been erected at Pamplemousses, as that district was, in those days, the most densely populated and the richest of the whole island. Still, Mr. Rae declares that this is a mere hypothesis of his, for although documents exist as to the project of raising such a monument, there is not the slightest evidence that it was built there in preference to any other locality. But, admitting that such was the case, how is it that it came to represent Paul and Virginia's tomb? Probably, answers Mr. l'Homme, because the Jacobins, desirous of blotting out the very remembrance of a tyrant, and, at the same time, moved by the propensity to idyllic and sentimental manifestation, so common in those days among the most bloodthirsty Maratists, may have decided that the structure should be thereafter dedicated to the memory of the two lovers in Bernardin de St. Pierre's story.

At a sitting of the Committee for Historical Researches, held on the 1st October, 1896, the Chairman, Mr. Albert Daruty de Grandpré, proposed the erection of a decent monument at Pamplemousses to perpetuate the memory of Paul and Virginia. It may be mentioned here that during his administration, and of his own accord, Sir George Bowen had also entertained a similar idea, as may be gathered from his book, *Thirty Years of Colonial Government*. Mr. Daruty de Grandpré's motion was unanimously adopted, but, unfortunately, never carried into effect.

II.—MADAME D'AUBAND.

(1728-59.)

It is generally known that the son of the Russian Emperor, Peter the Great, Tzarevitch Alexis, was a boor of the worst description, a violent, drunken and evil-tempered rascal, who had been married to Princess Charlotte Christine Sophia of Brunswick Wolfenbüttel, born on the 25th August, 1694, sister to Empress Elizabeth, the wife of Charles VI., Emperor of Germany, and being accordingly the aunt of the celebrated Empress Maria Theresa.

Either he was displeased with his young wife and wished to get rid of her in order to indulge in his degraded passions, or his constitutional brutal instincts, bordering on insanity, got the better of him, for he soon behaved with the utmost cruelty towards the Princess, and even attempted to poison her. One day, when she was in the eighth month of her pregnancy, he threw her on the ground without the slightest provocation, dragged her by the hair, kicked her in the abdomen, and left her bleeding and senseless. She was rescued by one of her attendants, Madame de Warbeck, a Countess of Koenigsmarck by birth, and aunt to the French Marshal de Saxe. This lady nursed her with the greatest devotedness, and a few days after, as the Princess had given birth to a dead child, occasion was taken of the circumstances to spread the report that the mother also had died. Tzarevitch Alexis, who probably was delighted to hear it, did not take the trouble to ascertain the truth, and information of the decease of the Princess was accordingly given to all the Courts in Europe.

Meanwhile, the young Princess had recovered, and, setting out in company of a single man-servant, who, she pretended, was her father, reached one of the French ports, where she embarked for Louisiana. There the two emigrants settled under the names of Mr. and Miss Wolf and lived in retirement. There she was met by a young French officer of fortune, going under the name of D'Auband, who at once recognised her, for he had formerly seen her at St. Petersburg. He, however, took good care not to let her suspect he knew the truth, but, deeply moved by her misfortune, he managed to be of some service to the old man, and soon gained his confidence to such an extent, that Wolf asked him to take lodgings in his own house. Some time after, it was announced that Tzarevitch Alexis was dead, and D'Auband then acknowledged that he had all along known the Princess, and proposed to take her back to Russia. This she stoutly refused and insisted upon his remaining on the same terms with her as before, provided he would not betray her secret. Hardly six months had elapsed when old Wolf died, and on D'Auband then pointing out to the Princess that he could no longer with propriety stay with her, she persuaded him by degrees to disclose his love for her and to marry her.

The couple lived in perfect happiness for some years, and their home was cheered by the presence of a baby girl. Eventually D'Auband fell ill and was obliged to return to Paris for his health. When he had recovered, the young officer offered his services to the French East India Company, and was appointed Major at the Isle of France. Whilst the preliminaries were in progress, Marshal de Saxe, happening to walk one day in the Tuileries Gardens, was surprised at hearing a lady talking German to her little daughter, and on looking at her, was amazed at recognising Princess Charlotte, who, everybody believed, had died so many years before. He went up to her and respectfully asked her to elucidate the mystery. Madame D'Auband had also recognised him, and, knowing she could rely upon his discretion, told him the whole story of her recovery, her flight to America, her wedding there, her husband's situation, and made him swear that King Louis XV. would not be informed of anything before three months. Marshal de Saxe promised and learned from her where she was living. After the three months were over, he called at her lodgings and found that she had just left for the Isle of France. He at once drove to Versailles and related the strange tale to His Majesty, who, being highly amused, and without explaining his reasons for so doing, ordered the Minister for the Colonies, M. de Machault, to inform the Governor of the Isle of France to behave most politely to M. and Mme. D'Auband.

Louis XV. was then at war with Austria and could not resist the malicious pleasure of informing Maria Theresa of the particulars about her aunt. The Empress was infuriated at first; but after she had cooled down, she invited her relative to come and stay with her at Vienna, where she would live a life in accordance with her rank, provided she abandoned her husband and daughter, who would be decently looked after. Madame D'Auband made no reply to that proposal.

OLD FRENCH GARDENS, TERRACINE, SAVANNE.

Now we come to the really authentic part of this most astonishing romance, the truth of which was arrived at by Mr. Albert Rae, who, after long and careful researches in the colonial records, published in 1891 an essay on the subject in a local magazine, the *Revue Historique et Littéraire de l'Ile Maurice*. From these sources, the actual name of the officer in question was Urbain Maldaque, as it appears from a deed of mutual donation drawn up by Mr. Notary Calbert, at the Isle of France, on the 10th September, 1736, between Urbain Maldaque and Charlotte Christine Wolfenbüttel, his wife; both parties therein declaring that they had been wedded for the previous fifteen years (consequently about 1721), without having drawn up any marriage contract, for reasons of a personal nature; that they had recently lost their only daughter and did not expect to have any more children; and that they, in consequence, mutually and reciprocally abandoned all their goods and chattels to the last survivor.

The couple appear to have arrived at the Isle of France in 1728; for the year after Maldaque, being Major in a regiment at Port Louis, was granted the concession of a plot of ground situated at the Grande Rue du Rempart de la Grande Montagne. In 1737, he figured as officer at Port South East. In 1740 his niece, daughter of his brother Guillaume Maldaque, was married to Nicolas Valentin Chautard, the notabilities of the island being present and setting their signature to the deed of marriage; from which fact it may be inferred that the situation of the ex-Princess was somewhat publicly known, or, at all events, that the Governor had received the Royal instructions above-mentioned. In 1757 Maldaque was Captain Acting-Major of the troops at Port Louis.

Maldaque being his true name, whence did he derive his surname of D'Auband? It may be that, as was the constant habit then among officers of inferior birth and small means, he adopted a *nom de guerre*, and made choice of D'Auband, this being perhaps the name of his own village or of some castle in its neighbourhood. It is certain, however, that he was generally known as D'Auband at the Isle of France, and only made use of his true name, Maldaque, when required to sign authentic documents.

With the year 1759, every trace of this officer is lost at the Isle of France; it is possible that he died and that Madame D'Auband then returned to Europe, for so the chronicle has it. (*Nouvelles à la Main pour 1771; Mémoires Secrets de Duclos; Correspondance de Grimm et Diderot; Souvenirs de Madame de Créqui.*)

That lady was, according to Baron Grant, who frequently visited her, a woman of high distinction, polite manners, and of an agreeable turn of conversation; by no means beautiful, but tall, exceedingly slender, and her face pock-marked all over. She was also, says the same author, of an astonishing fecundity—Grant remembered having seen her with child in 1745, when she was more than 50 years old. This is not substantiated by the declaration in the notarial deed already alluded to; but, anyhow, if she had other children they did not live long.

On her return to Paris, she stayed first at the *Hôtel du Pérou*, Rue Taranne, and endeavoured to get admitted to the Convent of Bellechasse. Not succeeding in this, she bought from President Feydeau, for 112,000 francs, his country residence La Meulière, near Vitry, where, under the name of Madame de Moldack, she dwelt with only two domestics and one black servant, till her death, in 1771.

It may easily be admitted that the Princess avoided preserving her name D'Auband as she came back to France, for her story must have been known at large. In our opinion, Maldaque and Moldack denominate the same person; Maldaque was evidently too plebeian for a person of her standing; de Maldaque was not possible, for the deception would have been too easily detected; whereas de Moldack was a genial invention, and by adopting that name she might as well have assumed the title of Duchess or Princess, without anybody objecting.

After her death the whole story was published in the *Nouvelles à la Main*. The Empress of Russia, Catherine the Great, thought herself bound to protest by a document from the St. Petersburg Chancery, giving the lie direct to the story and stating that the *mother* of Marshal de Saxe had never been in Russia. To this the editors replied that they had never spoken of the Marshal's *mother*, but of his *aunt*, Madame de Warbeck, etc.

"At all events," says Madame de Crébui, "opinions are divided; Madame d'Egmont never doubted that Madame D'Auband was the daughter-in-law of Tzar Peter the Great, and must have gathered this assurance from her father, Mr. Richelieu, who never was in the habit of deceiving her. Madame de Luxembourg, on the other hand, has always asserted that it was a mere fiction. As for me, I shall candidly tell you that I really do not know what to think of it."

III.—PRINCESS BÉTI.

(1742-54).

On the 30th day of July, 1750, France became the richer by a new colony, St. Mary's Island, on the east coast of Madagascar. Its annexation to the French Crown was brought about by a series of romantic events, which, apart from some fanciful details, are perfectly authentic, and not the less extraordinary. As the officer mentioned in the following narrative was a cousin of Baron Grant's, we may be excused for beginning with a few explanations concerning his genealogy.

The uncle of Baron Grant (or Mr. Le Grand Du Catalet, as the author was really called at the Isle of France), Mr. Grant, or Le Grand d'Anelle, had married Mademoiselle de Grenville, whose father had been compelled to fly to the colonies after an unlucky duel, in which he had killed his adversary under the King's very windows, at Versailles. Mr. de Grenville had settled at the Isle of France, where his simplicity of manners, his gravity and wisdom had won him the nick-name of "The Philosopher."

Under the government of La Bourdonnais, his second son, Mr. de Forval, was sent to Madagascar with the view of procuring slaves. Having landed at the Isle St. Mary, called by the natives *Nosse Ibrahim*, he was warmly greeted by King Tamsimalo, who, after having shown him his lands, his flocks and his wives, asked him whether he believed the King of France was his equal in greatness. Confident in this display of amity, Forval agreed to stay in his host's house for the night, keeping only a few soldiers with him, and sending the rest to camp on the shore at some distance.

In the middle of the night, some light footsteps roused him from his slumbers, and, on opening his eyes, he was surprised at seeing a young woman standing beside his couch. This was no other than Princess Béti, the King's own daughter, who came to warn him that his life was in danger. Before disclosing her secret, however, she inquired if he would be disposed to take her away with him, for at the news that she had saved the white officer's life, her relatives would not hesitate to make her a slave, in spite of her high birth. Forval, being moved by her frankness, swore that after having received such good service and such a proof of her sincerity, he would consider himself dishonoured were he to leave her at the mercy of her revengeful family; he promised accordingly to take her to the Isle of France, to make her his married wife, even should he undergo the displeasure of his friends. She then said that, at daybreak, her father would come to him with his body guard, and if Forval saw him break the stick he would hold in his hand, this would be the sign for the death of Forval and his men; if, on the contrary, the King threw off his hat, his followers would at once retire.

REMPART STREET, PORT LOUIS.

Forval instantly ordered his companions to get their arms ready, and he himself slept in a chair before a table, his hands resting upon his pistols. At dawn, as Béti had said, Tamsimalo came in, and whilst appearing to talk amicably, he broke his stick on his knee. Forval, who was on the watch, pounced upon him, seized him by the throat and pointed his pistol at him. The King, outwitted by the suddenness of the attack, threw off his hat, and his men, who were already advancing to the rescue, stopped and went away. Forval's soldiers then arrived from the shore and mastered the native chieftain, whilst the young officer was eloping with his copper-coloured bride. Tamsimalo was released when the couple had reached the vessel, which put all sails on and soon disappeared.

On his return to Port Louis, Forval fulfilled his promise, although he was remonstrated with and chaffed by his friends, who blamed his chivalrous spirit, and could not brook the idea of his wedding a Malagasy girl. The couple led a most happy life, however. The new Madame de Forval was distinguished by a fine figure and had an air of grandeur showing she was of noble birth and accustomed to be obeyed. She was most charitable and extremely kind to inferior people, but went on foot whenever she paid a visit to her husband's relatives, and was constantly followed by a slave who carried a light carbine, of which she made use in the most dexterous manner. Her education was, of course, very neglected, but she lacked neither wit nor judgment.

Some time after Béti, having lost her father, asked Forval's leave to return to her native country. He dared not refuse, although he consented with the greatest reluctance, for he really cared for his wife, and was pained by the idea of being separated from her. Still, the remembrance of her past services forbade his opposing such a reasonable wish. She accordingly set out, but soon came back followed by a numerous retinue, and informed Forval that, in compliance with her subjects' desire, she had conferred upon him the sovereignty of her kingdom of Foulpointe. She immediately proposed to Mr. David, who was then Governor of the Isle of France, to have a colony created there; to which the Governor consented, provided that the Isle of St. Mary would be officially ceded to France. At the close of July, 1751, the young Queen, with her family and followers, embarked on the *Mars*, commanded by Mr. de Villiers. On the 30th the vessel cast anchor before the island, which was solemnly taken possession of for the French Government, and entrusted to a commander, Mr. Gosse.

All went on smoothly at first; but Gosse, whilst treating Béti with the highest distinction, made the great mistake of overlooking the King's widow, a proud and vindictive woman, who sought to avenge herself for this offence. She succeeded in impressing the natives with the idea that the French had no other object, in settling there, than to get possession of fabulous treasures hidden in Tamsimalo's grave. Already averse to the presence of foreigners, the natives were exasperated by this story, and, on the 24th December, 1754, they rose and slaughtered the whole garrison.

The authorities at the Isle of France were quick in taking vengeance, and sent a vessel of war, which destroyed all the villages on the coast. During the bombardment, the queen mother endeavoured to make her escape to the mainland in a boat, which was, however, sunk by a volley from the ship. Among the prisoners was Béti herself, who was brought to the Isle of France, and had to appear before the Superior Council; her conduct being altogether blameless, she was acquitted and the Government conferred upon her, as an indemnity, several concessions of lands, both in Port Louis and the rural districts. In May, 1782, Mr. de Souillac went a step further, and granted her letters of naturalization.

Princess Béti is supposed to have brought from her country to the Isle of France the tuber which bears her name, a sort of sweet potato, commonly called *Cambarre Béti*.

There is not the slightest evidence that Forval and Béti were ever married; the registers of the Civil Status, which were regularly kept at that time by the curates of each parish, contain no entry concerning them. It is accordingly probable that they lived as man and wife, without having undergone any marriage ceremony. The story of Tamsimalo, too, is not supported by any authentic documents, although certain existing records show that, at her father's death, Béti conferred the sovereignty of the Isle of St. Mary upon the French Government. It is well established that, whilst at St. Mary, she actually was the mistress of Gosse, an ordinary sergeant in a regiment, and it has even been asserted that she had bestowed her favours upon him even before living with Forval.

From these contradictory accounts, it may be supposed that, as the story of her marriage was mentioned by Baron Grant alone, it may have been made up entirely by him, from strict family motives, and with a view of allaying in some measure the irregularity of his cousin's behaviour.

But, barring this romance of Béti with Forval, part of which is perhaps true, for all we know, the remainder of the narrative is perfectly trustworthy.

GRAND RIVER SOUTH-EAST FERRY.

PEOPLE AND POLITICS.

By The Hon. HENRI LECLEZIO, C.M.G.

THE HON. HENRI LECLEZIO, C.M.G.

MAURITIUS is a Crown Colony, which is governed by a Governor appointed by the King, on the recommendation of the Secretary of State for the Colonies. The Governor is assisted by an Executive Council, composed of the Officer commanding the troops, the Colonial Secretary, the Procureur and Advocate-General, and the Receiver-General. He has to consult it on all questions, but he is not bound to follow its advice; in this case he has to give in writing his reasons for dissenting.

From 1889 to 1911 two elected members of the Council of Government appointed by the King formed part of the Executive Council, and this was most useful to the Governors, who could ascertain from them the wants and wishes of the population; but this excellent measure was discontinued on the recommendation of the Royal Commissioners appointed in 1909 to report on the condition of the Colony. They were of opinion that the presence of independent members of the community in the Executive Council unduly influenced the mind of the Governors.

Strange to say, at the same time when these independent members ceased to form part of the Executive Council, an addition of two members of the Legislature was made to the Executive Council of another British Crown Colony. This is one of the examples of the strange ways in which Crown Colonies are managed by the Colonial Office.

To complete the political body of the Government, there is a Council called the Council of Government, composed of the Governor as Chairman, eight heads of departments called the official members, and appointed *ex-officio*, namely:—The Officer Commanding the Troops, the Colonial Secretary, the Procureur and Advocate-General, the Auditor-General, the Protector of Immigrants and Poor Law Commissioner, the Receiver-General, the Collector of Customs and Harbour Master, the Director of Public Works and Surveys—ten elected members, four official nominees appointed by the Governor, and five unofficial members also appointed by the Governor. The elected and unofficial members of the Council have thus a majority of two, but they very seldom out-vote the Government. The Council is renewed every five years by elections, and by the appointment of unofficial members.

The system is not perfect, but when a large majority of unofficial members oppose measures proposed by the Government, the Governor, unless such measures are imposed upon him by the Colonial Office, takes into account that strong opposition, and generally modifies his views accordingly. Surely it would have been desirable to have a more liberal constitution and a majority of elected members, but unfortunately the composition of the population does not permit it.

According to Froude (*The English in the West Indies*) there are colonies to which it is natural to give a self-government—those the population of which is of the same blood, same language, same habits, same traditions; on the other hand, there are colonies either as yet unripe for it or, from the nature of things, unfit for it.

Our population, being deficient in homogeneity, cannot aspire to be included in the first category of Froude. Can it be classified among those as yet unripe, or among those that are unfit for it "from the nature of things?"

The experiments made in the West Indies may serve as a guide; the case of Jamaica is particularly instructive. It possessed a liberal constitution. It had to give it up. Froude says that as it was assumed that it had failed before because the blacks were not properly represented, another experiment was made, a new constitution was given to the colony, but once more it had to be withdrawn.

INDIAN WOMEN.

Todd (*Parliamentary Government in the British Colonies*) says:—"The example of Jamaica in surrendering her free institutions and becoming a Crown Colony was afterwards followed in the West Indies, and the reason was the enormous disproportion between whites on one side and blacks and mulattoes on the other side."

Froude says:—"Nature has made us unequal, and Acts of Parliament cannot make us equal. Some must lead and some must follow, and the question is only of degree and kind. The blacks depend for the progress which they may be capable of making on the presence of a white community among them; and, although it is undesirable or impossible for the blacks to be ruled by the minority of the white residents, it is equally undesirable and equally impossible that the whites should be ruled by them."

INDIAN CAVADEE PROCESSION IN PRINCE REGENT STREET, PORT LOUIS.

Froude goes on to say:—"The theory of constitutional government is that the majority shall rule the minority, and as long as the qualities, moral and mental, of the parties are not grossly dissimilar, such an arrangement forms a tolerable *modus vivendi*. But, where in character, in mental force, in energy, in culture, there is no equality at all . . . . . to expect that the intelligent few will submit to the unintelligent many, is to expect what has never been found and what never ought to be found."

Referring to Trinidad, Froude adds that the relative members of the two races being what they are, responsible government means government by a black Parliament and a black Ministry. The negro voters might elect, to begin with, their half-caste attorneys or such whites (the most disreputable of the colour) as would court their suffrages, but gradually the black elector would only vote for black representatives. The future of the blacks, as our own influence over them for good, depends on their being protected from themselves, and from the schemers who would take advantage of them.

The riot in Port Louis of the 19th January, 1911, shows the correctness of Froude's contention that the blacks are not ripe for self-government. Thousands of them were mustered to await the arrival of the whites in Port Louis by the early morning train from Curepipe and other upland railway stations, with the intention of molesting and assaulting them. This projected attempt fortunately became known, and the whites generally abstained from coming to Port Louis. The few, however, who came received blows and had a very narrow escape. There can be no doubt that the movement was a political one, coming in the midst of the elections for the Council of Government, and after the candidate of the blacks in one of the most influential rural districts had been defeated; but, although an inquiry was held by a Commission appointed by the Governor, the leaders of the movement prudently kept back and could not be detected.

In Mauritius the situation is further complicated by the presence of a large Indian population, few members of which are as yet accustomed to European civilization and could properly make use of the right to vote for representatives.

We shall now consider the fabric of our population. The periodical census gives us a very imperfect idea thereof. It shows only the total number of the general population (whites, blacks, etc.), so many Indians born in India, and so many Indo-Mauritians, that is to say, Indians born in the colony, and so

THE PIAT FAMILY—ONE OF THE LARGE FRENCH-MAURITIAN FAMILIES.

(This group of 88 persons represents four generations. About 60 other members of the family were absent when the photograph was taken.)

many Chinese. We have tried to compute the several elements of the population, and we think that the following figures may be taken as a rough approximation. We have—

A. The white population, which may be estimated at about 10,000 persons (excluding the military) of French origin, and a small number of English or Anglo-Mauritian families. More than 70 per cent. of this category reside in Plaines Wilhems, or in Moka. Out of these whites, 544 were born in Europe. It is to be noted that as the Chinese population numbers 3,662, the white population would be exactly three times more numerous. This seems to indicate that a census of the whites would give rather more than less our rough estimate of 10,000. The white population is generally well educated and of high intellectual culture, and is the leading portion of the community.

B. What we can call the gentry of colour, composed of well-educated persons for the most part of an intellectual culture equal to that of the generality of the members of the white population. From this section of the population have grown men of high attainments who have done honour to their country. This section is rather exclusive, and may be reckoned at about 5,000 persons.

C. A coloured middle-class which has received a certain amount of instruction—in some cases of superior instruction—and which is generally well educated. This section, the members of which have an appreciable quantity of European blood in their veins, appears to be equal in number to A and B together, that is, 15,000 members. It has produced valuable men. A very strong caste spirit exists in this section, which is composed of clerks professors, accountants of sugar estates, railway employés, small traders, skilled artisans, milliners, etc.

D. The working classes—artisans, tailors, mechanics, printers, joiners. In this section there are also traces of European blood. It is intellectual to a certain degree, and is rather turbulent; the members thereof know how to read and write, and they are skilful—the Mauritian workman is very clever. This section may be estimated at 25,000 or 30,000 members. It is in this section, the partitions of which are more elastic than the preceding ones, that the Chinese get married and Indian infiltration takes place in its lower strata. When a leader issues from its ranks he will command the elections.

E. We have finally the inferior classes, which constitute an undefinable mixture, in which the Malagasy and African blood dominates, and which supply us with cooks, coachmen, carpenters, butchers, porters, fishermen, wood-cutters, bakers, cane-cutters, cartwrights, masons, etc., etc. They are the descendants of the liberated slaves. The majority of them do not know how to read and write This section is the most numerous of the general population. It certainly numbers 50,000 to 55,000 persons, that is to say, it constitutes nearly the half of our general population. It is not homogeneous, and it might be divided into several strata, of which the uppermost is represented by butlers of rich houses, who have their prejudices, their well-defined social circles.

To sum up, the 107,400 persons of the general population are composed roughly of—

A	10,000	= 9·3 %
B	5,000	= 4·7
C	15,000	= 14·0
D	25,000	= 23·3
E	52,400	= 48·6
	107,400	

that is to say, 10·7 of the black and coloured population to 1 white.

To pass on, the Indian population numbers 257,700, that is 2.4 Indians to 1 of the general population, and added to the coloured and black population, 35.5 to 1 white.

The 257,700 Indians, according to the last census taken in 1911, are composed as follows :—

Christians	14,100
Hindoos	202,750
Mohammedans	39,120
Others	1,730
	257,700

The census did not go further, but with the assistance of the Statistical Bureau of the Chamber of Agriculture we have been able to subdivide approximately the 202,750 Hindoos as follows:—

Of Calcutta origin	55 to 60%	let us say 55%	=	112,000
„ Madras „	33 „ 35	„ 35	=	70,500
„ Bombay „	9 „ 10	„ 10	=	20,250
				202,750

Those of Madras origin are divided into two principal classes, the Madrassees properly so-called, and the Coringhees.

Lastly, we have the Chinese, numbering 3,662.

The several elements of our population may, therefore, be summed up as follows :—

General Population ...	... A	10,000	=	2·7 %	of the total.
	B	5,000	=	1·3	,,
	C	15,000	=	4·0	,,
	D	25,000	=	6·8	,,
	E	52,400	=	14·2	,,
Chinese		3,700	=	1·0	,,
Indian Population —					
Christians		14,100	=	3·8	,,
Hindoos—Calcutta		112,000	=	30·4	,,
Madrassees ...		47,000	=	12·7	,,
Coringhees ...		23,500	=	6·4	,,
Bombay		20,250	=	5·5	,
Mohammedans ...		39,120	=	10·6	,,
Others		1,730	=	0·5	,,
	Total	368,800	=	99·9	

RENÉ MERANDON,
A well-known Politician.

Our population is, therefore, composed of a dozen elements quite different from each other by their ethnic character and by the social distinctions which keep them apart.

If Froude could describe the use which might be made of a liberal constitution in Jamaica, the population of which was composed of 700,000 coloured people, increasing rapidly, and of 15,000 to 16,000 whites, stationary if not declining, how much more complicated is the question in a country like Mauritius, composed of dissimilar elements, where the whites—less helpless, however, than in Jamaica—do not decline either in numbers or in influence, and are coolly resolved not to allow themselves to be swayed or submerged, while admitting that everybody has the right to claim a place in this world ?

Under a popular constitution, says Froude, the people are sovereign. In this country how would that sovereignty be exercised by the motley components of the people ? At first the coloured element would impose its sovereignty and upset the social strata, and afterwards they would fight one another ; then the Indian element would try to dominate, and a struggle for preponderance would take place.

If Jamaica, after having been provided with full plumage of parliamentary institutions, had to recoil, what would be the result here of self-government under the above circumstances ? Moreover, supposing we did obtain self-government, is it admissible that we could raise money, when we wanted it, on our own credit ? At present, England is practically responsible for the money we borrow, and it is on that account that we are able to obtain large sums on easy terms. Besides, we should have to provide for our internal order and security, and the lesson taught by the riot of the 19th January, 1911, proves that we want the protection of English bayonets.

No, we are not, and we are afraid we shall never be, ripe for free institutions, nor do we believe that we are fit for them.

DWELLINGS OF INDIANS ON BELLE VUE MAUREL SUGAR ESTATE.

POPULATION OF MAURITIUS AND ITS DEPENDENCIES.

SHOWING THE DISTRIBUTION OF THE POPULATION IN DISTRICTS, CLASS AND SEX, AS RETURNED AT THE CENSUS OF MARCH 31ST, 1911.

Districts.	General Population.			Indo-Mauritian.			Other Indians.			Chinese.			Total.		Grand Total.
	Males.	Females.	Total.	Males.	Females.	Total.	Males.	Females.	Total.	Males.	Females.	Total.	Males.	Females.	
Port Louis	13,419	14,743	28,162	8,720	8,419	17,139	2,278	1,010	3,288	1,290	181	1,471	25,707	24,353	50,060
Pamplemousses	3,722	3,509	7,231	13,751	12,688	26,439	2,241	1,230	3,471	228	12	240	19,942	17,439	37,381
Rivière du Rempart	2,739	2,525	5,264	11,173	10,712	21,885	2,409	1,337	3,746	146	10	156	16,467	14,584	31,051
Flacq	4,889	4,816	9,705	19,001	17,638	36,639	3,523	1,772	5,295	251	8	259	27,664	24,234	51,898
Moka	2,716	2,949	5,665	11,916	11,175	23,091	2,510	1,235	3,745	196	22	218	17,338	15,381	32,719
Plaines Wilhems	12,387	15,440	27,827	18,242	17,053	35,295	2,741	1,347	4,088	597	59	656	33,967	33,899	67,866
Grand Port	6,065	6,019	12,084	16,492	14,760	31,252	3,700	1,720	5,420	295	28	323	26,552	22,527	49,079
Savanne	3,270	3,201	6,471	11,340	10,518	21,858	3,627	1,627	5,254	194	15	209	18,431	15,361	33,792
Black River	2,601	2,422	5,023	4,581	4,122	8,703	729	360	1,089	116	14	130	8,027	6,918	14,945
Total	51,808	55,624	107,432	115,216	107,085	222,301	23,758	11,638	35,396	3,313	349	3,662	194,095	174,696	368,791
Military (in barracks)	1,263	149	1,412	36	24	60	124	6	130	...	...	...	1,423	179	1,602
Total population including Military	53,071	55,773	108,844	115,252	107,109	222,361	23,882	11,644	35,526	3,313	349	3,662	195,518	174,875	370.393
Dependencies.															
Rodrigues	2,422	2,245	4,667	54	48	102	29	7	36	18	6	24	2,523	2,306	4,829
Farquhar	44	35	79	10	8	18	2	...	2	...	...	...	56	43	99
Six Islands	82	67	149	5	1	6	1	...	1	...	...	...	88	68	156
St. Brandon	86	10	96	11	3	14	...	...	...	...	...	...	97	13	110
Peros Banhos	156	132	288	9	3	12	...	...	...	...	...	...	165	135	300
Diégo García	288	185	473	21	13	34	6	4	10	...	...	...	315	202	517
Agaléga	168	138	306	47	44	91	13	5	18	...	...	...	228	187	415
Eagle Island	55	46	101	3	...	3	...	...	...	...	...	...	58	46	104
Solomon Island	80	63	143	9	7	16	1	...	1	...	...	...	90	70	160
Total Population of Dependencies	3,381	2,921	6,302	169	127	296	52	16	68	18	6	24	3,620	3,070	6,690

SUMMARY OF CENSUS RETURNS 1846 TO 1911.

Date of Census.	General Population.			Indian Population.			Total.		Grand Total.
	Males.	Females.	Total.	Males.	Females.	Total.	Males.	Females.	
August 1846 ...	55,663	46,554	102,217	48,935	7,310	56,245	104,598	53,864	158,462
28 November 1851 ...	55,059	47,768	102,827	64,282	13,714	77,996	119,341	61,482	180,823
8 April 1861 ...	61,346	56,070	117,416	141,615	51,019	192,634	202,961	107,089	310,050
11 April 1871 ...	51,771	48,013	99,784	141,804	74,454	216,258	193,575	112,467	316,042
3 April 1881 ...	57,303	53,578	110,881	151,352	97,641	248,993	208,655	151,219	359,874
5 April 1891 ...	58,539	56,129	114,668	147,499	108,421	255,920	206,038	164,550	370,588
1 April 1901 ...	56,452	55,485	111,937	143,100	115,986	259,086	199,552	171,471	371,023
31 March 1911 ...	55,121	55,973	111,094	138,974	118,723	257,697	194,095	174,696	368,791

SCENERY.

By LEOVILLE L'HOMME. (Translated from the French.)

MR. LEOVILLE L'HOMME.

Port Louis.

FROM the deck of the steamer arriving in the harbour of Port Louis the visitor has before him the picturesque panorama of the island's capital, overshadowed by the grand range of serried mountains, in which the conical peaks of Pieterboth and the Pouce instantly attract attention. In November these mountains are of a uniform dark hue, and appear as though some great fire had swept over them ; but seen about the end of April, after the heavy rains of the intervening months, their chromatic aspect is entirely changed. Flooded by the sun, and standing out with remarkable clearness against the azure sky, the soft tints of their crevices and the lighter hues of their rocky projections harmonise with the green luxuriant vegetation rising from their base far up their precipitous sides.

Every Mauritian has, at one time or another, the eyes of the new-comer to the island. However familiar we may be with our little, sea-girt world, there was an hour when we "discovered" it—when, for the first time, we realised its beauties. To me, who was born in Port Louis, where all my youth was spent, it is only late in life that it has been given to know the charms of the city encompassed by the mountains and the sea. Its charms lie not only in its magnificent setting, but also in its highways and by-ways and in its secluded places, redolent of times and of people that have passed away. In the sleepy streets bordering the Champ de Mars, are tranquil enclosures with glossy-leaved badame trees or thick-set green mango trees, in the shade of which appear visions of former days to the eyes that see more than material things. The doors of the houses are left open so that the rooms may have fresh air; the verandahs are deserted; and the dreamful silence is only broken perchance by some forgotten water-tap dripping in the noonday heat.

The Champ de Mars never fails to fulfil the expectations arising from its well-merited scenic fame. The best time, however, to see it is about February, when the rains have carpeted it with new green grass. The great plain is almost encircled by the mountains; and what strikes one most is the majestic calm and the clearness of the atmosphere, whereby are seen all the details of the magnificent heights that have witnessed the passing of the nations in the harbour below, and that were of remote antiquity when other parts of the earth's surface were still in process of formation.

Is it possible to love scenery if we know not its associations? I venture to say no. A painter may reproduce it faithfully in its best aspect, and it remains only a picture to him; but it is only the dreamer who, with knowledge of its associations and possessed of a sympathetic imagination, can attain to the fullest realisation of all that it may have meant or may mean to the hearts that have joyed or sorrowed

SECTION OF HARBOUR, PORT LOUIS.

in its midst. I often told this to myself in my rambles through Pamplemousses, not merely in the famous garden laid out by Poivre and Céré, but through the whole of that district.

Pamplemousses.

Pamplemousses was, from the very beginning of French colonisation, the richest, most productive and most poetic part of the island. I like it especially for what it has been: what interests me most in it are its ruins, which are eloquently suggestive of the pathos and tragedy of the past. Whether we are walking along the main road or crossing some sugar-cane field, we may see ruins of foundations, broken steps or fragments of walls that were once those of handsome and happy homes. Often, too, amongst the vegetation may be observed traces of former lordly avenues of palm trees, through which drove splendid coaches up to the great verandahs that were full of life and beauty. Now silence reigns over all.

If on the way from Port Louis, as soon as Plaine des Calebasses is reached, you turn your back to the sea, you cannot fail to be elated by the scenery. In the background, the chain of mountains which surrounds Port Louis seems to have unfolded itself, culminating sharply with the tapering peak of Pieterboth. In the foreground, and almost at the foot of these mountains, there is nought but sugar-cane fields with clumps of trees and a few factory chimneys ; while towards the left the square and white steeple of the old church of St. Francis towers high above the green verdure. In the north the country fades away towards the sky warm with light.

ROYAL BOTANIC GARDENS, PAMPLEMOUSSES.

A foreigner, knowing nothing of our history and of the devastation wrought by fever in this fine plain once so thickly peopled, would not receive from the scenery the impression of sadness which it can convey only to a Mauritian. But he will certainly recall the sorrowful story of Paul and Virginia, who lived on these table-lands, and who on Sundays would cross on foot half of the district to worship at the church. It will be a revelation for him to go alone into the shadows of the garden, where their legendary tomb is in keeping with the strange melancholy pervading the silent, flower-bespangled groves and avenues, and the calm lakes that shimmer with the beauty of dreams. And he cannot fail to hear the wail of inconsolable grief of the streamlet flowing on its hidden way through the vegetation. In the garden of mysteries he is no longer alone. The Virginia whom he may have lost is with him again in spirit, and all the garden is illuminated with glory. Why look in this garden or its neighbourhood for the grave of the celebrated lovers? Their tomb, a single one, is everywhere—in all the hearts where has fallen the long twilight of regret.[1]

Baie du Tombeau.

The Baie du Tombeau (Bay of the Tomb) is interesting, because it was there that the sea cast up the body of Virginia, and there also, more than a century previously, the first European Governor of India, Pieter Both, perished. His body was never found, and his friends called the sublime peak, which commands all the scenery visible from the ocean, after him in order to render his name immortal.

Grand Baie.

The Grand Baie (Great Bay), which washes on the west the district of Pamplemousses and on the east that of Rivière du Rempart, supplies the best example of the Mauritian sea in its tranquil mood.

---

[1] I had not the pleasure of visiting the famous Royal Botanic Gardens with Mr. L'Homme, nor had we any conversation regarding their melancholic impressions. My verses on them were written before I received the talented littérateur's manuscript ; and I am delighted to notice the similarity of the thoughts and feelings with which the gardens inspired us both.—*Editor.*

WATERFALLS.

1. _EAU BLEUE.
2. _TAMARIN.
3. DEEP RIVER, BELOW OLIVIA DAM.
4. DIA MAMOUVE.
5. GRAND RIVER SOUTH-EAST.
6. RICH EN EAU.

This so-called *great buy* is not the largest of the island. Its opening and its depth are less than those of Mahébourg Bay. One is quite willing to believe that this ambitious name was given to it on account of its beauty. It looks more like a lake. Its shores are flat, its waters calm, and its neighbourhood almost, if not wholly, uninhabited. Of sufficient depth and harmoniously drawn, the bay narrows down towards its opening, through which, from certain points on the inner shore, one may see the lighthouse of the Pointe aux Cannoniers. Breaking on the reef far out at sea, the waves which reach the bay have practically no force.

Pointe aux Cannoniers.

The tranquil flow of the water as well as its murmur finds a fitting accompaniment in the eternal song of the filaos on the beach. Here and there are some fishermen's houses and a few bungalows (*campements*), which are only occupied for a month or two every year. There drought reigns supreme; but the place is delightful, although the sea is not such as I like it, or as many imagine it. I think, however, that it would be an acceptable abode, this maritime solitude, where the shadows of clouds fly, dragging white winding-sheets over the mirror of the sea, and blue ghosts on the grey furze or on the sugar-canes, which grow yellow up to the line of the wonderful azure sky.

BON ESPOIR SUGAR ESTATE AND FACTORY, RIVIÈRE DU REMPART.
(On the left in the distance is Coin de Mire, or Gunners Quoin Island; and on the right, Flat Island.)

Rivière du Rempart.

The district of Rivière du Rempart, formerly, with that of Pamplemousses, the most productive of the island, has fallen still lower than the latter from its splendour of old. It is inhabited chiefly by a few officials, fishermen, labourers, and the people employed on the sugar estates. Nearly everywhere within its borders are sugar-cane fields. The ground is by no means hilly, although here and there are some *buttes* (mounds). All the merit of the scenery in this part is in the coast, which is the most broken of the island.

Leaving Grand Baie, and following the coast, we soon reach the extreme north of the island. We have then, in front of us, at about three miles from the shore, a desolate and bare rock, known as the Coin de Mire or Gunners' Quoin, "which stands like a bastion in the midst of the waters." The sea, which is generally rough in this neighbourhood, breaks with violence against its steep side. A dense spray floats around the colossal granitic mass. The waves, like so many frenzied horses, strike it in a mad assault, and unceasingly, with a terrible noise, they renew their charge, breaking into spouting and streaming foam. Far away, enveloped by a

Gunners' Quoin.

mist, rounded off like a turtle-shell, the Flat Island is seen; and in the distance, when the sky is clear, appears the Gabriel Islet.

The sight of this turmoil carries our thoughts back to the calm of the Grand Baie, and rouses in us a vague feeling of wonder how, within so short a distance, this magician we call the sea can unfold two pictures so different from each other.

Still keeping to the coast and the regions not yet encroached upon by the sugar-cane, we meet within a fair distance from each other slightly undulating lands which, with their hollows hardly noticeable, their groves of tamarind and palm trees, their orchards so filled with shade as to look black, are suggestive of those Biblical country sides where the daughters of Israel used to come to draw water. But I do not think I am wrong when I see all the beauty of the district centred in its irregular coast.

Butte aux Sables.

It was here at the Butte aux Sables, some twenty years ago on a Sunday in midsummer, that I came upon the greatest collection of singing birds I ever saw. As my friend and I were rather tired, we came to rest among the filaos of the *butte*.

PORT LOUIS AND MOKA MOUNTAIN RANGE.

We had hardly arrived there when we saw a multitude of canaries, which were flying from one tree to another or suddenly coming down from the top of a filao to the ground, or again rising from the ground to the highest branches. One might have imagined that some gnomes hidden in holes, and some fairies concealed among the thin boughs of the filaos, were amusing themselves by throwing golden balls through the light. And all the neighbourhood was filled with the birds' loud sweet melody, which blended exquisitely with the low murmur of the sea.

Of all our maritime districts, that of Rivière du Rempart is the one with a coast which, although of less length than that of Pamplemousses and Flacq, has the greatest number of conterminous little islands. The most important is Amber Island, which is the largest of all those that almost touch the shore. It is well known that between this islet and the coast occurred, while La Bourdonnais was Governor, the wreck made famous by Bernardin de Saint Pierre. The sea here is always rough. Seen from the land, Amber Island rises steeply, a granitic mass above the waves; but the best time to view it is in the stormy season. On the one hand are the long lines of clouds which are tossed by the winds from the sea, and, after having been rolled and torn by the hills, are

Amber Island.

scattered upon the opposite shore; on the other the sun, falling perpendicularly from an opening in the clouds upon the sea, seems to burn it with silver flames. Formerly, when the island was cultivated, the waving cane-tops shone through the dark storm like a rainbow.

Islets are fairly numerous along our coast, but all of them are far from being green. Some are simply coral heaps;. others are mere rocks, covered with sea-weeds, and with cavities white with shells.

Grand Gaube.

It is a noticeable fact that these islets are scattered along the eastern coast of the island, from the neighbourhood of Grand Gaube (on the north-east of Rivière du Rempart) to that of the Souffleur (Blower) on the south-eastern coast of the Grand Port District. Fertile gardens, or barren rocks, they seem to have come to us with the light and with the breeze.

Coast of Flacq.

The prettiest of these little islands are on the coast of Flacq. The best time to see them is the afternoon, a little before the sun, in the long summer days, has disappeared behind the high central mountains. You take one of the fishermen's

CUREPIPE FROM THE TROU AUX CERFS.

small boats, so numerous in the bay of Trou d'Eau Douce (hole of fresh water), and row gently away from land. As soon as the eastern bend of the bay is reached, the islets appear in a long string, somewhat confusedly; but as soon as you are out at sea, they stand away clearly one from the other. The glimmering light of the West casts a golden hue on the tapering tops of the filaos which cover the Deer Island. The mighty shadows of the Grand Port Mountains throw upon the sea a sort of twilight, which improves the effect of the light of the dying sun amid the groves, upon the moss, and among the rocks of the lovely archipelago.

When the glorious orb has vanished, when the freshening breeze makes you think of returning to the shore, it seems, if you pass within a short distance of these Deloses already asleep, as if from them issues forth a secret voice of invitation to flee from the cares of the large island, to dream the livelong night under their shelter, where the gauze of the fairies is already floating in the thrill of eventide.

It is not only the Pamplemousses and Rivière du Rempart Districts which give this festival of light, poured unsparingly on the plain where man lives, and where the cane-fields, together with the factories, tell eloquently of his genius and of his labours. The north of Flacq, the whole district of Moka, and a part of Plaines Wilhems, present the same spectacle under more or less different aspects.

From Trou d'Eau Douce to Camp de Masque, we meet but with one hill of fair size. Everywhere we see only cane-fields and market gardens, little Indian villages, and the chimneys of sugar factories which stand up like lonely masts on a sea with long yellow and green waves.

Flacq.

It was in the district of Flacq that I really became acquainted with the life and the work of the planter. I was just coming out of adolescence. Having left the capital by one of the morning trains, I stopped at Quartier Militaire Station, on the boundary of Moka. At this time the railway line did not go farther. From there to the sugar establishment to which I was going the distance was about four miles. I spent the day at a friend's in the then thinly-populated village, which is near to the station. I took the road to Flacq, but in the afternoon. It was in July. To go four miles on foot, in bright, pleasant weather, was not a great undertaking. When I reached the sugar estate, the sun was almost disappearing. From some distance I had seen the chimney of the factory, high and smoking. On the road carts laden with sugar-canes and drawn by strong mules had passed quite close to me, on their way to the factory. The smell of the freshly-cut juicy canes was in the air.

CUREPIPE FROM THE TROU AUX CERFS.

Looking at the carts running under the last rays of the sun, hearing the cracking of whips with which the drivers were urging on the animals, seeing the flashes cast forth by the iron of the big wheels upon the rustic road, I received impressions which time has not weakened.

Indian labourers were coming along in groups; some of them were young men, and some were women who were clad in a *gony* like the men, and who had likewise been working in the fields. Laughter and calls were ringing joyfully in the evening air.

As I reached the road lined with sugar-canes, and leading to the factory, I met a young Creole girl. She was not what we generally call "a young lady" (*demoiselle*). She was walking barefooted. I deemed her the daughter of one of the poorest employees of the sugar estate. She was about twenty years of age. Her eyes, in which flames lurked, were of a deep brown, softened by shadowy eyelashes. Her hair, almost blue-black, was so long and thick that the girl, tired probably with combing it, had simply twisted it up, allowing the ample bulk to rest upon her neck. Overshadowed by this black mass, her golden nape was like dawn under the boughs of a forest. Her countenance was like in colour to a ripe peach. She was a perfect type of the mulatto Creole, a daughter of the sun and of the tropical earth. The sun was no longer visible; but the factory, the faggots, and the houses of the labourers were bathed in a golden light like to the colour of this beautiful girl, who thenceforth appeared to me as the image, the symbol, of all the scenery in which were united the eternal youth of the earth and the splendour of the sky.

There is something really poetic around our sugar factories, in the evening especially, and I am inclined to believe that the factories on a flat or slightly swelling land create a softer impression than those in the neighbourhood of mountains. When a solitary hill, with its blue basalt outlined against the sky, or on the sea, serves as a background to the factory, the impression received is certainly noteworthy; but it is not like that imparted by the factory chimneys standing out far away against the horizon in the evening glow.

The farewell of the sun as though tired of shining, the silence which pervades the fields, the weary oxen which the whip no longer urges on, all tell of the universal want of rest. The chimneys, which now appear taller, look black against the gold of the sky. Up the slope of the little path leading to the neighbouring river a labourer, the last one, with his pickaxe on his shoulder, is slowly climbing. And all the glory of the West, in the last reflection of the sun which has just sunk down, widens out like a crowning halo around the humble worker.

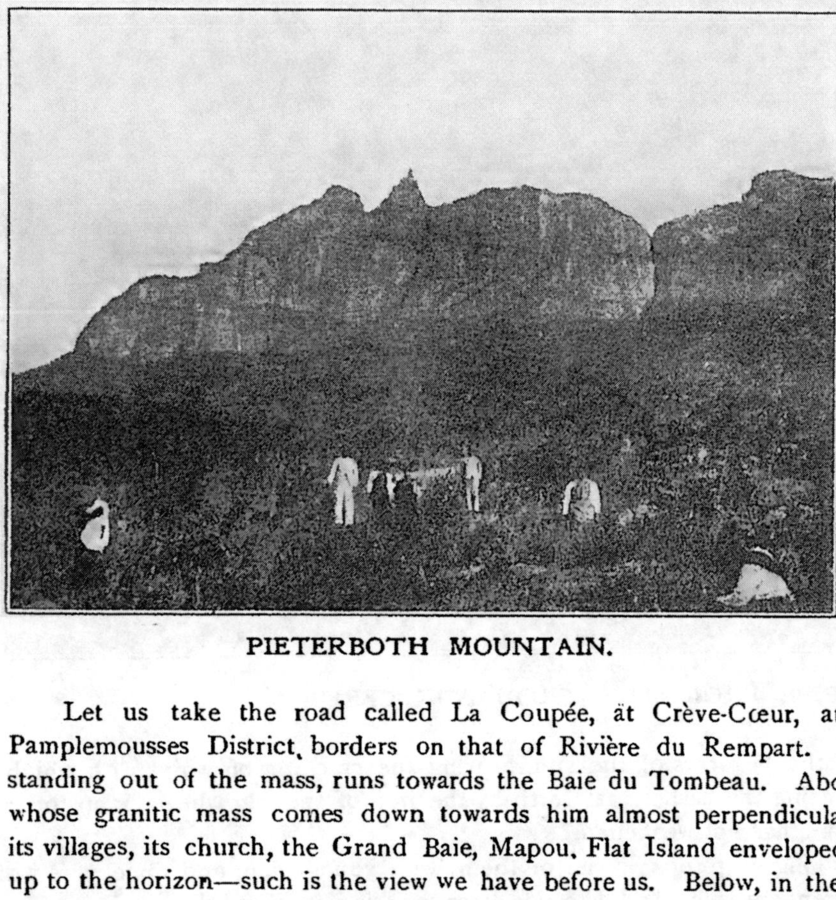

PIETERBOTH MOUNTAIN.

Moka. The district of Moka is still more level than that of Flacq, and towards the west are two or three low and isolated peaks which only half show themselves above the sugar-cane fields. The whole of the extensive plain of Moka is covered with sugar-cane, green towards October and yellowish in the first weeks of May. Here is the festival of the sun—a sun more gentle than that of Pamplemousses. This district is almost always cool. From the fields every morning rises a fog, which, on being dispersed by the sun, reveals in the foreground, on the left, the forest-clad mountains which separate Moka from Port Louis, and at the foot of which Moka has accumulated, as if at pleasure, the majority of its villas.

Let us take the road called La Coupée, ät Crève-Cœur, at the foot of Pieterboth, where the Pamplemousses District, borders on that of Rivière du Rempart. From this point the Long Mountain, standing out of the mass, runs towards the Baie du Tombeau. Above the spectator's head is Pieterboth, whose granitic mass comes down towards him almost perpendicularly. The Pamplemousses Plain, with its villages, its church, the Grand Baie, Mapou, Flat Island enveloped with spray, and the whole sea rising up to the horizon—such is the view we have before us. Below, in the narrow valley, the wild trees, banana-trees, letchis, and kitchen gardens, with some sugar-cane fields, blend in the brightest of green hues. The morning air is so still that the barking of a dog is heard on the plateau; and the voices of the children playing on the river banks echo on the woody slopes of the mountain.

Réduit. In Moka, in grounds of unsurpassed beauty, is Réduit, the residence of the Governor. The fine old mansion was built by the successor to La Bourdonnais, Mr. Barthélemy David, who wrote to the Secretary of State saying that if a war broke out between France and England, it would be necessary to have for the ladies of the colony a safe place of refuge in the midst of the ravines and forest behind the mountains overlooking Port Louis. It is asserted, however, that this was only a pretext for the erection of an abode, far from prying eyes, for himself and a very beautiful Moka woman with whom he had fallen deeply in love.

The spacious mansion stands amidst magnificent woods on land which converges towards a point forming the junction of two rivers. This jutting piece of land goes down steeply towards a hollow, woody in some parts, bare in others, and when seen from above it forms a separate scene in the picture. All the windows of the mansion command views of the most charming description; and Barthélemy David could not have chosen a more beautiful Eden for his lady-love. The sylvan retreats of Réduit are full of poetic inspiration, and dull indeed must the soul be which remains unmoved by them.

Pieterboth.

There are few places in Mauritius from which the sharp peak of Pieterboth is not visible; and it has not the same appearance when seen from Port Louis as from Pamplemousses or Rivière du Rempart. Its most wonderful aspects are seen from the plains of Moka, and it is, therefore, to this district that the imposing height belongs, although the boundaries of the three northern regions meet at its base. At Moka it is nearest to man, and it is by Moka that the mountain climbers go to it. If ever an earthquake were to bring it down, Moka would probably be the place where it would fall.

I cannot forget the impression it gave me some ten years ago. I had taken the train at Rose Hill before dawn to go to Flacq. After passing Réduit Station, I looked for my favourite peak. Twenty times before had I passed it on this very same railway, at the very same hour, and never had I made the discovery I am

CORPS DE GARDE MOUNTAIN.

going to tell you of. How many others have passed there more frequently than I, and yet have never noticed the change which takes place in the aspect of Pieterboth, as the train gradually advances towards the east!

A little after Réduit the peak had appeared to me like a monk seated in his sombre brown dress, with his back to me. He seemed to be reading, meditating or praying, and to have a book upon his knees. His elbow was clearly drawn under the granitic cloth. At a certain moment it appeared as if he had laid aside his book. As the train advanced, the rising sun was flooding the edge of the sky. We were at Verdun when the orb emerged completely from the horizon. I had stopped gazing at Pieterboth for some minutes, and was lost in rapturous contemplation of the grand bursting of light; when my eyes went up again towards the peak, the monk was no longer seated. Standing erect, as if moved by veneration of the ascension of day, he had let his long gown hang over the precipitous edge of his lofty pedestal; and I saw upon his face an ineffable smile greeting the luminary advancing towards him.

Plaines Wilhems.

Through the neighbourhood of the mountains which form nearly the whole district of Black River, Plaines Wilhems, especially from Grand Malabar Hill, is but one continuous sloping ground which reaches at Curepipe its culminating point. In the main, its name of "plain" is by no means a fitting one, and it is a remarkable fact that it is the only district of the island to which has been given this designation that is more appropriate to Moka, its immediate neighbour.

It is evidently to this gradual rising of the land that we owe the diversity of climates which has made of Plaines Wilhems the most valued and most thickly populated of all the districts. For the same reason, most of its landscapes unfold themselves from west to east, from the lowlands to the highlands. They are, in most cases, landscapes of details, of transition, if I may use the word. The land extends from the region of the plain, remarkable for its gracefulness, to the region of the mountains, where wild Nature is rampant, even in the neighbourhood of the towns.

SEPT CASCADES OR TAMARIN FALLS.

At Plaines Wilhems fine scenery is to be found, especially in the inhabited places, which are numerous. The most important, at first, is Beau Bassin, where the sections are better planted than those of Rose Hill. Nearly all of them are shaded by mango trees; so much so, that it might be called the town of the mango trees. A tree of comparatively recent introduction into Mauritius, the eucalyptus, is seen practically everywhere, with its slender leaves undulating like tresses of hair.

Beau Bassin.

This rustic town of Beau Bassin is pretty to look upon in the shine of the afternoon sun, when the rays begin to fall vertically upon the varnished leaves of the longan trees and palm trees, and on the few sugar-cane fields lying between humble cottages and rich villas, and bordering gardens, where the lilies dream in the perfume of the roses.

Rose Hill.

The main beauty of Rose Hill—separated from Beau Bassin only by a street—is its background formed by the long rocky Corps de Garde Mountain. If Beau Bassin commands a view of its environs, this is not the case with Rose Hill. Quatre Bornes, its other neighbour, has a vista of Moka, Black River, the plains of Flacq, whence every morning light comes to it, and the blue heights of Curepipe; but from Rose Hill nothing is seen of the neighbourhood, so that, as with Curepipe, its beauties are centred in itself. Some parts of it resemble places in Port Louis; others villages of Flacq; others again the most delightful spots of Curepipe.

Quatre Bornes.

Certain corners of Quatre Bornes have unsuspected charms. There are some streets which would tempt the painter's brush. They are lined with old walls or tall eucalyptus or badame trees, which cast their shadows upon the yards on each side. Sometimes, in the distance, a native hut is seen, under the broad leaves of a banana tree. Farther up a filao stands out of the row, or a crooked cocoa-nut tree inclines its leaves and its fruit towards the receding road. The perspective is enhanced when a cloud, passing slowly over the sun, casts a shadow on the foreground, but does not prevent the sun from lighting up the mountain; and the blue mass thus illuminated makes the shaded street and the verdure stand out more strongly.

Corps de Garde. The name of Corps de Garde is derived from the fact that the mountain, sloping towards the sea, reveals the outline of a reclining night watchman, beautiful, especially at sunset, silhouetted against the golden sky. But the sunset effects of the Corps de Garde are best seen in midsummer. Viewed from Rose Hill, the blazing orb seems to sink into the heart of the mountain, and forms a great fan of glory that, extending towards Curepipe on one side and the sea on the other, floods the town with golden light. Quatres Bornes, rather towards the eastern extremity of the mountain, knows something of this also. There, however, masses of clouds coming out of the East across great stretches of sugar-canes, are dispersed by the mountain in rain.

MAHEBOURG BAY.

Curepipe. Curepipe lies on the culminating height of the central table-land, and, through its lack of perspective, is poor in landscape—at least it does not present the great vistas characteristic of the other parts of the island. Its pleasant spots and delightful avenues are so wanting in character that they would be difficult to recognise in a painting. In Curepipe torrents of rain and blazing sunshine alternate with remarkable rapidity, so that the gardens are always green. The Mauritian people are reproached for not knowing how to cultivate flowers and for allowing their rose trees to grow wild as best they can. It seems contrary to our tastes to impose restraint upon our ornamental plants and trees; but surely their picturesqueness is by no means spoiled thereby!

Trou aux Cerfs. As has been already said, Curepipe, although on a table-land, entirely lacks perspective; but from the eastern slope of the Trou aux Cerfs—the wonderful extinct volcanic crater in the neighbourhood—the view obtainable is one of the finest and most extensive in Mauritius. Far away, the Moka chain extends to the boundary of Pamplemousses, and the highest summit, Pieterboth, seems like a gigantic eagle, with its wings folded, gazing down upon the great spaces.

Towards the West is the ocean, its blue outline broken by the Corps de Garde, the Rempart Mountain and the Trois Mamelles. In front, in the distance, the cane-fields of Flacq stretch away to the horizon.

I have done with the districts of the northern half of the island, those which are mostly level and where the immediate neighbourhood of the mountains is inhabited. Let us now consider the most mountainous regions.

Unfold a map of the island and you will see that Curepipe is exactly on the line which can be drawn horizontally from the Trois Mamelles to the mountain mass separating Flacq from Grand Port.

Tamarin Falls (Sept Cascades).

Leaving Curepipe, we turn towards the right. On the western boundary of Plaines Wilhems, within a few yards of the mountains of Black River, is the most original waterfall of the island, the Tamarin Falls, as the English call it; but it is better known under the name of the Sept Cascades (Seven Cascades). It is the fall into a deep ravine of the Tamarin River, which takes its source at about two miles from the Grand Bassin (great lake) near the boundary of Savanne. Before forming the seven waterfalls, the river crosses several miles of forests, and flows between open banks, then suddenly tumbles into the immense ravine, whence it runs for several miles through woods and between masses of rocks before reaching the sea.

I had left Vacoas, accompanied by a guide, for the express purpose of contemplating these falls, of which I had heard so much. A rumbling noise told me that they were near. I found myself suddenly in presence of a mighty funnel, the bottom part of which was not visible, so thickly woody are the banks which go down one towards the other. I followed for some time the eastern bank, and soon, on the other side, I saw the seven cascades, formed by a single flow of water, falling like liquid silver, the whiteness of the water contrasting strongly with the dark colour of the mountain banks.

MOUCHOIR ROUGE (RED HANDKERCHIEF) ISLAND, MAHÉBOURG.

The seven cascades are not all of the same height. It is said that the ravine is more than 400 feet deep. From one bank to the other one can hardly distinguish a man.

From the spot where I was, the last fall joining the bed of the torrent could not be seen. On descending I was enveloped in a bluish vapour in which I seemed lost. Instinctively I raised my head to the sky, and became enraptured with the wild tropical grandeur of the place.

In some parts are seen, above the perpendicular sides of the volcanic rock, the slopes covered with thick woods, where never a sunbeam finds its way. Against the dark green of the trees stands out the blue or yellowish-green of the sharply-pointed aloes.

It was useless to think of following the edge ot the water in the bottom of the hollow. This would not always be possible. The afternoon was nearly over. Raising my eyes, I could see well the aloes gilt by the rays of the setting sun, but around me, lower down, a violet mist—not the spray of the waterfalls—was now shrouding the trees.

I went up again to view "The Window," and advanced in the direction of the sea. In front a line of dark rock turned sharply and extended down the ravine obliquely. The opposite bank was similar. Through the opening thus made, bristling with aloes, the distant sea appeared. A little lower the gorge narrowed down. In the distance appeared the white glimmer of a lake, formed perhaps by the waters rolling through the ravine; and the setting sun lighted up a vista of the Black River District.

Mahébourg.

There is practically no scenery of special note in the extensive area between the Sept Cascades and Mahébourg, the capital of Grand Port. There are no more gardens, no more villas cowering in the chill air, under the shadows of the telfairias or the camphor trees. Here are undulating plains, fairly near to Curepipe, under a misty sky, where clumps of bamboos weep amid the longouzes. Here are the low hills covered right up to their summits with perennial plants, the forests haunted by the deer, the areas where the ravenules grow in clusters, and the rafias stand as if curdled by the cold; where the mists are born, and dissipating, under the least ray, reform immediately. Now and again may be seen some lonely talamaques without bark, all white, the last traces of the forests of old.

We have walked enough; let us take the train which has just blown its whistle. I long to warm myself under a more congenial sun. Mahébourg is near. I have just caught a glimpse of a portion of the sea between two forests of filaos. It disappears; there is another. I know this hide-and-seek play with which the ocean at this place teases the traveller. The first time I came here I grew rather impatient at its coquettish freaks as it appears, then steals away, appears a second time only to hide again behind the trees or some old wall, some Indian huts or rising ground, and finally and suddenly reveals itself in all its beauty.

Grand Port Bay.

Grand Port Bay with its wide opening is flooded with light; and this light is mingled with a radiance of glory. With the memory of the titanic struggle of a hundred years ago, the soul of every Creole expands before the bright immensity of the waves, the wide expanse of the heavens, the might of the mountains, and the archipelago of islets scattered from the coast to the high sea.

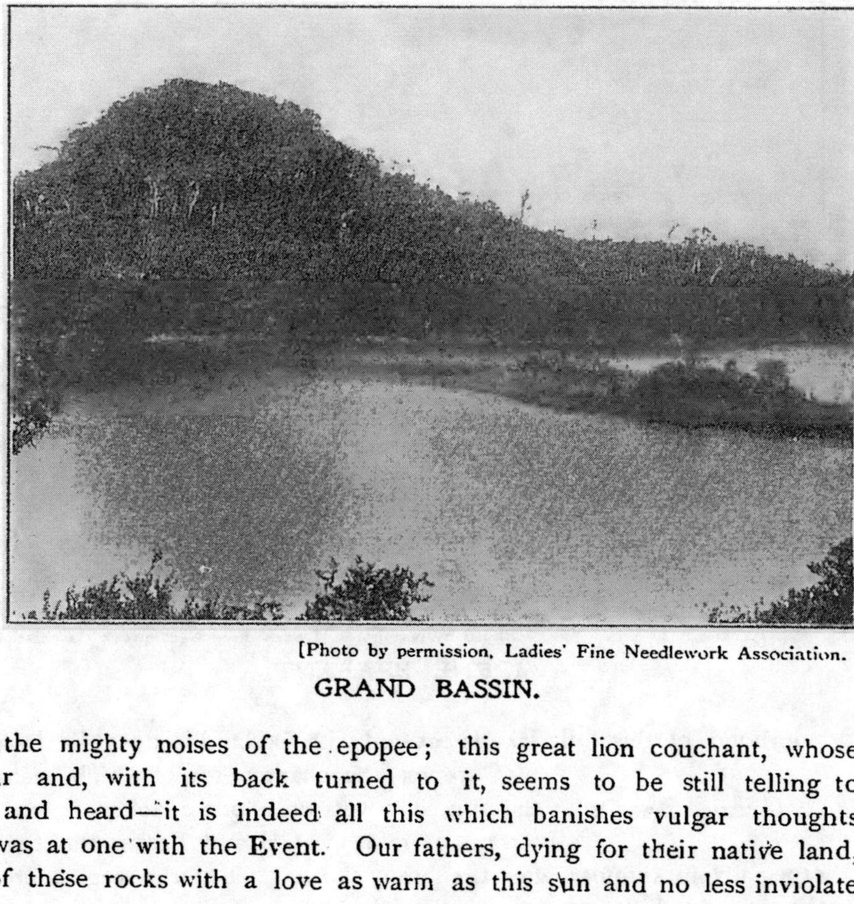

[Photo by permission, Ladies' Fine Needlework Association.

GRAND BASSIN.

In no other part of the island do we realise more than here the magic charm of the sea. Yet it does not show itself with all the force it displays on the cliffs in the neighbourhood of Souillac, but is manifested in simple and tranquil grandeur. On the north coast of the bay there is a little village sheltered by the trees and with an idyllic name, Bois des Amourettes (The Wood of Love Affairs). These words jar in their contrast with the gravity of the waves washing the Ile de la Passe. These mountains, whose basaltic sides echoed of yore the mighty noises of the epopee; this great lion couchant, whose granitic mass overlooks the harbour and, with its back turned to it, seems to be still telling to the whole island what it has seen and heard—it is indeed all this which banishes vulgar thoughts and unworthy desires. Here Nature was at one with the Event. Our fathers, dying for their native land, felt within their hearts the stoicism of these rocks with a love as warm as this sun and no less inviolate than this horizon.

Less than three years ago, on the day we modestly went to celebrate the glorious centenary and lay flowers and palms on the monument erected to the memory of those who died in the historic fight, I was thrilled exceedingly at seeing this ocean roll forth its yellow tides. A grey fog clothed the hills; the Ile de la Passe in the distance wore a crape of mist. All the scene had an austerity in harmony with the story of the past. On no other coast of the island is more beautiful marine landscape than here. One would like to see the bay absolutely deserted, free from the small boats which cross it in all directions. This sea has always looked to me like a widow to whom it is proper to leave to her grief. Our petty noises and agitations disturb her dream. What might please her, now and then, might be the presence among the batatran and mangrove trees of some enthusiastic spectator enamoured of her grand associations, or, under the summer moon, on the anniversary of the famous duel, a young couple, who, dreaming of sons as brave as their ancestors, might venture towards the Ile de la Passe, where amidst the spray they might see visions of the heroic spirits that, in sacrifice to the fatherland, went eagerly to the wedding of Death.[1]

On the coast, about eight miles to the south of Mahebourg, is the Souffleur (The Blower), a curious name, which describes exactly a remarkable spectacle. The coast there is uneven, bristling with rocks against which the waves break in perpetual foam. If Mahébourg shows the ocean in its majestic calm, the Souffleur displays it in its wrath. Immense basaltic blocks, telling of the terrific violence of the primeval volcanic eruption, are scattered about, black and slippery, in the eddy of the waves. The clouds rush in from the watery horizon, and sometimes, when torn open, the sun shines dazzlingly on the column of water spouting from the Souffleur, which falls back in foam that is scattered by the wind in the direction of the shore.

This column of water rises from the centre of a colossal black block half submerged in the sea, and joined to the shore by a line of smaller rocks. In the hollow of its back a cavity, about forty feet deep, goes down to the level of the sea, and there extending in a horizontal direction gives access to the sea, which rushes into it violently and spouts out at the top with great force and with the noise of a cannon. The Souffleur, which attracts swarms of seabirds, is seen to better advantage when the wind blows from the South-East; but even in the calmest weather this shore is never peaceful.

(Photo by permission, Ladies' Fine Needlework Association.

MORNE BRABANT.

Savanne.

Savanne is the best-watered part of Mauritius, and its rivers are numerous and beautiful. In this district is situated the Grand Bassin, the name of which, like that of Grand Baie, is deceptive. The reservoir of Mare aux Vacoas, south of Plaines Wilhems, is much more extensive than Grand Bassin, but the latter is of far greater beauty.

The way leading to it is fairly difficult, whether one goes by Curepipe or follows the roads and paths parallel with Rivière des Anguilles (River of Eels). In winter the neighbourhood of this little lake is covered with fog, and it does not look at all tropical. We are at the height of Curepipe, the phantom-town, which, seen from Vacoas Station, gently dreams in the sun, and yet, when one reaches it ten minutes later, has disappeared under a torrent of rain. At Grand Bassin the fog lasts longer. The view is really fine, especially in summer, after the heavy showers, when the vegetation has been rejuvenated and the slopes of the graceful hills surrounding the lake are covered with green velvet. Estimating the area of Grand Bassin roughly, it is not greater than that of the Champ de Mars in Port Louis. The water is wonderfully clear. In the centre is a diminutive island which lacks beauty with its common scrub and its ordinary aquatic plants. One would have liked to see there the delightful islet of the Mouchoir Rouge (Red Handkerchief)—situated a few yards from the shore of Mahébourg—with its rustic cottage, and its shading filaos and palm trees.

Grand Bassin.

But the poverty of the island is overlooked in the richness of the rest of the scenery. It is from the South-East that one enjoys the view most. In front, on the opposite shore, is a gently undulating hill, the

---

[1] It is fitting to recall here that my old friend George Gordon McCrae, the Australian poet, of Melbourne, who spent some months in Mauritius in 1890, and who is a great lover of the island, published at that time in *The Planters' Gazette* a fine poem entitled *The Legend of the Ile de la Passe*, in which he depicts the dead heroes rising suddenly on the desert islet under the light of the moon and shouting "Who goes there?" to a phantom enemy.—L. l'H.

outline of which is drawn on the lake, and in the distance towards the left is the blue Peak of Black River; otherwise the lake might seem some fairy region poised in space.

The woods around the Grand Bassin are very dense, and progress through them is slow and laborious. The brooding silence is broken now and again by the shrill note of the woodcock and the murmur of some invisible stream. Nature in these solitudes accomplishes its work, and I wonder if my profane steps have not disturbed some sacred mystery.

After a halt at the hut of a poor Creole labourer, we proceed on our way; and, coming again on the road which follows the coast, soon reach Baie du Cap, where before us is the basaltic pilaster of Macondé, which stands like a rough sentinel on the edge of the water.

Cape River.

The Cape River, which discharges its water here, has its source at the foot of the Peak of Black River, the highest mountain in the island. It is not the longest river of Savanne, but it is undoubtedly the most picturesque, and I am almost certain that it has the deepest ravine. Flowing down an inclined plane and along a winding course, its banks present the most varied aspects. Here it runs among black rocks; farther down it falls in a cascade, or rests and extends its mirror under steep banks from which hang creepers, and where thick-foliaged boughs swing in the air. It is indeed the most tropical of all the rivers of the island. At its mouth the water is wonderfully calm and limpid, but even there it is not so wide as the Rivière La Chaux, the mouth of which would look like that of a small European river, if there were not so many fine palm, rafia, filao and banana trees on its banks.

Morne Brabant.

We have crossed the bay, and are now in the district of Black River. On our left, the Morne Brabant, the mountain *par excellence*, outlines its dark mass on the double azure of the sky and the sea. In my opinion, it is not from here that it must be seen, but from farther away—from Case Noyale for example—at a distance of about four miles. From there it is seen advancing into the waves, as if to stand clear of the mainland, to be isolated; and one can hardly perceive the slightly swelling neck of land which unites to the mainland the mountain in which is found all that is poetic in the district. Perspective is necessary when giants are to be measured. Seen thus, Morne Brabant is in perfect harmony with the range of the horizon, the immensity of the sea, and the height of the sky, which enhance its colossal build; especially as I saw it, when the sun's rays, between the mountain and me, lent a silvery hue to the boundary line of the ocean and the sky, and seemed to make the mountain recede against the blue canopy of the horizon.

The Chamarel Waterfall in the Chamarel Plateau of Black River, is one of the finest in the island. It differs from the others by being a great unbroken column of water, and near it are the famous coloured earths. As

Peak of Black River.

already mentioned, the Peak of Black River is the highest summit in Mauritius, but I must confess that I do not admire it very much, notwithstanding its favourable position in the most rustic region of the island. The Peak bears some analogy to the mountains of Réunion. In the sister island the loftiest heights, the Piton des Neiges and the Grand Benard, among others, have no conical tops, but are flat and look like craters. The Peak of Black River is only twenty-six feet higher than Pieterboth, but cannot be compared to the latter so far as beauty is concerned. Figures here have no eloquence. Pieterboth may be regarded as the highest summit of Mauritius because it is the one which creates in the greatest degree the sensation of immensity and sublimity; moreover, it is seen from nearly every part of the island, and the farther away it is the grander it appears.

While going away from the Peak we saw the sun sinking behind rising ground planted with cocoa-nut trees. The kindled sky cast a golden light upon the forests sleeping in the bottom of the gorges, and soon a violet mist extinguished the gold. We were walking with difficulty in the gathering gloom, but at last the moon lent us its guidance and shed its soft white light on the solitudes, where the noise of the cataracts floated upon the breeze, sometimes like thunder and sometimes scarcely audible.

The scenery of Mauritius has been admirably painted by local artists, and amongst the finest of their pictures are those by Alfred Richard and La Géard de Cherval, all the works of the latter being signed "El Géardi." Both of those painters died some thirty years ago. More recently also died two other clever Mauritian artists—North Hall, whose productions were known in England, and Isis Boucherat, who was beginning to acquire some reputation in Paris. Amongst the native painters still living are Jules Lalanne, whose water-colour landscapes are in great demand, and Avice du Buisson, who, besides some very beautiful landscapes, has made exceptionally fine pictures of the fruits of the island.

SOIR RUSTIQUE.

PAR LEOVILLE L'HOMME.

Les charretiers ont vu les premières cabanes
Près du chemin qui court le long des champs de cannes :
Leurs fouets claquent plus fort; mais c'est en vain : les bœufs,
Sous le joug des grands chars lourds de feuillage et d'herbe,
Gardent la même allure en leur dédain superbe,
Le fanon blanc d'écume et les sabots bourbeux.

Le jour qui meurt sourit. La cloche de l'usine
Jette aux lointains l'appel de sa voix argentine.
Une rumeur s'accroît du moulin vers le camp.
Puis s'apaise. Partout s'étale un frais silence;
Et la terre, déjà prise de somnolence,
Savoure enfin l'oubli du long soleil piquant.

Des Indiens tardifs, la pioche sur l'épaule,
Chargés de rameaux secs, d'herbe, ou de quelque gaule,
Emergent du vallon plus ombreux qu'un ravin.
Nus, baignés d'or, jouant autour de leurs cahutes,
De beaux enfants rieurs aux syllabes de flûtes
Font de l'humaine voix l'écho d'un chant divin.

Et d'autres laboureurs accourent dans les sentes,
Avec eux des chokras et des adolescentes,
La botte de lastron, ou la faucille, au bras.
Pour arriver plus tôt ils ont pris par les cannes
Où le lièvre blotti laisse leurs caravanes
S'éloigner, et longtemps écoute encor leurs pas.

Au camp, le foyer luit. Montant de la ravine
Dans l'odeur du champac et de la balsamine,
Des femmes aux cils noirs d'un éclair étoilés,
Le vase en cuivre au flanc, ou posé sur la tête,
Profilent dans le ciel ambré la silhoutte
D'un galbe pur, de seins pudiquement voilés.

Madrasses et Bombays, leurs cheveux pleins de moire
Sur la nuque d'or clair ou sur la nuque noire
Sont tordus en nœuds lourds de jeune orgueil. Le poids
Du vase rempli d'eau laisse au cou droit et frêle
L'harmonieux contour d'un fin bronze de stèle
Où rien ne peut froisser la caresse des doigts.

Elles vont, pieds rêveurs, plis tombants, une à une.
L'éclat si pur dont flambe l'air sur leur peau brune
Semble un baiser d'amour du soleil expirant.
Tel un amant furtif, l'Esprit du soir vers elles
Se penche et, sous le lent flottement de ses ailes,
Rien que dans un soupir entre ses bras les prend.

L'une, avec ses longs yeux ne sourire et d'extáse,
A vu son jeune époux près du seuil de leur case :
Il s'arrête, et joyeux la regarde venir.
Une autre, cils baissés, peut-être en son silence
Compte les ans perdus dans la vaine espérance
D'entendre enfin l'appel qu'attendait son désir.

Et toutes dardent loin la prunelle. Le rêve
Grandit la vision qui les haute sans trêve.
Sur leur gorge s'endort le reflet du ciel roux
Dans un enivrement d'haleine chaleureuse.
Et l'ombre qui s'en vient déjà, l'ombre amoureuse
Fait leur chagrin plus tendre ou leur espoir plus doux.

RACING.

By MAURICE GALEA, Author of "The Mauritius Turf Club Centenary Book."

(Translated from the French.)

HISTORY.

MAURICE GALEA.

THE first race meeting ever held in Mauritius took place on June 25th, 1812, more than a century ago, and was destined to become an historic event in local annals. The sport itself was as novel as it was attractive to the inhabitants of the island. Horse-racing had its origin in England, where it was daily growing in favour; on the other hand, the "Isle of France" had only just been added to the overseas possessions of the British Crown after a long and heroic struggle, culminating in a desperate and truly glorious resistance against invasion by overwhelming forces. In these circumstances there would hardly be any hankering after public amusements among the colonists, still less after a pastime which might be described as peculiarly English. Painful memories were still rankling in their hearts, while many of them still cherished fond hopes of reunion at no distant date to the Mother Country of the past.

Their attitude towards the English civil and military officers in their midst was, not unnaturally under the circumstances, one of utter aloofness, if not of absolute hostility. Yet the event proved that it was no idle dream to appeal to the sporting instincts of both conquerors and conquered, and to call upon them to sink all their mutual rancour and rivalry in the common enjoyment of a noble pleasure. The task, doubtless, appeared uncongenial, but neither its inherent difficulties nor the uncertainty of its results discouraged the few Englishmen who, from the earliest days of their residence in the island, resolutely set their hearts on being the pioneers of racing in Mauritius.

The Mauritius Turf Club sprang into life as the result of their efforts. Theirs was truly an act of courage and a public benefit. One of them, a man of distinguished parts and wide sympathies, achieved well-deserved popularity; and his memory is still held in high respect and veneration. We refer to Colonel Edward A. Draper, who was in truth the father of the Turf Club, and who, to the end of his days, spared no effort to promote the development and prosperity of the institution, in the creation of which he had taken a leading part. With Colonel Draper's name should be associated, in this connection, those of Mr. Reader, Registrar of the Vice-Admiralty Court, who proved a right worthy helpmate, and of Sir Robert Farquhar, the first English Governor of Mauritius. The club was founded during the latter's tenure of office, and throughout its nascent stage, when it had but a precarious existence, it owed much to the Governor's patronage and material assistance.

The first meeting was held on the Champ de Mars—the present race-course in Port Louis—in presence, if we believe contemporary accounts, of a large gathering, representative of every district of the island. A second day's racing was immediately organised to take place forty-eight hours later; and from 1813 regular yearly meetings were arranged, each comprising three days' racing in the course of the same week. Apart from this, matches were frequently organised and run during the winter months or on New Year's morning.

The early performances accomplished on the Port Louis Race-course, more especially those of the first year (1812), do not seem to have been at all brilliant. Indeed, no sport really worthy of the name, from the point of view of racing, appears to have been held during the period of 1812—1832. Even the principal events were run for by Arab ponies, belonging to English officers and civil officials; and the hacks thus made to do duty, on occasions, for race-horses, were ridden by their owners or friends of their owners—gentlemen, no doubt, of high sporting qualities, but mostly of a bodily weight which was as little conducive to the exhibition of "form" as it must have been uncomfortable to their mounts. Such was what we might call the primitive stage of racing in Mauritius (1812—1832).

Prominent among the gentlemen riders were Colonel Draper and Mr. Reader, and among the winning ponies during the same period the following may be mentioned:—Fanny (winner of the Gold Cup, offered by Lady Farquhar in 1812), Rondeaux, Sportsman, Haphazard, Nabob, Little John, Violincello, Nimrod, Little Mark, Streatham Lass, Woodpecker, Bird of Paradise, Restoration, Mahomet, Mauritius Kennet, Saxe-Coburg, Enniskillen, Radamanthus, Charley I., Anti-Racial, Tripod, Ranger, Ganymede, Jester, Milkmaid, Snake, Sir Lawrence, Fitz-Orville, Pirate, Humbletonian—which died on the course from bursting a blood-vessel—Moscow, Cæsar, Coxcomb, and Robin Red Breast.

From 1833 to 1835 a serious political crisis prevailed in connection with the abolition of slavery, and no races were held during that troubled period. On the restoration of public harmony, in 1836, the institution was revived, and, in fact, was given a new impetus, for it was then that the Arab ponies, ridden by gentlemen riders, made way for thoroughbred horses, ridden by professional jockeys. The interest taken in the races was naturally quickened by this change, and the twenty-three years which followed formed a brilliant period in

GRAND-STAND, CHAMP DE MARS RACE-COURSE.

the turf history of Mauritius. This was especially so in the first part of the period in question, when the famous competitions occurred between, on the one hand, Lord John Chichester's dark bay Cape horse Faughaballah, and, on the other hand, Pauline, Aveline, Bolivar and Patriot, the latter being thoroughbred, of English or French origin, imported at a high price by Messrs. Adrien d'Epinay, Dumèe, Damain and Gonard. In many a contest Faughaballah got the better of his formidable rivals, all of higher breed and possessed of more pace, but endowed with less spirit and stamina, at a time when severe performances taxed a horse's grit and powers of "staying" to the utmost. Faughaballah, indeed, stands out decidedly as a "great horse" in the annals of Mauritius racing; and after this long lapse of well-nigh three-quarters of a century, his name is still one to conjure with among racing men.

The leading owners between that time and the year 1858 were Captain Yates, the Hon. W. R. Kerr (Auditor-General), Messrs. C. Bourgault du Coudray, D. Galea (for many years President or Steward of the Mauritius Turf Club), A. Prud'homme, a Persian merchant named Aga Hassen, Captain Bowers, Messrs. E. Oliver, de la Roche, and H. Hardy; while the most prominent winners were:—Creeper, Sylphide II., Chanticleer, Grey Momus, Brush, Bedlamite, Sir Peregrine, Sting, Montague, Little Montague, Whalebone, Lad of Stellenbosch, Charley II., Creeper III., Seth, Fearnot, Partisan, Sam Sly, As-de-Pique, Sir William, Californian, Surveyor, Casuarius, Royal Oak, Orlando, Traverser, Fleur-de-Lys and Garnet. All the last-named horses were Cape-bred, as the Cape had then become our only source of supply of horses. In 1859, however, an event of great significance occurred. Mr. E. Couve, having formed a powerful racing stable, started the practice of regularly importing thoroughbred horses direct from England; and up to 1866, with the exception of one year, this stable brought out every year a champion of such a class as to leave no chance to any competitor. As rival owners proved either unwilling or unable to follow Mr. Couve's example, the result was highly detrimental to the sport. The Mauritius Turf Club subsequently took certain steps to discourage the further importation of thoroughbreds from Europe, and the "premier stable" having become dissolved after some years, there was no more talk for a time of introducing great cracks from England. Yet the evil was done already. Many owners had retired disheartened from the turf, and it took many years to retrieve the position and overcome the deplorable effects of Mr. Couve's importations.

"CYRANO" OWNED BY MR. G. R. LAGANE, AND WINNER OF THE MAIDEN PLATE, 1902.

The English horses introduced by him were truly high-class animals, costing, on an average, $5,000 to $6,000 each, landed at Port Louis. The best-known were Tormentor, Honey-Tree, Tyrant, Croagh-Patrick, Dr. Rook, and Wolf Dog. Moreover, Mr. Couve and his associates had first call on the services of Adrien Scott, one of the best jockeys of the period, who helped most materially in making them practical masters of the race-course during seven years.

When the Couve stable ceased to exist, the future of racing in Mauritius, as already stated, had been much jeopardised. The old owners had been frightened out of competition and new-comers were shy of entering the lists. The turf remained in a depressed condition until 1882, when some good horses were imported and furnished fields of fairly equal merit. During the period of 1882–1890 some of the most noticeable performances on record were accomplished. In 1889 the Australian gelding, Elti, established a record (still unbeaten) in the Turf Club Plate (thrice round the course, equalling 19 furlongs 60 yards, in 4 min. 32 sec.), and, in the same year, another Australian gelding, Lord Sutton, by running twice round, equalling 12 furlongs 190 yards, in 2 min. 56 sec., made a further record, only to be beaten last year (1912).

"GRACE" OWNED BY MR. J. GANACHAUD, AND WINNER OF THE MAIDEN PLATE, 1908.

From the dissolution of the Couve stable to 1890, the chief winners were:—Brimstone, owner Mr. A. Couve and later Mr. Hewetson; Merry Monarch, Major J. C. Robinson and later Mr. A. Barbé; Coventry and Monitor, Mr. T. C. Bradshaw; Shadow, Mr. Franklin, Malabar, Major Robinson; Satan and Self-Reliance, Mr. Sers; Sam Sly II., Mr. Franklin and later Mr Barbé; Partisan II., Mr. Bradshaw; Detective, Mr. Joshua; Chorister and Proto-Martyr — the last two English race-horses imported into Mauritius—Mr. Barbé; Lancewood and Doctor, Mr. Bradshaw; Avernus and Wentworth, Mr. H. Barnard; Emperor, Mr. G. Pastourel; Band-Albion, Mr. J. Langlois; Valentine, Mr. J. Martin; Greyhound, Mr. L. Couve; Bouquet, Mr. A. Brouard; Beadsman, Mr. J. Langlois; Linda, the Wharf Society; Dukedom, Mr. A. Couve; Drummer, Mr. Brouard; Little Jack, Mr. P. Langlois; Don Quixote, Mr. A. Couve; Nora, Mr. Tarnec; Méléagrida, Mr. J. Martin; Discoverer, Mr. A. Brouard, later Mr. L. Couve; Combatant, Mr. T. C.

Bradshaw, Junr.—this horse was first fifteen times and second thrice out of a total of twenty races run; Lord Sutton, Mr. Barbé; Elti, Mr. Ch. Jacobs.

In 1893 it was forcibly realised that, to secure the future prosperity of the turf, it was necessary to devise an effective remedy against the chronic evil existing in connection with the introduction of horses. Under these circumstances, the Mauritius Turf Club took the right course by reserving to itself a monopoly for importing horses to be entered for the main races held under its rules and regulations—a certain number of such horses to be received annually and distributed among owners. The good effects of this most desirable reform were not slow to assert themselves; racing men readily took advantage of the fact that they could thus procure horses at a reasonable cost, without incurring the risks inseparable from importation on their own account; new racing stables were formed, and larger

From left to right: "MIREILLE," "ZELIE," "KING LEAR," P. GOUPILLE, Owner and Trainer: CUP WON BY "MIREILLE," JOCKEY VIC; "REVENGE," "CLOTH OF GOLD," "VICTORY."

fields took part in almost every race. The slackening interest in the races was immediately revived, and it was felt that at length a satisfactory and permanent solution had been found for a problem of primary importance, with which racing men had been faced for upwards of thirty years. The regeneration of our turf was thenceforward an accomplished fact.

Among the best performers received from Australia through the agency of the Mauritius Turf Club should be mentioned Lawyer and St. Albans, purchased in 1894 by Mr. E. Sauzier; Drummer II., of the same batch, Mr. L. Couve, later Mr. C. Antelme. In 1896 Marengo and Tom Trick, Messrs. P Langlois and Co. In 1897 Mercury, Messrs. G. Tostée; Earl of Montrose, winner of the Maiden Plate in the following year, under the colours of Messrs. P. Langlois and Co.; Mikado, owned successively by Messrs. C. Dumat and Co., A. Duclos and Co. and G. R. Lagane—winner of nineteen races and one second prize (Rs. 15,200) out of twenty-four appearances. In 1898 Clairon, Messrs. Dumat and Co., Duclos and Co., A. Esnouf. In 1901 Cyrano, Mr. G. R. Lagane. In 1903 Orion, Mr. A. Esnouf. In 1904 King of the Ring, Damoo. In 1905 Tahara Maid, Mr. M. Larché, imported *via* Réunion. In 1906 Gay Lad, Mr. H. G. Robinson, later Mr. M. Boullé. In 1908 Grace, Messrs. Larché, J. Ganachaud, P. Poupard, G. M. Ajum, Damoo; Cassy, G. M. Ajum, Damoo; Noonet, Mr. E. Lincoln, G. M. Ajum, Damoo. In 1909 Charley, Mr. P. Poupard, Mr. P. Goupille. In 1910 Majestic, Mr. R. Pitot. In 1911 Aeroplane, Gujudhur; Santa Claus, Mr. G. Rousset; Basso, Mr. L. Harel. In 1912 Straightshot, Mr. G. Rousset.

Within the past twelve years a great extension has been given to race meetings in the island. In 1901 the Mauritius Turf Club, in addition to the time-honoured and classic August meeting, started the practice of holding two days' racing in the month of July, and the popularity of this latter-day creation has remained very great. In 1906 sprang into existence a new club, the Mauritius Jockey Club, whose inaugural meeting was held on Mangalkhan Race-course (Vacoas) on January 3rd, 1906. In 1910 the Mauritius Jockey Club began importing horses from Australia, and of the string of griffins then received, two animals have stood out very prominently—You-You and Don José. The former, a dark bay mare, has, indeed, proved to be a performer of unusual merit, having hitherto achieved sixteen wins out of twenty-two races, and having established a fresh record by running twice round the Port Louis Course (12 furlongs 190 yards) in the very creditable time of 2 min. 53 sec. Both clubs have now joined hands for the importation of horses in common.

The welcome innovations we have outlined have done much to develop and popularise racing in Mauritius. Before 1901 about twelve races were run yearly in August on the Port Louis Race-course; there are now over fifty events included in the several Mauritius Turf Club and Mauritius Jockey Club meetings; the average fields have nearly doubled; the total stakes, amounting formerly to about Rs. 10,000, are now nearly Rs. 35,000.

CENTENARY OF THE MAURITIUS TURF CLUB.

The Mauritius Turf Club reached the hundredth year of its existence in 1912, and never had the old institution been more prosperous, never had its vitality been greater nor its prospects more brilliant than at this stage. Moreover, the Centenary Meeting was signalised by some of the best racing performances ever witnessed in the island. In view of the honourable traditions of the club, and the place it had ever held in the social life of the colony, it was but proper that its Centenary celebration should form one of the most memorable local events in the year 1912. Indeed, the hundredth anniversary of the club's foundation was commemorated in most brilliant fashion, amidst the greatest enthusiasm of all sections of the community, and as a truly national occasion. The week occupied by the August meeting was set apart for the celebrations. These began on the Monday, when the Maiden Plate, the traditional *classic race* under the Mauritius Turf Club rules, was competed for by a remarkably even field of six and yielded exceedingly good sport. On Tuesday the stewards and members of the club gave a ball in the Union Catholique Rooms, the principal guests being His Excellency the Governor and Mrs. Chancellor, the civil and military authorites, and the *élite* of Mauritian society.

The second day's racing took place, as usual, on Wednesday. On Thursday a banquet was held at the Club House, and those present included the Governor, the leading members of the civil and military establishments and of the professions, the members and officials of the club and of the sister society (the Mauritius Jockey Club), owners past and present, etc.

On Friday a deputation, headed by the stewards, went on a pilgrimage to the resting-place of the unforgotten founder of the club, in the ancient, and now deserted, cemetery of La mi Voie (Black River). After a well-deserved tribute had been paid to the memory of Colonel Draper in the speeches delivered by His Excellency the Governor and the President of the Mauritius Turf Club, and an *Ode to Draper*, composed by the distinguished local poet—Mr. L. L'Homme—a marble tablet, recording the feelings of gratitude and reverence cherished by the club towards the memory of its founder, was laid on Colonel Draper's tombstone.

On Saturday, August 31st, 1912, the week's celebrations closed with brilliant racing and popular rejoicings on a scale hardly ever paralleled in Mauritius. Not only was the attendance at the races unusually

"NOONET" OWNED BY MR. G. M. AJUM, AND WINNER OF THE MAIDEN PLATE, 1909.

large, but a unique feeling of joyous elation visibly and audibly pervaded all classes of the people—from the well-dressed crowd which filled the stands and the paddock, to the motley multitude thronging the meadow. It was apparent, even to the casual observer, that this was no ordinary gathering bent on mere amusement, but a historic event, almost a national function, in which each human unit claimed a share of hearty participation. The chief contest of the day was the Centenary Cup, for which, in addition to the stakes, a beautiful gold trophy was offered by subscription among the members of the Civil Service, on the initiative of the Hon. John Middleton (then Acting), Colonial Secretary. You-You, the property of Mr. A. Harel, ridden by Jack Moncrieff, carried off this coveted prize, as the result of an exceedingly good race, in which she beat all preceding records by running 12 furlongs 190 yards in 2 min. 53 sec., as already stated. The trophy was handed to Mr. Harel by Mrs. Chancellor amidst thundering cheers.

In the evening, a magnificent display of fireworks afforded a fitting termination to these memorable festivities.

The club may well look back with pleasure and pride upon the success of its Centenary week, favoured by King's weather, marked by excellent sport, and, above all, signalised by a universal display of public affection and loyalty towards itself. Nor is this affection or loyalty misplaced or exaggerated; it is but the well-merited recognition of an institution which, throughout three generations of men, has ministered to the public's liking for the noblest of sports, and provided a haven of reunion where dissensions have been effectively silenced and forgotten, and mutual understanding and hearty good fellowship promoted with the most gratifying results.

One hundred years is a long period of life for a sporting club in a small colony like Mauritius. It will remain to the credit of the Mauritius Turf Club that it has outlived many similar institutions and that, with whatever difficulties it may have been confronted at various stages of its career, it has reached this honourable anniversary in a state of great vigour and prosperity. This is due to the high traditions which the club has inherited from its founders and has studiously kept intact; moreover, there is a further reason for the success of the institution, and a further guarantee for its continued prosperity in years to come, to be found in the deep-rooted and ever-increasing love of racing that is instinct in the population of Mauritius. In this sense, it may be said that the club will maintain itself and thrive increasingly, because it supplies a public need. Racing and race-going are the social pleasures *par excellence* with the Mauritian public, and there has of late been a remarkable tendency on the part of all sections of the community to take more than a *dilettante* interest in the sport. The ranks of owners are open to honourable men of all classes, and now include Englishmen, French-Mauritians, coloured men, and Indians.

GOLD CUP

Presented in 1912 by the Members of the Mauritius Civil Service on the occasion of the Centenary of the M.T.C. and won by Mr. A. Harel's "You-You."

THE AUGUST RACES ON THE CHAMP DE MARS.

No right idea can be conceived of race-going as a *popular* pleasure in Mauritius without being present at Saturday's races during the August meeting. In fact, a stranger desirous of obtaining a bird's-eye view of the population could adopt no better method than merely to be a spectator on that occasion. Business is at a standstill in the towns; banks and offices are closed; while up-country agricultural work is stopped and a general holiday given to all estate hands. Long before daylight the coolies, in their best clothes, begin to arrive in Port Louis; some drive down in mule-wagons, the *paterfamilias* tramping steadily at the bridle, and the women folk and children huddled up in amazing promiscuity with a whole farmyard of goats and chickens—for the Indian is chary of leaving his possessions out of sight. Others come in covered with

A RACE DAY ON THE CHAMP DE MARS, PORT LOUIS.

dust from a twenty-mile walk overnight, man and wife each carrying a child, and, as often as not, leading a couple of goats. It is yet too early to proceed to the race-course, so that most of the Indians spend the first part of the morning in the Bazaar and the native shops, where various refreshments are partaken of, about which the less said the better. About ten o'clock they take possession of the meadow, their numbers swelled by fresh arrivals bv train—for estate owners frequently provide their labourers with free passages by special trains on "Race Saturday." A little later, the society people from up-country begin to make their appearance. The railway station becomes thronged with the country folk; there is a rush and scramble for carriages and taxi-cabs; the streets leading to the race-course are congested with vehicles and pedestrians; along the pavements may be seen an extraordinary confusion of office clerks, merchants, mechanics, shop-keepers, planters, hawkers, labourers, ladies and "slavies," and, above all, sellers of native delicacies—cakes, ground nuts, lemonade and fresh water! All the offices and stores, save refreshment bars and Chinese grocery shops, have long been closed, and all thoughts of the serious cares of life banished for a while. And still the long trail of pedestrians glides endlessly towards the race-course, as vehicles of all sorts and descriptions drive past, ranging from the native pony "carriole" to the latest model of 40-h p. Panhard or Daimler motor car.

The Champ de Mars now presents truly a striking spectacle, its meadow-crowded with some 25,000 to 30,000 spectators of all ages, nationalities, and castes, clad in garments of many hues; the Indians exhibiting on their clothes persistent traces of the bright purple liquid with which they sprinkle each other on all festive occasions—in a word, a kaleidoscope of seething humanity, raising a very Babel of Eastern tongues. Scarcely can one move twenty yards without encountering a miniature open-air emporium of native refreshments, set in a wicker basket or spread over a piece of matting on the grass; Indian cakes of disquieting shapes and colours, redolent of rancid vegetable fat, ground nuts, lemonade, cocoa-nut milk and other popular drinks. On the left-hand side, across the road, stands a Chinese pagoda, its courtyard, verandah and roof occupied by the sons of Confucius in serried ranks, intent on the gambling aspect of the sport. Farther up is the spacious and crowded Grand-stand, whence a good view may be obtained of the whole meadow and its thousands

MANGALKHAN RACE-COURSE.

of human heads, undulating with many coloured kerchiefs; while it is an exquisite pleasure to turn away at times from the contemplation of this scene of dazzling animation and gaze at the severe and beautiful profile of the surrounding mountains, or refresh one's eyes on the more composed demeanour of the well-dressed and refined public of the enclosure.

A few hours later the Champ de Mars is deserted; the evening has come down with its stillness, and widely-scattered lamps shed an uncertain light over the solitary field, so lately trodden by so many feet and resounding with the countless noises of the multitude. Empty is the meadow, where stood and gossiped and shouted the native throng; empty the Grand-stand, where beauty smiled; empty the Pari-mutuel booths, where the wagers were laid with trembling hand and throbbing heart. The track itself, so carefully trimmed during the past months, is now handed over as a prey to the luxuriant grass of the impending tropical summer.

The Champ de Mars occupies a charming situation, in the midst of magnificent scenery forming a vast amphitheatre, bounded by the Moka chain of mountains with its two famous peaks—the Pouce and Pieterboth. A visitor seeing the Champ de Mars for the first time, as he emerges from Pope Hennessy Street, cannot fail to be impressed with the beautiful prospect before him, more especially if he visits the spot towards evening, when the rich hues of sunset are reflected with an infinite variety of tints on the hill sides.

During the summer, when no races are held and the meadow is allowed to bear its natural crop of turf, the Champ de Mars looks like some gigantic emerald. In the middle the noble statue of the late King Edward VII., by the Mauritian sculptor, Prosper d'Epinay, an artist of world-wide fame, and who was a personal friend of his late Majesty, rears its striking lineaments. In the background appears the monument of General Comte de Malartic, the last but one of the French Governors of Mauritius, who died in 1804 during his tenure of office.

The track is in the shape of an oval. It occupies almost the same ground as in 1812, when our first races were held. Its total length was then 1,445 yards; it is now shorter by thirty yards. From the starting-post it rises slightly for a short distance, then it descends from the first curve to the end of the straight, where the final hill begins. From the last corner before entering the straight leading to the winning post, this hill is exceedingly steep, affording in many cases a severe test of a horse's powers of staying and strength of sinews.

On the extreme left of the meadow the Grand-stand is erected across the road, in a position permitting a full view of the whole course. This stand was built by Mr. Maurice Loumean, a local architect, in 1909, in place of the old wooden structures which were then done away with. It is made of stone and reinforced concrete, large enough to contain 2,000 spectators, and is of good architectural design. At the back is a sheltered courtyard and flower garden, beyond which a temporary café-restaurant provides refreshments during the race days. On the left is the paddock, fenced away from the courtyard, and in the centre of the latter the Pari-mutuel totalizators.

EUGÈNE ROUSSET,
President of the Mauritius Turf Club.

MANGALKHAN RACE-COURSE.

Nearly as extensive as the Champ de Mars, and also very picturesque, is the Mangalkhan Race-course, where the Jockey Club meetings are held. It is situated about half-way between Curepipe and Vacoas, in the heart of a locality destined to grow into a fashionable residential centre, but now having only a few disseminated houses amidst the cane-fields. Yet Mangalkhan Race-course forms, six or seven times a year, the rendezvous of all who are keen on the races—and we have seen that, in Mauritius, rich and poor take an equal share in the enjoyment of this pleasure, although they may not participate therein in quite the same way.

The lane leading from the railway platform to the stand has quite a rural aspect, as it extends between cane-fields on either side. The first noteworthy object on arriving is the paddock, where the horses are being walked round a sand track by the lads. It is pleasing to observe the behaviour of the animals, and to watch how the tyro goes round unmoved, while the veteran performer, knowing what these preliminaries mean, exhibits a highly nervous strain in his every action. Critical eyes rest on each horse as it passes by, and friendly discussions are not wanting about "form" and "condition." The owners are there, too, some making no attempt to conceal their nervous expectancy; others mastering their emotions and veiling their keenness under a look of unconcern. Their friends are eagerly interrogating: "Will he win?" Such is human nature that almost invariably the reply is an unquestioning affirmative; few and far between are those owners who can make prudent reservations a quarter of an hour before the horses line up. Yet there are a few such wise men who can retain an inscrutable expression of mystery under these circumstances.

Meanwhile, jockeys are fussing to and from dressing-room, weighing-room and stable, occasionally pulling up short to hear a parting instruction from an owner or to commit the *straight tip* to some friendly ear. The crowd thickens in the enclosure and on the course; now is the time to besiege the totalizators, while the horses entered in the first event are already saddled up and coming out on parade.

The track is comparatively wide, and can give ample space for starting a field of ten. It has a length of

1,400 yards, and is covered with native turf, clipped quite short. Although not absolutely flat, it possesses but slight undulations. The shape of the track is oval. It encloses a spacious meadow, where the Indians station themselves during the races. The stand is well placed for affording a complete view of the running, and commands beautiful scenery, extending over a large valley to the Moka and Black River Hills and including a "silvery streak" of sea in the gap between them. The valley is covered with verdant cane-fields, studded here and there with sugar-factory chimneys. The stand, made of iron on a high concrete substructure, was built in November, 1907. Across the track, facing the stand, are the stewards' box and an enclosure containing totalizators and a refreshment room. A flower garden has also been created, affording a pleasant "promenade" for the ladies.

A RACE DAY AT MANGALKHAN.

TURF CLUBS AND RACE MEETINGS.

The Mauritius Turf Club usually organises its July Meeting for the first week in that month, its August Meeting for the last week. The July Meeting comprises two days, Monday and Saturday; the August Meeting three days, Monday, Wednesday and Saturday. The Mauritius Turf Club has fifty "foundation" members; it is governed by an executive, composed of a president, two other stewards and a secretary—all office-bearers being selected from among the "foundation" members. The president in the Centenary year was the Hon. J. A. Duclos; the other two stewards were the Hon. L. Souchon and Mr. Eugène Rousset, while the secretary was Mr. Edouard Rousset. This year (1913) the executive is made up of:—Mr. Eugène Rousset, president; The Hon. E. Sauzier, K.C., and Mr. Edouard Rouillard, stewards; and Mr. Edouard Rousset, secretary.

DUCHESS OF CORNWALL AND YORK SQUARE, CHAMP DE MARS.

The Mauritius Jockey Club usually holds three meetings a year, each comprising two days' racing. These meetings take place in January, May or June, and November. Its present executive comprises:—Mr. Paul Baissac, president; Messrs. G. R. Lagane, H. G. Robinson, T. C. Bradshaw and P. Marion de Procé, stewards; and M. Boullé, secretary. It numbers 100 "foundation" members.

Both clubs are governed by the Newmarket rules and regulations.

HUNTING.

By HENRI ANTELME. (*Translated from the French.*)

HENRI ANTELME.

THE deer is unquestionably the finest game which exists in Mauritius, and is supposed to have been introduced into the island by the Portuguese or the Dutch. During the French occupation it was found in countless numbers on the mountains of Port Louis, where the settlers used to organise frequent battues. Nowadays this game is localised, more especially on the high table-lands of the island or in the deep gorges of the Black River Mountains.

It was from 1860 to 1880 that the number was the greatest in the forests of Curepipe and Fressanges. Unfortunately a terrible epidemic, which broke out in 1880, nearly wiped out all the herds. The sanitary authorities, justly moved by the spread of the fearful epizooty, organised gangs of men whose duty was to bury the putrefied bodies which were found in all the forests.

Unquestionably the finest private hunting grounds of the colony belonged to one of the best-known merchants of the time, a Scotch gentleman, Mr. James Currie, whose partners were the Hon. John Fraser and Mr. Stein.

When H.R.H. the Duke of Edinburgh visited Mauritius in 1890, it was Mr. James Currie who had the honour of organising a hunting party for the royal visitor. More than eighty deer were shot, amongst which was an exceptionally fine "three-cornicled" specimen shot by the Duke, who was stationed not far from the River Eau Bleue.

Although devotees of the hunt had not then at their disposal the rifles and quick-firing arms of the present day, no less than thirty or forty units were regularly shot at each battue.

CHASSE GIVEN BY MR. A. LAGESSE AT PARCE AUX CERFS.

CAPTIVE DEER AT PLAISANCE ESTATE, GRAND PORT.

Apart from the lordly estates of Messrs. Currie, Fraser, and Stein, mention may also be made of those of Messrs. Montocchio, at Flacq; Vuillemain, Constantin, Henri Pitot, Lucas Brothers and Eynaud, as well as the magnificent private hunting-ground of Sir Celicourt Antelme at Plaine Sophie, which had the reputation of harbouring the finest specimens of the island.

A battue was, at all times, the only mode of hunting in Mauritius, and it is only during the last few years that stalking has been finding favour in the colony. This new method was introduced by Admiral Kennedy, one of the most brilliant and distinguished officers of the British Navy, who reckons many sincere friends among the Mauritians. Each time he visited the island the Admiral was the guest of Sir Célicourt Antelme. He always went in for stalking rather than a regular battue, and being an experienced hunter and a dead shot he secured many splendid trophies of his prowess.

Stalking nowadays is considered a favour specially reserved for visitors of note. When King George V., as Duke of Cornwall and York, visited Mauritius in 1901 he was lucky enough to meet, on the lands of Mr. L. Antelme at Plaine Raoul, a deer of great magnificence, but, unfortunately, it slipped away through a dense fog which materially interfered with the Royal visitor's shooting.

The colony is still very rich in deer, and every year, as soon as the season opens, the Mauritians who have had the good fortune of retaining possession of their forests, organise parties in honour of the Governor and other gentlemen of note.

A battue is carried on in the following way:—When all the hunters are assembled at the hunting camp, the head gamekeeper distributes the pack of dogs, while the owner himself, or through his friends, assigns different stations to the hunters along four parallel lines, forming a square so as to avoid all accidents. The game is thus completely hemmed in, and it is quite rare that any animal succeeds in crossing the lines without being seen. The battue over, the hunters again assemble at the hunting camp, and there, after the lunch, the owners distribute the trophies.

As a rule, the Mauritian hunter is well equipped and well trained. He only wants the horn, which is the instrument of venery, just as the bugle is that of military life. As, however, coursing is impracticable in Mauritius, the hunters would not have many opportunities of sounding the death of a deer or the rally of the pack which have lost the scent.

The stranger who attends one of our hunting parties is generally struck by the disparity between the

RENÉ RAFFRAY, WITH SEVEN STAGS SHOT BY HIM IN TEN MINUTES.

various units composing the pack, in which all the breeds are badly represented. Here are dogs having the appearance of the fox-terrier, the fox-hound or the wolf-dog; some are of better appearance, with finer head and longer ears, but even these include such a mixture of breeds that it would be difficult for the cleverest expert to classify them accurately.

SPECIMENS OF NATIVE DEER IN THE MUSEUM, PORT LOUIS.

Those nondescript dogs, however, are all that can be wished, so far as training and natural qualities are concerned; they are thoroughly broken for hunting big game, and some are even found possessing very great stamina.

A sight which generally amuses the foreigner who attends our hunting parties is the great number of young vagabonds who put themselves at the disposal of the hunters. Being generally well paid by the visitors, they are seen sometimes hanging like bats on the hood of a carriage or a motor car, jostling and abusing each other, sometimes even fighting fiercely to secure a place.

It is indeed a fine sight to see before dawn the line of carriages on the roads, their lights, as they move along, giving sometimes the illusion of innumerable will-o'-the-wisps succeeding each other without interruption, while the profiles of the merry youngsters appear and disappear like spirits of the darkness.

Along the road the beaters, who look like so many ghosts, lead packs of many-coloured dogs that would undoubtedly create a sensation at any canine show. Under the jokes and quibbles of the boys, who are the gun-bearers of the hunters, the hawkers of cakes and monkey-nuts (pistachios) follow as best they can laden with their wares.

DINING-ROOM OF "LES FOUGÉRIES," FOREST SIDE, RESIDENCE OF MR. GEORGE ANTELME.

The deer at certain periods of its existence, more especially when the new horns are growing, is rather suspicious and shy, and makes of its distrust one of the conditions of its security; on the other hand, it becomes, at the time of its love-making, very bold and rash. While the roes fly disorderly at the approach of man, the big stag, during the rutting season, looks upon the hunter without fear, and sometimes even bellows at him in defiance. Sometimes even he is so wild, owing to his numerous fights, that he is no longer conscious of any danger. One of my friends, a fervent disciple of St. Hubert, once fired, during one of our stalking parties, at a splendidly antlered stag which he missed. The animal took a few leaps and disappeared in a thicket, but stopping immediately, he began to bellow angrily. We ran towards the corner of a wood to wait for him, and as he emerged my friend dropped him with a bullet in the shoulder.

There is also the "waiting" hunting, which is hardly in vogue among our hunters on account of the great patience it requires. During the rutting season, the stag in quest of a roe sometimes covers many miles at a gentle trot, stopping now and then to bellow or break down branches in the way. Success depends on lying in wait for him with the intelligence of a clever and experienced hunter, who must always manage to fix upon a place in harmony with the surrounding scenery, in order not to attract the attention of the deer.

Other game may often appear when the hunter least expects it. Thus it was that, while practising the "waiting" hunting once on the plains of La Grande Chartreuse, all covered with jungle, I was agreeably surprised to see, coming out of a thicket, at hardly ten metres from me, not a stag, but an enormous boar, which I stopped short with my rifle, as I would a rabbit.

MARBLE SCULPTURE OF CREOLE HUNTER AND STAG, BY PROSPER D'EPINAY.

The stag in Mauritius is called by different names, according to his age. The one-year old is known as the *soldier;* the animal of about eighteen months is the *brocket* (*daguet*); the three-year-old is the *three-cornicled* (*trois cornichous*); then come the *first great horns* (*premier grand bois*) and the *big stag*, the latter also going by the name of *cornard* (literally *horned one*), when its antlers are exceptionally fine.

The captive deer can be easily tamed, although the male is sometimes very dangerous. The roe, on the other hand, is gentle and caressing, and even becomes a faithful friend of man. A noteworthy fact is that she rapidly becomes familiar with the hounds, which instinctively distinguish her from the deer in a wild state. My father had a roe which was so fond of me that, one day, when I had left for the forest, she came to join me there about an hour later, following my footprints just as a dog would have done. She even accompanied me sometimes at the hunting parties; and I shall never forget the astonishment of some of my friends when she ran with the hounds in pursuit of a stag.

Undoubtedly the horns of our deer are not so grand as those of the deer in the Scottish Highlands, nor the ten-horned French deer, nor even, perhaps, as those of a certain variety of deer of the West Indies; but I fully believe that, so far as elegance is concerned, ours excel all the others.

The finest collection of hunting trophies which existed in Mauritius was certainly the one that belonged to Sir Célicourt Antelme. It included antlers which measured, from base to extremity, fifty-four inches; and I think that this is the extreme limit in length of the finest horns to be found in the island. This head, which came into the possession of Mr. Leopold Antelme after the death of his brother, Sir Célicourt, was presented by my brother to King George V. when, as Duke of Cornwall and York, he visited Mauritius.

Now that, in the near future, the destruction by the mongoose of our hare and feathered game is most probable, we shall be left with the deer only in our forests. That is why this noble and proud animal is the object of special protection by our forest authorities, who have organised gangs of men to prevent its destruction by the numerous poachers in the island.

We shall be left, it is true, with the wild boar as well, but this is a mammal whose capture is very difficult. It defends itself splendidly when attacked, and is met only occasionally after heavy rains, when it is busy digging the soil.

Big game was at one time so abundant in Mauritius that a good number of my countrymen, during their career as hunters, have shot more than 1,500 units, although this may seem incredible to those who have never visited the island.

Our forests are also inhabited by monkeys, which usually travel in troops with one of their number in advance to give due warning of the approach of any danger. Failing to do so, he is generally beaten to death. The deer is very familiar with them, for more than once, while stalking, I have seen monkeys astride stags, whose hair they were turning up in search of parasites. The operation seemed quite pleasant to the deer, for they went on grazing, without being in the least disturbed by their strange riders.

I have likewise seen the *Pastor tristes*, commonly known in Mauritius under the name of *martin*, engaged in the same way on the back of a deer. This bird often gives the signal of the approach of the hunter or the dog by uttering a cry of alarm and flying away rapidly.

The "white bird" (*Zosterops Mauritiana*) also gives evidence by a peculiar cry of the presence of the hare or the deer; and many a time have I shot game betrayed by these little birds. They become daily rarer owing to the introduction of the mongoose, which destroy them on a considerable scale.

The monkey has sometimes recourse to very clever tricks to procure for himself the delicacies he likes. For example, when he goes to a river to catch small shrimps, he takes his seat on some big stone, just above the level of the water, into which he lets his tail drop perpendicularly. After a certain time, the shrimps begin to swarm around the tail and hang on to it. When the monkey is of opinion that they are in sufficient number, he catches hold of his tail with both hands, pulls it suddenly out of the water, and, laying it down on the stone, succeeds in securing a good number, which he hurriedly swallows. When he comes upon a hive in the trunk of a tree, he manages to obtain some honey in the following manner:—Procuring a stick of dry wood, he climbs the tree gently, in order not to frighten the bees. As soon as he is within reach of the hive, he suddenly dips the stick into it and quickly decamps to enjoy the honey he has thus stolen, not without receiving, however, many stings during the flight; but they do not prevent him from renewing his artifice as often as possible.

Sportsmen in Mauritius sometimes shoot the monkeys on the immense sloping banks of the rivers; but this they do merely to test the precision of their rifles.

There are in the island two varieties of partridges—the reddish-brown (*Perdix Striata*), imported from India, and the "*pintadée*," (*Francolinus Perlatus*) imported from China. The latter, however, is in reality a sort of big quail, of which proof is afforded by the way it is hunted.

The reddish-brown partridge, generally found amongst short sugar-canes or in uncultivated fields, runs before the pointer just like the grey partridge of France. It is, therefore, necessary to hunt it with a dog which beats about the field rapidly and possesses a very good sense of smell. These partridges are generally found in coveys, and, when stopped by the setter, fly away one after another, so that the hunter may sometimes make several doubles.

A long time ago Mauritius was very full of these birds, and they were exceptionally numerous at Mont Choisy, in the Mapou region. The *Francolinus Perlatus* is scattered all over the island. It was specially abundant at Cluny when Mr. Edouard Hardy administered that estate. At Henrietta, during the lifetime of the Hon. George Robinson, who made it a point of inviting the foreigners temporarily resident in Mauritius to hunting parties, it was rare that, at such gatherings, more than sixty of the birds were not shot.

I was for a long time a hunter of this partridge, and more than once I bagged thirty of them in a single morning, with the co-operation of one or two friends. It is indeed sad that such interesting game is doomed to destruction by the depredations of the mongoose, which devour all the eggs and young ones.

There also exist in Mauritius several varieties of small quails, one of which was recently imported from Madagascar.

Our hare has rather the habits and the shape of the wild rabbit. Unlike the French hare, which runs several kilometres in a straight line, it doubles and runs in many directions within a limited circle. Hare hunting, which is really a science, is in great favour in Mauritius. Nothing interests a follower of this sport more than to see some spirited dogs finding out the track and sticking to it gamely, or a well-grouped pack starting again the game which had given them the slip.

The hare is found all over the island. There are some even in the town of Curepipe, where they are sometimes seen in the private gardens.

FISHES AND FISHING.

By W. WADE WEST.

SEA FISH.

THE sea round Mauritius abounds in fish of many beautiful species, most ot which are of excellent quality, only a few being poisonous. The *vieille,* or rock-cod, is very widely distributed, and many varieties of it attain great size. The best are the *vieille grise* (genus *Serramus*), a dark brown-spotted fish which varies from a quarter of a pound to three pounds or more in weight, and the *vieille rouge* (*Serramus Salmanoides*), which is vermilion-red in colour. Most varieties of this family are excellent table fish; two, however, called *le croissant* and *le cheval du bois* (*Serramus diacope*) are poisonous.

The *carangue* (genus *Scomberoïdes*) is a deep-sea fish of great size. It resembles tunny, but its flesh is somewhat coarse. The *gueule-pavée,* so called from the peculiar formation of the mouth, which has a coral-like plating, is a fine fish, taken in deep water; it is silver-scaled, and much esteemed for the table.

SECTION OF PORT LOUIS HARBOUR.

There is also the *Capitaine* (*Chrysogoprys belotula*), which is caught by the line in deep water; but, as this variety feeds on the young madrepora on the reefs, it often has a disagreeable taste of coral.

The mullet is very plentiful, and is caught in nets in large numbers when it comes into the bays and estuaries, with the tide, to feed. It is a fine silvery-scaled fish, and reaches a considerable size. There are two varieties of it, the *mulet voleur,* which is excellent, and the *mulet gros caille* (*grosse ecaille*). The latter is much inferior, the flesh being coarser and dry. It can be easily distinguished from the former variety by the larger size of its scales; besides which the *mulet voleur* has a peculiar jelly-like veil over the eyes.

The Creole fishermen have a very clever method of taking the mullet, by means of a large floating net, called a *canard,* which is spread on the farther side of an ordinary submerged net. The shoals of mullet travel at great speed, and when the fish detect the presence of the submerged net, they jump out of the water to avoid it, often covering a considerable distance, and fall on to the *canard* spread for their reception. A mullet drive of this nature is an interesting sight. The fishermen, who are in about a dozen pirogues, get round the incoming shoal and, by beating the sides of their boats, frighten the fish towards the nets. Then the mullet jump out of the water in large numbers, making a silvery cascade, falling on the unsuspected *canard*, in the meshes of which they become entangled.

Other fine table fish, which are frequenters of the channels and passes, coming in with the tides to feed, are the *cherugien* (*Acanthurus Chinensis*) and the *Dame Berry*, a silver-scaled fish, with a delicate firm flesh.

Lurking in the shallows and much dreaded by the inshore fisherman, is the *trembleur* (*Torpedo marmorata*), which lies low under the surface, and when trodden upon administers a sharp shock.

The *raie*, or sun-fish (*Rhinobatus*), is frequently obtained in great size. The *raies* are terrible foes to many of the denizens of the deep, for they are furnished with a long whip-like tail having bony excrescences which cut like a razor. It is with this formidable weapon that the *raie* holds its own against attack, and secures its prey. It is a flat, turbot-like fish, round in shape, furnished with powerful fins all round the body, with which it propels itself with incredible speed. Its mode of attack is to throw itself out of the water, and falling on its foe from above lacerates him with the whip-like tail. The flesh is sold in the markets, but is coarse. The fins, however, are very delicate if the fish is in good condition.

TROU FANFARON, PORT LOUIS HARBOUR.

There are many varieties of the thorny species of fish, the most common being the *boule-tangue* (*Tetraodon argontius*), which on being brought to land inflates itself, when it resembles a football covered with shark-teeth-like scales. There are also several varieties of the coffin fish, which is formed like a small box, and retains this shape when preserved.

A delicious but somewhat rare fish (*Platax Balochii*) bears the peculiar name of *poule-d'eau*, or "water fowl." It is turbot-shaped, of a dull greenish colour. The flesh is dark and firm, the choicest portion being the immense dorsal fin.

The *dilard* is another very delicate fish, which is caught in basket-traps near the reefs. In life it is very beautiful, the predominating colour being bright blue banded with brilliant yellow streaks.

A very common, and perhaps one of the best, table fish is the *cordonnier*, obtained in large quantities in basket-traps. It is dark slate colour with blotches of yellowish-white. The flesh is firm, flaky, and greatly resembles that of the English plaice or sole.

The sole is to be found in sandy bottoms, but is rare and a small variety, and in no way to be compared with the European species. Sardines or sprats, much used for bait, come in at certain seasons in large shoals, as well as a species of mackerel, which is one of the most common fish on the coast.

The octopus, known as *ouritte*, and the squid (*moorgatte*) form no small item in the food of the poorer classes. The former is speared in its retreat among the crannies of the reefs, and the bag of colouring matter or sepia, with which it generally discolours the water in order to effect its escape, is removed. It is eaten fresh, but requires a lot of beating to make the flesh tender, when it is made into curries. It is, however, generally dried in the sun, and makes an excellent chutney with lemon juice and chillies. It, as well as the squid, forms the principal bait for the fishermen, both for deep-sea lines and for basket-traps.

The repugnant looking *bambaras*, or sea slug, abounds all round the island in sandy bottoms inside the reef. It resembles a big black German sausage, but is not now used for edible purposes or for any other in the island, though it would certainly be of utility if collected for manure. It, nevertheless, used to be a favourite dish with the Chinese, who formerly carried on a regular industry in curing *bambaras*, the curing consisting in first boiling them, and then drying them in the sun, after which they were exported in large quantities to China. This industry has, however, completely died away, owing probably to the fact that cured *bambaras* can now be procured much cheaper in China and elsewhere.

Star-fish are plentiful, and some of them very curious in shape.

The *oursins*, or sea-urchins, infest the reefs and shallows, and their needle-like spines are a constant danger to the bare-footed wader and fisherman.

Besides the edible fish already mentioned, there are many others of inferior quality; in fact the daily harvest of the deep is very plentiful in the fine weather which generally prevails around Mauritius, and fish of all kinds form one of the staple items of food for all classes.

It is a very beautiful sight to watch from a boat the numerous varieties feeding among the corals and weeds along the reefs, many of the fish being most brilliantly coloured, notably the good edible *cateaux*, or parrot fish, which are of vivid blues, greens, and reds.

Of shell-fish there are several varieties, notably, *homards*, or cray-fish, which differ from the lobster by the absence of large flesh-filled claws. Crabs are represented by hundreds of varieties, some of which are minute, and many are very beautifully coloured. The large edible green crab is very delicate. There are some varieties, however, which are poisonous, but care is taken by the inspectors at the landing stations and at the markets that no poisonous fish of any kind is offered for sale. Eels are plentiful, and of several varieties, including the big conger.

Perhaps the most dangerous fish is the *laff* (*Synanceia bracchiata*), of which there are several varieties. These are armed with a deadly spike in the dorsal fin. The fish lies concealed in the sand, mud, or the sea-weed on the reefs at low tide, and on being alarmed raises its dorsal spike. Should an unwary fisherman tread barefooted on this hidden danger he receives a deep poison-charged wound, which, unless immediately attended to, often causes fatal results. The remedy is a drastic one—the spike has to be at once cut out, and the wound dressed with fomentations of a kind of creeper which grows on the seashore.

Sharks of great size abound around the coasts, and are often caught by fishermen at the entrance to Port Louis Harbour.

Oysters are found in several parts of the coast, the fat, juicy ones coming from Grand Port being considered the best, but no regular system is practised for oyster breeding; those obtained are found promiscuously on loose stones, and sometimes on the roots of the mangrove bushes which grow in the estuaries. The price of oysters is about R.1 a hundred, and there is a closed season for them.

Various kinds of shell-fish are edible, among them the mussel, and some varieties of the *nerita*, large numbers of which are found on the rocks. The *hache d'armes* is a kind of mussel, shaped like an axe, which is found buried in sandy bottoms near the shore. The broad ends of the shells are as sharp as razors, and inflict a bad wound if trodden on by bare feet.

On the shore large numbers of "soldier crabs" come out of their hiding-places at night; they are used as bait by the fishermen. There are also land crabs, or *tourlouroux*, which are amphibious, and live in long holes or burrows which they tunnel in the sandy soil, thus making it somewhat dangerous to ride near the shore, which is undermined by their activities.

Turtle were very plentiful in the early days of the colony, but are now very scarce. The turtle flesh, sold on Fridays in the market, is brought to Mauritius from the outlying dependencies, where the turtles are still fairly plentiful. The valuable hawk's-bill, or tortoiseshell turtle, is now hardly ever caught in Mauritian waters.

The fisheries of the island are regulated by law, by which the young fish are protected, it being unlawful to take them under certain specified dimensions. Moreover, in order to allow fish to breed, certain bays and creeks mostly frequented by them are declared to be "Reserves," and no nets are ever allowed to be used therein without the Governor's authority. This, however, does not prevent the Creoles, sometimes on a dark night when fish are coming in with the tide, and when the Inland Revenue Officers are supposed to be out of the way, from running their chance of making a good haul without detection. But sometimes the officers obtain information, which leads to capture of the fishermen, who are then liable to imprisonment and to the confiscation of all their nets, pirogues, and gear.

FRESH-WATER FISH.

These are somewhat scarce in Mauritius, for the reason that the rivers are very rapid and generally shallow. The best variety is undoubtedly a species of trout known locally by the name of *chite*, which is found in some of the rivers, notably Black River, and the mountain streams of Savanne. It is an excellent sporting fish and can be taken with a "fly." As a table-fish it is unsurpassed, but should be cooked as soon as possible after capture.

A fine variety of carp is also to be caught with a "fly," after patient whipping, in the Grand River or in the River des Créoles. It greatly resembles English carp in appearance, size, and taste.

A remarkably fine fish is the *gourami* (*Cyprimus auratus*), which is found in still water, the marshes at Flacq and Poudre d'Or containing large numbers; but the finest are to be seen at the Royal Botanic Gardens at Pamplemousses, where the fish are very tame, and readily come close to the edge of the pond in search of bread thrown to them by visitors. The *gourami* is a broad fish with coarse scales of a dark greyish hue. It was introduced into the colony and very easily acclimatised. Like other fresh-water fish, it should be cooked as soon as possible after capture. The flesh is delicate but not very firm. The French cooks excel in serving it as a *béchamel*—a really delicious dish. The *gourami* lives many years, and attains considerable size, up to about 8 lbs. or more.

NORWEGIAN WHALING VESSELS IN PORT LOUIS HARBOUR.

Gold-fish are found in the ponds and streams. Eels are also taken in the rivers and sometimes are very large. When young they are excellent eating. They do much harm in the streams as they feed upon the young fish and *camarons*.

Amongst the greatest delicacies in Mauritius are these same *camarons*, a kind of giant fresh-water shrimp; the older males are armed with long claws. The colour is blue-black, with red blotches. They are found in most of the streams and were at one time very abundant; but, owing to the destruction of the forests and the poaching proclivities of the Creoles and Indians, the *camaron* is not nearly so plentiful as it was formerly.

The manner of its capture affords much amusement, and requires a certain amount of skill, only acquired by practice. The "sporting" method is to noose the cautious *camaron* as he slowly and suspiciously emerges from the retreat under a sheltering rock in some deep pool, into which suitable bait, consisting of grilled maize, finely ground, has been previously introduced. The noose is made from the strong, flexible root of a small kind of orchid, which is securely fixed to a long slender stick or bamboo. The science of *camaron* catching consists in being able to gently pass the noose under his very sensitive tail, to bring it round his equally sensitive body, then by a sure and rapid jerk of the rod to tighten the noose, whereon the surprised *camaron* finds himself struggling on the bank. But care must be taken in handling him in order to disengage the noose, because in his desperate fight for life he can inflict a nasty pinch with his far-reaching, powerful claws.

The bodies of fully-grown *camarons* average about four to six inches, but the stretch of the claws doubles their length. They are most delicate eating, and with the heart of the palmiste make a mayonnaise which cannot be equalled. The poachers, however, take them wholesale by more expeditious methods. They let down into a deep pool where *camarons* abound an iron hoop, or *chevrier*, to which is attached a piece of fine netting, and made tempting by bait. The *camarons* crawl over the hoop, and when a good number are there gathered together, the poacher pulls up the *chevrier*, and is soon rewarded by a catch which would have taken some hours by the more sportsmanlike methods of rod and running noose. *Camaron* poachers when caught are severely punished.

METHODS OF FISHING.

Having given a description of the principal sea and fresh-water fish, it may not be out of place to describe how they are caught.

Deep-sea fishing is carried on by the Creoles and Indians, mostly from Bombay, in pirogues, or dug-outs, outside the reefs, or in the deep passes at night when the tide is rising, and the deep-sea fish approach the land to feed. The crew of a pirogue consists generally of two, three or even four men, who put out lines with several hooks attached to each, baited usually with octopus or squid. The catch is generally a profitable one, depending a good deal, however, upon the weather, but is also open to disappointment, when, for instance, after feeling a big fish on the hook, and hauling in a fathom or two of line, only the head and shoulders of the catch come over the side, the remainder of the fish having being carried off *en route* to the surface by a voracious *tazard*, a large fish always waiting for unsuspecting prey in the passes.

CAMARON.

Net fishing is carried on within the bays and shallows at certain periods when the fish come in; the size and meshes being strictly regulated by law (Ord. No. 21 of 1902). By this ordinance the following nets can be legally used:—

1. The large net, of any size as regards length and width, may only be used for fishing in the high sea outside the reefs.

2. Large nets, not longer than 1,000 metres (3,000 feet) nor wider than 10 metres (30 feet), may be used for fishing in places within the reefs or in bays or creeks which are not part of the Reserves.

3. The sprat net must not be more than 40 metres long and 5 metres wide, and must have square meshes measuring not less than 4 centimetres from knot to knot, or 4 centimetres round each mesh.

4. Mosquito net can only be used for taking bait.

5. Basket-traps, of several dimensions, made of rattan.

Reference has been made in this article to the method of catching mullet by the *canard* net. This net, by law, can only be used from the 15th May to the 15th July, and only for mullet fishing.

Any person contravening the ordinance regarding the size of nets is liable to a fine not exceeding Rs.100 and forfeiture of all nets, lines, and other tackle used in the commission of the offence, and of all fish illegally caught.

The poor crab cannot escape the wily Creole fisherman. On leaving his comfortable retreat under the coral or stones his appetite will be attracted by some tempting morsel, perhaps the intestines of the octopus, waiting for him, round which is, however, a suspicious-looking hoop. This is the insidious *carlet*, and stretched across it is a piece of old net, ready to entangle the clumsy, hair-covered claws of Cancer as soon as he allows his hunger to gain the better of his discretion, and he over-steps that treacherous little iron frontier which separates him from his rocky home and liberty and consigns him to the saucepan. In fact, the *carlet* for the crab is on the same principle as the *chevrier* used for the capture of the fresh-water *camaron*, to which reference has already been made.

Fishermen are obliged to pay licenses to use nets, and the following are the rates of such licenses for six calendar months :—

Fishing for sprats and small fish, with or without boats	Rs.2.25
Fishing with large nets (*grande seine*)	14.25
(An additional duty of Rs.2 per half year for every additional boat used.)	
Fishing with only one net without boat, whatever the number of fishermen may be	6.00
The fish traders who buy the catches from the fishermen at the private landing places (*barachois*) and resell to retailers have to pay a license of ...	15.00

The fish caught at sea on the western side is generally collected by one fast sailing boat, which conveys it to the nearest market—Port Louis; whilst that taken on the eastern coast is landed at Mahébourg, and thence forwarded by train to Curepipe and the other townships in the centre of the island. There are, however, many other authorised landing stations round the coast. The fish taken to the northward are for the most part forwarded to Port Louis in carrioles (light two-wheeled vehicles), drawn by fast mules or ponies. The catch on the Black River side and in the neighbourhood of the Morne Brabant is conveyed by the same means to Rose Hill, as well as by runners who carry heavy baskets of fish on their heads for considerable distances and with great rapidity. A few years ago an attempt was made to convey the fish more expeditiously by motor car, but apparently this did not succeed, for the motor car service was discontinued.

PETITE RIVIÈRE LIGHTHOUSE.

Except in the markets at Mahébourg, Curepipe, Rose Hill, and Port Louis, there are no fishmongers' shops, but fish hawkers sell from house to house. Fish is retailed by the packet, not by weight, and being generally very cheap, is within the means of even the poorest classes. On Fridays, however, it is dearer owing to the fact that Mauritius is practically a Roman Catholic colony.

The boats used in the fisheries are of two kinds, the pirogue or "dug-out," used chiefly for fishing inside the reefs, but in fair weather they also go some distance from land. They carry one mast on which is hoisted a jib and a main-sail, with which they go at great speed. For deep-sea fishing pinnaces, or *peniches*—half-decked boats, rigged in the same fashion—are used. These are larger and broader and better fitted for heavy seas, and are also very fast sailers. There are no regularly organised fishing fleets, each boat working more or less on its own account, except when deep-sea nets are used.

Formerly the boats were generally the property of the Creole fishermen, each man having his own boat, but at present at the different fishing stations there are proprietors of several boats, who either work them on their own account, or let them out on hire.

The fisheries furnish occupation and the means of livelihood to a very large number of Creoles and Indians, who may be divided into two classes—those who risk their lives in catching the fish, and those whose business is to sell it. For want of statistics it is not possible to ascertain the quantity taken annually, or the value of it, but it must be considerable, when it is borne in mind that fish enters very largely into the daily dietetic supply of a large portion of the population. Some idea can, however, be obtained of the importance of the fishing industry when visiting the sea-border of the island, where each bay or inlet has its fishing village, in front of which, when the day's catch has been landed, may be seen several pirogues and boats moored.

The Creole fishermen are, however, unfortunately for themselves, a thriftless set, and what they earn, with so many dangers and hardships, is soon spent, and goes mostly to the Chinamen who have shops in the fishing villages. But it must be said in favour of the Creole fishermen that they are brave and enduring; their lives are hard ones, and are in constant danger. There are many instances of the remarkable courage of these men, who are ever ready to put off in bad weather to give assistance to boats or other vessels in distress, a notable example of which occured in 1874, off Grand Port, when the barque *Chrysolite*, with a cargo of bullocks on board, went ashore in a cyclone and was lost. In gallantly attempting to rescue the crew of this vessel five fishermen of Mahébourg lost their lives. A monument to their memory stands in the square behind the railway station, and is the first object to attract the attention of the visitor when leaving the train at that terminus.

LAKE IN THE GROUNDS OF BARKLY ASYLUM, ORIGIN OF THE NAME OF THE TOWN OF BEAU BASSIN.

CONCHOLOGY.

By W. WADE WEST.

IN close connection with the icthyology of the bright seas which wash the fertile shores of Mauritius is the interesting study of its conchology. Mauritius is wonderfully rich in conchological specimens, most of them being of remarkable beauty and some of great rarity; but very little attention is paid now to this most fascinating and interesting science, although about twenty years ago or more there were in the island many ardent collectors of shells, by whose lavish expenditure on rare or new specimens numerous unknown varieties were in due course discovered, classified, and added to museums.

The first who really took a serious and scientific interest in Mauritian conchology was Mr. Elizé Lienard, who made the collection and classification of the local marine and land shells the occupation of his great intellectual powers during a long life; and it is his fine collection, brought together and classified with such affectionate care, from which the catalogue of the malacological fauna of Mauritius and its sister islands of the Dependencies was compiled by the celebrated French naturalist Professor Crosse, and was published in Paris in 1877 by the firm of Jules Tremblay. It includes the names of specimens of shells from Mauritius, the Seychelles, the Chagos group, Rodrigues and far-distant St. Brandon; that is, the greater part of the South Indian Ocean has been called upon to yield the treasures contained in its islands, reefs, and sands, for this really fine collection, which was left to the colony by Mr. Lienard's widow, and is now in the Museum, Port Louis, where it still is the type collection for reference in the classification of shells of these seas.

CRANE WHARF, PORT LOUIS.

Professor Crosse in publishing the catalogue found it necessary to add a preface thereto, in which he states that when inspecting for the first time, "about ten years ago" (that is about 1867) the collection of shells of Mr. Lienard, he was astonished to notice the number of species included in the malacological fauna of Mauritius, and he appears to have been lost in admiration of the patience, knowledge, and ability displayed by Mr. Lienard in making this remarkable and valuable addition to the general science of conchology.

Mr. Lienard at first opened his cabinets to shells from all parts of the Indian Ocean, but later, as the number and variety of specimens brought to his notice rapidly increased, he appears to have preferred to specialise in the shells found in Mauritius; and in this he was ably seconded by correspondents and friends, besides which he employed a considerable number of native fishermen. In this manner, and after incurring no small outlay, he succeeded in bringing together a collection of Mauritius shells which at that time certainly could not be matched in France, England, or elsewhere. It was whilst working on a complete catalogue of the result of his long researches that Mr. Lienard died in 1876, but his widow, who during the lifetime of her husband had shared his labours, afterwards completed the task.

This catalogue comprises 981 numbered and typed varieties for Mauritius alone, but since it was published the researches of other local collectors have very greatly added thereto; and if a really complete collection were made the number of specimens would far exceed that number.

There is also in the Museum, Port Louis, another rather large collection of shells, which was originally brought together by Monsieur Julien Desjardins, who may be said to have been the founder of the Museum.

He was a member of an old French family which owned "Argy" Estate, in the district of Flacq; and being a born naturalist he there created a small natural history museum which attracted at the time considerable attention. This gentleman died in 1840 at Paris, whither he had proceeded in order to publish his work *Zoologie de Maurice*, and he left his fine collection to his native land. It was in 1842 that this collection was transferred to a wing of the Royal College, and again transferred to its present home in 1885.

But the Desjardins collection has suffered by various removals. Although kept in several glass cases the specimens have deteriorated, and been damaged, and cannot be regarded now as of any scientific value.

Such is the history of the two local collections of Mauritius shells, but it may be interesting to students of conchology if some details are given here as to the most noteworthy varieties which can be found in the island.

As regards marine varieties Mauritius is remarkably rich. Beginning with the *Muricidæ*, including sub-genera, there are about thirty varieties, embracing the beautiful *Murex palma-rosæ*, the *M. Crosseii*; which is very rare, and was described by Professor Crosse in the *Journal de Conchylogie*, 1871, a fine specimen of it being in the Lienard collection. Another extremely rare one is *M. Clavus*. "Dead" specimens of this shell had been found, but the first "live" specimen was picked up on Barkly Island – a reef brought to the surface during the hurricane of 1863 —and has been very seldom found since. The delicate *M. Tenuispina* is also to be found, but rarely in perfect condition, one or more of its beautiful spines being broken in handling.

POINTE AUX CANONNIERS' LIGHTHOUSE.

Of *Pleurotoma* there are about forty varieties, of which *P. Allovirgulata* was classed by Sowerby and described in *Le Journal de Conchylogie*, Vol. VIII.

The genus *Tritonidæ* is represented by about eighty varieties; amongst which can be noted the *T. Anus* (*Lam.*) and *T. Clavator.* (*Lam.*).

The genus *Ranella* comprises about twenty varieties, some of which are notable for their curious formation.

Of the *Purpuridæ* the most common is *P. Persica*. There are only about fifteen varieties of this genus.

The curious coral shells, the inmates of which embed themselves in the soft coral of the reefs, are common; there being several species of *Coralliophila*, *Magilus*, and *Leptochonchus*.

We next proceed to that beautiful family the Olives. Although Crosse only catalogues some twenty species, there are many varieties of this shell; for, as a matter of fact, it is difficult to find two alike—the beautiful markings are so varied that each shell appears to be an individual species in itself. The method for catching these shells is ingenious. At low tide a long floating line is paid out of a boat, from which hang at a certain distance apart a number of smaller lines baited with a piece of octopus. The bait lies on the sandy bottom frequented by the Olives, which come to the bait and begin to feed. The lines are after a time taken up very carefully, one by one, and should a shell be adhering to the bait, the fisherman passes his hand under it before it reaches the surface, for if allowed to leave the water the Olive at once lets go of the bait and falls back into the sea.

In the genus *Conus* Mauritius is very rich, some of them being much prized, such as the *Conus Julii*, found for the first time on Barkly Island after heavy weather. . Lienard gives one hundred varieties in his catalogue, but many new species have been since found and described.

The Mauritius genus *Cypræa* is much diversified. The types vary from the tiny pearl-like *C. Tremeza* to the fine *C. Mauritiana*, which is very common on all the reefs, and to the very rare *C. Testudinaria* (*Lin.*). The *C. Tigris* is also found in many varieties, most of them very finely marked. There are at least 150 species of this most interesting family, which the French call *porcelaines*.

The genus *Mitra* always offers great attractions for the conchologist in all parts of the world, and Mauritius is no exception, there being over 200 varieties, including the brilliantly marked *M. Papalis* and *M. Episcopalis*.

But, perhaps, the most beautiful is the Harp Shell (genus *Harpa*), of which there are seven kinds, the most prized being *H. Imperialis* and *H. Ventricosa*. This shell is most elaborately marked and pencilled with delicate rose, and ribbed over its whole length, the ribs meeting round the apex and forming a coronet of fragile points. It is on account of these points that it is very difficult to obtain a really perfect specimen, as the fishermen take no pains to prevent injury to the shells. It is found in sandy bottoms and can be taken in the same manner as is adopted for Olives.

TOP OF SIGNAL MOUNTAIN, PORT LOUIS.

Coming to bivalves, there are not many species, but the *Pectens* are well represented, some of the smaller ones being brightly coloured.

For the specialist in land shells there is much of interest in Mauritius. There are two varieties of *Achatina*, namely, *A. Fulica* (*Morelet*), peculiar to the island, and *A. Panthera* (*Ferr.*), which found its way from Madagascar. These are terrible enemies of the garden, and voraciously devour plants and vegetables indiscriminately. The Creoles, however, turn them to some value by boiling them and feeding ducks therewith—apparently a very fattening régime.

Now and then specimens of *Tourne-à-Gauche Achatina* are found. As its name implies, the mouth of the shell turns to the left instead of to the right, a very rare and remarkable malformation. During the first wet weather the *Achatina* come out from hibernation in thousands, and it is then that they are most destructive. They lay their eggs in large quantities under stones and leaves.

Perhaps the next most destructive snail is the homely English garden snail, which has found its way across the world and settled here. It is a persistent enemy of the vegetable garden.

Of the genus *Pupæ* there are many very interesting living species, but from the large number of semi-fossil extinct varieties found in various parts of the island, it is evident that this genus was far more numerous prior to the destruction of the original forests. But with *Pupæ*, as with every other living thing, there are survivals of the fittest, of which there are about twenty species.

Of the genus *Gibbus* there are only four varieties, of which *G. Pagodus*, a large shell, was once common in the higher parts, but is becoming extinct. The most remarkable variety is the *G. Lyonetianus* (*Pallas*), an exceedingly rare shell, only found on the banks of a small stream in the district of Savanne, and nowhere else. So rare in fact had it become, owing to the denuding of the land, that it was considered to be extinct, until after some years, a Creole, who had been sent to try and find some "dead" specimens, found about twenty beautiful live ones. At one time live specimens of this shell were very valuable, and, as a matter of fact, it is not to be found in many large collections. But apart from its extreme rarity the shell is remarkable for its shape. It is about an inch in length and of a dull yellow, the mouth of the old shell being thickened into a lip. Instead, however, of being cylindrical like most shells, this *Gibbus*, which is rectangular in shape, looks as if it had been subjected to pressure and flattened.

The *Helices* comprise about forty species, some of them, such as the *H. Duponti*, being sub-fossil. The finest is *H. Uversicolor*, a bicolored shell, brown above and black below, with a rose-coloured mouth.

The *Cyclostomæ* are fairly numerous, but are not very remarkable except *C. Michaudi* (*Grat.*), a brown shell with a white lip; but here again we find one of these vagaries of Nature. There is a variety, *C. Barclayanum* (after a former resident who was an ardent collector), with a red lip, which is only found on the Corps-de-Garde Mountain. This limitation of certain shells to certain spots in such a small island as Mauritius is certainly peculiar. There are several sub-fossil varieties, of which *C. Tricarinatum* is the most noteworthy for its size, and the three sharp bands which encircle it.

We have in this article briefly indicated the points of greatest interest to the shell collector, from which it will be seen that there is vast scope in Mauritius for the researches and activities of the naturalist.

CATTLE ON BELLE MARE ESTATE, FLACQ.

CATTLE ON MESSRS. MERANDON'S ESTATE, BLACK RIVER.

CLIMATE.

By A. WALTER, F.R.A.S., Director of the Royal Alfred Observatory.

A. WALTER, F.R.A.S.,
Director of the Royal Alfred Observatory.

MAURITIUS is situated on the northern edge of the great high-pressure belt which extends over the South Indian Ocean from the Cape to Australia. The seasonal variations of weather are controlled for the most part by the annual migrations of this belt, north and south. During the winter months of the southern hemisphere its central position is in latitude 25° S. As the sun travels south, bringing with it the equatorial belt of low pressure, the high-pressure area also retreats southward, its central position during the month of February being in latitude 30° S Between these two systems there is a continual interchange of air. The surface winds which form the S.E. trade current flow from the anticyclonic areas toward the equatorial low pressure Rising throughout their journey by convection as they penetrate the warm tropical regions, they finally return as the N.W. upper current to the regions of high pressure.

As will be seen from the table giving the mean values of the principal meteorological elements, these migrations give rise to a progressive increase of pressure and decrease of temperature between the months of February and July. If the isobaric lines —or lines of equal pressure—for these two months of the year are drawn on a chart of the Indian Ocean and the adjacent land areas, it will be seen that, whereas during the month of July the closed isobaric system of low pressure extends over the ocean areas due north of Mauritius, during the month of February two such areas exist, one over each of the continents of Africa and Australia.

The positions of these systems relative to the high-pressure area south of Mauritius determine the variations in the mean wind direction —in accordance with the well-known rule that the surface wind blows out from the area of high pressure toward the nearest area of low pressure. We find in consequence that the direction of the wind, which is about S.E. during the winter months, steadily backs to east, blowing toward the continental low-pressure area which exists over Africa in February.

The wet season begins in December, the rainfall reaching a maximum in March, then gradually decreasing till June, with a second maximum in August. The dry season may be considered to extend from September to November.

LAKE IN THE ROYAL BOTANIC GARDENS, PAMPLEMOUSSES.
(Before the cyclone of 1892, which destroyed many of the beautiful Palms surrounding the Lake.)

Monthly Normals of the Meteorological Elements at the Royal Alfred Observatory.

(180 feet above sea-level.)

Month.	Mean Barometric Pressure.	Temperature of the Air. Mean of Daily Maxima.	Mean of Daily Minima.	Mean of Daily Ranges.	Mean.	Degree of Humidity (Saturation =100).	Elastic Force of Vapour.	Rainfall.	Duration of Rainfall.	Daily amount of Evaporation.
	ins.	°	°	°	°		ins.	ins.	mins.	ins.
January ...	29·750	86·1	72 9	13 2	78·9	75·1	·737	8·39	2,266	·243
February ...	29·730	85 6	73·0	12·6	78 5	77·7	·757	7·68	2,030	·214
March ...	29·766	84·0	72·1	11·9	77·3	80·2	·747	9·87	2,946	·183
April	29·822	82·0	70·1	11·9	75·3	80 9	·704	4·71	1,708	·166
May	29·890	79 0	66·3	12·7	72·1	79·3	·625	3·08	1 335	·144
June	29·965	76 2	62·6	13·6	68·7	76·4	·538	2·08	1,275	·125
July	30·004	75·2	61·5	13·7	67·5	75·7	·507	2·24	1,494	·135
August ...	30 010	75·7	61·8	13·9	68·0	74·5	·508	2·71	1 696	·158
September ...	29·993	77·6	62·4	15·2	69 6	71·9	·522	1·34	934	·191
October ...	29·942	81·0	64·7	16·3	72·1	70·1	·552	1·27	835	·228
November ..	29·877	84·1	67·2	16·9	75·2	68·4	·603	1·89	906	·267
December ...	29·811	85·7	71·1	14·6	78·0	70·9	·676	4·88	1,502	·254
Year	29·880	81·0	67·1	13·9	73·4	75·1	·623	50·14	hours 315·5	·192
Maximum ...	ins. 30·274 June 20, 1877	° 94·7 Dec. 23, 1900	—	° 27·8 Aug. 12, 1902	° 75·0 — 1875	98·5 Jan. 12, 1901	ins. 1·077 March 6, 1905	ins. 19·318 in 24h. Feb. 1896	—	ins. ·370 Dec. 31, 1907
Minimum ...	ins. 27·780 April 29, 1892	—	° 50 6 June 10, 1894	° 2 0 June 14, 1891	° 72 4 — 1893	34·0 Nov. 26, 1896	ins. ·321 June 10, 1894	—	—	ins. ·025 June 23, 1905

Month.	Mean amount of cloud (scale 0·10).	Daily duration of Sunshine.	Temperature of the Soil. 5 feet.	10 feet.	Wind. Direction.	Velocity.	Number of Days of Clear Sky.	Overcast Sky.	Rain.	Thunder Storm.	Lightning.
		hours.	°	°		miles per hour.					
January ...	6·4	7·69	79·92	77·12	East	11·07	1	11	19	4	2
February ..	6·3	7·21	80·74	77·64	E by S	10·99	2	11	18	4	2
March ..	6·4	6·72	81·15	78·06	E by S	10·42	1	13	21	4	2
April ...	5·7	7·31	80·82	78·31	E S E	10·51	2	9	18	3	1
May	5·1	7·37	79·71	78·39	E S E	10·27	7	7	15	1	0
June ...	4·9	7·43	78·09	78·25	S E by East	11·19	6	6	16	1	0
July ...	5·1	7·65	76·38	77·82	E S E	11·96	5	6	20	0	0
August ...	5·5	7·49	75·28	77·25	E S E	12·34	4	8	20	0	0
September ...	5·6	8·01	75·14	76·69	E S E	12·02	3	7	15	1	0
October ...	5·7	8·14	75·79	76·35	E by E	11·00	2	7	14	1	0
November ...	5·5	8·59	77·02	76·34	E by S	10·70	2.	7	12	1	1
December ...	6·1	8·27	78·55	76·60	East	10·79	2	10	16	2	1
Year ...	5·7	7·66	78·22	77·40	E by S	11·10	37	102	204	22	9
Maximum	—	hours. 2·15 Dec. 9, 1889	° 82·7 Feb. 13, 1892	° 79·99 May 13, 1898	—	121·2* April, 1892	13 Aug. 1902	25 Jan. 1905	31 Jan. 1905	19 Jan. 1898	9 Jan. 1863
Minimum	—	—	° 74·0 often in Sept.	° 75·00 Oct. 28, 1906	—	—	—	—	4 June, 1900	—	—

* For 5 minutes.

Station. / Element.	Port-Louis (Sea-level).	Observatory (altitude 180 ft.).	Beau Bassin (altitude 750 ft.).	Military Camp Vacoas (altitude 1350 ft.).	Alma Estate Moka (altitude 1500 ft.).	Curepipe Gardens (altitude 1850 ft.).
Temperature of the Air. Mean	° 77·1	° 73·4	° 71·7	° 69·7	° 69·3	° 67·5
Temperature of the Air. Mean of Daily Maxima	83·7	81·0	78·8	76·9	75·3	73·9
Temperature of the Air. Mean of Daily Minima	71·4	67·1	64·6	62·5	63·3	61·2
Temperature of the Air. Mean of Daily Ranges	12·3	13·9	14·2	14·4	12·0	12·7
Temperature of the Air. Absolute Highest	—	94·7	91·7	86·0	88·7	86·2
Temperature of the Air. Absolute Lowest	—	50·6	50·0	48·8	·46·4	44·0
Degree of Humidity (Sat=100)	71%	75%	—	80%	—	87%
Rainfall	ins. 38·2	ins. 50·1	ins. 50·5	ins. 86·8	ins. 126·0	ins. 124·4

For the purpose of describing the mean seasonal variations of weather it is convenient to refer to the high and low-pressure systems as permanent areas, but it must be understood that on these regular seasonal changes are superposed the variations due to the passage of well-formed anticyclonic and cyclonic circulations. The high-pressure area to the south is produced in reality by a series of rapidly moving anticyclones travelling from west to east, and we note in consequence a periodic variation of about ten to twelve days in nearly all elements—pressure, temperature, wind direction, and velocity. The sequence of weather is generally as follows:—

As the anticyclone approaches the meridian of Mauritius the wind veers towards the south, the barometer rises rapidly to about one-tenth of an inch above normal, the temperature falls, and the sky takes a deep blue tint, flecked here and there with white fleecy cumuli clouds. During these spells of fine weather in the cool season the conditions, especially in the higher portions of the island, resemble closely those of a fine sunny day, intermediate between the spring and summer, of the South of England.

As the anticyclonic conditions recede the barometer falls, the temperature increases, and the wind steadily backs to E.N.E., and sometimes N.W., to ultimately fall calm. This constitutes what is known as a V-shaped depression between two anticyclones, a name which describes the wedge form which the isobaric lines take in this intermediate position. There is hence a complete cessation of the trades for a few days until the arrival of the next anticyclonic area, when the same sequence of weather is observed.

In the summer months the same type of weather continues, although the sequence of the anticyclonic systems is less marked. Occasionally the island is brought under the direct influence of the tropical calms, which, apart from the conditions obtaining in cyclones, is the most objectionable of all the types of weather in these latitudes.

CYCLONES.

Since the days when the early navigators rounded the Cape of Good Hope in search of the treasures of the East, the violent storms which traverse the Indian Ocean both north and south of the Equator have been a source of terror and anxiety. The loss both of life and property which they have occasioned, on land as on sea, is untold. Previous to that period in the history of meteorology which witnessed the development of the laws governing the motion of these tropical storms, hardly a year passed without leaving behind it a dark page in the annals of the mercantile marine. With the advent of steam and a wider knowledge of the rules for avoiding the zone of dangerous winds, the losses have steadily diminished until, at the present day, a captain who allows his ship to suffer damage by a too near approach is looked at askance.

While, on the one hand, the constantly changing position of the ship greatly increases the probability of encountering a cyclone, it also, on the other hand, decreases the probability in the direct ratio to the extent of the commander's acquaintance with the law of storms. On land the conditions are different; the only advantage which can accrue from a knowledge of these laws is the possibility of taking precautions for the closing of buildings, etc. Apart from this the landsman has to suffer the full brunt of the storm. Very great interest to every section of the community centres, in consequence, round the determination of the frequency with which the colony comes within the zone of dangerous winds. The records of the Royal Alfred Observatory provide detailed information in this connection, extending over a period of more than fifty years:—

List of Hurricanes and Cyclonic Storms previous to 1857.

Date.	Date.	Date.
1695 ... February 9	1814 ... February 3	1834 ... April 30
1723 ... December 23	1814 ... April 19	1835 ... January 20
1731 ... February	1815 ... February 6	1836 ... March 5, 6
1734 ... March 13	1815 ... February 17	1837 ... February 15
1743 ... March 8	1816 ... January 22	1840 ... April 10
1748 ... February ?	1817 ... February 14	1841 ... January 16
1754 ... April 19-21	1818 ... March 1	1843 ... January 16, 19
1759 ... ? ?	1819 ... January 25	1844 ... January 4
1760 ... January 18	1819 ... March 29	1844 ... February 20, 23
1761 ... ? ?	1820 ... December 15	1844 ... March 20
1766 ... ? ?	1823 ... February 21	1844 ... December 20
1771 ... February ?	1823 ... March 6	1845 ... March 8
1771 ... March ?	1824 ... February 23	1847 ... January 28
1772 ... March 1	1824 ... April 11	1847 ... February ?
1773 ... April 9	1824 ... December 6	1848 ... March 8
1786 ... December 15	1825 ... March 10	1850 ... February 28
1788 ... December 31	1826 ... February 24	1850 ... March 1
1789 ... January 1	1826 ... December 27	1851 ... March 20, 21
1790 ... ? ?	1827 ... January 8	1852 ... January 9, 10
1795 ... March 14	1828 ... March 6	1852 ... January 23, 24
1800 ... February ?	1828 ... March 25	1853 ... January 14, 16
1806 ... ? ?	1829 ... February 7, 10	1853 ... March 5, 10
1807 ... February 3	1830 ... March 27	1854 ... February 10, 13
1807 ... February 28	1830 ... April 4	1855 ... January 22, 24
1811 ... March 6	1832 ... March 4	1855 April 27 to May 3
1811 ... March 21	1833 ... April 10	1856 ... February 2, 5
1812 ... February 26	1834 ... January 20	1856 ... April 3, 6
1813 ... February 19	1834 ... February 21	

Particulars of Cyclones which have passed within One Hundred Miles of Mauritius since 1857.

Date.	Maximum hourly velocity (miles per hour).	Date.	Maximum hourly velocity (miles per hour).
1857 ... January 28 ...	70	1881 ... January 21 ...	50
1857 ... December 5, 6 ...	80	1882 ... February 7 ...	24
1859 ... March 9 ...	36	1883 ... December 6, 7 ...	45
1860 ... January 12, 13 ...	33	1885 ... January 18 ...	28
1860 ... February 27 ...	33	1888 ... January 5 ...	41
1860 ... March 22, 23 ...	37	1892 ... February 12 ...	47
1861 ... February 11, 16 ..	75	1892 ... April 29 ...	103
1861 ... March 2, 3 ...	?	1893 ... January 21, 22 ..	35
1862 ... December 1 ..	32	1894 ... January 13 ..	41
1863 ... January 13, 14 ...	80	1894 ... February 21, 22 ...	62
1863 ... February 20 ...	80	1895 ... January 13, 14 ...	39
1866 ... April 16 ...	37	1896 ... February 19, 21 ...	51
1868 ... January 16 ...	30	1897 ... December 5, 6 ...	71
1868 ... March 12 ..	85	1899 ... March 6 ...	44
1871 ... January 5 ...	60	1901 ... January 12, 13 ..	72
1872 ... February 15 ...	60	1902 ... February 5, 6 ...	78
1874 ... March 26, 28 ..	80	1902 ... February 9, 10 ...	54
1875 ... December 21 ...	32	1904 ... March 21 ...	42
1876 ... January 8 ...	30	1905 ... January 23 ...	49
1877 ... February 10 ...	65	1908 ... March 1 ...	63
1879 ... February 26 ...	64	1910 ... January 11, 12 ..	45
1879 ... March 20, 21 ..	80	1911 ... March 29 ..	48
1880 ... December 18, 19 ...	39		

The damage caused to the crops by cyclones has been dealt with in the chapter on the Sugar Industry, and it will be remarked that very few cyclones give rise to serious loss.

Cyclones form, as a rule, to the north or north-east of Mauritius, between the latitudes of 8° and 12° south, in the belt which exists between the S.E. trade current and the N.W. monsoon. These two currents, rising by convection throughout their journey, give birth to a vortex motion in the superheated area of tropical calms. The direction of rotation of this vortex is determined by the rotation of the earth on its axis, the direction being clockwise in the southern hemisphere and anticlockwise in the northern hemisphere. The path described by these tropical storms is, as a rule, parabolic.

After their formation they usually travel on a west-south-westerly course until they reach the eighteenth to twenty-fifth degree of latitude. Betweens these parallels a curve, more or less sharp, occurs, and the cyclone then starts on the second branch of its parabola. The initial rate of translation varies from two to twelve miles, but this is invariably accelerated after curving.

The sequence of weather at Mauritius as the centre of a cyclonic storm approaches is as follows:— The normal direction of the wind during the hurricane season, which lasts from December to April, is from E. to E.S.E. The first indications of an approaching storm are: a veering of the wind to the south-east, an unsteady or falling barometer, and large amounts of fine wispy cirrus or cirro-stratus.

FOREST AFTER THE CYCLONE OF 1892.

As the storm approaches, the sky becomes covered with a thin, watery stratus, and the wind blows in irregular fitful gusts, which gradually increase in force and frequency. Shreds of low, neutral-tinted scud are driven rapidly across the sky, and rain falls at frequent intervals. The barometer now falls rapidly, and wind and rain increase in velocity and intensity until the centre of the storm is reached.

The wind then drops suddenly to a velocity of eight or ten miles an hour; the sky becomes clear, and a strong smell of the sea is carried even into the interior of the island, where large numbers of sea-birds take refuge.

The barometer, after falling in some instances one-and-a-half to two inches in a few hours, now begins to rise rapidly; and the wind, slowly turning through 180°, blows from a direction opposite to that in which it blew during the first half of the storm, the velocity slowly decreasing as the centre recedes.

The conditions which obtain in the cyclonic area vary considerably in different storms. Even when the centre passes over the island—and this is an event of rare occurrence—the result is not always disastrous from an agricultural point of view.

The mean values of the meteorological elements at varying altitudes in Mauritius will be seen from the following table:—

Station. / Element.	Port Louis (Sea Level).	Observatory (Altitude 180 ft.).	Beau-Bassin (Altitude 750 ft.).	Military Camp, Vacoas (Altitude 1350 ft.).	Alma Estate, Moka (Altitude 1500 ft.).	Curepipe Gardens (Altitude 1850 ft.).
Mean	77·1	73·4	71·7	69·7	69·3	67·5
Mean of Daily Maxima	83·7	81·0	78·8	76·9	75·3	73·9
Mean of Daily Minima	71·4	67·1	64·6	62·5	63·3	61·2
Mean of Daily Ranges	12·3	13·9	14·2	14·4	12·0	12·7
Absolute Highest	—	94·7	91·7	86·0	88·7	86·2
Absolute Lowest...	—	50·6	50·0	48·8	46·4	44·0
Degree of Humidity (Sat=100) ...	71%	75%	—	80%	—	87%
Rainfall	38·2 ins.	50·1 ins.	50·5 ins.	86·8 ins.	126·0 ins.	124·4 ins.

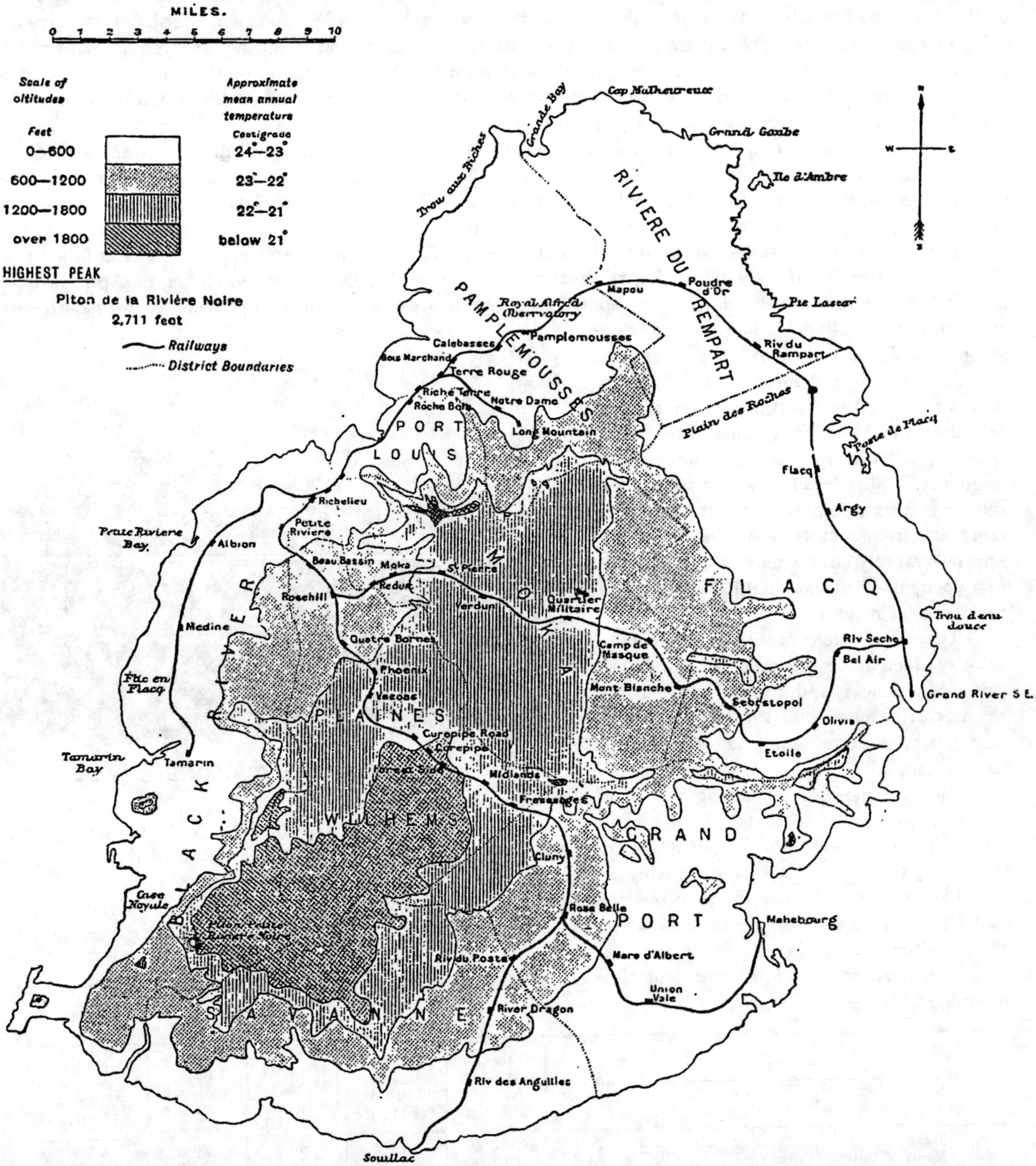

CONTOUR MAP OF MAURITIUS.

By A. WALTER, F.R.A.S., Director of the Royal Alfred Observatory.

It will be noticed that the range is considerable. The mean annual temperature decreases from 77.1° Fah. at sea level to 67.5° Fah. at Curepipe, while the humidity increases by 15 per cent. and the rainfall by over eighty-six inches between these limits. Under these circumstances, in spite of the unhealthiness of the low-lying districts, it is always possible to recuperate one's health to a certain extent by migration to the higher localities. It is principally on this account that Europeans find it possible to reside for long periods in Mauritius without being forced to return to Europe because of ill-health.

Rainfall at Ten Stations in Mauritius, 1871-1912.

Year.	Labour-donnais.	Observa-tory.	Botanic Gardens.	Beau Séjour (Salency).	Trianon.	Cluny.	Beau Vallon.	Gros Bois.	St. Aubin.	L'Union.	Means.
	ins.	ins.	ins.	ins.	ins.	ins.	ins.	ins.	ins.	ins.	ins.
1871	50·92	42·62	55·57	45·96	47·44	133·71	58·38	99·25	82·00	71·26	68·71
1872	44·20	47·75	53·99	62·68	62·70	146·82	53·99	90·08	76·10	78·59	71·69
1873	70·04	75·54	81·39	82·89	84·49	171·32	65·27	98·09	89·08	90·55	90·87
1874	64·48	64·82	73·77	110·36	102·41	177·59	71·86	120·26	88·68	94·31	96·85
1875	76·00	49·98	56·05	60·92	66·63	133·36	67·64	110·78	84·94	86·03	79·24
1876	70·60	41·87	50·23	58·29	64·09	146·42	50·90	74·45	67·92	71·35	69·61
1877	103·34	71·36	87·69	92·91	86·13	203·50	77·39	110·60	117·97	120·43	107·13
1878	52·86	43·25	52·44	63·65	55·79	133·10	59·00	112·06	92·58	76·00	74·07
1879	62·80	49·16	59·23	62·89	53·70	132·36	61·25	91·98	75·26	57·14	70·58
1880	40·79	34·03	43·33	43·43	36·90	107·44	41·10	82·59	64·53	49·51	54·36
1881	55·62	45·32	62·35	60·44	47·78	109·45	50·83	101·68	76·51	58·27	66·82
1882	75·98	56·06	75·87	71·60	63·18	181·18	95·24	126·40	104·17	109·86	95·95
1883	70·08	47·69	69·90	77·84	71·04	119·09	67·78	102·14	93·54	67·20	78·63
1884	56·36	45·80	70·59	60·69	54·75	117·40	55·34	80·96	56·24	58·02	65·61
1885	57·44	44·61	85·68	55·64	52·29	122·65	54·18	82·49	59·25	58·79	67·30
1886	33·18	29·74	46·26	31·06	30·68	95·16	31·49	54·40	47·28	49·68	44·89
1887	59·03	46·64	85·12	51·91	52·92	139·64	63·62	94·56	78·30	63·87	73·56
1888	75·53	52·81	66·23	79·61	71·69	194·36	93·24	128·97	130·66	125·48	101·86
1889	75·08	56·19	58·46	71·30	67·73	173·96	92·82	112·19	104·84	92·50	90·51
1890	64·79	53·17	60·55	73·29	64·05	133·75	57·78	90·77	74·98	76·26	74·94
1891	67·01	44·63	58·08	67·89	59·59	152·25	71·65	108·60	85·54	80·96	79·62
1892	77·18	59·12	69·99	93·09	72·04	165·93	70·55	84·44	80·87	85·65	85·89
1893	61·63	48·33	56·77	80·02	65·72	131·24	55·49	76·18	68·42	65·79	70·96
1894	55·37	48·91	53·70	76·28	69·17	147·59	67·65	88·25	79·59	67·70	75·42
1895	67·36	54·16	62·29	81·77	76·42	167·29	71·24	91·74	78·35	71·27	82·19
1896	94·94	68·17	73·63	88·12	78·19	163·34	69·04	103·71	103·39	99·10	94·16
1897	42·49	27·26	32·93	52·82	50·13	118·42	47·26	75·96	55·38	58·94	56·16
1898	63·05	47·76	49·72	52·53	55·27	139·73	66·64	97·07	79·63	78·09	72·95
1899	57·64	42·82	53·49	63·07	71·06	130·94	55·69	87·30	66·11	83·58	71·17
1900	35·34	31·28	36·96	41·89	41·69	109·66	39·43	74·62	59·56	60·07	53·05
1901	73·55	56·47	63·37	77·09	81·07	157·15	55·71	108·86	80·37	91·62	84·53
1902	51·46	47·11	56·79	55·52	59·17	134·95	56·12	96·76	72·49	74·00	70·44
1903	38·52	41·69	50·34	46·87	52·78	119·66	46·09	87·45	66·38	57·67	60·74
1904	31·97	43·11	48·17	42·24	51·40	120·45	53·72	91·30	74·12	65·06	62·15
1905	70·54	67·90	81·14	87·10	97·81	172·30	82·45	142·31	105·59	107·36	101·45
1906	47·98	41·67	43·86	43·39	43·32	145·45	55·04	107·65	75·64	63·02	66·70
1907	49·36	44·19	49·85	66·98	59·59	96·27	54·54	62·98	56·83	55·87	59·65
1908	70·68	62·43	65·66	73·61	55·90	154·70	72·79	95·87	66·60	70·22	78·84
1909	47·59	47·83	58·12	77·86	74·29	187·25	71·12	108·82	92·78	89·31	85·60
1910	36·38	38·79	42·16	54·39	50·75	143·29	47·37	80·87	67·32	56·08	61·74
1911	41·95	46·41	53·88	61·11	59·04	169·29	59·96	102·91	90·74	77·71	76·30
1912	72·01	72·88	73·41	61·15	58·81	200·27	—	140·27	107·78	103·51	—

In the central portions of the island an average annual rainfall of over 175 inches is recorded.

THE ROYAL ALFRED OBSERVATORY, PAMPLEMOUSSES.

The first Observatory was established in Port Louis in 1851 by the Meteorological Society of Mauritius, by which it was maintained with the assistance of a small Government grant. The observations made at this Observatory were analysed by Dr. C. Meldrum, who was then a professor of mathematics at the Royal College. The result of his labours was instrumental in bringing to the notice of mariners and others the marked incurving tendency of the winds in tropical cyclones; and he showed that the rules for avoiding the centre, based upon a circular theory, were not applicable in every quadrant of the cyclonic area. This work proved of such immense value to the shipping interests that the local Government agreed to the proposals of the Meteorological Society to establish a more suitable Observatory, and the present building was erected at Pamplemousses, the foundation stone being laid by His Royal Highness the Duke of Edinburgh in 1870.

THE ROYAL ALFRED OBSERVATORY.

The establishment is about three miles from the west coast, and five miles from Port Louis. The main building is a handsome stone structure standing in eleven acres of Crown land, tastefully laid out with palms and other tropical trees.

The Observatory is well equipped as a meteorological, magnetical and seismological station. Its unique position in the South Indian Ocean renders it of great importance, not only to the shipping which frequents these seas, but to the meteorological organisations of other countries, and especially to those of Africa and India, to which weekly cablegrams are forwarded in connection with the monsoon predictions. Its principal local work is the determination of time and the issue of storm warnings for the railway and for the shipping in the harbour.

The instrumental equipment consists of barometers, thermometers, anemometers, rain-gauges, etc., for meteorological work; a complete set of magnetic instruments, which has recently been supplemented by an earth inductor and Eschenhagen vertical force magnetometer, the gift of the Carnegie Institute of Washington; a Milne seismograph for recording unfelt earth tremors, a 6-inch equatorial telescope, and two 3-inch transit instruments.

The time service is very complete. It was inaugurated under the superintendence of the late director, Mr. T. F. Claxton—now Director of the Hong Kong Observatory—who set up electric transmitters in the underground magnet chamber, by which the various dials and clocks of the Observatory are controlled and the time-ball on the Port Tower dropped.

The present director is now superintending the erection of a new clock basement, as the electric transmitters are a source of trouble in the magnet basement. The astronomical work is, at the same time, undergoing development; the transit instruments are being mounted on suitable foundations in a room adjoining the clock chamber; a petrol gas-lighting plant has just been set up, and a well is being sunk for providing an efficient water supply.

CHAMBER OF AGRICULTURE.

By HENRI ROBERT,

Secretary, Chamber of Agriculture; Chevalier de l'Ordre National du Merité Agricole (France); Editor of "Bulletin Agricole."

HENRI ROBERT

THE Chamber of Agriculture was founded at a general assembly of the planters, held in the Masonic Lodge of the "Triple-Esperance," on the 16th October, 1853. It has had a succession of twenty-two Presidents, the first of whom was the Hon. (later Sir) Gabriel Fropier, and it has held over six hundred meetings, of which several may be said to have been of historic importance. It has always numbered among its members a majority of the leading men in the colony. The office of Secretary has been held by the following: Messrs. E. Baudot, Loïs Raoul, Finniss, Herchenroder, Clare Bernard, Gabriel Bouic, and Henri Robert.

Sir Robert Farquhar, the first English Governor of Mauritius, had created a Society of Agriculture (28th April, 1814); but that body had died out without effecting anything of note, and the same may be said of various local Societies which came into being prior to 1830. One of the latter, however, the Society of Rivière du Rempart, appears to have laboured actively towards the introduction of steam mills. Its existence was cut short when, on the 16th September, 1833, Lord Goderich, then Secretary of State for the Colonies, ordered the Governor of Mauritius to dissolve all the Societies and Associations existing in the island, including Societies of Agriculture.

Going back still further, it may be interesting to mention that, in the time of the French occupation, Cossigny had asked the French Minister of Colonies (1773) for permission to set up a Chamber of Agriculture at the Isle of France. The application was denied unconditionally, Cossigny being looked upon by the authorities in Paris as an agitator, and the colonists themselves as "hot-headed people, who dabbled excessively in politics."

No sooner was the present Chamber of Agriculture in existence than it adverted to numerous questions of importance, such as labour, irrigation, reafforestation, harbour improvement, overseas postal service, etc. In fact, it may be said without exaggeration that the history of the Chamber is intimately bound up with that of the economic life of the colony during the past sixty years. It was in the Chamber that the idea of building the railways in Mauritius was first mooted, and the ultimate carrying-out of the project was due to the persistent efforts of the Chamber in the face of numerous financial and other difficulties and objections. Strange to say, in Mauritius, as elsewhere, the establishment of the railways had its opponents. In his Annua Report for 1865 Dr. Icery, then President of the Chamber, stated that the Chamber had taken a leading part in the creation of our railways, and that he could assert, without fear of contradiction, that this body was entitled to claim the initiative in this important matter.

The following fact will illustrate the practical interest which planters had in the creation of a system of transport by rail. Mr. Longridge, an engineer, sent from England (1858) to study and report upon the matter, mentions that a planter wished to transport three boilers from the wharf at Port Louis to his estate, and called for tenders from job contractors for the purpose. The boilers weighed six to seven tons each, and the distance by road was some eighteen miles. The lowest tender was £1,200!

When one reflects that there were at the time 255 sugar-houses in the island, one may gain an idea of the capital sunk in these enterprises, and of the energy which planters must have displayed to have kept their business going in the face of such extraordinary economic conditions.

The Chamber was also the first to advocate the installation of the telegraph within the island. The Colonial Secretary, in reply (letter of the 28th July, 1859), informed the Chamber that *"it was not the intention of the Government to undertake such works."* The Chamber thereupon requested the Governor to lay the matter without delay before the Secretary of State, and added that it was not too ambitious to hope that, at no very distant date, this colony would be placed in the midst of a vast system of electric telegraphy, enabling the outlying possessions of Her Majesty to establish almost instantaneous communication with the mother-country.

In a Memorandum dated 1862, Mr. H. Barlow, one of the most active members of the Chamber, recalled the fact that the Chamber had already more than once reported to the Government on the preservation of the forests and rivers. Reference was made, in pointed terms, to the enormous quantity of water resulting from the heavy summer rains, all of which is allowed to flow down to the sea after washing away part of the most fertile lands, and a suggestion was put forward that, in the opinion of specialists familiar with irrigation works in Italy and in India, it would be feasible to retain the benefit of such water by means of dams built at suitable intervals along the principal streams in Mauritius.

In his report for 1862 Sir Gabriel Fropier again dwelt strongly on the "highly important question of irrigation and of the preservation of the hydraulic resources supplied to us by Nature every year."

In 1866 the Chamber addressed a letter to the Governor, suggesting a study of the question of damming the rivers, or adopting such other device as might furnish a practical means of irrigating those parts of the island which suffered most from the drought. On the 16th August, 1866, the Governor replied promising to give attention to the matter, and the Chamber from time to time reverted to it. On the 14th January, 1867, the Government informed the Chamber that the question of establishing a system of irrigation by means of "reservoirs" had had due consideration, but that such a scheme was open to serious practical difficulties, and, further, involved considerable outlay.

So early as 1859 (Memorial of the 27th February) the Chamber had insisted on the necessity of preserving the forests and retaining the flowing waters. "Thirty or forty years ago," the Memorial stated, "all our cane-mills were worked by water power; a stream which at the time kept ten or fifteen mills going would not now suffice to work even a single one."

In 1871 an exchange of views took place between the Government and the Chamber touching a scheme of irrigation by means of the waters of the Mare aux Vacoas, but the scheme came to nothing.

On a previous occasion, in reply to a Government query, the Chamber had pointed out that Rivière du Rempart was the district where irrigation could produce the most useful results; various difficulties, however, caused the project to be dropped. At the present time, more than fifty years after the first initiative taken by the Chamber, the Government is awaiting the arrival of an irrigation expert from India!

In spite of all mishaps and disasters—hurricanes, drought, cattle diseases, financial collapses, diseases of the cane, cholera, etc.—the Chamber remained untiring in the defence of the interests of the planters and of the colony in general.

In 1868 it went so far as to remonstrate with the Government on the inordinate amount of the public expenses! The colony had just been visited by a destructive hurricane, following upon an epidemic of fever, which had carried off thousands of people in the preceding year. The Government having at first paid no heed to the representations of the Chamber of Agriculture, Mr. MacPherson, a Scotchman by birth, owner of Cluny Sugar Estate, in the district of Grand Port, declared, at the meeting held on the 29th October, 1868, that, in these circumstances, the duty of the Chamber was to appeal not to the Governor nor the Secretary of State, but to the Queen herself, as Her Majesty would certainly entertain the just grievances of a people over-burdened with public obligations. There was no country in the world, he said, which proportionately had so enormous a public expenditure as Mauritius (£600,768 per annum).

The Secretary of State, on the other hand, having awakened to the gravity of the position, and being desirous of alleviating the burden of colonial liabilities, had requested the Lords of the Treasury to reduce the military contribution of Mauritius by £15,000 per annum during three years, but the request had been met with a blank refusal. It was on the announcement of this refusal that Mr. MacPherson suggested a direct petition to the Sovereign.

The newspapers then took up the agitation and advocated the idea of holding a vast public meeting. The Government realized that public feeling was becoming dangerously excited, and issued a proclamation appointing a committee, composed partly of official and partly of unofficial members, under the chairmanship of the Honble. C. Antelme, to investigate and report on such measures of retrenchment in public expenditure as might be conveniently carried out.

It is interesting to note that, among the steps advocated by the Chamber, it was suggested to make over the railways to a private company, "which would show a greater spirit of initiative than the Government." The Government, in reply, stated that they would favour the transfer of the railways to a company, but on condition, *inter alia*, that arrangements would be made for the repayment of the debentures; that the Crown Agents for the Colonies had, in fact, been instructed to accept any suitable offer, but that it might be detrimental to the credit of the colony to offer our railways for sale on the English market.

At the same time Mr. J. Yates Stevens, a former auditor of the Government railways, and some time connected with the management of an English railway company, in a letter dated 23rd May, 1868, unequivocally accused the Government of having made its own arrangements so as not to receive any offer.

The effects of this crisis, as of many others that Mauritius has undergone, passed away very rapidly, and

TROIS MAMELLES AND RÉUNION SUGAR FACTORY.

when the late Duke of Edinburgh visited the island in 1870, the Chamber could address His Royal Highness in these gratifying words: "Although of late years the agriculture and commerce have suffered severely from unforeseen calamities, Your Royal Highness visits the colony when our prospects are reviving."

About the same time (1st December, 1868) Dr. Icery, President of the Chamber of Agriculture, made to the Chamber an important communication on the subject of a new process of sugar manufacture by the use of mono-sulphite of lime, which he had lately adopted with success in his factory at La Gaîté (Flacq District). The subject excited much interest in all sugar-growing countries, and another member of the Chamber, Mr. (later Sir) Virgile Naz, was enabled to say that they had reason to feel proud that such cardinal improvements, of paramount importance to sugar manufacture, took their origin in Mauritius. Simultaneously, the transactions of the Chamber show that its members were giving attention to various other industrial problems of fundamental importance, *inter alia*, to the question of passing the cane megass through a second set of rollers—*i.e.*, double pressure. The matter had first been mentioned in the Chamber of Agriculture on the 9th April, 1857. Since then experiments had been made on several estates, with highly promising results.

The planter's life, as is well known, is not free from adversity; and of the difficulties which faced the sugar industry of Mauritius in the period with which we are dealing, none were more serious than those connected with the degeneracy of varieties of cane and the ravages of the *Borer*

Dealing with the first point, the Chamber at great cost imported new varieties of canes, and prevailed upon the Government to send the Director of Forests and Gardens, Dr. J. C. Meller, on a mission, with the object of procuring an extensive range of new specimens and creating a cane nursery at Pamplemousses Botanic Gardens. It may be of interest to remark, in passing, that these were the earliest Botanic Gardens founded in the tropics, having been created by *Intendant* Poivre in 1769.

It needed a hard fight on the part of the Chamber to bring about the mission entrusted to Dr. Meller. When the suggestion was first put forward (1862), the Government replied (7th May) that they were sceptical as to the results hoped for from the introduction of canes from abroad. As for the creation of a cane nursery in the Botanic Gardens, the Colonial Secretary intimated that the Gardens were designed to promote the introduction of "other plants" than those already existing in the colony, notably of "useful and ornamental trees." The Government's reply concluded with an expression of opinion that no appreciable results could be anticipated from the proposed scheme. After much controversy, however, the Chamber at length carried its point, and the Government, in 1868, agreed to send Dr. Meller on a mission for the purpose indicated.

[Photo by permission, Ladies' Fine Needlework Association.

SECTION OF MARE AUX VACOAS RESERVOIR.

Dr. Meller was a distinguished naturalist, and had been a companion of Livingstone in his travels in Africa, whence he had returned in a much impaired state of health. He, unfortunately, died in New South Wales in the course of his mission, at the early age of thirty-three, and his untimely end caused widespread regret among the planters of Mauritius, by whom he was held in high esteem. Yet he had had time to forward a number of important specimens, more especially from Penang. These were cultivated in the nursery at Pamplemousses Gardens, and we read in the President's report for 1875 that they produced "some of the cane varieties most successfully cultivated in Mauritius."

After Dr. Meller's death the Chamber prevailed on the Government to send out Mr. Caldwell, Assistant Colonial Secretary, who was a skilled botanist, and through him a good number of interesting new varieties were obtained. Then came the turn of Mr. J. M. Horne, most of whose highly interesting *Letters on Fiji* were addressed to the Chamber of Agriculture.

From the 13th April, 1869, when the first distribution of imported varieties of canes was made, to the end of December, 1875, the planters bought £3,890 worth of canes from the Pamplemousses Nursery. After meeting the expenses connected with the mission of Dr. Meller (£390), and of Mr. Caldwell (£565), the cost of cultivation, ground rent and water dues for irrigation of the nursery, there was left a profit of £1,600, out of which the Chamber voted a substantial remuneration to Mr. Horne, and presented Mr. Caldwell with a handsome cheque.

Many years previously (1850), the havoc done by the "white disease" in the sugar-cane had caused dismay, and the planters had chartered the ship *Reliance* to fetch from Batavia a full cargo of cane cuttings, obligingly sent by Mr. P. Diard, a Frenchman, then Inspector of Cultivations in Java.

The main trouble was now occasioned by the ravages of the *Borer* grub. So early as 1855 the Chamber had induced the Government to promise a sum of £2,000 as a reward for the discovery of an effective and reliable method of doing away with this pest. Hundreds of suggestions came from every quarter of the globe, and one of the competitors, Count Van Ranzow, of Java, set high influences at work, both in Holland and in England, in favour of his much-advertised process, consisting of an application of quicklime and arsenic; but none of the methods advocated was found to fulfil the object in view, and the prize was never awarded.

About the same period the practice was recommended by the Chamber, and generally adopted with fairly good results, of removing the straw from the growing canes when the latter had attained a certain size. As a means of obviating degeneracy in canes, we find in Sir Gabriel Fropier's report foı 1862 a recommendation to "exchange the plants from one district to another of different climate and soil properties." This measure had been advocated in 1847 by a distinguished foreign naturalist, Wenceslaus Bojer, who had settled in Mauritius. Since then the method has been from time to time *rediscovered* by many a leading agronomist in various parts of the world.

Among the canes imported at that time, mention may be made of the *Uba*, a "variety of no value," wrote Mr. Horne in 1870. Our friends in Natal are much mistaken when they say, according to a legend which is current in South Africa, that the name *Uba* was improvised in Durban on the receipt from overseas of a case of cane-tops, the label on which had been so much defaced that only the three letters U . . . B . . . A remained legible.

FILTER BEDS OF MARE AUX VACOAS RESERVOIR.

The Chamber also made representations to the Government on the need for an adequate control over the introduction from foreign parts of cane-tops, in view of the importation of the *Borer* grub through the medium of tops received from Ceylon. The circumstances of this unfortunate addition to local pests are worth recalling. In 1849 the ship *Elizabeth* arrived with cane-tops from Ceylon. These looked so seedy that the cases containing them were thrown overboard outside the harbour. A coasting schooner, belonging to Capt. the Hon. Wade West, on her way from Port Louis to Grand Baie, where Capt. West's estate was, picked up the cases, and on his arrival the skipper made a plantation of these tops. Soon after, the *Borer* showed itself at Grand Baie, created havoc in Capt. West's plantations, and thence spread over the whole island.

In reply to the Chamber's representations on this all-important subject, the Government merely stated that they were afraid they could render but little assistance in a matter which was one of "purely agricultural experience" (Colonial Secretary's letter of the 18th December, 1863).

Another important matter, of a different order, in which the Chamber showed great energy and perseverance, was that of the differential duties on sugar in England, established on the 9th May, 1854. In a Memorial addressed to Lord Stanley, then Secretary of State for the Colonies, in 1858, the Chamber observed that the imposition of such a tariff was in glaring opposition to the principles of Free Trade, and placed obstacles in the way of improvements in fabrication, as the enhancement of the duty on high-grade sugars made it more profitable to turn out a lower article. The inferior sugars from the West Indies were thus placed in possession of an undue advantage over our own high-class produce, and all the expenditure incurred by Mauritius planters, with a view to the constant improvement of the staple manufacture, was thus rendered unproductive. In a letter to Cobden (1st October, 1859) Sir Gabriel Fropier, addressing him as "the most illustrious advocate of commercial and industrial liberty throughout the world," was "ashamed to state" that our planters, on account of the duty, were compelled to debase their high-grade sugars by means of an admixture of low produce. It amounted, he said, to "putting a tax on progress and science." In conclusion, Sir Gabriel Fropier reminded Cobden that the latter had, two years previously, intimated to the Hon. C. Antelme, in London, that he might have taken up the matter in Parliament, had it not been for an unexpected dissolution.

In the same month the Chamber addressed a Memorial to the Duke of Newcastle, Secretary of State for the Colonies, on the same subject, reminding His Grace of the representations previously made, and insisting on the well-founded proposition set forth in the original Memorial of the 25th October, 1855, that such a tariff penalized the producer of good sugar fit for direct consumption. In 1862, in a fresh Memorial to the Secretary of State, the Chamber charged the Home Government with favouring those who "had shown less decision and enterprise" than the planters of Mauritius.

The Chamber of Agriculture had at the time in London a representative of high standing and distinguished merit, in the person of Mr. James Morris, some time Senior Professor of the Royal College, and brother of Dr. Morris, O.S.B., late Catholic Bishop of Port Louis. It would take many pages to record the numerous and excellent services rendered by this ardent friend of Mauritius, who looked upon himself as an adopted son of the island. His feelings were shared by his wife. When that large-hearted lady died, she left by her will a large sum to be permanently applied to charitable purposes in Mauritius. Mr. Morris, to whose memory more than this passing tribute should be due, was a man of vast learning and conspicuous ability; his equally distinguished wife, *née* Carolina Campbell, was, in addition to her numerous other attainments, a musician of unusual merit, and had been Music Mistress at Court.

Never had Mauritius a truer friend or more devoted champion of its interests than Mr. James Morris. His untiring efforts and the constant energy which he expended in our behalf were all the more admirable in view of his weakness of health. It is said of him that when he died, at the age of fifty-nine, he had never been a whole day without ailing; yet in him bodily weakness was overcome by extraordinary strength of will, and he achieved more than what many a stronger man would have been able to do.

"Our zealous agent and champion, Mr. J. Morris," wrote Sir Gabriel Fropier, in his presidential report for 1862, "had in the meanwhile ventilated the matter (*of differential tariff*) in England by every possible means at his disposal—the Press, public lectures, and official and private negotiations; and you will have noticed that, as the result of his efforts, the matter has moved forward appreciably, and we may now hope for a successful issue at no very distant time."

Mr. Morris waited in person on the chief statesmen of the time, and actively kept up the controversy in the leading London newspapers. He succeeded in quickening what he termed "the inert mass of public opinion," and in forming a group of merchants and City men, whom he introduced in deputation to Mr. Gladstone, then Chancellor of the Exchequer, with the result that Mr. Gladstone appointed a Committee to investigate and report upon the matter.

Cobden, in reply to pressing representations, wrote to Mr. James Morris that he "did not see *very clearly* how he could interfere in the matter." This astounding statement, under the pen of the Apostle of Free Trade, occurs in a letter dated Paris, 11th January, 1860. Unfortunately we have only a translation of it preserved in our printed records; the original perished in the fire of 1877, which destroyed a great part of the archives of the Chamber of Agriculture.

Mr. Stephen Cave, Chairman of the West India Committee, was secretly undermining our contentions. Mr. Morris cleverly compelled him to throw off the mask by writing a public letter inviting his support. The Hon. L. Arnaud wrote to the Chamber from London (25th May, 1862) that Mr. Cave was a man of distinguished parts and great energy; that Demerara was our chief opponent in the matter.

A keen fight was then set up between Mr. Cave and Mr. Morris, in which Mr. Morris showed the most admirable spirit and ability in the defence of his "dear adopted land." At the same time, he was constantly endeavouring to create an interest in the resources of Mauritius. On the 12th March, 1862, he lectured on Mauritius before the Royal Society of Arts, and his pamphlet, *Floreat Mauritia*, won him the coveted distinction of one of the Royal Society of Arts' annual prizes. Mr. Morris was also largely instrumental in bringing the question of our railway establishment to a successful issue; in the latter enterprise he shared with Dr. Ulcoq, one of the founders of the Chamber of Agriculture, the credit of having succeeded.

In the annual report for 1865 Dr. Icery, President of the Chamber, paid a high tribute to the eminent services rendered by Mr. Morris: "It was my privilege to see him at work in London, and I take great pleasure in stating that it would not have been possible for anyone to evince greater zeal, ability, and devotion to our interests than Mr. Morris did in carrying out the mission entrusted to him by this Chamber (*abolition of the preferential tariff*). Moreover, his intelligent endeavours to promote the interests of our colony, his perseverance in advocating all measures calculated either directly or indirectly to benefit our sugar industry, have long been appreciated by the members of the agricultural body."

It is matter for regret that considerations of space do not permit recording in this article the controversy which Mr. Morris had with the Commissioners of the London Exhibition of 1862 on the subject of our sugars—the "finest and the best," he wrote to them. The latter had been circumvented by Mr. Stephen Cave and other interested advocates of high duties on white sugars, and Mr. Morris, after a hard fight, finally carried his point by dint of energy and fearless perseverance. Never was Mauritius so prominently kept to the front of public attention in England as during the few years when Mr. Morris was our representative in London.

When he died—*multis flebilis ille bonis*—his distinguished widow acted, during the remainder of her own life, as correspondent of the Chamber in England, and acquitted herself with consummate ability and tact.

So early as 1855 Mr. Morris informed the Chamber from London that the supply of raw material for the manufacture of ropes and also of paper was steadily falling short of the demand, and suggested the utilization of our numerous textile plants. The Chamber, much impressed by Mr. Morris's communication, appointed a Committee to enquire into "the advantages of cultivating fibre plants in Mauritius." The Committee recommended that a prize of £1,000 be given for the introduction into the colony of an apparatus capable of turning out one hundred tons of good fibre in one year. Mr. Henry Labouchère, then Secretary of State for the Colonies, to whom the Governor transmitted the report, caused the Chamber of Agriculture to be informed, in reply, that "the Lords of the Treasury, to whom he had referred that document, were not of opinion that public funds could receive the proposed application."

About the same time an incident occurred which well illustrates the courageous and practical manner in which the Chamber of Agriculture has ever espoused the cause of the planters. Mauritius had been among the first countries in the world to recognise the agricultural value of Peruvian guano. A first trial was made in 1843, and so early as 1850 this guano was in favour on all estates. The subjoined figures, showing the increasing imports of Peruvian guano from 1851 to 1855, are all the more significant if it be noted that the total area under cane was then barely, if at all, in excess of 80,000 arpents (1 arpent = 1·043 acre):

	Tons guano.		Tons guano.
1851	8,229	1853	4,656
1852	10,980	1854	11,708
1855	30,169		

giving a total of 65,742 tons, or a yearly average of 13,148 tons.

On the other hand, the total sugar output of the island and its general imports show the following progress during the decade 1849-1858:—

	Sugar exported.		Sugar exported.
1850	lbs. 110,937,000	1853	lbs. 184,024,000
1851	„ 133,329,000	1854	„ 170,623,000
1855	lbs. 253,892,000		

General Imports.

1849	£719,000	1854	£1,269,000
1850	909,000	1856	1,430,000
1853	1,092,000	1858	2,089,000

It is worthy of note that the figures of general imports for 1854 show no decline, in spite of the terrible epidemic of cholera which took place in that year, an epidemic so deadly that the *Government Gazette* of the 12th June, 1854, published the text of a special prayer to be recited all over the island, imploring God's mercy on Mauritius.

No doubt the constant stream of Indian immigration, enhancing the labour facilities of the sugar industry, accounted in a measure for the rapid economic development evidenced by the above figures; yet there can be no doubt as to the fact that the application of guano was the chief factor in the steady and marked increase of the sugar output, by giving the necessary stimulus to vegetation in the higher plateaux, where cane cultivation had hitherto proved unremunerative.

Now, in 1857, just when the use of guano was most widespread in the island, a curious incident occurred. Through some misunderstanding, or otherwise, the planters were charged with having conspired to keep down the prices of this fertilizer, and the Peruvian Government threatened to prohibit exports of it to Mauritius. The Chamber at once took up the matter and memorialized the Home Government, proving the utter groundlessness of the accusation launched against the planters, and requesting the intervention of the Foreign Office. In this Memorial facts were adduced showing that, far from any artificial depreciation having been compassed in Mauritius, Peruvian guano was actually made the subject of keen speculation, prices having rapidly passed from $60 to $75 and $80 per ton. In one instance, Messrs. Blyth Bros. & Co., an English firm trading in Port Louis, being unable to meet the demands of their clients out of the limited stock in their hands, had put up the lot to auction, when it had fetched $102 per ton. Other sales were made at prices ranging from $90 to $120.

The late SIR CELICOURT ANTELME, K.C.M.G., Chevalier de la Légion D'Honneur.

The Memorial pointed out that what the planters of Mauritius required, in this matter, was equal treatment with the farmers of Great Britain, and that they offered to take yearly a certain stock at a fixed price. These representations were backed in London by several Mauritians then resident in England, headed by the Hon. Mr. Guthrie, a leading estate owner, and Chairman of the Mauritian Association in London.

Finally, the planters gained their point, and, as the result of representations made by H.M. Chargé d'Affaires at Lima, the shipments of guano to Mauritius were soon resumed.

We may add, for the sake of completeness, that the use of guano in Mauritian agriculture was first initiated by Messrs. Henry Barlow, Frederick Dick, and H. Gonin. The former two gentlemen were English merchants and planters in Mauritius; the last-named, a Mauritian by birth, was at the time a leading lawyer. He subsequently entered into the religious life, became a most distinguished and pious Dominican, and died Archbishop of Trinidad.

At the same time, it may be mentioned that consignments of Peruvian guano formed the medium for the introduction of a large and peculiarly voracious red ant, which long remained an object of execration to grocers and housewives alike.

It is hardly necessary to state that the Chamber had more than once to defend the interests of the planters in the matter of Indian immigration. So early as 1859, in a Memorial addressed to the Duke of Newcastle, then Secretary of State for the Colonies, the Chamber felt called upon to explain the true position of the Indian labourers in Mauritius. "The Indian immigrants, who make up the agricultural population of this island," the Memorial stated, "are as well treated and as contented as the most favoured of agricultural workers in any other part of the world. Owing both to local custom and to the special laws passed for their protection, these people enjoy a better guarantee of fair treatment than could be dreamed of by the corresponding class in England. None of these immigrants could ever have aspired to an equal share of well-being in his country of origin; in a word, it was an act of real kindness to have given these men an opportunity of leaving their native villages and emigrating to our shores. On the other hand, the facilities thus afforded to the Indian immigrants imply no detriment to the Creole natives, as the latter have no inclination to cultivate the soil; those of them who are employed on the estates work as mechanics, etc., and, in these capacities, receive higher wages than those given to the Indian labourers."

Yet, at a meeting held on the 13th November, 1871, the Chamber of Agriculture felt impelled to call upon the Governor, the Hon. Sir A. Hamilton Gordon (later Lord Stanmore), either to express repudiation of the aspersions made on the planters by a foreign adventurer named Von Plevitz, or else to request the appointment of a Royal Commission to inquire into the allegations contained in a document which Mr. MacPherson did not hesitate publicly to describe as "the miserable libel written by Plevitz."

In the course of the debate which took place at the Chamber on that occasion, the Hon. Célicourt Antelme (later Sir Célicourt Antelme, K.C.M.G.) quoted the opinion of the celebrated Dr. Livingstone on the treatment of Indian immigrants in Mauritius. While in London on a mission entrusted to him by the Chamber, he had sought the opinion of the great traveller and philanthropist on the subject. Dr. Livingstone had then stated in a letter to Mr. Antelme that "not only were the Indians well treated in Mauritius, but they were much happier there than in their native land." Dr. Livingstone had spent two months in Mauritius, where he had been the guest of Major-General Hay, Acting Governor, at Government House, "Le Réduit." He had arrived from Kilimane (12th August, 1856) in H.M. brig *Frolic*, commanded by Commodore (then Captain) Peyton, R.N., and before leaving he presented the Botanic Gardens at Pamplemousses with seeds of many interesting African plants.

This was a troubled period in the history of Mauritius. The Secretary of State had meanwhile been informed of the incident, and, a few weeks later, at a dinner at Government House, presumably given for the purpose, the Governor drew aside the Hon. J. Currie, President of the Chamber of Agriculture, and stated that, as regarded repudiating the allegations made by Plevitz, it was difficult for him to do what the Chamber had desired, but that he thought it his duty to caution the planters against the agitation which investigation by a Commission of Inquiry might create among the population. He gave Mr. Currie to understand that he was prepared to make certain declarations and give certain assurances, and begged him privately to ascertain the views held by members of the Chamber. That body assembled on the 18th March, 1872, and declined to reconsider the position it had taken up. The members were remarkably outspoken. Mr. Edward Hart said the Governor had failed to do justice to the agricultural interest; Mr. MacPherson stated that His Excellency had tried to discredit the laws of the colony; the Hon. Virgile Naz asserted that Sir Arthur Gordon had not arrived at an impartial decision; while Mr. Louis Rouillard (a distinguished member of the Chamber and later one of its Presidents) pointed out that the Secretary of State (Lord Kimberley) had made a vain attempt to uphold, at the same time, both the views expressed by the Governor and those held by the Chamber.

The late SIR VIRGILE NAZ, K.C.M.G.

In the end, the Royal Commission was appointed and came to Mauritius. The two Commissioners, Messrs. Frere and Williamson, appear to have been gentlemen of a somewhat suspicious and irritable disposition, and it certainly taxed all the powers of persuasion and the unrivalled knowledge of the subject of the Hon. Virgile Naz (later Sir Virgile Naz, K.C.M.G.), to dispel some of their prejudices and bring them round to a clearer perception of the merits of the case. Twenty years afterwards, when speaking on the subject of Indian immigration in the Chamber of Agriculture (on the 16th November, 1891), Sir Virgile Naz made the following remarks: "It is needless at this time to refer to the details of that inquiry. Yet, out of mere regard for truth, I am compelled to say that it was not always conducted in the proper spirit. I had the honour, which I shared with other gentlemen, members of this Chamber, to assist in dispelling certain misunderstandings and in defending the colony against unjust accusations. Unfortunately, the Chairman of the Commission was stricken by disease during his stay in Mauritius, and, in his long report of 592 quarto pages, more than one passage still bears the trace of the nervous irritability from which he suffered."

Sir Virgile Naz was kindness itself, and was as just as he was kind; and the irony and censure underlying the above words, even in such studiously mild form, are a proof that the manner in which the Commission did its appointed work was open to serious criticism in more respects than one.

Later, Sir Arthur Hamilton Gordon, who had meanwhile been created Baron Stanmore, became a firm friend of Mauritius, and even acted as the representative of the Chamber of Agriculture while the question of the sugar bounties was under discussion at home. Once the differences which had arisen were over, the Plevitz affair was settled and forgotten, he seemed anxious to carry out the undertakings given when, on his first arrival in Mauritius, he had replied (31st January, 1871) to the address of welcome presented by the Chamber of Agriculture, in the following terms: "Moved by the same spirit and pursuing the same object, we will work in hearty and ever-increasing harmony, for the French blood which has for centuries flowed in the veins of my ancestors binds me by a special tie to a country where I find so numerous and influential a population of French origin."

It is worthy of note that, even while the Commission of Inquiry was sitting in Mauritius, certain attacks were publicly made in London on the colony. These were easily refuted by certain distinguished Englishmen well acquainted with the island, amongst them being Bishop Ryan, Messrs. Anderson and Sandwith, the latter an eminent naturalist and some time Colonial Secretary of Mauritius.

While the inquiry was in progress, the Chamber of Agriculture was represented before the Commission by two brilliant young lawyers, Mr. W. Newton (now Sir William Newton, K.C.) and Mr. G. Guibert (now a K.C.). In his presidential address for 1872, Mr. J. Currie said of these two gentlemen: "I need not add that this mission has been fulfilled by them with perfect tact and discretion, and that, in every circumstance, this Chamber was worthily represented by them."

In the course of time Sir William Newton, having himself engaged in sugar growing, became a prominent member of the Chamber of Agriculture. He was President of this body when, in consequence of the political crisis which had resulted in the suspension of Governor Sir John Pope Hennessy, he was entrusted with an important public mission to England. He naturally acted at the same time as Delegate of the Chamber of Agriculture, and, in that capacity, he succeeded in persuading the Secretary of State to authorize the establishment, at the expense of the planters, of the Station Agronomique, the creation of which he had himself advocated some time previously in a pamphlet on the sugar crisis. When that pamphlet was read before the Chamber on the 22nd January, 1885, Mr. J. Currie, one of the oldest and most distinguished members, voiced the general feeling by observing that "it would be difficult to find a more remarkable or more complete work."

This work had first been submitted to the Council of Government on the 13th February, 1885, and the Council had given an unanimous vote in favour of awarding a suitable prize for a prompt and economic method of extraction, permitting a larger percentage of both juice and sugar being recovered from the available contents of the cane. The matter was subsequently referred home by the Government, and, upon consultation, Sir Joseph Hooker, of Kew Gardens, deprecated the advertising of such prizes to inventors, as they were generally found to appeal chiefly to the "least practical and most visionary class of inventors."

On his return to Mauritius Sir William Newton, who had been worthily replaced during his absence by the Hon. Henri Leclézio (now C.M.G.), replied in the following terms to an address of welcome presented by his colleagues of the Chamber of Agriculture: "I had no difficulty in persuading the Secretary of State to accede to our representations, and for the ease with which I succeeded in carrying that point I am indebted to yourselves. I was listened to with attention, because I had the honour to speak on behalf of an institution which, whatever may have been said by some people, is acknowledged to have rendered, and to be still rendering, the greatest service to the sugar industry, and therefore possesses a considerable and well-merited influence." And Sir William Newton read out the following letter, which had been addressed to him by Sir Henry Holland (later, Lord Knutsford), then Secretary of State for the Colonies:—

DEAR MR. NEWTON, *10th May, 1887.*

I am gratified that the Chamber of Agriculture are satisfied with the action taken upon the representations brought by you on their behalf under my notice.

I can assure them, through you, that I am quite alive to the importance of these representations, which will continue to receive my very careful consideration.

Believe me, etc.,

(Signed) H. HOLLAND.

The "representations" in question dealt mainly with the creation of the Station Agronomique, and with the need of some official action from London to rebut the libellous stories then circulated in India in relation to the alleged use of animal charcoal in the manufacture of our sugars.

Although the space allotted to the present article does not enable us to deal exhaustively with the all-important question of indentured labour, the following remarks, quoted from the address delivered before the Chamber by Sir Virgile Naz in 1891, will be found interesting, as giving an exact insight into the real position of affairs. What Sir Virgile Naz could say with justice in 1891 applies with still greater force to the present circumstances :—

"If we deduct," he said, "the decrepit men from the number of old immigrants, and the children from the Indo-Mauritians—if, moreover, we make due allowance for the percentage of vagrants and more or less incorrigible idlers—the number of efficient grown-up labourers will be found to be far from exceeding the manifold labour requirements of the colony. Apart from the workers indentured on the estates, the cultivation of vegetables and fruit, the production of milk, and the hawking of all these necessaries of life, are

INDIANS AND THEIR HUTS AT ANTOINETTE SUGAR ESTATE, RIVIÈRE DU REMPART.

exclusively in the hands of the Indian population. Without them, the prices of vegetables, fruit, milk, etc., would rise considerably, and the cost of living in Mauritius would become much greater. As carters, cabmen, and in cognate capacities, the Indians play a most useful part, and can claim credit for the cheapening of the cost of transport. The same people form the vast majority of domestic servants and washermen throughout the island. It cannot, therefore, be contended that those of the Indians who are not employed on the estates (leaving out, of course, the vagrants and habitual idlers) constitute a burden on the Colonial Treasury, or even that those people do not fulfil a useful part in life. During the past years, a very large number of them have become landowners or lessees of agricultural lands. . . . . The best proof of the proposition that the supply of efficient agricultural labour is in no wise in excess of the requirements may be found in the fact that, in spite of the favourable treatment indisputably extended by the estate owners to their own labourers, and in spite of their preference for men already acclimatized and used to the work to be done on estates, the planters find it impossible locally to procure the labour they absolutely require, and are compelled each year to resort to the importation of new immigrants, although the latter, through desertion, disease and lack of experience of sugar estate works, cost much more than old immigrants and are a frequent cause of annoyance to their employers."

The immigration of indentured labourers was abruptly discontinued in 1910, in consequence of the report of the Committee presided over by Lord Sanderson. The recommendations made by that Committee were themselves based on incomplete knowledge of the subject and erroneous evidence. Mainly through the exertions of the Hon. Henri Leclézio, C.M.G., who has laboured untiringly and with singular ability to dispel the ignorant prejudice with which the matter was wrapped up, and thanks also to the enlightened impartiality of His Excellency Major Sir John Robert Chancellor, R.E., C.M.G., D.S.O., the present Governor of Mauritius, there are now good grounds for hoping that immigration will soon be resumed on a scale sufficient to meet the legitimate exigencies of the sugar and other industries of this colony.

The foregoing remarks will, it is hoped, have shown conclusively that the Chamber of Agriculture, during the sixty years it has been in existence, has been unremitting in its efforts to defend the agricultural interests of the island, and that it has keenly interested itself in the possibilities of every agricultural industry attempted in Mauritius.

Among the numerous subject-matters of discussions, lectures and reports of which a record is found in its Minutes of Proceedings, we meet with the following: Vanilla, aloe, tobacco, forage and rotation crops, foodstuffs, cocoa-nut (so early as 1859), coffee, silkworms, epizooty, diseases of plants, tramways (so early as 1858), fertilizers, the rice supply, the manufacture of paper from cane-megass (1862), pollution of streams, irrigation, agricultural chemistry, loans on standing crops, telephone extension over the rural districts, railway tariffs, immigration, vagrancy, reafforestation, etc.

In 1875 the Colonial Secretary and the Procureur-General attended a meeting of the Chamber and invited an expression of its opinion on the most important question of changing the money standard.

In 1856, in deference to representations made by the Chamber, the Government suggested to Dr. C. Meldrum, then Professor of Mathematics in the Royal College, the formation of a class for natural history and agricultural chemistry in that institution.

The Chamber of Agriculture, after creating its own laboratory of microbiology on a small scale, was largely instrumental in the establishment of the Colonial Laboratory of Bacteriology, founded after the introduction, through the steamer *Naseri*, from India, in 1901, of a most destructive and ruinous cattle-plague known under the name of "Surra."

It took a keen and practical interest in the question of imposing countervailing duties on sugar in India, and petitioned Queen Victoria in this vital matter. At the meeting of the Chamber on that historic occasion, Mr. Quintin Hogg, a distinguished planter of Demerara, then a visitor to Mauritius, was present as a guest, and delivered an interesting address (27th October, 1898).

Among other distinguished persons whom the Chamber of Agriculture has had the honour of receiving as its guests, allusion may be made to Mr. Hubert de Lisle, Governor of Réunion, to whom a banquet was given in 1855; Mr. Diard, Superintendent of Agriculture in Java (1858), who, a few years previously, had rendered inestimable service by sending, on board the ship *Reliance* chartered by the planters, a shipment of upwards of a million cuttings of sugar canes, at a time when all the varieties locally cultivated were dying away; Mr. Minchin, manager of the *Aska* Factory (Madras Presidency), who read a paper on the diffusion process in 1882; Herr Herbst, an eminent German botanist, who came to us in 1858 from Rio de Janeiro with a large collection of Brazilian plants contained in glass cases—a present from the Emperor of Brazil, who requested to be favoured in return with cuttings from our best varieties of sugar-cane, etc. Without being ungracious, it is permissible to suppose that with these new plants we received into the colony many a new insect pest, so that the gain was not always on our side.

It is worthy of note—and it may be said without undue boasting—that the Government never had cause to regret having followed the advice of the Chamber of Agriculture on any subject on which that body was competent to give an opinion or enter a protest; and instances are not wanting, on the other hand, of the detriment that has more than once resulted from setting aside its well-founded observations. A case in point is that of the introduction of the mongoose, now a most serious pest in Mauritius. When consulted about the expediency of importing mongooses from India with a view to destroying the rats, the Chamber, on the

16th March, 1899, by a large majority deprecated the experiment. The Government disregarded the advice, and a certain number of mongooses—*a few males*, it was stated with the usual official dogmatism—were imported and let loose for purposes of experiment. These *few males* bred with prodigious rapidity; their descendants now overrun the whole island, and, having naturally discovered a more toothsome prey than the rat, turn by preference to partridges, quails, hares, pigeons and chickens. The Government has now for several years been giving rewards for their destruction, and a few thousand rupees go out of the Colonial Treasury each year on this item, while small game continues to diminish in number at a disquieting rate.

For many years the Chamber of Agriculture had been advocating the establishment of an organized Bureau of Agriculture in Mauritius. A formal resolution to that effect was adopted on the motion of Mr. G. Regnard, and at a meeting held on the 16th August, 1906, the Hon. C. Dumat said: "Our main object should now be the following up of the idea put forward by our colleague, Mr. Regnard, *i.e.*, the creation of

IMMIGRATION SQUARE, PORT LOUIS.

a Department of Agriculture." Some delay was caused by a reference to Sir Daniel Morris, who had been requested to "recommend a botanist," and who (30th March, 1907) replied that the only suitable person he could recommend was Mr. F. A. Stockdale, but that he was himself in need of the services of that gentleman and could not possibly spare him. Finally, it is Mr. F. A. Stockdale himself who has just taken up the organization of the Department.

Yet, apart from the serious difficulties which arose under the governorship of Sir Arthur Hamilton Gordon, and a few minor skirmishes with some of his predecessors and successors, the relations between the Chamber of Agriculture and the Governors of Mauritius have on the whole been friendly and even cordial. A most popular Governor with the planters was Sir William Stevenson, K.C.B., himself a colonial by birth, having been born in Jamaica. His genial manner and sterling honesty endeared him in a peculiar degree to the planters. He died at "Le Réduit," on the 9th January, 1863, and his demise was widely and sincerely mourned in Mauritius. A handsome bronze statue of him, the masterly work of a distinguished Mauritian sculptor (Prosper d'Epinay), now stands in the courtyard of Government House, Port Louis, having been erected by public subscription in the island.

A few weeks before his sudden and untimely death, Sir William Stevenson, in reply to the congratulations of the Chamber of Agriculture on the birth of his son, said (1st December, 1862) that the child could learn "to glory in looking upon himself as a true Mauritian," and that the auspicious event to which they referred would tend to enhance the constant interest which he took in everything that concerned this island. On the 22nd January, 1863, it was Lady Stevenson's sad duty to reply to an address of condolence from the Chamber on the sudden death of her distinguished husband. Her reply showed a spirit of fortitude worthy of ancient Rome. The main object of her life, she said, would thenceforth be to ensure that her infant son, should God be pleased to spare him, should follow in the footsteps of his father; her most ardent desire would be to inspire in him the most earnest and lively sentiments towards this island of his birth, and towards its inhabitants, who had evinced so much respect for the memory of his father, and so much sympathy and kindness to his widow and orphan child.

This child (Francis Seymour Stevenson) has now had a distinguished career in England. He sat in the House of Commons for North-East Suffolk from 1885 to 1906, and is well known as the writer of standard historical works: *Historic Personality*, *Life of Robert Grosseteste*, etc. He has just published a *History of Montenegro* (Jarrold and Sons). His Declaration of Birth states that he was born at Moka, Island of Mauritius, on the 24th November, 1862, the son of Sir William Stevenson, K.C.B., and of Carolina Olivia Briscoe, his wife; the witnesses being Captain William Plumer Gaskell, A.D.C., 24th Regiment, and Surgeon-Major Francis (later Sir Francis) Reid, M.D., 2nd Batt. 5th Fusiliers. Sir Francis Reid was subsequently Chief Medical Officer of Mauritius. Curiously enough, the name of Lady Stevenson was wrongly given in the Declaration of Birth, and certain formalities had to be gone through in order to rectify the error and alter the name *Carolina Olivia Briscoe*, as originally registered, to *Carolina Octavia Briscoe*.

As already stated, the relations between the Chamber and the Government have, on the whole, been friendly and cordial. It is pleasing to note, at the same time, that the Governors of Mauritius have more than once placed on record their appreciation of the spirit of industry and enterprise, and of the fortitude and resourcefulness, exhibited by the planters of Mauritius in the face of numerous mishaps and even disasters.

In an Administrative Report, dated the 10th July, 1864, Sir Henry Barkly, K.C.B., wrote: "I cannot refrain from describing the first impression produced on my mind by my introduction to Mauritius. It is one, in the main, of unbounded surprise and admiration. That such a mere speck on the ocean should have become the most prosperous and important of the sugar-growing colonies of the British Crown, that an area of scarcely 400,000 acres should, through the enterprise and industry of its inhabitants, annually export from two to three million pounds of produce, are facts well worthy of attention."

It may be remarked that at that time the average sugar output of the colony was 190 tons per square mile, and that this has now attained to 350 tons—an average far ahead of that of Barbadoes (181 tons), Martinique (92 tons), Porto-Rico (80 tons), Hawaii (75 tons), etc.

Sir George Bowen, K.C.M.G., in the course of a paper read before the Royal Colonial Institute (18th April, 1882), said: "With regard to its colonial importance, I need only remark that the public revenue of this little island, which is not larger than a simple average-sized English county, amounts to above £750,000—that is, it is equal to what was the public revenue of the entire kingdom of England in the reign of Charles II. Moreover, the trade of Mauritius, including exports and imports, amounts in value to £6,000,000 sterling yearly—that is, it is equal to the entire trade of Great Britain in the reign of Queen Anne. . . . I think that all will agree that the facts which I have mentioned amply prove the importance of Mauritius . . . . as, for its size, the richest colony of the Empire—perhaps the richest country in the world of similar extent."

Sir George Bowen proceeded to relate that, on his arrival in Paris in the preceding year, the Mauritians then residing in that city had entertained him at "a very brilliant public banquet. The toasts and speeches were all in French; but, when the health of the Queen was proposed, Her Majesty's loyal Mauritian subjects made the gilded and vaulted roof of the great hall of the Hôtel du Louvre, where the banquet was held, ring with cheers as enthusiastic as could be heard in Canada or in Australia. The demonstration made a deep impression in Paris, and especially on the leading French statesmen. One of them (the great Gambetta) remarked to me that 'we in France see that England is indeed a great colonising power when it can make the French in Mauritius so loyal to its Crown and Government.'"

Speaking of the Labour Law, proposed and carried by his immediate predecessor, Lieut.-General Sir Arthur P. Phayre, K.C.M.G., K.C.S.I., C.B., and brought into full operation under his auspices, Sir George said: "I wish to bear my testimony publicly, not only to the loyal co-operation of the entire body, but to the sincere desire of the planters generally, to go even beyond the proposals of the Government in securing the welfare and comfort of the Indian labourers."

Sir Henry Barkly was present and said: "I shall never cease to remember the courage and equanimity with which the planters of Mauritius bore up against the almost overwhelming misfortunes which seemed at one time to threaten them with ruin; nor shall I ever forget the many kind friends with whom I became acquainted during my six years' residence on that beautiful and romantic island."

It was in the course of a speech delivered on the same occasion that Sir George Bowen recalled an interesting historical fact, which it may not be out of place to mention here. It was through the merest accident that the "Iron Duke" (then Sir Arthur Wellesley) did not come to us as the first English Governor of Mauritius in 1810. Sir Arthur Wellesley, who held a command in India at the time, was appointed by his brother the Viceroy "to command the expedition and, after the conquest, to be the first English Governor of Mauritius." A sudden and dangerous attack of fever compelled Sir Arthur Wellesley to return home, where other and more momentous enterprises lay in store for him.

BACTERIOLOGICAL LABORATORY, RÉDUIT.

In an address given before the Scottish Geographical Society (January, 1908), Sir Charles Bruce, K.C.M.G., also a former Governor, said: "When the Prince of Wales returned from his colonial tour, he declared with perfect felicity of phrase that Mauritius had preserved many charming characteristics of Old France."

But the encomium does not come from Governors alone. In *A Transport Voyage to Mauritius* (Murray, 1851), the supposed work of Capt. Wallond, the planters are described thus: ". . . . To the natural civility of the French manner, the *habitants* (planters) of the island have added a frankness and *bonhomie* peculiarly their own. Unlike the farmers of other countries, the Creole Frenchman is always a gentleman. . . ." Of the natural scenery of the island, the same author writes: "The scenery of Port Louis harbour is very beautiful, and of a character totally unlike anything in Europe."

This leads us to recall the remarks made by the great Darwin: "29th April, 1836.—In the morning we passed round the northern end of Mauritius, or the Isle of France. From this point of view the aspect of the island equalled the expectations raised by the many well-known descriptions of its beautiful scenery. . . . The whole island, with its sloping border and central mountains, was adorned with an air of perfect elegance; the scenery, if I may use such an expression, appeared to the sight harmonious."

In conclusion, we may be allowed to quote the following passage of *Floreat Mauritia*, by that eminent friend of Mauritius and the Mauritians, James Morris:—

"The beauty of Mauritius as an island has long been proverbial. . . . Every traveller has been enchanted with the loveliness and picturesqueness of its scenery. . . . In no colony is civilization and intellectual pursuits more vividly prominent. . . ."

Speaking of the Chamber of Agriculture, after mentioning the various public bodies, he states: "This is one of the most important bodies in the island, and its members are men of large landed property, and of great experience, who naturally, having the real welfare of the colony at heart, interest themselves zealously in all that concerns the agriculture of the colony, Indian immigration, and all those questions which have such necessary relation to the best and most scientific cultivation of the sugar-cane, and its after-manipulation into sugar."

THE SUGAR INDUSTRY.

By A. WALTER, F.R.A.S., Director of the Royal Alfred Observatory.

THE cultivation of the sugar-cane in Mauritius, commercially speaking, dates from the administration of La Bourdonnais, who took over the reins of government for the French East India Company in 1735.

The cane appears to have been introduced by the Dutch at a very early period of their colonisation, but the necessity for the production of food-stuffs, such as rice, maize, corn and other grains, together with the immense profits derived from the cultivation of various spices, indigo, etc., and the exploitation of the ebony forests, retarded the development of an industry in which the manufacturing methods were extremely primitive.

In 1776 the colony possessed only three sugar factories; in 1789 the production amounted to 600,000 lbs. of sugar, and in 1816 had risen to 8,858,600 lbs. (French), harvested from about 11,688 acres, according to the statistics published by Baron d'Unienville.

The condition of the other crops will be gathered from the following *résumé* :—

	Arpents.	lbs.
Cotton ...	5,631	259,750
Coffee ...	2,449	324,450
Indigo ...	388	11,700
Cloves ...	1,194	66,400
Grains ...	24,318	11,376,075
Others ...	33,397	450,000

From the date of the British occupation in 1810 up to the epidemic of malarial fever in 1867, the output of sugar rose steadily to a normal yield of nearly 130,000 metric tons (260,000 000 lbs.). With the temporary abandonment of the low-lying estates and the extension of cane cultivation to the higher and cooler regions, there was a decided decrease in the total yield of sugar, and the industry appears to have stagnated for many years under the adverse conditions which originated with the over-production of the bounty-fed Continental beet sugars. The terrible cyclone of 1892, fearful as its immediate consequences were, marked the commencement of a new era in the industrial life of the colony. The rebuilding of the damaged mills, with money obtained at a relatively low rate of interest, offered exceptional opportunities to the planters, of which the great majority were not slow to take advantage. The normal output of sugar, which had fallen to 120,000 tons, and had remained at this low ebb for the previous twenty-five years, rose steadily between 1892 and 1909 to the phenomenal yield of nearly 250,000 tons. The variation in the total yield of sugar will be more readily appreciated with the aid of the accompanying diagram.

The Exportation of Sugar from Mauritius for each year from 1810 to 1910.

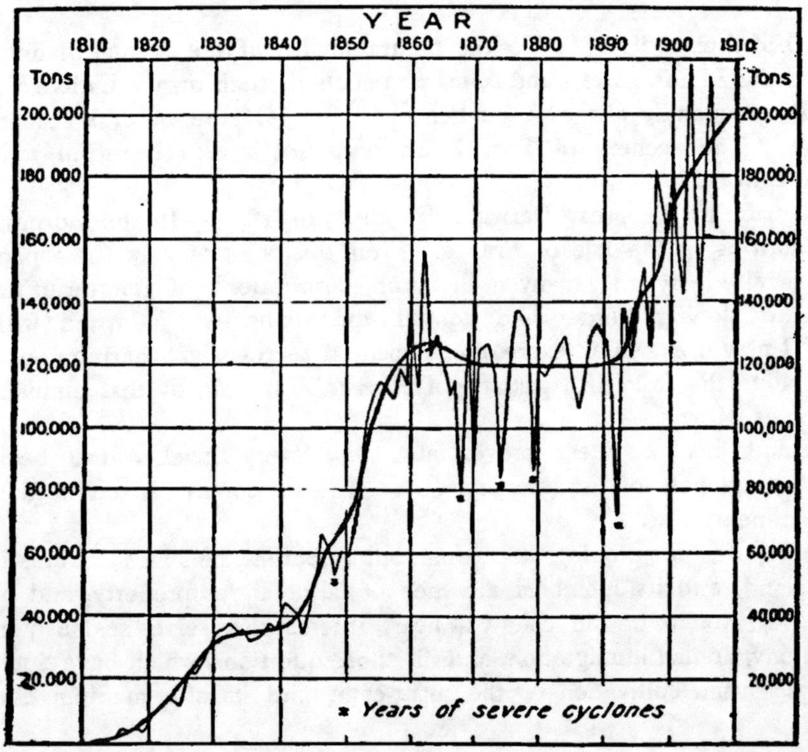

SOME REPRESENTATIVES OF THE SUGAR INDUSTRY.

1. EDGAR DE ROCHECOUSTE, Proprietor of Rich-en-Eau Estate and Factory, Grand Port.
2. BARON D'UNIENVILLE, Proprietor of La Lucie Estate, Flacq.
3. HENRI HAREL, Manager of Belle Vue (Mauricia) Estate and Factory, Pamplemousses.
4. A. J. WILSON, Proprietor of Bel Air Estate and Factory, Savanne.
5. ARTHUR J. BROAD, General Manager in Mauritius of the Mauritius Estates and Assets Company, Limited.
6. The Hon. J. J. GIBSON, General Manager in Mauritius of the Anglo-Ceylon and General Estates Company, Limited.
7. The Hon. GASTON ANTELME, Manager of Stanley Estate, Plaines Wilhems.
8. RAOUL RAFFRAY, Manager of Medine Estate and Factory, Black River.
9. W. DESPLACES, Manager of Beau Champ Estate, Factory, and Annexes, Flacq.
10. T. W. INNES, Manager of Britannia Estate and Factory, Savanne.
11. PAUL ADAM, Manager of Mon Loisir Estate and Factory, Rivière du Rempart.

THE CULTIVATED AREAS.

The Island of Mauritius is of volcanic origin. In appearance it forms a rough triangle with its apex toward the north. The central plain, bounded on the north and south by rugged mountain ridges, rises in the vicinity of Curepipe to a height of 1,800 feet.

From Curepipe toward the east an irregular range of mountains, known as the Bambou Range, runs right up to the sea and forms the principal water-shed, while from the Moka Range, which constitutes the northern boundary of the central plateau, the land slopes gradually to the coast toward the north. As a consequence of this distribution of the mountain ridges and the direction of the prevailing wind, the northern districts of Pamplemousses and Rivière du Rempart, and certain portions of Black River, are badly served by the river system, thus determining in great measure the distribution of the cultivated areas.

Originally the whole island was under forests, which, either for the exploitation of the valuable essences they contained, or to permit the extension of cane cultivation, have gradually dwindled down to a bare 60,000 arpents at the present day.

The progress of deforestation and the corresponding extension of the cultivated areas will be gathered from the following table:—

Date.	Area under Forests.
1753	406,157
1770	388,705
1836	300,000
1846	142,000
1874	85,526
1880	35,000

In addition to the main water-shed, the island is divided naturally into thirteen minor river systems, and it has been found convenient, in dealing with agricultural questions, to refer them to these divisions. The first, which includes the districts of Pamplemousses and Rivière du Rempart, has an area of 56,000 arpents (excluding mountain and river reserves), of which about 26,000 are uncultivated, but capable of being cultivated. The area under cane is about 30,000 arpents; while of the 26,000 arpents uncultivated the greater part is either under wild aloes (*fourcroya gigantea*) or kept as a fuel and fodder reserve.

The uncultivated soil is of a gravellous nature, and for the most part quite unsuitable for cane cultivation, although other crops requiring less water appear to grow well. The average yield from this area varies from twelve to twenty-four tons per arpent.

Area No. 2 includes a large portion of the district or Flacq, about 46,000 arpents in extent, of which, approximately, 17,000 arpents are under cane and 10,000 uncultivated, but capable of being cultivated. About one-sixth of the total area (7,500 lying near the coast of Quatre Cocos) consists of rock or sand, while half of the uncultivated area of 10,000 arpents is kept as a fuel and fodder reserve. The average yield of cane from this area varies from about eleven to twenty-four and a half tons per arpent.

Area No. 3 is a small section of nearly 9,000 arpents, of which about 3,500 arpents are under cane and about 1,500 still capable of being cultivated. On the remaining land, the soil is shallow and rocky. The average yield of cane is high, from twenty to twenty-four tons per arpent.

Area No. 4 is bounded on the south by the Bambou Range. It has an extent of about 46,000 arpents, with nearly 15,000 under cane; about 8,000 arpents are uncultivated, but capable of bearing cane. The higher portions, amounting to a quarter of the whole area, the climate of which is cold and damp, consist of Crown Lands, while the soil along the valley known as Quatre Sœurs is "black soil"; both areas are unsuitable for cane cultivation. The general average yield in this section is also high, giving about twenty-three tons of cane per arpent.

Areas Nos. 5 and 6.—These two most important cane-bearing districts comprise the whole of Grand Port and a large portion of Savanne. The total extent is about 106,000 arpents, of which at least 45,000 are under cane and 16,000 capable of being brought under cane. About one-eighth of Area No. 5 possesses a black soil in the portion known as Vieux Grand Port, and is quite unsuitable for cane cultivation, while all the upper portion of both sections has a very heavy rainfall. The general average yield per arpent is about twenty-three tons.

Areas Nos. 7 to 10, inclusive, forming the south-eastern portion of Savanne and the southern portion of Black River are, for the most part, mountainous and rugged. Nearly all the large estates have been parcelled out to peasant proprietors. About half of No. 9 is either under permanent forest or possesses a stiff black clay soil, while practically the whole of No. 10 serves as a grazing ground. A certain amount of maize is grown as a "shifting" crop.

Area No. 11.—The upper part of No. 11, lying in the district of Plaines Wilhems, comprises about 7,000 arpents of permanent forest land, while a large proportion of the lower part consists of soil unsuitable for cane cultivation.

At least 10,000 arpents at present not under cultivation might be profitably worked with irrigation. The total area amounts to nearly 32,000 arpents, barely 3,000 of which are under cane. The yield of the cultivated lands reaches about twenty-two tons per arpent.

Area No. 12, which comprises a little over 56,000 arpents, is highly cultivated in the highlands and includes portions of Moka and Plaines Wilhems. At least 17,000 arpents are under cane. The lower portion requires copious irrigation before it can be profitably worked.

Area No. 13 includes the district of Port Louis and the lower portions of Pamplemousses. The latter is cultivated by peasant proprietors and suffers from a state of chronic drought.

The cultivated soils of Mauritius consist either of laterite (red soil) or alluvium.

The total area under cane at the end of 1911, according to a return published by the Bureau of Agricultural Statistics, is shown in the following table :—

Total Area in Canes at the end of 1911.

DISTRICTS.	Area cultivated on Estates with Factories. 1	Area cultivated by small Planters on Estates with Factories. 2	Area in Canes on Estates with Factories. 3	Area cultivated on Estates without Factories. 4	Area cultivated by small Planters on Estates without Factories. 5	Area cultivated on Estates with or without Factories. 6	Area in Canes outside Sugar Estates. 7
Pamplemousses ...	7.024.56	2.108.40	9.132.96	650.90	400.00	10.183.86	4.656.00
Riv. du Rempart ...	8.688.18	989.81	9.677.99	4.322.43	341.00	14.341.42	3.229.00
Flacq	8.403.43	1.740.00	10.143.43	8.682.53	3.346.28	22.172.24	6.775.00
Moka	10.172.80	7.25	10.180.05	2.815.02	601.00	13.596.07	3.721.41
Plaines Wilhems ...	2.382.43	1.200.00	3.582.43	2.111.97	873.97	6.568.37	6.914.00
Rivière Noire ...	1.182.85	300.00	1.482.85	679.95	—	2.162.80	734.00
Savanne	15.005.59	3.175.00	18.180.59	1.237.75	—	19.418.34	3.556.60
Grand Port	12.925.06	2.597.91	15.522.97	6.389.76	144.90	22.057.63	4.393.00
Port Louis	—	—	—	—	—	—	—
	65.784.90	12.118.37	77.903.27	26.890.31	5.707.15	110.500.73	33.979.01
Preceding year ...	69.506.12	10.929.64	80.435.76	24.029.59	5.529.46	109.994.81	34.302.00

DISTRICTS.	Area in Canes in each District. 8	Total area of each D.strict. 9	Percentage of each District in Canes. 10	Total area cultivated in Canes by Indians on or off Estates. 11	Percentage of Plantations owned by Indians. 12	Percentage of Plantations not owned by Indians. 13
Pamplemousses	14.839.86	42.339	35.05%	6.901.83	46.51%	53.49%
Riv. du Rempart	17.570.42	34.303	51.22	5.083.71	28.93	71.07
Flacq	28.947.24	70.255	41.20	11.939.28	41.25	58.75
Moka	17.317.48	54.611	31.71	3.802.25	21.96	78.04
Plaines Wilhems	13.482.37	47.862	28.17	7.334.97	54.40	45.60
Rivière Noire	2.896.80	61.807	4.68	594.00	20.50	79.50
Savanne	22.974.94	57.373	40.04	6.166.60	26.84	73.16
Grand Port	26.450.63	61.844	42.77	5.920.49	22.38	77.62
Port Louis	—	9.057	—	—	—	—
	144.479.74	439.451	32.88%	47.743.13	33.04	66.96
Preceding year	144.296.81	439.451	32.83%	45.914.14	31.82	68.18

The estimated area under cane at different epochs during the British occupation, together with the approximate average yield per arpent, is as follows:—

Year.	Tons of Cane per Arpent.	Acres.	Year.	Tons of Cane per Arpent.	Acres.
1812–20	16	9,300	1861–70	15½	129,000
1821–30	16	27,000	1871–80	15	128,000
1831–40	15½	42,000	1881–90	15	128,000
1841–50	15½	61,000	1891–1900... ...	16	128,000
1851–60	15½	114,500	1901–09	17	132,000

The low yield of cane as compared with that derived from the large estates, to which reference will be made later, is due to the defective methods of cultivation practised by the Indians, who hold considerable areas.

The Indians purchase their holdings on a principle known locally as that of "morcellement," consisting of the sale of land on a deferred payment scheme with the produce as a guarantee. It would appear to have developed out of a pure metayer system, which still exists on most estates, under which the proprietor permits his labourers to cultivate on estate lands, after their usual working hours, the proprietor advancing the necessary material and buying the produce at a reduced rate.

Under the morcellement system the freehold is purchased, the capital being paid in annual instalments together with interest, usually at the rate of nine per cent. per annum, extending over a large number of years. In this way about 40,000 arpents of land have been acquired by Indian planters.

Cultivating without capital, without foresight and without instruction, the yields are not infrequently excessively low both in cane and sugar; and yet even this low yield appears to bring a return adequate to the simple requirements of the Indian planter, who, it should be stated, has usually many other resources—hawking, milk selling, cattle and poultry rearing, etc., all on a small scale—with which to supplement the revenue derived from his land.

CLIMATIC CONDITIONS AS AFFECTING CANE CULTURE.

Mauritius is situated just within the tropics south of the Equator, and, owing to its insular position, its climate is mild and equable. The mean annual temperature at varying altitudes is given in the table in the article on "Climate." The critical temperature for the cane appears to be about 70° Fah., below which there is a distinct retardation of growth. The virgin canes in the lowlands come to maturity in about thirteen to fifteen months, while in the highlands nineteen to twenty-four months are required. When to these favourable temperature conditions is added a copious and regular rainfall the growth of the cane is phenomenal.

The rainfall in the centre of the island is frequently too heavy to permit the cane to develop normally, the higher portions of the south-eastern districts receiving an average yearly rainfall of 175 ins. If this amount were evenly distributed at the rate of about half an inch per day, the effect would be most beneficial, but a large proportion is derived from cyclonic rains, which at times yield twenty or thirty inches, and have been known to exceed fifty inches in one day.

The cane suffers to a considerable extent on account of these heavy rains. On the other hand, the lowlands are often deprived of water for weeks at a time, and the shortage causes much damage, as for instance, in the case of the severe drought of 1897, when the crop on some estates was seventy-five per cent. below normal. It should be remarked, however, that these conditions are very unusual. The climate, as a rule, is highly favourable for the cultivation of sugar-cane except in so far as it is influenced by cyclones.

It has been shown that the effect of high wind velocities on the growing cane, even in those cases in which the cane is not entirely uprooted or broken, produces a complete temporary cessation of growth, owing to the tearing and stripping of the leaves, as well as to damage done to the tender growing point of the stem by bending. Winds of under forty miles per hour do not, as a rule, except when they occur late in the season and the cane is well advanced, cause any serious damage.

The losses suffered by the planters from 1857 until 1911 on account of high wind velocities have been calculated as follows:—

Date.		Damage to Crop.	Date.		Damage to Crop.
1857	January 28th ...	2·8%	1881	January 21st ...	0·5%
—	December 5th ...	1·0	1892	February 12th	48·3
1861	February 13th ...	7·2	—	April 29th	
1863	January 13th	13·8	1894	February 21st ...	3·6
—	February 20th		1896	February 19th ...	1·1
1868	March 12th ...	32·5	1897	December 5th ...	0·5
1871	January 5th ...	0·2	1901	January 12th ...	6·2
1872	February 15th ...	0·9	1902	February 5th	18·2
1874	March 27th ...	19·0	—	February 9th	
1877	February 10th ...	1·8	1908	March 1st ...	9·3
1879	February 26th	29·2	1911	March 29-30th ...	10·0
—	March 20th				

From this table it will be seen that violent cyclones are extremely rare. If the unprecedented storm of April, 1892, is omitted, there are only two which have caused damage of about thirty per cent. of the total crop in fifty-six years, and three others under twenty per cent. It should be possible under these conditions to effect an insurance on the crops against serious damage from cyclonic winds, and several attempts have been made to devise a satisfactory scheme on which to assess the damage.

It can be easily understood that the damage sustained falls principally under the heading of invisible damage. Fields which have suffered a serious check often recover completely to the eye during the ten or fifteen days following the cyclone, and it has been necessary to prosecute an elaborate statistical inquiry into the yields of cane over a considerable period in order to determine the real damage caused to the standing crops. This statistical analysis revealed a close numerical relation between the variations of temperature and rainfall and the yield of cane—a relation so close, indeed, that it was found possible to actually estimate the crop from these elements by multiplying the departures from normal conditions by a suitable factor. The difference between the harvested crop and the yield, estimated from the effect of temperature and rainfall in years of cyclone, indicated the loss caused by the high wind velocities. This loss bears a very close relation to the wind velocity, and a simple formula has been derived for the conversion of wind velocities into loss of cane.

It will be seen in consequence that, although it is impossible to determine the damage to the crop by inspection of the cane-fields, a close approximation can be arrived at when the wind velocity is known. The basis of insurance thus established eliminates entirely the personal element, and risks can be covered by the adoption of a scale for the payment of premiums dependent on the probability of the occurrence of a given wind velocity. The details of the scheme have been very carefully worked out, but underwriters have not yet acquired sufficient confidence in meteorological statistics to give it a fair trial.

IRRIGATION.

Closely associated with the sharply-contested question of the influence of forests on rainfall, the possibility of irrigation in Mauritius has provided a subject of perennial discussion for many years past, and it now appears to be universally admitted that large irrigation works affecting extensive areas are doomed to financial failure. For the most part, the only chance of success would appear to turn on the possibility of the co-operative application of the existing water-courses to the lands lying immediately along their banks. The key-note to the whole problem undoubtedly lies in this word "co-operation," but it is difficult to make a planter realise that it is to his personal advantage to permit the conduct of water over his lands for his neighbour's benefit, even though he should be unable to personally utilise the water running to waste. Until this question has been satisfactorily solved co-operative schemes become impossible.

As will be seen from the previous section, the rainfall in the central portions of the island is copious and regular, but the possibility of storing it with a view to its distribution to the low-lying lands during the dry season has not yet been demonstrated. Of the large reservoir schemes several have been considered in the island, and two at least promise to yield a satisfactory return. Both, however, deal with the irrigation of the district of Black River, and up to the present time no plausible plan has been devised for bringing the much-needed water to the rich plains of the north of the island.

Little or nothing has been done on the other hand to utilise the subsoil reservoirs. In several localities in the north underground supplies have been tapped fully adequate to the requirements of small areas of from five to ten acres. A well recently sunk in the Observatory grounds at Pamplemousses revealed the existence of two impermeable layers of basaltic rock at depths of thirty and forty feet respectively, between which several fairly large springs were discovered. Other wells in the north are giving permanent yields of from 500 to 3,000 cubic feet per day according to depth, and it appears likely that the benefit to the virgin canes would at least pay for the cost of sinking the wells.

The whole question is about to be studied by an irrigation expert from India.

Some extremely interesting statistics were published in the Report of the Mauritius Royal Commission in 1909 concerning the effect of rainfall of various intensities, and the excess of the yields on the irrigated over those of the non-irrigated estates. These statistics are reproduced in the following tables. It will be noticed that the yields per arpent increase up to about 100 ins. a year and then decrease, while the excess of the yields on the irrigated estates amounts to more than fifty per cent. on the general average of all ages.

Rainfall.	Virgin Crop.		Ratoon Crop.		All Crops.	
	Average Yield per Arpent.	Mean departure from Average.	Average Yield per Arpent.	Mean departure from Average.	Average Yield per Arpent.	Mean departure from Average.
	Tons.	Tons.	Tons.	Tons.	Tons.	Tons.
Below 50 inches	(4) 19·2	+2·7	(4) 14·5	+2·2	(6) 16·3	+2·3
50 inches to 75 inches ...	(19) 27·9	+2·9	(19) 20·9	+2·9	(22) 22·4	+2·5
75 " " 100 " ...	(8) 32·5	+3·2	(8) 21·2	+3·1	(11) 24·2	+2·1
100 " " 125 " ...	(4) 29·9	+3·7	(4) 19·0	+1·5	(6) 21·4	+2·4
125 " " 150 " ...	(4) 29·9	+4·5	(4) 19·7	+2·1	(4) 21·8	+1·9

N.B.—The figures in parentheses over the yields indicate the number of estates from which the average has been derived.

Age of Cane.	Yield of Cane on Non-irrigated Estates with Rainfall below 50 ins. per year.	Yield of Cane on Irrigated Estates with Rainfall below 50 ins. per year.	Percentage excess on the Irrigated Estates.
Virgin	19·2	32·3	+68
Ratoons	14·5	22·4	+54
All ages	16·3	24·8	+51

LABOUR.

In common with most of the other British cane-growing colonies, prior to the abolition of slavery, the sugar estates in Mauritius were worked by African negroes.

In 1829 the value of the slaves on the estates was estimated at about £4,000,000, of which the planters received a little more than one-half as compensation. The emancipation was declared on February 1st, 1835, and the final liberation effected in 1839. A system of seven years' apprenticeship was established as a transitional measure.

Number of Apprentices and their Children as enumerated at the Census of 1841.

District.	Males.	Females.	Total.
Port Louis	5,788	5,192	10,980
Pamplemousses	4,748	3,658	8,406
Rivière du Rempart	1,467	1,179	2,646
Flacq	3 508	2,785	6,293
Grand Port	3,014	2,365	5,379
Savanne	1,666	1,421	3,087
Black River	1,946	1,499	3,445
Plaines Wilhems	2,957	2,285	5,242
Moka	1,559	1,293	2,852
TOTAL	26,653	21,677	48,330

This step on the part of the British Government, essential as it was in the interests of civilisation, spelt ruin for the sugar planters, as the liberated blacks abandoned agricultural pursuits entirely. Even to the present day, more than half a century later, their descendants still retain a very strong prejudice against this form of labour. The total number of persons returned as agricultural labourers at each census enumeration since 1871 will be seen from the following table, from which it is evident that the general population, of which the negroes or their descendants form the great majority, are very feebly represented :—

Proportion of each Class of the Population working as Agricultural Labourers, shown as a Percentage of the Total Population under each Class.

General Population	Males	3·37	Percentage of the total population under each class and sex at the census of 1911.
	Females	0·35	
Indian Population	Males	41·13	
	Females	5·62	

Locally the term "Creole" applies only to that class of the general population, the origin of which has been referred above to the African slaves. They work principally as carpenters, masons, mechanics, artisans, etc., but there is a marked tendency for the Indian to replace the Creole, not only in agricultural pursuits but in every branch of industry. This was very clearly shown by a comparison of the returns from the last two censuses, the numbers of each class employed in industrial, agricultural, and professional callings being returned as follows :—

Occupation of the Population as returned at the Census of 1911 under Five Main Orders.

Occupation.	General Population.		Indian Population.		Chinese Population.	
	Males.	Females.	Males.	Females.	Males.	Females.
Professional	2,598	881	1,417	162	9	...
Domestic	2,088	3,789	4 079	1,217	25	1
Commercial	3,514	211	8,688	1,464	2,901	7
Agricultural	5,073	176	62,948	7,264	6	...
Industrial	16,653	2,319	7,462	281	73	4

There can be little doubt that much of the uneasiness in the labour market at the present time is due to this.

Fortunately for the planters, on the abolition of slavery it was found possible to substitute Asiatic for African labour.

The first Indian immigrants, amounting to seventy-five in all, were introduced in 1834, and from 1834 to 1845 a further addition of 83,073 was made. The number introduced into the Colony each year will be seen from the table given below, as extracted from *The Mauritius Almanac* for the year 1913:—

Arrivals and Departures of Indian Immigrants, 1834 to 1912.

Year.	Arrivals.		Departures.		Year.	Arrivals.		Departures.	
	Males.	Females.	Males.	Females.		Males.	Females.	Males.	Females.
1834... ...	75	—	4	—	1874... ...	4,818	2,234	2,874	1,201
1835... ...	1,182	72	25	1	1875... ..	1,996	923	2,368	1,055
1836... ...	3,639	184	187	3	1876... ...	330	172	2,354	917
1837... ...	6,939	353	114	20	1877... ...	1,528	659	1,794	623
1838... ...	11,567	241	148	6	1878... ...	3,203	1,623	1,835	527
1839... ...	933	102	170	3	1879... ...	2,013	1,066	1,926	629
1840... ...	107	9	394	23	1880... ...	371	213	1,731	614
1841... ...	499	43	995	94	1881... ...	—	—	1,180	371
1842... ...	73	10	2,021	94	1882... ...	805	436	1,466	397
1843... ...	30,218	4,307	2,884	108	1883... ...	1,283	632	1,766	640
1844... ...	9,709	1,840	2,312	149	1884... ...	4,450	1,939	1,362	491
1845... ...	8,918	2,053	1,492	170	1885... ...	246	112	2,891	1,110
1846... ...	5,718	1,621	2,556	204	1886... ...	511	235	1,649	671
1847... ...	5,174	656	1,651	133	1887... ...	191	73	1,707	643
1848... ...	4,739	656	2,639	376	1888... ...	482	231	1,283	448
1849... ...	6,378	1,047	4,298	594	1889.. ..	3,244	1,298	990	329
1850... ...	8,436	1,594	3,283	442	1890... ...	2,152	873	827	228
1851... ...	8,257	1,763	2,895	374	1891... ...	713	278	716	184
1852... ...	13,671	3,814	2,034	392	1892... ...	—	—	1,129	349
1853... ...	9,877	2,267	1,767	261	1893.. ...	353	132	1,197	457
1854... ...	14,995	3,489	3,166	509	1894... ..	758	268	754	214
1855... ...	9,645	3,270	3,702	565	1895... ..	1,249	485	860	275
1856... ...	9,130	3,523	4,220	677	1896... ...	593	208	858	297
1857... ...	8,640	4,085	3,794	809	1897... ..	314	112	671	248
1858... ...	20,932	9,014	6,707	1,458	1898... ..	—	—	842	264
1859... ...	31,643	12,754	4,146	971	1899... ...	—	—	564	182
1860... ...	9,070	4,216	2,290	543	1900... ...	2,094	796	858	293
1861... ...	10,232	3,753	1,786	471	1901... ...	3,265	1,309	469	162
1862... ...	7,440	2,453	1,752	460	1902... ...	1,875	690	462	186
1863... ...	3,667	1,587	2,553	667	1903.. ...	374	134	383	140
1864... ...	5,626	1,926	2,692	721	1904... ...	1,513	544	413	148
1865... ..	14,910	5,373	2,854	667	1905.. ...	534	186	314	105
1866... ...	3,702	1,894	2,925	890	1906... ...	463	155	435	180
1867... ...	317	33	2,571	827	1907... ...	439	147	366	145
1868... ...	1,968	640	1,880	664	1908... ...	—	—	775	266
1869... ...	1,182	590	1,684	636	1909.. ...	—	—	512	174
1870... ...	2,831	1,245	2,172	670	1910... ...	397	135	403	182
1871.. ..	2,318	974	2,369	705	1911... ..	—	—	364	127
1872... ...	4,015	1,759	2,788	1,031	1912... ...	—	—	338	119
1873... ...	5,226	2,388	2,160	875					

The system of immigration at first adopted was not carried on under Government control, the only action taken by the authorities being to insist upon intending emigrants appearing before a magistrate in India in order to ascertain whether they thoroughly understood the conditions of their contracts and were emigrating entirely of their own accord.

It soon became evident, however, from various reports of neglect or ill-treatment, either during the voyage or on arrival in the Colony, that more stringent Government supervision was required, and in 1837 several special emigration laws were passed by the Indian Government (Acts V. and XXXII. of 1837). In the same year questions concerning the condition of the Indian immigrants were brought before the English Parliament by Buxton, Lord Brougham and others, and a Commission of Inquiry was appointed in India. Their report was submitted in 1840, and although there was but little evidence in support of the rumours of ill-treatment in Mauritius, still it was recommended that the conditions under which emigration was carried on should be more strictly supervised.

In accordance with these recommendations an Order in Council in Mauritius in 1842 made provision for the appointment of emigration agents in India and a Protector of Immigrants in the Colony.

The introduction of a new Labour Law in Mauritius, in 1867, imposing certain new restrictions on the whole of the immigrant population, gave rise to the appointment of the Frere-Williamson Commission in 1872. This Commission denounced the Ordinance of 1867 and the spirit in which it was administered. Several reforms were recommended, and steps were immediately taken to put them into force, with the result that an amended Labour Law was passed in Mauritius in 1878, the principal provisions of which are summarised below:—

THE HON. B. A. FRANCIS,
Protector of Immigrants and
Poor Law Commissioner.

(*a*) The Protector is authorised to visit estates employing immigrants, to take cognizance of complaints made by labourers against their employers, to conduct investigations and institute legal proceedings against the latter as circumstances may require; to assist the Stipendiary Magistrates in the estimation of wages; to inspect estate camps, hospitals and asylums, including their books and registers; to intervene in the case of appeals against any judgment of the magistrate; to prosecute employers on behalf of the immigrants and institute actions for damages against employers for breach of contract; to inspect immigrant ships on arrival and departure. In addition to such duties he is the official guardian of orphans, minors and lunatics of Indian origin.

(*b*) The medical officer is required to visit every estate in the Colony at least every six months, and to report to the Protector on its condition and management.

(*c*) Immigrants are engaged by the Emigration Agency in India only on the receipt of a written requisition from a planter or employer of labour, such requisition being accompanied by a bond, duly signed by the requisitionist and two sureties.

(*d*) Wages, not exceeding one month's pay, are advanced to intending emigrants in India prior to embarkation if they require it.

(*e*) Provision is made in the law for regulating the proportion of females to males introduced (50 females to 100 males being the regulation minimum limit). In distributing the immigrants to the various estates precautions are taken to avoid, as far as possible, the separation of friends and relatives.

(*f*) Provision is also made in the law to prevent the illegal introduction of immigrants from India, and for handing such immigrants, if introduced, over to the Protector.

(*g*) Special licenses are necessary for the introduction of immigrants from places other than British India.

(*h*) Contracts of service are limited to one month, unless made in writing before a Stipendiary Magistrate, otherwise they may extend to five years, but not longer.

(*i*) After the completion of their five years of service immigrants who have no visible means of subsistence are required to re-engage, or are sent to the vagrant depot. If, after three months, they still refuse to work, they are dealt with as incorrigible vagrants. (See *n*.)

(*j*) Provisions are made in the law for the transfer of contract on the part of either employers or employees.

(*k*) Field labour is limited to nine hours, and provision is made for the payment of additional salary for extra work. The Sunday work, or "corvee," is regulated by Art. III., as follows:—

"No servant engaged for field labour shall be compelled to perform any work on any Sunday or Public Holiday save only such as shall be of immediate necessity for the care and feeding of animals, the cleanliness of yards, sties, stables, folds, manufactories and buildings, and other work indispensable for the preservation of the estates, which work, moreover, shall not be of more than two hours' duration, nor be continued after the hour of eight in the morning; and any employer contravening the provisions of this article shall be liable to a penalty not exceeding Rs.100."

(*l*) Illegal absences are now punished by a deduction of one day's pay for each day's absence; the labourer is, moreover, required to make good his absences by a prolongation of his contract, and the law provides for the application of certain penalties in case of refusal.

The amendment of Article 113 of Ordinance 12 of 1878, referring to this question, is as follows (13 of 1908):—

"Any servant under written contract of service who has, without lawful excuse, been absent from his work for one or more days from Monday to Saturday inclusive in any week, exclusive of estate holidays, shall be guilty of an unlawful absence, and shall, in addition to the loss of his wages and rations during such days of unlawful absence, forfeit his wages for Sunday, and he shall be liable to the prolongation of his contract for the number of days that he has been illegally absent, including Sunday, if he did not attend the corvee on that day, in which case he shall further forfeit his rations. The prolongation of his contract shall be made by order of the Stipendiary Magistrate."

Habitual idlers are treated in accordance with the provisions of Article 116, as follows:—

"Any servant under contract of service who shall be unlawfully absent from work for ten or more days in a month, including Sundays and estate holidays, shall be deemed an habitual idler, and shall be liable to a fine not exceeding Rs.5, or to imprisonment with hard labour not exceeding one month. He shall also be liable to a prolongation of his contract for the ten or more days that he has been unlawfully absent and for such period as he may be sentenced to punishment. Every charge for any offence committed under this Article shall be made in the form of Schedule No. 1, and shall be entered within six clear days from the end of the month in which the offence has been committed, so that the servant may have every opportunity to defend himself."

G. LINCOLN,
Assistant Protector of Immigrants and Poor Law Commissioner.

(*m*) Any labourer absconding from his dwelling for three consecutive days is considered, in the terms of the law, a deserter, and is reported to the police as such. Provision is made for the issue of a free warrant for the apprehension of deserters, who are required to make good their absences by a prolongation of service, and are liable to three months' imprisonment.

(*n*) Immigrants convicted of incorrigible vagrancy (*i*) are liable to twelve months' imprisonment, and, if twice convicted, to deportation.

(*o*) An immigrant may redeem his "Industrial Service" at the rate of Rs.24 per annum; but provision is made in the law for discharge from service of exemption from "Industrial Residence" in cases of infirmity, accident, sickness, etc.

(*p*) Old immigrant tickets are issued to immigrants completing their term of "Industrial Residence," and provision is made for the payment by Government of the return passage to India of immigrants and their families who may be in distress or necessitous circumstances.

Penalties are imposed for the employment of false tickets or certificates.

(*q*) Labourers' wages are paid monthly and rations issued weekly. Officers belonging to the estate are not allowed to keep shops.

In the event of non-payment of the labourers' wages, the Stipendiary Magistrate may order the seizure and sale of the estate and standing crops.

(*r*) All estates employing twenty or more servants are required to provide adequate accommodation, and special provisions are made in the law for : Efficient construction and maintenance, regulating hospital dietary, provision of proper bedding, drugs and medicines, engaging duly qualified medical officers, keeping correct registers of illness, the imposition of penalties in case of improper treatment of sick immigrants.

(*s*) Employers of labour are required to provide efficient and wholesome lodging, and to prevent immigrants from keeping animals in the camp or dwellings, special localities being set apart to the leeward of the camp for such purposes.

(*t*) The law also provides for the formation of special Stipendiary Courts, and the powers of the Stipendiary Magistrates are set forth in Articles 249-253 of the Labour Law, which give them "exclusive jurisdiction for the enforcement of all contracts of service and for imposing all penalties for the breach, neglect, or non-performance thereof."

Although in the early days the lot of the Indian immigrant appears to have been little better than that of the negro slave, he is at the present time, owing to the intervention of the Colonial and Indian Governments, in a far more prosperous condition than he could ever hope to attain in his native land.

The care and protection accorded to the immigrant commences long before his arrival in Mauritius.

From the day that he evidences a desire to emigrate from India as an engaged labourer the special emigration agents attend to his wants, make advances of money if he requires assistance, and superintend in detail the circumstances of his embarkation and transport, which can only be effected under special and stringent conditions.

VACOAS TREE.
From the leaves of which Sugar Bags are made.

On arrival in Mauritius the immigrants are photographed for purposes of identification, and distributed to the various estates, special care being taken to avoid separating members of the same family. Should any case of infectious disease have occurred on the voyage from India, the labourers are despatched to one or other of the quarantine stations for supervision, during which time they are under the special care of a qualified Government medical officer.

The Indian labourer is generally engaged for a period of five years, and during the whole time not only has the right of appealing to the Protector whenever he considers that he has a grievance against his employer, but is the object of continued supervision on the part of the officers of the Immigration Department.

On the estates the site of the camp is carefully chosen, and frequently inspected by the Government inspectors and medical officers ; the dwelling houses are properly constructed and efficiently ventilated, also under their supervision ; estate hospitals are erected and placed under the care of qualified medical practitioners and trained dispensers.

By a recent ordinance, the powers of the Protector have been extended to include the care of all labourers living in estate camps, whether under contract of engagement or not.

All this care on the part of Government has, in many instances, rendered the estate camps the healthiest localities in their respective districts. But in addition to the care of their persons and surroundings, the nature and duration of their work are carefully controlled, and they enjoy many facilities for earning revenue in excess of their wages by planting cane on estate lands, rearing cattle and poultry, etc.

For the field work on the estates the labourers are divided into three gangs:

(1) "La Grande Bande," consisting of the able-bodied men, perform all the heavy work, such as clearing the ground, digging the holes for planting, cutting the canes, carting, and charging and emptying carts and waggons, etc.

The wages of this gang amount to Rs.9 per month, with rations of:—

Rice	12½ lbs. per week,
Dholl	2 " " "
Oil	¼ " " "
Salt	¼ " " "

"La Petite Bande," composed of the weaker men, generally clean, guano and manure the canes, and aid the "Grande Bande" in the lighter tasks when necessary; they receive from Rs.7 to Rs.8 per month, with rations similar to those noted above.

The third gang consists of the boys—"chocras"—who perform a variety of light tasks, cutting out *borers*, guanoing the young canes, etc., and receive from Rs.3 to Rs.6 per month, with rations of:—

Rice	10½ lbs. per week,
Dholl	2 " " "
Oil	¼ " " "
Salt	¼ " " "

In addition to the above, the women and young girls work more or less irregularly—never under contract—and receive Rs.0.25 to Rs.0.40 per day. The tasks allotted to them are of the simplest and lightest nature.

It should be remarked that the rations indicated above are invariably exceeded on nearly all estates.

Work begins at about 6.30 a.m. or 7 a.m., and, as the field work is performed by task, the best men are generally free by 11.30 a.m. or noon.

When all the circumstances under which the Indian labours on the sugar estates in Mauritius are considered, the prosperous condition of the Indian community at the present time is easily accounted for. The estimated value of immovable property held by the Indians amounts to nearly Rs.20,000,000, and this is increasing yearly. Large sums are transmitted annually to India, and about Rs.400,000 a year deposited in the banks. The last return of the Protector gave the value standing to their credit in the banks of the Colony at Rs.1,148,161.

In addition to the labourers under contract of service, monthly and day labourers are also employed on the estates, especially for field work. The work performed by them is, however, far from satisfactory, and the rate of wages at the present time is much higher than the profits from the industry can well afford. The total number of labourers in these classes at the recent census amounted to:—

	Males.		Females.
Day Labourers	18,647	...	6,351
Monthly "	6,661	...	507
	25,308	...	6,858

They are not provided with rations and quarters, but are often granted medical attendance. They earn normally from Rs.1 to Rs.1.25 a day, but whenever there is a dearth of labour, or an excess of work owing to heavy crops, this is considerably exceeded.

CULTIVATION.

As was stated in the introductory paragraph of this chapter, the sugar-cane appears to have been brought to Mauritius during the Dutch occupation, but was not systematically cultivated until the French took possession of the island.

The nature of the plant will be seen from the accompanying illustration. It can be propagated either from cuttings or seeds. Commercially the tops of the canes are used. Three or four of the tops are laid in small holes (fossés) about ten inches deep, from ten to 'twelve inches wide and two feet long. These holes are generally arranged in long straight lines with about six inches between the holes and four to five feet between the lines. In consequence of the labour difficulties at the present time, there is a growing tendency to adopt the use of ploughs, and to plant the canes in continuous furrows instead of in the holes referred to above ; but, unfortunately, a not inconsiderable extent of the area under cane is covered with huge boulders, so that in these cases the ploughs are unserviceable.

The canes in the lowlands are planted in April or May, and harvested in August or September of the following year, the period of growth being about fifteen or sixteen months. In the higher and colder districts

CUTTING THE SUGAR-CANES.

the plantations are made in November or December, and the canes cut after eighteen or twenty months' growth.

The canes cut from the plantations constitute the virgin crop, after which, both in the highlands and lowlands, the canes are harvested every twelve months as ratoons, the rotation going up to the third, fourth, and in some cases fifth or sixth ratoon without replanting. The Indian planters carry the ratoons very much further, and often do not replant for ten or even twelve years.

The methods of cultivation vary considerably on the different estates and according to climate, but most planters, whether in the highlands or lowlands, consider it advantageous to plant on stable manure. On some estates the plantations are made on a mixture of manure, molasses and ashes, and some very high virgin yields have been obtained by this method. One estate obtained an average virgin yield from a large area of over forty-seven tons per arpent.

The average virgin yield on the large estates amounts to a little over twenty-eight tons, while the average ratoon yield for all ages (first, second, third, etc.) is about twenty tons. The average of all crops amounts to about twenty-one tons and a half. These yields are naturally only obtained by the employment of adequate cultural methods. The Indian planters have been known to obtain yields as low as two or three tons per arpent from their ratoon crops, and seldom exceed fifteen tons even for the virgin crop.

The average yield of cane per arpent in each of the different districts, as derived from the large estates, is given in the following table :—

District.	Yield of Virgin Crop.	Yield of Ratoon Crop.	General Average Yield of all Crops.
	Tons per Arpent	Tons per Arpent	Tons per Arpent
Pamplemousses	24·3	17·1	19·1
Rivière du Rempart	21·8	16·9	18·2
Flacq	29·7	20·2	22·8
Grand Port	27·8	18·8	21·5
Plaines Wilhems...	31·1	18·6	21·9
Black River	33·3	24·9	26·4
Moka	34·6	21·4	24·7
Savanne	29·1	23·1	24·8

Under normal conditions the average cost per arpent for a full rotation—virgin and ratoons up to the fourth—varies between Rs.130 and Rs.150. In the first year the costs are naturally heavier, as the expenditure of clearing and holing has to be met.

During the period of growth cultivation consists of frequent cleanings of the soil to free the young plants from the effect of the rapidly-growing grass and weeds.

As a rule the growing cane is guanoed or manured early in summer, so as to supply an adequate quantity of food for the vigorous growth of the rainy season. The flowering canes send up a central sheath or flower —known as arrowing—as soon as the cold winter temperature sets in; the colder and drier the season the earlier the canes flower. From this time there is an almost complete cessation of growth, and the cane slowly ripens ready for the harvesting, which begins some time in August.

The canes are cut with small hatchets—billhooks—and transported to the factories either in carts, or by means of wire ropes or light tramways. Mechanical transport has been extensively introduced since the outbreak of the epizooty known as surra in 1902-03. Many thousand head of cattle were destroyed during harvest time of that year, and a loan was raised by the local Government to assist the planters in purchasing the tramway material. Since this date the great advantage of mechanical over animal transport has been fully appreciated, and every year has witnessed a considerable extension of the network of tramways which is rapidly covering the cane-bearing areas.

There are a great many varieties of cane. The most important of those cultivated commercially in Mauritius are given in the following table, together with the results of the analyses performed at the Station Agronomique with a view to the determination of their richness in saccharine matter. This list is by no means exhaustive. There are innumerable seedling canes, most of which have little or no commercial value :—

Nos.	Variety.	For 100 c.c. of Juice.		For 100 of Canes.		Purity.	Glucose Co-efficient.
		Sugar.	Glucose.	Sugar.	Glucose.		
1	Port McKay	18·35	0·45	14·28	0·34	87·8	2·4
2	Lousier Ordinaire	20·93	0·23	16·20	0·17	93·0	1·1
3	Lousier Rayé	20·31	0·37	15·75	0·28	92·1	1·8
4	New Caledonian Queen or Kavenger ...	21·56	0·24	16·65	0·18	93·6	1·1
5	Iscambine Rouge	18·61	0·24	14·60	0·18	91·3	1·2
6	Iscambine Rayé	19·76	0·29	15·32	0·22	89·6	1 4
7	Big Tanna	20·57	0·22	15·89	0·17	89·3	1·5

Nos.	Variety.	For 100 c c. of Juice.		For 100 of Canes.		Purity.	Glucose Co-efficient.
		Sugar.	Glucose.	Sugar.	Glucose.		
8	Fotiogo	21·28	0·17	16·41	0·13	90·4	0·8
9	Bellouguet	20·39	0·54	15·75	0·42	88·4	2·6
10	Sandal	21·46	0·13	16·56	0·10	92·1	0·6
11	Borneo	15·68	0·55	12·33	0·43	87·5	3·4
12	Bois Rouge	19·95	0·26	15·45	0·20	90·0	1·2
13	Branchu	20·84	0·15	16·07	0·11	92·8	0·6
14	Bambou Rayé or Guinghan	10·06	0·23	14·83	0·17	93·4	1·1
15	Lahinia	18·17	0·40	14·15	0·31	88·1	2·2
16	Reine	20·57	0·19	15·93	0·14	92·4	0·9
17	Tambiapin	20·57	0·16	15·93	0·12	92·4	0·7
18	Grosse Blanche	21·10	0·28	16·30	0·21	92·6	1·2
19	Vilaine	22·98	0·14	17·62	0·10	91·1	0·5
20	Setters	23·78	0·12	18·25	0·09	94·4	0·5
21	Tamarin	23·06	0·10	17·72	0·07	93·3	0·4
22	Mignonne	18·20	0·11	14·20	0·08	89·4	0·6
23	Diard	21·46	0·28	16·57	0·22	92·1	1·3
24	Meera	21·02	0·38	16·25	0·29	91·5	1·7
25	Penang	20·84	0·37	16·04	0·28	92·6	1·7
26	Black Java	18·79	0·91	14·64	0·70	90·0	4·8
27	Fiji Rayé	18·88	0·25	14·70	0·19	92·8	1·3
28	Otamiti	18·34	0·22	14·33	0·17	91·4	1·1
29	Galaga M.	17·28	0·44	13·54	0·34	89·7	2·5
30	Mapou	17·28	0·45	13·95	0·42	90·1	3·0
31	Galaga C.	21·28	0·19	16·47	0·14	93·5	0·8
32	Sèche or Morte	21·56	0·17	16·64	0·12	91·7	0·7
33	Verte Jardin	15·94	1·22	12·49	0·95	81·6	7·7
34	Brea	20·59	0·33	15·91	0·25	90·4	1·6
35	Trinidad T.	16·65	0·99	13·00	0·77	83·9	5·9
36	Rat (Gros Ventre)	19·86	0·34	15·41	0·26	91·2	1·6
37	Verte Pays	15·81	1·00	12·34	0·78	79·7	6·3
38	Mignonne Rouge P.	17·01	0·77	13·27	0·59	84·6	4·5
39	Graine Rouge	20·03	0·31	15·50	0·23	89·0	1·5
40	Graine A	20·40	0·38	15·85	0·29	90·7	1·8
41	„ B	19·78	0·30	15·36	0·23	91·9	1·5
42	„ C	19·68	0·61	15·27	0·47	90·3	3·0
43	„ D	18·07	0·75	14·08	0·58	88·7	4·1
44	Graine de Rouge	20·84	0·30	16·11	0·22	91·5	1·3
45	„ Blanche	20·57	0·20	15·96	0·15	93·4	0·9
46	Fraser 1	21·02	0·22	16·28	0·17	94·4	1·0
47	Keni Keni	20·39	0·13	15·80	0·10	92·5	0·6
48	Lousier Rouge	19·60	0·38	15·22	0·29	91·1	1·9
49	Lousier Rayé Rouge	21·28	0·24	16·45	0·18	93·4	1·1
50	Lousier Rayé Vert	20·49	0·19	15·88	0·14	92·9	0·9
51	Horne	20·99	0·19	15·20	0·14	91·1	0·8
52	Knox	18·35	0·15	14·34	0·11	93·8	0·8
53	Tiambo	15·85	0·78	12·46	0·60	88·3	4·8
54	Port McKay (Noire)	19·24	0·39	14·95	0·30	89·4	2·0
55	Striped Java	19·86	0·34	15·39	0·26	90·1	1·7
56	Black Java	18·61	0·15	14·54	0·11	93·8	0·8
57	Purple Jamaica	19·14	0·78	14·88	0·60	90·4	4·0
58	Fraser 2	19·95	0·52	15·48	0·40	91·5	2·6
59	Natal	16·03	0·40	12·52	0·31	89·2	2·4
60	Chine Pamplemousses	20·67	0·11	10·02	0·07	93·8	0·4
61	Chine Natal	17·90	0·71	13·94	0·54	86·7	3·9

Of these canes the most in demand at the present time are:—Big Tanna, Fotiogo, Port McKay, Iscambines, Lousiers, Petite Senneville. Canes formerly cultivated extensively, but now almost entirely abandoned, are: Sandal, Borneo, Lahinia, Reine, Tambiapin, Grosse Blanche, Vilaine, Meera, Black Java, Fiji Rayé, Otamiti, Galaga M, Mapou, Galaga C, Sèche or Morte, Verte Jardin, Brea, Trinidad T, Rat Gros Ventre, Verte Pays, Mignonne Rouge P, Fraser 1, Keni Keni, Lousier Rouge, Lousier Rayé Rouge, Lousier Rayé Vert, Knox, Tiambo, Port McKay (Noire), Striped Java, Black Java, Purple Jamaica, Fraser 2, Natal.

A great many varieties which were formerly cultivated on an extensive scale have now entirely disappeared, on account of their having been attacked by one or other of the many cane diseases. The principal of these varieties of canes are:—Bellouguet, Setters, Tamarin, Mignonne, Diard, Penang Blanche d'Otaiti, de Batavia, Bambou Rose, Horne.

One of the most deadly of the cane diseases—the gumming disease, Maladie de Gomme—has been known to diminish the yield of cane by more than thirty per cent. over the whole of an estate.

In addition to these cane diseases, the depredations of insects cause considerable damage. The several species of *borer* are responsible for the destruction of large numbers of canes, and quite recently, in 1911, the larva of a coleoptera, since designated *Phytalus Smithii,* destroyed whole fields of plantations over a restricted area in the north of the island.

MANUFACTURE.

OLD METHOD OF BRINGING SUGAR-CANES TO THE FACTORY.

During the past century the details of factory work have undergone a very radical and complete change, although the principles of the manufacture of sugar have remained practically unaltered. The four principal steps in the production of sugar are:

(*a*) Crushing or extraction of the juice.

(*b*) Purification, chemically and mechanically.

(*c*) Crystallisation.

(*d*) Separation of the crystals from the non-crystallisable matter.

The original mill consisted of a heavy, oblong stone slab, along the sides of which two canals were worked. Three or four of the canes to be crushed were laid on this stone, and a heavy stone roller dragged over them backwards and forwards two or three times. One of these mills is on exhibition in the grounds of the Mauritius Institute Museum in Port Louis. The extracted juice was then collected in buckets, placed in a suitable position near the stone. The operation was repeated with other canes until sufficient juice, or vesou, as it is then called, had been collected to fill the evaporating plant. This consisted of a row of five large open pans—batteries *a feu nu*—of varying sizes. The juice was first discharged into the largest of these cauldrons. The furnace was placed under the fifth and smallest cauldron.

As soon as the juice became warm in the large pan, which served the purpose of the modern defecator, a thick creamy film of wax and other impurities rose to the surface. After the removal of these first impurities the heated juice was transferred to the second pan, in which, being nearer the furnace, it began to boil. The heavy froth which rose to the surface during this operation was removed by means of long wooden laths about five inches in width.

In each of these first two pans lime was added; in the third pan the juice reached a syrupy condition, was concentrated in the fourth pan, and finally cooked or crystallised in the fifth.

When this process was completed the massecuite was sent into the cooling pans, and finally placed in wooden cases, through which the uncrystallised matter percolated, leaving the sugar crystals behind. This was completed in about fifteen or twenty days, when the crystals were placed on large mats in the sun to be dried. The sugar resulting from these primitive methods was a brown sticky mixture of molasses and crystals.

The final process of drying the crystals demanded very careful supervision, and the whole personnel of the estate had to answer the factory bell, whenever a shower of rain occurred, to place the drying produce in safety. But in spite of these methods large fortunes were realised by the planters during those early days, as the selling price of the sugars was excessively high.

Although the underlying principles remain the same in the modern factory, the single stone crusher actuated by animal traction is now replaced by a twelve or fourteen roller steam mill. The juice is pumped from the mill into the measuring tanks. From these tanks it is sent to the sulphur apparatus for bleaching, and thence to the clarifiers. From the clarifiers, with their automatic skimmers, it is pumped into the multiple effect, where it is condensed and then sent into the vacuum pans for boiling until the proper crystals are formed.

The crystals are still further built up by the malaxeurs, or crystallisers in motion, from which the massecuite is sent into the centrifugals. Here the crystals are steam-washed and separated from the molasses.

The sugar thus obtained is the first grade or vesou. The rich runnings from the centrifugals are reboiled and again treated in the centrifugals, producing the first syrups; and so on for the lower syrups until the process of crystallisation no longer yields a sugar product of commercial value.

[Photo by permission, Ladies' Fine Needlework Association.

NEW METHOD OF BRINGING SUGAR-CANES TO THE FACTORY.

The following is a brief description of the various apparatus employed at the present time in treating the juice extracted by the mills, with special reference to the methods adopted in the Mauritius factories.

The Sulphur Apparatus.—After the juice extracted from the cane by the mill has been strained, it is sent through an apparatus known as the sulphur box. There are several different forms of this apparatus, but they all serve more or less efficiently to thoroughly impregnate the juice with the sulphur fumes. The object of this process is twofold; it is claimed that it bleaches the juice and produces pure white sugars, and facilitates the precipitation of impurities, besides rendering the juices easier to work.

The most common form of sulphur box consists of an upright chamber about twelve feet high, carrying internally a series of perforated plates at distances of about one foot apart. The sulphur fumes enter at the bottom, while the juice flows through suitable pipes into the top of the box and is broken into numerous jets by the perforated plates. This is the primitive sulphur box; but several other apparatus have been devised to insure the absorption by the juices of a measured quantity of the sulphur fumes, and to free the fumes from all traces of sulphuric acid and other impurities which they contain.

After sulphuring, the juices are generally "limed"—that is to say, a certain measured quantity of lime is added in order to render the juice neutral, or give it a faint alkaline reaction. The juice is subsequently raised to a temperature of about 150° Fah. in a juice-heater, and then discharged into tanks to allow the impurities which have been precipitated by the combined action of the sulphur, lime, and heat, to settle. In some cases the juice is kept in tanks at a high temperature and drawn off automatically in such a way that the heavy impurities are left at the bottom, while the top scum remains unbroken. These tanks, or clarifiers, consist of large open iron pans containing a coil of copper tubes, through which steam is passed for the purpose of heating the juice.

Juice Filters.—After the process of clarification and the precipitation of the heavier particles of non-saccharine matter, the juices are sometimes filtered, but the process of filtration is generally confined to the scums removed from the top of the clarified liquid. This filtration consists of forcing the liquid to be filtered through strong cloth bags, and there are various apparatus by which this is effected.

Triple Effect.—The next process after clarification and filtration consists of reducing the juices to syrup. This is performed in an apparatus known as an "effect." The effect consists of a large upright cylindrical vessel of height a little more than twice its diameter. The lower portion carries two plates connected by a series of copper tubes. The juice is run into the effect above the top plate, and flows through the tubes, filling them and the space below the lower plate. Exhaust steam, at a pressure of about five lbs. per square inch, is admitted into the space between the plates, and completely surrounds the tubes through which the juice has flowed. In this way the juice becomes heated, and as the pressure in the vessel containing the juice is considerably reduced, it boils at a very low temperature. Two, three, and sometimes four effects are employed; the vapour of evaporation from the juice of the first effect being admitted to the space between the tube-plate of the second, and that from the second to the third, in such a way that the vapour condenses on the surface of the tubes and heats them by the liberation of its latent heat of condensation. In this way the only steam required for heating all the system of effects is that which enters the first cylinder, and an enormous economy of vapour is thus realised.

Vacuum Pan.—When the juice has been reduced to syrup it is "cooked," the object being to form the sugar crystals. It is on the man in charge of the "cooking" that the success of the whole process of sugar making depends. The apparatus used for this purpose is known as the *vacuum pan*. It consists of a large iron pan hermetically closed by a spherical or conical cover. The lower portion of the pan contains a series of copper pipes through which steam is passed for heating the juice. The boiling is effected, as in the case of the "effect," under reduced pressure.

The process of boiling may be divided into three stages: the granulation, the growing of the crystals, and the bringing up to strike. Granulation consists of the formation in the syrup of very minute, almost invisible, crystals, which have subsequently to be built up by judicious boiling.

One of the most fascinating of all the various branches of physical science is that dealing with crystallography. Not a few scientists consider that the crystal forms a connecting link between the inorganic and the organic world. Whether this is so or not, it is certain that the crystal possesses a curious faculty closely resembling the power of growth in the organic world, and is even able to repair damage sustained by it. There is, in consequence, a certain degree of scientific romance associated with this final process in the treatment of the juice. The sugar-boiler, all unwittingly perhaps, is controlling and directing one of the most marvellous of all Nature's processes, and one on which science has had, and probably still has, much to say.

Granulation, or the birth of the sugar crystal, is generally determined by a sudden cooling of the syrup. When once this substratum of crystals has been formed, the whole attention of the sugar-boiler is directed to building them up to the required size, and the prevention of the formation of new ones, which any unnecessary cooling would at once give rise to.

Cooling Tanks.—When the crystals are formed to the satisfaction of the boiler, the "masse cuite," as it is termed, is discharged into the cooling tanks. If the cooling of the mixture is not very carefully controlled there is a danger of the formation of a false grain, due to a too rapid cooling of the non-crystallised and super-saturated syrup. It is evidently the object of the manufacturer to extract the maximum amount of crystallisable matter from the juice; but he endeavours, as far as possible, to form crystals of the same size in the same "cuite." In order to determine that the fresh deposits during the process of cooling shall go to increase the size of the crystals already formed, and not give rise to new ones, an apparatus known as a "malaxeur" has been devised.

This consists of a cooling tank in which revolves a spiral of tubes into which steam or water can be admitted, so that the rate of cooling can be very readily controlled, and the formation of this false grain avoided. When the mixture is thoroughly cooled it is conducted to the centrifugals, in which the crystals are separated from the syrup.

TRIPLE EFFECT, BEAU CHAMP FACTORY.

VACUUM PANS, BEAU CHAMP FACTORY.

TRIPLE EFFECT, BRITANNIA FACTORY.

DRIVING ENGINE, BRITANNIA FACTORY.

Centrifugals.—The centrifugals consist of vertical cylindrical perforated baskets, to which a fine wire-gauze strainer is fitted internally. The basket is revolved at a high speed, and the mixture of sugar and syrup thrown against the strainer, which allows the syrup to run through and arrests the crystals.

In Mauritius these crystals are then treated with high-pressure steam in order to wash away every particle of syrup clinging to them. The syrup, which still contains some crystallisable matter, is sent back to the factory for reboiling, and the clean crystals are transported to the packing branch, where they are discharged into suitable sacks for export.

From this brief description of factory work it is not difficult to see how much the whole process of the manufacture of sugar lends itself to constant and progressive improvement. There is so much scope for the use of automatic and labour-saving devices—so many details, mechanical and otherwise, on which the ingenuity of both chemist and engineer can be exercised—that each year sees some change for the better in every branch of the work; and the Mauritian planter at the present day is fully alive to the necessity for keeping his factory up to modern standards.

EVOLUTION OF THE FACTORY.

The various stages in the evolution of the Mauritian factory occurred approximately as follows: During the period 1806-1845 the primitive stone slab and roller was generally abandoned for three *vertical* roller mills worked by animal traction, or by wind or water power. From 1846 to 1855 the vertical roller mills were replaced by triple horizontal mills worked by steam, although there still remained a few which were worked by water or wind. This period also witnessed the introduction of vacuum pans and centrifugals, as well as the Wetzell crystallising apparatus, a machine somewhat similar to the now universally employed malaxeur.

From 1856 to 1865, the vacuum pans became universal, and there were still a few water-mills remaining. It would appear that during this period the mill employed was a larger and more powerful single-roller mill instead of the small triple-roller mills.

From 1865 to 1875 there was little improvement in factory work. Some double mills were in use, and imbibition—watering the bagasse between the mills—was tried on several estates. The principal advance during this period was in the chemical treatment of the juice.

During the next ten or twelve years there was a general awakening to the necessity for improved methods, but the industry was passing through the most critical period of its history. The bounty-fed beet sugars, the outbreak of malaria in the colony, and the gumming disease on the cane, reduced the profits from the industry to such an extent that the planters found it impossible to lay out the capital which the improved factory methods demanded—a condition which was more or less chronic up to the year 1909, when an exceptionally heavy crop and high selling prices enabled most of the planters to place their factories on a more modern footing.

The extraction of commercial sugar per cent. weight of cane at the various epochs referred to above will be gathered from the following table:—

Decennial Period.	Approximate Average Extraction (per cent. weight of Cane).	Decennial Period.	Approximate Average Extraction (per cent. weight of Cane).
	%		%
1811–20	5·00	1881–90	8·30
1821–30	6·00	1891–1900 ...	8·70
1831–40	6·75	1901–08	10·10
1841–50	7·10	1908–09	10·56
1851–60	7·60	1909–10	10·50
1861–70	8·10	1910–11	10·62
1871–80	8·20	1911 12	10·66

COIL CENTRIFUGALS, LA BARAQUE FACTORY.

WATSON-LAIDLAW CENTRIFUGALS, LA BARAQUE FACTORY.

DOUBLE TURBINES, BELLE VUE MAURICIA FACTORY.

THE MOUNT FACTORY UNDER RECONSTRUCTION.

During the last three years practically the whole manufacturing plant of the colony has been re-modelled with capital derived from the profits of the industry alone; several new mills, the most powerful which modern sugar machinery manufacturers construct, have been introduced, and every branch of the factory work has been enlarged and modernised.

Heat economisers, bagasse furnaces, large vacuum pans, Weston centrifugals, and automatic appliances of every description are being ordered and fitted by estates proprietors all over the island. Chemical control is no longer regarded as a fad, but is rapidly being recognised as the most essential part of the whole factory work. The capital expenditure has of course been heavy, but the increased yield and diminishing cost of production have already amply repaid the initial outlay.

MARKETS.

The principal market for the Mauritian sugars at the present day is India. Formerly large consignments were disposed of in Australia and South Africa; but both of these countries have now developed a sugar industry of their own, sufficient not only to supply their local requirements, but to permit them to carry on a growing export trade.

The Mauritian industry is specially handicapped by its insular position and the great distances which separate it from the important sugar-purchasing centres, and there can be little doubt that a co-operative shipping concern would be an immense advantage to the industry.

The quantities of sugar exported from the island to various countries during the last twenty-nine years will be seen from the following tables:—

Comparative Returns of the Exports of Sugar from Mauritius, 1884 to 1912.

Year.	India.	South Africa.	Madagascar.	Europe.	Australasia.	China.	America	Other Countries.	Total.
	kilos	kilos	kilos	kilos	kilos	kilos	kilos	kilos	kilos
1884 ...	56,551,487	5,680,660	42,209	15,417,709	41,207,943	—	6,598,579	157,357	125,655,946
1885 ...	56,925,489	3,718,621	89,739	14,237,731	29,787,039	376,216	10,340,773	180,488	115,656,096
1886 ...	68,391,916	4,766,627	83,188	15,183,641	23,499,150	687,571	5,136,269	259,392	118,007,754
1887 ...	51,885,275	3,725,842	110,428	7,135,070	25,515,590	308,741	7,805,435	441,778	96,228,159
1888 ...	68,806,234	8,501,311	113,565	11,955,405	31,601,956	2,401,839	6,269,837	416,371	130,066,518
1889 ...	65,000,261	10,633,344	94,682	14,437,566	41,396,880	174,337	9,417,895	628,469	141,783,434
1890 ...	68,664,084	11,742,966	84,808	14,867,982	29,800,236	788,624	1,792,439	664,799	128,405,938
1891 ...	73,754,882	14,292,079	84,684	11,645,897	19,217,225	441,346	4,148,689	596,178	124,180,980
1892 ...	59,900,285	7,728,296	82,665	13,983,652	8,533,167	534,019	—	2,329,172	93,091,256
1893 ...	50,146,834	11,669,809	210,483	14,890,919	7,114,642	1,507,179	—	527,975	86,067,841
1894 ...	87,514,989	12,386,185	144,906	11,941,115	19,248.329	2,354,388	3,898,806	943,015	138,431,733
1895 ...	66,514,193	17,054,232	529,831	6,684,332	13,270,196	1,417,175	9,861,144	1,123,477	116,454,600
1896 ...	81,651,142	25,448,503	386,743	1,173,973	28,452,806	2,136,525	13,617,782	707,941	153,575,415
1897 ...	73,977,218	31,751,351	330,566	1,040,869	15,999,686	3,355,877	10,946,212	677,921	138,079,700
1898 ...	83,707,707	30,966,602	888	5,641,652	9,466,047	1,228,640	22,838,811	698,310	154,548,657
1899 ...	83,345,307	26,972,200	—	7,402,073	11,130,557	925,733	33,928,421	1,207.542	164,911,833
1900 ...	104,381,693	30,633,703	—	11,265,758	10,367,690	478,302	16,289,215	349,424	174,765,785
1901 ...	91,256,758	33,660,792	—	15,227,732	8,791,547	1.134,007	6,517,851	428,289	157,016,976
1902 ...	92,718,031	26,673,615	1,790	16,618,900	6,512,595	7,458,325	—	322,422	150,305,678
1903 ...	121,503,570	20,030,999	—	18,681,730	4,888,497	4,951,803	—	359,941	170,416,541
1904 ...	115,666,665	49,156,056	—	26,409,059	3,546,594	1,465,898	—	1,581,394	197,825,666
1905 ...	95,096,166	40,310,350	—	7,701,980	3,471,835	6,407,521	10,038,237	1,118,766	164,194,858
1906 ...	113,188,249	38,028,049	—	10,311,038	4,761,325	15,906,072	3,446,491	748,015	186,389,239
1907 ...	125,745,932	30,701,551	—	29,003,617	4,448,752	1,578,531	4,460,185	807,488	195,746,056
1908 ...	137,847,310	23,547,136	—	19,109,988	2,803,110	—	12,990,067	751.328	197,048,909
1909 ...	116,382,761	12,440,529	—	20,770,164	3,456,004	—	15,762,892	10,437,121	179,249,471
1910 ...	140,584,193	19,878,299	—	47,368,022	1,860,243	3,854,242	—	2,198,243	215,743,242
1911 ...	106,192,634	18,991,634	—	103,777,234	1,499,644	**882,751	4,642,570	1,063,581	237,050,048
†1912 ...	143,361,055	11,879,666	—	21,046,269	26,273,078	2,016,733	—	1,490,088	206,066,889

† The values for 1912 are tentative.

** Hong Kong.

The above values refer to the calendar year.

Crop Values and Average Price of Sugar from 1885 to 1913

Year ending July 31st.	SUGAR.				Year ending July 31st.	SUGAR.			
	Total produce (English tons).	* Total produce (1,000 kilos to ton).	† Average price per 1,000 kilos.	Monetary value of Crop Unit Rs.1,000,000.		Total produce (English tons).	* Total produce (1,000 kilos to ton).	† Average price per 1,000 kilos.	Monetary value of Crop Unit Rs.1,000,000.
			Rs.	Rs.				Rs.	Rs.
1885	124,357	126,347	171·4	21·7	1900	154,926	157,404	163·0	25·6
1886	115,763	117,615	198·2	23·2	1901	180,543	183,433	175·0	32·0
1887	98,793	100,381	188·4	18·9	1902	151,220	153,639	145·0	22·3
1888	119,118	121,024	184·6	22·3	1903	139,452	141,684	145·0	20·5
1889	128,285	130,337	186·4	24·3	1904	212,300	215,697	135·0	29·1
1890	125,703	127,714	208·6	26·5	1905	140,012	142,253	194·0	27·5
1891	124,491	126,483	183·0	23·1	1906	183,078	186,007	140·0	26·0
1892	112,779	114,583	191·4	21·9	1907	211,318	214,699	132·0	28·3
1893	67,950	69,044	240·8	16·7	1908	161,330	163,911	153·0	24·9
1894	136,776	138,965	204·2	28·4	1909	188,458	191,482	152·0	29·1
1895	115,035	116,874	193·8	22·6	1910	242,666	246,560	168·6	41·6
1896	140,607	142,857	195·0	27·6	1911	210,987	214,372	141·8	30·4
1897	148,375	150,749	164·8	24·8	1912	163,047	165,663	193·6	32·1
1898	119,854	121,772	163·0	19·9	1913**	—	205, ...	152·0	31·2
1899	180,733	183,624	142·4	26·2					

* The above figures are exclusive of local consumption, which amounts to about 6,000 to 7,000 metric tons. The values of total produce are derived from the returns of the Chamber of Commerce corrected for balance in store.

† Net selling price. ** Estimate only; figures not available at the time of writing.

There can be little doubt that the sugar industry in Mauritius is still capable of great extension. The resources of the colony are far from being completely utilised, and the profits from the industry are sufficiently great to attract the European capitalist if only local information were more accessible.

First, the fertility of the soil is almost proverbial, and everything in the colony seems to mark it out as the acme of sugar-producing countries. There are still extensive areas awaiting cultivation, if sufficient capital can be obtained to carry the much-needed water to them. The greatest enemy of the planter is, beyond all doubt, shortage of rain; but in the central portion of the island the rainfall never falls below eighty inches a year, while many less favoured countries are considered well-watered with one-half this yearly supply.

Secondly, it has hardly yet been realised to what extent the water-power of the rivers can be developed. There are some forty waterfalls in various parts of the colony, most of which are susceptible of utilisation for electric power generating stations. Some of them are already so utilised on a small scale.

It is not by any means impossible that, as the centralisation of the factory work progresses, sufficient power may be available for the electrification of the mills, and the consequences would be very far-reaching.

BUREAU OF AGRICULTURAL STATISTICS.

Previous to the publication of the information collected for the Royal Commission in 1909 reliable agricultural statistics were entirely wanting in Mauritius except from a few isolated estates.

The work of the Bureau of Agricultural Statistics, which was inaugurated while the Royal Commissioners were still in the colony, has made it possible, under the able direction of Mr. Henri Robert, to keep at least a portion of the information then collected up to date. The publications of this Bureau since its inauguration are as follows:—

Local Sugar Consumption in Regard to Local Production.
Nos Epizooties.
Le Nouveau Procédé Javanais.
The Labour Supply.
The Last Crop (1909-10).
Average Sale Prices of Crop 1909-10.
Les Fluctuations des Cours du Riz et l'Industrie Sucrière.
Estimation de la Coupe 1910-11.
Les Effets du Cyclone du 3-7 Février 1911.
La Culture Cotonnière.
Estimated Total Area in Sugar-cane.
La Dernière Coupe (1910-11).
Moyenne des Prix de Vente des Sucres de la Coupe 1910-11.
La Coupe 1911-12—Estimation.
La Superficie Cultivée en Cannes.
Le Recensement et la Main d'Œuvre.
Moyenne des Prix de Vente des Sucres de la Coupe 1911-12.
L'outillage de nos Usines.
La Coupe 1912-13.

All the available information concerning the condition and progress of the sugar industry in the island since the British occupation up to the year 1908 has been collected and published in book form, under the title of *The Sugar Industry in Mauritius*, by Mr. A. Walter, F.R.A.S., Director of the Royal Alfred Observatory.

REPRESENTATIVE SWORN AND EXCHANGE BROKERS.

1. RENÉ RAFFRAY.
2. EDOUARD ROUILLARD.
3. HENRI GIBLOT DUCRAY.
4. OCTAVE COUVE.
5. GABRIEL REGNARD.
6. A. DE MAROUSSEM.
7. LÉOPOLD ANTELME.
8. GUSTAVE LABAT.
9. JULES REGNARD.
10. C. F. SHAND.

THE SUGAR FACTORIES.

By HENRI ROBERT.

THE following is a list of the fifty-nine sugar factories in active operation in Mauritius. These factories crush their own canes and those of the estates without factories, as well as the canes grown by small planters.

In order to show at a glance the increasing capacity of the factories, their average annual output before and after the economic crisis of 1907-08 is given in columns 3 and 4.

Column 5 does not indicate the *full* capacity of the factories, but the maximum output of each of them recorded during any of the years under review. In most cases that maximum was reached in the "banner year," 1909-10; which signifies that it might be exceeded as things now stand, considering the many improvements effected in the factories since 1909-10, and the consequent increased production of sugar in most of them. For instance, factories which had attained their record total production for one season in 1909-10 with, say, a daily output of thirty-five tons of sugar as a general average, now produce well over forty tons per working day.

FACTORIES.	Total Acreage.	Approximate acreage under Sugar-cane.	Average Annual Sugar Production in Tons. 1902-7	1909-12	Maximum Output in one year.	PROPRIETORS.	ESTATE MANAGERS.
	arpents.				tons.		
Alma	3,221	1,960	5,200	5,450	6,638	Hon. H. Leclézio, C.M.G.	Louis Leclézio.
Antoinette	2,155	1,275	2,550	2,850	3,440	G. Martin & Cie.	Michel Martin.
Argy	3,200	1,150x	1,380	2,760	3,142	Baschet & Cie.	Louis Baschet.
Bassin	3,000	1,100x	1,740	2,520	3,000	Bassin Sugar Estate Co.	Raoul d'Unienville.
Beau Champ and annexes	5,682	3,075	6,350	7,925	9,137	Mauritius Estates and Assets Co.	W. Desplace.
Beau Plan	710	650	3,175	3,940	4,865	Beau Plan Sugar Estate Co.	Robert Piat.
Beau Séjour	2,530,76	1,575	2,550	3,180	4,022	Beau Séjour Sugar Estate Co.	W. P. Ebbels.
Beau Vallon (R.) ...	3,121,17	1,825x	2,525	3,400	3,736	de Rouchecouste & Cie.	F. Coombes.
Bel Air (W.)	647	580	1,230	1,475	1,655	A. J. Wilson.	A. J. Wilson.
Bon Air	1,600	1,400x	1,490	2,200	2,625	A. G. Ossen & Co.	Edg. Chelin.
Belle Vue S. Estate ...	3,032	1,695x	2,000	2,900	3,505	Belle Vue Sugar Estate Co.	H. Rousset.
Belle Vue (Mauricia) ...	1,550,70	825	1,750	2,900	3,605	Nemours Harel.	Antoine Harel.
Belle Vue (Maurel) ...	3,652,21	1,100x	2,100	2,250	2,752	Léon Maurel.	A. Maurel.
Bel Ombre	6,327	2,400x	1,950	2,675	3,232	Bel Ombre Sugar Estate Co.	R. Desvaux.
Bénarès	1,812,52	1,275	2,230	2,900	3,350	Lady Naz.	E. Constantin.
Britannia	3,708,68	2,575	4,750	6,125	8,250	Anglo-Ceylon General Estate Co.	T. W. Innes.
Cent Gaulettes	1,482	815x	1,240	1,720	2,154	Dalais & Cie.	Arth. Dalais.
Constance (La Gaieté)...	3,132,76	1,450x	3,550	4,630	5,240	Constance-La Gaieté Sugar Estate.	Jules Rousset.
Côte d'Or	1,245	975	1,780	1,830	2,561	Charles Castel.	C. Castel.
Deep River	1,947,25	1,120	2,100	2,100	3,172	Deep River Sugar Estate Co.	Raoul Dalais.
Deux Bras	1,365,35	1,120	2,075	2,820	3,133	R. de Rochecouste & Cie.	Edg. Wilson.
Etoile	2,670,83	1,360x	2,260	2,680	3,375	Mauritius Sugar Estate Co.	R. Hein.
Ferney	3,395,73	850x	830	1,530	1,824	Heirs Dumontet.	A. Rey.
Grande Rosalie	1,612,80	1,060	1,780	1,950	2,285	Mauritius Sugar Estate Co.	Geo. Lorans.
Gros Bois	—	2,175	3,425	5,350	7,128	Gros Bois Sugar Estate Co.	Ed. d'Unienville.
Highlands	521	350	2,880	4,800	5,500	Anglo-Ceylon & General Estate Co.	J. Nichols.
Ile d'Ambre	3,138	1,575	2,250	3,160	4,100	Ile d'Ambre Sugar Estate Co.	Maurice Giraud.
Industrie...	—	425	990	1,360	1,565	Atchia Bros.	Atchia.
La Baraque	2,109,98	1,215	3,120	4,690	5,156	A. d'Arifat & Co.	Raoul d'Arifat.
Labourdonnais	2,924,58	1,800	3,150	4,390	5,500	L. Souchon.	Adrien Wiehé.
Le Vallon	4,111,95	1,300x	1,650	2,300	2,689	Le Vallon Sugar Estate Co.	Robert Lagesse.
Médine	3,814,88	550	1,640	2,480	3,029	Médine Sugar Estate Co.	Em. Pastor.
Minissy	1,430	1,025	2,030	2,375	2,851	Hardy & Co.	A. Hardy.
Mon Désert (M.) ...	2,738	2,060	4,750	5,750	7,165	Mon Désert Sugar Estate Co.	Abel Ducray.
Mon Désert (C.) ...	2,748,86	1,525	2,140	4,510	5,483	Ed. & P. Carie.	H. Cuquet.
Mon Loisir (S.)	1,591,51	775	1,230	1,550	2,074	Mon Loisir Sugar Estate Co.	Paul Adam.
Mount	1,620,05	1,185	2,300	2,400	2,745	The Mount Sugar Estate Co.	Roger de Brugada.
Pieterboth	2,228,50	1,475	—	2,430	3,348	Crédit Foncier of Mauritius, Ltd.	Geo. Mackie
Plaisance	1,953,50	1,260	1,890	2,750	3,373	Amd. Hugnin.	Am. Hugnin.
Queen Victoria	2,708,90	1,530	3,000	4,870	5,360	Queen Victoria Sugar Estate Co.	F. Dalais.
Réunion	272	185	2,250	2,250	3,057	Heirs Langlois and others.	Shand Harvey.
Riche Bois	1,671,53	1,440	—	3,550	4,640	Mauritius Sugar Estate Co.	Gaston Harel.
Riche-en-Eau	1,860	1,400	2,675	3,325	3,853	Edg. de Rochecouste.	Em. Voïart.

1 arpent = 1·043 acre. Ton of 1,000 kilos. x Indian plantations on the Estate.

FACTORIES.	Total Acreage.	Approximate acreage under Sugar-cane.	Average Annual Sugar Production in Tons. 1902-7	1909-12	Maximum Output in one year.	PROPRIETORS.	ESTATE MANAGERS.
	arpents.				tons.		
Rich Fund ...	1,196,79	750	4,020	4,560	5,511	Cie. Sucrière de Rich Fund.	Joseph Joly.
Rivière des Anguilles ...	673,01	575	1,620	1,850	2,012	Senneville & Co.	Jules de Senneville.
Rosalie-Constance ...	1,295,75	1,105	1,775	2,310	2,660	Antoine Ulcoq.	Geo. Hardy.
Rose-Belle	2,858,37	2,025x	3,660	4,475	5,241	Mauritius Estates and Assets Co.	T. A. Johnson.
St. Antoine	3,700	1,350	2,800	6,640	7,441	de Chazal & Co.	Francis Rouillard.
St. Aubin	2,927,17	2,000	3,400	4,230	4,756	Gustave Guimbeau.	Emile Labat.
St. Hubert	1,957,31	1,175x	2,000	2,050	3,048	St. Hubert Sugar Estate Co.	Marcel d'Unienville.
Savannah	2,307,27	1,600	3,180	4,075	4,633	Savannah Sugar Estate Co.	Ant. Le Breton.
Sans Souci	6,088	3,700x	5,125	11,650	13,302	Sans Souci & Bel Etang Sug. Est. Co.	Maurice Lagesse.
Solitude (St. André) ...	3,700	1,250x	1,775	2,500	3,205	Le Court de Billot Frère.	J. Le Court de Billot
Tamarin	6,194	900x	1,760	1,975	2,504	Mauritius Estates and Assets Co.	Chalain.
Terracine	1,213,45	1,100	3,170	3,625	4,212	Terracine Sugar Estate Co.	Maxime Rey.
Trianon	2,275	1,550x	2,400	3,640	4,407	de Belzim & Harel.	Am. Carbonel.
Union Beau Bois ...	1,695 61	1,425	2,250	6,400	7,615	Union Beau Bois Sugar Estate Co.	Ray d'Unienville.
Union (S.)	820	700	1,930	2,950	3,383	Union Sugar Estate Co.	Eug. de Senneville.
Union-Bel Air	2,180	1,100x	2,040	3,375	4,616	Union-Chamouny Sugar Estate Co.	G. Mayer.

1 arpent = 1 043 acre. Ton of 1,000 kilos. x Indian plantations on the Estate.

Two factories (Valetta and St. Félix) were closed down at the end of last year (1912); they had together an average annual output of over 4,000 tons of sugar.

Since the 1909-10 record crop (252,000 tons of sugar) the following factories, in addition to the two just named, have been closed down: Jolibois, Union Vale, Chamouny, Espérance (*T.*), and Constance (*M.*), the last having been destroyed by fire.

Of the foregoing fifty-nine factories,

1	(Sans Souci) has actually produced			over 100 tons (115·6 tons) of sugar per working day, average of a whole season.		
5	(*a*) have	do.	do.	60 tons	do.	do.
5	(*b*) ,,	do.	do.	from 51 to 60 tons	do.	do.
9	,,	do.	do.	,, 41 ,, 50 ,,	do.	do.
14	,,	do.	do.	,, 31 ,, 40 ,,	do.	do.
22	,,	do.	do.	,, 20 ,, 30 ,,	do.	do.
3	,,	do.	do.	under 20 ,,	do.	do.
59						

(*a*) Beau Champ, Britannia, Highlands, St. Antoine, Gros Bois.

(*b*) Alma, Mon Désert (Moka), Mon Désert (*C.*), Queen Victoria, Union (*R*).

One of the three factories under 20 tons (Bel Air, *W.*) will this year (1913) double its daily capacity.

The fifty-nine factories can easily give a daily output of 2,350 tons of sugar, that is, can bag an over-normal crop of 235,000 tons of sugar in 100 working days, general average.

The 1910-11 crop (222,837 tons of sugar) was turned out by sixty-four factories in 98.5 working days; whereas, at the rate of 2,350 tons, the fifty-nine factories remaining are capable, in the same number of days, that is, 98·5, of dealing with 231,475 tons of sugar.

The 1903-4 bumper crop of about 224,000 tons of sugar (factory figures) was dealt with by seventy-nine factories in 123 working days; that is, 1,821 tons per day, which means that though the planters have closed down, from 1903-4 to 1912-13, no fewer than twenty of their factories (79-59), the general working capacity has been improved by more than 500 tons of sugar per day. The industrial effect of centralisation is thus strikingly manifested.

SOME OF THE SUGAR FACTORIES.

1. BELLE VUE (MAUREL), RIVIERE DU REMPART.
2. ANTOINETTE, RIVIÈRE DU REMPART.
3. UNION BEAU BOIS, FLACQ.
4. RÉUNION, PLAINES WILHEMS.
5. CONSTANCE (LA GAIETÉ), FLACQ.
6. BEAU CHAMP, FLACQ.
7. ST. AUBIN, SAVANNE.

SOME OF THE SUGAR FACTORIES.

1. BEAU VALLON, GRAND PORT.
2. BRITANNIA, SAVANNE.
3. MONT DÉSERT (C.), GRAND PORT.
4. SOLITUDE (ST. ANDRÉ), PAMPLEMOUSSES.
5. DEUX BRAS, GRAND PORT.
6. UNION (S.), SAVANNE.
7. GROS BOIS, GRAND FORT.

SOME OF THE SUGAR FACTORIES.

1. FERNEY, GRAND PORT
2. BÉNARÈS, SAVANNE.
3. RICHE-EN-EAU, GRAND PORT
4. ALMA, MOKA.
5. MON LOISIR, RIVIÈRE DU REMPART.
6. ARGY, FLACQ
7. LABOURDONNAIS, RIVIÈRE DU REMPART

SOME OF THE SUGAR FACTORIES.

1. RICH FUND, FLACQ.
2. THE MOUNT, PAMPLEMOUSSES.
3. CÔTE D'OR, MOKA.
4. DEEP RIVER, FLACQ.
5. UNION VALE (DISMANTLED), GRAND PORT.
6. MINISSY, MOKA.
7. BEL AIR (W.), SAVANNE.

SOME OF THE SUGAR FACTORIES.

1. RIVIERE DES ANGUILLES, SAVANNE.
2. BELLE VUE (MAURICIA), PAMPLEMOUSSES.
3. RICHE BOIS, SAVANNE
4. TERRACINE, SAVANNE
5. SANS SOUCI, MOKA.
6. BEAU SÉJOUR, RIVIÈRE DU REMPART.
7. SAVANNAH, SAVANNE.

LA BARAQUE, GRAND FORT.

HIGHLANDS, PLAINES WILHEMS.

MEDINE, BLACK RIVER.

ILE D'AMBRE, RIVIÈRE DU REMPART.

AFTERNOON TEA AT BRITANNIA SUGAR ESTATE HOUSE, SAVANNE.
T. W. INNES, THE HON. J. J. GIBSON, A. MACMILLAN, MRS. INNES.

THE ALOE FIBRE INDUSTRY.

By PHILLIP GALEA.

ALOE fibre occupies second rank in the list of the industrial products of Mauritius. Although from various causes referred to in the course of the present article, it is still a long way behind sugar in point of economic importance, its possibilities are admitted to be great, and it is not altogether vain to hope that, with proper attention and stimulus, it may speedily attain a high degree of prosperity.

Mauritius hemp, extracted from the fibre of the aloe plant known under the scientific appellation of *furcræa gigantea,* is already a well-appreciated product on the world's market, and fully holds its own in commercial favour against sisal (the fibre of the Central American *agave*). Although the output of Mauritius hemp is at present somewhat limited—the exports for 1912 being 2,249 tons, representing a money value of Rs. 682,000—the future of this industry is one of great promise, and a few words as to its history and prospects will not, it is hoped, be out of place.

Whether the plant from which our fibre is extracted was originally of indigenous growth in Mauritius and, if not, when and by whom it was first introduced into the island, are matters of uncertainty. It is commonly believed that the *furcræa gigantea* was imported, for ornamental purposes, in 1790, its origin being traced by some to India, by others to Madagascar. On the other hand, we have it on record that, as early as 1701, Deodati, the Dutch Governor of Mauritius, was able to supply an English vessel calling for repairs with, *inter alia,* rigging and cordage apparently of local manufacture. If the Dutch had at their disposal on the island the raw material for making ropes, it seems admissible, to say the least of it, that this early specimen of Mauritius hemp was derived from the *furcræa,* as this is the only plant of the aloe family that has been observed to thrive in a wild state in the island. Be this as it may, the question, after all, is one of academic interest; and it is sufficient for our purposes to record the fact that the *furcræa* thrives remarkably well in Mauritius, requiring practically no cultivation and no attention at the hands of man, and that, even if it was originally imported from elsewhere, it has certainly found here its most congenial *habitat.* So much is this the case that attempts to acclimatize the plant in other fibre-producing centres have never yet proved entirely successful. From all accounts the plantations of Mauritius aloe made on a large scale in South and East Africa, as well as in the Federated Malay States, have not exhibited in the same degree the hardiness of growth and industrial qualities of the parent stock derived from this colony.

NEW MILL ALOE FIBRE FACTORY, PAMPLEMOUSSES.

As at present constituted, the fibre industry of Mauritius may be said to be, in many respects, in a primitive condition. It is, indeed, in its infancy; and, although it undoubtedly has a prosperous future before it, much time and energy will have to be expended ere it attains its legitimate development. The total area under aloe exploited by the estates does not at present exceed 20,000 acres—a noteworthy feature, in view of the fact that aloe grows luxuriantly on vast areas in the low-lying and intermediate districts, which are unsuited to cane cultivation through lack of water. Add to this that, with a few exceptions, there are no fibre *estates* properly speaking, and that regular plantations of aloe are practically unknown, the manufacturers, in most cases, being content to get the leaves they require from the more or less inaccessible places where the plant grows wild. Indeed, the extraordinary ease and abundance with which the aloe thrives in indifferent soil, reproducing itself and becoming luxuriant on the bare hill-sides and in the midst of the thickest brushwood, uncared-for and unheeded by man, seem to have blinded many fibre manufacturers to the practical advantages of establishing regular plantations, laid out within striking distance of the factory and kept up with due attention to the necessary rotation of crops. It is but just to add, however, that this defect is also in a large measure ascribable to lack of capital—perhaps the most severe handicap under which our fibre industry labours; yet, in this as in numerous other cases, it would seem that the required goad has not been applied to man's ingenuity through Nature having proved over-bountiful.

The fibre content of the *furcræa* is inferior to that of the American sisal. Whereas the latter is stated to exhibit an absolute fibre content of ·5 per cent., our aloe leaf contains about 3.5 per cent. of fibre; and, out of this, the primitive machinery we use extracts, on an average, not more than 2.5 per cent. of commercial fibre on the weight of leaf manipulated; so that it takes practically forty tons of leaf to turn out one ton of commercial fibre. In view of these figures, it is evident that the question of the transport of such a large mass of raw material is one of the chief economic problems with which the industry has to contend. Even allowing, on the one hand, for improved machinery enabling a larger proportion of the available fibre to be extracted, and, on the other hand, for any enhancement of the absolute fibre content that rational cultivation and timely harvesting may induce, the ratio between the weight of leaf to be carried to the factory and the ultimate commercial output must in the nature of things remain such as to render the material difficulties and the actual cost of transport a permanent problem of the industry. An obvious remedy would be to lay out regular plantations within easy distances from the factories, and, in districts where natural conditions make the transmission of driving power feasible and comparatively cheap, the solution of the problem might be made more complete by having scutching machines disseminated over the estates. By this means only the "green" fibre (*i.e.*, the fibre as it comes out of the scutching drum more or less mixed with moist pulp, and to which the ratio of commercial fibre stands as 18 : 100 to 20 : 100) would have to be carried over any distance to the factory, where the complementary operations of washing, drying, beating-out and baling the fibre would then be performed. Aloe plantations, where they have been attempted, have involved but little outlay, and the return has been highly encouraging in itself, besides mitigating the difficulties of transport just alluded to. The *furcræa* reproduces itself, not by suckers as does the sisal, but by means of bulbs forming an efflorescence along the stalk which shoots up from the plant when the latter has reached the climax of its growth. The bulbs soon put out little leaves, and they are detached by Nature from the parent stalk when sufficiently developed to vegetate for themselves. The wind carries them "where it listeth," and where they fall they take possession of the soil and soon become healthy and luxuriant plants, however rocky and parched with drought the land may be. As already stated, the *furcræa* is phenomenally hardy. Of natural conditions it resents only excess of cold or moisture; it requires little nourishment from the soil and practically no cultivation. No doubt it will grow more luxuriantly if well looked after; but care must be taken not to "kill it with too much kindness," as, if nursed like more delicate plants, excess of vegetation will cause the fibre content to fall off. As a rule, it will be quite sufficient to weed out the plantations and remove young trees, thorns, etc., about twelve months after planting. The growth up to the time of making the first harvest of leaves occupies about five years; and several successive crops may be harvested from the same plants at intervals of about eighteen months.

In his annual report for 1912, the then President of the Mauritius Chamber of Agriculture, Mr. E. Carcenac, himself a prominent and progressive fibre manufacturer, was able to state from actual experience that the expense of planting 100 acres of *furcræa* in 1906 and cultivating the same up to the end of 1912 amounted, including all costs of upkeep and compound interest at 9 per cent. per annum on all disbursements, to Rs. 2,250. The 100 acres were giving a yearly return of fifty tons of fibre, or, at a minimum profit of Rs. 100 per ton, Rs. 5,000 a year net income. It is true that, after yielding a succession of crops, the actual number of which fluctuates largely according to weather conditions, the

SCENES AT
ALBION ALOE FIBRE FACTORY,
BLACK RIVER.

1. Aloe Plant, *Furcræa Gigantea.*
2. Pits for Washing the Fibre.
3. Drying the Fibre.
4. The Fibre about to pass through the "Battéuse" before being packed for shipment.

plants will give out stalks and thereafter perish; but their reproduction is so easy and inexpensive that, with a little attention, a reliable rotation can be regularly established.

Next comes the question of machinery. This is truly in a most primitive state. Not only is an inordinate proportion of the fibre content lost, but the call made on human labour is so great that the cost of production is far above what it should be. The process followed may be briefly summed up as follows. The leaves, cut by hand in the more or less outlying spots where they are generally harvested from the wild state, are carted to the factory—only a few estates possess tramways. No weighing is done; both the leaves themselves, unless reaped from the home fields, and the cartage being paid for at so much per *bundle;* the number of leaves in each bundle naturally varying with the size and weight of the individual leaves. The fibre is first extracted by means of small scutching drums, generally of two feet diameter. The scutching station consists of from two to six drums. Each operator inserts the leaves, two or three at a time, into the drum in front of which he stands; one half of the leaf goes in and is scraped, the operater holding the other end in his hand; when he feels, from the diminished pressure, that the part inserted is scraped fairly clean, he draws it out, grips the fibre and inserts the other end of the leaf. The fibre, as it comes out of the scutching drum, is of a greenish colour and still has a quantity of moist pulp adhering to it. It is next washed in soap and water and subsequently in clear water, and spread out to dry in the open air on parallel racks. There it remains during a period varying from ten to forty-eight or even seventy two hours, according to the temperature, the degree of sunshine, and the characteristics of the season. When dry it is beaten in a machine called "batteuse," to clear it of the fragments of pulp still clinging to it in the form of a bran-like powder, and finally baled at the rate of 200 to 250 kilos per bale. The baling is done by means of hand-presses, so that much space is wasted and freight expenses are correspondingly heightened.

The main point requiring attention and reform is the scutching, because it is at that stage that the largest wastage occurs and that the use of human labour most severely affects the cost of production. On the one hand, an appreciable percentage of fibre is lost owing to mechanical defects; on the other, the scutching hands are practically specialists and command an excessive wage. They are paid from R. 0.60 to R. 0.80 per cent. kilos of fibre scutched (green), and when the ratio of green to commercial fibre is borne in mind, a simple calculation will show that the cost of scutching alone works out at about Rs. 30 per ton of fibre ready for export. The use of automatic defibrating machines, similar to those employed for sisal in America, would induce a large saving on this score. Such machines are worked by two boys, and, allowing for a minimum output of half a ton of commercial fibre a day, and counting the day's work of boys at R. 0.40, the labour expenses incidental to the scutching of one ton of fibre would thus be reduced from Rs. 30 to R. 1.60. It is, therefore, highly desirable that an effort should be made with a view to finding a defibrating machine suitable for *furcræa.* The question, however, is not free from difficulty. Of the standard models employed with good results in other countries, none has hitherto been experimented with in Mauritius. Perhaps the most celebrated of these machines, the Krupp *New Corona,* is now stated to have proved disappointing with Mauritius aloe, although it is admittedly doing splendid work so far as sisal is concerned. A trial made with Mauritius aloe on a plantation in the Federated Malay States is said to have ended not quite satisfactorily for the *New Corona;* and the Krupp Works recently informed one of our own planters that they were unable, as then advised, to give a guarantee of successful working with *furcræa.* It is highly probable, however, that the makers will be studying the necessary modifications to be effected, and that, ere long, the difficulties encountered on a first trial will be surmounted. On the other hand, the *Ajax* Defibrating Machine, manufactured by the Alma Works, Liversedge, Yorks., is claimed to be suitable for *furcræa* as well as sisal; this model is simple and attractive, and the manufacturers are offering it on trial on exceedingly generous and tempting terms. Again, a local contrivance, invented by Mr. D. J. Macgregor and improved by Messrs. Genève and Hall, engineers, of Port Louis, is working with fair success and may, with further improvement in the course of time, form a substantial contribution towards the solution of this interesting problem. What is required, in a word, is a reliable machine, giving a good extraction in clean fibre, without entailing too much driving power, and enabling the fibre manufacturer to dispense with the onerous and none too satisfactory assistance of the specialised scutching hands. To attain this object the co-operation of the Government seems to be needed. It is not suggested that the Government should give a direct or an indirect subsidy to any particular industry or any particular class of people; but that it should encourage and practically assist experiments and trials conducted for the benefit of the whole country. We are here dealing with an industry requiring stimulus, having an undoubted future before it, but still struggling with difficulties which the majority of those engaged in it are not in a position to overcome. There could be no suggestion of undue interference if the Government took an active and a *practical* part in the trial or conditional purchase of specimens of improved machinery. Much may be hoped, in this connection, from the recent appointment of a Director of Agriculture, who is said to take a lively interest in the possibilities of secondary industries in Mauritius.

Further improvements would be needed in the other stages of manufacture, including the substitution of hydraulic for hand-presses in connection with the baling process. Again, the continual uncertainty of the weather in Mauritius, where there is no season of *absolute* drought (a circumstance, by the way, which has gone far to occasion the recent failure of Sea-Island Cotton), has suggested the desirability of setting up hot-air furnaces for drying the fibre in rainy weather. It is true that sun-dried fibre will always remain the "prime" article, owing to the bleaching action of the sunlight; but it is equally true that the varying periods during which fibre is left to dry in the open air, and the vicissitudes through which it passes meanwhile, cause irregularities of colour which act as a severe handicap on the prompt disposal of Mauritius hemp.

GENÈVE AND HALL'S DEFIBRATING MACHINE AT ALBION ALOE ESTATE, BLACK RIVER

(From left to right: L. HAREL, Jun., Factory Manager; F. V. HALL, C. H. GENÈVE.)

In spite of the difficulties under which it labours, the fibre industry in Mauritius yields profitable returns wherever properly managed. According to a report prepared by Mr. A. Walter and submitted to the Royal Commission in 1909, there were at the time thirty-four aloe factories, fourteen of which were worked by water power, thirteen by steam, three by water and steam combined, one by petroleum motor, and one by electricity. [According to *The Mauritius Almanac* list of factories at the end of this article, the number is now fifty-three.—*Editor*.] The average *inclusive* cost of producing one ton of fibre ready for export was calculated to be Rs. 189, and the average price paid by local merchants for first-grade fibre during the past three years has been slightly over Rs. 300 per ton. On the other hand, London market statistics show conclusively that Mauritius hemp is enjoying a sustained and high degree of favour in competition with sisal and kindred produce; the demand is firmly established, and its decided tendency to become regularly enhanced justifies sanguine expectations as to the future of the industry.

At present there are only 20,000 acres under aloe exploited by the factories. The exports of fibre during the last fourteen years has been as follows:—

	Kilos.	Rs.		Kilos.	Rs.
1899	2,249,809	588,671	1906	1,949,878	737,602
1900	3,105,341	978,049	1907	2,879,685	986,403
1901	1,242,998	353,444	1908	2,141,901	623,655
1902	2,144,609	937,876	1909	1,878,599	530,697
1903	1,518,684	551,233	1910	2,021,226	627,501
1904	1,920,078	627,519	1911	2,129,330	603,490
1905	1,673,922	564,548	1912	2,249,047	679,729

These figures show what remains to be done for the development of this industry. What it requires most of all is intelligent attention from the point of view of technical progress and, especially, capital. The Government should certainly assist in supplying the former requirements—if not, the creation of a Department of Agriculture will have been little more than an idle multiplication of dusty papers and red tape; capital is a matter for private enterprise. When one thinks of the almost unique natural advantages enjoyed by the fibre industry—the abundance of the raw material, the hardiness of growth of the aloe plant, its practical immunity from damage by cyclones, the comparatively trifling outlay involved in its cultivation and manipulation, and the commercial favour with which the produce is meeting, there is every reason to feel confident that, when it is placed on a sound and economic footing, Mauritius hemp will magnificently repay those who engage in it, and hold high rank as one of the world's principal textile products.

One word as to other fibre plants will suffice. *Sisal* has been found to grow well in Mauritius; it requires too much cultivation, however, to become truly an *industrial* plant in this island, so long as the present acutely-felt want of labour lasts, and even were this effectively mitigated, it is a question whether it will pay as well as the hardy *furcræa*, which grows practically uncared for—an immense superiority in any circumstances.

Abaca, or *musa textilis* (Manila hemp), was planted experimentally in the seventies and eighties of last century; the manufactured product was exceedingly fine, but the commercial results poor in proportion. *Ramie* does not appear to have any future before it, and *sansiviera*, which certainly has the advantage of growing naturally and well, remains to be tried industrially.

LIST OF ALOE FIBRE FACTORIES.

Name of Factory.	Name of Owners.
Pamplemoussses.	
Richeterre ...	Genève and Hall
Massilia	Kaylaissin
New Mill	Heirs Atchia
Les Moulins ...	Mamode Hossen
L'Amitié	Mme. Duvivier
Balaclava	S. Mayer
Ville Valio ...	Do.
Bel Air	Do.
Léonbourg ...	Aboo Bakar
Mon Choisy ...	Belle Vue Sugar Estate Co.
Le Hochet ...	Là Société du Hochet.
Rivière du Rempart.	
Melville	Société de Melville
Mare Sèche ...	A. Duclos
L'Union	Asquaciati and Co.
Le Vale	Soc. Boullé and Leclézio
Roche Noire ...	J. Darné
Flacq.	
La Caroline ...	
Providence ...	E. Tostée
Petite Victoria ...	Heirs E. Baschet
Grande Retraite ...	Union Beau Bois Sug. Est. Co.
Plaines Wilhems.	
Stanley	Stanley Sugar Estate Co.
Plaisance	A. Duclos
Chébel	O. Maingard
Solférino	Heirs Mungra
Richelieu	E. Tostée
Grand Port.	
Anse Jonchée ...	Parumputh
Moka.	
Ste. Marie ...	Arnut and Co.
Savanne.	
Choisy	Dr. Lincoln
Black River.	
Beau Songe ...	Bassin Sugar Estate Co.
Sea Side	Atchia Bros.
Goblet	
Mon Repos ...	Mme. F. D'Unienville
Belle Isle	
La Ferme	Heirs Vigoureux
Médine	Médine Sugar Estate Co.
Constance Kahin ...	L. Hardy
St. Antoine ...	Max Poupinel de Valencé
Bosquet	Bosquet Aloe Fibre Co.
Palmyre	Mme. E. Loumeau
Anna	Desmarais Bros.
Yemen	Chalain and Co.
Les Rochers ...	
Gros Cailloux ...	
Cazoté ...	E. Tostée
Albion	
Rivière Noire ...	R. Pitot
Walhalla	E. de Carcenac
Mon Vallon ...	M. McGregor
Petit Verger ...	Vve. C. Nayl
Belle Vue ...	Mamet and Co.
Barachois ...	Sumchund Kistoo
Bernica ...	J. Ganachaud
Port Louis.	
Grand River ...	Grand River Aloe Fibre Co.

THE RUM INDUSTRY.

By JAMES BAX, of the Central Rum Warehouse.

(*Translated from the French.*)

THE rum produced in Mauritius is obtained by the distillation of the molasses which form the residue of the manufacture of sugar.

In spite of careful researches it has not been possible to discover at what period the first distillery was established. It would seem that the distilling industry was contemporaneous with that of sugar making. According to *The Mauritius Almanac* of 1873, edited by Mr. J. B. Kyshe, who was acting as Receiver-General, we find that, in fact, there were then no less than seventy-seven distilleries at work, which seems to indicate that at that time a distillery formed an integral part of most of the sugar factories. The number of distilleries has, however, since greatly diminished. In 1878 there were only thirty-seven distilleries, and this number has to a certain extent been maintained up till now, with this difference, that there are but few distilleries annexed to sugar-factories—in fact, there are only three, namely: "Beau Champ," belonging to the Mauritius Estates and Assets Company, "Ile d'Ambre," belonging to the Ile d'Ambre Sugar Estates Company, and "Beau Vallon," belonging to Messrs. R. de Rochecouste and Company. The other distilleries, which belong to private owners, are distributed in the various districts of the island, and represent a capital of at least Rs. 2,500,000.

L. A. CÉLESTIN,
Superintendent of Inland Revenue and Distilleries.

Prior to the conquest of Madagascar by France (1895), the distilling business was justly considered to be the second industry of Mauritius. The distilleries produce annually about five million litres of rum of various degrees. The rum thus produced is partly consumed in the Colony, the rest being exported to the markets of Madagascar, London, the East Coast of Africa, Seychelles and Aden. The exports of rum to these various markets are subdivided as follows:—The Madagascar market, which is by far the most important, alone takes 1,200 casks of 220 litres per annum, or a total of 2,500,000 litres at 22° Cartier, representing about the half of the output of the island; London takes 3,000 casks of 240 litres or 720,000 litres at 30° Cartier; the African Coast takes about 2,000 casks, or 500,000 litres at 17° Cartier; and Seychelles and Aden together take a little over 40,000 litres at 30° and 36° Cartier, per annum. The local consumption is about 100,000 litres at 23° Cartier monthly, or 1,200,000 per annum.

One of the first measures adopted by the French Government after the conquest of Madagascar was to levy a prohibitive duty on rum coming from Mauritius, and this market is now completely closed to the colony.

As regards the English market it is only open occasionally. The increased price of molasses, together with the difficulty in procuring freight for London, only allows of exportations to that market when the quotations for rum reach 1/6 a gallon at 22°, which occurs but rarely. Thus it is that the average exportation to London during the last ten years was only about 148,000 litres yearly, or about 700 casks.

The East African Coast is also a market completely closed to Mauritius rum, which used to be sent there in exchange for palm oil, elephants' tusks, etc. Messrs. Menthe Bourelli, of Marseilles, who were the only buyers for the African market, and who were represented in Mauritius by the firm of Elias

Mallac and Co., had to give up the business on account of the difficulty they met with in finding vessels to undertake these voyages, which lasted sometimes a year, and also perhaps owing to the rise in the price of rum (Rs. 0·09 per litre of 17° Cartier). Seychelles and Aden therefore remain the only markets, and even the first of these is likely to be lost. The Messageries Maritimes Co., which constitutes the only regular line of communication with Seychelles, generally refuses to take goods, and even passengers, from Mauritius, owing to the epidemics which have been prevailing in the island—first the plague, and just recently smallpox.

It will accordingly be seen from the foregoing how precarious is at present the situation of the distilling industry in this island. Having lost all its means for exportation, Seychelles and Aden alone excepted, the industry is reduced to supplying the local consumption and to the manufacture of denaturalized spirit. Furthermore, the Government has increased so much the Excise dues (as a matter of fact these have risen in thirty years from Rs. 0.96 to Rs. 1.67 per litre at 23° Cartier), that the consumption has weakened, and has dropped from 100,000 litres to 65,000 litres per month. Thus it is that whereas in 1883, with a population of 359,874 inhabitants, the duty being Rs. 0.96 per litre, the consumption was 1,842,690 litres, bringing in to the Government Revenue Rs. 1,772,355; in 1912, that is to say, thirty years later, the

SECTION OF CENTRAL RUM WAREHOUSE, PORT LOUIS.

duty being Rs. 1.67, the local consumption does not exceed 797,070 litres for a population of 368,791 souls, bringing in to the Revenue only Rs. 1,332,107. The consequence is that of the thirty-seven distilleries which were at one time working in the island, only one, that of "Phœnix," situated at Flacq, is working now fairly regularly.

When the heavy loss of capital, which has been the result of the closing down and abandonment of these various distilleries, is considered, one wonders how their owners could have accepted it; for instead of having sought to improve their plant and machinery and their methods of production in order to lower the cost price of the litre of rum, as would have been possible by introducing into their distilleries the progress achieved in Europe in the fermentation of molasses, and in the methods of distillation, which would have brought about a considerable increase in the yield from the molasses (fifty per cent. instead of thirty per cent.), and would have placed them in a position to produce rum of a superior quality, they believed it more profitable to agree to raise the price of rum for local consumption—Rs. 0.42 per litre at 23°—thus calling upon their only outlet to compensate them, if not entirely at least in part, for the losses incurred by the closing of the export markets.

The result was that the Chinese shop-keepers, who have long been established in the Colony, monopolised the retail consumption of rum, and on their part came to an understanding among themselves, and refused to buy rum at this price. They formed a syndicate, known under the name of "Var Siong Kwong Saw," which was authorised by its members to purchase rum by contract only from one distiller. This contract has been in force for five years, and was made on the basis of Rs. 0.17 per litre of 23°.

Such, briefly stated, is the present position of the distilling industry in Mauritius, and it can be seen that it is not over brilliant. It would appear to be without remedy, but such is not the case. It has already been stated that it was only necessary for the distillers of this Colony to apply to the fermentation of their molasses, and to their distilling apparatus, the requisite ameliorations in order to restore to their industry its former prosperity.

MOLASSES.—On an average Mauritius produces annually 400,000,000 pounds of sugar. Formerly it used to be calculated that a million pounds of sugar left 400 half-casks (tiercons) of molasses Some years ago the factory owners resolved to enter on a path of progress. The factories are being every year improved, and at present one can only reckon on 250 tiercons of molasses for each million pounds of sugar, which brings the total number of available tiercons of molasses to 100,000.

Of these 100,000 tiercons, susceptible of producing 6,000,000 litres of rum at 30° Cartier if they be distilled, 20,000 tiercons only find their way to the distillery. The syrup for distilling weighs 40° Beaumé, and is at present worth from Rs. 6 to Rs. 7 for two tiercons delivered at the distillery. The 80,000 tiercons of molasses remaining are either exported to India or employed on the estates for manurial purposes.

INTERIOR OF CENTRAL RUM WAREHOUSE, PORT LOUIS.

FERMENTATION.—The process of producing fermentation in molasses is carried on in a very haphazard manner, the employment of pure ferments being unknown. Suffice it to say that, to obtain ferment, a certain quantity of molasses at 40° Beaumé is placed in a vessel to which water is added to reduce it to 10° Beaumé, and there it is left to ferment.

When the first ferment is obtained, no matter what may be its alcoholic density, it is gradually added to until a sufficient quantity is obtained for charging the basins.

These basins are leaded receptacles, rectangular in shape, in which the molasses are diluted down to 10° Beaumé. When the dilution has been thoroughly made, the ferment is introduced. Fermentation soon spreads throughout the mass of liquid, and lasts from thirty-six to forty-eight hours according to the season and generally falls to 3° or 4° Beaumé.

DISTILLATION.—After the fermentation is over the must is sent to the distillery. The apparatus in use is somewhat primitive, and the principal parts of it are :—

2 Heaters in copper or in wood,
1 Copper distilling column,
1 Copper column, locally known by the name of "Trois Six,"
2 Horizontal circular rectifiers, and
1 Receptacle with double bottom into which the rum descends, called "Florentin."

The distillation is effected by means of steam. The apparatus makes rum in one process, the rum running generally at 30° Cartier. There is not a single rectifying apparatus in the Colony. On leaving the "Florentin" the rum is conducted by pipes to the store, where it is placed in vats.

The distillation is carried on under the control of Government. An inspector is for this purpose attached to the distillery, which is opened, worked and closed in his presence. The day's work is of twelve hours (6 a.m. to 6 p.m.). In order to be allowed to distil, a license of Rs. 550 for six months must be paid, and a guarantee of Rs. 15,000 has also to be furnished. The cost price of a litre of rum varies according to the price of molasses, of fuel, the yield from the molasses, and especially according to the amount of work performed. The following is a rough estimate of the cost of a litre of rum at a distillery capable of turning out 6,000 litres of rum daily, working twenty days in the month :—

Purchase and transport of 2,000 tiercons @ Rs. 7 for 2 tiercons	Rs. 7,000·00	
Fuel - 20 days @ Rs. 40 *per diem*	800·00	
License—Rs. 550 for six months = for one month ...	91·66	
Transport of rum, 500 casks @ Rs. 1...	500·00	
Warehousing	1,200·00	
Upkeep and repairs	300·00	
		Rs. 9,891·66
Staff—1 distiller	Rs. 50·00	
1 cooper	30·00	
2 stokers @ Rs. 20	40·00	
1 assistant stoker	16·00	
1 man in charge of the basins	30·00	
3 men working the basins @ Rs. 16	48·00	
1 watchman	15·00	
10		229·00
		Rs. 10,120·66
Expenses in town—cost of office, clerk, messenger, etc.		200·00
		Rs. 10,320·66

which brings the cost price of the rum at Rs. 0.08$\frac{3}{5}$, but if to this be added the loss by evaporation (2%), the cost price can be put down at Rs. 0.09.

Once the rum has been distilled it is despatched to Port Louis to be stored, at the cost of the distiller, in the vats of the Central Rum Warehouse, a building belonging to a company to which the Colonial Government has granted the monopoly of the storage of all the rum made in the Colony. It receives from the distiller a storage fee, or rent, equivalent to about one cent. per litre of rum stored per month, broken periods included.

Further information about the Central Rum Warehouse will be found in the section of this volume devoted to the local business concerns.

The following table gives the consumption and the duty levied from 1883 to 1912 :—

Years.	Excise Duty.	Home Consumption	Total of Duty Levied
	Rs.	Litres.	Rs.
1883 ...	0·96	1,842,696	1,772,355
1884 ..	0·96	1,784,546	1,715,891
1885 ...	0·96	1,324,583	1,273,614
1886 ..	0·96	1,390,387	1,336,940
1887 ...	1·00	1,300,199	1,302,402
1888 ...	1·00	1,273,235	1,275,179
1889 ...	1·05	1,450,613	1,532,505
1890 ...	1.11	1,379,466	1,533,018
1891 ..	1·21	1,289,370	1,566,998
1892 ..	1.21	1,147,684	1,394,528
1893 ...	1·21	1,083,053	1,321,756
1894 ...	1·32	1,026,839	1,358,634

Years.	Excise Duty.	Home Consumption.	Total of Duty Levied.
	Rs.	Litres.	Rs.
1895 ...	1·32	891,365	1,152,492
1896 ...	1·21	1,052,648	1,274,808
1897 ...	1·32	936,422	1,239,775
1898 ...	1·32	801,488	1,067,604
1899 ...	1·32 & 1·45	978,128	1,359,677
1900 ...	1·45	1,004,903	1,462,485
1901 ...	1·45	1,012,831	1,475,880
1902 ...	1·45	1,008,440	1,463,589
1903 ...	1·45	948,341	1,376,253
1904 ...	1·45 & 1·67	895,195	1,362,447
1905 ...	1·67	781,454	1,305,836
1906 ...	1·67	778,169	1,300,044
1907 ...	1·67	651,994	1,089,140
1908 ...	1·67	447,146	747,031
1909 ...	1·67	580,256	969,336
1910 ...	1·67	806,833	1,347,464
1911 ...	1·67	840,110	1,382,984
1912 ...	1·67	797,070	1,332,107

Thus, therefore, in thirty years the consumption dropped from 1,842,696 litres a year to 797,070, due entirely to the surcharge of duty. Mauritius rum is perhaps that which is the most heavily taxed in the world. In France the duty per hectolitre of pure alcohol is frcs. 493·85, which, with exchange at 52½%, is equivalent to Rs. 308·65; whereas, in Mauritius the duty is Rs. 1·67 the litre at 23°, plus 8 cents for each supplementary degree. But as 100° of the alcometre of Guy Lussac equals 44° of that of Cartier, there is therefore a supplement of 21°, which gives Rs. 1.68 in excess by litre. Therefore the litre of pure alcohol pays Rs. 1.67 plus Rs. 1.68 = Rs. 3.35 the hectolitre of pure alcohol.

From the point of view of public hygiene the result is satisfactory enough; in fact, the following tabular statement shows the consumption per head from 1861 to 1911:—

Date of Census.	Consumption of Rum.	Imported Alcohol.	Total.	Population.	Average Quantity.
	Litres.	Litres.			Litres.
1861	1,465,266	212,244	1,677,511	310,050	5·73
1871	1,293,100	153,715	1,446,815	316,042	4·57
1881	1,419,508	164,830	1,584,338	359,874	4·40
1891	1,289,370	99,622	1,388,992	370,588	3·74
1901	1,012,831	132,083	1,144,914	371,023	3·08
1911	840,110	178,827	918,937	368,791	2·50

From this table, therefore, we find that the average local consumption per head is 2 litres, 50 centilitres, at 23° Cartier, which represents in pure alcohol: $x = \frac{2\cdot50 \times 23}{44} = 1\cdot30$ litre pure alcohol per head; whereas the average consumption of alcohol per head in France is 4.56, England 3.56, Sweden 3.53, and Norway 1.33 litres, from which it can be seen that Mauritius is one of the countries least addicted to alcoholism.

Retail Sale of Rum.—Rum for local consumption is delivered at 23° by the distillers to the traders on "Request Notes" on the Rum Warehouse. Provided with a "Request Note," the trader goes to the Rum Warehouse with his cask, which is weighed and measured by the Government Inspector. After all the fiscal formalities, namely: Rs. 1.69 per litre duty, storage, and fees for diluting included, have been complied with, this cask, accompanied by a transport permit, is removed to the shop, and the rum retailed to the public by the dozen bottles, single bottles, or by "grogs."

SALE BY DOZEN.—Sales by the dozen leave but small profits:—

The dozen of rum is sold at present at ... ... Rs. 16·80

But the trader has to pay:—

To Government	Rs. 1·69	
To the Distiller	0·17	
	Rs 1·86 per litre	

or for 9 litres, or one dozen bottles, Rs. 16.74, which only leaves a profit of six cents a dozen. Thus it is that the traders who sell by the dozen regard this business as being not so much one of profits as being a means of attracting to their stores a number of small customers who, at the same time as they buy their rum, purchase also other articles.

SALES BY THE BOTTLE.—Rum is sold by the bottle or by "grogs" ("toppette") at 20° Cartier. The retailer who, as has been shown above, buys his rum direct from the Warehouse, pays Rs. 16·74 per dozen bottles, that is to say, per 9 litres; and to reduce it to 20° Cartier he adds 2 litres of water. Accordingly, 11 litres of rum of 20° cost Rs. 16.74, which brings the price of a litre of rum at 20° to Rs. 1.52, or, for 9 litres, Rs. 13.58, which, divided by one dozen bottles, gives the price of a bottle at Rs. 1.13. A bottle of rum is retailed at Rs. 1.35, and, therefore, leaves a profit of 22 cents net per bottle.

SALES BY "GROGS."—It has been seen that the litre of rum at 20° costs Rs. 1.52. The "grog" is equivalent to a half decilitre, and is sold at 10 cents The retailer consequently makes Rs. 2.00 on his litre at 20°, or a profit of 48 cents per litre. If the retailer buys his rum by the dozen (Rs. 16.80) his profits are evidently one rupee less, but still they are considerable.

EXPORTATION.—The exports, as has already been pointed out, are now limited to shipments to Seychelles and Aden, and occasionally to London.

The following statement shows clearly what were the exports prior to the taking of Madagascar by the French in 1895, and what they have been since:—

Year.	Amount Exported.	Year.	Amount Exported.
	Litres.	(After the French occupation of Madagascar).	Litres.
1878 ...	4,329,998	1896 ...	2,536,866
1879 ...	3,848,628	1897 ...	528,546
1880 ...	3,099,275	1898 ...	831,067
1881 ...	3,795,909	1899 ...	1,431,599
1882 ...	4,119,622	1900 ...	1,917,081
1883 ...	2,363,938	1901 ...	785,810
1884 ...	3,193,085	1902 ...	155,917
1885 ...	3,693,399	1903 ...	47,381
1886 ...	3,350,355	1904 ...	97,020
1887 ...	3,234,836	1905 ...	53,763
1888 ...	2,371,543	1906 ...	50,421
1889 ...	3,293,103	1907 ...	219,475
1890 ...	3,412,501	1908 ...	656,731
1891 ...	3,815,516	1909 ...	240,881
1892 ...	2,738,505	1910 ...	168,761
1893 ...	2,606,980	1911 ...	248,451
1894 ...	3,078,186	1912 ...	87,474
1895 ...	3,026,372		

DENATURALIZED SPIRIT.—At last, after some years, attention was turned to the denaturalization of rum which is used for lighting purposes. This is known in the Colony as "alcool dénaturé," the consumption of which has reached 4,000 litres a month, the price being 25 cents a litre. The Government exacts a minimum duty of 2 cents on each 5 litres, or less than 5 litres withdrawn from the local consumption, to meet the cost of denaturalization; and a further charge of 2 cents per degree for each 115 litres or fraction thereof thus denaturalized.

LEGISLATION.

By E. ROGER PEZZANI, Barrister-at-Law.

"Every cog of every wheel in the complicated machine of State has been placed there by law. The dignity of the law overshadows it all, providing for everything and justifying everything."
—SWETTENHAM (on Mauritius), *Also and Perhaps, p. 177.*

E. ROGER PEZZANI,
Barrister-at-Law.

THE Mauritius Legislature, which has brought upon itself the foregoing sarcastic and not altogether unjustified criticism from Sir Frank Swettenham, is yet young. Its present constitution dates from 1885, but it traces its origin back to the early thirties of last century.

Indeed, a small Council had been established under Letters Patent of February 9th, 1825; but it consisted of the Governor and four officials—the Chief Justice, the Chief Secretary, the Officer Commanding the Troops, and Mr. A. W. Blanc, Collector of Customs; and although one can still read in the archives of the colony a Government Notice of August 19th, 1825, setting forth in its peculiar wording that on the Wednesday previous "the members of His Majesty's *Council* were sworn in, the customary oaths having been administered to the members thereof by His Excellency the Governor, in presence of the chief authorities of the settlement and under a royal salute from the batteries on the occasion," it can hardly be said that such an exclusively official body was in any way the parent of the present semi-elected Chamber.

It was only in 1832, on 18th January, to be precise, that the admission of a number of unofficial members to the Council table in virtue of Letters Patent of June 24th, 1831, laid the foundation of the present Legislature.

The sequence of events leading up to this important political happening was briefly as follows: Some twenty years had elapsed since the French reverses culminating in the Treaty of Paris and the surrender of Mauritius to Major-General Henry Warde and Commodore Josias Rowley. The colony, or rather the settlement, to repeat the expression of the Government Notice of 1825—an uncomplimentary expression indeed to the French colonists, who had materially advanced the prosperity and degree of civilisation of the island from 1721–1810—had, during those twenty years, benefited by the wisdom of the rule of some enlightened Governors, more especially Sir Robert Farquhar, Bart., under instructions from Lord Minto, Viceroy of India; the Hon. Sir G. Lowry Cole, and the Hon. Sir Charles Colville, K.C.B.

Their well-intentioned efforts on behalf of the island had, however, been persistently opposed and counteracted at home by the ebullient activities of the Anti-Slavery Society. That body, in its attempts to rouse feeling in England and obtain the emancipation of slaves without regard for vested rights, had forgotten itself so far as to defame the colonists by recklessly publishing perverse accounts of the condition of slaves in Mauritius. Slaves were represented as the victims of a "series of cold, calculating, deliberate, bloody-minded ferocity," dictated by "the cruel and sanguinary cupidity of the planters"; it was said they were whipped until their bodies were a "bloody mass of lacerated flesh, and to this was added the further excruciating torture of the application of lime juice or salt or pepper," and that "the so-called ladies (of the colony) often hired their women slaves out to the soldiers for the purpose of prostitution" (*Souvenirs d'Adrien d'Epinay*, pp. 54, 55).

Such ghastly fabrications, redolent of Chinese barbarism, and such scurrilous attacks on what the colonists held most dear, created a storm of indignation among them and a sense of insecurity which they felt they must remedy without delay under pain of annihilation. The importance of the liberty of

ELECTED MEMBERS OF THE COUNCIL OF GOVERNMENT.

1. THE HON. HENRI LECLÉZIO, C.M.G. (Moka).
2. THE HON. Dr. EUGÈNE A. O. LAURENT (Port Louis).
3. THE HON. G. EDOUARD NAIRAC (Port Louis).
4. THE HON. V. AMAND ESNOUF (Plaines Wilhems).
5. THE HON. FREDERIC MELCHIOR LOUIS ROUILLARD (Savanne).
6. THE HON. E. EMILE SAUZIER, K.C. (Pamplemousses).
7. THE HON. JOSEPH A. DUCLOS (Flacq).
8. THE HON. JOSEPH ANTOINE MAURICE MARTIN (Rivière du Rempart).
9. THE HON. GASTON GÉBERT (Grand Port).
10. THE HON. GASTON ANTELME (Black River).

the Press, then unknown in the colony, and the necessity or obtaining a share of control in the affairs of their native land, came home to them as some means of relief.

They accordingly deputed one of themselves, Mr. Adrien d'Epinay, a stout-hearted man and a powerful advocate and jurist, to vindicate their honour and voice their grievances. He left for London on 10th October, 1830, and returned in October, 1831. His success had been complete. Lord Goderich, who was then in charge of the Colonial Department of the War Office, had shaken himself free, for a while, of the intrigues and wire-pulling of the powerful abolitionist party, and had agreed to give the colonists the right of free speech, in the Press and at the Council table.

Under instructions embodied in L. P. of 24th June, 1831, rendered public in the colony by Government Notice of 18th January, 1832, the Governor (Sir Charles Colville) was empowered "to establish and constitute a *Council of Government* composed of certain officers of the Crown and of *an equal number* of other persons to be taken from the chief landed proprietors and principal merchants of the colony, and to nominate and appoint the latter by commissions to be issued by him."

Thus it may be said that by yet another curious effect of poetic justice, Mauritius received its impetus in the direction of political reform and advancement by operation of the intrigues and machinations of its calumniator, The Anti-Slavery Society.

The nefarious political events that followed the grant of that restricted constitution to the colony are beyond the scope of this essay. The verdict of history stands out in heavy type even now against the share which John Jeremie took in attempting to undo what the charter of 1831 had done, and in sowing, between the conquerors and the conquered, those seeds of distrust, the vigorous roots of which it may yet take another generation to completely eradicate.

GOVERNMENT HOUSE, PORT LOUIS.

Suffice it to say that the first legislative body, representative to some limited extent of local public opinion, met for the first time on January 25th, 1832. The Government Notice issued on that date recites that "at the levee held at Government House . . . . . . the Royal Commission to His Excellency the Governor was read with the accustomed honours, and His Excellency and the Members of the *Council of Government* then present took the prescribed oaths in the presence of the Public Authorities and principal inhabitants of the colony." They then adjourned to the banqueting room at Government House, where the first meeting was held, and a Committee appointed to frame rules and regulations for the conduct of business in the Council. It was styled, as has been seen, the *Council of Government*, and by that name it has been known ever since, even after further changes in 1885. It consisted of the Governor and seven officials—the Chief Judge, the Officer in Command of the Forces, the Colonial Secretary, the Collector of Customs, the Advocate-General, the Procureur-General, the Protector of Slaves, and of "an equal number" of unofficial members—Pierre Lucas, Adrien d'Epinay, Laurent Barbé, Jacques Gaillardon, Edouard Pitot, Charles Millien, Antoine Bestel. The public was not admitted, and d'Epinay's attempt to obtain full public discussion was abortive (see his letter of 14th May, 1832, to Sir Charles Colville and the latter's reply at the meeting held on 5th June). None of the seven official or seven unofficial members had any powers to originate discussion—that lay exclusively with the Governor; but the Government had under the new régime the benefit of the advice and opinion of prominent members of the community, whilst dexterously humouring its impatient French subjects' legitimate demand for recognition.

The advent of those advisory bodies in the field of legislation (1825-1832) brought into being the method of legislating locally by ordinances, and did away with the rough-and-ready practice that had as yet obtained, ever since the surrender of the island, of legislating by proclamations issued in virtue of Royal instructions by the Governor, who united in his person until then all executive and legislative powers.

Most of those proclamations are now inoperative. Meant as expedients to bridge the inevitable gulf that had at first estranged the conquered from the conquerors, they are now spent; they are known as the Code of Farquhar, and their perusal is instructive of British direct and tactful methods to win the confidence of hostile subjects; but also, it must be admitted, of blunt and tactless attempts at absorbing them.

MAJOR-GENERAL CHARLES RUDYERD SIMPSON, C.B., General Officer in Command of the Troops.

In like manner the ordinances passed before 1832 are now, with very few exceptions, mere fossils on the statute book of the colony. As an apt and historically interesting illustration, the very first ordinance that was enacted in the island was passed on 8th September, 1825; it commuted the sentence of death of "one Rémy, a negro slave of the widow Robert, for robbery and house-breaking, into that of twenty-six years' chains." Such a reprieve would now of course be decreed by the Executive, *i.e.*, the Governor in Executive Council.

From 1832 onwards, on the other hand, a considerable number of enactments were promulgated, the great majority of which are yet extant, some in an altered or amended form, as part of the law of the land. The more important amongst those which immediately engaged the attention of the newly-constituted Council of 1832 were: The Penal Code, The Press Ordinance, The Abolition of Slavery Ordinance.

From 1832 to 1885 no change is worthy of note except that the number of members was increased to sixteen.

In 1882, after a vigorous campaign led by Messrs. Lois Raoul and Newton (now Sir William Newton) with a view to obtain a semi-elected Council, a monster petition was sent to the Queen, because, in the words of Governor Hennessy, "it was recognised that a Council entirely nominated by the Governor or by the Secretary of State was unsuited to so enlightened a population as that of Mauritius. Nor could it be denied that a purely nominee Council was at variance with the genius of the British Constitution, which associates the principle of representation with the power of levying taxes and of spending public money.

On December 21st, 1884, Mr. Raoul carried a resolution to the same effect in Council. The reform movement was opposed with considerable energy by Mr. (afterwards Sir) Célicourt Antelme, but the reformists won the day owing to the powerful assistance of Sir John Pope Hennessy, and after some correspondence with Lord Derby and his successor, Colonel Stanley, the final change came with despatch No. 89, of 19th September, 1885, and an elected element was introduced.

Letters Patent of 16th September, 1885 (modified by L.P. of 23rd September, 1894, 14th August, 1901, and 19th November, 1904), radically altered the constitution of the old Council of 1832. By operation of these charters the Council of Government now consists of the Governor, who has an original and a casting vote, ten elected members, eight ex-officio members, and nine nominated members, one-third of whom at least must be, and five of whom have hitherto been, in practice, "persons not holding any office in the public service of the colony." The elected element is returned by the nine districts of the colony, Port Louis returning two members and every other district one. Every candidate must be an elector, but he cannot be a minister of religion or the holder of an office of emolument under the Crown.

Every elector must be a British subject, sane, and of age. He must be a male, and may that qualification long stand in Mauritius! He must not have been on the rates within a certain period of his intended registration, nor have been sentenced for perjury; and having been convicted for certain specified periods, he must first have secured. his pardon. He must have resided in the colony for three years at least previous to the date of registration. It was held in 1911 by the High Court in *Lacaze* v. *de Ranville* that these words did not mean the three years immediately preceding registration. The soundness of that decision may, however, be doubted.

MAJOR-GENERAL CHARLES RUDYERD SIMPSON, C.B., AND HIS STAFF OF OFFICERS.

(Reading from left to right, standing:—Major A. G. PRATT, Essex Regiment; Major O. STRIEDINGER, A.S.C.; Major S. H. DUXBURY, A.P.D.; Lieut. H. A. L. ROSE, R.A. (A.D.C.); seated, Lieut.-Colonel INNISS, R.A.M.C.; Lieut.-Colonel C. W. RICHARDSON, R.A.; Major-General C. R. SIMPSON, C.B.; Lieut.-Colonel H. PRENTICE, R.E.)

The other franchise qualifications are based on realty of the net value of £20 per annum; payment of rent of the like amount; personalty of the value of £200; the quality of husband or eldest son of a female possessing any of the foregoing qualifications; salary of £40 a year; payment of license duty of £14 per annum. These qualifications are to be kept up within specified periods previous to the 1st January of the year of registration, and within the district in which the elector seeks to obtain a vote. Plural voting exists, but in a restricted sense. The number of registered electors on 31st December, 1910, was 6,399; the number of votes polled in January, 1911, was 4,357. These figures afford an interesting comparison with those of 1886—4,059 and 3,886 respectively. Further provision has been made for those elections by Ordinances Nos. 5 of 1887, 6 of 1889, 22 of 1895, and 13 of 1912.

Members are elected for five years. The Governor may at any time by proclamation prorogue or dissolve the Council. There must be "at least one session in the Council in every year," and the Governor fixes by proclamation the time and place where it is to be held. The Council as a matter of practice meets in the Council Room at Government House, Port Louis. It sits on an average twice a month from May to December in every year. The Governor, or his deputy, presides at the head of a horseshoe table covered with green baize. The officials and nominees occupy the rest of the table. In the centre is another rectangular table. The Clerk sits with his back to the President, with a silver mace (presented in 1886 by Sir John Pope Hennessy) in front of him at the head of that table, and the elected members occupy the three other sides.

HONG KONG AND SINGAPORE BATTALION, ROYAL GARRISON ARTILLERY, LINE BARRACKS, PORT LOUIS.

At the opening of the session, pursuant to a proclamation, new members, if any, are sworn in. The Governor reads the Speech from the Throne in the Throne Room and declares that the session is open. A Committee of Council, composed of all its members down to 1906, and since of the unofficial members only, then retires to the Council chambers, and prepares an Address in reply to the Speech. The reply is subsequently read to the Governor in the Throne Room.

Any member of Council, if seconded, may propose practically any question for debate, so long as it does not involve expenditure or is not meant to recall expenditure already approved, nor does not aim at bringing about the suspension of Standing Orders. In such cases the Governor's sanction or consent must first be obtained.

Any such question may be pressed to a division and decided by a majority of the votes of the members present. Bearing in mind the figures already given, it may appear that the position of the Government is insecure—the non-official vote being fifteen strong, while the officials can only muster thirteen votes. The non official supremacy is, however, purely nominal, and the Government is taking no actual risk; so much so, indeed, that it has never deemed it necessary to resort to the strict letter of the Charter of 1885, by the enforcement of which the tables might be turned and the present unofficial majority of fifteen against thirteen reversed into the inverse minority.

The explanation is simple enough. The Government expects, and not unreasonably, that parochial interests, always rife in a colony, will create a division among the elected members. In the second place, should they present a serried and united front, then it is very likely that the unofficial nominees, who take their seats on the assumption that they are in sympathy with the broad lines of the Government's policy, will be hand and glove with the elected opposition on any one occasion. The vote of even one of the present five nominees in favour of the Government would divide the Council equally, and the

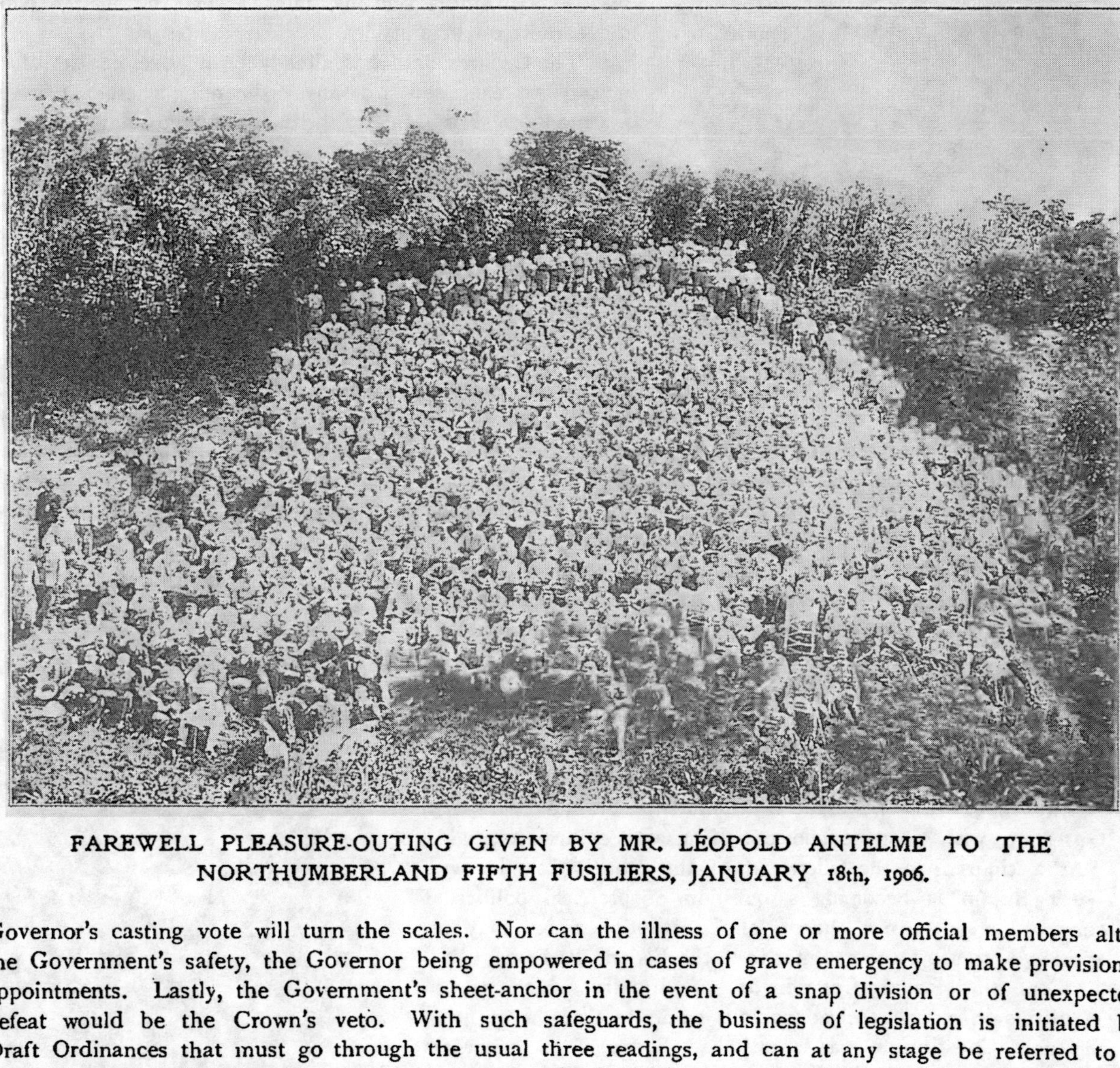

FAREWELL PLEASURE-OUTING GIVEN BY MR. LÉOPOLD ANTELME TO THE NORTHUMBERLAND FIFTH FUSILIERS, JANUARY 18th, 1906.

Governor's casting vote will turn the scales. Nor can the illness of one or more official members alter the Government's safety, the Governor being empowered in cases of grave emergency to make provisional appointments. Lastly, the Government's sheet-anchor in the event of a snap division or of unexpected defeat would be the Crown's veto. With such safeguards, the business of legislation is initiated by Draft Ordinances that must go through the usual three readings, and can at any stage be referred to a Committee. Standing Committees are appointed at the beginning of each session. After the third reading the Ordinance is enacted as it stands, by the Governor assenting thereto in writing "with the advice and consent of the Council of Government." Ordinances come into operation on the day of their publication in the Government Gazette. They must be assented to by the Governor in the year in which they have been passed by Council (*semble* the Governor has a discretionary power to reserve or assent to, with reservations, *any* ordinance), unless they require to be reserved for the signification of His

L. L. KERR,
Inspector-General of Police.

Majesty's pleasure. Of such a class are those dealing with divorce; donations to the Governor; status of public officers; currency banking; differential duties; treaty obligations of Great Britain; His Majesty's sea and land forces; the Royal prerogative; rights and property of British subjects absent from the colony; British shipping; differential caste or race treatment; matters already disallowed by the Crown. Such ordinances can only take effect in the usual way when His Majesty's pleasure has been made known. Indeed, in certain extreme cases, they may be brought into immediate operation by the Governor, but he must report the matter home at the earliest opportunity.

The Crown's veto has already been adverted to; of course it can be exercised on any ordinance, whether reserved or assented to. His Majesty's disallowance of any enactment is notified by proclamation, and from the date thereof the enactment ceases to have effect. Lastly, it should be said, that the Crown has the "undoubted right, by and with the advice and consent of. Parliament, or with the advice of . . . . the Privy Council, to make from time to time all such laws as may . . . . appear necessary for the peace, order, and good government of the colony."

Such then, synoptically, is the history, and such the powers of that legislative instrument, the offspring of which has been the target of Sir Frank Swettenham's sarcastic and gifted pen—a single semi-elected Chamber so constituted that the elective and nominated elements can in full liberty of speech denounce any abuse, call for official and authoritative statements, riddle any Government measure with criticism that may lead to its being dropped, that can be most damaging, but can never be destructive supposing the Government is bent on seeing it through.

Through its labours a considerable portion of French Law (Code Napoleon) preserved by Art. 8 of the Capitulations (1810) has been amended or repealed; and it is doubtless only fair to record the talent and credit with which men like Sir Célicourt Antelme, Mr. G. Guibert, Sir Virgile Naz, Sir William Newton, and Messrs. Ritter and Leclézio have discharged themselves of their duties as lawgivers.

The Reformed Council met for the first time on 19th April, 1886. In his speech from the Throne the then Governor, with characteristic optimism and enthusiasm, said: "At a time when the federation of the British Colonies with Great Britain is becoming a question of practical politics, I congratulate you on a change of Constitution which may yet entitle you to send a representative to the Federal Parliament."

Yet the Royal Commission of Inquiry which sat in Mauritius in 1909 received copious evidence that the grant of the new Constitution was a mistake. Some of the witnesses were men of weight, and they earnestly advocated the reversion to the old Constitution of 1832.

The question of further political change is thus once more at issue.

It must be admitted that the Election Rabble Riots of 1911, which were underrated in London, are some indication

C. W. DUNCAN,
Deputy Inspector-General of Police.

of the worst kind of political unrest in a small colony with a heterogeneous population. It must be remembered that all through 1908, 1909, and 1910, the lowest classes were kept on the *qui vive* of political agitation by "patriots," avowedly inflamed with the civic desire to have the leading men of the colony belittled by Royal Commissioners, but secretly bent on burrowing their way to the Council table. The question is whether such agitation if renewed could have any other effect for a sugar-producing colony like Mauritius than dangerous ebullition among the class from which are recruited idlers, criminals, and labourers.

MILITARY BARRACKS, VACOAS.

The Royal Commissioners in their report agree that the present Législature is not "under the circumstances . . . . . the best form of government." From a perusal of their report it would appear that they felt, during their very short stay in Mauritius, disquieting political symptoms; that they realised that, although the Reformists had not made the best of their opportunities, they had not shown themselves quite unworthy of political emancipation; and that being unable, for want of maturer consideration, to advise a retrograde or progressive policy, they recommended the *statu quo*.

One expected more than such *aurea mediocritas;* but they could not do better (and they have done some good) with their departmental and one-sided knowledge, and their over-diligent inquiry into the other side of the question.

Truth to say, there appear now and then in the report such paternal recommendations as regards the Asiatic element in Mauritius that the hostile critic might wonder if the Indianisation of Mauritius was not an unconscious alternative in their minds to the recommended *statu quo*.

TREASURY BUILDING, PORT LOUIS.

Of course, it would be mere affectation to pretend that the "redistribution of seats on a numerically fairer basis, which, if seriously demanded, the Government could not reasonably refuse"—Report of the Mauritius Royal Commission, sec. 284—would render the task of the Government much easier. The question is, however, for how long? Indo-Creoles are not the meek lambs that the armchair politician takes pleasure in picturing to himself; those whose life has been spent chiefly in Mauritius know how fractious they are becoming daily. To such people the policy of distrusting collaborators one hundred years old, and of attempting to oust them in favour of a servile horde yet unreclaimed from heathendom and barbarism, is the unstatesmanlike policy of the blind-alley, to say nothing of its unfairness. It is also as well to quote Lord Derby's words in his despatch of 12th April, 1884: ". . . . . . Her Majesty's Government would not object to . . . . . constituencies enjoying such a franchise as would include those persons of every race who would be *capable of exercising it with intelligence and responsibility.*"

Moreover, although the situation is clearly not satisfactory, there is every indication of coming improvement. The liberal policy followed so far is every day bearing fruit and daily paving the way to a better understanding between the Government and the inhabitants. All the youths of the colony get the benefit of an English education nowadays, and act as a buffer state between their elders and what is too frequently the rough-and-ready way of the administration. Surely a little discipline and tolerance in the ranks of the Service, a little cheerfulness and self-restraint on the part of the public, would do much definitely to bury the hatchet; and another generation would do the rest.

What then is the need of a political change? There can be no satisfactory system of Government without a healthy and sensible opposition. That system is fully capable of doing ample justice to any legitimate grievance on the part of any section of the community, as witness, to quote the latest enactments (1912)—The Money Lending Relief Ordinance; The Civil Status (Indian Marriages) Ordinance; The Donations and Wills Ordinance; The Companies' Ordinance. Lastly, that system is capable not only of social pleasantness and educative intercourse, but of strong moral help and assistance whenever appealed to in the difficult task of administration.

The irresistible conclusion tends therefore towards the *statu quo*, but towards a level-headed, well-intentioned, not a vacillating, malevolent *statu quo*. Then, and then only, will be solved in hearty co-operation such besetting problems as those of primary education, franchise, and Imperial decentralisation. Then, too, Mauritius will doubtless humbly ask to help and pay its tribute of flesh to the greed of the war-god in any Imperial crisis, and then, to adapt to the new situation d'Epinay's words to Mr. Secretary Stanley in 1833: "Mauritians having become Britishers by conquest will desire to be treated as Britishers," with all their rights, but all their duties too.

GYMKANA CLUB-HOUSE, VACOAS.

from 1909 to 1912.

Head of Revenue.	1908-09	1909-10	1910-11	1911-12
	Rs.	Rs.	Rs.	Rs.
Customs	3,225,512	3,956,174	4,059,116	3,841,091
Harbour Dues...	234,855	528,091	213,259	206,931
Licenses, Excise and Internal Revenue	1,846,841	2,287,394	2,558,911	2,545,369
Fees of Court or Office ...	355,933	399,334	368,790	340,871
Post Office and Telegraph ...	131,499	173,776	210,275	217,604
Rent of Government Property	67,449	67,004	74,179	70,466
Interest	858,888	829,546	844,120	828,363
Miscellaneous Receipts ...	32,125	54,433	281,589	47,352
Land Sales	664	1,140	515	2,619
Total	6,753,766	8,296,892	8,610,754	8,100,666
Railway Traffic	2,070,698	2,502,831	2,519,235	2,334,982
Grand Total	8,824,464	10,799,723	11,129,989	10,435,648

from 1909 to 1912.

Expenditure.	1908-09	1909-10	1910-11	1911-12**
	Rs.	Rs.	Rs.	Rs.
Personal Emoluments	3,546,091	3,480,220	3,432,404	...*
Public Debt, Pension, &c. / Defence	2,451,818†	2,522,159†	2,557,505†	2,429,777
Administration	425,424	411,399	440,549	445,206
Revenue Departments	2,233,625	1,995,668	2,034,751	2,134,475
Law and Justice	1,215,278	1,147,520	1,141,927	1,088,158
Medical and Sanitary	770,709	741,766	687,283	718,537
Plague Services...	113,426	133,913	123,796	110,553
Education	627,697	591,600	606,877	604,277
Ecclesiastical	152,689	152,721	152,696	152,718
Immigration	91,719	88,291	95,876	84,596
Poor Law	282,810	261,237	224,395	230,511
Public Works Department ...	114,504	113,754	111,918	111,623
Public Works Recurrent ...	425,329	471,923	496,270	547,477
Public Works Extraordinary ...	46,569	152,292	193,526	154,046
Forests and Gardens	169,624	161,544	165,316	217,996
Observatory	20,932	19,766	19,928	15,684
Public Library and Museum ...	8,155	8,118	8,263	8,136
Miscellaneous	417,470	421,587	463,501	734,449†
Dependencies	53,676	54,003	53,866	55,760
Total	9,621,454	9,449,261	9,578,244	9,843,980
Expenditure from Loan Funds.	...	114	1,611,481	1,066,962

* Not published. † Includes Interest and Exchange. ** From the Government Gazette.

TABLE OF PRECEDENCE FOR GOVERNMENT OFFICIALS IN MAURITIUS.

CLASS I.

Governor.
Lieutenant-Governor (if there is one).

General in Command of Troops (if there is one) Admiral.	According to dates of Commission.

Bishop of Port Louis Bishop of Mauritius	According to dates of appointment.

Chief Judge.
Officer Commanding the Troops (if a Colonel or a Lieutenant-Colonel).
Puisne Judges of the Supreme Court—According to dates of appointment
Colonial Secretary.
Procureur-General.
Receiver-General.
Auditor-General.
Other Members of the Executive Council—According to dates of appointment.
Collector of Customs.
Protector of Immigrants.
Director of Public Works and Surveys.
Other Members of the Council of Government—According to dates of appointment or election.

CLASS II.

<table>
<tr><td>Colonels in the Army,
Post Captains in the Navy above three years' standing.
Director of Medical and Health Department not being a member of Council.
Director of Public Instruction.
Mayor of Port Louis.</td><td>According to dates of nomination.</td></tr>
<tr><td>President of the Chamber of Agriculture.
President of the Chamber of Commerce.
President of the Royal Society of Arts and Sciences.
Substitute Procureur-General—not being a member of Council.
Master and Registrar of the Supreme Court.
Inspector-General of Police.
Rector of the Royal College.
Archdeacon } According to dates of appointment.
Vicar-General }
Assistant Colonial Secretary.
General Manager of Railways.</td><td>To rank with Lieutenant-Colonels and Post Captains in the Navy under three years' standing according to dates of Commission.</td></tr>
<tr><td>Receiver of Registration Dues and Conservator of Mortgages.
Storekeeper-General }
Receiver-General } Not being members of Council.
Director of Observatory }
Colonial Postmaster }
District Magistrate, Port Louis, 1st Division.
District Magistrates—According to dates of appointment.
Stipendiary Magistrates.
Superintendent of Prisons.</td><td>To rank with Majors in the Army and Commanders in the Navy.</td></tr>
</table>

CLASS III.

Additional Substitute Procureur-General. Clerk of the Councils and any Officer who has previously held the Office permanently. The Clergy according to dates of appointment. Medical Inspector. Sanitary Warden. Crown Attorney. Crown Prosecutors. Government Notary. Deputy Mayor of Port Louis. Superintendent of Museum. Custodian of Archives.	To rank with Captains in the Army, and Lieutenants in the Navy.

CLASS IV.

Inspector of Schools.
Inspectors of Immigrants.
Medical Superintendents—According to dates of appointment.
Chief Officer of Police in charge of Port Louis.
Inspectors of Police.
Director of Forests and Gardens.
Health Officer.
Curator of Vacant Estates.
Assistants in Departments.
Landing Surveyors of Customs.
Chief Clerks of Departments.

Ex-Officio Members of the Executive Council.

Name.	Date of Appointment.	Position.
His Excellency Major Sir John Robert Chancellor, R.E., C.M.G., D.S.O.—*President*	November 13th, 1911 ...	Governor and Commander-in-Chief.
Major-General Charles Rudyerd Simpson, C.B.	March 8th, 1912 ...	Commanding H.M. Troops.
John Middleton	August 13th, 1913 ...	Colonial Secretary.
Etienne Kœnig	January 1st, 1913 ...	Procureur and Advocate-General.
Edward Allan Grannum	January 19th, 1912 ...	Receiver-General.

Members of the Council of Government.

Name.	Date of Appointment.	Position.
Ex-Officio Members.		
His Excellency Major Sir John Robert Chancellor, R.E., C.M.G., D.S.O.	November 13th, 1911 ...	Governor and Commander-in-Chief.
Major-General Charles Rudyerd Simpson, C.B.	May 28th, 1912... ...	Commanding H.M. Troops.
John Middleton	August 13th, 1913 ...	Colonial Secretary.
Etienne Kœnig	January 1st, 1913 ...	Procureur and Advocate-General.
Edward Allan Grannum	May 28th, 1912 ...	Receiver-General.
Harold Charles Scroggs	November 1st, 1910 ...	Collector of Customs and Harbour Master
Bertram Alexander Francis ...	July 2nd, 1912	Protector of Immigrants.
Paul Le Juge de Segrais	November 22nd, 1904 ...	Director of Public Works and Surveys.
Dr. Robert Denman	October 31st, 1911 ...	Director of Medical and Health Department.

Elected Members.	Date of Election.	Electoral Districts.
Dr. Eugène A. O. Laurent ...	January 17th, 1911 ...	Port Louis.
G. Edouard Nairac	January 17th 1911 ...	Port Louis.
V. Amand Esnouf	January 18th, 1911 ...	Plaines Wilhems.
Henri Leclézio, C.M G.	January 19th, 1911 ...	Moka.
Frederic Melchior Louis Rouillard	January 28th, 1913 ...	Savanne.
Joseph A. Duclos	January 27th, 1911 ...	Flacq.
E. Emile Sauzier, K.C.	January 26th, 1911 ...	Pamplemousses.
Gaston Antelme	January 31st, 1911 ...	Black River.
Joseph Antoine Maurice Martin ...	November 5th, 1912 ...	Rivière du Rempart.
Gaston Gébert	No election took place in this District ...	Grand Port.

Nominated Members.	Date of Nomination.
William Thomas Alder Emtage, M.A., Director of Public Instruction	May 15th, 1911.
Léon Emile Pitot, General Manager of Railways	do.
Martial Louis Auguste Noël, Registrar General	do.
Edward Cleather Fraser	do.
James John Gibson	do.
Robert Balfour Graham	do.
Gustave Albert Ritter, C.M.G.	do.
Hassan Sakir, M B.	do.

By reference to the index at the end of the volume portraits will be found of all the Members of the Council of Government, with the exception of the Hon. John Middleton, Colonial Secretary, and the Hon. John Léon Emile Pitot, General Manager of Railways, whose photographs were unobtainable.

TREASURY BUILDING, SIGNAL MOUNTAIN, BANK OF MAURITIUS, LTD., PORT LOUIS.

GOVERNMENT DEPARTMENTS.

TREASURY DEPARTMENT.

THE office of Receiver-General was inaugurated in 1874, under the provisions of Ordinance 17 of 1873, by which all the powers of the Colonial Treasurer and Collector of Internal Revenues were transferred to him.

The Hon. A. GRANNUM,
Receiver-General.

J. PILOT,
Assistant Receiver-General.

The Receiver-General is the Head Accountant of the Colony and has charge of all public money. By Government Notice 95 of 1876 he was created *ex officio* manager of the Government Savings Bank.

The Treasury Department comprises the Inland Revenue Branch and the Distillery Branch. The stamping and examination of weights and measures and all stamped paper are performed under the control of the Receiver-General, who also has charge of, and issues to the Post Office Department as required, all postage stamps, postal orders, etc.

A. G. BIDEN,
Auditor.

AUDIT DEPARTMENT.

THE powers, authority and duties vested in or imposed upon the Auditor-General under certain Ordinances were vested in and are exercised by an Auditor under Ordinance No. 3 of 1912.

The accounts of the Colony are, since the promulgation of the above Ordinance, audited on behalf of the Secretary of State, by the Auditor, acting under the supervision of the Director of Colonial Audit, who is assisted in London by a central establishment connected with, but not forming part of, the Colonial Office.

In the work of examination and inspection of accounts the Auditor is assisted by a subordinate staff recruited from the local general clerical staff, for whose efficiency and discipline he is responsible to the Governor and the Director of Colonial Audit.

THE MAURITIUS GOVERNMENT SAVINGS BANK.

THIS Bank was established on May 1st, 1837, under the provisions of Ordinance No. 13 of 1836. The head office is in Port Louis, but there is a branch office in each of the eight rural districts and one at Curepipe. The depositors for the financial year ending on the 30th June, 1911, numbered 28,032, and the sum deposited amounted to Rs. 1,295,865 and the withdrawals to Rs. 1,131,063. The total amount at the credit of depositors amounted to Rs. 3,253,494.

The rate of interest allowed on deposits has since the 1st of January, 1899, been reduced to 3 per cent. per annum in virtue of Ordinance No. 45 of 1898.

The expenditure of this branch of the Receiver-General's Department for the financial year ending June 30th, 1911, amounted to Rs. 98,593, including the amount paid for interest on deposits. The Revenue was Rs. 102,022.

The invested funds amounted to Rs. 3,494,171.

Financial Condition of the Government Savings Bank, 1902 to 1910.

Year.	Assets.	Liabilities.	Balance.	Depositors.		Total Deposits.		Amount to Credit of Depositors.	
				General Population.	Indian Population.	General Population.	Indian Population.	General Population.	Indian Population.
	Rs.	Rs.	Rs.					Rs.	Rs.
1902–03 ...	3,134,997	2,825,859	309,138	15,284	10,384	590,122	299,224	1,584,996	1,138,598
1903–04 ...	3,141,650	2,832,512	309,138	15,946	10,545	670,019	428,163	1,664,198	1,222,582
1904–05 ...	3,138,360	2,837,663	300,698	16,299	9,498	633,490	327,512	1,724,662	1,120,430
1905–06 ...	3,211,350	2,931,175	280,175	17,629	10,054	662,363	333,131	1,669,038	1,181,196
1906–07 ...	3,130,970	2,830,272	300,698	15,712	10,802	617,860	330,396	1,571,330	1,183,433
1907–08 ...	3,171,294	2,817,705	353,589	15,631	10,767	721,751	289,023	1,561,418	1,131,377
1908–09 ...	3,180,822	2,827,266	353 556	15,728	10,849	644,020	326,654	1,555,431	1,161,171
1909–10 ...	3,353,598	3,000,038	353,560	16,097	11,219	741,801	492,626	1,673,135	1,326,893

THE HON. MARTIAL NOËL,
Registrar-General, Receiver of Registration Dues, and Conservator of Mortgages.

REGISTRAR-GENERAL'S DEPARTMENT.

THIS department was amalgamated with that of Registration and Mortgage under one head during the year 1912.

The law relating to the Civil Status was promulgated under Ordinance 26 of 1890 (repealing 17 of 1871) as amended by Ordinance 23 of 1912. This Ordinance provides for the establishment of a Central Civil Status Office in Port Louis, and one or more in each of the rural districts.

Yearly indexes of all births, deaths and marriages are forwarded to the Central Office, and copies kept at the Rural Offices. The printing of Decennial Tables has been discontinued and replaced by annual Alphabetical Indexes drawn up and printed under the direction of the Registrar-General.

The Central Office is situated at the Treasury Buildings in Intendance Street.

REGISTRATION AND MORTGAGE DEPARTMENT.

THE systems of registration and mortgage in Mauritius are entirely of French origin. The fundamental law dates from the Arrêté Decaen 36 of the 16th, Frimaire An XII. The Registration Office is a revenue department, and the dues are fixed or proportional according to the nature of the deeds and of the transactions embodied therein.

The tariff of registration dues in the rupee currency was abolished under Ordinance 19 of 1877, to which several amendments have, however, since been made (Ordinance 16 of 1895).

The Mortgage Office is not primarily a revenue department, but is intended to protect vendors, purchasers, and creditors. The principal Ordinances dealing with transcription and mortgage are 36 of 1863, 15 of 1878, 24 of 1898, and 21 of 1912.

The two branches are united into one department under the direction of the Receiver of Registration Dues and Conservator of Mortgages.

T. AVICE,
Assistant Registrar-General.

POST AND TELEGRAPH DEPARTMENT.

A POST OFFICE was established in Port Louis soon after the capitulation of the island in 1810, and the District Offices were inaugurated on the 1st of July, 1847. By 1858 their number had increased to 16, and at the present time there are 68.

The telegraph service, which was originally under the control and supervision of the Railway Department, was transferred to the Postal Department in 1876. There are now 375 miles of telegraph wire and 87 miles of telephone wire in the island.

Some idea of the development in the postal service of Mauritius may be gathered from the fact that in 1844 inland and foreign letters transmitted through the Post Office amounted to only 65,638, and newspapers to 39,898, whereas in 1910 they reached 1,566,835 and 1,334.423 respectively.

The Central Post Office is in Port Louis at the entrance to the Customs yard.

W. C. RAE,
Colonial Postmaster.

R. H. STOCKDALE,
Government Electrical Engineer and Inspector of Telegraphs.

PORT AND CUSTOMS DEPARTMENT.

PORT OFFICE.

THE Port Office is situated on the upper part of the harbour and forms part of the Customs House. It is a two-storied building and is easily distinguished by a flagstaff, eighty feet above the sea-level, from which all signals are made in and off the Port. The whole establishment is under the direct control of the Harbour Master.

1. The Hon. H. C. SCROGGS (Lieut. R.N., retired), Collector of Customs and Harbour Master.
2. W. G. OLDERSHAW (Lieut. R.N.R.), Assistant Harbour Master.
3. R. LEJEUNE, Deputy Collector of Customs.
4. A. S. THOMPSON, Pilot. 5. N. CAUVIN, Pilot.

This Department is equipped with a steam life-boat, a rocket apparatus for saving life, and sailing and rowing boats for harbour and sea service.

All hurricane signals are made from the Port Office, which is in telegraphic communication with the Observatory at Pamplemousses, and are repeated from Fort George. The Pilot Staff is composed of three pilots, who are on duty from 1st October to 31st March between the hours of 5.45 a.m. and 6.45 p.m., and from the 1st April to 30th September between the hours of 6.15 a.m. and 5.45 p.m. Candidates for the pilot service have to be in possession of a 1st or only Mate's certificate or one of a higher grade. The pilots, who are all master mariners, are under the orders of the Harbour Master. Ships of war are piloted free of charge.

CUSTOMS DEPARTMENT.

THE Customs Department, the staff of which is divided into an indoor and an outdoor branch, occupies the building which faces the landing stage of the harbour. During the year 1911 this Department was amalgamated with the Port Department, the duties of Harbour Master and Collector of Customs being performed by the same officer. Since then numerous changes have been made in the staff, and the number of officers employed has been greatly reduced. The approved estimates on personal emoluments for the service 1912-1913 amounts to Rs. 191,541 for the combined departments. The Towing Branch and Lighthouse Establishment are also under the control of the Collector of Customs and Harbour Master.

THE HARBOUR OF PORT LOUIS.

THE harbour of Port Louis is about a mile in length from the Custom House Wharf to a line drawn between the two forts at its entrance; it is almost as broad. It is of irregular form and is bounded on the north by a stone causeway known as "Chaussée Tromlin," which separates the harbour from a large lagoon known by the name of Mer Rouge. The depth of water in this part of the harbour is not more than four feet at its deepest part. The south side of the harbour is bounded by a shelf of rocks which extends from the shore for about a quarter of a mile. The bottom of this side is of coral, with not more than three or four feet of water over it, and suddenly deepens to fourteen feet. The harbour itself varies in depth, but it has accommodation for 150 vessels drawing from fifteen to thirty feet, not including coasters, or vessels under one hundred tons register, for which accommodation for about sixty more can be found. The harbour entrance is now marked by red and white chequered buoys with ball on the left hand coming in, and black with ball on the right hand side. A patent Wigham Buoy is also there, carrying a thirty-one day occulting white light, visible on a clear night about five miles, but it has been sighted at eight miles from a steamer's bridge.

There is one small dredger employed to dredge the mouths of the streams that run into the harbour.

There are moorings laid down for ships of war drawing respectively from twenty-six to thirty-five feet. There are also two sets of moorings for large merchant steamers with a span of 400 feet each. Cargoes are loaded and unloaded by means of lighters varying in size from twenty-five to seventy-five tons. The anchorage in the roadstead ranges in depth from eight to thirty fathoms. It is at this latter depth that vessels are allowed to heave ballast overboard. The holding ground is excellent. The best anchorage is about a quarter of a mile to the northward of the light buoy in from twelve to fourteen fathoms.

The quarantine anchorage is about a mile westward of the spot where the light-ship "Beacon" was formerly anchored, and which has now been replaced by the light-buoy, the depth of water being from ten to eighteen fathoms with fairly good holding ground. The rise and fall of tide is two feet nine inches full and change. Vessels having small cargoes to land, or not being desirous to receive pratique, are allowed to anchor between the forts or in the inner harbour, where they discharge cargo into large lighters.

LIGHTHOUSES.

THERE are four lighthouses on the coast of Mauritius. The first in starting north from Port Louis is that erected on Canonniers' Point at right angles to the existing reef. It is a fixed catoptric light of the first order, and is situated in latitude 19° 59′ 54″ south and longitude 57° 32′ 34″ east. Its elevation above the mean level of the sea is eighty-nine feet six inches, and it can be seen from the deck of a vessel fourteen feet above the water at a distance of ten nautical miles. This light is a perfectly safe guide in working a vessel up or down the coast between Canonniers' and Grenadiers' Points, and gives admirable warning by turning red when the vessel is standing into danger.

The lighthouse placed on Flat Island is situated at the south-west or highest part of the island, in latitude 19° 54′ 26″ south and longitude 57° 41′ 12″ east as determined by triangulation; its elevation above the mean sea-level is 366 feet. Flat Island is about six miles distant from the northern extremity of Mauritius and is used as a quarantine station. The light is a revolving catoptric of the first order, and is visible from the deck of a vessel thirteen feet above the sea at a distance of twenty-five nautical miles; the rise and fall of the tide at this place is the same as at Ile aux Fouquets, three feet at full and change. There are two landing places at Flat Island—one is called the Pass, the other the Palissades; both are difficult and sometimes dangerous. The anchorage is not very secure, and on signs of a heavy sea, or rollers setting in, ships must immediately get under weigh.

Grand Port Lighthouse is built upon a small island called Ile aux Fouquets, in latitude 20° 23′ 34″ south and longitude 57° 46′ 12″ east; it marks the southern entrance to Grand Port Bay, and is 800 yards to the east-north-east of Ile de la Passe; there is a small islet between them called Ile aux

Vacoas. The light apparatus is dioptric of the first order, showing a fixed white light from sunset to sunrise visible in every direction from seaward, but dark on the land side. This light is 108¾ feet above mean sea-level, and in clear weather can be seen at a distance of sixteen nautical miles from the deck of a vessel twelve feet above water. The lighthouse, as well as the adjacent buildings, is white; its ground-line is thirty-nine feet above the mean sea-level. It forms a most conspicuous object which cannot be mistaken, and serves as a guide for vessels passing by day or by night.

Pointe des Cavernes Lighthouse, on the coast of Petite Rivière, was built under the government of Sir Cavendish Boyle, K.C.M.G., and inaugurated in October, 1910. Its light is visible at a distance of more than 29 kilometres.

POOR LAW DEPARTMENT.

THE Poor Law Department was created by Ordinance No. 17 of 1902. The head of the Department is called the Poor Law Commissioner, and his duties are: (*a*) To direct and control the administration of relief to the poor. (*b*) To establish almshouses, workhouses, infirmaries, and other asylums for the poor, and to direct the management of such institutions. (*c*) To receive and disburse the amount voted annually by the Council of Government.

The Government Medical Officers in the districts are Poor Law Officers subject to the control of the Commissioner. All persons who, through advanced or tender age or infirmity of mind or body, are incapable of working for their livelihood, and have no relatives liable to support them, are considered as paupers and entitled to relief. The Commissioner also provides for the protection and care, and for the instruction and employment, of destitute orphans and of children whose parents are paupers. Paupers of unsound mind are also maintained at the expense of the Department. The expenses for the re-conveyance to Mauritius of distressed natives of the colony are repaid by the Treasury, subject to the subsequent recovery of such expenses either from the person so sent back or from any relative liable in law to support such person. In-door and out-door relief is granted. In-door relief is given only to sick paupers who require hospital treatment. They are sent to the Government Hospitals or to Canal Street Convent Hospital, Barkly Asylum, St. Lazare (lepers), and the Lunatic Asylum.

Several Convents are authorised to receive infirm paupers, payment being made by Government at the following rates:

Boys or girls below 10 years ...	Rs. 6	per month.
Boys from 10 to 12 years ...	7	„
Girls from 10 to 14 years ...	7	„
Adults ...	10	„

The lepers at St. Lazare, under the care of the Roman Catholic Sisters, cost the Government Rs. 0.66 per head per day.

Out-door relief consists of the distribution of money, food or medical comforts, or medical attendance to such persons who, in the opinion of the Commissioner or medical advisers, are *bona fide* destitute.

IMMIGRATION AND POOR LAW RELIEF.

FROM the 1st July, 1912, the Poor Law and Immigration Departments have been amalgamated, and the Hon. B. A. Francis appointed Protector of Immigrants and Poor Law Commissioner, with Mr. G. Lincoln as Assistant Protector of Immigrants and Poor Law Commissioner.

The Clothing Branch of the Storekeeper-General's Department (since abolished) has also been transferred to this Department. The post of Medical Officer has been abolished. All medical duties in connection with estate hospitals have been transferred to the Medical and Health Department, and are to be performed by such Government Medical Officers as may be designated by the Medical Director. For the present these duties are performed by Dr. Momplé for the Northern and part of the Eastern Districts, and by Dr. Milne for the Central, Southern and South-Eastern Districts.

Information regarding the Immigration Department will be found on pages 215 to 220.

THE MEDICAL AND HEALTH DEPARTMENT.

L. G. BARBEAU, M.B., C.M.Edin., D.P.H.Lond., Assistant Director and Chief Sanitary Officer, Director of the Bacteriological Laboratory.

The Hon. R. DENMAN, M.R.C.S.Eng., D.P.H.Cantab., Director of the Medical and Health Department.

A. F. G. MASSON, M.B., Ch.B.Edin., Health Officer and Assistant Government Medical Officer, Port Louis.

THE Medical and Health Department, which was created under Ordinance No. 32 of 1894-5, is primarily divided into two branches—Medical and Sanitary—under the control of a Director. The Medical Branch deals exclusively with the various hospitals and medical institutions—asylums, dispensaries, prison hospitals, etc. The Sanitary Branch deals with the general sanitary conditions of the colony—the application of antimalarial measures, plague prevention, inspection of buildings, slaughter-houses, rural drainage works, etc.

By Ordinance 4 of 1912 "all the powers, authority, and duties attached to the office of Medical Officer to the Immigration Department shall vest in and be exercised by the Director of the Health Department, or such other officer or officers of the Health Department as may be appointed in writing by the Director for the purpose."

A Bacteriological Laboratory, under control of the Medical Department, was created in August, 1907, and work in connection with it was begun at Malmaison St. Pierre as a provisional measure; but in 1908 was transferred to the new and commodious establishment at Réduit. The building, which was designed and executed by the Director of Public Works, is constructed in concrete and consists of six large rooms which serve for library, laboratory and offices for the Director and his assistants. Close by are quarters for the Director and stabling for a number of horses; also buildings for animals undergoing treatment or under observation. Dr. Barbeau performs the duties of Director concurrently with those of Assistant Director of the Health Department. The institution is called upon daily to make analyses of blood, detection of microbes, etc., for local medical practitioners. The Quarantine Stations, under the control of the Medical Department, are at Cannoniers' Point and Flat Island. The Health Officer, who is attached to the Medical Branch, visits every incoming vessel, examines the crew and passengers, and orders the disinfection of such personal effects and cargoes as he considers necessary.

J. L. NAZ, A.C.G.I., M.I.C.E., F.I.S.E., Sanitary Engineer.

MARE AUX VACOAS WATER WORKS.

THE reservoir at Mare aux Vacoas, where the average annual rainfall is 137 inches, has a catchment area of about five square miles. The top water-level is 1,840 feet above the mean sea-level, and the reservoir has a maximum capacity of 570,000,000 gallons. The water flows from the reservoir for 4,900 feet in an open channel, and for a further distance of 7,700 feet is taken in a 16-inch cast-iron pipe to the filtering establishment at La Marie, which is 1,645 feet above sea-level.

J. W. DAWSON,
Assoc.M.Inst.C.E., F.I.S.E., Assistant Director of Public Works and Surveys.

P. LE JUGE DE SEGRAIS,
M.Inst.C.E.,
Director of Public Works and Surveys.

At the filtering establishment there is a depositing reservoir with a capacity of 1,300,000 gallons, and a covered service reservoir with a capacity of 500,000 gallons. Owing to the water being at times heavily charged with organic matter, the "Anderson Process" for the purification of water was installed, and concrete partitions were erected in the depositing reservoir to improve the settlement of solids. Originally there were only four filter beds, with a superficial area of 6,720 square feet, but five additional filter beds have since been constructed with a superficial area of 18,000 square feet, and extra aerating trays have been added. These additional works and the increased filtration area enable two filters to be always left exposed to sun and air, and with a slower process of filtration there are few complaints of the quality of the water.

E. D. POUGNET, A.C.G.I., A.M.I.C.E.,
Government Surveyor.

The daily consumption of water exceeds 1,600,000 gallons, and, with the exception of the supply to the town of Curepipe, the water flows by gravitation to the lower districts. The supply for Curepipe is pumped by means of hydraulic rams to two reservoirs standing 368 feet above the filtering establishment, the motor being driven by water power from the 16-inch supply main. The increase in the population of Curepipe has necessitated additions to the pumping plant and the reconstruction of the reservoirs. A masonry building was erected at the filter beds for the pumping machinery, and a second 16-inch cast-iron pipe has been laid to supply the motive power. The open conduit from the reservoir to the filter beds, which was liable to pollution, has been replaced by a concrete conduit with a ferro-concrete covering.

RAILWAYS.

THE Mauritius Railways, the first branch of which was opened in 1864, consists of two main lines —the North and the Midland—having a common terminus in Port Louis, and of four branch lines, the Moka-Flacq, the Savanne, the Black River and the Long Mountain.

The North Line is thirty-one miles in length and runs through the districts of Port Louis, Pamplemousses, Rivière du Rempart and Flacq to Grand River S.E. It was the first one opened to traffic. The maximum gradient is 1 in 77, and the highest level attained is 326 feet above sea level.

"DOUBLE DECKER" RAILWAY TRAIN OF MAURITIUS.

The Midland Line, which is thirty-six miles in length, traverses the centre of the island running through the districts of Plaines Wilhems and Grand Port to Mahébourg. It reaches a height of 1,822 feet in the vicinity of Curepipe, and the gradients are of exceptional steepness, 1 in 27 occurring several times.

The Moka-Flacq Line, twenty-six miles in length, joins the Midland Line at Rose-Hill, and runs through Plaines Wilhems, Moka and Flacq to Rivière Seche, where it forms a junction with the North Line. The ruling gradient is 1 in 70.

The Savanne Branch, eleven miles in length, joins the Midland Line at Rose Belle and runs through the district of Savanne to Souillac, at the extreme south of the island. The ruling gradient on this line is the same as that on the Moka-Flacq, about 1 in 70.

In the year 1903 a branch line, four miles in length, was opened from Terre Rouge on the North Line to Long Mountain; and another, thirteen miles in length, joining the Midland at Richelieu, was carried through the Black River district to Tamarin in the following year.

The total length open to traffic at the present time is 120 miles. The gauge throughout these lines is 4 ft. 8½ ins.

A small gauge line of 2 ft. 6 ins., known as the Bois Chéri Line, runs from Rivière du Poste Station on the Savanne Branch line to Mexico, a station in the vicinity of the Government Forest at Kanaka.

CENTRAL RAILWAY STATION, PORT LOUIS.

In 1894, after the Pailles Bridge accident, a petition was sent to Government, signed by a large number of passengers on the Midland Line, asking that the Grand River Bridge be rebuilt at a much lower level, and the line correspondingly altered so as to diminish the danger in the event of an accident similar to that which occurred at the Pailles Bridge. The petition was referred to the consulting engineers in England, Messrs. Hawkshaw and Hayter,

GRAND RIVER RAILWAY BRIDGE, NEAR PORT LOUIS.

who reported against the proposed scheme—which could only have been carried out at a prohibitive cost and would not have materially lessened the danger—but they suggested certain modifications to the existing bridge with a view of increasing its stability in a heavy wind. The two cylinders constituting each of the piers (cylinders being about four feet apart) were accordingly enclosed in iron sheeting up to the height of twenty feet, the space between the cylinders and the sheeting being filled in with concrete. It was considered that by thus binding together the two cylinders, which were independent of each other, the structure would offer much greater resistance to a gale. The girders themselves are strutted to the top of the piers by wrought iron struts, so as to diminish the risk of the wind upsetting them. The total cost of these works amounted to about Rs. 10,000.

The deviation line is to join the main line at Richelieu Station.

Owing to the development of the traffic it became necessary to increase the capacity of the engines, and, in place of the old engines weighing fifty-six tons, there are now in use new ones of eighty-five tons, for which, of course, all the bridges have had to be renewed, as they were constructed to carry only the old and lighter locomotives. As all the railway lines in the island are single, it was found to be practically impossible to renew the girders of the Grand River Bridge without stopping the traffic completely for a long time. A new bridge is, therefore, now in course of construction a little farther down the river, and differs considerably in design from the old one. The piers are of stone instead of iron, and the trains will run between the girders instead of on top as in the old viaduct. The total span is 626 feet 3 inches, or 6 feet 3 inches longer than that of the old bridge. The height of the new structure, however, is 52 feet less, being about 87 feet from the water level to the rail level.

The bridge has seven spans of 83 feet 4 inches formed of six piers, which are composed of carefully cut stones embedded in cement, no lime being used in building them. The first and last piers are built on solid ledges of rock; those in the bed of the ravine are on large masses of cement concrete about 35 feet long, 22 feet wide, and from 10 to 14 feet in thickness, resting on the compact rock boulders that fill up the bed of the gorge. The piers are

GRAND RIVER NEW RAILWAY BRIDGE.
In process of construction, showing the old one in the distance.

B. K. ADAMS,
New Works Engineer.

J. S. MORRISON,
Head Accountant.

A. J. DYKES,
Locomotive, Carriage and Wagon Superintendent.

85 feet in height from the top of the concrete to the bed-stones upon which the girders rest, and are 24 feet long by 10 feet wide at the bottom, tapering to 21 by 7 feet at the top.

To build these piers economically a steel wire cableway, capable of lifting a load of three tons from the bottom to the top of the piers, was erected across the ravine. All the men and the building materials are lifted up by means of this cableway, which is operated by a steam winch on one side of the gorge.

The greatest difficulty to be overcome in the construction of high bridges of this description is that of getting the heavy girders, weighing in this case twenty-five tons each, on to the piers when they are built. Owing to the enormous quantity of timber required, it was not practical to build up a temporary staging, or false-work as it is technically termed, as is usually done for smaller bridges, and it became necessary to devise some other method. After considerable investigation a plan was adopted which,

G. LATTER,
Maintenance of Way Inspector.

C. A. A. STANDLEY,
Senior Railway Audit Examiner.

H. KOENIG,
Acting Chief Clerk.

although involving careful calculations and nice adjustments, has proved very satisfactory in practice. It is generally known as the launching method, as it has some similarity to the launching of a ship. Four old girders, taken from another bridge, were joined together so as to form a pair of girders 186 feet in length. These, weighing eighty tons, were pulled forward so as to project rather more than half way across the opening to be spanned and thereby form a cantilever. Between this pair of girders or cantilevers was placed the girder to be launched, or, in other words, carried forward. It was picked up in the middle by means of a hydraulic jack capable of lifting fifty-six tons and mounted on a frame which ran on rails fixed to the top of the cantilever girders, the jack and girder weighing together fifty tons.

A steel wire rope running to a winch on one side of the ravine was attached to the frame carrying the jack, and by this means the jack with its load was pulled forward until the projecting end of the girder reached the pier, where it was lowered down on packings placed ready to receive it, the whole operation occupying not more than an hour.

The work of building the new bridge was commenced in November, 1911, and is expected to be completed about January, 1914. The deviation is to join the main line at Richelieu Station.

The traffic of the railway is at present worked on the train-despatching system. As the line is a single one loops or sidings are provided at nearly all the stations to allow the trains to pass each other. Each train is known by a number (No. — up or No. — down) and is scheduled to pass other trains at certain points only. So long as all the trains are running to time this system is highly satisfactory; but it can be readily understood that if a train loses time, as is daily the case with one train or another, it will delay the other trains that must pass it. To obviate this the running times of all trains are telegraphed from each station to the Traffic Superintendent's office at Port Louis. It is the duty of that official to keep a close watch on the times the trains are keeping, and, when a train has lost time and is likely to delay another, to telegraph instructions for the passing to be effected at another station. It is only on receipt of such instructions that trains pass each other at any other than the appointed stations. As might be expected, this system does not answer very well where the traffic is considerable, and the time taken up by telegraphing greatly increases the delay.

In order to obviate this unsatisfactory state of affairs Mr. R. H. Stockdale, Telegraph Inspector, invented in 1911 a unique "lock and block" system for single line railways, and specially designed to meet the peculiarities of the Mauritius railways. In 1912 he proceeded to England to develop his invention and superintend the manufacture of the apparatus on behalf of the Mauritius Government. He returned in April of this year (1913), and is now engaged in applying his invention to the local railway line, which will, instead of having a central control, be split up into "block" sections, each of which will be under the joint control of the station-master and signalman at each end of the block. By this means the trains will not be required to pass at any stipulated place, but will automatically pass wherever convenient and will not delay each other. The sections will be protected by locked signals, which can only be unlocked at the proper time, this locking and unlocking rendering it impossible for more than one train to occupy a section at one time.

The administrative work of the railway is carried on from Port Louis, the head office of the General Manager being on the first floor of the Central Railway Station.

The total cost of the Mauritius Railways, so far as it has been possible to procure information on the subject, has amounted to £1,878,183, the funds being derived from loans as follows:—

Loans under Ordinance 19 of 1862 and 15 of 1864 including premium ...	£1,066,795
Contributions from General Revenue 1862-67 } North and Midland Lines ...	377,058
Loans under Ordinance 1 of 1869 } North and Midland Lines ...	100,000
" " 10 of 1876 Savanne Branch	100,000
" " 2 of 1887 Moka Branch	102,900
" " 4 and 12 of 1892 (Hurricane Loan)	57,831
" " 19 of 1903 Black River Branch	40,000
" " 51 of 1904 Long Mountain Branch...	7,973
" " Bois Chéri Light Railway	16,759
" " 39 of 1905 Black River Branch	8,867
	£1,878,183

The capital expenditure incurred year by year does not, however, appear to have been included in the foregoing.

The total revenue and expenditure of this department for the last nine years for which figures are available up to the time of writing has been as follows :—

Financial Year.	Expenditure.		Revenue.
	Personal Emoluments.	Other Charges.	
1901-02	Rs. 555,459	Rs 1,032,659	Rs. 1,927,273
1902-03	569,358	1,314,126	2,377,495
1903-04	262,434	2,144,623	1,809,104
1904-05	270,530	1,601,728	2,657,596
1905-06	630,553	1,110,720	2,437,511
1906-07	639.145	1,500,776	2,500,409
1907-08	645,213	1,115,807	2,039,326
1908-09	662 943	1,063,736	2,070,699
1909-10 ...	652,367	889,676	2,502,831

Table of Distances from Port Louis, and Altitude above Sea Level of Stations on the North, Midland, Savanne, Moka, and Black River Lines.

North Line. Stations.	Miles from Central Station, Port Louis.	Height of Rails above Mean Sea Level.	*Midland Line.* Stations.	Miles from Central Station, Port Louis.	Height of Rails above Mean Sea Level.	*Savanne Branch.* Stations.	Miles from Central Station, Port Louis.	Height of Rails above Mean Sea Level.
	Miles.	Eng. feet.		Miles.	Eng. feet.		Miles.	Eng. feet.
			Port Louis	—	8	Rose Belle	25	874
			Cassis ...	1	19			
			Pailles ...	2	165	Riv. du Poste ...	28	920
			Coromandel	3	175			
			Petite Rivière ...	5	392	,, Dragon ...	30	753
Albion Dock	1	20	Beau Bassin	7	737			
Roche Bois	2	44	Rose Hill ...	9	923	,, des Anguilles ...	32	426
Riche Terre	3	106	Quatre Bornes ...	10	1.083			
Terre Rouge	4	137	Phœnix	12	1,311	Souillac	36	42
Mont. Longue	8	450	Vacoas	13	1,371			
Notre Dame	7	420	Curepipe Road ...	15	1,784	*Black River Branch.*		
Calebasses	6	192	Curepipe	16	1,806			
Pamplemousses	7	208	Forest Side	17	1,812			
Mapou	10	296	Midlands	19	1,467	Richelieu	4	218
Poudre d'Or	13	172	Fressanges	20	1,313			
R. du Rempart	17	134	Cluny	23	1,000	Albion	9	72
Flacq	22	78	Rose Belle	25	874			
Argy	24	147	Mare d'Albert ...	27	559	Medine	12	284
Rivière Sèche	29	100	Union Vale	30	253			
Gd. River S.E.	31	38	Mahébourg	36	4	Tamarin	17	155

Moka Branch. Stations.	Distance from Central.	Height of Rails above Mean Sea Level.	*Moka Branch.* Stations.	Distance from Central.	Height of Rails above Mean Sea Level.
	Miles.	Eng. feet.		Miles.	Eng. feet.
Rose Hill	9	923	Camp de Masque	23	995
Réduit (Pass. Platform) ...	11	1,030	Montagne Blanche	25	906
Moka	12	1,130	Sébastopol	27	641
St. Pierre	14	1,210	Etoile	29	418
Verdun	15	1,420	Olivia	31	376
Alma Siding	17	—	Bel Air	33	242
Quartier Militaire	19	1,337	Rivière Sèche	36	100
Providence Siding	21	—	Port Louis (Circular Journey)	65	—

THE ADMINISTRATION OF JUSTICE.

By G. RONDEAUX DE COURCY, Barrister-at-Law.

G. RONDEAUX DE COURCY,
Barrister-at-Law.

IT was in the course of those glorious times in the history of France, when the Indian Ocean resounded with the names of Suffren, d'Estaing, La Motte Piquet, d'Entrecasteaux and their emulators, that du Fresne, in conformity with Royal instructions, took possession, on September 20th, 1715, of Mauritius, and gave it the name of Ile de France. Some time afterwards du Fougerai-Garnier hoisted the fleur-de-lys over the newly-occupied territory, and also erected a cross whereon was carved the coat-of-arms of France, with the following inscription—"*Lilia fixa Crucis capiti Mirare sacratae Ne stupeas jubet hic Gallia stare Crucem,*" reminiscent of the proud title of *Fille Aînée de l'Eglise* which France had achieved by centuries of chivalry and heroism.

In 1722 de Nyon, under a recent appointment, assumed the government of the island, and ruled with a free hand until the following year, when a Council was instituted to assist the Governor. That Council was styled *Conseil Provincial*; its powers were legislative, judicial, and administrative, but only the judicial powers will be dealt with here.

Thenceforth l'Ile de France was possessed of a Court of Justice, and out of that first judicial institution gradually grew a system which, being subsequently transformed and invested with powers similar to those exercised by certain of the Courts of England, has developed into our present judicature.

The Court exercised full original jurisdiction in criminal as well as civil matters. The enactments which created the *Conseil Provincial* also established in the neighbouring island of Bourbon a *Conseil Supérieur*, and that Court was given appellate jurisdiction over the *Conseil Provincial de l'Isle de France.*

In 1734 the *Conseil Provincial* was abolished, and a *Conseil Supérieur* established, independent of the *Conseil Supérieur* of Bourbon, with full original and final jurisdiction over *l'Isle de France.*

In 1738 the judgments delivered in the Colony were made subject to a right of appeal, by way of *pourvoi*, before the *Cour de Cassation.*

In 1766 another Court was instituted to take cognizance of matters concerning "concessions" (grants of land and of water from rivers). It was given the name of *Tribunal Terrier.* In the same year the *Conseil Supérieur de l'Isle de France* was abolished. It was replaced by a *Conseil Supérieur* differing from the former Court of the same name, and was invested with a restricted original jurisdiction.

In 1771 the *Conseil Supérieur* was also abolished, and another Court of original jurisdiction, criminal and civil, was established under the name of *Cour de Juridiction Royale*; a *Conseil Supérieur* was created to sit as a Court of Appeal over the former Court.

THE SUPREME COURT, PORT LOUIS.

In 1776 Admiralty jurisdiction was granted to the *Cour de Juridiction Royale.*

In 1791 after the overthrow of the French Government, the *Conseil Supérieur* and *Cour de Juridiction Royale* were abolished. Magistrates *(Juges de Paix)* were appointed; they exercised a limited jurisdiction, both civil and criminal.

During the period which elapsed between the constitution of the *République (Une et Indivisible)* and the eleventh year of the revolutionary calendar (1803), extraordinary agitation was manifested in the contrivance of substitutes for the Courts of Justice and other institutions. Several of those innovations were in the form of unprecedented tribunals and committees—*e.g.*, *Tribunaux de Famille, Conseil des Trois, Comité du Salut Public.* As regards the last-named improvement on the evolution of the national traditions, it is noteworthy that the *Comité* did not, in spite of the existence of the local *Club des Jacobins* and *Club des Cordeliers,* follow suit with its cognomen of France. Indeed, during the Reign of Terror, only one revolutionary murder was committed in *l'Ile de France.* No Mauritian, thank God, participated in that deed. The episode deserves a short digression. An officer, Comte de Macnemara, had been summoned before the *Assemblée Coloniale,* which at the time sat permanently within the walls of the Church. As he was wending his way thence to the barracks under an escort of soldiers, the procession came up to a *lanterne,* the sight of which reminded Macnemara of the methods which of late had been obtaining in France. Fearing a similar fate, he endeavoured to escape, but was pursued by several soldiers, who shot him dead, after his pistol, with which he had endeavoured to defend himself, had missed fire. His head was severed from his body, and promenaded on a pike through the streets, to the disgust and horror of the population. His mangled corpse was buried by a sailor.

MR. JUSTICE FURCY ALFRED HERCHENRODER,
Chief Judge.

MR. JUSTICE CHARLES S. DAVSON, B.A., LL.B.,
Puisne Judge.

MR. JUSTICE THOS. WAGSTAFFE HAYCRAFT, B.A.,
Puisne Judge.

In 1803, good order having been restored in France, the office of *Juge de Paix* and the various tribunals created during the revolutionary period were abolished at *l'Ile de France* and the *Tribunal Terrier* was re-established, as well as the *Cour de Juridiction Royale* and *Conseil Supérieur*, the former under the appellation of *Tribunal de Première Instance*, the latter under that of *Tribunal d'Appel.*

The *Tribunal de Première Instance* was granted original jurisdiction in all cases, civil, commercial, admiralty, criminal and police, whilst the *Tribunal d'Appel* was invested with appellate jurisdiction over the former.

In 1808 the *Tribunal d'Appel* was styled *Cour d'Appel.* Those were, with the exception of several petty courts which it is unnecessary to mention here, the judicial institutions which were in existence in 1810, when the island capitulated to the British.

The Hon. ETIENNE KOENIG, Procureur and Advocate-General.

On December 28th, 1810, Sir Robert Farquhar, the first Governor appointed by the British Crown, proclaimed that the Courts would continue in existence and exercise, *durante bene placito*, the same jurisdiction as was then in vogue. The only alteration which the cession effected in the administration of justice was that the judgments of the Courts of Mauritius were ordered to be pronounced in the name of His Britannic Majesty, and that appeals from Mauritius were thenceforth no longer to be made to the *Cour de Cassation*, of France, but to the King in Council. In 1812 the denomination of the island was changed to "Mauritius." In 1814, in terms of the Treaty of Paris, Mauritius and its dependencies were ceded in full right and ownership by His Most Christian Majesty to His Britannic Majesty.

L. A. HUGUES, Master and Registrar of the Supreme Court, Acting Puisne Judge.

Between 1803 and 1814 Admiralty jurisdiction had continued to be exercised by the *Tribunal de Première Instance.* In the latter year a Vice-Admiralty Court was established. In 1832 the *Tribunal Terrier* was abolished and its jurisdiction transferred to the Governor in Executive Council. The jurisdiction of the other Courts remained unchanged up to 1850.

Then the system of judicature in the island underwent a complete transformation. The *Tribunal de Première Instance* was abolished. Subject always to a right of appeal from its decisions to the Privy Council, the *Cour d'Appel* was styled "The Supreme Court of the Colony of Mauritius." Its appellate jurisdiction, as then existing, was withdrawn, and it was invested with an original, as well as with an appellate, jurisdiction, which, with subsequent extensions and modifications, the Court has preserved to this day and still exercises.

E. SERRET, Additional Substitute Procureur and Advocate-General.

JURISDICTION OF THE SUPREME COURT.

Since 1850 the criminal side of the Court has borne the style of "Court of Assizes." It is the superior Court of original criminal jurisdiction, and is held by one or more judges of the Supreme Court; questions of fact are decided by the jury. Four sessions are held yearly—once every three months from January 1st, or oftener if found necessary.

The civil side has been invested, ever since 1850, with all the powers, authority and jurisdiction of the then existing Court of Queen's Bench and with equitable jurisdiction. The Court consists of a Chief Judge and two or more Puisne Judges, and at public sittings is composed of not less than two judges. The Court has the discretion of ordering that any case be heard by a jury. The judges may also refer, for decision, to the Master any such cases as they may be advised.

Divorce suits are within the jurisdiction of the Supreme Court, so also are suits in judicial separation.

The Hon. G. A. RITTER, C.M.G., Attorney-at-Law.

The Court likewise exercises Admiralty jurisdiction, that jurisdiction having been transferred from the Vice-Admiralty Court to the Supreme Court in 1863. The Court, when exercising Admiralty jurisdiction, bears the title of "Colonial Court of Admiralty," and is presided over by the Chief Judge. The judgments of the Court are liable to appeal before the King in Council.

The Court is further in- which is peculiar to Mauritius jurisdiction which may be said rivers and streams of the Colony property. In 1872 the jurisdic- was withdrawn and vested in inferior ordinary tribunals, the

HENRY BERTIN, Attorney-at-Law.

LEON HUET DE FROBERVILLE, Acting Chief Clerk of the Supreme Court.

vested with "Land" jurisdiction, of all other British Colonies—a to be *sui similis*. In 1863 the were declared to be public tion of the Governor in Council the Supreme Court and the Governor in Council retaining only the power of deciding certain questions for the public benefit.

The Court has a Bankruptcy Division. A Court of Bankruptcy, to be held by any one of the judges of the Supreme Court, had been constituted in 1853. In 1887 the Master of the Supreme Court was made Judge of the Bankruptcy Court. In 1899 the Bankruptcy Division of the Supreme Court was created, and the Master ceased to exercise bankruptcy jurisdiction, which was vested in the judges of the Supreme Court, any one judge sitting alone. The Bankruptcy Division is further vested with jurisdiction in insolvency and the winding-up of companies, which jurisdiction had previously been exercised by the Master.

The judges also exercise a jurisdiction in Chambers. The Judge in Chambers has power to finally dispose of certain matters specified by law, with the discretion of referring the case to the Court. He can grant a Writ of Injunction, but the Court is empowered, on motion, to dissolve or modify the writ. The Judge in Chambers can decide all matters which were formerly settled in Chambers by the President of the *Cour d'Appel* or the President of the *Cour de Première Instance*, and can give any order which was previously within the jurisdiction of either of them. The judge of the Bankruptcy Division may exercise in Chambers the whole or any part of his jurisdiction in bankruptcy, except in certain matters specified.

The Master also holds a Court, and the Master's Court has original jurisdiction in matters concerning probate of wills, judicial sales, and in certain other matters. The probate of wills, mentioned in the Charter of Justice, is not that which is known in English law under the same name. The Court, in accordance with its statutory powers, sits as a Court of Appeal over the following tribunals:—The Bankruptcy Division, the Master's Court, the District Courts, the Benches of Magistrates, the Stipendiary Courts, the Supreme Court of Seychelles. As regards Seychelles cases, the right of review by Writ of Certiorari was expressly withdrawn in 1903, when Seychelles was made a separate Colony and the Supreme Court of Seychelles created.

When sitting as Colonial Court hears appeals from cer- Court. There also exist the District Courts, the Benches and the Stipendiary Courts the Dependencies, there is a magistrates are appointed, as over the Oil Islands.

JACQUES GANACHAUD,
Attorney-at-Law.

Court of Admiralty, the Supreme tain decisions of the Marine Courts of inferior jurisdiction, of Magistrates, the Marine Court for Mauritius itself. As regards Court in Rodrigues, and two a rule, to exercise jurisdiction

EDGAR DE ROBILLARD.
Notary Public.

[Since the foregoing was written an enactment (Ordinance 36 of 1912), affecting the Supreme Court, has been unexpectedly put into force by proclamation. By that statute claims not exceeding Rs. 3,000, suits for divorce or judicial separation, motions and rules returnable, will in future be susceptible, at the discretion of the judges, of being heard and determined by one judge sitting alone. In this connection it may be as well to observe that in 1850 there was created a branch of the Supreme Court, subsequently known as the "Bail Court," which was composed of one judge, and exercised a limited original, as well as an affillate, jurisdiction that was abolished in 1881.]

INFERIOR COURTS OF MAURITIUS.

The District Courts are Courts of Record. They were created in 1850, and their jurisdiction has been modified by subsequent enactments. They are presided over by a District Magistrate, who has similar powers, privileges and functions, and exercises the same jurisdiction under any Act of Parliament extending to the Colony as those of a Justice of the Peace, or

PAUL BAISSAC,
Notary Public.

two Justices sitting together. The law expressly provides that the Magistrates shall exercise such jurisdiction in connection with the Merchant Shipping Act of 1894 (57 and 58 Vict., c. 60). The Magistrate also decides certain questions formerly within the jurisdiction of the Land Court.

The District Courts exercise original jurisdiction, both civil and criminal. The Magistrate has, in certain cases specified in the law, the powers originally granted to the *Juge de Paix.* He exercises jurisdiction over civil claims of minor pecuniary importance, but certain matters are expressly excluded from his jurisdiction.

The Court exercises summary jurisdiction over certain minor criminal offences. The District Magistrate also holds preliminary inquiries into crimes over which he has no jurisdiction, and is also invested with certain other powers defined by law; such, for instance, as the investigation of cases of death by violence.

At Port Louis the District Court sits in three "Divisions" The First Division hears civil, and the two others criminal, matters, the Magistrate for the Third Division trying offences of a minor degree, and acting, in addition, as Police Magistrate. He is also commissioned as Stipendiary Magistrate for Port Louis. As Police Magistrate the last-named official exercises the jurisdiction which had been conferred on the Municipal Tribunal of the Capital, when it was created in 1852. In 1860 the Municipal Tribunal was abolished, and its jurisdiction transferred to the Police Magistrate for Port Louis.

L. A. AIMÉ DUVIVIER,
Custodian of the Archives.

The Benches of Magistrates are composed of three District Magistrates sitting together. The Court exercises an original criminal jurisdiction intermediate between that of the Court of Assizes and the summary jurisdiction of the District Magistrate sitting alone.

As regards the Marine Court, a Marine Board was created in 1856 for the purpose of investigating cases of wrecks and other casualties affecting ships. In 1902 the jurisdiction was transferred to the Marine Court, which was composed of the Magistrate for the First Division of the District Court of Port Louis, sitting with no less than two "assessors" possessing certain qualifications. In 1910 the Magistrate sitting alone was invested with the jurisdiction of the Court, and his powers were defined by enactment; the jurisdiction extends to shipwrecks and other casualties, incompetency or misconduct on the part of masters, mates, or engineers of ships, in certain cases enumerated in the statute.

The Magistrates for the Second and Third Divisions are granted concurrent jurisdiction. On the occurrence of a casualty a preliminary inquiry may be held, and the Court holds that inquiry with the assistance of one or more assessors, who must be experts possessing specific qualifications.

The Stipendiary Courts have existed on their present footing since Ordinance 12 of 1878 (The Labour Law) was passed, remodelling the former law as to the relationship between employer and servant. Stipendiary Magistrates had been appointed ever since the Order in Council of 7th September, 1838. These are Courts of petty jurisdiction applying the Labour Law, and are mostly engaged in punishing indentured labourers for breaches of their contracts with their masters.

COURTS OF THE DEPENDENCIES.

Most of the Dependencies were occupied between 1742 and 1758. The original jurisdiction of the then existing Courts extended to them until special enactments were passed to provide them with Courts of inferior original jurisdiction. In 1814, when Mauritius was ceded to the British Crown, it was so ceded with its Dependencies.

As regards Rodrigues, a Judicial and Police Establishment was created there in 1843. In 1866 the

Police Magistrate of Rodrigues was invested with powers similar to those of the District Magistrates of Mauritius, as their jurisdiction then existed and under certain reservations.

In 1883 certain additional powers, resembling those of notaries public, were conferred on the Magistrate. He also acts as Civil Status Officer. In 1890 the Police Magistrate's appellation was converted into that of Magistrate.

As regards the Oil Islands, His Excellency the Governor may appoint two Magistrates for them, and in special circumstances three. These Magistrates are to visit the islands at such times as they are requested to do so by the Procureur-General, and cumulate the powers and authority of the District and Stipendiary Magistrates of Mauritius, subject to the modifications set forth in the law. They may exercise their jurisdiction in Port Louis, and, in the event of impediment, the Magistrates for Port Louis are empowered to act in their stead. Their jurisdiction is final, and an appeal lies only on an *ex parte* order of a Judge in Chambers that a question of law is involved in the issue which "deserves and requires" to be considered by "a higher tribunal"—an expression understood to designate the Supreme Court of Mauritius.

DISTRICTS OF MAURITIUS.

For administrative and political purposes Mauritius is divided into nine districts, the names of which are given below together with the principal towns and villages, that in which the Courthouse is situated being printed in italics.

PORT LOUIS, 16½ sq. miles—*Port Louis*, Grand River, Roche Bois, Vallée des Prêtres. (10,560 acres.)

PAMPLEMOUSSES, 69 sq. miles—*Pamplemousses*, Long Mountain, Pieter Both, Callebasses River, Piton, Bois Rouge, Mapou, Tombeau, l'Arsenal, Pointe aux Piments, Trou aux Biches. (44,160 acres.)

RIVIERE DU REMPART, 57 sq. miles—*Poudre d'Or*, Bois Rouge, Grand Baie, Mapou, Piton, Plaines St. Cloud, Rivière du Rempart, Plaines des Roches. (36,480 acres.)

FLACQ, 115 sq. miles—*Flacq*, Mares aux Lubines, Quatre Cocos, Trou d'Eau Douce, Rivière Sèche, Mare Fougères, Trois Ilots, Camp de Masque. (73,600 acres.)

GRAND PORT, 100½ sq. miles—*Mahébourg*, Mare d'Albert, Plein Bois, Mare Tabac, Cent Gaulettes, Rivière La Chaux, Rivère des Créoles, Les Anses. (64,320 acres.)

SAVANNE, 94½ sq. miles—*Souillac*, Grande Savanne, Petite Savanne, Jacotet. (60,480 acres.)

PLAINES WILHEMS, 78½ sq. miles—*Rose Hill* and *Curepipe*, Bas du Quartier, Terre Rouge, Beau Bassin, Quartre Bornes, Phœnix, Le Bassin, Vacoas, Mesnil. (50,240 acres.)

MOKA, 89 sq. miles—*Moka*, Les Pailles, Terre Rouge, Quartier Militaire, St. Pierre. (56,960 acres.)

BLACK RIVER, 100 sq. miles—*Bambous*, Petite Rivière, Plaines St. Pierre, Tamarin, Black River, Coteau Rafin, Chamarel, Gorges du Cap. (64,000 acres.)

In the areas given above the following islands are included :—

PORT LOUIS.	Acres.
Flat Island	626
Gabriel Island	104
Pigeon Rock Island ...	2
Barkly Island	3
Tonneliers Island ...	60
	795

RIVIÈRE DU REMPART.	Acres.
Round Island	417
Serpent Island ...	78
Gunner's Quoin Island	188
Ile d'Ambre and Pointe Bernache	339
	1,022

FLACQ.	Acres.
Ile aux Cerfs	323

GRAND PORT.	Acres.
Mouchoir Rouge ...	1
Ile aux Aigrettes ...	61
Ile de la Passe ...	5
Ile Vacoas	2
Ile aux Fouquets ...	8
Ile aux Fous ...	1
Ile Marianne	10
Ile des deux Cocos ...	10
Ile Brocus and Lafond	39
	137

BLACK RIVER.	Acres.
Ilot Fourneaux ...	31
Ilot Bénitiers	125
Ilot Malais	3
Ilot Fortier	16
	175

CHIEF JUDGES AND COMMISSARIES OF JUSTICE from 1814 to 1913.

George Smith	30th October	1814
Edward Berens Blackburn ...	10th January	1824
James Wilson	1st October	1835
Sir J. Edward Remono—*acting*—6th March to 20th June and 1st November, 1858, to ...	20th August	1860
Sir Stevenson Villiers Surtees—*acting*	31st January	1857
Sir Charles Farquhar Shand ...	30th May	1860
Sir Nicolas Gustave Bestel—*acting*—19th January, 1868, to 4th June and April, 1875, to 6th June, 1876, and 11th September, 1878, to ...	31st August	1879
Sir Adam Gib Ellis	1st September	1879
Sir E. P. J. Leclézio	22nd November	1883
F. T. Piggott—*acting*	7th April	1895
Sir E. P. J. Leclézio	25th May	1897
L. V. Delafaye	30th April	1898
Sir L. V. Delafaye	1st December	1899
F. C. Moncrieff—*acting*	16th February	1900
Ernest Didier St. Amand—*acting*	24th April	1900
Richard Myles Brown—*acting* ...	31st August	1906
Louis Arthur Thibaud—*acting* ...	5th October	1908
Richard Myles Brown—*acting* ...	23rd October	1908
Furcy Alfred Herchenroder, K.C. —*acting*	2nd September	1912
Sir L. V. Delafaye, K.C.	12th November	1912
Furcy Alfred Herchenroder, K.C.	1st January	1913

BENCH AND BAR.

By E. ROGER PEZZANI, Barrister-at-Law.

> "The talents, the merits, the genius of the Colonial (Mauritius) Bar I do not mean to dispute, nor would I have the presumption to contend that I am equal to compete with them."
>
> JEREMIE.—*Speech in Council (9th July, 1832).*

THE subject of these short and unpretending jottings is one of those nearest to a barrister's heart. After a while the Court-house becomes a second home to him, and he feels unhappy if through illness or otherwise he has to keep away from it for any length of time. It does not matter one whit whether or not he is personally engaged in the case; he will devote any little leisure in watching with delight a witness's finesse, or note at once the judge's almost imperceptible yawn or impalpable smile; and should he think himself justified he will be happy to help his fellow-barrister with some useful item of information or with a decision in point. Indeed, he would rejoice to take up the cudgels at the slightest intimation for the love of the thing.

SIR WILLIAM NEWTON, K.C.

SIR VICTOR DELAFAYE, K.C.

In Mauritius it is all the more so. Seldom has the full-fledged (but what a pitiable fledgeling!) young counsel to wait long for briefs on his return from his "dinners." He has to win his spurs at the Assizes, where he appears with a brief assigned to him by the Chief Justice and marked with the assurance of his pauper client's gratitude. If successful, as he is certain to be, owing to his legitimate assurance and ambition, but especially thanks to the invariable courtesy of his trained opponent and the charming manner of the presiding judge and interested jurymen, the young débutant will soon have enough briefs to make many an old "junior" at home envious indeed.

G. GUIBERT, K.C.

Unfortunately the medal has its reverse side. After a few years' practice the junior barrister realises that he has reached the top of his tree; and long will he stay there at an average considerably under £1,200 per annum, which is about the yearly maximum of the busiest man. The reason is that there is in Mauritius an abnormally large number of small cases, and big cases are few and far between.

No barrister is now allowed to practise in any of the inferior Courts of the Colony or in the High Court who has not been called to the Bar in the United Kingdom, and almost every barrister now in practice has eaten his dinners in the Middle Temple Hall. It may be that they have thus imbibed the true spirit of confraternity from the same time-honoured loving cup, but the fact is that there cannot be a more congenial Bar, on the whole, in the world. Speaking as a member of the Junior Bar, I am hopelessly in the debt of the pleasant, able and learned friends and "silks" at the Bar, whose kindness to me has been untiring and whose assistance I have often found invaluable. Long may such traditions be handed down to the never-failing array of yet younger men.

The Hon. EMILE SAUZIER, K.C.

Professional etiquette, however, is far from being so satisfactory, and a Council of the Bar when it is established will supply a long-felt want. On the other hand the Procureur-General is by statute the guardian of the Bar's professional honour, and it is certainly gratifying that not once, during at least the last two or three decades, did a member of the Bar render himself amenable to the jurisdiction of the High Court.

The Hon. LOUIS ROUILLARD, Barrister-at-Law.

There is little doubt that both now and in the days gone by the Bar in Mauritius is and has been represented by men of exceptional attainments. It may be many a long day before we can once more boast of men of the eminence of Mr. G. Guibert, K.C., and of Sir William Newton, K.C., to speak only of those whom it has been my privilege to know and listen to, and whose venerable age permits mention of them without creating invidious distinctions. Their presence at the Bar would surely have been an ornament in any part of the world ; and to them the Junior Bar must be thankful indeed not only for their unbounded assistance, but for the countless important decisions to which they have contributed their share of legal acumen and learning by means of searching and lucid arguments. Similarly we have been taught to lay much store by the names of Adrien and Prosper d'Epinay (father and uncle of the celebrated sculptor), and Evenor Dupont, as the fathers of the Bar in Mauritius. The Government also has more than once benefited by the discretion, devotion, and talent of Mauritians like them. Others who have held with distinction the post of Procureur and Advocate-General are Mr. E. Pellereau, Sir Lionel Cox, who were both promoted to other Colonies, and Mr. F. A. Herchenroder, whose distinguished services have lately been rewarded with the Chief Justiceship of the Colony. The Hon. E. Koenig is now the holder of the much-coveted post vacated by Mr. Herchenroder, and there is not, I fancy, a more justly popular man at the Bar, which he now leads.

ERNEST LECLÉZIO, Barrister-at-Law.

The High Court Bench consists of a Chief Judge, with two or more Puisne Judges. Of late years three Puisne Judges have been found necessary to overtake arrears and keep the Cause List in a businesslike condition. Justice to be sure must be slow, and certainly there was occasion to say not very long ago that the judges were evidently attempting to make assurance doubly sure; but there seems to have been no justification whatsoever for the abolition of the fourth judgeship on the recommendation of the omniscient Royal Commission of 1909. Opinion is certainly hardening at the Bar against that abolition and against the inconvenience that flows from it for the profession, especially when the unworthy plea of economy is put forward. Only quite recently Lord Shaw said that no judge could hope to do justice without the splendid and able help of the Bar. The Bar of Mauritius is, I believe, fully worthy of similar praise, and it is to be hoped that, when the present inadequate system has once again been voted a failure, in spite of the energetic efforts of the Chief Justice and his two brother judges, the Bar's respectful representations will not be abortive.

EDOUARD AMAND ESNOUF,
District and Stipendiary Magistrate, Port Louis.

LOUIS ULCOQ,
District Magistrate, Flacq.

The greatest of the judges sent been Sir Eugène Leclézio, jurist and highly-esteemed gentle- Leclézio. Considerable weight of Mr. Gustave Colin, Sir Charles

in Mauritius has by common con- C.J., the father of another able man, his Honour Mr. Léon also attaches to the judgments Farquhar Shand, Sir Victor Delafaye, and Mr. R. M. Brown.

L. LECONTE,
Acting District Magistrate, Port Louis.

The constitution of the Supreme Court has lately been modified. It shall now be lawful for one judge to sit alone (Ord. 36 of 1912) instead of sitting with a brother judge without a jury as he had to formerly in all matters not exceeding Rs. 3,000 in value.

The abolition of the third Puisne Judge created the necessity of that ordinance, and the Bar will watch its development with interest. There can be no objection, it seems, to the new departure; on the contrary it should, I think, be welcomed; but the public may not unreasonably ask that, as is the case in England, there should be an appeal from the one judge's decision to a full Bench of three judges, and that will necessitate the presence of four judges at the High Court.

In all coming changes I am confident that the Mauritian Bar, if lacking in the lustre and talent to which even John Jeremie had to pay homage, will yet keep up the standard of ability of a profession to which, as Prosper d'Epinay said: "l'Etat a toujours du et principaux sontiens et homme le plus illustre."

ECCLESIASTICAL.

By ALBERT PITOT.

THE last decennial census for 1911 sets down the population of Mauritius as follows:—

General population (Europeans, coloured and mixed)	107,432
Indians	257,697
Chinese	3,662
Total	368,791

out of which 122,586 are Christians of different denominations. As for the balance, it may be roughly estimated that about 90,000 are Mohammedans, 3,000 Buddhists and followers of Confucius, and the rest, represented chiefly by Indians, are members of various Hindu sects.

We shall only deal here with the Christian element, which, according to the same authority, is thus composed:—

Roman Catholics (including about 12,000 Indians and Chinese) ...	115,984
Protestants of various creeds	6,602
Total	122,586

His Lordship the Right Rev. J. R. BILSBORROW, O.S.B., Bishop of Port Louis.

Of the latter, 2,315 belong to the Church of England; the others to several dissident congregations of the Church of Scotland, and a few hundreds to the New Jerusalem Church.

From this it may be inferred that over $94\frac{1}{2}$ per cent. of the Christian population of Mauritius are followers of the Church of Rome.

It may be of interest to place before the reader a brief historical outline of the different phases which the religious establishments of this Colony have gone through before settling in the present state of things.

The first occupants of the island—the Dutch—after having settled here on two consecutive occasions for about sixty-five years in all, finally retired, leaving the island uninhabited. As far as can be gathered from authentic sources, the number of the Dutch colonists, all belonging probably to the Reformed Church, was so small indeed that it was not deemed worth while having a clergyman attached to the establishment. The first number, twenty-five, landed in 1638, and were soon increased to eighty, a figure which in no case was to be exceeded. In 1652 the Commander, Reynier Por, prayed the Governor-General at Batavia for his transfer to some other Colony, on the ground that, under the present circumstances, he was unable to comply with the dictates of his religion, and was conscience struck at seeing his two youngest children grow up without having been christened. In reply to his request a minister was sent over, who, during a stay of three months, baptised about a dozen children; and it was understood that such visits would be renewed periodically. In July, 1658, the Colony was abandoned, but reoccupied in 1664. The only mention concerning religion thenceforth found in official records is contained in the instructions for Governor Lamotius (1677-92), in which he is directed to say prayers in public every morning and evening, and to preach to the inhabitants on Sundays.

Matters changed altogether when the French settled here in 1721 under Mr. de Nyon, on behalf of the East India Company. The King had made a private arrangement with the congregation of

BISHOP'S PALACE, PORT LOUIS.

St. Lazarus to the effect that a few missionaries were to be sent out to the island, under the direction of an Apostolic Prefect; those priests were to be entirely independent of local authorities, and responsible only towards the Cabinet and their own General, as the Superior of their Order was called.

Four of them arrived with the Governor, and took up their dwelling in the only two ports then existing—Port South-East (or Port Bourbon) and Port North-West Over the more respectable inhabitants they very soon acquired considerable influence, which proved a great boon in those troubled and unruly times; for it must be remembered that the original few settlers, mostly rough and uneducated people, sent from the neighbouring island of Bourbon, were composed of the laziest and most undesirable persons who had not succeeded in making a living there. Things were altered, of course, when the population increased by the introduction of a better class of colonists emigrating from France with their families.

According to the Letters Patent putting in force the *Code Noir*, that is to say, the legislation applicable to slaves, every master was compelled to see that his blacks were taught the principles of religion, that they were regularly married among themselves, and that their children were duly christened. This gave rise to much discontent amongst the colonists, who resented the interference of the clergy in what they considered their private affairs, and so grievously insulted the priests that the latter complained to the Prefect, Father Borthon, with the result that the inhabitants of Port Bourbon Parish were excommunicated. For two years no divine service was performed there; but things somehow amended afterwards, through the intervention of the civil authorities.

THE CATHEDRAL, PORT LOUIS.

When a Provincial Council was established at the Isle of France, in 1725, the Ecclesiastic Superior became *ex officio* a member of that assembly, and likewise sat in the Superior Council, which replaced it in 1735, till 1772, when an Edict of King Louis XV. forbade priests from being appointed to such offices. The influence of the Superior was manifested many times, when he protested against the encroachment of the authorities, or the indifference of some inhabitants for the most elementary precepts of morality. For instance, in 1730, at the request of Father

Borthon, the Council sentenced one François Marteau, *alias* Dragon, to dig up the body of his dead child, which he had buried in a field of sweet potatoes without any religious rites having been performed, and to carry it in his own arms to the church, so that prayers might be said over the corpse. Nevertheless, religious influence had progressed in other parts. In 1729 the inhabitants of Flacq and Savanne approached the local Government with a petition demanding that two Capuchin Fathers, who happened to visit the Isle of France on their way to India, should be prevailed upon to settle in these two districts.

In 1734 we find Abbé Igou, Vicar-General and a highly popular priest, complaining to the Council of there being no church at Pamplemousses, although the population of that district was rapidly increasing. This was taken into consideration; but it was not until eight years later that a house belonging to one Mr. Boucher was purchased for the purpose. The present church of St. François was built some fifteen years after, when Governor Magon personally shared in the expense.

ST. JAMES'S CHURCH (Protestant), PORT LOUIS.

When La Bourdonnais had transferred the seat of the Government to Port Louis, a small chapel was attached to the newly-built hospital, in addition to which a large stone building was provisionally appropriated for divine service, its site being now comprised in the block between Royal and Queen, Church and Bourbon Streets. There, on February 16th, 1738, was interred the Governor's infant child, François Gilles, aged twenty-two months; there also, three months later, on May 9th of the same year, was buried his first wife, Marie Anne Josèphe Le Brun de La Franquerie, who had died suddenly at Monplaisir of indigestion, caused by eating a loaf of millet flour just after coming out of the oven. On her death-bed she had asked that her son's corpse should be laid beside her in the same coffin, and further, that her heart should be severed from her body and deposited in the new Parochial Church, which was about to be erected half-way between Government House and the Champ de Mars. Her requests were duly complied with.

In the following year new use was made of an old building then occupied by the Superior Council, close to Government House, at the corner of Royal Street and a small lane called Rue des Bons Enfants, which disappeared in the conflagration of September, 1816, and, at that time, ran along Government House Gardens, parallel with Church Street, ending at the square where now stands the theatre. After having been used in succession as Registry Office, retail shop for the East India Company's Indian goods, Treasury Office, and residence of the officer commanding the troops, the building in question was turned into a chapel, and consecrated to St. Anne in 1739, after Madame de La Bourdonnais' name, when the remains of that lady and her child were transferred to a vault in the chapel, at the foot of the wall facing Royal Street.

Eighty-eight years later, in December, 1827, after the building had undergone a strange series of transformations—viz., Controller's Office, Justice of the Peace Court, Municipality under the French Revolution, Police Office under General Decaen, and, finally, Government printing office under the British rule, it was partly demolished in order to accommodate the offices of the Colonial Secretary. It happened that the vault was then discovered, and the coffin brought up and opened; its contents, having been identified, were transferred in great pomp to the Cathedral.

Previous to 1771 the site of the present Company's Gardens was a cemetery of the worst possible description, for it was a low marshy lagoon, partly covered by the sea when the tide set in, and exposed to the rays of a burning sun when it receded. The Chaussée, which originally was nothing but a narrow causeway, did not then exist, and was built only in 1780, in order to avoid the encroachments of the sea and secure a direct communication between Government House, the Barracks, and Rempart Street, where stood the richest dwellings. The authorities had long before decided to transfer that cemetery outside the limits of the town, but as it was necessary to remove also the dead bodies interred there, they had dreaded the opposition of the inhabitants and clergy. In 1771, however, Governor Desroches, during an outbreak of smallpox in the Colony, caused a new burying ground to be prepared at Cassis, and ordered the removal of the corpses, notwithstanding the charges that were brought against him of irreverence towards the dead; and his praiseworthy behaviour doubtless saved Port Louis from a most dreadful pestilence.

The Cathedral, or Parochial Church as it was called under the French administration, was also built in La Bourdonnais' time, at a period between 1740 and 1746, although the exact date of its construction cannot possibly be ascertained, through lack of documents to that effect. Its southern transept was occupied by a chapel dedicated to St. Anne, Madame de La Bourdonnais' patroness, where now is St. Louis' Chapel. There, at the foot of the wall, close to the choir, was deposited the heart of Madame de La Bourdonnais, inserted in a leaden casket bearing an appropriate inscription. In the wall itself, at the height of about six feet, was a recess containing an urn of carved stone, resting on four lion's claws and terminated by the representation of an undulating flame. Above this a polished flagstone displayed in colours the arms of La Bourdonnais and his wife.

The Venerable Archdeacon
H. H. BUSWELL.

This stone disappeared during the Revolution, probably through the dislike of the Sans Culottes for heraldic emblems. The above-mentioned urn was thrown outside the church, where it still remained forgotten some twenty years later, during the re-edification of the building, probably on account of the architect's ignorance of the particulars we have related. After a long time, however, it was placed in the Presbytery, facing the north aisle of the Cathedral, in Dauphine Street. As for the heart of Madame de La Bourdonnais, it is impossible to say whether it still lies where it had been originally placed, or whether it was thrown away by the fury of the Jacobins.

The Parochial Church, however, was doomed to undergo extraordinary vicissitudes. It was first totally wrecked by a hurricane on April 9th, 1773. In the next year its reconstruction was entrusted to Mr. Dayot; but with the view of sparing the Colonial finances, the authorities insisted upon making use of the former understructures, although the architect objected to their resting partly on a huge rock and partly on soft ground, which might affect the solidity of the building. The preliminary operations were not completed till 1780, when Vicomte de Souillac, then Governor, was called upon to lay the foundation-stone of the new church, which was inaugurated six years after, and was very similar to the one now existing, except that its roof was a terrace, or an *argamasse*, as it was termed in the Colony.

When the French Revolution broke out, and the Isle of France elected a Colonial Assembly, the Apostolic Prefect, Mr. Darthé, granted this body, in order to hold its sittings and keep its records, the use of two-thirds of the church, comprising the gallery above the main entrance and the one on the right-hand side, running above part of the nave. The church had been already badly treated by successive storms, when, on November 29th, 1793, a solemn funeral service was held in honour of Marat—a most eccentric idea, it must be confessed! A battery of field-pieces, placed on the porch, fired a volley at the moment of consecration, with the result that the walls were rent in several places. The building being no longer considered safe, divine service was afterwards performed in the chapel of the hospital.

For some time the Assembly persisted in holding its sittings in the less ruinous part of the structure, but was soon compelled to dislodge also, and the tottering church was used as a central store, where goods were deposited against a receipt from the authorities, which, on account of the depreciated finances, were used as a fiduciary instrument of exchange in daily transactions.

Some time previously the Ecclesiastic Superior, Mr. Darthé, had left the Colony and resigned in favour of the curate of Pamplemousses, Abbé Durocher, an aged man who died within a few months of his appointment. The supreme ecclesiastical authority was accordingly vested in Father Hofmann, chaplain of the hospital, an Alsatian by birth, and a former corporal in the French army, a worthy and an excellent man in all respects, who probably, from the bluntness of his ways and crude speech, gained great influence over the most zealous of Colonial Jacobins, so as to prevail upon them to join the procession on Corpus Christi Day, and even to kneel down and make the sign of the Cross as he passed before them carrying the pix

On July 28th, 1800, Governor Malartic died, and his body having been embalmed, was on the next day exposed in the chapel of the hospital till August 16th, when it was buried in the Champ de Mars.

On the arrival of General Decaen in 1803, the Concordat passed between Napoleon I. and the Holy See two years before came into force at the Isle of France; but, as it merely affected the relations of the clergy with the French Government, it brought no change whatever in local circumstances. Ministers of the Church still continued to be very few in the island—so few, indeed, that in rural districts only three churches existed: one at Pamplemousses, the present St. François; one at Moka, which by no means resembled the St. Pierre Church of our days; and one at Flacq, St. Julien, which was then but an old stone magazine dating from Abbé Igou's time, covered with shingles, which, as they were rotten, had been economically thatched over with a layer of vetiver straw. In 1806, General Decaen having created the small town of Mahébourg, a very modest chapel was opened there, in a house hired from Mr. Bertrand for twenty dollars a month. As for the Parochial Church of Port Louis, it was nothing but a crumbling heap of ruins.

STE. CROIX CHURCH, PORT LOUIS.

Such was the state of ecclesiastical affairs in Mauritius when the Colony passed under the British rule in December, 1810. According to the terms of the Capitulation, the inhabitants were to preserve their religion, laws, and customs, which accordingly remained unaltered. But, on the other hand, it happened that most of the authorities and the garrison now belonged to the Reformed Church. At first the military chaplains held services at the Line Barracks till June, 1812, when it was decided that a more spacious building should be appropriated, and the Government made choice of the old French powder magazine in Poudrière Street, which of late had accommodated the English prisoners of war, and was hastily turned into a Protestant Church, the military being employed in demolishing the bomb-proof casemate covering it, and replacing this by a vault in masonry; a porch was also added to the front entrance. Governor Farquhar had noticed at Villebague, on an estate formerly belonging to the French Governor Magon, now *La Rosalie*, a tower that had contained a large clock, the only remnant of which was a big bell, which he purchased and sent to Port Louis. This was provisionally placed on a scaffold, close to the church, to be used as a belfry.

The vault does not appear to have been properly constructed, for fifteen years later it had cracked to such an extent that it was deemed of the utmost urgency to close the church at once, and services were temporarily performed in a store on Place d'Armes, facing Government House, somewhere about the site of the present Bank of Mauritius. The repairs were steadily carried on under the supervision of the Rev. A. Denny, who changed the vault into a shingle roof and built over the porch the octagonal steeple which still exists, and where Governor Magon's bell was hoisted. Nevertheless, that church was not entirely completed till June, 1850, when it was consecrated, as well as other Protestant churches in the island, by Dr. James Chapman, Bishop of Colombo, the first prelate of the English Church who ever visited Mauritius, and the building received, after him, the appellation of St. James.

MARBLE BUST OF THE
REV. FATHER JEAN DESIRÉ LAVAL,
By Prosper d'Epinay.

About 1814 the London Missionary Society sent to this Colony a young minister from Jersey, Rev. J. J. Le Brun, to catechize the black population; the first place of his meetings was a small house in St. George's Street, on the very site now occupied by the Roman Catholic Church of the Immaculée Conception. In 1826 this clergyman opened another chapel at Rivière du Rempart, from funds collected among his co-religionists. His proselytic enthusiasm was great and met with fair success; but, not satisfied with addressing grown-up people, and being fully aware of the influence of religious instruction on young children, he devoted considerable attention to school-teaching, and had the supervision of a few institutions carried on in the Mico Charity system—these institutions having since developed into the present Government schools.

As for the Roman Catholics, Mr. Farquhar got the Governor-General of Bengal, Lord Moira, who visited Mauritius in 1813, to lay the first stone of the Parochial Church, which had been entirely demolished, and was then reconstructed on the same spot for the third time.

The Colonists also petitioned the home Government for the resumption of an ecclesiastical hierarchy and for a sufficient number of priests, so that the districts might have their own parishes. This was not entirely granted at first; but the Rev. Dr. Slater was sent out as Vicar-Apostolic. Though this prelate was Bishop *in partibus* of Ruspa, he was not officially recognised as such for Mauritius, and the Colony did not become an episcopal see till some twenty-six years later, when one of his successors, Dr. Collier, was regularly appointed in December, 1846, Bishop of Port Louis, a title which has since been held by the first dignitaries of the Roman Catholic Church in Mauritius. Dr. Slater belonged to the English Order of St. Benedict, from which the ecclesiastical superiors here have been constantly recruited—the only exception being made for Bishop Meurin, who was a Jesuit.

TOMB OF THE REV. FATHER JEAN DÉSIRÉ LAVAL,
STE. CROIX CHURCH, PORT LOUIS.

Of the Bishops of Port Louis only two died during their tenure of office ; those were Bishops Hankinson and Meurin, who were buried in the choir of the Cathedral. In 1911 Bishop O'Neill also died in the Colony, and his body was placed beside his two colleagues. He had left for England some time before, and had resigned his office on account of ill-health, when his successor, the present Bishop, his Lordship the Right Reverend J. R. Bilsborrow, O.S.B., who was his intimate friend and had for years assisted him in his episcopal duties as his Vicar-General, prevailed upon him to return to Mauritius and settle among his former flock, who held him in great veneration. Shortly after his arrival, however, Bishop O'Neill fell dangerously ill and was carried off, in spite of the most devoted efforts to save his life. The Colony at large was deeply grieved by this melancholy event.

The first Bishop of the Church of England in Mauritius was the Rev. Dr. Ryan, appointed in 1854. The present Bishop is the Right Rev. F. A. Gregory, M.A., D.D., appointed in 1904. [It is regrettable that a photograph of his Lordship was unobtainable.—*Editor*.]

Churches and chapels gradually rose over the island, and more decent structures replaced the hastily utilised buildings. One of the first was Ste. Philomène, at Poudre d'Or, built in 1848, and it was a great boon to the inhabitants of Rivière du Rempart, who had been, up to that time, compelled to travel many miles to attend services at Pamplemousses Church. Then Plaines Wilhems and Moka had their own churches—St. Jean in 1850 and St. Pierre in 1852; next St. Jacques was inaugurated at Souillac in 1855. Soon after, religious buildings were erected at Flacq, Petite Rivière, Bambous, Mahébourg and other localities. A number of Protestant churches were also built, such as St. John's, in Poudrière Street, Port Louis; St. John's, at Moka, near Réduit; and St. Thomas's, at Beau Bassin. Meanwhile Port Louis possessed only one Roman Catholic church when, in 1845, came a Jesuit missionary, Father Mazuy, who soon gained great influence over the well-to-do citizens. After ten years' stay in the island he took a twenty-four months' leave, and proceeded to Rome with the view of advancing the interests of his faith. On his return, in 1857, he persuaded the Mauritians in general to unite for the purchase of a piece of ground in St. George's Street—on the very spot where the Rev. Le Brun had first assembled his followers—and a provisional wooden structure was erected and consecrated on August 15th, 1859; this was the Immaculée Conception, the second parish church of Port Louis, of which Father Mazuy was deservedly appointed curate.

FUNERAL OF HIS LORDSHIP, BISHOP O'NEILL, AT THE CATHEDRAL, PORT LOUIS, NOV. 8th, 1911.

Father Mazuy had, however, ambitions for a finer and more enduring edifice, and by means of subscriptions he began to raise the walls of a splendid basilica. When the work had proceeded for some time it had to be abandoned through lack of funds, and in spite of the worthy curate's repeated efforts, in spite of lotteries and all possible ways of raising money, the attempt had to be relinquished, and the modest wooden structure stood, towered over on all sides by the unfinished lofty walls. No change took place until the dreadful cyclone of April 29th, 1892, completely wrecked the timber church, after which part of the stone walls were utilised in rebuilding the Immaculée Conception Church as it now stands.

What public enthusiasm had failed to perform, private generosity succeeded in accomplishing. A wealthy physician, Dr. Thomy d'Arifat, undertook to build a church out of his own personal funds.

For some reason or other the spot chosen was Cassis, on the outskirts of the western suburb of Port Louis. Having died, however, before his object could be attained, he entrusted his widow with the care of completing the undertaking. Cassis Church is a really fine Gothic structure, which reflects much credit on the architect who planned it, but it is scarcely adapted to the locality. More recently, St. Thérèse Church was built at Curepipe, and a neat little church, St. François Xavier, erected at Plaine Verte.

We have spoken of the Rev. Le Brun's missionary achievements, and it is only fair to mention the wonderful progress accomplished in catechizing a large part of the general population by one man alone, a Roman Catholic missionary, the Rev. Father Jean Désiré Laval, of the Congregations of the Holy Ghost and Holy Heart of Mary, who arrived in this Colony with the Rev. Dr. Collier in 1841, and consecrated his whole life to the religious education of the lower classes. His success was so enormous, his influence over the multitude so amazing, that he was soon looked upon as an apostle and admired by all. When he died, on September 9th, 1864, his body was buried in the churchyard of Ste. Croix, in the eastern suburb of Port Louis, where he had mostly exercised his ministry. Although nearly half a century has elapsed his grave is, on the anniversary of his death, still the object of a pilgrimage in which all classes, even pagans, respectfully join.

CHURCH OF THE IMMACULÉE CONCEPTION, PORT LOUIS.

His example was followed, on a smaller scale but with no less success, by others, especially by Rev. Father Faduilhe, a Mauritian, whose memory will ever be blessed by his countrymen as a model of pious zeal and unbounded charity. About the same time, Father Pucinelli was busy converting Indians to the Roman Catholic doctrines; but the most extraordinary achievement was, perhaps, accomplished by a woman, Mother Barthélemy, Superioress of a convent at the foot of Signal Mountain which, on that account, goes under the name of Convent de la Montagne. She was a Mauritian lady by birth, and belonged to the best society, when she willingly renounced the world for a higher ideal. Her sphere of action, strange to say, was mostly directed towards the Chinese; and one can hardly realise what a woman, aided by a few diligent priests, did for the conversion of these people, who, from their particular turn of mind and their circumstances in Mauritius, appeared to be the last who would be disposed to embrace Christianity.

Throughout the island are numerous convents, originally founded by another Mauritian lady, out of her own personal finances, who took the veil and became, in course of time, Superioress of the Convent de Bon Sécours, under the name of Mother Augustine. In these convents Sisters of Mercy devote their lives to the nursing of the sick, to the rescuing of orphans and the education of young girls. Besides this they visit, comfort, and assist the poor by connection with private charitable institutions, the most important of the latter being the highly beneficial Société de St. Vincent de Paul, which has adherents in all classes of the population. A number of these pious women, headed by Mother Augustine, created, some forty years ago, a house of refuge known as Hospice St. Lazare, now patronised and assisted by Government, where lepers are attended to with never-failing zeal and devotedness, and their condition amended within the limits of possibility. In this noble work of mercy the Sisters are encouraged and assisted by persons belonging to the best society. The names of the late Dr. Charles Poupinel de Valencé and Mademoiselle Clémentine Déroullède, both related to the oldest families of the Mauritian community, will ever stand out brilliantly in the annals of the efforts made to ameliorate the sad lot of lepers in the island.

For the present, the only ecclesiastical establishments of education for boys are those managed by the Brethren of the Christian Doctrine—one at Curepipe and the other at Port Louis. There existed in the latter town, some thirty years ago, a college under the supervision of Marist Fathers, at the corner of Pope Hennessy Street and Champ de Mars, which, after having met with considerable encouragement, declined and had to close its doors, chiefly through the exodus of the population to the uplands, due to the malaria epidemic of 1867. This college is now occupied by the Brethren.

Although not strictly considered as a Government department, the cost of the clergy is supported by the Colonial Government in the following proportion:—

	Personal Emolument.	Other Charges.
Roman Catholic	Rs. 89,700	... Rs. 21,806
Church of England	34,500	... 43
Church of Scotland...	6,500	... —

It may seem somewhat strange, at first sight, that the Roman Catholic Church should figure in the Colonial expenditure for over Rs. 100,000; but it must be borne in mind that the arrangements resulting in this expenditure were made with the clergy by the French Colonial Government at the Revolution, as an indemnity for the confiscation of curial manses and ecclesiastical properties, and this having been tacitly recognised by the Capitulation, the local Government is accordingly bound, in all justice, to defray these expenses. Such being the case, it may be questioned, on the other hand, whether, in spite of such apparent liberality, Roman Catholics in Mauritius stand in a fair situation as compared with the other Christian communities, if we impartially consider the following figures:—

The regular Roman Catholic clergy is composed of the Bishop of Port Louis, a Vicar-General, fifteen first-class, sixteen second-class, and sixteen additional priests, or, in all, forty-nine ministers for a population of about 116,000 Roman Catholics—*i.e.*, roughly one minister for every 2,400 persons; whereas the Church of England possesses the Bishop of Mauritius, an archdeacon, and ten clergymen, or twelve in all, for 3,465 adherents (including 1,150 soldiers of the garrison)—*i.e.*, one minister for every 300 persons.

Remonstrances have often been respectfully addressed to the home Government on that subject, but have proved of no avail.

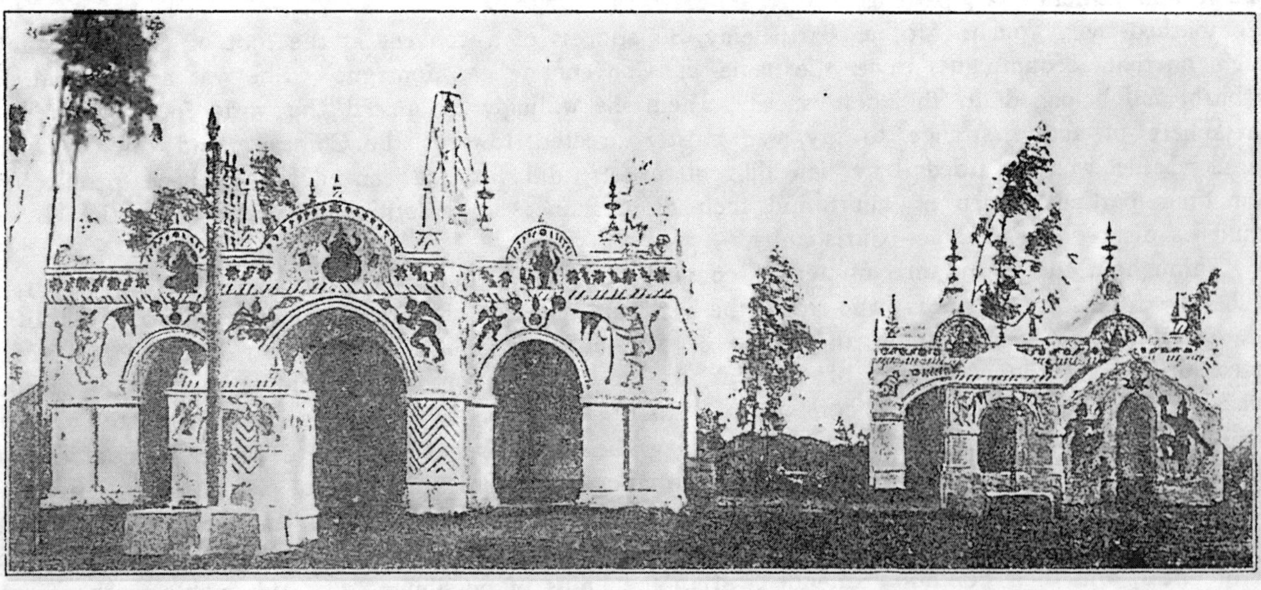

INDIAN TEMPLE, VACOAS.

THE MUNICIPALITY OF PORT LOUIS.

THE existence of the Municipality under the French dates so far back as 1790. It was then called *Municipalité du Canton du Port Louis,* and was instituted, as were other local Municipalities, by the *Assemblée Coloniale.* These institutions are mentioned in the constitutive law of the Ile de France promulgated by the *Assemblée Coloniale* on the 21st of April, 1791. Sixteen prominent men of the city acted as Councillors of the *Municipalité du Canton du Port Louis,* and were called the *Conseil des Notables,* which was dissolved in 1792. It was, however, reconstituted at the end of the eighteenth century under the denomination of the *Conseil de Commune,* and abolished on the 18th February, 1820.

THE TOWN HALL, PORT LOUIS.

The present Municipal Corporation dates from 1850, the first elections taking place at the Masonic Lodge *La Triple Espérance* on the 21st, 22nd, and 23rd of February. Two eminent Mauritians, Adrien d'Epinay and Remy Ollier, appear to have been the principal agents in determining the re-establishment of the Corporation. The former on the occasion of his two visits to London made strong representations to the Secretary of State for the Colonies, and the latter carried on an active campaign in the local press. No definite action appears to have been taken, however, until the year 1848, when the political troubles in France roused the colonists from apathy; and a public meeting was held at the *Hotel d'Europe,* on the site of which the present Town Hall of Port Louis was subsequently erected. The meeting was stopped by the police, and the leaders then carried their grievances to the Governor, Sir William Gomm, who, although he approved the action of the police, received the deputation and promised to forward their request to the Secretary of State for the Colonies, which resulted in the wishes of the colonists being acceded to; and the Municipal Corporation of Port Louis was constituted by Ordinance No. 16 of 1849.

THE TOWN HALL, CUREPIPE.

The roll of electors numbered 600, and the eighteen elected candidates were proclaimed on the 26th February, 1850. On the 4th March Sir George Anderson selected Mr. Louis Léchelle as Mayor and Mr. Félix Kœnig as Deputy Mayor.

Under Ordinance 23 of 1903 the number of Councillors was reduced to twelve, including the Mayor and Deputy Mayor, three for each of the four Wards of the city.

At the time of the establishment of the Corporation Port Louis appears to have been in a deplorable condition. The main streets were so badly kept that it was somewhat difficult to walk upon them. The alleys and smaller streets had never been metalled and were full of refuse. Paved gutters were unknown; and although some underground drainage for rain water existed—built in the time of the French—the gully holes had never been cleaned. The task which faced the new Corporation was in consequence a heavy one, and it is evident that the improvements which have been effected in the central part of the city are considerable, although there is still a great deal to do on the outskirts.

At the present time the finances of the Corporation are in a flourishing condition: it possesses properly controlled slaughter-houses, markets, a modern fire-brigade, and electric lighting stations.

The powers invested in the Municipal Corporation by the constituting Ordinance of 1849 have been considerably modified, and many of them repealed by various ordinances up to the present day; so much so that the exact limitations of their jurisdiction appears to be a somewhat complicated problem.

[Our information regarding the Municipality of Port Louis has been taken from *The Mauritius Almanac* for 1913].

LIST OF MAYORS AND DEPUTY-MAYORS from 1850 to 1913.

Year.	Mayors.	Deputy-Mayors.	Year.	Mayors.	Deputy-Mayors.
1850	Hon. Louis Léchelle	Félix Kœnig	1882	Alfred Lavoquer	Dr. Léonce Allas W. Standley
1851	Hon. Louis Léchelle	Félix Kœnig	1883	Alfred Lavoquer	C. E. Thomy Pitot
1852	Hon. Louis Léchelle	Félix Kœnig	1884	C. E. Thomy Pitot	Dr. W. A. T. Edwards
1853	Hon. Louis Léchelle	Félix Kœnig	1885	Alfred Lavoquer	G. V. K/Vern
1854	Hon. Sir Gabriel Froppier	Félix Kœnig Alfred Besnard	1886	Hon. Alfred Lavoquer	G. V. K/Vern
1855	Hon. Sir Gabriel Froppier	Emile Pipon	1887	G. V. K/Vern	Edgar Aubert
1856	Hon. Louis Léchelle Hon. Emile Pipon	Emile Pipon Hon Hippolyte Le Mière	1888	G. V. K/Vern	C. E. Thomy Pitot
1857	Hon. Hippolyte Le Mière	Arthur Edwards	1889	G. V. K/Vern Edgar Aubert	Edgar Aubert E. Duponsel
1858	Arthur Edwards	F. N. Jouanis	1890	Edgar Aubert	Eliacin François (*junior*)
1859	Pierre Nelsir Charon	Désiré Sicard	1891	Edgar Aubert	E. Duponsel
1860	G. de Courson	Arthur Edwards	1892	Edgar Aubert E. Duponsel	E. Duponsel Eliacin François (*junior*)
1861	G. de Courson	J. Mallac	1893	Eliacin François (*junior*)	Evenor Ganachaud
1862	G. de Courson	Eugène Marie	1894	Eliacin François (*junior*)	Evenor Ganachaud
1863	Hon. Hippolyte Le Mière	Charles Pitot	1895	Eliacin François (*junior*)	Evenor Ganachaud
1864	Hon. Hippolyte Le Mière	Charles Pitot	1896	C. E. Thomy Pitot	Robert Aldor Rohan
1865	Pierre Nelsir Charon	J. Brodie	1897	C. E. Thomy Pitot	Robert Aldor Rohan
1866	Charles Pitot	Eugène Laurent	1898	C. E. Thomy Pitot	Charles Olivier
1867	Charles Pitot	Eliacin François	1899	C. E. Thomy Pitot	Dr. Louis Joseph Pétricher
1868	Hon. Eliacin François	Emilien Ducray	1900	C. E. Thomy Pitot	Dr Louis Joseph Pétricher
1869	Hon. Eliacin François	A. Letard	1901	Hon. C. E. Thomy Pitot	Robert Aldor Rohan
1870	Emilien Ducray	Jules Barbeau	1902	Robert Aldor Rohan	Amédée Poupard
1871	Hon. Emilien Ducray	Jules Barbeau	1903	Robert Aldor Rohan	Amédée Poupard
1872	Hon. Emilien Ducray	Dr. W. A. T. Edwards	1904	Robert Aldor Rohan	Amédée Poupard
1873	Hon. Eliacin François	A. C. Macpherson	1905	Dr. Eugène Laurent	Dr. Louis Joseph Petricher
1874	Hon. Eliacin François	William Hazlitt	1906	Amand Esnouf	Dr. Louis Joseph Petricher
1875	Hon. Eliacin François G. F. Poulin	G. F. Poulin Adolphe Rolando	1907	Hon. Dr. E. A. O. Laurent	Dr. Louis Joseph Petricher
1876	G. F. Poulin	William Hazlitt	1908	Hon. Dr. E. A. O. Laurent	C. E. Thomy Pitot
1877	L. Hily	Emile Bazire	1909	Hon. Dr. E. A. O. Laurent	C. E. Thomy Pitot
1878	Emile Bazire	L. Hily	1910	Amand Esnouf	Robert Aldor Rohan V. Ducasse
1879	Emile Bazire	Dr. Léonce Allas	1911	Hon. Dr. E. A. O. Laurent	Goolam Mamode Issac
1880	Emile Bazire	C. E. Thomy Pitot	1912	Hon. Dr. E. A. O. Laurent	Goolam Mamode Issac
1881	Emile Bazire	Dr. Léonce Allas	1913	Hon. G. Edouard Nairac..	V. Ducasse

THE COUNCIL OF THE MUNICIPAL CORPORATION OF PORT LOUIS, 1913.

The Hon. G. E. Nairac—*Mayor*. V. Ducasse—*Deputy-Mayor*.

WARD I.	WARD II.	WARD III.	WARD IV.
The Hon. Dr. E. A. O. Laurent,	The Hon. G. E. Nairac,	R. Noël,	J. D. Mélotte,
J. D. Mélotte,	A. A. Piperdy,	J. P. Goupille,	M. Edouard,
E. M. V. Laurent.	G. M. Issac.	V. Ducasse.	L. Baudot.

MUNICIPAL COUNCILLORS OF PORT LOUIS, 1913.

1. THE HON. DR. E. A. O. LAURENT, Mayor, 1912, 1911, 1909, 1908, 1907, 1905.
2. GOOLAM MAMODE ISSAC, Deputy-Mayor, 1912, 1911.
3. E. M. V. LAURENT.
4. J. D. MÉLOTTE.
5. THE HON. G. E. NAIRAC, Mayor, 1913.
6. R. NÖEL
7. J. P. GOUPILLE.
8. V. DUCASSE, Deputy-Mayor, 1913.
9. A. A. PIPERDY.

Photos of the other Councillors were unobtainable.

THE TOWN AND DISTRICT BOARDS.

The Town Boards are all corporative bodies, and as such may acquire and hold real and personal property and sell, lease, alienate or otherwise dispose of any property, and may contract, sue, or be sued.

They have the power of taking measures within the prescribed limit of the township for the making, arrangement, maintenance, etc., of roads, sewers, bridges, canals and other works of public utility; for the prevention of fires; the proper paving and lighting of the town, and the supply and distribution of water, providing that no such arrangements contravene the existing sanitary rules and regulations made by the sanitary authorities.

Curepipe.—A Board of Commissioners was established for the Town of Curepipe under Ordinance No. 12 of 1889. It consists of six members nominated annually by the Governor; the first Board was appointed by virtue of Proclamation No. 9 of March 28th, 1890.

The taxable property in the Town of Curepipe was estimated in 1911 at Rs. 5,096,076, giving a revenue at ½ per cent. of Rs. 25,480.38. Revenue from other sources—taxes on animals and vehicles, license duties, etc., fees, permits for buildings, night soil service—amounted to Rs. 43,029.90, giving a total revenue of Rs. 68,510.28. The expenditure for the financial year 1910-11 amounted to Rs. 72,008.54.

MAIN STREET, CUREPIPE.

In 1900, under Ordinance No. 39, a loan of Rs. 70,000, was raised upon Debentures—re-imbursible in 28 years, and bearing interest at 5 per cent.—for the erection of the Town Hall, and in 1902 a further loan of Rs. 25,000 was authorised by Government payable in ten years without interest.

Rose Hill and Beau Bassin.—The Board of Commissioners of the Town of Rose Hill and Beau Bassin was constituted under Ordinance No. 31 of 1895. It consists of eight members, and enjoys the same powers and privileges as that of Curepipe, except that the licenses are not refunded by Government as is the case at Curepipe. The total taxable property in 1911 was estimated at Rs. 3,442,898, yielding a revenue of Rs. 17,214.49. The total revenue from all sources amounted in 1909-10 to Rs. 36,995.84, and the expenditure to Rs. 36,651.70. In 1911-12 the total revenue from all sources amounted to Rs. 36,565.93, and the expenditure to Rs. 36,506.94. The debt of this Corporation at the end of June, 1912, amounted to Rs. 4,100.

Quatre Bornes.—Quatre Bornes was formed into a township, and a Board of Commissioners appointed under Ordinance No. 32 of 1895. The Board consists of six members. The revenue in 1911-12 amounted to Rs. 13,374.32, and the expenditure to Rs. 11,720.44. The total debt amounts to Rs. 615. The Board's credit in the Commercial Bank amounts to Rs. 3,539.

In addition to the Town Boards, District Boards were constituted under Ordinances 9 of 1900 and 35 of 1902, and are called the "Branch Roads Boards" for each district. The Boards consist of the Director of Public Works, the Elected Member of the Council of Government for the District, and three other members appointed annually by the Governor.

These Boards are empowered to pass resolutions for the making, maintenance, and improvements of branch roads and footpaths.

The funds are provided (1) by a contribution from the Treasury of an annual sum equivalent to 10 per cent. of the direct taxes collected during the preceding year in each district, (2) by an addition of 10 per cent. to the direct taxes to be levied in each year in each district, exclusive of Port Louis and other townships.

[The above information regarding the Town and District Boards has been taken from *The Mauritius Almanac* for 1913.]

EDUCATION.

By T. W. EYRE, B.A. (Cantab.), Professor of the Royal College.

T. W. EYRE, B.A. (Cantab.),
Professor of the Royal College.

THE sight of the word "Education" at the head of a chapter nerves the ordinary reader for some strenuous skipping. Why this almost universal shrinking from the topic? Well, it is possibly due to the fact that many of the serious gentlemen who compile the standard works on education think it respectable to be dull, just as some of my northern compatriots deem it honest to be rude. That dulness is a pledge of respectability is, of course, a wide-spread belief. Earnest Conservatives of Mid-Victorian days found it hard to reconcile Disraeli's leadership with his novels, and rather thought that a serious statesman ought not to be witty; and the electors of Oxford considered Thackeray too humorous a person to represent them with due gravity in Parliament.

Whatever the cause, the fact remains that books on education are usually deadly dull; and though I cannot guarantee that the present chapter will not fall under the same condemnation, I can at least assure the hesitating reader that nothing will here be said of the percentage of passes, or average cost per head; my modest aim in these pages being merely to offer a few notes on the local educational system in general, and on the Royal College in particular, and to jot down some personal reminiscences drawn from twenty-three years' experience of teaching in Mauritius.

Education in Mauritius is organised as a Government Department under the control of the Director of Public Instruction. Primary education is provided by Government schools and by schools assisted by Government. In both these categories Government pays the salaries of the teachers and also grants for pupils who pass the various standards.

Primary education is free, although not yet compulsory; and a system of scholarships and free tuition connecting the primary schools with the Royal College enables a clever boy not only to get his whole education for nothing, but to make money by it as well. Such a pupil may pass through the Royal College without costing his parents a penny, and even, eventually, win the educational *grand prix* of Mauritius—the English scholarship, of which I shall have something more to say later.

The worst fault of almost all the schools in Mauritius is the system of cramming, and cramming is likely to continue in full force while grants are paid "by results"—that bad old practice which has so long been abolished in England.

If a man's salary depends on the number of boys he can force through a given standard by a given date, education will always degenerate into unintelligent cramming for that standard. The tree is known by its fruits; and the fruits of cramming are an overtaxed memory, parrot-like learning by rote, and the habit of reading without really understanding what is read—and of being content not to understand it.

Extraordinary results of this cramming system are frequently supplied, alike by boys and girls, in the various local examinations. Stock essays are written by masters on subjects thought likely to be set, and these productions are committed to memory and reproduced word for word in the examination room—but often with some blunder that shows the candidate has completely failed to grasp the meaning of what he has so carefully transcribed; whole pages of history and geography, too, are thus learned by rote and faithfully reproduced—sometimes with similar slips that make nonsense of the passage.

What has been said of cramming in the boys schools of Mauritius applies with equal force to the schools for girls. There exists a local scheme for the higher education of girls, and as grants are paid by Government for pupils passing in the various standards, the temptation to cram the girls proves irresistible to their teachers.

While acting as examiner in English under this scheme, I was always impressed by the retentive memories of the girls, and was equally struck by the fact that, like the boys, they had often no idea of the meaning of the passage committed to memory. I still remember a girl's explanation of Gray's well-known lines:—

> "Full many a gem of fairest ray serene
> The dark, unfathom'd caves of ocean bear,"

in which she mistook the "ocean bear" for an ursine quadruped, and "the dark, unfathom'd caves" for its place of abode.

However, the Director of Public Instruction is doing his best, in the face of strong opposition, to abolish the system of grants for passes in the Primary and Associated Schools, and when that goes, the cramming system will not long survive it.

Secondary Education is provided by the Royal College and a preparatory school attached to it, and by numerous private schools associated with the Royal College and drawing Government grants.

THE ROYAL COLLEGE.

The Hon. W. T. A. EMTAGE,
M.A. (Oxon.),
Director of the Department of
Public Instruction.

The Royal College of to-day is the lineal descendant of the French *Ecole Centrale des Iles de France et de la Réunion*, founded in 1800, and known later as the Lycée Colonial. Its original site was naturally in Port Louis, the capital, and at that time the abode of most of the inhabitants of the Colony—a state of things brought abruptly to an end by the great outbreak of malarial fever in 1866.

We read that in 1806, at Dr. Caen's instigation, the school buildings were enlarged and a swimming bath and riding school provided for the use of the pupils—luxuries, alas! conspicuously absent in these less spacious times of economical reform. After the British occupation, the school was reopened in 1811 as the Colonial College, which title was changed to that of the Royal College in 1817, by special authorisation of the Prince Regent.

The two English scholarships, those glittering objects of the young Mauritian's ambition, were founded in 1815; and in 1852 the College was first thrown open to the sons of the coloured population.

Since 1852 boys of every class, race, colour, and religion have been admitted with absolute impartiality to the Royal College, which is thus in a very real sense the *Alma Mater* of Mauritius.

As we have seen, the College possesses a respectable pedigree; and for over one hundred years the intellectual *élite* of the Mauritian youth has passed through the hands of its professors and masters. But as regards the material college of wood and stone—the body of the educational soul—both teachers and pupils have been extremely ill-provided since 1892.

A plain substantial-looking building composed of a central wooden structure with two stone wings, and situated in a network of mean streets, through which masters and boys had to pass on their way to and from the railway station—such was the Royal College in 1889 when I first saw it, and such it must have been for some sixty or seventy years. It was surrounded by a high wall in those days; and the courtyard in front of the main building was overshadowed by enormous banyan trees, their branches haunted by some particularly noisy mynahs. A quaint little porter's lodge with domed-shaped roof stood at the gate—the porter himself a strangely garrulous little man devoured by an insatiable curiosity. The chemical laboratory was situated in an orchard which yielded delicious mangoes and cocoa-nuts in their season.

The premises were commodious. Each member of the staff had his own class-room; equipped with a large cupboard, wash-hand-stand and so forth, in addition to the regulation black-board ; there was a large central hall, a fair library, and a gymnasium and playing field for the boys.

The gymnastic classes were held during the recreation time—from one to two—the hottest time of the day. Imagine the results of violent gymnastic exercise during a Mauritian summer, with the thermometer at 92° in the shade! The boys used to return to class dripping with perspiration and steaming with heat. *Horresco referens!*

The building described was completely destroyed by the great cyclone in 1892, when only the wrecks of the two wings were left standing.

The chance of transferring the Royal College to cooler and more sanitary surroundings was unaccountably lost; and in spite of the opposition of the more enlightened members of the community, it was decided to rebuild the College on the old site.

To the argument that Port Louis was extremely hot, dirty, and unhealthy, and therefore an unsuitable site for the principal school of the Colony, the partisans of the *status quo* were wont to reply, "I stood it when I was a boy, so my son ought to stand it too."

Such reasoning as this appears to have decided the matter, combined with some jeremiads about "decapitating the capital," and similar clap-trap. The real interests at stake—those of the boys and their teachers—were completely left out of the question.

While the new College was building, work was temporarily carried on in the Line Barracks, Port Louis, in small, dark rooms most ill-suited to the purpose—an uncomfortable period for boys and masters alike, though tempered to the latter by the privilege of obtaining good draught beer from the canteen at moderate prices.

Hardly had the new College buildings been completed, and pupils and teachers once more comfortably installed, when a strange thing happened. Plague broke out in Port Louis: people lost their heads in panic and "surexcitation:" and the building that had been erected a few years before expressly to fulfil the special functions of a College was annexed by the medical and health department and converted into a hospital. Boys and masters were adrift again.

Thus, in 1899, the College was hurriedly transferred to Curepipe and located in the quiet inadequate buildings of the Royal College school, eked out by a derelict hotel on the other side of the main road.

This makeshift arrangement has lasted from that day to this; and it was only in 1912 that Government finally decided to settle the Royal College permanently at Curepipe and to start the work of erecting suitable buildings. At the date of writing this (April, 1913), the walls are already rapidly rising, and the new Royal College bids fair to be opened before the end of the year. Curepipe is far from being an ideal site for the Royal College, as it is by no means central and has a colossal rainfall; on the other hand—and this is of vital importance—it is far cooler and healthier than Port Louis. The boys who come to Curepipe from Port Louis form but a small proportion of the total number of pupils, and it is clearly preferable for them to come up to Curepipe for their education than for the Curepipe boys to go down into the hot, unhealthy town. The working conditions are incomparably better in the hills than on the coast, particularly in the hot season; and the disadvantage of the continual showers will be in great measure obviated when all the College buildings are again under one roof, and boys and masters have no longer to cross a road to get from one class-room to another.

THE STAFF.

After the British occupation of Mauritius, when the Lycée Colonial was reopened as the Colonial College in 1811, the staff appears to have been composed entirely of those French professors who had previously taught at the Lycée. The most conspicuous members of this band were MM. Lorquet and Bernard, who were not merely professors but poets, and sometimes recited their own verses on College prize days.

M. Lorquet's muse inspired him to write a poem on Napoleon, which lost him his appointment at the Royal College, though happily only for a time; for he lived to be triumphantly reinstated and to recite a long poem of his own composition at the distribution of prizes on October 14th, 1836.

There seems to have been difficulty at times in obtaining suitable teachers, and strangers arriving in the Colony with any flavour of mathematics or tinge of the humanities about them were usually welcomed on the staff.

From 1858 to 1868 Mr. Redl, an Austrian ex-sergeant, was Rector of the Royal College, a fact which seems to point to a dearth of competent applicants for the post. As might have been expected, under Redl's régime the status of the College declined, teaching deteriorated, and the number of pupils fell off—a condition of things to which the great outbreak of malarial fever, in 1866, materially contributed.

From this period of decay the College was rescued by the appointment of Mr. Bruce as Rector in 1868. Mr. Bruce introduced many reforms; among others, he confided the examination for the English Scholarships to the syndicate of Cambridge University, affiliated the College to the same University for the Cambridge Local Examinations, and restored the practice, which had fallen into disuse, of sending the Laureates to England. Mr. Bruce, now Sir Charles Bruce, K.C.M.G., returned to Mauritius as Governor in 1897.

Another member of the staff, Mr. Sweet-Escote, afterwards Sir Ernest Sweet-Escote, K.C.M.G., became successively Governor of Seychelles, of British Honduras, and of the Leeward Islands, and several other ex-Professors of the College have filled high positions in the Colonial service.

W. F. RUSSELL, B.A. (Oxon.), Rector of the Royal College.

But by far the best-known name on the roll is that of Mr. Besant, afterwards Sir Walter, the successful novelist of the later Victorian era, and inspirer of the People's Palace, in the East End of London, who taught mathematics at the Royal College in the sixties.

Besant's local knowledge is shown in an early work, *They Were Married*, which I have heard of but never seen, appears incidentally in *Ready-Money Mortiboy*, and plays an especially important part in *My Little Girl*. In the last-named work Mauritius, with its heterogeneous population, its colour question, its Press, its social life, its planters, and its Government, is portrayed under the pseudonym of Palmiste Island; and the opening chapter, devoted to a description of the Colony, may be received as substantially true to-day.

The chief changes since Besant's time are due to the introduction of electric light, to the laying of the cable that supplies Mauritius with its daily modicum of the news of the world, and to the advent of the motor car. Besant's pictures of Mauritius and its natives were drawn with no sympathetic hand, and I have never heard his name mentioned by a Mauritian or seen an allusion to him in the local Press.

When Mr. Messervy became Rector in 1880, he strengthened the teaching staff by obtaining the appointment of several English graduates of Oxford and Cambridge, including Mr. Hamley, afterwards Rector from 1901 to 1909; Mr. Roberts, who acted as Rector on several occasions, and Mr. Russell, the present Rector of the Royal College, all of whom I found here on my arrival in 1889.

In those days practically all the Mauritian professors and masters were dressed in black broadcloth from head to foot—the "only wear" regarded as correct by the profession at that period. The more ambitious wore frock coats and top hats, but most contented themselves with morning coats and "bowlers." This habit has lingered on in professional circles, but is dying out now.

In recent times the Rector has always been an English University honours man, and the staff has consisted partly of Oxford and Cambridge graduates in honours, partly of teachers recruited locally—a combination that appears to give satisfactory results.

When Sir Charles Bruce returned to Mauritius as Governor in 1897, he at once proceeded to reorganise the Education Department, under a Director of Public Instruction with a salary of Rs. 12,000 per annum.

The new Director was appointed in 1900, and as a natural consequence the College fell to a subordinate position; the Rector ceased to be a head of department and his salary was reduced first from Rs. 10,000 to Rs. 9,000, and subsequently to Rs. 8,000, at which sum it stands to-day.

The reorganisation of the Royal College has now been under consideration for some fifteen years (1898-1913). There appears some likelihood of its attaining a final settlement this year (1913).

The Royal College contains a classical and a modern side. The highest class, that of the English Scholarship, corresponds to the sixth form of an English Public School; and before entering it pupils on the classical side have to pass the London Matriculation Examination, and those on the modern side the Senior Cambridge Local Examination in five subjects.

The English Scholarships themselves, of which two are given annually to the best boy on the classical and on the modern side respectively, are probably the most valuable prizes offered by any school in the world, as each is of the value of £1,150, and to win the English Scholarship is naturally the ambition of every clever pupil of the Royal College.

The examination for these scholarships is in most respects up to the scholarship standard of Oxford and Cambridge, and the examiners are appointed by the Cambridge University Syndicate. Perhaps the best way to form some idea of the progress made at the Royal College during the last forty or fifty years is to compare the curriculum of Besant's time with that in force to-day. Before 1865 all the College examinations were conducted locally, and often under very unsatisfactory conditions; now the examinations, not only for the English scholarships but also for many minor scholarships and exhibitions tenable at the Royal College, are conducted by examiners appointed by the Cambridge University Syndicate.

The Laureates for 1865 were appointed on passing the London Matriculation Examination, then just introduced into the schedule of studies; now boys on the classical side have to pass this examination before entering the English Scholarship class; while, since 1873, the Cambridge Local Examinations have also been passed annually by large numbers of pupils.

The standard of teaching has been raised all round. The number of classical authors read during the year has been much increased, and an equally great extension has been given to the range of mathematics, physics, and chemistry. It is in the last-named subject that the English Scholarship programme has in recent years shown, perhaps, the greatest development, especially on the quantitative side of practical chemistry. Special attention is also paid to the study of French and English literature.

The College has been accused of maintaining a curriculum of cram, to the detriment of a sound educational system; but this charge is certainly unfounded as regards the senior classes. That a boy cannot cram Latin prose, or the Higher Mathematics, or the niceties of the English and French languages, is obvious enough to anyone with the smallest practical experience of teaching.

But probably the best proof of the essential soundness of the education provided by the Royal College is to be found in the achievements of the Laureates themselves. These young Mauritians, who must be under nineteen years when they sit for the English Scholarship Examination, going straight from the Royal College to London, meet youths of the same age from English schools and colleges, and frequently defeat them in open competition for scholarships, exhibitions and prizes.

A long list might be made of the victories thus won, especially in the medical schools but in the limited scope of this article room is only found for two of the most recent successes:—

Messrs. Leblanc and Dyson, the Laureates of December, 1911, both achieved high distinction last year (1912), Mr. Leblanc winning the Entrance Scholarship of £50 at Guy's Hospital, and Mr. Dyson the Entrance Scholarship of £100 at Middlesex Hospital.

It may be added that Mr. Dyson was originally a pupil of the Government schools.

RELIGIOUS INSTRUCTION AT THE ROYAL COLLEGE.

Serenely regardless alike of the Zeitgeist, Mr. Lloyd George, and the example of the great self-governing Dominions, Mauritius boasts no less than three State-supported churches, and pays subsidies to Roman Catholic, Anglican, and Presbyterian establishments.

Although the Royal College is as impartial in the matter of religion as in that of race or colour, and welcomes the young Hindu or Mohammedan as freely as his Christian schoolfellow, it yet provides instruction in the tenets of the State-supported churches for such pupils as wish to receive it.

Once a week a Roman Catholic priest and an Anglican clergyman are in attendance to instruct classes in their respective creeds; and were there sufficient Presbyterian pupils to justify such a course, doubtless the services of a Presbyterian minister would likewise be engaged. The course observed by the Royal College with regard to religious instruction is so obviously rational and satisfactory that one wonders some similar plan has never been adopted to end the bickering over this question in the English rate-supported schools.

PRIVATE TUITION.

Almost every schoolboy in Mauritius takes private lessons, and almost every adult seems to give them. Men and youths of all classes and of the most varied qualifications ply the trade of the private tutor.

Large numbers of the junior clerks in Government and merchants' offices and in the two banks of the Colony thus increase their scanty incomes. Some professors and masters of the Royal College make from £100 to £200 a year by private tuition.

Efforts have at different times been made to limit the number of hours that the staff may devote to private lessons. The Director of Public Instruction has suggested eight hours a week as the allowable maximum, and the Rector has power to intervene if he considers the privilege is being abused.

In 1901, Mr. Hamley, then Rector, stated that private tuition in Mauritius takes the place of preparation, and owned that he "felt helpless" to prevent it. There the matter rests for the present. We read indeed in the *Archives Coloniales* of July, 1889, of a time "when pupils laughed at private lessons and at those who relied on them, and strove to deserve real crowns." But this refers to the golden age when poets upon the College staff, like M. Lorquet, still sang, and I have described the state of things existing to-day.

After all, as the Mauritian schoolboy demands private tuition, who are so fit to supply it as the members of the College staff? To prevent the professors and masters of the Royal College from giving private lessons would not stop the demand, but would merely ensure an inferior supply.

GAMES.

No games are played at the Royal College. Since 1899 the boys have possessed no playing field worthy of the name. Although the College buildings at Curepipe stand in a fair-sized field, nothing has been done to prepare it for cricket or football, and the live rock still crops out here and there on the surface.

Physical drill was started a year or two ago under a competent instructor, and was taken up by the boys with a zeal which promised well for the future; and in our new usher, Mr. Lamb, an ex-N.C.O., we have an able exponent of every manly sport, who is anxiously awaiting a chance of turning this athletic zeal in the direction of cricket and football.

It is not, I hope, unduly optimistic to look forward to a time when the Royal College will be able to put into the field both a cricket and a football team.

PRIZE DAY AT THE ROYAL COLLEGE.

Prize Day at the Royal College was at one time a popular fête, attended not only by the parents and relations of the pupils but by Heads of Departments, Judges of the Supreme Court, Members of Council, and other notabilities of the island, most of whom were old boys; and the distribution was presided over by the Governor, whose speech was eagerly expected and attentively heard.

We read of pupils being told off in the early years of last century to collect greenery wherewith to decorate the College Hall for this function, and to make laurel wreaths for crowning the brows of the Laureates, and we have heard how their own verses were recited by gifted members of the staff.

The first English Governor, Sir R. T. Farquhar, took a great interest in the Royal College, and used to deliver remarkably long orations at the distribution of prizes.

In later times Sir John Pope Hennessy reserved his most striking pronouncements of policy for such occasions, a habit which ensured a crowded attendance and gave a special interest to prize days. His successor, Sir Charles Lees, I saw preside at a prize distribution in 1890; and witnessed (and, perhaps I should add, shared) the general disappointment when he refused, on being approached by a senior boy, to grant the customary half-holiday in honour of the event.

After the destruction of the College in 1892, and again on the annexation of the new building by the Medical and Health Department in 1899, the annual distribution of prizes was held in all sorts of odd places—in the theatre, in the grounds of Government House, and more recently in the stifling atmosphere under the glowing tin roof of the Union Catholique.

Here I heard Sir Graham Bower, early in this century, assure the staff that teaching was not a profession but a religion; and it was here too, in the normal conditions of heat and discomfort, that H.E. Major Sir John Robert Chancellor, at the distribution of prizes last year (1912), touched on two subjects of prime importance to the Royal College.

Speaking first of the value of *esprit de corps* among school boys, His Excellency expressed the hope that sentiments of loyalty and affection would not fail, in course of time, to gather about the walls of the new Royal College at Curepipe; and next urged upon the boys the practice of courtesy and politeness, by calling their attention to the good old maxim—" Manners makyth man."

The French rightly draw a strong distinction between instruction and education. For them instruction means merely the knowledge acquired from the official curriculum of a school or college; while education covers a much wider ground, and includes manners, morals, and general tone. The Royal College provides satisfactory instruction, but is less successful with education, regarded from this wider point of view. The College suffers in this respect from the disadvantages inherent in all day-schools.

Day-boys can hardly imbibe the same feelings of loyal affection for their school as spring up so naturally among the boarders of our great English public schools. A boy who joins such a school steps at once into an atmosphere of tradition that has been accumulating, perhaps, for several hundred years. The school has a tone, a code of manners, often a language of its own, which the new-comer is quick to assimilate. Above all, the influence of the masters is all-pervading and is equally felt in the class-room, at meal times, in the school chapel, and on the playing fields.

What a strong man can effect in this way is well shown by the extraordinary influence exerted by Dr. Arnold, the famous Headmaster of Rugby; and *Tom Brown's Schooldays* remains, perhaps, the highest tribute ever paid to a former master by an old pupil.

But, besides the disadvantages common to all day schools, the Royal College suffers from many peculiar to the local conditions. Its pupils differ in race, religion, and social standing; and many live at such a distance from the school that they are compelled to leave their homes at an early hour and can only reach them again after nightfall. Boys who have to spend more than three hours daily on the railway naturally hurry from the College to catch the next train as soon as school is over, and the absence of playing field and games has also its inevitable effect.

For but five hours daily for five days a week in term time can the master's influence be brought to bear upon the boys—a small period, indeed, compared with their out-of-school existence. How, in these conditions, to foster *esprit de corps* and encourage politeness and courtesy among the pupils of the Royal College are problems waiting to be solved.

With the opening of the new buildings at Curepipe, a fresh page will be turned in the annals of the Royal College, and a new era will begin.

All interested in the future of the youth of Mauritius—and which of my Mauritian readers is not here included?—will join me in hoping that it may prove an era of progress, prosperity, and successful effort, and that courteous and well-behaved pupils may loyally co-operate with a contented staff to sustain and raise still higher the prestige of the new Royal College.

LAUREATES OF THE ROYAL COLLEGE
from 1818 to 1912.

Year.	Names.	Remarks.
1818	Bigot, A.	—
1821	Faduilhe, Félix	Barrister-at-Law, Procureur du Roi.
1822	Dupont, E....	do.
1823	Geffroy, H....	do.
1839	Soubrié. Joseph	—
1840	Kœnig, Alfred	Barrister-at-Law.
1841	Garreau, V.	do and District Magistrate.
1842	Fressanges, H. F.	Doctor in Medicine.
1843	Meistre, A....	Notary Public.
—	Longueville, A.	—
1844	D'Emmerez de Charmoy, P.F.O. ...	Barrister-at-Law, was Registrar, Supreme Court.
1845	Colin, Jules	do. was Procureur-General.
1846	Barbeau, A.	Doctor in Medicine.
1847	Tourrette, C.	do.
—	Dick, Charles	Joined the Army, Director of Prisons, England
1848	Dupuy, A.	Barrister-at-Law
1849	Bardet, T	Roman Catholic Priest.
1850	Leclézio, Eugène	Barrister-at-Law, was Chief Judge of Mauritius.
—	Beaugeard, Onésiphon	Doctor in Medicine.
1851	Allas, Léonce	do.
1852	Brunet, Fulcher	Barrister-at-Law.
1853	Rouillard, John	do. was Judge, Supreme Court.
1854	Barraut, A. Rodrigues	Doctor in Medicine.
—	Rogers, Henry P....	do.
1855	Beaugeard, Horace ...	do.
—	Mayer, George	Barrister-at-Law, was District Magistrate.
1856	Pellereau, Etienne...	do. was Procureur-General.
—	Laconfourque, N.	do.
1857	Cox, George	Doctor in Medicine.
—	Coignet, Charles	do.
1858	Leclézio, Henri	Did not avail himself of the privilege; is Member for Moka, and C.M.G.
—	Rogers, William	Doctor in Medicine.
1859	Guibert, George	Barrister-at-Law.
1860	Didier, St. Amand	do. was Judge, Supreme Court.
—	Chastellier, Evenor ...	Doctor in Medicine, was Director, Med. and Health Dept.
—	Newton, William	Barrister-at Law.
1861	Trouche, William	do.
—	Dick, George Royer	do. was Auditor-General.
—	Jenkins, T. L.	do.
1862	Cox, Lionel	do. is Chief Judge, Straits Settlements.
—	Legrand, Louis	Did not return to Mauritius.
1863	Galéa, Henri	Barrister-at-Law.
—	Forder, Joshua	Doctor in Medicine.
1864	Hermans, Jean	Barrister-at-Law.
—	Lemière, Hippolyte ...	do. was District Magistrate.
—	Dubois, Victor	Doctor in Medicine.
1865	Hobbs, William	Was Professor at the Royal College.
—	Le Bobinnec, F.	Doctor in Medicine.
1866	Brown, Richard Myles	Barrister-at-Law, was Judge, Supreme Court.
—	Pellereau, Elie	Doctor in Medicine, practising in Paris.
1867	Forget, Arthur	Barrister-at-Law.
—	Thibaud, A. L.	do. was Judge, Supreme Court.

Year.	Names.	Remarks.
1869	McDonald, Peter	Passed into the Civil Service of India.
—	Hullard, Jean Arthur	Doctor in Medicine.
—	Crétin, Eugène	do. was Lieut.-Col. 1st Bengal Infantry.
1871	Dick, Frederick C. V. de G. ...	Professor and Examiner, London.
—	Bouchet, Louis V. Geo.	Doctor in Medicine, was Member for Flacq.
1873	Paddle, James Issac	do. in charge of Lunatic Asylum.
—	Anderson, Daniel Elie	do. practising in Paris.
—	Jean, Louis Nemours	Doctor in Medicine.
—	Cantin, Louis Alfred	do.
1875	Bell, Herbert Irving	Was Assistant Director of the Observatory.
—	Whornitz, Ferd. B.	Doctor in Medicine.
1876	Laurent, Eugène	do. Senior Member for Port Louis.
—	Hullard, George	do.
1877	K/Vern, Victor F. G.	Barrister-at-Law.
—	Rohan, Virgile	Doctor in Medicine.
—	Newton, Charles	Barrister-at-Law, Editor of newspaper.
1878	Boucherat, Julien	Professor, Royal College.
—	Suzor, Jean Renaud	Doctor in Medicine, practising in Paris.
—	Dumat, Frank C.	Barrister-at-Law, Natal.
1879	Bell, John Ackroyd	Doctor in Medicine, Hong Kong.
—	Despleissis, Louis Henri	Civil Engineer, South Africa.
1880	Bonnefin, Henri	Doctor in Medicine, Australia.
—	Laurent, Octave	Barrister-at-Law.
1881	Despleissis, Anthony	Civil Engineer, Civil Service of India.
—	Kœnig, Etienne	Barrister-at-Law, Procureur-General.
1882	Bonnin, Louis	Agricultural Chemist.
—	Croft, James	Died whilst studying at Cooper's Hill.
1883	Rouillard, John	Doctor in Medicine, Natal.
—	Rouget, Auguste	do. Medical Supt., Civil Hospital.
1884	Serret, Eugène	Barrister-at-Law, Add. Substitute Procureur-General.
—	Pitot, L. Emile	Civil Engineer, General Manager of Mauritius Railways.
1885	Herchenroder, Alfred	Barrister-at-Law, Chief Judge, Mauritius.
—	Cochemé, A. E.	Civil Engineer, Indian Civil Service.
1886	Standley, A.	do.
—	Rouillard, Louis	Barrister-at-Law.
1887	Barbeau, Gabriel	Doctor in Medicine, Asst. Med. Director.
—	Lejuge de Segrais, Paul	Civil Engineer, Director of Public Works.
1888.	Martin, Charles	Doctor in Medicine.
—	Jacques, L. V.	do.
1889	De Chazal, René	Civil Engineer, Indian Civil Service.
—	Chastellier, Gustave	Barrister-at Law.
1890	Pitot, Ch. A. Robert	do.
—	Kœnig, Paul	Agricultural Chemist, Director of Forests and Gardens.
1891	Monplé, E. Robert	Doctor in Medicine, Sanitary Warden.
—	Perdreau, J. A	do. in Europe.
1892	Giraud, P. L.	Agricultural Chemist.
—	Duclos, Joseph A....	Barrister-at-Law, Member for Flacq.
1893	Mélotte, J. B. D.	do.
—	Rowell, Percy Fitz Patric... ...	Merchant's Clerk, London.
1894	Louis, Jean Léon	Doctor in Medicine.
—	D'Avray, Edouard Alfred ..	Civil Engineer, Professor at Royal College.
1895	Nairac, Edouard	Barrister-at-Law, Junior Member for and Mayor of Port Louis.
—	Desenne, Henri	Civil Engineer, Indian Civil Service.
1896	Bolton, John Douglas	Doctor in Medicine, Mauritius.
—	Masson, Gaston	do.
1897	Galéa, Philippe	Professor and Journalist, Mauritius.
—	Savrimootoo, N.	Civil Engineer, Mauritius.

Year.	Names.	Remarks.
1898	Ferrière, J. Anthony	Doctor in Medicine.
—	Félix, J. Raoul	do.
1899	Esnouf, Auguste	Civil Engineer, Mauritius.
—	Cantin, P. Léon	do. Indian Civil Service.
1900	Leconte, Louis	Barrister-at-Law, Magistrate.
—	Rampal, Maxime	Civil Engineer.
1901	Mayer, Clifford	Doctor in Medicine, in India.
—	Vandermeerch, A.	Civil Engineer.
1902	Thompson, Percy	do. Indian Civil Service.
—	Baissac, Maurice	Agricultural Chemist.
1903	Giraud, George	Professor of Mathematics in England.
—	Perdreau, René	Student in Medicine.
1904	Duvivier, Emile	Doctor in Medicine.
—	Catto, William Henry	do.
1905	Genève, H.	Civil Engineer.
—	Pezzani, E. Roger...	Barrister-at-Law, England.
1906	Perdreau, Raoul	do.
—	Genève, Antoine	Civil Engineer.
1907	Maingard, Fernand	Barrister-at-Law.
—	Barnard, E. O.	Law Student.
—	Curé, Maurice	Student in Medicine.
1908	Mayer, Norman	Reading for the Civil Service.
—	Moreau, Jules	Engineering Student.
1909	D'Avray, Alex. D....	Student in Medicine.
—	Leblanc, Gaston	do.
1910	Herchenroder, Philippe	Law Student.
—	Baylis, Joseph Anno	Engineering Student.
1911	Mayer, Frank Chazal	—
—	Celestin, Louis Abel	Student in Medicine.
1912	Dyson, J. D.	do.
—	Leblanc, J....	do.

Although not Laureates, the following distinguished gentlemen were pupils of the Royal College:—

Dr. Brown-Sequard, who was a Professor at the "Royal de France."

Prosper d'Épinay, who was Procureur-General.

Adrien d'Epinay, his brother, whose statue is in the Company's Gardens.

Prosper d'Épinay, his son, the famous sculptor.

Eloi Mallac, who was Prefet de la Nièvre during the government of Louis Philippe.

Eugène Poujade, who was Ministre Plénipotentiare de France in Extreme Orient during Guizot' Ministry.

Dr. Tholozan, Physician to the late Shah of Persia.

Sir Gabriel Fropier, was Mayor of Port Louis and District Magistrate.

Hyacinthe Gonin, at first an Attorney-at-Law, became a Roman Catholic Priest, and died as Archbishop of Trinidad. He came out first in the Examination of 1830.

Sir Victor Delafaye, was Chief Judge.

Dr. Joseph Rivière, Knight of the Legion of Honour; he founded the "Institute Physico-Thérapique de Paris" at his own expense, and is the Editor of *Les Annales Physico-Thérapiques de France.*

1. Residence of Mr. H. M. Blyth, Vacoas.
2. "Benares," Savanne, Residence of Lady Naz.
3. Residence of The Hon. F. M. Louis Rouillard, Forest Side.
4. "Richmond Lodge," Residence of Mr. Alexander Taylor, Curepipe.
5. "Belvédère," Curepipe, Residence of Lady Naz.
6. Labourdonnais House, Labourdonnais Sugar Estate, Rivière du Rempart.
7. "Beau Séjour," Residence of Mr. George Aubin, Curepipe.

1. "Kingston," Residence of Mr. A. J. Broad, Quatre Bornes.
2. "Benares," Savanne, Residence of Lady Naz.
3. "Les Palmiers," Residence of the Hon. J. J. Gibson, Phœnix.
4. "The Castle," Residence of the Hon. E. C. Fraser, C.M.G., Beau Bassin.
5. Residence of Mr. H. Fraise, Forest Side.
6. Riche Bois House, Riche Bois Sugar Estate, Savanne.
7. "Marly," Residence of Mr. Pierre Adam, Forest Side.

1. Mon Rêve House, Residence of Mr. A. Cayeux, Flacq.
2. Residence of Dr. F. M. Aimé Lesur, Flacq.
3. Residence of Mr. H. Fraise, Forest Side.
4. Mon Loisir House, Mon Loisir Sugar Estate, Rivière du Rempart.
5. "Ulverton," Residence of the Hon. H. C. Scroggs, Phœnix.
6. "The Lodge," Residence of Mr. J. Brodie, Beau Bassin.
7. The Mount House, The Mount Sugar Estate, Pamplemousses.
8. Constance-Manes House, Constance-Manes Sugar Estate, Flacq.

THE FAMOUS STAMPS OF MAURITIUS.

By ALBERT RAE.[1]

ALBERT RAE.

First "Post Office" Issue, September 21st, 1847 :—Diademed head of Queen Victoria, on ground of crossed lines, in rectangular frame ; lettered *Post Office* reading upwards on left side, *Postage* at the top, *Mauritius* on right side reading upwards, and full value beneath ; two values : *One die for each value ;* one penny, orange-vermilion ; twopence, dark blue. Mr. James Stuart Brownrigg was Postmaster-General at the time of this issue.

It was in 1846 that the question of postage stamps was first raised in Mauritius. In the first draft of an amended postage law submitted to the Council of Government in 1846, it was proposed that the charge on a single letter from abroad should be 6d., and on the same forwarded to a foreign country 3d. ; but, after a prolonged debate in Council, it was decided that the charge outward ought to be so reduced as to offer no temptation to evade the postage, and an Ordinance was passed in Council on the 1st December, 1846 (Ordinance No. 13 of 1846), which fixed the inland mail at 1d., and the outward one at 2d. ;[2] newspapers were free of postage.[3] The two stamps, however, served indistinctively to prepay both postages.[4]

The stamps were to be provided by the Government (Art. 9 of the Ordinance), and a very severe penalty was enacted for persons forging or counterfeiting them, *i.e.*, transportation for a period not exceeding three years (Art. 10).

In order, therefore, to carry out the provisions of the Ordinance, stamps of the value of 1d. and 2d. had to be provided, and the Postmaster-General was accordingly instructed to attend to this matter. He entrusted the engraving of the dies to one Mr. Joseph Barnard, a watchmaker, residing on the Chaussée, and the *only engraver at the time in the island,* who undertook to perform the work for £10.

The stamps were engraved in *taille douce* on copper plate, with diademed head of Queen Victoria looking left, in rectangular letter frames and on ground of crossed diagonal lines ; having at the top the word *Postage,* at the bottom the full value, on the left hand side the words *Post Office* reading upwards, and on the right *Mauritius* reading also upwards.

Mr. Barnard was, however, unable to complete his work in time,[5] some delay in the delivery of the stamps having unavoidably occurred in consequence of the engraver having been for some time under medical treatment for his sight, which had become impaired.[6] On the 20th September 700 copies had been struck off and were ready for issuing.[7] The issue must have taken place on the 20th or 21st September.[8]

[1] I have to thank His Excellency the Governor for the highly-appreciated favour bestowed on me in authorising me to have access to the official records kept in the Archives Office, whereby I have been enabled, not only to correct many errors in the dates and number of stamps issued, but also to add some very valuable notes hitherto unknown to many collectors concerning these most interesting stamps.

[2] By Ordinance No. 1 of 1850 that rate was raised to 4d.

[3] Appendix A shows the different tariffs provided by that Ordinance.

[4] This is evidenced by the letter addressed to Thomas Jerome, Esq., Secretary to the Bombay Auxiliary Bible Society, found by Mr. Haward in India, and which was franked by means of two 1d. *Post Office* stamps. These two stamps are Nos. 18 and 19 on Mr. Lemaire's list on page 318.

[5] By a proclamation at Réduit on December 28th, 1846, the Ordinance was to take effect on January 1st, 1847.

[6] Letter of Colonial Postmaster to Colonial Secretary of May 2nd, 1848.

[7] Letter of Colonial Postmaster to Colonial Secretary of September 20th, 1848.

[8] The letter addressed to Mr. Edmond Duvivier, as shown by the illustration on the following page, was post-marked September 21st, 1847.

There was only one die for each value, and only one impression could, therefore, be taken at the same time.

When these stamps were first introduced, 1,000 were struck off—500 orange-vermilion *One Penny* and 500 blue *Two Pence*—and so desirous was the public of procuring them, particularly for town, that in a few days they were all disposed of. The whole issue was limited to 1,000 owing to the fact that any great number could not be printed in sufficient time. In order to supervise the process of working the plates, a press for that purpose was erected in the Post Office.

THE RAREST STAMPS IN THE WORLD.
The 1d. and 2d. of Mauritius of 1847.
(Reproduced by permission of Somerset House.)

Out of the number issued twenty-two specimens are known to exist. On the following page is a tabular list which appeared in 1899 or 1900 in *Le Philateliste Français* a stamp magazine, edited by the well-known stamp dealer of Paris, Mr. Lemaire, showing all the *Post Office* stamps known to exist at that time, and indicating that there were two unused and ten used *One Penny;* and three unused and five used *Two Pence*. A very interesting detail can be noticed on the edge of the neck of the illustration on the stamps; Mr. Barnard, the engraver, had the fanciful idea of engraving thereon the initials of his name and surname (J.B.). These letters can be easily seen, even without the help of a magnifying glass.

The *Post Office* stamps of Mauritius are considered to be the rarest stamps known, and the reason of their scarcity is due to their destruction by white ants, one of the plagues in this country; the many great fires which have ruined so many valuable properties in the island; the exposure of the stamps to moisture; the fact that at least half of the issue served to prepay letters of invitation to a ball given at Réduit by the Governor, Sir William Gomm, K.C.B., in October, 1847, the envelopes enclosing the invitations being, naturally, destroyed with the stamp affixed thereon. Two of these letters were found with the invitation enclosed in them—the first, in 1896, by the widow of the late Mr. Edmond Duvivier; the envelope was post-marked in red, September 21st, 1847,[9] and is franked by means of a *One Penny Post Office* stamp.

Envelope, found in Mauritius in 1896 by the widow of the late Mr. Edmond Duvivier, bearing one of the 1d. "Post Office" stamps of Mauritius of 1847, which was sold for Frs.15,000.

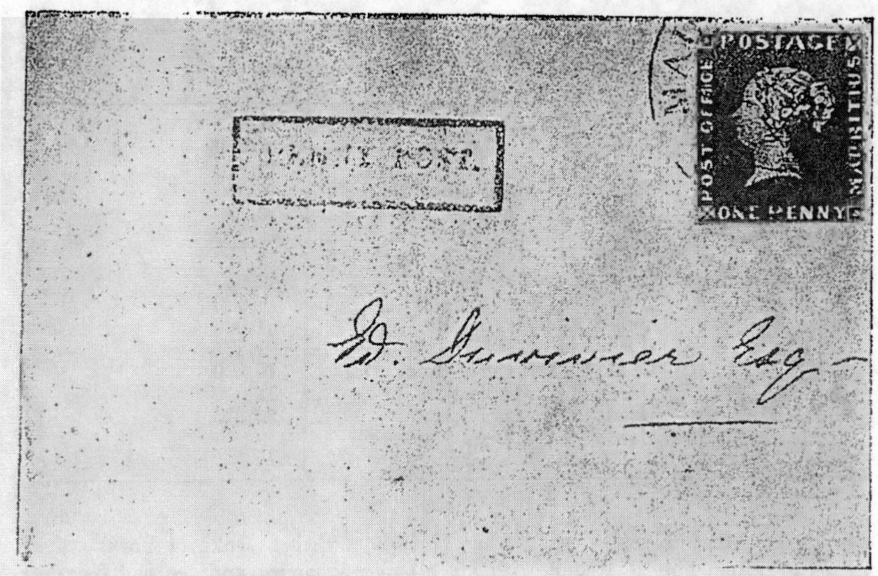

(Reproduced by permission of Somerset House from a photo supplied by Mr. L. A. Aimé Duvivier, Custodian of the Archives, Mauritius, and nephew of Mr. Edmond Duvivier, addressee of the above envelope, which contained an invitation to the famous ball given at Réduit in October, 1847, by the then Governor, Sir William Gomm, K.C.B.)

The accompanying illustration is a photographic reproduction of that envelope and stamp. The stamp was sold by cable to Mr. Peckitt, stamp dealer, in London, for the sum of Frs. 15,000. Mr. Peckitt is said to have resold it for Frs. 25,000 to an English gentleman, who asked that his name should not be mentioned.[10] The second stamp was found by the late Hon. C. F. H. Adam, who was a well-known merchant in Port Louis, and a member of the Council of Government, and was sold by him in 1898 to Mr. Lemaire for a sum unknown.[11]

---

[9] This date is a most conclusive proof that the issue took place on the 20th or 21st September, and not on the 1st October as is generally believed.

[10] Stamp No. 17, on Mr. Lemaire's list.

[11] Stamp No. 20, on Mr. Lemaire's list.

Another *One Penny Post Office* stamp was lost in the following manner :- A Mr. Noirel had the good luck of discovering two *One Penny Post Office* stamps affixed to some old newspapers purchased by him at a public sale;[12] he sold one of the stamps to Mr. Rotchild for the sum of 500 rupees, but the second one, left by him absent-mindedly in the pocket of a white linen waist-coat, was sent with other clothes to the river to be washed, and was lost for ever. I have been given to understand that, since the publication of Mr. Lemaire's list, a *One Penny* and a *Two Pence*, on the same envelope, have been discovered at Bordeaux, which would bring the number of known existing specimens up to twenty-two, as already indicated. Of these mention may be made of (*a*) the pair which is in the collection of His Majesty King George, who is an enthusiastic philatelist;[13] (*b*) five *Post Office*, of which three unused, were, I understand, in one of the best collections in Paris some years ago—if my memory serves me well, the Ferrari collection; (*c*) two are reported to be in the collection of the Emperor of Russia; (*d*) the stamp (a *Two Pence* blue) which I purchased in Mauritius for the trifling sum of 300 rupees from Mr. Henri Adam, Junior, and which I sold to Mr. Le Roy d'Etionnel (of Paris).

I have had occasion several times to see very clever forgeries of both *Post Office* stamps affixed to parts of envelopes having every sign of old age and duly post-marked with the proper date. They were so well executed that they would have deceived any unexperienced collector, and especially beginners.

Imitations of the two *Post Office* stamps made and sold as such by Mr. Moens, of Bruxelles, are far from resembling the originals.

The dies from which the two *Post Office* stamps were printed had disappeared and were considered as lost, when unexpectedly they turned up at the Stamp Exhibition, held on the 7th October, 1912, at the Horticultural Hall, Westminster. They were exhibited by Mr. Sydney Loder, who had purchased them from Mr. D. Field, the well-known philatelist, of London. The latter in his turn had bought them from the son of a gentleman who had resided in Mauritius, but whose name, unfortunately, has not been ascertained.

List of "Post Office" Stamps known to exist, from "*Le Philateliste Français*," edited by M. Lemaire, of Paris.

No.	Date of Last Sale.	Face Value.	Used or Unused.	Last Purchaser.	Price Paid.
					Frs.
1 and 2	1881	1d. and 2d.	Used	Mr. La Renautiere ...	1,000
3 and 4	1893	1d. and 2d.	Unused	Mr. Avery	17,500
5	1870	1d.	Used	Mr. Rotchild[14] ...	500
6	1890	2d.	Used	Mr. Mirabaud[15] ...	3,750
7 and 8	1897	1d. and 2d.	Used	Mr. Bernichon ...	46,500
9 and 10	1881	1d. and 2d.	Unused	Mr. La Renautiere ...	5,500
11 and 12	1896	1d. and 2d.	Used	Mr Moens	42,000
13	1872	2d.	Used	Mr. Rotchild... ...	600
14	1890	2d.	Unused	Mr. Tapling[16] ...	1,000
15	1892	1d.	Used	Mr. Tapling[16] ...	1,875
16	1897	1d.	Used	Mr. Kirchner ...	10,000
17	1898	1d.	Used	Mr. Peckitt[17] ...	15,000
18 and 19	1898	One pair 1d.	Used	Mr. Peckitt[18] ...	34,375
20	1898	1d.	Used	Mr. H. Lemaire[19] ..	?

[12] Stamp No. 5 on Mr. Lemaire's list.

[13] It is a pleasant recollection for me to mention here that in August, 1901, when His Majesty (then Duke of York) visited Mauritius, he did me the great honour of asking me to call on him at Réduit with my album of stamps, and we had together a most interesting and instructive talk about stamps.

[14] One of the two found by Mr. Noirel.

[15] This was the stamp I purchased for Rs.300 from Mr. Henri Adam, junior.

[16] These two stamps are now in the British Museum, to which Mr. Tapling bequeathed his collection.

[17] This is the stamp found by Mrs. Duvivier in 1896 on an envelope enclosing an invitation to the ball given by Governor Gomm.

[18] Resold for Rs.45,000.

[19] This was the last *Post Office* stamp discovered in Mauritius. It was also on an envelope conveying the invitation to the famous ball, and was sold by the Hon. C. F. H. Adam to Mr. Lemaire.

Second Issue "Post Paid," (?) May, 1848:—Diademed head of Queen Victoria, as in the first issue; the words *Post Office* are replaced by *Post Paid* in this issue. The ground has crossed diagonal lines, coloured impression on white paper;[20] two values—1d. vermilion, 2d. dark blue. Engraved by Joseph Barnard. Samuel Stuart Brownrigg, Postmaster-General.

As already stated, the difficulties in the printing of the first issue were so great that it was found advisable to have recourse to a second issue. The new engraving was again entrusted to Mr. Barnard, who this time engraved the stamps in a block or plate containing twelve specimens, in four rows of three stamps. The 1d. stamp is, as in the first issue, orange-vermilion, and the 2d. of a brilliant blue. The first impressions were clear and fine, but in process of time the details got worn out. The later impressions are very inferior, and have given rise to many striking varieties of colour and paper. The stamps have the same lettering as in the first issue, with the exception of the words *Post Office* having been replaced by *Post Paid;* the background has crossed diagonal lines.

The plates were completed ready for working on the *2nd May, 1848.*[21]

Mr. Barnard's price for engraving and printing the stamps was 10s. per 100; and he undertook to supply 1,000 to 1,500 impressions per hour.

Third Issue, 1854.—Britannia Seated. On engine-turned ground; coloured impression, rectangular. Engraved by Messrs. Delarue & Co., of London.

Owing to the Ordinance No. 7 of 1850 stipulating that two distinct rates were chargeable on letters conveyed by private ships, viz.: on a single letter and under ½ oz., despatched, 4d.; on a single letter and under ½ oz., received, 6d., it was found necessary to have recourse to stamps printed in England. The first stamp received (*i.e.*, the green *Britannia Seated*) bore no face value, and it was therefore necessary to have the stamp surcharged with the number "Four" to execute the provisions of the said Ordinance. Mr. Sherwin, already referred to, was entrusted with this work, and the words *Four Pence* were surcharged in a semi-circle over the head of Britannia by means of a hand stamp.

On the 1st and 2nd February, 1854, 10,153 of these stamps had been surcharged, and with the exception of forty-one, which were unfit for use owing to the words *Four Pence* on them being illegible, were issued on the 4th April, 1854.[22] They were, I believe, the first surcharged stamps of the world.

This issue served for ships' letters, and in 1854 no less than 31,895 of them passed through the Post Office.[23]

On May 23rd, 1858, a special Committee was appointed to examine a box of stamps which had been received and deposited in the Treasury Vault. On examination it was found to contain 50,000 of the red-brown *Britannia Seated* (*without value*) series, intended to serve as 6d., on paper blued by the gum, and 100,000 blue ones, on white paper, also without value, to be used as 1s.; but these stamps were never issued.[24] This box was lost sight of until 1872, and, as the stamps had become obsolete, they were sold to the public, in 1872, under their face value.[25] A large number of them was purchased by Mr. W. J. Ausorge (Professor at the Royal College), who, instead of disposing of them by small quantities, committed the mistake of putting the whole stock at once on the London market, with the result that these stamps are still sold at a ridiculously low price. Some remnants of these *Britannia Seated* stamps were also sold at the Treasury in 1877, or 1878, under the same conditions as in 1872.

On March 31st, 1859, the Colonial Postmaster informed the Colonial Secretary that, on examination of a lot of stamps received from England, it was noticed that they differed from those in use in the colony, and that the red stamps bore no mark by which their value might be known; also that

---

[20] In the later issues impressions were taken on *blue* paper.

[21] Letter of Colonial Postmaster to Colonial Secretary, dated May 2nd, 1848.

[22] Government notice of May 4th, 1854. Letter of Colonial Postmaster to Colonial Secretary, March 24th, 1854.

[23] Letter of Colonial Postmaster to Colonial Secretary, July 30th, 1855.

[24] Pemberton, *Stamp Collector's Handbook*, and nearly all the Standard Catalogues of Stamps, such as Stanley Gibbons', Scott's, Moen's, Lemaire's, Yvert & Tellier's, etc., etc.

[25] Postal Regulations, No. 38 of 1877.

stamps similar in colour had been received bearing the words *One Shilling* to be sold at that price Blue stamps had likewise been received, which were to be substituted for those sold at 6d. A large bundle of purple stamps was also found, and the Colonial Postmaster recommended that these should be impressed with the words *Nine Pence*, as the 9d. stamp would be useful to enable persons to prepay with it long-rated letters for the United Kingdom, *via* Marseilles. These recommendations were not put into execution, so far as the *Britannia Seated* series are concerned, another type (series of 1860 without watermark) being adopted.

The last stamps of the *Britannia* series received have been :—

In 1859. The 6d. grey-blue and the 1s. brick-vermilion, *with value*, unperforated.
In 1861. The 6d. brown-lilac and 1s. yellow-green, *with value*, unperforated.
In 1863. The 6d. slate-lilac and 1s. dark green, *with value*, perforated.

The red-brown, red and blue of the issues of 1856–59, and also the *Six Pence* brown-violet and dark-slate of the 1862–63 issues, have been forged.[26]

A curious error in the engraving took place in the plate of the 2d. blue; the first stamp in the third row, *i.e.*, the seventh of the plate, reads *Two Penoe* instead of *Two Pence.*

In order to be able to execute the printing without delay, as the demand for the stamps was very great, an ordinary table for holding the steel and other matters used by the printer when working the postage-stamp press was purchased for £1 4 0, as well as several other articles. However, as the printing of the stamps gave also considerable trouble, particularly in the gumming, it was decided to order better stamps from England;[27] but as a considerable time would have elapsed before any supply could be received, it was found advisable to continue, in the meanwhile, to print stamps from the 1848 plates.

After the introduction of the "Penny Post" in Mauritius, the town delivery was unquestionably most successful and a great boon to the people, who were not, as formerly, under the obligation of sending to, or calling at, the general office for their letters.

In 1852 the demand for postage stamps had so greatly increased that the Postmaster-General applied for a fresh supply of the 1d. and 2d. ones, the plates of which had been deposited in the Colonial Secretary's office.[28]

In 1854 the stamping press then in use had deteriorated and was repaired by Mr. Barnard for £43 12 0.[29]

A new stamping press was, in consequence, ordered from England, from Mr. Henry Hide, for £144 12 0, exclusive of the stand and lath on which it was fixed; but it was nearly lost, as the *Gladiator*, the vessel on which it had been shipped, was wrecked in 1855 at Cannoniers' Point, Mauritius. The ship, however, with its cargo, was purchased by a Mr. Paillotte, who resold the stamp press to Government for £100.[30]

Fourth Issue, 1858.

In 1858 the plate of the 2d. had become almost worn out through long use, and it was decided that a new one should be prepared. The work was entrusted to Mr. Sherwin, an usher of the Royal College and an engraver,[31] who agreed to do the work for £7.[32]

Mr. Sherwin, however, through pressure of his other duties, was unable to finish the plate by

---

[26] "*Album-weeds or How to Detect Forged Stamps*," by Revd. R. B. Earée. London, Stanley Gibbons & Co. (1882).

[27] The first stamps printed in London by Messrs. Delarue & Co. were received in March, 1853; they were the *green*, *vermilion*, and *violet*, *Britannia Seated*, without value.

[28] This information was supplied to me by the late Mr. Gustave Rose, who was a clerk (in 1848) in the Colonial Secretary's office. He joined the Post Office in July, 1852, and he informed me that the early *Post Paid* stamps were printed in his presence.

[29] Letter of Colonial Postmaster to Colonial Secretary, dated May 7th, 1848.

[30] Letter of the President of the Stamping Committee of December 3rd, 1855, to the Colonial Secretary.

[31] Letter of the Colonial Postmaster to Colonial Secretary of February 10th, 1858.

[32] Letter of the Colonial Postmaster to Colonial Secretary of February 24th, 1858.

the stipulated time, April 29th, 1858,[33] and his operations on it were still uncompleted when he returned it on September 2nd.[34]

The stamps printed from this plate are known to collectors as *The Small Fillet;* the head, which has been compared to that of Marat, has a fillet and is smaller than the one in the next issue; it is also called *Tête de Mozambique,* and is the ugliest stamp ever printed. The background is composed of scratched crossed lines; the letters are the same as in the previous issue, but with Mauritius in the right hand side reading downwards.

Fifth Issue, 1859.—Plate of twelve varieties of *Two Pence,* blue. Engraved by Mr. Lapirot.

As Mr. Sherwin's work was so unsatisfactory, the plate was entrusted, for the purpose of being properly finished, to Mr. Lapirot, who was a member of a theatrical troupe performing in Port Louis at the time. Mr. Lapirot found, however, that the plate was beyond redemption, and from a new one which he made, and for which he was paid £10,[35] 5,000 stamps were printed by the Government printer; but the work was so badly executed that a great number had to be destroyed.

The stamps in this issue are known as *The Large Fillet,* or *Grand Bandeau.* They are the rarest Mauritius stamps next to the *Post Office.* The design is the same as that of the *Post Paid,* but the head is larger and finer, and the word *Mauritius* reads upwards, as in the second issue.

In November, 1859, the Colonial Postmaster furnished a list of stamps required for the service of 1860. On his suggestion 20,000 1d., 300,000 2d., 150,000 4d., 100,000 6d., 50,000 9d., and 50,000 1s. were ordered from England. The stamps of this issue were printed in London by the firm of Messrs. Delarue & Co., and were issued in 1860–63. Diademed head of Queen Victoria, coloured impression in rectangular frame, paper without watermark; the design is the same for all the values—the 1d. is brown, the 2d. sky-blue, the 4d. pale pink, the 6d. green, the 9d. lilac (issued in 1863), the 1s. yellow-brown (issued in 1863), the 1s. blue (1870), the 5s. red-lilac, and the 5s. mauve.[36]

The cost of printing by Messrs. Delarue & Co. was, for six new plates £480, and for 650,000 stamps, printed, perforated, gummed, and packed for transmission to Mauritius, 1s. 6d. per 1,000.[37]

Sixth Issue, 1859.—Diademed head of Queen Victoria on solid ground, *Mauritius* above, and value below, with a Greek border on each side. Lithographed by Mr. Dardenne. One variety for each value. Two values—1d. vermilion, 2d. blue. Henry Hamilton Cook, Colonial Postmaster.

In November, 1859, the plates from which the *Post Paid* stamps had been printed were so worn that it was found indispensable to replace them by new ones. As the stamps ordered from England would take some considerable time before reaching Mauritius, Mr. Dardenne, a lithographer on the Chaussée, was commissioned to lithograph the two stamps for 7s. per 100, and to supply as many as 5,000 per day.

The two values—1d. vermilion and 2d. blue—bear the same design of the diademed head of Queen Victoria turning to the left on solid ground, *Mauritius* on the top, and the full value below, with Greek ornaments on each side. There was only one variety for each value, and this arrangement was to continue until a supply of stamps could be obtained from England.[38]

In the beginning of December, 1859, Mr. Dardenne had completed his work,[39] and on the 5th December, 30,000 (1d. vermilion) and 40,000 (2d. blue) had been struck off, and supplied to the Colonial Postmaster. Instructions were given to him that the lithographic stone should remain in the

---

33 Letter of Colonial Postmaster to Colonial Secretary, April 29th, 1858.

34 Letter of Colonial Postmaster to Colonial Secretary, September 4th, 1858.

35 Letter of Colonial Postmaster to Colonial Secretary, March 19th, 1859.

36 It is to my personal knowledge that in 1878 Mr. Thompson, Colonial Postmaster, had the plate of the 1d. cleaned and impressions in *black* taken therefrom. This work was entrusted to Mr. Alcide Lafleur L'Orlanz, a clerk in one of the Chaussée shops, and an engraver in his leisure hours, who performed it in the Church Street shop of a jeweller named Groeme, under the immediate supervision of Mr. Thompson. Mr. Groeme, who is still alive, and whom I have interviewed about this matter, informs me that he recollects perfectly these facts and that he knew well Mr. Thompson. The plates, he says, were so worn out that only very defective impressions could be taken, about a dozen in all, in black, all the bad ones being destroyed immediately by Mr. Thompson himself.

37 Archives.

38 Letter of Colonial Postmaster to Colonial Secretary, November 5th, 1859.

39 Letter of Colonial Postmaster to Colonial Secretary, December 3rd, 1859.

hands of the Stamping Committee, in whose presence alone the stamps were to be printed.[40] *These stamps were the last of the native series.*

List of *Post Paid* and *Britannia Seated* Stamps issued from 1853 to 1859.

(There is, unfortunately, no record of the stamps issued from 1848 to 1852).

Date of Issue.	Post Paid. 1d. Vermilion.	Post Paid. 2d. Blue.	Britannia Seated.	Remarks.
1853.—May 14	—	—	8,000 (red)	
,, ,, 25, 27, 28	8,004	8,004	—	
1854.—January 16 & 19	8,004	—	—	
,, ,, 26 & 29	—	8,004	—	
,, ,, 30 & February 7	—	—	5,000 (4d.)	Surcharged "*Four Pence.*"
,, ,, 1 & 2	—	—	5,000 (4d.) 10,112 (4d.)	
,, May 15	10,000	10,000	—	
,, ,, 19	625	—	—	
,, ,, 23	—	3,500	—	
,, ,, 25	—	3,696	—	
,, ,, 26	—	3,808	—	
,, August 7	10,000	10,000	—	
,, November 1	3,912	—	—	
,, ,, 6	1,608	—	—	
,, ,, 7	—	5,808	—	
,, December 30	—	4,200	—	
,, ,, 31	456	—	—	
1855.—	—	—	—	There is no record for that year.
1856.—January 1	—	10,008	—	
1857—October 29	4,000	12,000	—	
1858.—April 29 & May 5	—	—	10,000 (4d.) 2,000 (6d.)	
,, ,, 22	—	—	—	A box was found at the Treasury, containing 50,000 (red) and 100,000 (blue) B.S., *never issued.*
,, September 16	10,000	—	—	
,, November 2	—	—	5,000 (4d.) 2,000 (6d.)	
,, ,, 7	—	—	10,000 (6d.) 50,000 (1s.)	Blue. Red.
,, ,, 23	10,000	—	—	
1859.—January 28	10,000	—	—	
,, March 19	—	4,959*	—	*Engraved by Lapirot.
,, ,, 25	2,000	5,000*	—	
,, ,, 26	10,000	5,000*	—	
,, May 6	5,000	10,000	—	
,, June 11	12,000	12,000	—	
,, August 6	—	10,000	—	
,, ,, 10	10,000	—	—	
	115,609	125,987		
,, December 12	30,000†	40,000†	—	†Lithographed by Dardenne.

GOVERNMENT NOTICE, No. 40 of 1858.

His Excellency the Governor directs it to be notified that Her Majesty the Queen having been pleased to confirm and approve Ordinance No. 23 of 1855, cited as *The Postage Amendment Ordinance*, 1855, Postage Stamps of the colours *red* and *green* respectively, for the prepayment of letters under the Ordinance, will be sold at the General Post Office and Branch Post Offices on every business day between the hours of 10 a.m. and 3 p.m.

The *red* stamps do not bear any money value; they will be sold for *Six Pence* each. The *green* stamps are each marked *Four Pence* and will be sold at that price, and these stamps will be received at the Post Office as of the value of *Six Pence* and *Four Pence* respectively when affixed to any letter, packet, or parcel, and intended to be prepaid in terms of the Ordinance aforesaid.

[40] Letter of Colonial Postmaster, December 3rd, 1859.

POST OFFICE NOTICE.

Notice is hereby given that Ordinance 23 of 1855 having come into operation, the following charges, with regard to the weight of letters and parcels for transmission abroad, will come into operation from and after the *6th day of May next*:—

I.—Every letter posted for transmission to any part of the United Kingdom by any private vessel shall be charged the full rate:

If not exceeding ½ oz. ... ... 6d.
If exceeding ½ oz., but not exceeding 1 oz. ... ... 1s.
If exceeding 1 oz., an additional 6d. for every additional ½ oz. or fraction thereof.

II.—All letters subject to the rate above-mentioned, if prepaid, must be paid by postage stamps.

III.—All parcels containing books or pamphlets (whether written, printed, plain, or a mixture of the three) posted for transmission to any part of the United Kingdom shall be charged the following rates:

If not exceeding ½ lb. ... ... 6d.
If exceeding ½ lb., and not exceeding 1 lb. ... ... 1s.
If exceeding 1 lb., an additional 6d. for every additional ½ lb. or fraction thereof.

IV.—Letters and sealed packets for transmission abroad, by private vessel, to any part of the United Kingdom must be prepaid by postage stamps, and if not so prepaid, will be treated as dead letters.

They shall be liable to the following rates:

If not exceeding ½ oz. in weight ... ... 4d.
If exceeding ½ oz., but not exceeding 1 oz. ... ... 6d.
If exceeding 1 oz., an additional 4d. for every additional ½ oz. or fraction thereof.

V.—*Red stamps* of the value of 6d. each, and *green stamps* of the value of 4d. each, for prepayment in terms of this notice, will be sold at the General Post Office and Post Offices on every business day between the hours of 10 a.m. and 3 p.m.

(Signed) CAMILLE GEBERT,
Acting Colonial Postmaster.

GENERAL POST OFFICE,
30*th April*, 1858.

POSTAL REGULATION, No. 38 of 1877.

Notice is hereby given that Mauritius Postage Stamps, design *Britannia Seated*, unperforated, *sold in the year 1872*, as specimens below their nominal values, and upon the distinct understanding, under bond, that they should not be used in Mauritius for postal purposes, are, on and after this date, declared *Obsolete*, and that any letter or paper posted with such stamps will be treated as *Unpaid*.

Passed at a meeting of the Executive Council, held at Government House, Port Louis, Mauritius, this 13th day of February, A.D. 1877, and ordered to be laid before the Council of Government.

Laid on the table at a meeting of the Council of Government held on the 20th day of February, 1877.

STATUES.

MAHÉ DE LA BOURDONNAIS.

THERE are few towns in the small British colonies which possess so many statues as does Port Louis. The first which attracts the attention of the stranger is the one facing the landing-place, at about two hundred paces from the water's edge. It represents Mahé de La Bourdonnais, who, to a great extent, was the founder of the French colonisation of the island, and who was one of the most remarkable seamen France has ever produced.

It may well be said that among the great French mariners La Bourdonnais was pre-eminently the one of whom England would have been envious, had she not been so rich herself in equally celebrated contemporaries.

When La Bourdonnais reached Mauritius on the 5th June, 1735, Port Louis was only an encampment consisting of a few huts. The capital of the island was at that time on the northern shore of the Bay of Grand Port, which is situated on the south-east of the island. With the acumen for which he was distinguished La Bourdonnais at once saw that, owing to its advantageous situation facing the Cape of Good Hope, and to its chain of mountains which would shelter shipping from the easterly and southerly winds, the north-west bay was the best place for the capital of the island, and, therefore, to him the foundation of the capital was due; although, as Mr. Albert Pitot points out on page 18, the transference of the capital to that locality had already been recommended by Mr. de Maupin, the previous Governor.

MAHÉ DE LA BOURDONNAIS.
Statue in Place d'Armes, Port Louis.

It was about 1737 that the site of the capital was cleared. Bernardin de Saint Pierre writes: "Everything that I have remarked in this island as being of the greatest utility and done best has been the work of Mons. de La Bourdonnais." Lord Macaulay speaks of him as being a "man of eminent talents and virtues." James Mill, in his *History of British India*, says that when La Bourdonnais arrived in the Isle of France, "so little had been done for the improvement of the island that the people, few in number, were living nearly in the state of nature. They were poor, without industry and without the knowledge of almost any of the useful arts. They had neither magazine nor hospital; neither fortification nor defensive force, military or naval. They had no roads; they had no beasts of burden and no vehicles. Everything remained to be done by La Bourdonnais; and he was capable of everything. With the hand to execute, as well as the head to contrive, he could construct a ship from the keel; he performed the functions of engineer, of architect, of agriculturist; he broke bulls to the yoke; constructed vehicles, and made roads. He apprenticed blacks to the few handicraftsmen whom he carried out with him; he prevailed upon the inhabitants to cultivate the ground, and introduced the culture of the sugar-cane and indigo. To introduce any degree of order and vigilance into the management even of the hospital which he constructed for the sick, it was necessary for him to perform the office of superintendent himself. During the eleven years La Bourdonnais was Governor there was but one law suit in the Isle of France, he himself having terminated all differences by arbitration."

It can, therefore, be understood that among Mauritians the memory of this man is very dear. In 1853 a Committee was formed for the purpose of erecting a statue to him, and the Committee, at the suggestion of the Governor, Sir William Stevenson, K.C.B., fixed upon the landing-place as the site for it. This spot had been indicated twenty years previously by one of the most remarkable of Mauritian patriots, Mr. Adrien d'Epinay. Governor Stevenson, when speaking on the subject, said: "The statue of the founder of the town should face the sea, and appear to be welcoming strangers."

The statue is of bronze, and is by the French sculptor, Augustin Dumont. There are two other similar statues, one at St. Denis, the capital of Réunion, and the other in one of the public places of Madras, which was captured in 1746 by La Bourdonnais, with the frigates and troops from the Isle of France under his command.

La Bourdonnais is represented in ordinary costume, holding in his left hand an unfolded chart of the Isle of France, and with his right hand he points to the sword with which he conquered the enemies of his country. What is most admired in this work of Dumont, one of the finest of the many statues executed by him, is the happy union of force and elegance; thus it is that in this bronze of one of the men who did most honour to the French race is a true representation of a French gentleman of the eighteenth century; that period when France, both at home and abroad, displayed the greatest energy, and displayed also, under its most charming aspect, that elegance which was the proudest and most captivating ever known.

The inauguration of the statue took place on the 30th of August, 1859. Governor Stevenson on that occasion thus terminated his speech: "We now see before us the figure of him who may justly be styled the Founder of this Colony and the Founder of this City. We have hailed the presence of his effigy with the same earnest enthusiasm with which we should have greeted his personal return. . . . . I hope, so long as the monument endures, so long as its history is recorded, so long as its subject is remembered, that it will always be regarded by the successors of La Bourdonnais as an admonition to them to imitate his example and to emulate his character."

In 1899 the colony celebrated the second centenary of the birth of La Bourdonnais, and an impressive demonstration was then made around his statue.

QUEEN VICTORIA.

On leaving La Bourdonnais' statue, the stranger naturally directs his steps through the avenue of fine trees, bordered by half-buried French cannon, towards Government House, which faces the sea at the other end of the square. He will observe there, at the entrance, a marble statue of Queen Victoria, which was erected in 1902. The first stone of the pedestal was laid at the beginning of August, 1901, by H.R.H. the Duke of Cornwall and York (now His Majesty King George V.) when he visited Mauritius accompanied by the Duchess (now Her Majesty Queen Mary). The name of the sculptor has not been ascertained; no one in Mauritius, except perhaps some officials, seems to have ever heard it mentioned; and this is not to be wondered at, for the statue is lacking in artistic beauty, and the marble does not appear to be of the best quality. Some persons believe that it is the work of an Italian artist; others consider that it evolved under the chisel of an English sculptor. It was erected, we understand, by the Government conjointly with the Municipality. An illustration of it appears on page 255.

There is another statue of Queen Victoria in front of the Central Railway Station. It was erected and unveiled in 1897 on the occasion of Her Majesty's Diamond Jubilee; but the less said about it the better from an artistic point of view.

SIR WILLIAM STEVENSON, K.C.B.

Behind this statue of Queen Victoria, at the end of the courtyard formed by the wings of Government House, in a group of palms, is a lofty and martial figure in bronze representing Sir William Stevenson, K.C.B. Little did this Governor think, when eulogising La Bourdonnais at the foot of the statue which the Mauritians had erected to the great French sailor, that a few years later a statue would be erected in his own honour by the public officials of the colony. Sir William had assumed the reins of government in September, 1857. He died at Réduit in the early days of January, 1863. As his administration had proved most prosperous he was able to adopt a more equitable system for the payment of the Civil Service than that which had been in existence since the taking of the island by England. Suddenly the salaries of the officials were augmented, and they saw before them the prospect of further increments. Consequently, when Sir William died they agreed among themselves to erect a statue to his memory. Funds were quickly forthcoming, but soon the subscribers were greatly embarrassed on learning that no portrait of him existed, and that it would, therefore, be impossible for a sculptor to design and execute the statue. Owing to this difficulty the subscribers would probably have abandoned their project had not someone remembered having seen somewhere a statuette of him, modelled in clay, by a young Mauritian named Prosper d'Epinay, aged about twenty-seven, who has now become one of the most famous sculptors of the present time.

The statuette was found to be a perfect likeness, but the shrewd artist would not sell it, still less lend it. The subscribers, therefore, had to entrust to him the execution of the statue, for which purpose he left for Rome, where he opened his first studio. The statue, when completed, was exhibited in England, and *The Athenæum* said that the work was "really superior to any bronze statues such as we are accustomed to see," and added: "If it be considered that this is the work of a young artist, it will be found to be most remarkable."

Statue by Prosper d Epinay of
SIR WILLIAM STEVENSON, K.C.B.,
At Government House, Port Louis.

Sir William Stevenson is represented in a general's full uniform. The martial character, devoid of stiffness, which the artist has given to his work is specially to be admired. The inauguration took place on the 20th June, 1867. It is unfortunate that so fine a statue should have been erected in such an entirely unsuitable place, where it is almost completely hidden.

ADRIEN D'EPINAY.

Sir William Stevenson's statue was ordered before that of Adrien d'Epinay, which is to be seen in the Company's Gardens (the Company referred to being *La Compagnie Française Orientale des Indes*); nevertheless the statue of Adrien d'Epinay was inaugurated nearly a year before it.

Mauritius is indebted to Adrien d'Epinay for many signal services rendered by him as a great citizen. Immediately after the conquest of the island by England, in 1810, the new Metropolitan Government, which had promised to treat Mauritians as most favoured subjects, manifested towards them feelings of the greatest hostility, and they were accused of disloyalty. The political constitution of which they had made such noble use from 1791 to 1803, and which the despotism of Napoleon Bonaparte had suspended for ten years, was not restored. Mauritius, in short, was treated as a conquered country. In 1830 the colonists sent d'Epinay to England to defend their interests. He succeeded, but not without difficulty, in obtaining the creation of a Legislative Council, the members of which were appointed by the Governor. In 1833 d'Epinay again went to England to defend the rights of his country. Since 1832 the Anti-Slavery party desired the liberation of the 60,000 slaves in the colony, without according any indemnity to their owners, the pretext being that the slaves had been introduced into the island in defiance of the English prohibitory laws of 1813. The Abolitionists nearly succeeded in their project. Even after the general abolition of slavery, in 1834, in the British colonies, they maintained that Mauritius had no right to an indemnity, and several times asked Parliament to distribute the share due to Mauritius, namely, two millions sterling, amongst the West Indian colonies.

d'Epinay was once more in London, in 1834, when the Abolition Bill was discussed in Parliament. By his counsels he gave enlightenment on the subject to Mr. Stanley, who was then Minister for the Colonies. If d'Epinay had not happened to be in London at that time, the Abolitionists would certainly have succeeded in depriving the Mauritians of their share of the indemnity.

Adrien d'Epinay had also succeeded in obtaining a semi-elective Council for his country; but the Anti-Slavery party snatched this concession from the Mauritians. He was, however, able to return in triumph to the island, for he had obtained authority to create a bank at Mauritius, and had secured from some large capitalists in England the loans necessary for the opening of this bank. Furthermore, he had, since 1827, persuaded the Ministry to allow Mauritius sugar to enter the English market on the same footing as that of the West Indies, and through his efforts the Customs tariff of the colony was modified for all kinds of goods.

He was the first to introduce into the island steam-engines for the manipulation of the sugar-cane; and he greatly encouraged arts and sciences. He had the honour of drafting the only plan for the abolition of slavery which any British colony ever presented to Parliament (1832); and many of the ideas embodied in this plan were adopted by Mr. Stanley in 1834. He was passionately fond of sport, and was the first to introduce English horses on the race-course at Port Louis.

In gratitude for so many signal services rendered by him, the Mauritians erected the fine bronze statue in question, which was inaugurated on September 26th, 1866. It is a work of admirable simplicity. The patriot is represented with his left hand placed over his heart, as if to express the sincerity of his devotion to his countrymen, to whom he is addressing himself. Attention is at once attracted and retained by the energy and indomitable force of character expressed in his face.

Speaking at the inauguration of the statue, the Governor (Sir Henry Barkly) said: "As Her Majesty's representative in this colony I am here to frankly and cordially associate myself with the honours offered by one of his own sons to Adrien d'Epinay.

"Although during the greater part of his life he was the ardent adversary of the local Government, although he professed opinions which I can in no way share, I, nevertheless, experience no difficulty in uniting myself to those who are rendering homage to the eminent intellectual qualities which he displayed. I have no hesitation in recognising the independence and loftiness of his character, the purity and disinterestedness of his patriotism. In a word, the imposing spectacle now before my eyes proves to me that the services he rendered to his country are held in the same esteem after more than a quarter of a century."

Statue by Prosper d'Epinay of his Father,
ADRIEN D'EPINAY,
In the Company's Gardens, Port Louis.

PAUL AND VIRGINIA.

About 1880 the Mauritians were inspired with the idea of acquiring a purely artistic work by their celebrated countryman. The Municipality of Port Louis headed the movement, and asked Mr. Prosper d'Epinay to execute a marble group of Paul and Virginia, whose story has made the island famous in the world of romance.

PAUL AND VIRGINIA.
(Original Marble by Prosper d'Epinay in possession of the Royal Family of Braganza.)

The sculptor first thought of representing Paul, overcome with grief, lifting up the body of Virginia, which he had just discovered on the sea-shore. It certainly was an admirable and touching subject; but the Municipality disagreed with the artistic conception and said that as this was not according to Bernardin Saint Pierre's tale, they wanted him to confine himself to the idea of the passage of the torrent. Although that subject did not offer much scope to the artist, he produced a masterpiece unrivalled for its exquisite grace and beauty. Paul has steadied himself on his right foot on a rock in the middle of the rushing water, and, bending forward on the other foot, he balances himself preparatory to crossing the torrent. The great anxiety which he is feeling is wonderfully depicted on his face.

Virginia, carried in the arms of Paul, is leaning on his shoulder. Her eyes, fixed on the torrent, tell also of her fear; but her hand placed on the young lad's shoulder, her feet modestly drawn up out of reach of the water, eloquently express her confidence in the strength of her loving companion. In a word, it is a drama of love, admirably represented and beautifully executed, and is considered by many as the sculptor's finest work. Mr. d'Epinay, however, has always regretted that he was not allowed to give effect to his first conception, in which were united, at the final dramatic scene, all the great emotions of the immortal romance.

The original marble group of natural size is in the possession of the Royal Family of Braganza. A replica in marble was executed for the Municipality of Port Louis, and is at the top of the stairs in the Town Hall.

The bronze replica in the grounds of the Town Hall at Curepipe has the additional merit of having been cast from the original wax model moulded by the artist himself.

[Photo, Ladies' Fine Needlework Association.

BRONZE FROM THE ORIGINAL WAX MODEL OF PAUL AND VIRGINIA, Town Hall Gardens, Curepipe.

KING EDWARD VII.

It is regrettable that what is probably the finest statue in Mauritius was not erected in one of the public places in the centre of Port Louis. The one in question is that of King Edward VII., also the work of Mr. Prosper d'Epinay. It stands in the Champ de Mars, and although of considerable dimensions it is dwarfed by the plain, more than an English mile in diameter, and the semicircle of the over-looking mountains.

It was during 1908 and 1909 that the Municipality of Port Louis (during the Mayoralty of the Hon. Dr. E. A. O.

Laurent) caused the sum of Rs. 500 to be inserted in the Budget for a bust of the King, but this was soon increased to Rs. 1,000 for a complete statue, the balance of the sum required to be obtained by public subscription. It is worthy of remark that Mauritius did not wait for the death of the King in order to erect a statue to him. Money poured in, and it was at first suggested that the execution of the statue should be entrusted to an English artist; but in 1910 Mr. V. A. Esnouf, who was then Mayor, commissioned Mr. Prosper d'Epinay to execute this work for his native land. The great sculptor was all the more delighted at undertaking it, as he had long been the personal friend of King Edward. Then occurred the death of the King, and the artist wrote to Queen Alexandra asking for a photograph which Her Majesty considered to be the best likeness of the lamented sovereign. It was by using this photograph, and trusting to his memory, that Mr. d'Epinay modelled the magnificent work of art. Having no longer a studio at Paris, he went to work on it in his spacious establishment at Rome, where he had already produced the statues of his father and of Governor Stevenson. The following was the artist's conception, which he communicated to one of his local friends:—Mauritius is an island of volcanic formation in the Indian Ocean, placed like an outpost on the great ocean routes between India, Australia, East Africa, Egypt, and China. This statue, which is more than life size, on a stone pedestal, stands, therefore, in the midst of the ocean which bathes the most ancient and most celebrated of the dependencies of the British Crown. Furthermore, the population of Mauritius, which is so heterogeneous —where the white man elbows the Chinaman, the Indian, the Arab, the African—is like an agglomeration of the races sheltered by the British flag in every latitude. It was necessary, therefore, to give to the statue of King Edward an attitude in which each of these races, so different in thought and custom, would contribute a symbolical attribute of the power of Great Britain. Edward VII. is consequently represented as a sovereign animated by the desire for peace; his physiognomy, proud and dignified, well expresses the serenity of him whom men call the "Peacemaker." But as concerns the peoples of Africa and Asia who are subjects of the British Empire, the sentiment expressed is equally noble. The King's right hand gathers round him the ample Imperial mantle, as though to shelter and protect; whilst the left hand, resting on the hilt of his sword, seems to signify that Great Britain, when called upon, can defend all those who appeal to her for protection, and who live under the shadow of her flag.

KING EDWARD VII.
Statue by Prosper d'Epinay in the Champ de Mars, Port Louis.

INAUGURATION OF THE STATUE OF KING EDWARD VII., JUNE 24th, 1912.

The artist has fully succeeded in giving expression to his ideas in this admirable work, which he executed in the finest bronze. The inauguration of the statue took place on June 24th, 1912, in presence of an enthusiastic gathering, which saluted with the sincerest fervour the image of a sovereign who had done so much to foster friendship between France and England.

On Christmas Eve of 1912 Mr. d'Epinay forwarded as a present to Her Majesty Queen Alexandra a miniature replica in clay of the statue. The Queen immediately replied by telegram, couched in the most gracious terms, saying that the sculptor could not have offered a more acceptable gift.

RÉMY OLLIER.

About a hundred paces from the statue of Adrien d'Epinay is a very modest monument—a bronze bust of a Creole journalist, Rémy Ollier, who died at the age of twenty-seven years. He was born in 1816, in the district of Grand Port, on the south-east of the island. He was a half-caste; his father was a retired officer of the French army, and his mother belonged to a respectable middle-class family. The coloured population, which had been emancipated by the Revolution, had seen its rights trodden underfoot by Bonaparte. It was only twenty years after the taking of the island that England restored to the mulattos the political rights which they had enjoyed under the French domination. In 1830, however, the social inequality weighed heavily on them, and it was with difficulty that the Government was prevailed upon to accord to them their rights. Ollier founded a journal, *La Sentinelle de Maurice*, for the purpose of claiming from the Government the realisation of its promises. His task was extremely arduous. After a struggle lasting for two years, he succumbed under the heavy burden he had undertaken.

STATUE OF SIR JOHN POPE HENNESSY, K.C.M.G., AND THE THEATRE, PORT LOUIS.

Sixty years later, when apparently forgotten, his fellow-countrymen erected to his memory the modest monument referred to, which is the work of a Mauritian artist, Mr. Maurice Loumeau. The bust is of bronze, cast at Paris, and is said to be a good likeness. Its inauguration took place at the end of 1908, and was attended by representatives of all the political parties of the island. Ollier was no longer looked upon as a partisan, but as a patriot gifted with the greatest disinterestedness and loftiness of soul.

SIR JOHN POPE HENNESSY, K.C.M.G.

In the square in front of the theatre is to be seen another of Mr. Maurice Loumeau's works, in the form of a bronze statue of Sir John Pope Hennessy, K.C.M.G., who was Governor of the island from 1883 to 1889.

Sir John Pope Hennessy, an Irishman of mark, was one of Disraeli's friends, and a well-known speaker in the House of Commons even at an earlier period. When he came to Mauritius there happened to be here an advanced party which claimed a reform of the Constitution, and endeavoured to obtain a semi-elective Legislative Council. When their petition had been first presented it was refused by the Colonial Office somewhat curtly. Sir John Pope Hennessy revived the hopes of this party by his encouragement, and finally he lent his support to a new demand, which he forwarded to Downing Street, for a new legislature by which the nine districts of the island should be represented by elected members. Lord Derby, who was then Minister for the Colonies, granted to the Mauritians that which had been denied them a few years before. Sir John Pope Hennessy had desired that Mauritius should be for the Mauritians. He considered it unjust that the highest posts of the administration should be reserved for Englishmen coming from the United Kingdom, whereas there were many Mauritians who could fill those posts with distinction. When it became a question of the election of members to the Council of Government, in conformity with the new Letters Patent, political divisions, which degenerated into dissensions, broke out all over the colony. Sir John Pope Hennessy was held responsible for this and was suspended from office. An inquiry was instituted, and the Home Government was obliged to reinstate him. In spite of the dissensions which his liberal policy had caused in the island, his memory has remained dear to Mauritians, even amongst his opponents.

The inauguration of the statue took place in December, 1909; and although it leaves much to be desired from an artistic point of view, it testifies that Sir John Pope Hennessy's mission in Mauritius was not altogether in vain.

PROSPER D'EPINAY.

PROSPER D'EPINAY,
The Famous Mauritian Sculptor.

Mr. Prosper d'Epinay was born in Mauritius on July 13th 1836, and, when scarcely three years of age, was taken by his parents to France. After the death of his father, which occurred at Paris, he returned with his mother to his native island, where he soon gave ample evidence of the ability that was eventually to make him famous. In 1857 he again left Mauritius to study in the atelier of the sculptor Dantan at Paris, and afterwards in that of his contemporary Amici at Rome. In 1864 he went to London, where he attained great success, and one of his humorous caricatures at that time, entitled *Entente Cordiale*, and representing Napoleon III. and Lord Palmerston, caused much amusement both in France and England.

In 1865 he executed a bust of the Princess of Wales (now her Majesty Queen Alexandra), which was preferred to one of the same subject by the English sculptor Gibson. Since then Mr. d'Epinay has made several likenesses of the gracious spouse of King Edward VII.; and the friendly interest in him manifested by his late Majesty, when Prince of Wales, was in no way diminished when he became King.

One of the chief works exhibited in England by Mr. d'Epinay was his *Hannibal Enfant*. When the jury of the Royal Academy halted before this beautiful production, representing the young Carthagenian struggling with the eagle, they could not restrain their applause—an incident without precedent in the history of the Royal Academy, so wrote the President to the Duke of Buccleuch, who is the owner of the splendid marble.

In 1874 Mr. d'Epinay left London to establish himself at Paris, where in the same year he added to his fame by his exquisite female statue, *Ceinture Dorée*. Thereafter Mr. d'Epinay included amongst his patrons Sovereigns, the nobility, and many celebrated men and women. An instance of the great appreciation in which his productions are held was afforded by the successful action which he brought against a dealer in objects of art at Rome for clandestinely reproducing some of his finest works. Amongst those most admired are his *Sappho Jalouse*, *Bacchantes*, *Paul et Virginie*, and *Jeanne d'Arc au Sacre*. The latter is a magnificent polychrome statue which has been placed in the Cathedral at Rheims, on the spot where Joan of Arc stood during the consecration of Charles VII. At the Anglo-French Exhibition of 1908 in London his superb marble bust of Queen Alexandra and a work by Mons. M. de Saint Marceaux alone appeared in the place of honour in the Central Hall. That marble by the gifted Mauritian now graces the reception chamber of the British Embassy at Paris.

Mr. d'Epinay is a member of the well-known clubs, *Cercle de l'Union Artistique*, Paris, and *Circolo della Caccia*, Rome, which he was instrumental in founding with a few friends in 1860 and 1870 respectively.

He has received decorations from several Sovereigns of Europe in token of their high appreciation of his talent. He is a Knight of the Royal Victorian Order, Commander of the Order of Isabella the Catholic, Officer of the Golden Lion of Nassau, Chevalier of the Legion of Honour, Chevalier of St. Maurice and St. Lazarus, Officer of the Rose of Brazil, etc.

THE CIVIL HOSPITAL, PORT LOUIS.

F. A. ROUGET, M.D. Edin.,
Medical Superintendent, Civil Hospital.

THE Civil Hospital, a purely state institution and the largest of the kind in the island, stands in spacious grounds in the south-eastern part of Port Louis, at the foot of Signal Mountain.

The buildings were originally intended for the Royal College of Mauritius. The central block and the two southern wings were designed by the Hon. Léon Emile Pitot, at present General Manager of Railways, and were erected in 1893 in place of the old wooden pile (dating from the French occupation), which was blown down by the great cyclone of 1892. The two northern wings are all that remain of the Old Royal College.

The Civil Hospital was originally situated near the wharf behind the Post-Office, and in the proximity of the Meat and Fish Market and the Customs Warehouses. For more reasons than one the building, which is now used as Government Offices, was unsuitable and the site objectionable.

In April, 1899, a few months after the breaking out of plague in the island, the old Hospital became infected by plague-stricken rats, so that it was considered necessary to transfer the patients at once to the Royal College buildings, and the College to Curepipe, schoolboys from Port Louis being granted free railway tickets as a compensation.

This measure, which was at first intended to be purely provisional, was rendered permanent in December, 1905, by a vote of the Council of Government.

From that time alterations and additions have been, and are still being, made to adapt the Royal College buildings as far as possible to the requirements of a modern hospital. As a matter of fact the new Hospital is provided with well-ventilated wards, including one for maternity cases, also an up-to-date operation room, mortuary, clinical laboratory, powerful X-Ray apparatus, and even a small Radium tube.

The institution is a general hospital intended for the reception of all surgical and medical diseases, except leprosy, which is treated in a special lazaret.

Infectious cases are kept in isolated wards or, in the case of epidemic diseases, transferred to any special hospital that may have been provided for them.

The Medical Staff comprises:—F. A. Rouget, M.D. (Edin.), Medical Superintendent; E. M. G. Sénêque, M.D. (Paris), Resident Medical Superintendent; and J. Crétin, L.R.C.P. and S. (Edin.), L.F.P. and S. (Glasgow), Police and Prison Surgeon.

The Medical Superintendent has the general management of the Hospital from both the medical and administrative points of view. The general staff numbers about eighty persons.

The nursing in the male department is done entirely by male nurses, designated warders; and those only are appointed who are holders of certificates of competency, obtained after a sufficient hospital training and an examination, conducted on theoretical and practical lines, according to a prescribed curriculum.

Formerly the nursing in the female department was entirely in the hands of Sisters of Mercy, as the young women of the island had some prejudice against the nursing profession. This, however, no longer exists, for since 1904 a scheme has been in force whereby local nurses are trained in the Civil Hospital, and granted certificates of competency after an examination similar to that laid down for male

E. M. G. SÉNÊQUE, M.D. Paris,
Assistant Medical Superintendent, Civil Hospital.

nurses, with special reference to midwifery.

In connection with this scheme, four scholarships of the value of Rs. 250 per annum each (open only to female candidates) are granted every year by the Government to the most successful candidates at an entrance examination, on condition that they undergo a two years' training at the Civil Hospital.

About twenty thoroughly trained and competent nurses, prepared under the above scheme, have hitherto been granted certificates with very encouraging results. These are employed in Government Hospitals, and the others are very successful as private nurses.

OLD ROYAL COLLEGE AFTER THE CYCLONE OF 1892: REBUILT AS THE CIVIL HOSPITAL.

The Hospital with its present arrangements has accommodation for about 250 patients, not including the isolated wards for infectious diseases.

The total number of patients treated in 1912 was 5,894, viz.: 4,541 males and 1,353 females. Special wards are provided for members of the Police and for Prison Warders.

The surgical operations at the Hospital (963 in 1912) comprise the whole range of operative surgery, including abdominal sections.

No private rooms have as yet been fitted up for paying patients desirous of privacy; but the question of providing for such rooms is embodied in the general scheme of adaptation, which has been in operation for some years past, and will receive consideration at no distant date. The tariff of charges is as follows :—

A. Private patients :—

(1.) In-door patients :—

Class I. 2 Rupees per diem. | Class II. 1 Rupee per diem.

(2.) Out-door patients (limited to casualties, emergencies, and special surgical dressings) :—

For each attendance, Rs. 1 | For radioscopic examination, Rs. 5 | For radiography, Rs. 10

THE CIVIL HOSPITAL.

B. Special terms for Government servants, who are charged one-quarter, one-third, one-half, three-quarters of the rate fixed for private patients, or the full rate, according to their salary. When a private ward is available patients may be admitted thereto on payment of an additional charge of one rupee per diem.

C. Labourers under written contract from sugar estates are charged 50 cents; and ordinary servants under verbal contract are charged 33 cents.

Paupers, and Government servants drawing Rs. 300 and less per annum, are admitted free of charge.

The above tariff in the case of Government servants applies also to their wives and children.

THE BARKLY ASYLUM, BEAU BASSIN.

J. I. PADDLE, F.R.C.S. Engl. and M.D. Lond., Medical Superintendent, Lunatic Asylum.

A. B. Y. JOLLIVET, L.R.C.P. and S. Edin. and Glasgow, Medical Officer, Barkly Asylum.

THE Barkly Asylum is a Government institution consisting of infirmary wards, where paupers are received and maintained, an orphanage with a school attached, a separate compound where all the harmless patients from the Government Lunatic Asylum are maintained, and a hospital for the sick inmates of the institution as well as those of the district. The sections for the paupers, orphans, and imbeciles are under the control of the Protector of Immigrants and Poor Law Commissioner, and the hospital under that of the Medical and Health Department.

In the Poor Law branch there are six wards—two for female and four for male paupers—containing 133 beds. In the imbeciles' compound there are 100 beds—68 for males and 32 for females. Three buildings in the middle of the grounds form the orphanage, where 42 orphans are maintained and educated.

In connection with the institution there is a sewing class, under the direction of a seamstress, composed of all the able-bodied female paupers, who help in the production of the clothes for the inmates of both the Poor Law and Medical branches.

The hospital has four wards containing 153 beds, a maternity ward of six beds, and a ward with forty beds for females, the latter two wards being separate buildings away from the main structure. At the extremity of the grounds are five wards with eighteen beds for contagious diseases.

The staff of the Poor Law branch numbers fifty-one persons, and that of the hospital thirty-five persons. The buildings include two chapels, one for Roman Catholics and the other for Protestants.

The grounds of the institution (about 80 acres) formed part

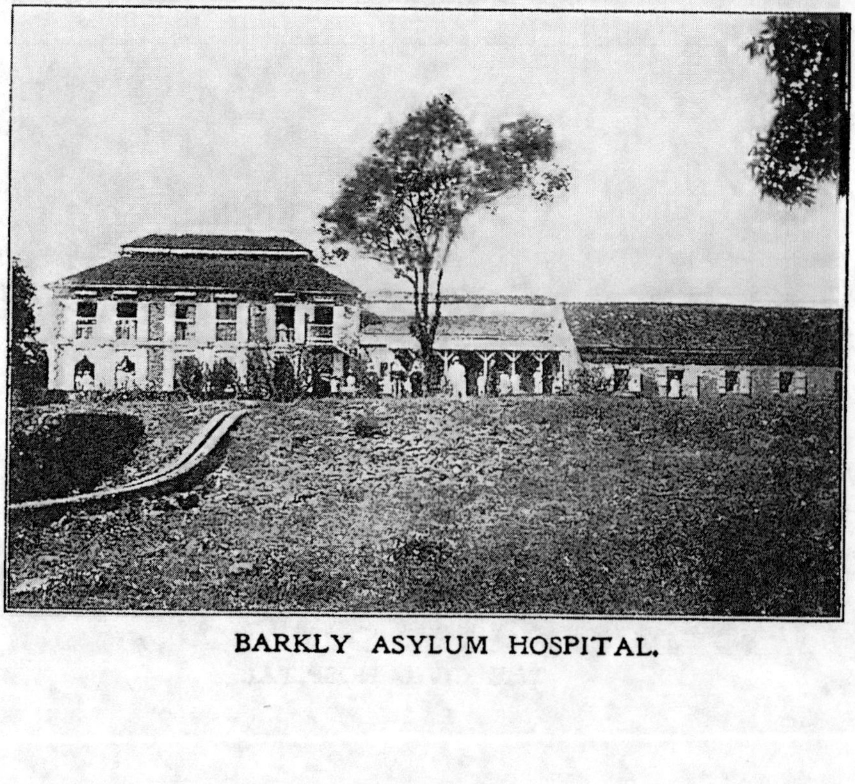

BARKLY ASYLUM HOSPITAL.

of an old sugar estate, which derived its name from the beautiful pond now bordered by the vegetable garden of the Asylum; so that this pond, of which an illustration appears on page 180, is the origin of the name of Beau Bassin District. The estate belonged to Colonel Metcalffe, an officer in the Indian Army, and was bought by Government in 1868. Part of the hospital building was formerly the sugar factory of the estate, and another part was rebuilt in 1895, after having been destroyed by the cyclone of 1892.

The establishment is lighted by electricity, and, with its roads and the cottages of the resident officers, has the appearance of a village of about 620 souls. It was named after Sir Henry Barkly, K.C.B., who at the time of its inception was Governor of Mauritius.

SOME MAURITIAN DOCTORS.

1. J. C. H. GENTIL, L.R.C.P. and S. Edin., L.F.P. and S. Glasgow.
2. L. J. LOUIS, M.B., Ch.B. Edin.
3. J. A. RAFFRAY, M.D. Paris.
4. C. J. PÉPIN, M.D. Paris.
5. H. G. LAMBERTY, L.R.C.P. and S. Edin., L.F.P. and S. Glasgow.
6. HASSAM SAKIR, M.B., C.M. Edin.

THE MAURITIUS INSTITUTE, PORT LOUIS.

DR. W. T. A. EDWARDS, C.M.G.,
Chairman of the Board of Directors of the Mauritius Institute.

In 1880 an Ordinance was passed for the erection, establishment, and regulation of a Mauritius Institute, a Museum, and a Library. This Ordinance (No. 19 of 1880) authorised the Governor, with the advice of the Executive Council, from such sums as should be voted for the purpose by the Council of Government, to erect within the city of Port Louis a building to be called the "Mauritius Institute," in which a Museum and a Library should be established.

The Military Government having put at the disposal of the Civil Government certain portions of land and buildings, some of these were sold, and the proceeds of the sale, together with an additional vote of the Council of Government, were employed to purchase the piece of land where stood the Hotel de l'Univers, and some buildings of minor importance which were burnt in 1877.

All the back part of the Institute yard then formed Malartic Street, which ran parallel to that part of Intendance Street now separating Government House from the Audit, the Treasury, and the Registrar-General's Offices.

The Museum, which existed already, containing the collection given to the colony by the late Julien Desjardins and called the "Museum Desjardins," was removed in 1885 from the Royal College, where it had been first established, to the new building.

But no public library had yet been formed when, at the instigation of Dr. W. T. A. Edwards, C.M.G., Ordinance No. 37 of 1900 was passed, repealing Ordinance No. 19 of 1880 and placing the Institute under the care and management of a Board of Directors.

THE MAURITIUS INSTITUTE, PORT LOUIS.

The Museum, at first composed only of the collection of the late Julien Desjardins, already referred to, was gradually increased by acquisitions made by Government and by donations from Mr. and Mrs. Liénard and sons, Mr. Albert Daruty de Grandpré, The Hon. Christian Wiehé, Messrs. Donald d'Emmerez de Charmoy, Théodore Sauzier, George Antelme, Paul Carié, etc.

The Mauritius Public Library is now composed of 13,927 catalogued volumes, as follows:—

1. Catalogued volumes belonging to Sir V. Naz's Library 5,958
2. Catalogued volumes belonging to the Royal College Library 3,823
3. Books belonging to the Dromart Library 887
4. New books, purchased in Europe or in Mauritius, or presented to the Library 3,138
5. Volumes of French Reviews (such as *Revue de Deux Mondes*, *Revue Rose*, *Revue Bleue*, *Annales de l'Institut Pasteur*) 121

13,927

In this total (which is continually increasing, as the mean number of books purchased by or presented to the Library in a year exceeds 300) are not comprised hundreds of volumes in bad condition, incomplete, duplicates—many of which are superseded editions—scientific, commercial, administrative and other reports, old periodicals, reviews, annuals, guides, etc., which are not considered as Library works.

The foregoing information on the Mauritius Institute has been taken from *The Mauritius Almanac* for 1913.

THE MAURITIUS CRICKET CLUB.

According to the booklet containing the rules and regulations of the Mauritius Cricket Club, the first historical record of cricket in Mauritius is to be found in the *Mauritius Gazette* of May 21st, 1831, where the following notice appears:—

"A Grand Match for £500 will be played on the Champ de Mars between eleven gentlemen of the Mauritius Club and eleven gentlemen of the 29th and 82nd Regiments, on Monday, the 23rd May. Wickets to be pitched at half-past eight."

It is supposed that the "Mauritius Club" referred to in the above notice is the present Mauritius Cricket Club, although no minute-book of the club can be found prior to May 14th, 1856, when a meeting was held at the Hotel d'Europe, Port Louis, "for the purpose of uniting the Union Cricket Club and the Mauritius Cricket Club into one club, and also to appoint office-bearers for the season."

MEMBERS OF THE MAURITIUS CRICKET CLUB.

The Union Cricket Club was founded in the year 1849 at a meeting held at the Hotel d'Europe on August 2nd. Of this club Mr. E. Chapman was the first president, and Mr. R. Leishman, hon. secretary. Of the combined clubs (called the Mauritius Cricket Club) Lieut.-Col. H. F. F. Johnson, 5th Fusiliers, was the first president, and Mr. T. Ambrose, hon. secretary.

Until the cyclone of April 29th, 1892, when the pavilion was blown down, the headquarters of the club were at the Champ de Mars, where from six to twelve matches were played during the winter season. So far back as the year 1877 the question of acquiring a cricket ground in Plaines Wilhems was raised, and Sir Célicourt Antelme offered to sell a portion of Stanley Estate for that purpose; but the committee considered that the ground was too far from the railway station. A similar offer of ground at Beau Bassin from Mr. E. C. Fraser (now the Hon., C.M.G.) could not be accepted on account of the prohibitive cost of clearing and levelling.

In the year 1892, however, Sir Célicourt Antelme's offer of 4½ acres of land adjoining Stanley Estate for Rs. 1,350 was accepted. The members of the club subscribed Rs. 1,688, and a loan of Rs. 3,500 was contracted to defray the cost of clearing, levelling, planting the ground, etc., and for building the pavilion. On January 12th, 1901, not long after this debt was paid off, the pavilion was badly damaged by a cyclone, and a loan of Rs. 6,500 was contracted to rebuild and enlarge it. By April 15th, 1909, the debt had been reduced to Rs. 3,366·38, and on April 1st, 1912, stood at Rs. 2,500.

CLUB DE CUREPIPE.

CLUB DE CUREPIPE.

CUREPIPE is the principal residential centre of the white population of Mauritius, and in this bracing town, 1850 feet above the level of the sea, is situated the Club de Curepipe, which is the only institution of the kind in the island.

The first meeting in connection with this club took place in November, 1900; the first President of it was the late Mr. Louis de Rochecouste; and the first club-house was a dwelling utilised for the purpose not far from the present establishment. The latter was acquired in 1909, and, standing on the summit of spacious and artistically laid-out grounds, commands an excellent view of a portion of the charming garden town.

The members of the Club de Curepipe, numbering about one hundred of the leading men of the island, are to be congratulated on the metamorphosis through which the institution has passed and the attractive combination of utility, comfort and elegance which it now exemplifies. Merchants, planters, Government officials, men of law and men of medicine meet in it and enjoy its amenities; and the hearty welcome and kind hospitality which they accorded to the editor of this volume during his sojourn in the colony will ever be amongst his most pleasant memories. The Club de Curepipe may be termed the hub of the local male social world, and is an admirable institution in every way, with ideals in accordance with the splendid characteristics for which the Mauritian gentleman is noted

The Committee of the Club is as follows:—The Hon. Emile Sauzier, K.C., President; Mr. F. V. Descroizilles, Vice-President; Mr. Edgar de Robillard, Secretary; Mr. J. Ganachaud, Auditor; Messrs. J. H. Adam, T. L. d'Arifat, E. Marrier d'Unienville, G. Rousset, A. Ulcoq, P. Goupille, and A. Lagesse.

CLUB DE CUREPIPE AND SOME OF THE MEMBERS.

CABLE COMMUNICATION.

J. R. SMITH,
Manager of the Eastern and South African Telegraph Co.'s Station in Mauritius since 1900.

THE Eastern and South African Telegraph Company has a station at Mauritius through which direct communication is maintained with Durban, Seychelles, Rodrigues, and Réunion.

The Company started operations so far back as 1870 with only a few stations and an insignificant mileage. At the end of 1903 the total length of the cables of the Eastern Telegraph Company associated with the Eastern Extension and Eastern and South African Telegraph Company exceeded 100,468 miles, exclusive of 1,528 miles of land lines and 2.300 miles leased to the Company.

The length of the line from Zanzibar to Seychelles is 1,017 knots, or 1,173 English miles, and from Seychelles to Mauritius 1,066 knots, or 1,229 miles

The deepest repairs that have yet been made were in 1874, when the Madeira cable was raised from a depth of 2,900 fathoms, or 17,400 feet (about 3½ miles), and repaired.

The annual subvention at present paid for the Mauritius-Seychelles-Zanzibar line is £28,000, divided as follows :—English Government, £10,000 ; Indian Government, £10,000 ; Seychelles Government, £1,000 ; Mauritius Government, £7,000.

The subsidy began on the 23rd November, 1893, and will end on 23rd November, 1913.

The greatest depth in which the cable from Zanzibar to Seychelles lies is 2,650 fathoms, or 15,900 English feet ; Seychelles to Mauritius 2,300 fathoms, or 13,800 feet.

The following are the names of the ships of the Company :—"Amber," "Electra," "John Pender," "Recorder," "Sentinel," "Sherard Osborne," "Duplex," "Levant I," "Levant II.," "Britannia."

The Zanzibar-Seychelles cable was completed on the 11th November, 1893, and the Seychelles-Mauritius cable on the 22nd November, 1893.

The cable between Natal and Australia, touching at Mauritius, Rodrigues, and Cocos-Keeling Island, was successfully laid in November, 1901. Its length is from Mauritius to Rodrigues 404 knots, thence to Cocos-Keeling Island 2,150 knots, and from Cocos-Keeling Island to the mainland at Perth 1,500 knots. The actual length of cable on bottom is 4,054 knots, a knot being equal to 2,028 English yards.

The Mauritius-Réunion-Madagascar cable was opened for traffic on the 13th October, 1906. The total length of this cable, which belongs to the French Government, is 132 knots from Mauritius to Réunion, and 435 knots from Réunion to Tamatave.

PORT LOUIS DRAINAGE WORKS.

THE Port Louis drainage works were begun in 1895, the sewers being designed on the separate system, and the surface drainage being carried in the street gutters to the various streams which flow into the harbour. The town is divided for drainage purposes into four districts, three of which drain by gravitation sewers into separate collecting wells, which are connected by means of syphon pipes with the pumping station near Caudan Basin. From there the sewage is pumped through cast-iron pipes for 7,000 feet to the sea outfall at the mouth of Grand River North-West, and is discharged in ten feet of water at low tide, 1,000 feet from the shore. Sewers have been laid in districts Nos. 2 and 3 ; the laying of sewers in district No. 4 is being proceeded with ; the enlargement of the pumping station has been completed ; and the additional pumps have been installed. The total length of sewers laid is 19 28 miles, and 732 properties have been connected. The amount expended on construction works in districts Nos. 2, 3, and 4 is Rs. 796,740, and on house services Rs. 470,000.

BRIDGES.

PREVIOUS to 1905, most of the road bridges of the colony were built in timber, nineteen only out of 189 being constructed in masonry or steel. The sums spent annually for maintaining these timber bridges in good state of repair have amounted to about £4,000, and, with the object of doing away with this large recurrent expenditure, the policy of replacing gradually all the timber structures in material of a durable character has, on the suggestion of Mr. P. Le Juge de Segrais, the Director of Public Works, been adopted by the Colonial Government.

GRAND RIVER SUSPENSION BRIDGE, WITH KOENIG TOWER ON THE RIGHT.

As a result, three bridges have been entirely rebuilt in masonry (arches) and three with steel super-structures. Over thirty have been rebuilt in reinforced concrete, which has proved cheaper than either masonry or steel, and practically requires no maintenance. All the ferro-concrete bridges are periodically examined and show no sign of cracking anywhere.

The existing abutments or piers of the timber bridges are generally of substantial basalt masonry, so that the super-structure only requires renewal, and this is done by blocking the road, if there is another road available within some reasonable distance, or the work is done by halves, which is naturally not so satisfactory, and is also more costly.

In some cases, however, it is necessary to rebuild the bridge entirely, either because there are no satisfactory abutments or piers, or because the position of the existing bridge is dangerous and difficult of approach, especially with the motor traffic, which is daily largely increasing.

The longest bridge in the colony is Cavendish Bridge, called after Sir Cavendish Boyle, K.C.M.G., the former Governor of the island, and completed in August, 1911. The old structure, built about the year 1856, consisted of thirty-five pairs of timber piles, spaced eighteen to twenty feet apart, across the estuary of River La Chaux, to connect the town of Mahébourg with its suburb of Ville Noire, and to establish communication between Mahébourg and an important section of the district of Grand Port.

Only light traffic, such as carts and carriages, was permissible, and now and then a roller, not exceeding five tons in weight, was allowed to be dragged over the bridge by men with the greatest precaution. Traction engines were, of course, prohibited from going over, so that those conveying sugar from the three sugar factories had to stop at the end of the bridge and transfer their loads from trailers into

CAVENDISH BRIDGE, MAHÉBOURG.

light carts carrying half a ton, which took the sugar across the bridge, either to a wharf on the opposite bank of the river for shipment in coasters to Port Louis, or to the railway station for conveyance by rail to the same place. A similar process had to be gone through again for all the estates' stores and provisions coming from Port Louis.

The new bridge was designed with a view to facilitate the traffic, and to carry a moving load of one ton per foot run, which is more than ample for the local requirements. The bridge has seven flat arches of 62 feet 6 inches span each, the piers at the springings of the arches being five feet thick, and the abutments twenty feet deep, giving a total length of 507 feet 6 inches for the portion of the work done in reinforced concrete. The approaches, measuring 82 feet and 177 feet respectively, are made in coursed rubble masonry with a finely dressed ashlar parapet.

Three years were occupied in building the bridge, at a cost of £8,637. The work was started on the 17th February, 1908, and the bridge tested on the 28th March, 1911, when, on passing a traction engine weighing seventeen tons and three trailers loaded with bags of sugar, each trailer weighing nine tons, a maximum deflection of one twenty-fourth of an inch was obtained.

The old timber bridge was built originally for a contract price of 47,000 dollars, equivalent to £9,400; the timber was naturally periodically renewed. The sums spent for repairs to the bridge for a period of nine years, from 1895 to 1904, amounted to Rs. 36,425, giving an average sum of Rs. 4,000 in round figures, or £266, for annual maintenance.

ALLISTER MACMILLAN AND HIS ASSISTANT, MAURICE GALEA, IN THE GARAGE MERVEN MOTOR CAR USED IN THE COMPILATION OF "MAURITIUS, ILLUSTRATED."

THE FAMOUS CHINA TEA-CLIPPER "SIR LANCELOT."

THIS celebrated yacht of the Indian Ocean was built in 1865 at Greenock, and proved the fastest sailing ship that ever sailed the sea. Of 886 tons register, she had a length of 197 feet 7 inches, and the depth of her hold was 27 feet. Her framework was of iron and her sheathing of wood. Everything in her construction was made subservient to speed. Before the fixing of her copper bottom, her planks from the water-line downwards were planed off, and the hard teak rendered as smooth as a ball-room floor. In order to give the vessel greater stability, and enable her to carry her immensely long masts, nearly 100 tons of "pig" iron, or "kentledge," was fitted into the open spaces along the keelson between her frames. The necessity for this deadweight may be understood by the fact that, when in racing trim and under all sail, the *Sir Lancelot* spread upwards of 46,000 square feet of canvas—probably the greatest area ever shown by any full-rigged ship. In 1869, during the fourth season of her running, she made the swiftest passage on record of any sailing ship between China and England. According to the entries made in her logbook, she left Foonchoofoo on the 17th of July; on August 7th made Anjer Light; on the 28th of the same month sighted the African coast somewhere to the east of Buffalo River; on September 11th made her number off St. Helena; passed the Lizard on October 10th; and on the 14th was berthed in the West India Docks, having made a passage of 14,000 miles in eighty-nine days against the prevailing monsoon. Her most remarkable run was while crossing the Indian Ocean, when she did by observation 354 statute miles in twenty-four hours; and this upon a westerly course in which she was meeting time, and must have gained, during that one day's work, on the parallel she was then traversing, at least twenty minutes, which would represent the equivalent of another five miles to add to the distance covered. For a consecutive week, with fresh beam winds, she kept up an average daily run of 300 miles. The most remarkable point about this vessel's extraordinary sailing qualities was her capacity of maintaining her high speed in the very lightest breeze, and the power she had of fore-reaching against an almost dead head wind.

THE "SIR LANCELOT."

The *Sir Lancelot* was often moored in Port Louis Harbour. She sailed from Muscat in September, 1892, for Calcutta, and never reached her destination, having, it is supposed, foundered in a cyclone in the Bay of Bengal.

Particulars of Captain Murdo Stewart Macdonald and Captain C.W. Brebner, F.R.G.S., F.R S.A., who, at different periods, commanded the *Sir Lancelot*, will be found amongst the biographies at the end of the volume.

CAPTAIN C. W. BREBNER, F.R.G.S., F.R.S.A.,

Former Captain of the *Sir Lancelot*, and now Captain of S.S. *Secunder*, plying between Madagascar, Réunion, Mauritius, and Rodrigues.

CAPTAIN MURDO STEWART MACDONALD,

Former Captain of the *Sir Lancelot*, and now Surveyor to *Lloyd's Register* and the Vice-Admiralty Court, Mauritius.

MAURITIUS CHAMBER OF COMMERCE.

THE Mauritius Chamber of Commerce was formed on January 22nd, 1850. Its object and duties are to receive and collect information on all matters of mercantile interest bearing upon the removal of evils and the redress of grievances so far as commerce is concerned; to communicate with authorities and individuals thereupon; to form a Code of Practice whereby the transaction of business by all engaged in it may be simplified and facilitated; and finally, to arbitrate between disputants wishing to avoid litigation, and willing to refer to and abide by the judgment of the Chamber.

According to its rules, the composition of the Chamber is thirty-six members, elected by ballot by the commercial subscribers to the Exchange Rooms. Five members form a quorum, and no member can serve for a period exceeding three years unless he be elected by ballot at a general meeting of the commercial subscribers to the Exchange Rooms specially called for that purpose. Any of the members going out may be re-elected, but no person absent from the colony is eligible for election or re-election.

The Chamber elects annually from its own body its President, Vice-President, Treasurer, and two Auditors, and has power to appoint other officers. In case of death or departure from the colony of the President or Vice-President, a special meeting of the Chamber is held to elect an acting Vice-President during the absence of the President or Vice-President. The President and Vice-President cannot be elected for two consecutive years to the same office. In all cases the President or Chairman of Committees has a casting vote.

Committees of Arbitration are formed by the President and Vice-President, composed each of five members of the Chamber, and serve in rotation every week; three members of such Arbitration Committees forming a quorum. The Committees of Arbitration hear and decide on all commercial matters submitted to them. Any party whose case has been judged by a Committee of Arbitration has the right of afterwards appealing to the whole Chamber against the decision of the Committee; but no member of a Committee of Arbitration serving in its turn can be objected to by the parties requiring judgment. The notice of appeal must be given within forty-eight hours of the delivery of the copy of decision of the Committee of Arbitration.

Where parties resorting to the Committees of Arbitration, for the settlement of questions in dispute, are not satisfied to refer their case to the Committee serving in turn, a Special Committee is called, and is formed by each party naming two members from the Chamber, these four choosing a fifth, and if they cannot agree on their choice, the fifth member is named by the Committee of Arbitration serving in its turn. The Committee so formed judges the special case, and no appeal is allowed from the decision of such Special Committee.

Applicants submitting for arbitration questions in which both parties interested are subscribers to the Exchange Rooms pay a fee of ten rupees to each member of the Arbitration Committee for his attendance, and in all other cases the fee is twenty rupees.

The President and Vice-President have the power to name a Committee for the management of the affairs of the Chamber, and another Committee for the examination of stores, each composed of five members, three of whom form a quorum.

At the Annual General Meeting, held on a day fixed within the month of January, the Annual Report of the Chamber and the Financial Statement of the Treasurer, duly audited by two Auditors, are submitted to the commercial subscribers to the Exchange Rooms.

The funds of the Chamber are applicable for the general expenses; and in case of a balance remaining with the Treasurer to the credit of the Chamber, the Committee of Management has power to direct that such balance or any portion thereof be placed in any Bank or Banks of the colony.

Books of reference, records and decisions of the Chamber are duly kept, and open at all times to members of the Exchange Rooms.

No two members of the same firm can be elected members of the Chamber nor vote at any general meeting of subscribers. But the elected member of any firm who is unable to attend any general or special meeting of the Chamber may be represented at such meeting by another member of the firm, or by a person holding the procuration of the firm.

In case of death or resignation of any member of the Chamber a general meeting of the commercial subscribers to the Exchange Rooms is called by the President to replace him by election in the usual way.

On a month's notice duly recorded in the minutes of the Chamber at any of its meetings, any member has the right of proposing to rescind, add to, or modify any of the existing Regulations, the Code of Practice, or the Commercial Tariffs; such proposition being decided by a majority of *three-fourths* of the members attending such a meeting and being in number not less than *two-thirds* of the total number of the members of the Chamber.

The Committee of Management has power from time to time to modify the Tariff of Charges to be paid by the different applicants for decisions or extracts from the Archives of the Chamber. It also has power to frame, modify, or repeal by-laws for the carrying into execution of the foregoing Regulations; such by-laws to be approved by the majority of the members of the Chamber, and, according to law, to be submitted for approval to the Governor before they are carried out.

The Chamber has power to remove the Committee of Management, the Treasurer, the Auditors, and other officers; and any difference which may arise between the Chamber and any of its members, or any person's claim by or through any member, is settled by the Committee of Arbitration.

COMMERCIAL COMMISSION,

As revised by the Chamber of Commerce of Mauritius, September, 1868.

Art. 1.—	On sales of Goods imported of all descriptions, on the nett amount if sold by auction, and on the gross amount of all other sales	5 per cent.
Art. 2.—	On sales of Colonial sugar and Colonial produce	2½ "
Art. 3.—	Purchase of Goods:	
	On Purchase effected when the Agent is in funds	2½ "
	On Purchase effected when funds are provided by the Agent	5 "
Art. 4.—	On the sale of Specie or Encashment of Bills of Exchange	1 "
Art. 5.—	On remittances of proceeds on the sale of Goods, Specie, Bills of Exchange, etc.	1 "
Art. 6.—	On Goods consigned and afterwards withdrawn, on Invoice value	2½ "
Art. 7.—	On Goods landed on account of damage incurred by the vessel and reshipment of the same—	
	When the value does not exceed Rs. 20,000	2½ "

Exceeding Rs. 20,000 and not exceeding Rs. 50,000	Not less than Rs. 500 or 2 per cent.	At the option of the consignees.
" 50,000 " " 100,000	Not less than Rs. 1,000 or 1½ per cent.	
" 100,000 " " 200,000	Not less than Rs. 1,500 or 1 per cent.	
" 200,000 " "	Not less than Rs. 2,000 or ¾ per cent.	

(The Chamber of Commerce consider the sliding scale not as a commission, but as a means of fixing a fair remuneration for the risk and trouble incurred.)

Art. 8.—	On Freight or Passage Money	5 per cent.
Art. 9.—	For collecting Freight or Passage Money	2½ "
Art. 10.—	On ships' disbursements, when the Agent is in funds	2 "
Art 11.—	On ships' disbursements, when the Consignee furnishes the funds	5 "
Art. 12.—	On disbursements, for vessels under repairs	5 "
Art. 13.—	On letters of credit and advances of funds from which no other Commission is derived	2½ "
Art. 14.—	On effecting Marine Insurance on the amount issued	½ "
Art. 15.—	On sales or purchase of houses, or other immovable property, under power of attorney	5 "
Art. 16.—	On sales or purchase of vessels whether abandoned or whether purchased or sold under power of attorney	5 "

Art. 17.—For recovery of rent ... ... 5 per cent.
Art. 18.—On affairs in dispute ... ... 5 „
Art. 19.—On affairs before the Courts and attended with legal proceedings, according to the delay and trouble, but not less than 5 per cent. on the amount received.
Art. 20.—On affairs in dispute and withdrawn before being brought to a settlement upon the actual value of claim ... ... 2½ „
Art. 21.—On protested Bills returned for recovery on the amount recovered ... ... 2½ „
Art. 22.—On funds employed at interest for parties absent, on the amount of interest received ... ... 10 „
Art. 23.—On guarantee of sales (del credere) when the term does not exceed six months, 2½ „ and ½ per cent. additional on each month beyond six months.
Art. 24.—Indorsement of Bills of Exchange or Local Bills ... ... 2½ „
Art. 25.—For the delivery of Goods from a cargo when the freight has been paid beforehand ... ... 2*s.* per ton.

N.B.—Brokerage and Auction dues are a separate charge.

The following is an extract from the Annual Report of the Chamber of Commerce for 1912:—

"A legislative event of considerable importance, and worthy of note, has been the passing of an Ordinance regulating companies and other associations. Prior to its discussion in Council a draft of the proposed Ordinance was submitted to the Chamber for consideration. A Special Committee having examined the various clauses more directly affecting commerce, recommended that the Ordinance, as a whole, should be supported; and it is satisfactory to note that several amendments suggested by the Chamber were adopted, and now form part of the law.

"In August last the Chamber received official intimation from Government that Great Britain had decided to withdraw from the Brussels Sugar Convention on the 1st September, 1913. The announcement of this decision was received with regret; and without discussing such a complicated question of economics, it seems difficult to share the optimism of the Home Government 'that the interest in the sugar-producing colonies will not be affected materially.' The decision will perhaps not tell against Mauritius as much as against some of the other colonies, but we cannot but deplore the necessity under which the Ministry felt themselves to be obliged to adopt 'a policy which does not commend itself to the inhabitants of the sugar-producing colonies.'"

B. I. S. N. CO.'S STEAMER "QUERIMBA," 4,937 tons.
Completing in Port Louis Harbour intake of a record cargo of 137,601 bags of sugar and 402 packages, totalling altogether 11,000 tons, on December 21st, 1912.

VESSELS ENTERED AND CLEARED.

Number and Tonnage of British and Foreign Vessels from various Countries ENTERED with Cargoes and in Ballast at Port Louis, Mauritius, from 1900 to 1911.

Years.	British.				Foreign.				Total.				Grand Total.	
	With Cargoes.		In Ballast.		With Cargoes.		In Ballast.		With Cargoes.		In Ballast.			
	Vessels.	Tons.	Vessels.	Tons.	Vessels.	Tons.	Vessels.	Tons.	Vessels.	Tons.	Vessels.	Tons.	Vessels.	Tons.
1900 ...	158	194,097	24	35,754	76	96,691	8	11,292	234	290,788	32	47,046	266	337,834
1901 ...	171	221,441	40	67,765	70	103,371	11	8,829	241	324,812	51	76,594	292	401,406
1902 ...	164	233,628	25	43,541	63	89,492	13	11,353	227	323,120	38	54,894	265	378,014
1903 ...	171	253,637	13	23,746	55	96,185	13	17,969	226	349,822	26	41,715	252	391,537
1904 ...	154	248,096	22	45,001	60	104,057	8	11,010	214	352,153	30	56,011	244	408,164
1905 ...	133	220,718	16	24,360	61	116,179	2	3,778	194	336,897	18	28,138	212	365,035
1906 ...	150	247,496	11	18,717	80	141,686	3	2,141	230	389,182	14	20,858	214	410,040
1907 ...	139	241,924	8	17,956	75	115,120	3	514	214	357,044	11	18,470	225	375,514
1908 ...	128	242,289	8	15,948	61	112,833	6	12,728	189	355,122	14	28,676	203	383,798
1909 ...	125	237,982	15	34,982	48	104,096	3	1,103	173	342,078	18	35,085	191	378,163
1910 ...	154	336,109	18	41,713	54	108,218	8	2,711	208	444,327	26	44,424	234	488,751
1911 ...	136	281,421	21	49,127	53	98,382	7	9,151	189	397,803	28	58,178	217	433,081

Number and Tonnage of British and Foreign Vessels from various Countries CLEARED with Cargoes and in Ballast at Port Louis, Mauritius,* from 1900 to 1911.

Years.	British With Cargoes Vessels.	Tons.	British In Ballast Vessels.	Tons.	Foreign With Cargoes Vessels.	Tons.	Foreign In Ballast Vessels.	Tons.	Total With Cargoes Vessels.	Tons.	Total In Ballast Vessels.	Tons.	Grand Total Vessels.	Tons.
1900 ...	134	154,482	50	69,214	48	57,371	37	52,039	181	211,853	87	121,253	268	333,106
1901 ...	145	183,389	58	102,015	45	68,603	34	43,585	190	251,992	92	145,600	282	397,592
1902 ...	143	178,774	49	100,933	59	82,253	16	18,074	202	261,027	65	119,007	267	380,034
1903 ...	139	184,766	46	89,195	53	94,290	15	19,991	192	279,056	61	109,186	253	388,242
1904 ...	128	193,467	46	98,721	47	84,092	20	29,555	175	277,559	66	128,276	241	405,835
1905 ...	107	175,908	44	78,655	43	86,481	21	34,654	150	262,389	65	113,309	215	375,698
1906 ...	120	205,045	40	58,479	47	91,810	33	50,186	167	296,855	73	108,665	240	405,520
1907 ...	111	200,603	32	50,334	46	84,419	33	32,607	157	285,022	65	82,941	222	367,963
1908 ...	110	210,428	29	48,879	45	93,327	23	32,617	155	303,755	52	81,496	207	385,251
1909 ...	92	170,721	47	101,767	38	79,474	12	25,025	130	250,195	59	126,792	189	376,987
1910 ...	117	251,831	51	134,133	36	54,605	26	56,947	153	306,436	83	191,080	236	497,516
1911 ...	101	220,650	54	111,950	37	57,936	23	49,074	138	278,586	77	161,024	215	439,610

* Port Louis is the only Port in the colony at which an import trade is carried on.

BANKING.

THE first attempt to establish a Bank in Mauritius was made by the Colonial Government in the early days of the British administration. Governor Farquhar, in an order dated July 23rd, 1812, appointed a committee composed of the chief members of the Civil Service, under the presidency of Mr. A. Barry, Chief Secretary, to consider whether it would prove useful to establish a Bank for Mauritius, Bourbon, and Dependencies. In March, 1813, a Government Notice appeared to the effect that "The Colonial Bank of Mauritius, Bourbon, and Dependencies" was under consideration, and that a prospectus was then in the Press. In this prospectus the Governor informed the inhabitants that in establishing the Bank he had in view the active prosperity of agriculture, the development of internal as well as external commerce of these islands, and the recourse to new taxation.

THE MAURITIUS COMMERCIAL BANK.

On April 10th the Bank opened for business, and on July 1st the first bank-notes were issued in crowns of the current value of 10 Colonial livres each. It began with a capital stock of 2,000,000 livres in hard metallic money known and current in these islands, equal to 400,000 sicca rupees or 200,000 dollars. This sum was advanced by Government for the account of the Colonial revenue, and the public were allowed to purchase to the extent of an equal sum in shares of 10,000 livres, or 1,000 dollars each, but no individual was allowed to hold more than ten shares. The Charter of this Bank, dated September 17th, 1813, authorised it to carry on business for a period of five years, reckoned from June 30th, 1813; but just when its credit had met with general confidence, it ceased operations on October 31st, 1813, on account of the refusal of the Secretary of State to sanction its establishment. Immediately afterwards Messrs. Pitot, Wiehé, Roble, Bousquet, Carcenac, Gaillardon and other shareholders of the concern, joined together, and a co-partnership for the establishment of a new Bank, under the name of "La Banque de l'Ile Maurice," was formed. The deed was drawn up by Notary Amand on November 6th, and received Government sanction by a proclamation dated December 2nd, 1813. The capital was 200,000 dollars, divided into 200 shares of 1,000 dollars each,

INTERIOR OF THE MAURITIUS COMMERCIAL BANK.

THE BANK OF MAURITIUS, LTD.

and it began business on December 20th, 1813, in the building which had been the Internal Revenue Department, and is now the central Police Office. The new establishment gradually increased in prosperity and public confidence until the disastrous fire of 1816, when such heavy losses were sustained by the greater number of persons connected with Port Louis, that public credit was shaken to its foundations, and the Bank found it necessary to call upon Government for assistance.

In a proclamation, dated October 11th, 1816, the Charter was modified, and a loan of 100,000 dollars was made to the Bank by Government on a satisfactory report of a special committee of civil servants appointed to examine into the standing and solidity of the Bank.

The Charter of the Bank expired on June 30th, 1818, but, to enable it to liquidate its business the Governor, by special proclamation of November 12th, 1817, extended it for two years. The liquidation, however, lasted till about 1826.

After the liquidation of "La Banque Gaillardon," as the Bank was familiarly called, and the cessation of business of the "Chambre d'Assurance"—an establishment which also lent money to the extent of 150,000 dollars—the want of banking facilities was felt, and several of the partners of the old Bank joined together and decided on the formation of a new Bank.

The scheme was submitted to the Secretary of State, and on October 30th, 1831, a notice by Messrs. Adrien d'Epinay and Laing appeared, announcing the authorisation given to Messrs. John Irvine, Reid, and others to establish a Bank, and stating that part of the capital should be subscribed in the Colony.

It was, however, only on June 20th, 1831, that by Letters Patent of King William IV. the Bank was granted a Charter.

On December 8th the Act was signed, and "Le Banque de Maurice" was formed. Mr. Adrien d'Epinay was appointed President; the other Directors in Mauritius were Messrs. Gaillardon, Delisse, R. Pitot, Adam, and Lagane, with Mr. H. Ritter as Secretary.

On December 24th a notice of the Secretary appeared calling upon the shareholders to pay into the hands of the cashier three-fifths of their shares in specie before January 9th, 1832.

The capital was 300,000 dollars, divided into 300 shares of 1,000 dollars each, a third of which was subscribed by the Calcutta firm of Curtenden, MacKillop and Co., who introduced 100,000 dollars in hard metallic money as their share. The office of the Bank was in the building on the Place d'Armes now occupied by Messrs. Ulcoq and Montocchio.

G DICKSON,
Manager in Mauritius of the Bank of Mauritius, Ltd.

THE MAURITIUS COMMERCIAL BANK.

F. P. MURRAY,
Managing Director of the Bank of Mauritius, Ltd.

The question of the necessity of having a new Bank concurrent with the present one having been favourably resolved by the Governor in Executive Council, a deed of partnership was drawn up by Notary Maingard on June 12th, 1838, to constitute the "Mauritius Commercial Bank," which establishment was authorised by proclamation on July 6th, 1838. Amongst the chief shareholders of the Bank then were:—Messrs. J. Blyth, H. Hunter, J. E. Arbuthnot, H. H. Griffiths, A. Garreau, H. Koenig, T. Lavergne, and E. Leclézio.

The Bank started business in the property opposite the Roman Catholic Cathedral, now belonging to Mr. Nalletamby, and then occupied by lawyers. It was there that took place the famous robbery by Chinese, who managed to obtain access to the vault by the drain (running from Poudriere Street through Hazard Street), which passed along the Bank's premises. In 1860, or thereabouts, the Bank purchased and moved into the premises it now occupies.

The first Directors of the Bank were Messrs. J. Blyth, J. E. Arbuthnot, F. Barbé, R. Bullen, G. C. Bourguignon, A. H. Giquel, H. H. Griffiths, Y. J. Jollivet, and Henry Koenig.

From the time that "La Banque de Maurice" ceased operations till 1894, the Mauritius Commercial Bank was the only local banking institution in the Colony. Branches of foreign Banks were from time to time opened. The one which met with perhaps the greatest support and certainly benefited the Colony by the amount of fresh capital it introduced, much of which was never destined to be withdrawn, was the Oriental Banking Corporation, which for many years exercised a considerable influence on the agricultural and financial affairs of the Colony. Its failure in 1885 caused great inconvenience to the planting and commercial community. It was succeeded by the New Oriental Banking Corporation, which closed its doors in 1892, after an existence of only six years.

P. R. CHALMERS,
Director of the Bank of Mauritius, Ltd.

During its long career the Mauritius Commercial Bank has rendered invaluable service to agriculture, commerce, and the Colony in general, and has passed through many a crisis successfully. It has now a capital of Rs. 2,000,000, and the fact that its reserve fund of Rs. 1,280,000 is invested in London in sterling securities has considerably strengthened the position of the Bank, as up till 1909 its reserve was invested in Mauritius. The wisdom and foresight of this action of the Directors has been amply justified by the fact that for some years past, owing to the abundance of money in the Colony, the Banks have had difficulty in finding remunerative employment for their surplus funds. An average dividend of 9½ per cent. has been distributed by the Mauritius Commercial Bank since its inception. Its agents are as follows:—

London: Lloyd's Bank, Ltd.
Paris: Mallet Fréres et Cie.
India: National Bank of India, Ltd.
Cape Colony: National Bank of South Africa, Ltd.
Australia: Union Bank of Australia, Ltd.

The Mauritius Commercial Bank sells drafts upon its agents at sight, or at thirty, forty or ninety days at the current rate of exchange. It also buys drafts upon Great Britain, France, Australia, South Africa, India, etc., and issues Letters of Credit for these countries. It likewise makes advances secured by Dock Warrants of sugar deposited in duly licensed warehouses, and, in fact, transacts banking business of all kinds.

THE BANK OF MAURITIUS, LTD.

The Bank of Mauritius, Ltd., was incorporated in London in 1894, its head office being then as now at 10, George Yard, Lombard Street, E.C.

Those chiefly responsible for its inception were the late Right Hon. the Lord Stanmore, G.C.M.G. (Chairman of the Board of Directors from 1894 to 1911), Messrs. G. W. Davidson and Maurice Ulcoq—two more of the four original Directors—and Messrs. J. A. Ferguson and Alexander Wemyss, Managers respectively in London and Mauritius.

The Late Right Hon. the LORD STANMORE, G.C.M.G.,

As Sir Arthur Hamilton Gordon, K.C.M.G., was Governor of Mauritius from 1871 to 1874, and Chairman of the Board of Directors of the Bank of Mauritius, Ltd., from 1894 to 1911.

The Bank was floated with a capital of £200,000, of which £125,550 was subscribed in fully-paid shares of £10 each, about £30,000 having been raised in Mauritius. It is governed by a Board of Directors in London, who are assisted by a local Board, or rather Advisory Committee, selected from the leading residents in the Colony.

Its premises in Mauritius are the finest commercial structure in the business centre of Port Louis.

The personnel of the Bank as at present constituted consists of four Directors—Mr. Graham Lloyd, Lord Stanmore, Mr. P. R. Chalmers, and Mr. F. P. Murray (Managing Director); Mr. W. L. MacLaren being Secretary. The local Board in Mauritius comprises the Hon. E. C. Fraser, C.M.G., the Hon. R. B. Graham, and Mr. Pierre Adam. Mr. George Dickson, the Mauritius Manager, has also a seat on the local Board.

The Bank has, since its inception, given ample evidence of the excellence of its management. The conservative and businesslike policy of the Directors has enabled them to build up a reserve fund of £90,000, while a pension fund has been started for the benefit of the staff. The report of the Royal Commission, held in the Colony in 1909, commented most favourably on the general conduct of the Bank and the policy it had pursued.

The Bank transacts the usual banking business, the purchase and sale of drafts, discounting and advances against security. Its principal bankers and agents are as follows:—

London: Barclay and Co., Ltd.
Paris: Offroy, Guiard and Co.
India and the East: The Chartered Bank of India, Australia and China.
South Africa: The Standard Bank of South Africa, Ltd.
Australia: The English, Scottish, and Australian Bank, Ltd.

COMMERCIAL PORT LOUIS.

BLYTH BROTHERS and Co., General Commission Merchants, etc.

H. M. BLYTH.

In the year 1835 an English gentleman, Mr. James Blyth, was cruising in his yacht for the benefit of his health about the Mascarenes, and called at Mauritius. To that circumstance is due the existence in the island to-day of the great business of Messrs. Blyth Brothers and Co. It is curious how apparent trivialities lead to results of the most surprising and enduring character. When Mr. Blyth landed at Port Louis he was so impressed with the opportunities it presented for commercial enterprise that he lost no time in starting a general merchandise business, which, under his able direction, made rapid progress, and which now, after seventy-eight years, has attained dimensions probably far beyond the greatest expectations of its founder.

The extensive three-storied establishment on the western side of the harbour where Messrs. Blyth Brothers and Co. conduct their numerous affairs was built in 1856, and is the largest mercantile structure in Port Louis. The impressive aspect of the counting-house, which gives employment to forty clerks, not including the wharf staff, is eloquent of the status of the business and the part it plays in local commerce. To do the right thing in the right way, to do some things better than they have been done before, to eliminate mistakes, to know both sides of a question, to anticipate requirements, to develop resources, and to act with ever-ready initiative rather than by hard-and-fast rule, are evidently the methods which Messrs. Blyth Brothers and Co. endeavour to exemplify throughout all the ramifications of their extensive trade. To detail that trade within the limits of space at our disposal is impossible. It covers every field of mercantile activity; it embraces all classes of merchandise. The annual statistics of the island show that the firm are amongst the largest exporters of sugar. The list of their agencies at the end of this sketch indicates something of the wide scope of their operations. Although far from the great European centres of manufacture and distribution, the business has advantages which many of its contemporaries do not possess. Since its commencement it has been established in London, where its interests are looked after by experts in the fluctuations of demand and supply—keen, shrewd men, who are ever on the alert for opportunities of extending its influence and activities.

The London house was originally known as H. D. and James Blyth. This title was changed in 1839 to Blyth, Greene and Co., which gave place in 1874 to Blyth, Greene, Jourdain and Co, and in 1894 it became Blyth, Greene, Jourdain and Co., Ltd. The capital of the company is £250,000, and an average dividend of 10 per cent. has been paid on the Ordinary shares, and 6 per cent. on the Preference shares.

The Chairman of the London concern is Mr. H. D. Blyth, and the Managing Directors, Messrs. J. W. Hollway and J. B. Currie.

The Directors of the Mauritius business are Messrs. H. M. Blyth

BLYTH BROTHERS AND CO.'S PREMISES.

(son of the Chairman of the London Company), H. C. Wynne and F. J. Elyard, each of whom is very popular amongst all classes of the community. Mr. H. M. Blyth is Consul for Belgium, Austria-Hungary, and Vice-Consul for Italy. Mr. Elyard is Consul for Italy and the Netherlands. The partners in Mauritius always have one of their number a member of the Board of the Mauritius Commercial Bank, in the formation of which in 1838 Mr. James Blyth was instrumental, and of which Mr. H. M. Blyth is President.

BLYTH BROTHERS AND CO.'S PREMISES FROM THE HARBOUR.
Signal Mountain in the Background.

The following are some of the concerns represented by Messrs. Blyth Brothers and Co:—

BANKS.

King, King and Co., London and India.
The Mercantile Bank of India, Limited, London and India.
Grindlay and Co., London and India.
London and County Banking Company, Ltd., London.
The Union Bank of London, Ltd., London.
German Bank of London, Ltd., London.
Samuel Montagu and Co., London.
F. Huth and Co., London.
Bank of Montreal, London and Canada.
The London City and Midland Bank, Ltd., London and Birmingham.
The Union Bank of Australia, Ltd., London and Australia.
Bank of Australasia, London and Australia.
Bank of New South Wales, London and Australia.
Antony Gibbs and Sons, London and Australia.
The Commercial Bank of Tasmania, Ltd., London and Hobart.
Brown, Shipley and Co., London and the United States.
Brown Brothers and Co., London and the United States.
The Standard Bank of South Africa, Ltd., London and South Africa.
Royal Bank of Scotland, Edinburgh.
Dresdner Bank, Berlin.
Deutsche Bank, Berlin.
Bank of Genova, Genova.
André Neuflize et Cie., Paris.
Dreyfus Fréres et Cie., Paris.
Jacob E. Dybwad, Christiania (Norway).
Kountze Brothers, New York.
The Bank of New York, New York.
Union Trust and Loan Company, Ltd., Chicago.
The Merchants' Trust and Loan Company, Ltd., Chicago.
Continental National Bank of Chicago, Chicago.
Hong Kong and Shanghai Banking Corporation, Hong Kong.
De Nationale Bank der Zuid Afrikansche Republick Beperkt, Transvaal.

STEAMSHIP AGENCIES.

Messageries Maritimes—Chargeurs Réunies.
Union Castle S.S. Company, Ltd.
British and Colonial Steam Navigation Company, Ltd.
Orient Steam Navigation Company.
Asiatic Steam Navigation Company, Ltd.

FIRE, LIFE AND MARINE INSURANCE AGENCIES.

London Assurance Corporation, Fire, Life and Marine.
Guardian Assurance Company, Ltd., Fire and Life.
Phœnix Fire Office, Fire.
The Lancashire Insurance Company, now merged in the Royal Assurance Company, Ltd., Fire and Life.
The Swiss Lloyd Transport Insurance Company, Marine.
The Alliance Marine Assurance Company.
The Ocean Marine Insurance Company, Ltd.
Reliance Marine Insurance Company, Ltd.

GENERAL.

Colonial Sugar Refining Company, Ltd., of Adelaide, Melbourne, Sydney, Brisbane and Auckland.
Anglo-Continental (late Ohlendorff's) Guano Works, London.
Asiatic Petroleum Company, Ltd., London.
Orenstein and Koppel, Arthur Koppel, Berlin.
Daimler Company, Ltd., Coventry.
Crossley Brothers, Ltd., Manchester.
Mackie and Co.'s "White Horse" Whiskey.
Mirrlees, Watson and Co., Ltd., Engineers, Glasgow (the largest makers in the world of sugar-cane machinery).

IRELAND, FRASER and Co., General Merchants and Commission Agents, Bowen Square.

The Hon. EDWARD CLEATHER FRASER, C.M.G.

GEORGE HUGH IRELAND.

HITHERTO no attempt has ever been made to portray by descriptive letterpress and photographic reproduction the commerce and industry of Port Louis. Our efforts in that direction are confronted with no more meritorious subject of recognition than the prominent and extensive business of Messrs. Ireland, Fraser and Co. — a business that has its connections throughout the world, and has been one of the principal factors in local activity for upwards of half a century. Indeed, reference to the commerce of Mauritius is synonymous with reference to this well-known concern that inspires confidence and respect throughout all the ramifications of its far-reaching trade. Its influence permeates all branches of operation in the island, from the large sugar factories to the small retail establishments whose Asiatic proprietors regard the firm as an embodiment of the white man's integrity and ability in everything amenable to mercantile endeavour.

Messrs. Ireland, Fraser and Co.'s handsome offices, erected in 1879, are in striking contrast to many of the other counting-houses in Port Louis. Much of the sugar exported from Mauritius passes through the hands of this firm, who act as shipping, insurance, and general commission agents.

Removing from the Landing Stage, Port Louis, cases of the celebrated Kerosene and Motor-Car Spirit of the Vacuum Oil Co. of South Africa, Ltd., for which Messrs. Ireland, Fraser and Co. are Agents.

The history of the business goes back to 1850, in which year it was founded by Messrs. George Ireland, Hugh Hunter, and James Fraser, under the title of Hunter, Ireland and Co. Its present designation was assumed on the 1st July, 1860, after the retirement of Mr. Hunter. The following are the names of the various partners and the dates of their connection with the firm :—

	Entered partnership.	Retired.
George Ireland	July 1st, 1850	June 30th, 1878
Hugh Hunter	,, ,,	,, 1860
James Fraser	,, ,,	,, 1878
George Walter Davidson	,, 1862	March 30th, 1886
Thomas Dykes Campbell	,, 1873	June 30th, 1881
The Hon. Edward Cleather Fraser, C.M.G.	,, 1878	Present Partner
George Hugh Ireland	,, 1879	,, ,,
John Currie Fraser	,, 1884	June 30th, 1892
George Ireland Humphrey Davidson	,, 1895	,, 1910

IRELAND, FRASER AND CO.'S OFFICES.

With the exception of Messrs. Hugh Hunter and Thomas Dykes Campbell, all the partners have been relatives; and the Hon. John Fraser, C.M.G., brother of Mr. James Fraser, was for many years a partner in the firm of Currie, Fraser and Co.

The Hon. Edward Cleather Fraser, C.M.G., born in Mauritius, was educated at Blackheath, and, from 1872 to 1875 inclusive, at Merton College, Oxford, playing in the Rugby football teams of that College during the years mentioned, and in the English International Rugby Football team of 1875. He returned to Mauritius in 1876, and entered the business in the same year, becoming a partner, as already stated, in 1878. In 1902 Mr. Fraser became a nominated member of the Council of Government of Mauritius, and in 1912 received the honour of being made a Companion of the Order of St. Michael and St. George. He is Consul for Sweden, a director of the Bank of Mauritius, Ltd., a member of the Chamber of Commerce and the Railway Board, and President of the Meteorological Society.

Mr. George Hugh Ireland was also born in Mauritius and educated at Blackheath. He joined the firm in 1877 and, as already mentioned, became a partner in 1879. He acted as nominated member of the Council of Government from 1907 to 1909. With the exception of 1907, when he was away on holiday, Mr. Ireland has been President of the Mauritius Cricket Club since 1902, and is one of the best players in the island.

Practically all the shares in the Cold Storage Co., Ltd., described on pages 378 and 379, are held by Messrs. Ireland, Fraser and Co. They have been agents for Lloyds since 1850; and amongst many other concerns represented by them are the following:—

- Union-Castle Steamship Co., Ltd.
- Ellerman-Harrison Steamship Co., Ltd.
- Commercial Bank of Australia, Ltd.
- London Salvage Association.
- Liverpool Salvage Association.
- British and Foreign Marine Insurance Co., Ltd.
- Maritime Insurance Co., Ltd.
- South British Insurance Co., Ltd.
- Royal Insurance Co., Ltd. (Fire and Life).
- Vacuum Oil Co. of South Africa, Ltd.
- Burmah Oil Co., Ltd.
- Cox's Shipping Agency, Ltd.
- Geo. Wheatley and Co.

THE MAURITIUS FIRE INSURANCE COMPANY, Church Street.

THE Mauritius Fire Insurance Company was established in March, 1855, with a capital of Rs. 400,000, which was increased in October, 1863, to Rs. 2,000,000, of which Rs. 600,000 have been paid up. It has a reserve fund of Rs. 544,262. The great fire in Port Louis on October 24th, 1877, cost the Company Rs. 200,000. The still greater conflagration in the city in July, 1893, involved it in a loss of Rs. 600,000. An average dividend of 12 per cent. per annum has been paid during the last ten years.

The Company issues policies which include the risks of fire caused by lightning or the explosion of gas or steam, at premiums varying according to the nature of the risk. It also insures against risk of fire from neighbours—*risque du voisin*.

The Company renounces all claims and right of action against the insured when a fire accidentally begins on his premises, and shall cause to other premises damages for which the Company is responsible.

The insurance of the tenant's risk (*risque locatif*) is one-fourth of the ordinary premium when the property is already insured by the Company, and the whole when the property is not insured by the Company. The premium for the *risque du voisin* is fixed by mutual agreement.

Policies are delivered for a period of five years on the payment of all premiums for four years, and corresponding reduction is made on the premium for insurance effected for three or four years.

The present Board of Directors is as follows:—Mr. A. Larcher (President), Mr. W. H. Edwards, Dr. M. E. X. Nalletamby (Vice-President), Messrs. N. Couve, J. Hein, F. Descroizilles, E. D. de Spéville, A. Lagesse, and M. Montocchio. The Secretary is Mr. A. R. Pitot, B.A.

TAYLOR, SMITH and Co., Ship and Boat Builders, Engineers and Electricians, Ship Chandlers and Stevedores, etc.

ALEXANDER TAYLOR.

THE extensive business of Messrs. Taylor, Smith and Co. is one of the largest industrial undertakings in Mauritius, and is well calculated to dispel the erroneous ideas of those who, unacquainted with the island, consider local facilities and resources a negligible quantity. The premises of this prominent firm, very advantageously situated on one side of the harbour, occupy an area of between three and four acres, and their numerous departments, carefully and cleverly organised, afford instructive object lessons in the benefits of specialisation in materials, methods, and executive ability. Within this busy and important place are employed from 500 to 600 men, whose operations range through many branches of skilled work.

The large stacks of logs and planks in the lumber sheds are constantly replenished by shipments from overseas, and are requisitioned for the firm's activities. They are the principal builders of the lighters employed in the harbour for handling cargo, and also of the coasting vessels used for the transport of sugar from the various estates to the docks in Port Louis. The firm's patent slipway is continually employed in cleaning and repairing all kinds of craft; and their careening hulk is also kept busy taking out heavy lifts or heaving down ships, and by it vessels up to 500 tons can be easily dealt with.

Their equipment and position enable Messrs. Taylor, Smith and Co. to deal promptly and efficiently with all kinds of repairs to steamers and sailing vessels. The powerful machinery in their engineering section is made subservient to mechanical work of every description, and enables the firm to complete with economy and rapidity the largest contracts with which they may be entrusted.

The firm supply every shipping requisite from the proverbial "needle to an anchor" They are the leading local firm providing fresh water to the shipping, for which purpose they have two steam water-boats capable of supplying 400 tons daily. They are also stevedores to all the principal shipping lines using the port.

As electrical engineers Messrs. Taylor, Smith and Co. operate likewise with noteworthy skill and enterprise in everything associated therewith. Electric lighting has been in use in Mauritius for many years, but since the firm's introduction of electricity in 1909 for driving sugar-mill machinery, great economies have been effected in the various local factories where their work in that direction has been performed. They are local agents for the principal British manufacturers of electric and hydraulic machinery, of which they always keep on hand a large and well-assorted stock embracing everything of the kind that a sugar factory can need.

An addition to the business in 1912 was a motor garage, replete with all the best brands of tyres and accessories; while a competent staff of mechanics, aided by an excellently-fitted machine shop, look after the repairs to cars.

The firm's town office is situated near the Post Office. Their telegraphic address is "Blacksmith, Mauritius," and they use the 5th edition of the A B C code, Engineering code, etc.

The business was established about half a century ago under the title of Black and Smith, which was changed in 1908 to its present style of Taylor, Smith and Co. The original founders are deceased, and the personnel of the firm now comprises Mr. Alexander Taylor, principal; Mr. George Anderson Smith, Mr. John

JOHN GORDON SMITH.

GEORGE ANDERSON SMITH.

ERNEST DOUGLAS PEARMAIN.

TAYLOR, SMITH AND CO.'S CAREENING HULK.

MOTOR BOAT "MITE." Built by Taylor, Smith and Co.

Gordon Smith, and Mr. Ernest Douglas Pearmain, all of whom are actively engaged in the supervision of the business. Mr. Alexander Taylor is a native of Speymouth, N.B,, and his well-merited success testifies to the business enterprise and ability of the Scot. Mr. James Smith, one of the founders of the concern, was also a native of Speymouth, and his sons already mentioned have succeeded him in the business. Mr. Pearmain, who is in charge of the Electrical and Motor Departments, was born and educated at Richmond, Surrey, and is a member of the Institute of Electrical Engineers, London.

TAYLOR, SMITH AND CO.'S PATENT SLIPWAY.

We may add that Mr. Taylor's eldest son, George, served his apprenticeship in London as an engineer, and is now qualifying at sea for his B.O.T. certificate of chief engineer, with the intention of joining the firm in the near future. His fitness for that capacity is evident by the first prize awarded to him for his drawings and models of steamship machinery at the Founders' Exhibition, London, in 1910.

TAYLOR, SMITH AND CO.'S PREMISES.

ADAM and Co., Merchants and Commission Agents.

THIS business has the distinction of being the oldest in Port Louis. In Messrs. Adam and Co.'s offices is an ancient letter-book containing copies of the firm's correspondence so far back as 1802, and in which reference is made to the stirring events at the beginning of the nineteenth century, when Napoleon Buonaparte was making the French arms glorious, and the Isle of France had not yet passed into the possession of the British.

The business was founded by a Mr. Pipon, and when he was joined in partnership by a Mr. Bell it became known as Pipon, Bell and Co. Its title was next changed to Pipon, Adam and Co., which was continued until 1897, when the present designation was assumed.

Mr. Charles Felix Henry Adam, grand-nephew of the founder, and the gentleman who first gave the Adam name to the concern, had been a colonel in the French army, but became a British subject in Mauritius, and died in the island in 1854. After his death the business was conducted by his sons, Louis Gustave and Charles Felix Henry Adam. Mr. Louis Gustave Adam was an administrator of the Bureau Veritas of Paris, and died in London in 1894. His brother, Mr. Charles Felix Henry Adam, was decorated with the coveted French distinction of the Legion of Honour; and for his fervent Catholicism was also decorated by the Pope with the honour of

1. LOUIS GUSTAVE ADAM. 2. CHARLES FELIX HENRY ADAM.
3. CHARLES FELIX HENRY ADAM (Grand-nephew of Mr. Pipon). 4. OCTAVE ADAM. 5. PIERRE ADAM.

Commander of the Order of St. Gregory the Great. He was a very able and highly-respected member of the Council of Government of Mauritius, and was President of the Comité Commercial Consultatif Français, and was also Conseiller du Commerce Exterieur de la France. He died at Paris in 1903.

The present partners are his sons, Messrs. Pierre and Octave Adam. Mr. Pierre Adam is President of the Chamber of Commerce and is a director of the Bank of Mauritius, Ltd., the Albion Dock Co., and the General Electric Supply Co. of Mauritius, Ltd. Mr. Octave Adam is a director of the Mon Loisir Sugar Estate Co.

Messrs. Adam and Co. are general merchants and commission agents and extensive exporters of sugar. They are also importers of wines, chemicals, tramway materials, etc., etc., and are agents for the Clan Line of Steamers, Ltd., La Compagnie Havraise Péninsulaire de Navigation à Vapeur, the Bureau Veritas, La Banque de la Réunion, Le Comité des Armateurs de France, Les Assureurs Maritimes Français, the Alliance Assurance Co., Ltd., the Commercial Union Assurance Co., Ltd., the Union Marine Insurance Co., Ltd., La Foncière (Compagnie Lyonaise Réunie), the Sugar Machinery Manufacturing Co., and the Gandy Belting Co.

Messrs. Adam and Co.'s telegraphic address is "Adagio, Mauritius," and the codes they use are A1, A B C—4th and 5th editions—Scott's, Watkins', and Lieber's.

LES FORGES ET FONDERIES DE MAURICE, LIMITED,

Route Nicclay, Port Louis, and Rose Belle, Grand Port.

LLEWELLYN JONES,
Manager of Les Forges et Fonderies.

THE Forges and Foundries of Mauritius!—truly an imposing and comprehensive title, but one which is well justified by the wide scope and extent of the business so named. It has three establishments—two in Route Nicolay, Port Louis, and the other at Rose Belle—which combined occupy 10,000 square metres of land, and give employment to 400 men. The Company's chief establishment in the capital is prominent amongst the most noteworthy of the local undertakings The various buildings form a large square, in which are many Flamboyant (*Poinciana Regia*) trees, and a venerable Banyan with numerous long tendrils making their way slowly but surely from the leafy branches towards the sustenance of the ground. Around the trees, with their welcome, cool shade, pulsates the big business—brain and muscle and machinery, steam power utilised in many ways, and engineering knowledge and skill exemplified in keeping with the mechanical ingenuity of the age. This extensive establishment is a place of specialisation, where many crafts are in harmonious combination for the minimum expenditure of time and labour and the perfection of process and result.

Facing the entrance is the office, conterminous to which is the draughtsmen's department, where experts prepare drawings that show at a glance the outlines of the multifarious objects, great and small, made by the Company. In one of the buildings other experts fashion wooden patterns, which the moulders in the foundry use for forming in the mould the designs of the various castings that range in every conceivable shape up to six tons in weight. After the wooden patterns have been carefully extracted the moulds are ready for the molten metal. Out in the open is a great assortment of scrap iron—innumerable worn and broken things that await resurrection to new forms of utility by being melted in the intense heat of the two Thwaites cupolas, made by the well-known firm of that name at Bradford, England. Opposite to the cupolas is a building called the "Fan Department," in which a Robey portable steam engine of between fifteen and twenty horse-power operates a Roots blower beside it, by means of which a mighty air pressure is forced through underground pipes to the fires in the cupolas, and the necessary melting heat obtained. Through an aperture in each cupola the liquid metal is received in massive cauldrons, which are run on tramway trucks into the foundry, where movable cranes convey the cauldrons to the various moulds into which the liquid metal is poured, and where it solidifies quickly. One of the cranes in the foundry has a lifting capacity of twenty tons, which is considerably in excess of the capacity required, but is a wise provision against any likelihood of a breakdown and the calamitous results that might ensue through a cauldron of liquid metal falling amongst the men.

Although the Company can make, as we have said, castings up to six tons in weight, that does not limit, however, the weight and size of some of their enormous articles of manufacture. They have made three of the largest sugar-

OFFICES OF LES FORGES ET FONDERIES.

pans in Mauritius, each of them having a capacity of twenty-eight tons masscuite; indeed, there is probably not a single sugar factory in the island that does not include in its equipment something manufactured by this enterprising Company, who compete very successfully with their oversea rivals in the production of every kind of machinery required in the sugar industry.

FITTING AND ERECTING SHOP, LES FORGES ET FONDERIES.

But although the foundry is interesting and impressive, it is eclipsed in comparison with the perspective of the machine shop, where enormous lathes, drilling, boring, punching machines and other contrivances operate with wonderful power and precision. While specialising in sugar-mill requirements, the Company also undertake repairs to locomotives, traction engines, steamships' boilers and machinery, and, in fact, everything to which their splendid equipment can be made subservient. The premises have an excellent tramway system, and include various warehouses filled with the miscellaneous articles required on the estates.

A few yards nearer town, on the opposite side of Route Nicolay, the Company have a very large garage, which they opened in 1912, and which provides accessories of every description as well as all facilities for the renovation and storage of motor cars. In this section three pits have been constructed in such a way that repairs to the under parts of cars are very easily and readily effected. The branch at Rose Belle is similar to the chief establishment in Port Louis, but on a smaller scale.

The business is the oldest of the kind in Mauritius, and was established about 1850 under the designation of Barron Bros. It was afterwards carried on under the name of Autard de Bragard, which gave place in turn to Paturau, Fontaine and Smith. In 1879 it was taken over by a limited liability company, with a capital of Rs. 250,000, and its present title was then assumed. The average dividend paid is 10 per cent., and the Company have a Reserve Fund of Rs. 337,704. The directors are Mr. Geo. Dickson (President), the Hon. J. J. Gibson, Messrs. Louis Nöel, V. Huteau, M. Montocchio, and E. Rouillard.

SECTION OF MACHINE SHOP, LES FORGES ET FONDERIES.

The manager, Mr. Llewellyn Jones, a native of Yorkshire, is a member of the Institute of Engineers and Shipbuilders of Scotland, the British Astronomical Association, and the West India Committee. Before taking up his present position, in 1910, he was for many years engaged in connection with the sugar factories in Demerara and Trinidad.

SCOTT and Co., General Merchants and Commission Agents, Corderie and Church Streets.

History records that in former times the Book of Proverbs used to be published in separate form in Scotland and carried in the pockets of the merchants there. Whether or not the wise precepts of that inestimable compilation should be considered among the causes instrumental in the formation of the keen business acumen ascribed to the Scot, it cannot be denied that the men from northern Britain are to be found occupying many of the foremost positions in the commercial centres of the Empire, as well as in remote parts of the earth where civilisation has scarcely penetrated. Mauritius is not lacking in examples of Scottish enterprise and ability, and prominent amongst these is the business of Messrs. Scott and Co. — a business owned and managed by men born and bred in the land of the thistle and the heather. It was founded so far back as 1830 by two Scotsmen,

JAMES MARIE BRODIE.

The Hon. ROBERT BALFOUR GRAHAM.

Messrs. Scott and Bell, who have long passed away. The business has outlived nearly all its early contemporaries. Firmly established and ably directed it has withstood many seasons of commercial depression, the development of new rivals, and the growth of competition; and after its long existence it is to-day greater and more flourishing than ever, with a record of integrity behind it of which its proprietors may well be proud. These gentlemen are the Hon. Robert Balfour Graham—nominated member of the Council of Government, director of the Bank of Mauritius, Ltd., and Consul for Germany, Norway, and Denmark — who entered the business in 1879 and became a partner in 1887; Mr. James Marie Brodie, who joined the firm in 1887 and became a partner in 1907; and Mr. Arthur McIrvine, who also became a partner in 1907 after having served in the concern since 1891.

ARTHUR McIRVINE.

Messrs. Scott and Co. are one of the largest commercial houses in Mauritius, and they have nine warehouses containing extensive stocks of provisions, liquors, general hardware and estates' supplies, sugar-mill machinery, building materials, etc. One of their warehouses is devoted entirely to Gossage's soap, for which they are sole agents here, and of which they import on an average 3,500 boxes of 35 lbs. each monthly. Twenty-two persons are employed in the firm's commodious and well-appointed offices at the corner of Corderie and Church Streets.

Messrs. Scott and Co.'s telegraphic address is "Scott, Mauritius," and the codes they use are A B C —4th and 5th editions—Watkins', Scott's, Lieber's, Bentley's.

They are agents for the following:—

- British India Steam Navigation Co., Ltd.
- Deutsche Ost Afrika Linie.
- Germanischer Lloyd.
- Registro Italiano.
- Bank of Scotland.
- Hong Kong and Shanghai Banking Corporation.
- Commercial Banking Company of Sydney.
- Colonial Bank of Australia.
- National Bank of New Zealand.
- African Banking Corporation, Ltd.
- Vacuum Oil Company.
- Standard Life Assurance Co.
- New York Board of Underwriters.
- Verein Hamburger Assecuradeure.
- Bremen Assuranz Verein.
- Sweriges Angfartygs Assurance Forening (Goteborg).
- Italia Societa d'Assicurazioni Maritime Fluviale Terresti (Genova).
- North China Insurance Co.
- South British Insurance Company of New Zealand.
- North German Insurance Co.
- Assicurazioni Generali in Trieste.
- Triton Insurance Co., Ltd.
- Magdeburg Fire Insurance Co.
- Nord-West Deutsche Versicherung Gesellschaft.

TARDIEU and Co., "FORGES COLONIALES," Port Louis, and St. Pierre, Moka.

THE large business of Messrs. Tardieu and Co. is an admirable example of the engineering activity created and sustained by the extensive sugar and shipping interests of Mauritius. It is essentially a Mauritian undertaking that has always been supported by Mauritian capital, even through the severe financial crisis of 1910; and, managed by very able natives of the island, has performed noteworthy pioneer work in connection with every mechanical improvement tending to benefit the local sugar industry, particularly so in the introduction of green-megas furnaces, juice-heaters, crystallisers, etc.

LATHE DEPARTMENT, "FORGES COLONIALES."

The concern was started about 1870 by Messrs. E. de Rosnay and François, who carried it on until 1882, when it was formed into a company bearing the name of Les Forges, Fonderies, et Constructions Coloniales. Prosperous since its inception, the business has undergone steady development, and, besides the chief premises, which occupy nearly the whole of the square bounded by Bourbon, Rémy Ollier, Corderie, and Prince Regent Streets, the firm have now for their foundry an establishment about a mile away in Route Nicolay, as well as branch works at St. Pierre, in the district of Moka.

The aspect of their machine shops, with their numerous lathes—one of which will take gear wheels and calandrias, etc., up to fifteen feet in diameter—their radial and other drilling contrivances, their shears, punching apparatus, boring mills, planers, pipe and plate shapers, etc., demonstrates that no effort has been spared to keep pace with the latest progress in mechanical equipment and engineering skill.

In the blacksmiths' department the fires of many forges are seen, and the ringing of the sledge hammers and the heavy thuds of the steam hammers contribute to the industrial chorus of the works. Contrasted therewith the neighbouring pattern-makers' department appears less strenuous to the visitor, but probably not so to the dark-complexioned men who there cleverly fashion the wooden models of all shapes and sizes which the moulders in the foundry use for their castings. The excellent equipment of the foundry includes rotating cranes for dealing with castings up to six tons in weight, as well as for the conveyance to the moulds of the molten metal from the three cupolas that are operated by a Root's air blower.

The most impressive section of the works is doubtless the fitting and erecting shop, where every piece of machinery made by Messrs. Tardieu and Co. is assembled and tested in the most thorough manner under expert supervision. This department is furnished with a travelling crane of fifteen tons capacity, as well as with pits that make it possible for every apparatus emanating from the establishment to be erected and checked before delivery—a very commendable and successful method to which the firm strictly adhere.

FITTING AND ERECTING DEPARTMENT, "FORGES COLONIALES."

Messrs. Tardieu and Co.'s chief operations are devoted to the manufacture, supply, and repair of sugar-factory machinery; and while their versatility in this direction includes everything pertaining to the complete equipment of sugar production, mention may be made of their crystallisers, which have considerably increased the output of first sugars. Reference must also be made to their vacuum pans, of which they have supplied many to the local factories, and which have given in every case unqualified satisfaction. Large sugar-crystals are produced in these pans in minimum time, even when operated

MAURICE C. REGNARD. AUGUSTE ESNOUF.
ALFRED LECLEZIO. FERNAND PATURAU.

by waste steam only. They all have a patent large section door, and the bottom, cupola, and belt of each are made in one single solid casting.

Messrs. Tardieu and Co. have many clients in the shipping trade and, with their trained workmen and staff of skilled engineers, have repeatedly had opportunities of repairing large disabled steamers. Cases are on record of temporary repairs executed by them having been ultimately accepted as permanent.

They are also agents for several firms of machine-makers and other specialists in Great Britain and the Continent, and as such transact no small amount of import trade.

The general management of the business is vested in Mr. Fernand Paturau, the senior partner, who is assisted by the other technical partners, Messrs. Auguste Esnouf, Alfred Leclézio, and Maurice C. Regnard.

CURRIMJI JEEWANJI and Co., General Merchants and Commission Agents, Hospital Street.

Messrs. Currimji Jeewanji and Co. are the largest Mahommedan firm in Mauritius, and have been established here since 1892. Although importing goods of many kinds from England and Australia, their principal trade is in rice, grain, dholl, ghee, flour, lentils, oil, oats, bran, salt, etc., which they receive from India mostly, and supply in large quantities to the sugar estates. They are also general commission merchants and extensive exporters of sugar. They have six warehouses in Port Louis.

The business was founded by three brothers—Mr. Noorbhoy Jeewanji, who looks after their establishment at Calcutta; Mr. Currimji Jeewanji, who supervises the one at Bombay; and Mr. Hossen Bhoy Jeewanji, the partner resident in Mauritius. All of them are natives of Bora, Bombay, and of the Bora caste, of which there are only one or two others in the island.

Under the name of Currimji, Noorbhoy and Co. the firm have branch offices in Réunion. Their various telegraphic addresses are as follows:—"Currimji," Mauritius and Réunion; "Noorbhoy," Calcutta; and "Contrive," Bombay.

THE MAURITIUS ESTATES AND ASSETS COMPANY, LTD.,
Offices and Stores: Arabian Dock.

A BUSINESS that gives employment to about 10,000 people is certainly one worth talking about. Such is the Mauritius Estates and Assets Company, Ltd., the largest undertaking in the island. Formed in 1890 this concern took over the assets in Mauritius of the Oriental Banking Corporation which had gone into liquidation, these assets in land representing at that time one-tenth of the entire island. In 1892 the new undertaking was seriously handicapped by the terrific hurricane which has made that year ever memorable in the annals of Mauritius; and it is not to be wondered at that it took the Company about fifteen years to recover from the great misfortune it sustained.

The estates of the Company under cultivation are as follows:—

	Acres.
Beau Champ ...	2,843
Olivia and Beau Vallon ...	1,342
Belle Rive ...	2,108
Rose Belle and annexes, La Rosa, New Grove, and Mare d'Albert ...	2,858
Tamarin, Clarence, and Wolmar ...	6,194
Total acreage ...	15,345

The estates which the Company have abandoned, and which are in process of "morcellement," are Clemencia, Melrose, Midlands, Chamarel, La Louise, Bananes. Cressonville, Espérance, Rivière Créole, Bon Accueil, Mont Ida, Nouvelle Découverte, Triolet.

The Company's output of sugar during the last ten years has been as follows:—

	Tons.		Tons.
1903 ...	13,150	1908 ...	12,265
1904 ...	10,300	1909 ...	16,580
1905 ...	13,600	1910 ...	15,270
1906 ...	15,900	1911 ...	10,586
1907 ...	11,100	1912 ...	14,800

Forty thousand pounds are being spent by the Company in equipping their sugar factories at Beau Champ, Rose Belle, and Tamarin with new machinery of the latest type.

Illustrations of Beau Champ Factory appear on pages 227 and 235.

The Company has a share capital of £100,000 and Mortgage Debentures of £350,000.

The able and genial attorney and commercial manager, Mr. Arthur J. Broad, whose portrait appears on page 209, is one of the most prominent and popular men in Mauritius, and has been identified with the Company since 1894. The accountant and auditor, Mr. Charles W. Rock, F.S.A.A., is another well-known and esteemed Englishman.

CURRIE, FRASER and Co., General Merchants and Commission Agents,
33, Corderie Street.

LOUIS H. G. SCOTT.

DEMAND and supply are the two weights that keep the balance of trade at a proper and workable level, and adjust the scales of commerce in such a manner as to enable the people to reap the benefits of a fairly even level of prices for the various commodities they require. This law is part of our political economy, expressing the relation between production and consumption; and in the many ramifications of demand and supply the vocation of the commission merchant is one of the most noteworthy departments of modern activity. In Messrs. Currie, Fraser and Co. it has long-experienced representatives with thorough knowledge of local conditions and requirements. Their operations are not confined to any class of goods, but range through general merchandise of every description. They are agents for Messrs. A. and W. Smith and Co., Ltd., Glasgow, the well-known manufacturers of sugar-mill machinery; B. F. Avery and Son, New York, whose ploughs are held in great esteem throughout the world; Craigellachie-Glenlivet Distillery Co., Ltd.; Northern Fire Insurance Co., Ltd.; and many other notable concerns.

The business was first established as J. and A. Guthrie, and for many years carried on under that name until 1869, when it became Currie, Fraser and Co. The partners are Mr. Robert Heaton, who resides in Liverpool, and looks after its interests there; and Mr. Louis H. G. Scott, resident in Mauritius.

The firm's telegraphic address is "Currie, Mauritius," and the codes used by them are the A B C, 4th and 5th editions, and Watkins'.

ENTRANCE TO THE NEW MAURITIUS DOCK CO.'S PREMISES.

NEW MAURITIUS DOCK CO.'S PREMISES.

MIXING SUGAR AT THE NEW MAURITIUS DOCK CO.'S WAREHOUSES FOR MESSRS. JACOBS AND SONS, FOR SHIPMENT TO SOUTH AFRICA.

NEW MAURITIUS DOCK CO.'S COAL DEPÓT.

NEW MAURITIUS DOCK COMPANY.

In 1876, the year in which the New Mauritius Dock Company was founded, the sugar crop of the island was 115,000 tons. During the last three years it has been as follows:—1910, 242,666 tons; 1911, 210,987 tons; and 1912, 163,047 tons. This great increase has called into requisition corresponding development in storage accommodation in Port Louis, of which the extensive buildings and admirable resources of the New Mauritius Dock Co. are a fitting illustration.

This Company took over in 1876 the business that had been conducted for about fifteen years previously under the name of the Mauritius Dock Co., hence the word "New" in the title of the later concern. The additions and improvements which the New Mauritius Dock Co. have effected in their premises and equipment from 1876 to the present time have cost about Rs. 600,000, *i.e.*, 60 per cent. of the capital; and the costs of the up-keep of the establishment have amounted in the same period to upwards of Rs. 800,000. At the beginning of their operations the Company had accommodation for between 50,000 and 60,000 tons of sugar. To-day they have accommodation for 100,000 tons, or about double their former capacity. In 1876 they had one tug and twenty-four lighters. Now they have two tugs and thirty-six lighters capable of carrying 1,624 tons. By means of their excellent facilities, which include two cranes—one operated by steam—the Company can load or unload the cargo of a steamer with wonderful celerity, as was the case, for instance, with the S.S. *Bendu*, which they loaded with 3,200 tons of sugar in thirty hours. Another example of the rapidity of their work was afforded by the 700 tons of coal which they placed on board His Majesty's troopship *Dufferin* in sixteen hours.

P. EVANOR PIAT.

In 1876 the area occupied by the Company's buildings was three acres and a half. Their forty-nine stores now cover six acres and a half. Throughout the buildings is a tramway system of four kilometres, which was constructed in 1901, and greatly expedites the handling of the extensive shipments which pass through the Company's hands. On their thirteen large scales about 1,600 tons of sugar can be weighed daily.

The Company's premises are bounded on the western side by a stretch of water, or basin of the harbour, equal to three acres in extent, on the opposite side of which is the "Caudan," owned jointly by the New Mauritius Dock Company and the Albion Dock Company, where 80,000 tons of coal can be stored. This place, which comprises well-built stores and fourteen acres of land, used to be the locale of the Royal Engineers, and was purchased from the Government by the two Companies. It is very advantageously situated close to the railway station, with which it is connected by a branch line.

The taxes paid by the New Mauritius Dock Co. to the Government of Mauritius and the Municipality of Port Louis amount to about Rs. 20,000 annually. A very large number of mules and carts are employed in the business. The clerical staff numbers between fifty and sixty persons, and the Company give employment to about 200 indentured Indians, who are, of course, supplemented by hundreds of casual men according to the work in hand.

The capital of the Company is Rs. 1,000,000, and the average dividend paid is about 5 per cent. half-yearly. The Board of Administration is as follows:—The Hon. G. A. Ritter, C.M.G., President; Mr. G. V. de K/Vern, K.C., Vice-President; Messrs. A. Larcher, H. G. Ducray, J. Mallac, and A. Piat: The Manager is Mr. P. Evanor Piat, who has occupied that position since 1908.

It is interesting to note that the building in which the Directors hold their meetings was the first Observatory of Mauritius.

LEWIS P. ROGERS, General Import and Export Merchant, Warehouseman, Ship Owner, Cartage Contractor, etc., Church Street.

Mr. Lewis Rogers is one of the most prominent of the local merchants, and the scope of his operations is certainly wide and varied. Born in Mauritius in 1851, he began business here in 1882, and by his enterprise and ability has built up, from a small beginning, a concern that extends its influence in many directions and contributes materially to the commerce of Mauritius. He is, for instance, an extensive importer of provisions, hardware, textiles, wines and spirits, etc., and as a commission merchant operates with the success that comes through exhaustive knowledge and experience of local conditions and requirements. He is also a ship owner, coal and timber merchant, cartage contractor, and money lender. He holds large interests in the Diego and Peros Oil Company and the sugar industry of Mauritius. The bulk of the shares in the Ile d'Ambre Sugar Estate Co., Ltd., are owned by him, and he is agent for Grand Bay Sugar Estate and Aloe Fibre Factory, which used to be his own property, but which he sold. He is also agent for Joli Bois Sugar Estate. At Ile d'Ambre he has a rum distillery, which produces 5,000 litres of rum per day from December to May. In it is also made alcohol for lamps, etc., which is sold at the rate of fifty gallons for Rs. 55.

Mr. Rogers is owner of much property in Port Louis; and his warehouses in different parts of the city provide accommodation for 188,000 bags of sugar, his resources in this direction being well taken advantage of by local and foreign firms. Amongst his sailing ships are the *Jone*, trading between Singapore and Mauritius, and the *E. J. Spence*, which brings to him from Australia coal, flour, oats, etc.

Mr. Rogers is agent for many European firms, including the well-known German company, Sociedad Vinicola, whose wines and spirits afford a selection of the most varied description.

KEMPTON, WOOD and Co., successors to JOHN GODDARD and Co., Merchants, Port Louis and London.

MESSRS. KEMPTON, WOOD AND CO., with the original firm of John Goddard and Co., have been transacting an extensive trade with Mauritius for the last twenty-five years. Their business up till 1906 had been entrusted to local agents, but in that year they opened their own branch here under the management of one of their partners, Mr. Welby R. B. Read. Early in 1908 the firm sent out Mr. C. W. Jackson, who has since been in charge of this branch; and during the past three or four years their general trade has very considerably increased, not only in imports, but also in exports of local products, particularly sugar, of which they are now amongst the principal shippers.

C. W. JACKSON.

Going back to the earlier days of this firm's existence, when the business had been carried on by the late John Goddard at 81, Gracechurch Street, London, for some thirty years, the records show that their operations had been of a very varied nature, as they successively traded in widely different directions. For many years their attention had been chiefly confined to the Continental countries, where they obtained powerful connections about the time of the Franco-German War; and on the capitulation of Paris in 1871, Messrs. John Goddard and Co. were one of the foremost firms to run very large consignments of provisions and live stock into that city for its relief.

At a later date the firm were largely interested in the petroleum industry with the United States of America and in the importation of coffee, etc., from South America.

Mr. John Goddard amassed an immense fortune in the course of his commercial career, and on retiring in 1903 he left his business to Messrs. Alfred Kempton, Charles S. Wood, and Welby R. B. Read, who had all been associated with the firm for many years. Mr. Charles S. Wood is now the sole principal of Kempton, Wood and Co., whose head offices are at No. 15, St. Mary Axe, London. Their telegraphic addresses are "Goddard, Port Louis," and "Goddard, London," the codes used being Private, A B C—5th Edition—AI., and Lieber's.

Among their most important agencies are the following:—

Norwich Union Fire Insurance Society, Ltd.
State Assurance Co., Ltd.
Robert Barbour and Brother, Ltd., Manchester.
Kearley and Tonge, Ltd.
Lever Brothers. Ltd.
Vinolia Co., Ltd.
Blondeau et Cie.
Hodgson and Simpson, Ltd.
Benjamin Brooke and Co., Ltd.
Schweppes, Ltd.
Moses Risk and Sons, Ltd.
I. P. Clarke and Co., Leicester.
Schröder and Schlyer and Co., Bordeaux.
André Givelet et Cie, "St. Marceaux," Champagne.
L. T. Piver and Co., Paris.
P. F. Esbensen, Copenhagen.
James Buchanan and Co., Ltd.
Brush Electrical Engineering Co., Ltd.
B. F. Goodrich and Co., Ltd. (Motor Tyres).

A. LAGESSE, Grain Merchant, etc., Church Street.

A. LAGESSE.

WHEN attention is directed to the business of Mr. A. Lagesse an example is obtained of the class of undertakings that exemplify specialisation, which is the trend in every department of commerce and industry, science and art. Mr. Lagesse is a specialist in grain, and what he does not know about it may be relegated to the limbo of the negligible. His knowledge and experience of rice, oats, barley, beans, and other staple products have been acquired by a lifetime devoted to their importation and sale; and his extensive warehouses with their large stock in Church Street testify to the extent of his trade. But the distinctive feature of his business is that it is confined almost wholly to the supply of the sugar estates. It was established in 1852 under the name of Lagesse and Co. by his father, who died in 1904; and when Mr. A. Lagesse became its proprietor in 1885 he gave it his own name.

SECTION OF CHURCH STREET SHOWING A. LAGESSE'S PREMISES.

Mr. Lagesse is one of the most esteemed and influential merchants of the old French stock, and is Chairman of the Constance Sugar Estate, Managing Director of Le Vallon Sugar Estate, and a Director of the St. Barondon Fish and Manure Co. and the Mauritius Tea Estate. He also is a keen sportsman and is owner of several fine hunting grounds in the island. An illustration of one of his "chasses" appears on page 169.

THE MAURITIUS CENTRAL RUM WAREHOUSE CO.

THE Mauritius Central Rum Warehouse Co. was formed in 1882, and took over the business which had been founded in 1869 by Mr. Désire Maigrot. The premises occupy about an acre of land, and through the large storage warehouse passes most of the rum produced in Mauritius. They are under the supervision of Government inspectors, and provide great facilities and advantages for the levying of duty and the storage and dispatch of the output of the various distilleries.

The Company was granted the monopoly of the storage of all the rum made in the Colony in order to enable the Government to exercise an effective control on the deliveries of rum with a view to the prevention of fraud. Prior to the foundation of the Central Rum Warehouse each distiller had his own store, and delivered his rum to the public under the control of a revenue officer.

The rum exported from Mauritius during the last twelve years has averaged about 407,800 litres annually. The duty on the liquor delivered for local consumption is 1 rupee 67 cents per litre, and the monthly charges for storage in the Central Rum Warehouse are as follows:—For every 18 litres and 17 centilitres of spirits, or a proportional charge for every fractional part thereof, issued for home consumption, 25 cents, which is also the charge for every 109 litres and 4 centilitres of spirits per mensem, or a proportional charge for every fractional part thereof, whether the spirits are intended for home consumption or for exportation.

The Central Rum Warehouse has accommodation for about 550,000 litres in 55 vats having a capacity of from 3,000 to 11,000 litres each. The various distilleries have vats reserved for their own use. In front of the vats are glass tube indicators that show at a glance the contents of each vat, the rum being received from the vats in connected standard measurers.

The Manager of the Company is Mr. Lionel Lincoln, who has held that position since 1900. The Company's capital, fully subscribed, is Rs. 220,000, and the average dividend paid during the last ten years has been about 7½ per cent. The Directors are the Hon. G. A. Ritter, C.M.G., Chairman; Mr. Nemours Larcher, Vice-Chairman; Messrs. Frederick Rouillard, Edouard Rouillard, and André de Chazal.

Illustrations of the Central Rum Warehouse appear on pages 248 and 249.

THE ALBION DOCK COMPANY.

ERNEST ANTELME,
Manager of the Albion Dock Co.

THERE is no business in Port Louis that serves as a better index to the great trade of the island than that of the Albion Dock Company, whose premises occupy about fifteen acres of land, and comprise eighty-four warehouses having accommodation for about 1,200,000 bags of sugar. The admirable position and arrangement of these warehouses greatly facilitate the work to which they are devoted. The ground on which most of them stand slopes upward to the railway, which has several branches running into the premises. The bags of sugar received from the factories are placed on trucks, of which there are nearly one hundred, each truck carrying ten bags. Throughout the premises are about two miles and a half of rails, on which the trucks, propelled automatically by the incline of the ground, convey their loads to the Company's many buildings that line so large a portion of the basin of the harbour called Trou Fanfaron.

The Company's dock is 318 feet long, sixty feet broad, and has a depth of water of twenty feet. It is excavated in solid basalt, and is situated in Trou Fanfaron, the entrance to which is protected by a long breakwater. The average depth of water in the basin is from nineteen to twenty-four feet.

The business necessitates an extensive equipment of carts and mules, and gives employment to some hundreds of men. It was started about 1870 by a Mr. Hewetson, and was purchased in May, 1874, by the present Company, under whose *régime* it has undergone remarkable development, three-quarters of the buildings having been built out of the profits made by the Company. The capital of the Company is Rs. 900,000 in shares of Rs. 200 each. The reserve fund is Rs. 63,000, and the average dividend paid is about ten per cent.

The Directors comprise the Hon. H. Leclézio, C.M.G., Chairman; Hon. J. J. Gibson, Messrs. Maurice Montocchio, G. Regnard, Pierre Adam, L. Nöel, and J. Hein. The Manager is Mr. Ernest Antelme.

COIGNET BROS. and Co., The Central Printing Establishment, 23, Church Street.

IT is worth noting that while other British colonies impose a high duty on printed material other than books, goods of this class are admitted into Mauritius free. Although the competition which exists amongst the large foreign typographical firms, who are therefore benefited by this exemption, results in quotations providing only the barest margin of profit to themselves, they cannot compete in price with their local contemporaries, whose charges are certainly remarkably low. An instance of this is afforded

OFFICES OF THE ALBION DOCK CO.

SECTION OF THE ALBION DOCK CO.'S PREMISES.

SOME OF THE ALBION DOCK CO.'S STORES.

ALBION DOCK CO.'S WHARVES.

by the work and charges of Messrs. Coignet Bros. and Co, who place at the disposal of the community a printing service that calls for meritorious inclusion in our presentation of what is being accomplished commercially and industrially in the island. Although this firm's prices are, as we have indicated, much below those possible where high cost of living necessitates correspondingly high wages, they execute, in the ordinary branches of the vocation, work equal to the most acceptable canons of typographical utility and effect. These qualities are dependent everywhere upon the brain behind the machinery, upon the cultured taste of the designer, upon harmonious combination, "get-up," type arrangement, colour scheme, and proportions. In these directions Messrs. Coignet Bros. and Co. put forth their greatest efforts to excel; and the fact that they were awarded, for the excellence of their general printing, a bronze medal at the Universal Exhibition held at Paris in 1900, is eloquent of their ability, especially when the number of great contemporary firms who competed with them in that historic event is taken into consideration.

Messrs. Coignet Bros. and Co. used to do the printing for the Mauritius Government before it started its own establishment here. They also operate with equal skill as lithographers and bookbinders, and as stationers they take advantage of the entire resources of that trade, including also in their supplies wall-papers, of which they keep a greatly assorted stock.

In all the departments are ample evidences of the able manner in which the business, established upwards of a quarter of a century ago, is directed by Mr. Charles Coignet, who has for sleeping partners his brother, Mr. Noël Coignet, and Mr. Joseph Darne.

ANGLO-CEYLON AND GENERAL ESTATES COMPANY, LIMITED,

Rempart Street.

THE business of the Anglo-Ceylon and General Estates Co., Ltd., which has its London office at 20, Eastcheap, E.C., was formed in 1886, and has a paid-up capital of £250,000 in Ordinary Shares of £1 each, and £110,000 5 per cent. Mortgage Debentures. Its sugar estates in Mauritius are Britannia, Highlands, La Flora, Bagatelle, and Stanley, which represent a total of 6,000 acres. The Company are also the principal proprietors and managers of the Beau Séjour Sugar Estate Co., Ltd., which owns 2,500 acres. The combined yield of all these estates averages about 15,000 tons of sugar per annum. The Company have three excellently equipped factories —Britannia, Highlands, and Beau Séjour, illustrations of which appear on pages 227, 236, 239, and 240.

OFFICES OF THE ANGLO-CEYLON AND GENERAL ESTATES CO., LTD., REMPART STREET.

In Ceylon the Company possess fifteen estates, utilised as follows:—

	Acres.
Tea	7,153
Rubber	302
Cardamoms	377
Fuel Reserves and Nurseries	914
Forest, Chena, etc. ...	2,203
Cocoa	2,142
Total	13,091

The Hon. J. J. Gibson, manager of the Mauritius business, has been identified with it since 1895. He became a nominated member of the Council of Government on May 15th, 1911, and is a director of the Albion Dock Co. and Les Forges et Fonderies de Maurice. Mr. Gibson is a Scotsman and one of the most popular and prominent men in the island. His portrait appears on page 209.

ELIAS, MALLAC and Co., General Commission Merchants, Rempart Street.

THE ramifications of modern commerce are truly wonderful, and the intricate and numerous sub-divisions of labour provide a subject on which many volumes could be written. This is seen to better advantage in large cities, but is by no means lacking in Port Louis, which, although small, reflects in its mercantile establishments the busy activity of the great world beyond the sea. Its chief commercial firms carry through transactions for manufacturers and others in all parts of the globe, and mention of them must include the old-established business of Messrs. Elias, Mallac and Co.—a business that has its connections far and wide, and plays an important part in the import and export trade of Mauritius. It was founded about eighty years ago and carried on under the name of P. Elias and Tristan Mallac. This was changed in 1841 to P. Elias, Mallac and Co., which subsequently gave place to the present designation.

OFFICES OF ELIAS, MALLAC AND CO., REMPART STREET.

In 1893 the great fire which devastated the Chaussée district in the centre of the city included in its destruction the premises where the firm had been operating since the commencement of their business. Messrs. Elias, Mallac and Co.'s present premises were accordingly erected, and they are amongst the best-built mercantile edifices in Port Louis. In the excellent warehouses consignments of all kinds are handled, and in the large and handsome building where the offices

TRISTAN MALLAC.

JOSEPH MALLAC.

VICTOR HUTEAU.

are situated are recorded transactions of a magnitude that would surprise none familiar with the prominent position which Messrs. Elias, Mallac and Co. occupy amongst their local contemporaries.

Besides their extensive dealings as general commission merchants, the firm are money lenders, and their facilities in this direction have saved many a planter from financial embarrassment. They are managers of the Colonial Fire Insurance Company of Mauritius, which has well merited the confidence and support of the public during its existence of about fifty years.

The partners in the business are Messrs. Joseph and Tristan Mallac and Victor Huteau.

Born in 1871, Mr. Joseph Mallac was educated at the College of the Brothers of the Christian Doctrine and ultimately at the Royal College, successfully passing, at the latter institution, in the first division of the London Matriculation Examination of June, 1889. In 1891 he joined the business of which his father, Mr. Tristan Mallac, was then one of the managing partners, and succeeded to his father's place in the partnership in 1902. Mr. Joseph Mallac is a director of the following companies:—The Mauritius Commercial Bank, New Mauritius Dock Co., Société Huiliere d'Agalega, Nouvelle Société Huiliere de Diego et Peros, etc., etc.

Mr. Tristan Mallac was born in 1874 and educated at the College of the Brothers of the Christian Doctrine and also at the Royal College. In 1891 he became employed in the office of Mr. H. G. Ducray, where he remained until 1898, when he left for France. After serving in that country as managing partner of the firm of Messrs. Mallac and Edwards, he returned to Mauritius, and succeeded in 1893 his grand-uncle, Mr. Albert Mallac, as partner in the business of Messrs. Elias, Mallac and Co.

Mr. Victor Huteau was born in Mauritius in 1840, and joined Messrs. Elias, Mallac and Co. in 1859, becoming a partner in the business in 1881. He is President of the Mauritius Sugar Estates Co., Ltd., Mauritius Engrais Chimiques Co., and the Colonial Dock Co., and is a director of Les Forges et Fonderies de Maurice.

The firm's telegraphic address is "Compesco, Mauritius," and the codes they use are the A.1, A B C—4th and 5th editions—and Lieber's. They are correspondents for Le Comptoir National d'Escompte de Paris; La Banque de l'Indo-Chine; La Banque Transatlantique; La Société Bordelaise de Credit Industriel et Commercial et de Depôts, etc., etc.

COLONIAL ENGRAIS CHIMIQUES CO., Offices, Corner of Place D'Armes and Royal Street.

Mr. A. Ulcoq, the manager of this business, founded it in 1883. The nominal capital of the Company is Rs. 160,000, of which Rs. 120,000 have been paid up. It has a reserve fund of Rs. 145,000, and has since its inception paid an average dividend of 14 per cent. Its operations are in the importation of sulphate of ammonia, saltpetre, nitrate of soda, sulphate of potash, super-phosphate guano, and other chemicals and their preparation as fertilizers for the cultivation of the sugar-cane.

The Company occupies 15 acres of land at its works on the outskirts of the city. The chief building there has accommodation for 2,000 tons of chemicals, and is equipped with powerful Carr grinding machinery, including two crushing wheels five feet in diameter rotating in opposite directions at 500 revolutions per minute, by means of which the chemicals are ground and mixed into powder. A steam winch on the upper floor facilitates the handling of the materials, of which between 4,000 and 4,500 tons are mixed annually on the premises. Besides that large amount the Company sells every year about 500 tons of unmixed chemicals.

COLONIAL ENGRAIS CHIMIQUES CO.'S FACTORY.

The neighbouring building forms the laboratory, where the Hon. J. A. Maurice Martin and his assistant chemists, Messrs. Emile Sauzier, Junr., and Frederick Hertogs, analyse the soils of the different estates and determine the requisite proportion and character of the chemical manures necessary for the best results in each individual case, a warranted analysis being sent with each consignment of fertilizer from the factory. The laboratory is admirably equipped with all the appliances necessary for the clever scientific work performed in it, which includes also analyses of milk and animal secretions, etc.

The Company has in the city a number of other stores with accommodation for about 4,000 tons of its products. The Directors are Messrs. Emile Sauzier, Senr., Chairman; Louis Noël, Jules Hein, Maurice Montocchio, and Felix Montocchio. The Secretary is Mr. F. Hein.

Mr. A. Ulcoq, the Manager, is one of the prominent and influential business men of Mauritius. He is a member of the Chamber of Commerce and the Chamber of Agriculture, and is proprietor of Rosalie (Constance) Sugar Estate, 1,500 acres, and factory in the district of Pamplemousses. Mr. Ulcoq has been several times to Europe, and his agents in London are Messrs. Chalmers, Guthrie and Co., Idol Lane, E.C.

BOUIC, HAREL and Co., Hardware Merchants and Ship Chandlers, 8, 10, and 27, Royal Street.

THE hardware trade calls upon its exponents, whether wholesale or retail, for the maintenance of a more varied and comprehensive stock than almost any other specialised branch of business, as well as for a correspondingly diversified knowledge of the innumerable articles pertaining to its wide range. And the demands which this important trade makes upon its representatives grows greater year after year owing to its constant augmentation by the countless labour-saving devices—domestic, agricultural, and industrial — which scientific and mechanical ingenuity is ever producing. An illustration of this may be found in the premises of Messrs. Bouic, Harel and Co., whose stock is of the most comprehensive character, and embraces not only the many articles usually associated with general hardware and ironmongery but also the multifarious things which the exigencies of the sugar industry entail. There is also the local shipping to be considered, and in that direction, too, the firm keep all the goods pertaining to ship chandlery.

BOUIC, HAREL AND CO.'S WHOLESALE DEPARTMENT.

The business was established as a "civil partnership" in 1894. All the shares were eventually purchased by Messrs. Jules Bouic and Adrien Harel, under whose direction it has made excellent progress. In the beginning of 1913 they were joined in partnership by Messrs. Edouard de Rosnay and Georges Mamet, general hardware merchants, whose business at 27, Royal Street, under the supervision of Mr. Georges Mamet, is now Messrs. Bouic, Harel and Co.'s retail branch; the establishment at 8 and 10, Royal Street, of which we give an illustration, being devoted to wholesale trade. We may add that the firm's importations are conducted through Messrs. Ireland, Fraser and Co.

EDOUARD DE ROSNAY. GEORGES MAMET. JULES BOUIC.
ADRIEN HAREL.

ROGERS and Co., Import and Export Merchants, Bank, Insurance, Shipping and Commission Agents, etc., Quay and Church Streets.

L. GOUPILLE.

W. R. ROGERS.

THE great ramifications of modern commerce have developed the sphere of the commission agent to a degree as unlimited as human activities can make it. Indeed, there is no department of business more ubiquitous, nor one that contributes more to demand and supply, than th s somewhat indefinite but potential vocation; and it is impossible to consider the highly complex conditions of commerce at the present day apart from the influence exerted by the countless able and enterprising men who in general commission business have built and are building up concerns of the most successful and important character. General commission business may be said to be the chief feature in the operations of the leading mercantile firms in Mauritius; and a review of them necessitates, of course, reference to Messrs. Rogers and Co., who import merchandise of every description, and export sugar, hemp, timber, etc. Their two-storied premises, at the corner of Quay and Church Streets, facing the harbour, occupy an area of 12,000 square feet, and are well adapted to their purpose.

The business was established in 1895, and carried on under the name of Laroque and Co. until 1900, when it was taken over by Mr. W. R. Rogers, who is Consul for Siam. In 1909 Mr. L. Goupille, Consul for Russia, became a partner in the firm.

Messrs. Rogers and Co. are agents and correspondents for the following:—

ROGERS AND CO.'S PREMISES.

The Elands Laagte Collieries, Ltd., Durban.
Henckell Du Buisson and Co., London.
The London City and Midland Bank, Ltd., London.
The Eastern Bank, Ltd., London, Bombay, Calcutta.
Corn Exchange Bank, New York.
Banque Française Pour le Commerce et L'Industrie, Paris.
Société Bourbonnaise De Credit, Réunion.
Law Union and Rock Insurance Co., Ltd., London.
General Accident Assurance Corporation, Ltd., Perth.
The British Dominions General Insurance Co., Ltd., London.
The Upper Rhine Insurance Co., Ltd., Mannheim.
The General Insurance Co., Ltd., of Trieste, Trieste.
The World Marine Insurance Co., Ltd, London.

Messrs. Rogers and Co.'s telegraphic address is "Finance," Mauritius, and the codes they use are the A I; A B C, 4th and 5th editions; Lieber's, Premier, Watkins', Ira Scott's, Bentley's, and Whitelaw's Telegraphic Cyphers.

AUX MAGASINS REUNIS, Jewellery, General Fancy Goods and Dress Materials, etc., Port Louis and Curepipe.

NOVELTY is sought by countless designers in every material that lends itself to manufacturing purposes; and the unceasing efforts for new patterns and devices, whether for utilitarian or ornamental purposes, or for the mere manifestation of the uncommon or bizarre, exert an influence in commerce and industry that cannot be adequately appraised and that grows greater every day. The great variety of interesting things in the two-storied establishment of the above business in Rempart and Barrack Streets gives one the impression, from even a casual observation, that the firm have drawn upon the entire resources of European manufacture for their stock. A closer and more lengthened inspection demonstrates that the impression is founded on fact, for the arts and sciences are well represented by the multifarious goods in this store, filled, as it is, with articles that appeal powerfully to everyone, from unsophisticated childhood to fastidious old age. Novelty is the dominant feature of the assortment—novelty that instantly captivates by beauty of design, by ingenuity of construction, by imposing and artistic effect, and by intrinsic worth. So many classes of goods are shown here that it is difficult to say which are most worthy of mention. All kinds of watches, clocks, jewellery, vie with gold and silver plate and lovely bronze and other statues of exquisitely modelled human figures in graceful attitudes; handsome mirrors, pictures and table services compete with glittering cut glassware, delicately tinted vases and dainty household ornamentations; gramophones, toys, bonbons, allure towards purchase; and elegant handbags, photo frames, perfumery, and numerous other articles solve problems for those in search of inexpensive but tasteful and useful things to serve as gifts; while in dress materials, for both ladies and gentlemen, fashion and fancy are exemplified by the firm in goods well calculated to meet the most diverse as well as the most exacting demands. The variety of the stock precludes the possibility of our enlarging on any of its most noteworthy sections, but, taken altogether, the business may be said to represent, although, of course, on a much smaller scale, the large European departmental stores that cater for the general shopping requirements of the public. It has, we may add, a very attractive branch establishment at Curepipe.

AUX MAGASINS REUNIS, PORT LOUIS.

The concern was formed in 1911 by the amalgamation of the business of Mr. E. Vidal, which had been established in Rempart Street since 1852, and the business of Messrs Mautalent and Co., founded in 1860, and carried on in the premises now constituting the headquarters of the Company, under the name of "Aux Magasins Reunis." The managing director is Mr. Eugène Vidal, and the other directors are Messrs. F. A. Miquel, Alexis Coutanceau, Oscar Moizeau, and Gaston D'Hotman.

AUX MAGASINS REUNIS, CUREPIPE.

AUX MAGASINS REUNIS, Objets de Fantaisie, Articles de Toilette, etc., Port Louis et Curepipe.

La recherche de la nouveauté est le souci dominant d'innombrables inventeurs qui s'ingénient à tirer parti de tous les métaux pouvant se prêter à des fins de fabrication, et leurs efforts incessants vers la création de nouveaux modèles d'objets utiles ou agréables, ou d'objets devant simplement servir à la manifestation de l'original ou du bizarre, exercent sur le commerce et sur l'industrie une influence qui ne peut être exactement déterminée, mais qui s'accroît chaque jour. La très grande variété d'articles exposés dans l'immeuble à étage des "Magasins Réunis," à l'angle des rues du Rempart et des Casernes, donne l'impression, même au visiteur de passage, que l'établissement a mis à contribution toutes les ressources de la manufacture européenne pour la constitution de son assortiment de marchandises. Un examen plus attentif confirme la première impression; les arts et les sciences sont également bien représentés dans ce magasin si plein de choses à faire envie à tout le monde, depuis l'enfance naive jusqu'à l'exigeante vieillesse. La nouveauté est la qualité essentielle de cet assortiment—une nouveauté qui captive aussitôt par le bon goût de la conception, l'ingéniosité de la fabrication, un certain reflet artistique, et la valeur intrinsèque de l'objet. Tant de choses de catégories diverses sont ici offertes en vente qu'il nous serait difficile de dire lesquelles valent le plus d'être citées. Des montres de toutes sortes, des pendules et des bijoux rivalisent avec des objets d'art en or et en argent, avec des bronzes et d'autres statuettes représentant des formes humaines exquisement ciselées dans les attitudes les plus gracieuses; des miroirs, des tableaux et des services de table font concurrence aux étincelantes verreries, à des vases délicatement nuancés et à de frais objets d'ornement; les gramophones, les jouets et les bonbons invitent à l'acquisition; d'élégantes saccches, des cadres de photographie, de la parfumerie, et mille autres choses résolvent des problèmes pour les personnes en quête de présents peu coûteux, mais de bon goût et utiles; tandis que du côté des coupons et autres matériaux pour vêtements d'hommes et de dames, la mode et la fantaisie ressortent de marchandises destinées à satisfaire aux demandes les plus diverses et les plus exigeantes. Le caractère varié du stock des "Magasins Réunis" ne nous permet pas d'insister sur l'un ou l'autre de leurs rayons, mais nous pouvons dire que, pris dans l'ensemble, ils représentent, dans des proportions bien entendu réduites, l'un de ces grands magasins d'Europe qui vont au-devant des besoins généraux du public. Ajoutons qu'ils possèdent à Curepipe une succursale fort bien assortie.

La Maison actuelle a été fondée en 1911, à la suite de la fusion du magasin de bijouterie de M. Eugène Vidal, établi à la Rue du Rempart dès 1852, et du magasin Mautalent et Cie, fondé en 1860 et installé dans l'immeuble servant à la nouvelle Compagnie.

L'administrateur de la société est M. Eugène Vidal, qui fait aussi partie du Comité de direction, dont les autres membres sont: MM. F. A. Miquel, Alexis Coutanceau, Oscar Moizeau, et Gaston D'Hotman.

CRÉDIT FONCIER OF MAURITIUS, LTD., Rempart Street.

The Crédit Foncier of Mauritius, Ltd., was established in 1864 by Sir Célicourt Antelme, K.C.M.G. and member of the Council of Government of Mauritius. He was owner of Stanley Sugar Estate, and died in 1899.

SECTION OF THE PREMISES OF THE CRÉDIT FONCIER OF MAURITIUS, LTD.

The business of the Crédit Foncier of Mauritius, Ltd., consists in lending money on first mortgage to proprietors of sugar estates. Its authorised capital is £617,328.

The Mauritius Board of Directors consists of Sir William Newton, K.C., Chairman; Hon. J. A. Duclos, and Mr. Gustave Guimbeau; the local manager being Mr. Eugène Gallet, and the accountant Mr. Camille Rey. The London Board of Directors comprises Messrs. J. A. H. Macnair, Chairman; Guy Lushington, John Cross, and Louis Souchon; the manager in London being Mr. Alfred Graeme Dick.

The London office is at 12, King William Street, and the bankers of the concern are the Commercial Bank of Scotland, Ltd., 62, Lombard Street, E.C. The auditors in London are Messrs. Turquand, Youngs and Co., and the solicitors, Messrs. Thompsons, Quarrell and Jones.

COUTANCEAU and Co., Wine and Spirit Merchants, Commission Agents, and General Importers, Barrack and Rempart Streets.

ALEXIS COUTANCEAU.

WHATEVER ethical considerations be involved it cannot be denied that the prosperity of the wine and spirit trade is a fairly accurate index to the prosperity of a community. This branch of activity has in Messrs. Coutanceau and Co. a firm whose operations are directed with specialised knowledge and experience that are demonstrated by the nature of their supplies and the organisation of their business. As the Customs books show, they are the largest importers of wines and spirits in Mauritius; and their comprehensive stock, selected by their agent at Bordeaux, Mr. Edgar Couteau, wine broker, is not only the best factor in the retention and satisfaction of their customers, but also in the attraction of new clients and the spread of the firm's reputation as distributors of goods of the highest quality.

Messrs. Coutanceau and Co. are also general merchants and commission agents, handling large transactions in sugar, provisions, hardware, textiles, and goods of all kinds. To this section of their business is devoted the portion of their premises opening in Rempart Street, wherein may be seen samples of the multifarious commodities that pass through their hands for local indenters.

The business as at present constituted was started in 1905, the active partners being Messrs. Alexis Coutanceau and Léopold Lecornu. The former gentleman is Consul for Peru, Officier d'Académie, and member of the Chamber of Commerce. His brother, Mr. Maurice Coutanceau, is head of the firm's clerical staff.

Messrs. Coutanceau and Co.'s telegraphic address is "Coutanceau, Mauritius," and the codes used by them are A 1, Lieber's, A B C—4th and 5th editions, A-Z, France, and Western Union. Amongst the well-known houses represented by them are the following:—

Charles Heidsieck, Champagne, Rheims.
Léon Chandon, Champagne, Rheims.
J. Latrille Fils., Wines, Bordeaux.
Sicard and Co., Wines, Bordeaux.
Vianne Lazare, Wines, Bordeaux.
Louit Frères et Cie., Chocolate, Bordeaux.
Adet Seward and Co., Brandy, Bordeaux.
J. W. Burmester, Port Wine, Oporto.
Forestier Frères, Liqueurs, Oporto.
Harth and Co., Commission Agents, Paris.
L. Permezel and Co. Silk Manufacturers, Lyons.
J. B. and A. Artaud Frères, Spanish Wines, Marseilles.
Eugène Bardou and Co., Cigarette Paper, Perpignan.
Webcott and Co., Commission Agents, Birmingham.
J. B. Artaud, Oils, Marseilles.
O. Adelin, Cigarettes, Tobacco, Réunion.

COUTANCEAU AND CO.'S PREMISES.

COUTANCEAU et Cie., Négociants en Vins et Spiritueux; Agents-Commissionnaires, Importateurs de Marchandises Generales, Rue Barrack et Rue Rempart.

DE quelques considérations éthiques que l'on se prévale, il ne peut être contesté que la prospérité du commerce des vins et des spiritueux reflète celle d'une communauté. Cette branche de l'activité a en MM. Coutanceau et Cie. des représentants dont les opérations sont dirigées avec une connaissance et une expérience spécialisées que démontrent la nature de leurs marchandises et l'organisation de leur commerce. Leur assortiment vaste et varié de boissons alcooliques, qui comprend plusieurs des marques les plus réputées et connues, n'est point un stock constitué au hasard. Il est le résultat d'un examen attentif et de l'expérience, et le plus puissant facteur, non seulement de la rétention des clients actuels de la maison, mais encore, de l'attraction de nouveaux clients et de l'expansion de sa réputation de pourvoyeuse de marchandises de première qualité. Les boissons qu'elle vend et qui sont choisis par leur agent à

Bordeaux, M. Edgar Couteau, courtier en vins, occupent une place en vue à plus d'un fastin, de même que sur les tables de l'élite. Comme on peut s'en assurer en consultant les livres de la douane, MM. Coutanceau et Cie. sont à Maurice les plus grands importateurs de vins cerclés, de vins en caisse et de spiritueux.

Leurs spécialités sont citées avec entrain par des laïques comme par des ecclésiastiques; par des négociants et des clercs, par des commerçants et des artisans, en un mot par des gens de toutes les carriéres. MM. Coutanceau et Cie. sont aussi négociants commissionnaires, et ils assurent l'exécution de commandes considérables en sucres, comestibles, quincaillerie, articles textiles, et autres genres de marchandises. Ils consacrent à cette partie de leurs affaires la portion de leur établissement qui ouvre sur la rue du Rempart, et où l'on peut voir les échantillons de certaines des multiples marchandises qui passent par leurs mains pour le compte de leurs clients.

La Maison telle qu'elle est maintenant constituée fut crée en 1905 avec, comme associés responsables, MM. Alexis Coutanceau et Léopold Lecornu. Le premier est consul du Pérou, membre de la Chambre de Commerce, Officier d'Académie. Un de ses frères, M. Maurice Coutanceau, est le chef employé de la maison

L'adresse télégraphique de MM. Coutanceau et Cie. est "Coutanceau, Mauritius," et ils emploient les codes A1, Lièber, A B C, 4ème et 5ème éditions, A-Z, France, Western Union.

Au nombre des maisons bien connues qu'ils représentent, se trouvent les suivantes: –

Charles Heidsieck, Champagnes, Rheims.
Léon Chandon, Champagne, Rheims.
J. Latrille Fils., Vins, Bordeaux.
Sicard et Cie., Vins, Bordeaux.
Vianne, Lazare, Vins, Bordeaux.
Louit Frères, Chocolat, Bordeaux.
Adet Seward, Eau-de-vie, Bordeaux.
J. W. Burmester, Porto, Oporto.
Forestier Frères, Liqueurs, Oporto.
Harth et Cie., Agents-Commissionnaires, Paris
J. B. Artaud, Huiles, Marseille.
O. Adeline, Tabac a Cigarettes, St. Denis, Réunion.
L. Permezel et Cie., Soieries, Lyon.
J. B. et A. Artaud Frères, Vins d'Espagne, Marseille.
Eugène Bardou et Cie., Papier à Cigarettes, Perpignan.
Webcott et Cie., Agents-Commissionnaires, Birmingham.

COLD STORAGE COMPANY, LTD.

THE building in which the ice consumed in Mauritius is made was erected as a hospital some time in the eighteenth century when the island belonged to France. In 1902, when the Cold Storage Co., Ltd., was formed, a large part of the structure was demolished and reconstructed for the Company's operations.

The ice is made by the direct expansion ammonia system, and the duplicate machinery was supplied by Messrs. Arthur Enock and Co., of London and Durban. The two boilers, locomotive type, have each

PREMISES OF THE COLD STORAGE CO., LTD.

a capacity of 20 horse-power. The establishment is lighted by electricity generated by its own dynamo. At the time of writing the monthly output of ice from the factory is about thirty tons; but by the beginning of 1914 additions to the plant will have doubled its present capacity.

The water for the ice comes from Mare Aux Vacoas—the purest supply in the island—and is thoroughly filtered in the factory before being inserted into the twenty pans in the freezing tank, whence it emerges in blocks of clear, pure ice, each measuring 8 by 16 by 36 inches and weighing 112 lbs.

There are seven cold storage chambers in the factory with accommodation for 402 tons of beef, mutton, and other perishable commodities. The great advantages of these chambers are now being well utilised by the local fishing industry for its surplus, to the mutual benefit of both consumers and suppliers, fresh fish being, therefore, always available whatever the weather conditions may be.

The manager of the factory is Mr. A. H. P. Hugnin, who has been in charge of it since 1909, and the engineer is Mr. J. Jones, who has held that position since the commencement of the business. The establishment occupies about half an acre of land, and gives employment to sixteen persons. The capital of the Company is Rs. 250,000, and most of the shares are held by Messrs. Ireland, Fraser and Co., as stated in our reference to their business.

THE CENTRAL DOCK COMPANY.

ANYONE returning to Mauritius after an absence of a decade or two could not fail to be struck with the great additions and improvements which have been made in the stores and operations of the various dock companies in Port Louis, due, of course, to the remarkable development of the local sugar industry during recent years. The Central Dock Company is an instance of this metamorphosis, and a comparison between its negligible resources and business thirty years ago and the extent of its premises and operations at the present day affords a noteworthy indication of the vast increase in the storage accommodation and shipping facilities which have been effected by the expansion of the island's sugar trade.

OFFICES OF THE CENTRAL DOCK CO.

The Central Dock Company was formed in 1882 with a capital of Rs. 330,000, and took over the business which had been carried on by Mr. G. Barnard, who had died in that year, and Mr. G. Davidson, of Messrs. Ireland, Fraser and Co. The Company has twenty-three stores well built of stone and iron, with galvanised iron roofs, at a cost of Rs. 400,000; and the manner in which they are arranged and connected with each other considerably enhances their utility and the facilities for handling their extensive stock. One of the stores, with a capacity for 80,000 bags of sugar, is the largest in Port Louis, and was built in 1906. The latest building was erected in 1912. The Central Dock Company is the only concern of the kind in Port Louis admitting railway waggons inside its stores. The premises occupy about two acres and a half, and

SECTION OF THE CENTRAL DOCK CO.'S PREMISES.

LOUIS SAUZIER (Manager), and C. DE LA GIRODAY (Chief Clerk).

all the land and buildings are the property of the Company, which has also a steam tug and twenty-six lighters, each of the latter being capable of carrying fifty tons. The business has an extensive equipment of mules and carts, and gives employment to about 250 persons.

Mr. Louis Sauzier, the manager of the Company, was appointed to that position in 1902, and the development which the business has undergone since then is an eloquent testimony to his enterprise, ability, and indefatigable efforts for its welfare. He entered the concern when he was nineteen years of age.

The Board of Directors comprises the Hon. Emile Sauzier, K.C., Chairman; Hon. E. C. Fraser, C.M.G.; Edouard Rouillard, Louis Le Breton, A. de Maroussem, and Dr. M. E. X. Nallétamby.

A. G. HOSSEN and Co., General Merchants.

No review of the commerce and industry of Mauritius would be complete without reference to Messrs. A. G. Hossen and Co., whose extensive business, established upwards of sixty years, plays a noteworthy part in local activities. Its founder was Mr. Goolam Hossen Piperdy, who carried it on until his death in 1875. He was succeeded by his son, Mr. Ajum Goolam Hossen, who operated in his own name until 1891, when he was joined in partnership by Mr. Ahmodie Ajum Piperdy, and the present name of the concern was then assumed. In 1900 Mr. Cassim Ajum Piperdy was also made a partner.

Messrs. A. G. Hossen and Co. are extensive importers of all kinds of grain and foodstuffs, textile fabrics, timber, etc., and are exporters of sugar. They own the Bon Air Sugar Estate, of 1,500 arpents, at Pamplemousses, and have also a factory there capable of grinding between thirty and forty tons of sugar daily. The average production of sugar from their estate during the last ten years has been fifteen tons per arpent.

The firm have branches at Calcutta, Bombay, and St. Denis, Réunion.

A. G. HOSSEN AND CO.'S TRACTION ENGINE AND TRUCKS carrying Sugar from their Estate, Bon Air, to their Private Dock at Port Louis.

Mr. Ahmodie Ajum Piperdy, the partner resident in Mauritius, is a native of Rander, near Surat, Bombay Presidency, India, and first came to the island in 1883. Before becoming identified with Messrs. A. G. Hossen and Co. he was in business at Bombay, Calcutta, and Singapore. Mr. Piperdy, whose portrait appears on page 301, has been a member of the Municipal Council of Port Louis since 1909, and represents Ward No. 2. His brother, Mr. Cassim Ajum Piperdy, born in Mauritius, was also a member of the Port Louis Municipal Council before his departure for Bombay, where he and Mr. Ajum Goolam Hossen now look after the interests of the business.

The firm are owners of many houses and other property in Mauritius, and are agents for Le Comptoir National d'Escompte, of Paris and London, etc.

DAUBAN, DESVAUX and Co., Timber Merchants.

On the large piece of ground occupied by Messrs. Dauban, Desvaux and Co. are open sheds containing great stacks of timber that may be seen on the way to and from the neighbouring railway station; but, probably, not one of the busy business men who daily pass that large assortment of sawn wood ever thinks of its potentiality or is aware of the variety of the places whence it is obtained. What does the ordinary individual know or care about such prosaic things, and what material is there for descriptive writing in a timber yard? Nothing, of course, for the non-reflective mind, but much for the discerning eye and the mind where thought dwells. Planks upon planks, methodically arranged according to size, quality and kinship with each other. Some of them were hardy pines on the cold, wind-swept hills of Norway and Sweden; some have come from the timbered regions of Burma, India, the Malay States, Madagascar, and Australia in vessels chartered by the firm. All are the hearts of trees through which the rich sap flowed in the long ago when wild things rested and slept in the shade of their leafy branches. From life to death and then resurrection to greater utility than all earth's uncut timber could supply. Potential planks, only yet in the first stage of their varied destiny of manipulation and usefulness. Hissing saws are waiting for them. Turning, moulding, planing, and other machines will fashion them into many designs. Knives and nails will pierce their grain. Strength will be exemplified by some, ornamentation by others. They form the embryo of buildings, and boats, and boxes, counters, and shelves, and fittings, tools, vehicles, furniture and innumerable articles by which human activity and purpose will be demonstrated as diverse as Nature, as comprehensive as Life. *Verbum sat sapienti.*

SECTION OF DAUBAN, DESVAUX AND CO.'S PREMISES.

The firm have a sawmill opposite to their timber yard.

The business was established about a quarter of a century ago by Messrs. Auguste Dauban, his son Charles Dauban, and Ivanoff Desvaux. Mr. Auguste Dauban retired from it in 1902, and died in 1904. The other two gentlemen are now the sole proprietors.

The firm's telegraphic address is "Dauban, Mauritius," and the code they use is the 5th Edition of the A B C.

SECTION OF DAUBAN, DESVAUX AND CO.'S PREMISES.

DAUBAN, DESVAUX et Cie, Chantier de Bois.

Sur le vaste emplacement qu'occupent MM. Dauban, Desvaux et Cie, sont érigés des hangars contenant d'immenses piles de bois que l'on peut voir en se rendant à la gare de chemin de fer ou en en revenant; mais, très probablement, aucun des hommes d'affaires occupés qui passent journellement devant cet amoncellement de bois scié ne songe jamais à sa virtualité ou ne se rend compte de la variété des endroits d'où il provient. Que sait l'individu ordinaire, ou que désire-t-il savoir de ces choses prosaïques, et qu'y a-t-il à écrire sur un chantier de bois? Rien, évidemment, pour l'esprit éloigné de la réflexion, mais beaucoup pour ceux dont les yeux savent discerner et qui pensent. Il y a là des madriers sur des madriers, tous méthodiquement rangés suivant leurs dimensions, leur qualité et leur relation d'origine. Certains d'entre eux étaient de robustes pins sur les froides collines de la Suede et de la Norvège, balayees par les vents; d'autres ont été introduits dés régions forestières de la Birmanie, de l'Inde, des Etats Malais, de Madagascar et d'Australie, sur des navires affrêtés par l'établissement. Tous sont les coeurs d'arbres à travers lesquels la riche sève a passé dans les temps lointains où les plantes sauvages reposaient et dormaient à l'ombre de leurs branches touffues. Après la vie, la mort, puis la résurrection à un état d'utilité. Les puissants madriers, encore dans la première phase de leur destinée diverse de manipulation et d'emploi! De stridentes scies les attendent. Des tours et des machines à raboter et d'autres les transformenent de maintes façons. Des poincons et des clous perceront leurs veines. Certains représenteront la solidité, d'autres l'élégance. Ils sont l'embryon de futurs bâtiments, de navires, de pied-a-terre, de comptoirs, d'étagères, de véhicules, et d'innombrables objets par où il sera démontré que l'activité humaine et ses buts sont aussi variés que la Nature, aussi étendus que la Vie. *Verbum sat sapienti.*

L'établissement possède, de l'autre côté de la rue, une scierie mécanique.

Le chantier fut fondé il y a environ un quart de siècle, par M. Auguste Dauban, son fils M. Charles Dauban, et M. Ivanoff Desvaux. M. Auguste Dauban se retira en 1902 et mourut en 1904. Ces deux autres messieurs en sont donc maintenant les seuls propriétaires.

L'adresse télégraphique de MM. Dauban, Desvaux et Cie. est "Dauban, Mauritius," et ils emploient la 5ème. édition du code A B C.

IVANOFF MANUEL, Importer of Gramophones and Records,

Architect, Builder and Contractor, "GRAND DEPOT," 11, St. George's Street.

ALTHOUGH an extraordinary scientific achievement was accomplished by the production of the gramophone, the novelty of those first placed on the market was soon followed by universal dislike of the harsh, discordant notes which the best instruments of that time produced; and the possessor of one of those crude, nerve-trying machines not only quickly tired of it himself, but drew from his neighbours uncomplimentary and unparliamentary language of the most lurid and descriptive character. The beginning of most, if not all, things is accompanied by imperfection, and, like many other modern inventions, the gramophone has evolved from distressing limitations into the perfect product of creative genius. To-day, talking machines are procurable tnat imitate the human voice and musical instruments in all their range of cadence and expression with astounding fidelity and freedom from the former unpleasantness of mechanical reproduction.

The business in Mauritius specialised for the supply of gramophones and records is that of Mr. Ivanoff Manuel, in whose establishment, called the "Grand Depot," at 11, St. George's Street, is a stock of the most comprehensive description, including many thousands of records in English, French, Chinese, and Hindustanee, all being so systematically arranged and tabulated that any one can be obtained at a moment's notice. Mr. Manuel is sole agent for the London Gramophone Co., Ltd. (trade mark, "His Master's Voice"), 21, City Road, London, E.C., and the Fonotipia and Odeon Gramophone Companies of Paris. From the "Grand Depot" are obtained machines and accessories that bring back to many an exile the scenes and songs of childhood in lands far away, and that reproduce the voices of the greatest singers, orators, mirth-makers, and the music of the greatest instrumentalists whom few dwellers in this remote island can ever see.

But this interesting establishment is only one department of Mr. Manuel's business activity. He is the largest builder and contractor in Mauritius, and gives employment on an average to about 200 men. It was he who built, for the War Office, Fort Albert, Fort William, and Fort Victoria, as well as several large buildings at the Curepipe Camp. Amongst the many structures he has erected during the thirty years he has been operating here are the Mauritius Institute and the new Government Offices in Pope Henessy Street, Port Louis; the Town Hall and St. Therese Catholic Church, Curepipe; Anglican Church, Quatre Bornes; Notre Dame Catholic Church, Rose Hill; and the Church of the Immaculée Conception, Port Louis, besides numerous dwellings and business premises, the latter including those of Messrs. Elias, Mallac and Co. At the time of our visit to the island in the early part of this year (1913), Mr. Manuel was erecting all the new buildings in the Chaussée district of Port Louis, which had been devastated by fire in 1893. Amongst the new structures being built there were extensive premises for the Oriental Telephone and Electric Co., Ltd., which were expected to be completed by the end of 1913. The Nicolay Bridge, at the end of Royal Street, Port Louis, is another example of Mr. Manuel's work. This is the largest mono-arch stone bridge in Mauritius. He also constructed the chief main for the water supply from Grand River to Port Louis.

Mr. Manuel was born in Mauritius, but widened his knowledge and experience of things in general by residence in Paris and London; and his achievements in his native isle well merit his inclusion amongst its notable men.

THE MAURITIUS PHARMACY COMPANY, LTD., Port Louis and Curepipe.

P. LHOSTE.

E. LE CUDENNEC.

In the earliest periods of the world's history of which we have any record, the work of the pharmacist, like that of the perfumer, was practised by a special class of the priesthood. Egyptian inscriptions indicate that the physician-priests, when they visited the sick, accompanied by the charter of incantations and spells, sent their prescriptions to be dispensed by the priests of Isis. It is a far cry between those ancient times of superstition and the enlightened days in which we live; and probably no department of commerce stands for greater benefit to the human race than the modern pharmacy, with its comprehensive variety of everything that knowledge and experience have produced for the prevention and alleviation of pain and illness and the enhancement of physical well-being.

The pharmaceutical trade is excellently represented in Mauritius by the Mauritius Pharmacy Co., Ltd., who possess three establishments—one in Moka Street, one in Church Street, Port Louis, and the other at Curepipe Road. The great development which has attended the production of patent medicines during recent years is illustrated by the stock in these well-organised pharmacies. Their assortments embrace remedies for the entire range of physical ills; and amongst the numerous specialities mention may be made of the efficacious "Tortuol," or Turtle Oil Extract, prepared from the recipe of Mr. P. Lhoste, one of the managing directors of the business. "Tortuol" contains all the active principles of turtle oil and all the nutritive and analeptic principles of cacao. It agrees with persons exhausted by disease or excesses of every kind. It restores strength and speedily produces an obvious improvement. Free from any fatty, indigestible substance, "Tortuol" is superior to turtle oil because it gives increased activity to the functions of the stomach, stimulates the appetite, and is, during the hot summer days, a first-rate restorative especially for children, who readily take to it.

MOKA STREET PREMISES OF THE MAURITIUS PHARMACY CO., LTD.

CHURCH STREET PREMISES OF THE MAURITIUS PHARMACY CO., LTD.

The Company devote careful attention to the procuring of goods ot the best quality, and their importations, which include toilet articles and photographic materials, are regulated so as to avoid the staleness almost inevitable everywhere when additions are made in too large quantities. About half of the sugar estates of the island are supplied with pharmaceutical goods by this concern.

Accurate compounding of medicines is as important as accurate diagnosis of disease. The Company's dispensing departments are in charge of experts and conducted in a thoroughly commendable manner.

The Mauritius Pharmacy Co., Ltd., was formed in 1900 with a capital of Rs. 80,000 (increased after one year to Rs. 100,000), by the amalgamation of the business of Mr. P. Lhoste, whose pharmacy in Moka Street had been established by him since 1893, and the business of Mr. E. Le Cudennec, who had also been operating as a pharmaceutical chemist and druggist at Curepipe. The amalgamation was followed by the opening of the Company's establishment in Church Street, where Mr. Le Cudennec, who is a Pharmaceutical Chemist of London, with twenty-five years' experience of his vocation, now presides. Mr. Lhoste, who has had forty-five years' pharmaceutical experience, supervises the concern in Moka Street. Both gentlemen were born in Mauritius.

The directors are the Hon. G. A. Ritter, C.M.G. (Chairman); the Hon. Emile Sauzier, K.C.; Messrs. Edouard Rouillard, Henri G. Ducray, Gabriel Regnard, René Raffray, and Louis Goupille.

CHARLES JACOBS and SONS, Merchants, Place D'Armes.

THE well-known firm of Charles Jacobs and Sons have been prominently associated with the commerce of Mauritius for upwards of forty years. The headquarters of their extensive business are at present at Melbourne, but the concern was founded in the sixties of last century by Mr. Charles Jacobs in Adelaide, and afterwards extended to Melbourne, Mauritius, and South Africa. In the latter country the firm have branches at Durban, East London, Port Elizabeth, and Capetown, and agents throughout the Transvaal and Rhodesia.

C. A. BEARE.

The founder died in the eighties, and the present members of the firm are Messrs. M. C. Jacobs, S. J. Jacobs, J. Jacobs, and F. W. Jacobs. The senior partner is Mr. M. C. Jacobs, through whose remarkable ability and enterprise the business has attained a development probably far beyond the greatest hopes and aspirations of its originator when he laid its foundations so well and so securely.

The popular definition of the integrity of Messrs. Charles Jacobs and Sons is that their word is as good as their bond, and this will be found substantiated wherever the firm's influence and trade extend.

In Mauritius Messrs. Charles Jacobs and Sons deal chiefly in sugar and tea and have their own vessel, the *C. J. S.*, carrying their cargoes between this island and Australia. They are agents for Wright and Greig, Ltd., Whiskey Distillers, Glasgow; Bosanquet and Co., Tea Merchants, Colombo; Australian Alliance Insurance Co.; British Foreign Insurance Co.; and the Marine Insurance Co., etc., etc.

Mr. C. A. Beare, the manager of the Mauritius business, is one of the best known and most popular men in the colony. He has looked after the firm's interests here since 1893, in which year he came from their Adelaide house, where he had been since 1881. Mr. Beare is Vice-President of the Horticultural Society of Mauritius.

RAOUL RAFFRAY, Commission Agent, etc., Church Street.

MR. RAOUL RAFFRAY, whose portrait appears on page 209, started business in 1895 as a land surveyor. In 1903, when the surra decimated the draught animals on the sugar estates, he imported into the island £25,000 worth of tramway locomotives and materials from Messrs. Alexander Penney and Co., 16, Water Lane, London, E.C., the well-known firm who specialise in the manufacture of these goods. Mr. Raffray has been agent for them from that time, and he is also agent for Messrs. Harrods, Ltd., the celebrated London universal providers, whose name and goods are known in every part of the world.

He is manager of the Médine Sugar Estate Co., Ltd., which has at Black River 2,815 acres under cultivation and a factory capable, with its new improvements and additions, of turning out forty-five tons of sugar daily. There is also on the estate an aloe fibre factory.

The Médine Sugar Estate Co., Ltd., was formed in 1911, and has a nominal capital of Rs. 800,000, of which Rs. 300,000 have been paid up. The Board of Directors comprises Mr. J. G. Guibert, Chairman; Dr. Alphonse Raffray, Messrs. Nemours Raffray, and Philippe Raffray. The present output of the estate is between 4,000 and 4,500 tons of sugar and about 180 tons of fibre per annum.

THE MAURITIUS ENGRAIS CHIMIQUES COMPANY, 3, Prince Regent Street.

THE Mauritius Engrais Chimiques Company was established in 1876, and has a capital of Rs. 200,000 and a reserve fund of Rs. 250,000. During the last ten years it has paid an average dividend of about 10 per cent. The Directors are Mr. V. Huteau, President; the Hon. G. A. Ritter, C.M.G., and Mr. H. G. Ducray.

The Company manufactures and supplies chemical manures for the fertilisation of the sugar estates,

THE MAURITIUS ENGRAIS CHIMIQUES CO.'S FACTORY.

and at Roche Bois, on the outskirts of Port Louis, has two acres of land, where is situated its factory, which gives employment to about thirty men and is equipped with duplicate machinery of the most up-to-date character for the work performed. The plant is operated by a Robey steam engine of 40 horse-power, and the factory is capable of producing daily 100 tons of fertiliser.

The well-equipped laboratory is in charge of Mr. Volcy Goupille, the Company's chief analytical chemist. The Manager of the business is Mr. E. Goupille, and the Auditor, Mr. N. Larcher.

GARAGE MERVEN, Rempart Street.

THE development which has taken place in the local motor-car trade is certainly remarkable. Throughout the island is heard the horn of the vehicle that is everywhere synonymous with prosperity; while the facilities afforded by the numerous cars for hire in the streets of Port Louis and Curepipe need not be expatiated upon. This metamorphosis necessitates, of course, garages and workshops for repairs, etc., and one of the best of such establishments here is the Garage Merven, where operate men and machinery equal to the most diverse motor-car requirements. The machinery is of the latest type, and includes powerful lathes, boring, cutting, planing, punching, and other appliances of wonderful ingenuity and capacity. One of them is used for the manufacture of crank wheels, and is the only apparatus of the kind in Mauritius. It cost Rs. 8,000, and was made by the well-known firm of Messrs. Glaenyer, Perreaud and Thomine, Paris. The fine plant derives its motive force from electricity generated by the firm's own dynamo.

The premises are admirably adapted to their purpose, and include everything necessary for the perfection of process and result at the minimum expenditure of time and money.

The business is under the personal direction of Mr. Paul Merven, who established it in January, 1911, as a natural sequence to the Delahaye cars which he had already plying for hire in the island. Mr. Merven has augmented these by the importation of a number of Panhard-Levasor cars, one of which, shown on page 341, was used by the Editor in the compilation of this volume.

JOSEPH MERVEN, Commission Agent, Dumot Street.

MR. JOSEPH MERVEN, brother of the gentleman above-mentioned, has in Dumot Street a large shop for the sale of ladies' and gentlemen's outfitting and general fancy goods, etc., which are imported by him from Grand Magasins, Au Bon Marche, Paris, as well as from other French and English concerns represented by him. He is sole agent in Mauritius for Felix Potin, Paris, and Marius Toy Riont, Manufacturers of Lard, Oils, and Grease, Marseilles. We may add that he delivers the goods ordered by his customers throughout the island in motor vans constructed at the Garage Merven.

LE NOUVEAU CHANTIER, Rue du Quai.

ARTHUR SINGERY.

In 1911 it was stated in the French Chamber, by men who had made a long and careful inquiry into the subject, and corroborated in the British House of Commons, that the enormous and constantly increasing demands for timber would in twenty-five years exhaust the world's available supply. The remarkable and continual rise in the price of timber in all parts of the globe seems to confirm their prognostication; and the steps that are being taken by different Governments, especially that of the United States, for the development and preservation of the latent forestal resources of their countries indicate very eloquently the enhanced value of timber at the present day compared to what it was in the years before the growth of population and industry had so greatly depleted the earth of one of its most indispensable products. According to Mr. Arthur Singery, the able and well-informed manager of Le Nouveau Chantier, which we had the privilege of inspecting during the collection of the facts and figures relating to the sketches of the business activity of Mauritius, the cost of timber has increased 20 per cent. more than it was ten years ago, and, during the previous year, teak had increased by Rs. 20 per load of 50 cubic feet. Facts like these call for the consideration of those who may be finding a corresponding increase in the cost of buildings, furniture, and all those branches of productive effort in which timber is a *sine quâ non.*

Le Nouveau Chantier is one of the two principal establishments in Mauritius that meet the local requirements for timber, and to it come extensive shipments of pine deals from Norway and Sweden, teak planks and square pieces from Moulmien and Singapore, native wood from Madagascar, and square pieces, boards, and scantlings of the celebrated Swan River mahogany from Australia.

LE NOUVEAU CHANTIER.

The Company owning the business was formed in September, 1905, and its Directors comprise Messrs. Evanor Tostée, Chairman; Walter Rogers, Vice-Chairman; George Smith, and Arthur Singery, all well-known and influential Mauritian gentlemen. Mr. Singery, who has been identified with Le Nouveau Chantier since 1909, has spent most of his business career in the timber trade, both in Mauritius and Madagascar, and is an expert in everything pertaining thereto.

M. B. LABAT, Pharmacie Nouvelle, Royal Street.

Among the marvellous achievements which have made the last century the most wonderful since the birth of time, there are none that have benefited humanity more than the results obtained by scientific and medical men for the prevention and amelioration of pain and illness and the enhancement of physical welfare. If at the close of the twentieth century there will be corresponding progress in therapeutics, as well as in social and economic conditions, the millennium will not be far short of being an accomplished fact. Reference to the benefits conferred by scientific and medical research and experiment must include also the prominent part played by representatives of the pharmaceutical profession, whose knowledge and training are of an importance that cannot be over-estimated.

There are many pharmacies in Mauritius, and one of the best of them is the Pharmacie Nouvelle, which, as its name indicates, is a comparatively recent competitor in this branch of trade in the island. The elegant appointments of this establishment, and the artistic manner in which its comprehensive stock is displayed, are in keeping with the best ideals of the vocation. On the stock itself much could be written. The fluids in the handsome glass jars and the powders and crystals in the various receptacles embody the elements of life, strength, and freedom from pain and illness. The extensive assortment of patent medicines include many famous to the utmost corners of the earth, and of an efficacy tested and proved by generations of suffering humanity.

PHARMACIE NOUVELLE.

Amongst the pharmaceutical houses from whom the firm import their goods are the well-known English manufacturers, Baiss Bros., and Stevenson, Ltd.; Park, Davis and Co.; Burroughs, Wellcome and Co.; A. Wulfing and Co.; Burgoyne, Burbidges and Co.; Curling, Wyman and Co.; and the Parisian houses of Darrasse Frères; Adrian; Poulenc Frères; and Clin et Cie.

The most elaborate embellishment is negligible in every pharmacy in comparison with the superlative importance of careful and accurate dispensing of medicines, for a momentary lapse of attention or forgetfulness in the making up of a prescription may be followed by calamitous and irremediable results. This work in the Pharmacie Nouvelle is in charge of Mr. Raoul Rochecouste, a certificated practitioner, so that the utmost reliance may be placed on everything compounded there.

SECTION OF PHARMACIE NOUVELLE.

The systematic and pleasing manner in which everything is arranged in the public portion of the premises also characterises the departments at the rear, which include a laboratory where microscopic examinations and analyses are conducted by Mr. Raoul Rochecouste. Amongst the apparatus in the laboratory is a centrifugal machine operating with almost incredible speed, by means of which the sediment of liquids can be extracted without the delay otherwise necessary.

Above the Pharmacie Nouvelle are the consulting rooms of Dr. J. A. Ferriere and Dr. J. L. Louis. The establishment was opened in May, 1912, as an extension of the similar business started in 1911 at No. 19, Desforges Street, where Mr. J. A. Rochecouste, brother of the gentleman already mentioned, is in charge.

"FLORE MAURICIENNE," 19, Church Street.

ALTHOUGH Port Louis has been abandoned as a place of residence by the upper classes of Mauritius, business men must have their breakfast or lunch in the city, and for their requirements the "Flore Mauricienne" Restaurant in Church Street is all that could be desired. The admirable resources of this popular and high-class establishment are, therefore, well taken advantage of, especially from 10 a.m. to 1 p.m., and at its tables leading representatives of commerce and industry, Government officials, army officers, brokers, and men of law and science are to be found daily.

The front portion of the "Flore Mauricienne" consists of a commodious and attractive shop, excellently stocked with choice wines and spirits and the many delectable things such as cakes, pastries, confectionery, etc., that are made on the premises.

Behind the shop is a courtyard, furnished with tables and chairs, which is a favourite resort throughout the day for refreshments of every description. At the far side of the courtyard are the kitchens and bakery, where expert cooks, bakers and confectioners produce the delicacies for which the "Flore Mauricienne" is noted. The range of cakes, pastries, and confectionery of the finest quality made daily in this highly-commendable place is very extensive. For the manufacture of wedding and birthday cakes the proprietors have a large assortment of decorative materials. They make delicious jams and jellies from the fruits of the Colony, as well as pickles and preserves of all kinds from vegetables and other local products.

On the upper floor are situated the nicely-appointed dining-rooms, including private rooms for ladies and parties, the two chief apartments overlooking Church Street. The menu is as varied as possible, the dishes being well cooked and supplied at very moderate prices.

The business has been established in the same premises for about seventy-five years. It was taken

"FLORE MAURICIENNE."

ONE OF THE DINING ROOMS IN THE "FLORE MAURICIENNE."

over in 1862 from a Mr. Salaffa by Mr. S. Thomas, and from the latter gentleman in 1878 by the present Company, since when it has undergone considerable development and improvement.

The prosperity of the Company may be gauged by the fact that its original capital of Rs. 80,000 has been reduced to Rs. 30,000, and that the average dividend paid is 25 per cent. The "Flore Mauricienne" gives employment to about fifty people, and the directors are the Hon. Emile Sauzier, K.C., Messrs. T. J. Cowin, L. Le Breton, and Edouard Rouillard. The manager, Mr. Léon Lafitte, has been identified with it for thirty-six years.

E. MAYER, General Merchant, Auctioneer, and Government Vendue Master, Pope Hennessy Street.

WILFRED MAYER.

EDWIN MAYER.

DURING recent years every branch of commercial and industrial activity throughout the world has undergone an evolutionary process of transformation and development, which is still far from having reached its climax, for keen brains and unflagging energies are continually directed towards increasing the tide of discovery and improvement, nearly every day showing something better than its predecessor, and relegating to the past that which had formerly been considered the highest possible standard of attainment.

In Mr. E. Mayer's emporium productions representative of nearly every department of manufacture are displayed in a variety that creates a realization of new wants for the home, for personal outfit, and for many of the manifold directions in which utility and art are expressed. Boots and shoes, clothing for both sexes, furniture, crockery, glassware, literature in French and English, stationery, toys, beautiful ornaments, statues, pictures, jewellery, handbags, writing-cases, and general fancy goods, travelling and toilet requisites, perfumery, saddles, cycles, musical instruments, Peter Dawson's whisky, for which the firm are agents, and many other articles attract strangers and people from all parts of the island to this noteworthy establishment, where requirements innumerable are admirably met and where ample illustration is afforded of the evolution to which we have referred.

The business was started in 1836 by Mr. Edward Mayer, a native of Staffordshire, England, who was afterwards joined in partnership by his son, Mr. Edwin Mayer. The latter gentleman died in 1876, and Mr. Edward Mayer in the following year. Another of the founder's sons, Mr. Edgar Mayer, then carried on the concern until he, too, passed away in 1909. It is now controlled by Messrs. Edwin and Wilfred Mayer, sons of Mr. Edgar Mayer.

Mr. Edwin Mayer is a sworn auctioneer and Government vendue master, and sells by auction houses, land, furniture, and property of all kinds with manifest ability and knowledge of local values and conditions. He is also a general commission agent.

NOËL COUVE and Co., Ltd., late Minet and Co., Wholesale and Retail Chemists and Druggists, 18-22, Church Street.

NOËL COUVE.

All human progress is based on the fundamental process of alternately putting one foot in front of the other. Step by step we move—some faster, some slower. There are those who stand still; there are even those who step backward; but the tendency of all effort is forward, step by step, towards greater realisation and greater achievement. In no direction is this forward movement more beneficial than in the activities sustaining and enhancing the pharmaceutical trade, as is demonstrated in the premises of Messrs. Noël Couve and Co., Ltd., where a stock of remedial agents is held that covers the entire range of physical ills. It is confidently asserted by authoritative writers that the evolution towards perfection in everything human will eventually result in a race almost, if not totally, immune from the many weaknesses and diseases that are at present our unfortunate lot. Until that halcyon time arrives, however, the establishments of chemists and druggists must always be a *sine quâ non* in every centre of population. If one looks with discerning eyes at the display in the pharmacy of Messrs. Noël Couve and Co., Ltd., what potentialities are realised in the numerous glass jars and other receptacles filled with chemical compounds; what cures for obstinate and painful maladies there are among the fluids and powders; what interesting things could be written about the great variety of patent medicines, ointments, and surgical and medical appliances that add to the completeness of the large assortment! Then there are the varieties of perfumery—essences instinct with the life of things, souls of flowers wrested from the gardens of the world, and confined in the pretty little bottles that would be an acquisition without their fragrant contents. Ordinary, indeed, the establishment may appear to the non-reflective; but, to the observant and thoughtful, how pregnant it is with suggestions of the wonders and mysteries of the healing art and hygienic welfare!

NOËL COUVE AND CO.'S PREMISES.

The firm also deal in photographic materials of all kinds, and transact wholesale as well as retail trade. They employ fifteen assistants, including experts for the making up of prescriptions—that most onerous of all the work of a pharmacy.

The business was established in 1862 by Mr. A. Minet, who died in 1879. Its principal then became Mr. Noël Couve, a Pharmaceutical Chemist of London, who after some years relinquished his active interest in it, and devoted himself to the sugar industry of the island. In the beginning of 1912, however, he sold his estates, and once more assumed control of the concern in question, since when, under his skilful and enterprising direction, it has developed very considerably.

R CANABADY and Co., Importers of Gunny and Vacoas Bags, Rattan Cane, Salt, etc., etc. Hospital, Rémy Ollier, and Corderie Streets.

R. CANABADY.

THE extensive interests which the Hindoos have obtained in Mauritius and the influence they are exerting on its commerce are very noteworthy. Probably the largest local business owned and operated by men from the great land of India is that of Messrs. R. Canabady and Co., which has contributed to the welfare of the island's export sugar trade for about sixty years. It was established and carried on under the name of Messrs. I. Valadon and Co. until 1906, when, on the death of Mr. Valadon, its title was changed to Vve. I. Valadon and Co., under which it was directed until the beginning of 1912, when Messrs. R. Canabady and Co. became its proprietors.

We have said that the business contributes to the welfare of the sugar trade. The firm do so by their enormous importations of gunny and vacoas bags, these articles being essential, of course, for the exportation of the staple commodity that sustains the entire population of the island. In Hospital Street, Rémy Ollier Street, and Corderie Street the firm have six warehouses, the extent of which will be better understood by saying that they have accommodation for 200,000 bags of sugar of eighty kilos each. But instead of sugar they are often so filled with the goods in which the firm deal that other warehouses in the city have to be requisitioned for the overflow. At the time of our visit Messrs. R. Canabady and Co. had in stock in their Port Louis stores gunny and vacoas bags to the value of Rs. 300,000, besides Rs. 100,000 worth of the other articles in which they trade, such as oil, salt, rattan canes, maize, lead, old copper, twine, etc. They have also branch establishments at Souillac, in the district of Savanne; Plaine Magnien, in the district of Grand Port; and Rivière Sèche, in the district of Flacq. At the dock warehouses they do the mixing of the sugar into different qualities for Messrs. Blyth Bros. and Co., Charles Jacobs and Sons, Adam and Co., and Rogers and Co., and repack it for these firms in bags of fifty kilos each for export chiefly to the Cape, as well as to Australia and England.

R. CANABADY AND CO.'S OFFICES.

Messrs. R. Canabady and Co.'s capital, fully paid up, is Rs. 100,000, and their transactions average about Rs. 1,000,000 annually. A business like this necessitates, of course, a large equipment of mules, oxen, and carts, and the number of these employed by Messrs. R. Canabady and Co. contribute an ample share to the busy activity of the streets.

The partners in this important concern are Madrassee Hindoos and are as follows:—Mr. R. Canabady, a native of Karichal, near Pondicherry, the capital of French India, who has been thirteen years in Mauritius; Mr. Candassamy Pillay, born in Tranquebar, also near Pondicherry, who has been twenty years in Mauritius.

ROZIN and SUZOR, Aerated Water Manufacturers, Colonial Ice Works, Sir Célicourt Street.

THIS business was started in 1880 by Mr. Harry Smith, who died in 1902. It was conducted in Rempart Street until the great fire of 1893 destroyed its premises there, and the present establishment in Sir Célicourt Street was then erected. After Mr. Smith's death the concern was conducted for his heirs by Messrs. Ireland, Fraser and Co. until 1912, when it was taken over by its present proprietors, Messrs. G. Rozin and J. G. Suzor, who have entirely metamorphosed the manufacturing operations by the installation of a new plant of machinery of the most modern type, and by making improvements in many directions.

The firm import their essences from the leading manufacturers in England, and in the preparation of their syrups from their own boiled sugar they exercise the utmost precaution against contamination by flies by having their syrup department enclosed by metal gauze. The water for their beverages undergoes thorough filtration, and the greatest care is taken to ensure absolute purity in everything produced by them.

It is a noteworthy fact that the cavity at the top of the ordinary glass-stoppered bottle is eminently adapted for the collection of dust, and, however excellent the contents of the bottle may be, grave risks are incurred, especially in a place like Port Louis, by the possibility of microbes contaminating the beverage as it flows over the dust accumulated at the mouth of the bottle. The vulcanite screw cork with rubber washer is consequently a great improvement on the ordinary and familiar round glass ball cork, for it has no cavity for dust; and Messrs. Rozin and Suzor's adoption of it is certainly a very commendable innovation in the local aerated water trade.

COLONIAL ICE WORKS.

Amongst their fine new machinery is an apparatus which corks their bottles at the rate of between 700 and 800 per hour. The firm's new plant has, besides its great superiority for the perfection of process and result, six times more capacity than the former machinery, and with their increased resources the firm are able to turn out several hundred dozens of bottles of delicious, non-alcoholic drinks daily.

The business derives its name of Colonial Ice Works from the fact that it used to be devoted to the manufacture of ice, and this branch of it was discontinued when the Cold Storage Co., Ltd., was started in 1902.

In the front portion of the premises is a clean and attractive saloon for the use of the public, where the refreshing drinks made by the firm are nicely served with ice.

One of the partners, Mr.

J. GEORGE SUZOR, Commission Merchant, Place d'Armes,

deals in general merchandise, and has always in stock the well-known "Helvetia" belting and centrifugal linings. His buying agents in London are the Helvetia Leather Co., and in France Messrs. Mace and Co., Corbie.

J. COWIN and Co., "White Star" Lighterage Establishment.

T. J. COWIN.

THIS business was originally owned by Messrs. Blyth Bros. and Co., who sold it in 1859 to Messrs. Cooper and Ellis, by whom it was carried on until 1864, when the name was changed to Cooper and Co., which was altered to Cowin and Co. in 1891 and to J. Cowin and Co. in 1896.

The firm have an equipment of twenty-five lighters, capable of carrying 1,225 tons, a tug boat and all the necessities for the landing and shipping of goods.

The partners are the children of the late owner, Mr. John Cowin, who died in 1895, and who was the first surveyor to Lloyd's Register in Mauritius. The managing partner is Mr. T. J. Cowin, who is also a director of the "Flore Mauricienne."

DESCROIZILLES FRÈRES and Co., Importers of Chemical Manures, Church Street.

MANY industries create and sustain numerous branches of commerce that are as distinct and individual in their character and trade as specialisation can make them. One of these branches of mercantile activity, so far as the sugar industry is concerned, is exemplified by the business of Messrs. Descroizilles Frères and Co.—a business in which specialisation is demonstrated to a degree not found in any of the other local commercial undertakings.

DESCROIZILLES FRÈRES AND CO.'S PREMISES.

Messrs. Descroizilles Frères and Co., who have been established since 1906, are suppliers of chemical fertilisers for the sugar-cane, and in their six warehouses in various parts of Port Louis are held large stocks of sulphate of ammonia, saltpetre, superphosphates; precipitated phosphates, nitrate of lime, and Packard's patent phosphoric acid for the clarification of cane juice, for which the firm are agents, as well as other materials for the perfection of process and result in the island's staple commodity. The warehouses have accommodation for 2,000 tons of the goods in which the firm deal.

The active partners in the business are Messrs. M. F. V. and C. V. Descroizilles, sons of Mr. F. V. Descroizilles, who is a sleeping partner, and was formerly store-keeper of the Government supplies, from which position he retired with a pension. Mr. M. F. V. Descroizilles has, we may add, travelled very extensively throughout the world.

FORGET and Co., Ironmongers and Hardware Merchants, 15, Royal Street.

WERE it possible for a hardware merchant who lived a hundred years ago to return to life in a modern establishment representative of his trade, he would be at a great loss to know the use of a large number of the things forming the stock. During the last century the changes and improvements which have been effected in tools and fittings are greater than the uninitiated ever realise, and in Messrs. Forget and Co.'s premises, which present no distinguishing characteristic from those of their contemporaries, are numerous articles that have by their production entirely changed great industrial activities and helped materially in the creation of economic facilities and resources that were formerly unknown in many branches of skilled labour. And just as this evolution towards perfection in ways and means has relegated to the limbo of the obsolete the contrivances in which the hardware merchant and ironmonger of former decades dealt, so through the same progressive tendency the goods sustaining the vocation to-day will a hundred years hence be superseded by designs and patterns of which the most versatile and imaginative mind can at present have no conception.

MR. SUZOR,
Messrs. Forget and Co.'s Manager.

The business of Messrs. Forget and Co. was started about a quarter of a century ago by Mr. A. Forget as a saddlery and harness concern; for at that time the ubiquitous motor car was unknown, and in Mauritius, as elsewhere, horses and carriages were much more numerous than they are now. The craft of the saddler and harness maker is rapidly dwindling into such insignificance, as compared with its previous importance and prominence, that it provides little or no prospects of remunerative exploitation; and it was certainly fortunate that Mr. A. Forget soon after commencing operations added to his supplies general hardware and ironmongery, for it is these latter goods that constitute now the bulk of the firm's trade.

For their harness and saddlery the firm were awarded a gold medal at the Colonial Exhibition held in Mauritius in 1894, and they also received the Diplomé D'Honneur (the highest award) at the Mauritius and Reunion Exhibition organised by L'Union Catholique and held at Port Louis in 1907.

Messrs. Forget and Co. also deal in necessities for sugar estates and ships, and in domestic utensils of all kinds. Besides their well-stocked premises in Royal Street they have a warehouse in Bourbon Street.

They are agents for Messrs. J. Molle, Charleroi, Belgium, and Reckitt and Sons, Ltd., London, S.W. Their cable address is "Forget, Mauritius," and they use the A I code.

HENRI FRAISE, General Wholesale Merchant and Commission Agent, 4, Prince Regent Street.

WHOLESALE trading has ever been an indispensable factor in commerce. Without the services of its representatives the factories of the world would cease their operations, and famine and misery would spread everywhere. Wholesale merchants are the distributors of the manufacturers' goods, and their activity is the heart-beat of the world's trade. The largest mercantile firms in Port Louis are, of course, engaged in wholesale trade, and no review of them would be complete without reference to the business of Mr. H. Fraise. This flourishing concern was established in 1888 by Mr. P. Limonaire, of Paris, and was carried on in his name until 1893, when its title was changed to Limonaire and G. Papon, which, in 1904, gave place to Limonaire and Co. Eventually, in 1908, the business was taken over by Mr. H. Fraise, who had entered it as a clerk and had been partner in it for fifteen years. Under his capable and enterprising direction it has developed well.

HENRI FRAISE.

Wholesale trading necessitates, of course, considerable warehouse accommodation, and in Mr. Fraise's commodious premises are brands of wines, spirits, groceries, provisions, pharmaceutical goods, etc., that are famous to the uttermost corners of the earth.

Like his local contemporaries, Mr. Fraise is a general commission merchant, and holds himself ready at all times to carry through in the most satisfactory manner any commercial undertaking that may be committed to his trust. Mr. Fraise is a native of Bayonne, and spent his early career in commercial houses at Paris, where he gained the business knowledge and experience which he has exemplified so ably since he came to Mauritius. He is, we may add, a nephew of the afore-mentioned Mr. P. Limonaire, who is now established as a general commission agent at Paris.

Mr. Fraise's telegraphic address is "Fraise, Mauritius," and the codes he uses are the A B C—4th and 5th editions—and Lieber's. He is agent for the following:—

Th. Roederer, Champagne, Rheims.
Louis Roederer, Champagne, Rheims.
Marie Brizard and Roger, Liqueurs and Cognacs, Bordeaux and Cognac.
Eschenauer and Co., Wine, Bordeaux.
H. Thompson et Fils, Wine, Bordeaux.
Gibelin et Vieille, Tonic Wines, Marseilles.
J. and R. Tennent, Beer and Stout, Glasgow.
Wm. Foulds, "Castle" Whisky, Glasgow.
J. and R. Adamson, Salt Meats, Liverpool.
H. Salle and Co., Drugs, Paris.
Baiss Bros. and Stevenson, Ltd., Pharmaceutical and Chemical Goods, London.
Schloesing Frères & Co., Chemicals, Marseilles.
Ch. H. Seligmann and Co., Commission Agents, Glasgow.
P. Limonaire, Commission Agent, Paris.
J. Rouhier, Union Commerciale Française, Paris.
A. Jacquemin, Successor to Limonaire and Co., General Merchant, Réunion.
Baron et Fraise, General Merchants, Tamatave, Madagascar.
Bellanger and Co, Tobacco and Cigarettes, Réunion.
Plagniol de James, Oil, Marseilles.
Guilhoux et Fils, Soieries, Lyons.

Mr. Fraise is sole agent for the products of the Labourdonnais Dairy, Mauritius, of which an illustration appears on page 425.

HENRI FRAISE, Négociant-Commissionnaire, 4, Rue du Prince Régent.

LES TRANSACTIONS en gros ont toujours été l'un des facteurs indispensables du commerce. Sans l'intermédiaire de ceux qui s'y adonnent, les usines du monde cesseraient de fonctionner, et la famine et la misère se répandraient partout. Le négociant est le distributeur du produit du fabricant, et son activité représente les mouvements du coeur du commerce mondial. Les plus grands établissements de commerce de Port-Louis n'opèrent, bien entendu, qu'en gros, et en les passant en revue, nous ne saurions être complet sans mentionner celui de M. H. Fraise. Cette florissante Maison fut établie en 1888 par M. P. Limonaire, de Paris, et exista sous son nom jusqu'en 1893, où elle prit le titre de "Limonaire et G. Papon," qui en 1904 fut transformé en celui de "Limonaire et Cie." Plus tard en 1908 elle passa entièrement aux mains de M. H. Fraise, sous l'habile et entreprenante direction de qui elle s'est fortement développée. M. Fraise, qui avait débuté comme simple employé dans la Maison, y appartenait déjà comme associé depuis une quinzaine d'années.

Le commerce en gros exige, cela va sans dire, de vastes magasins. Dans ceux de M. Fraise sont logées des marques de vins, de spiritueux, d'articles d'épicerie, de comestibles et de produits pharmacetiques, connues dans le coin le plus retiré de la terre.

Comme ses confrères de Maurice, M. Fraise est aussi agent-commissionnaire, et il se tient toujours à la disposition du public pour assurer l'exécution de n'importe quelle commande qui lui serait confiée. M. Fraise est né à Bayonne (Basses-Pyrénées). Il fit la première partie de sa carrière dans des Maisons de commerce de Paris, où il acquit les connaissances et l'expérience des affaires dont il a donné tant de preuves depuis son arrivée à Maurice. Ajoutons qu'il est le neveu de M. P. Limonaire, dont nous avons déjà parlé, et qui est maintenant établi à Paris comme commissionnaire. L'adresse télégraphique de M. Fraise est "Fraise-Mauritius," et il emploie les codes A B C 4ème et 5ème éditions, et Liéber. Il représente les Maisons suivantes :—

Th. Roederer, Champagne, Rheims.
Louis Roederer, Champagne, Rheims.
Marie Brizard et Roger, Liqueurs et Cognacs, Bordeaux et Cognac.
Eschenauer et Cie., Vins, Bordeaux.
H. Thompson et Fils, Vins, Bordeaux.
Gibélin et Vieille Toniques, Marseille.
J. et R. Tennent, Bière et Porter, Glasgow.
W. Foulds, Whisky "Castle," Glasgow.
J. et R. Adamson, Salaisons, Liverpool.
Baiss, Bros. et Stevenson, Ltd., Produits Chimiques et Pharmaceutiques, Londres.
H. Salle et Cie., Droguerie, Paris.
Schloesing Frères et Cie., Produits Chimiques, Marseille.
Ch. H. Seligmann et Cie., Commissionnaires, Glasgow.
P. Limonaire, Commissionnaires, Paris.
A. Jacquemin, successeurs de Limonaire et Cie., Négociant, Réunion.
Baron et Fraise, Négociants, Tamatave, Madagascar.
Plagniol de James, Huiles, Marseille.
J. Rouhier, Union Commerciale Française, Paris.
Bellanger et Cie., Tabac à Cigarettes, Réunion.
Guilhoux et Fils, Soieries, Lyon.

M. Fraise est aussi seul consignataire des produits de la beurrerie de Labourdonnais, Ile Maurice, de laquelle une illustration paraît sur page 425.

J. HENRY ADAM, Mail Order Agent, 28, Rempart Street.

J. HENRY ADAM.

PORT LOUIS is essentially a commercial city, and while it represents every department of retail trade, it has, however, a remarkable absence of up-to-date establishments devoted entirely to ladies' outfitting. This is all the more noteworthy in view of the rich and stylish apparel always seen at every social function in the island; and the uninitiated might well speculate on the probable source of this perennial supply of the latest Parisian modes, as elegant and varied as may be seen at any assembly in the fair city on the Seine. Elucidation of the matter is found in the mail order business, of which Mr. J H. Adam is the most prominent local exponent; and without the excellent facilities which he places at their disposal, many people of the upper classes in Mauritius would experience inconveniences and limitations that would undoubtedly be manifested in their wardrobes. For nearly twenty years Mr. Adam has been affording to the inhabitants of the island the advantages accruing from direct trade with the European manufacturers and suppliers; and his activity in this direction is a subject of anathematization amongst the local retailers whom he so affects.

The two-storied establishment where he conducts his business gives little indication from its outward appearance of the part it plays in local commerce, and the extent to which Mr. Adam's operations have developed. Very interesting and instructive indeed is its interior, where numerous shelves and other fixtures are heavily laden with packages containing goods of the most varied character, all the packages being arranged in a system that illustrates the highest degree of clever and ingenious classification, and enables any particular one to be obtained at a moment's notice without any uncertainty as to its whereabouts. As the packages are delivered to the numerous customers, other packages, arriving by every mail boat, take their place, and so goes on the procedure that brings to the local community choice articles of dress, ornamentation, and utility from the leading sources of supply oversea.

From the illustrated catalogues, which Mr. Adam issues periodically, his many customers are given a range of selection of the widest possible description, and the only addition to the catalogued prices of the European suppliers is 15 per cent. for the cost of freight, Customs duty, and other incidental expenses; so that those who avail themselves of this straightforward and commendable method of procuring the best and the latest goods have the satisfaction of knowing that they are getting them at prices which would be otherwise impossible.

Mr. Adam is nothing if not thorough and up-to-date in his methods, and he is, we believe, the only business man in Port Louis using the card index system, which has elsewhere in the world relegated the old-fashioned ways of account-keeping to the limbo of the obsolete.

Being agent for Messrs. Laguionie et Cie., the great Parisian universal providers, who have branches at Hendaye, Cerbére, Irun and St. Sebastien, Lisbon, Turin, Avricourt, Bâle, Geneva, Brussels, Roosendal, Copenhagen, Constantinople, Bucharest, Alexandria, Cairo, Port Said, Buenos Aires, and Santiago (Chili), most of his trade is, of course, transacted with them, although there are no manufacturers in the world whose productions he is not ready at all times to make subservient to the requirements of his clients.

J. CLOSEL, Importer of Hardware and Estate Supplies, Glass and China Ware and General Domestic Goods, Royal Street.

NEARLY all the stores in Port Louis are lacking in the embellishments common to those in other cities, and anyone endeavouring to form an estimate of their trade by their outward appearance would receive a very erroneous impression indeed. Amongst those which convey externally little idea of their importance and status in local commerce is Mr. J. Closel's establishment, which, although sufficiently indicative of a comprehensive and prosperous business, has ramifications and resources not seen by the public that is apt to regard the concern only by its familiar retail section in front. Mr. Closel deals in ironmongery and hardware of every description, including paints, oils, building materials, and estate supplies, to which the various sections at the rear are devoted; and, although there are several other contemporary stores in the city holding very extensive stocks of these goods, there is none containing a larger assortment of crockery, glass, and china ware than is to be found on the upper floors of Mr. Closel's premises. Dinner and tea services from the famous potteries of Staffordshire and elsewhere, and glass ware, ranging from the daintiest samples for special occasions to the ordinary kinds for every-day use, are obtainable here in many choice patterns that are well calculated to satisfy the most varied requirements. Furniture and filters, bedsteads and sewing machines, stoves and wall-papers, brushes and picture-frame mouldings, cutlery and lawn mowers, guns and ammunition, lamps and "Tanglefoot" fly paper, and even cages and live canaries are amongst the many things which Mr. Closel supplies.

J. CLOSEL.

He is also a timber merchant, and has large interests in the timber plantations at St. Lucia, near Fort Dauphin, Madagascar. He is owner of the schooner *Greyhound*, 177 tons, plying between Mauritius, Réunion, Madagascar, and the Seychelles. His business in Port Louis was established by him in 1893, and has developed considerably.

On February 1st, 1913, Mr. Closel opened a branch at Curepipe, opposite to the Market. where goods similar to those in his Port Louis establishment are sold.

C. C. CROFT, "Star" Mineral and Aerated Water Works, General Mechanician, etc., St. George's Street.

THE great reduction during recent years in the consumption of intoxicating liquors, as shown by the statistics of the United Kingdom, is a source of gratification to every right-minded individual; for the benefits so long attributed to the use of alcoholic stimulants are now, in the light of fuller scientific and medical knowledge, proved fallacious. Consequently, the spread of education and the increasing disfavour and odium with which intemperance is everywhere regarded are, while reducing the output of distilleries and breweries, correspondingly enlarging the operations of mineral and aerated water manufacturers. In the tropics, especially, unwise indulgence in alcoholic liquors is fraught with the most serious consequences; and to make matters worse, the water supply of most places in the torrid zone is extremely bad, so that the safe and satisfactory quenching of thirst is often a problem not easy of solution. In Mauritius, however, this difficulty does not obtain, in demonstration of which we have only to refer to the business of Mr. C. C. Croft, whose well-appointed factory has a capacity of turning out daily 300 dozen bottles of non-intoxicating beverages of the finest quality that absolute purity of ingredients, elaborate mechanical and other equipment, and rigorous care in manufacturing processes can entail.

The water supply of Mauritius is good, but Mr. Croft takes no chances with its meritorious reputation. Typhoid and other germs are the embodiment of elusiveness, and the apparently purest water may be contaminated in countless ways. The supply that comes from the water pipes of the town into his establishment is guarded from all possible infection by sterilisation and non-contact with the atmosphere, or any material where bacilli may lurk. From the large hermetically-closed tank where it is first received it passes through filters of the celebrated Berkefeld make, and thence through the ingenious machinery used for its conversion, along with the necessary syrups, essences, and carbonic acid gas, into the numerous delightful and refreshing beverages for which the "Star" Mineral and Aerated Water Works are noted.

"STAR" MINERAL AND AERATED WATER WORKS.

Mr. Croft gets his essences from the well-known London manufacturers, Stevenson and Howell, for whom he is sole agent in Mauritius, and whose methods of packing are so admirable that during the four years since Mr. Croft started his factory and has been receiving their periodical shipments, not one of their large, familiar "Red Seal" bottles has arrived broken.

Mr. Croft manufactures his own syrups, using egg albumen for the clarification of the sugar, which, after boiling, is of the same quality as the best loaf sugar. The syrup is filtered slowly through conical cloth bags in the same manner as calf's foot jelly is made. The section where this operation is performed is carefully guarded by fine metal gauze against the intrusion of flies. All sweet substances are a powerful attraction to flies and other insects, and when one considers the places where the ordinary fly alights, and its dreadful potentiality as a disseminator of disease, the precautions taken by Mr. Croft for the purity of his productions are commendable indeed. This same fastidiousness for cleanliness is manifested in his bottle-washing department, where revolving brush machinery cleans the bottles inside and out with great efficiency and rapidity.

The syrups and essences are placed in closed receptacles connected with the wonderful bottling apparatus, which operates automatically and can fill and cork 800 bottles per hour. All the work in the factory, from the washing of the bottles to the fixing of the labels on those ready, with their delicious contents, for dispatch, proceeds in a chain of operations, each dependent on the other; so that a glance at the end of the chain, where the labellers are, shows at once whether or not the employees in each department are putting forth their best efforts.

In the organisation and control of his factory Mr. Croft has the advantage of being an expert engineer and mechanician; and conterminous with the "Star" Mineral and Aerated Water Works he has an establishment, equipped with powerful lathes, drilling, boring, turning, and other machines, where he executes all kinds of work associated with that branch of activity, including brass-founding and general blacksmiths' work. It was in this direction that Mr. Croft began business for himself in 1903, and the clever use he made of the one machine which then formed his entire outfit, and which is still in active use, led to the gradual acquisition of the rest of the plant and the development of his business into the important undertaking it is now. Mr. Croft makes a speciality of the repair of oil engines, and was the first to introduce into Mauritius the famous Crossley oil engines, for which he is also sole agent here.

R. de SPÉVILLE and Co., The Mauritius Stationery and Printing Establishment, Corner of Royal and Church Streets.

THE metamorphosis through which the art of printing has passed during recent years is manifested by countless examples of chromatic beauty and artistic effect in the most ordinary things as well as in those high phases of excellence that contribute so greatly to decorative and utilitarian purposes. It cannot, of course, be expected that the remarkable achievements of printers in the great cities of the world can be equalled by their contemporaries in Mauritius; but, nevertheless, for the ordinary and less-advanced processes Messrs. R. de Spéville and Co. possess facilities and resources in men, materials, and methods thoroughly adequate to local demands and necessities. Recognising the value of simple and dignified type-setting, they endeavour to make their work a continual advertisement of their ability. A very great deal can be effected by the judicious setting up of type. An announcement which looks commonplace and insignificant when set up by the ordinary compositor, can be made to look tasteful and artistic by one who has the capacity to rise above the level of ordinary arrangement. Such work will attract attention and produce far greater results than the same matter set up at the same cost in a commonplace fashion. It is Messrs. R. de Spéville and Co.'s aim to exemplify this quality in all their printing. They undertake jobbing work of every description, from visiting cards to posters and books, for which they have an excellent equipment of machinery. Amongst the volumes printed by them is the large and meritorious annual publication, *The Mauritius Almanac*, as well as Albert Pitot's *Ile Maurice*, and Dr. Clement Darntz's *Plantes Medicinales*.

R. de SPÉVILLE AND CO.'S PREMISES.

As lithographers and bookbinders they also operate very commendably, turning out work that is a credit to themselves and a source of pleasure and satisfaction to those for whom it is performed.

Their comprehensive stock of stationery meets the most varied requirements. They are also suppliers of wall-papers and makers of picture frames, their assortments in these directions being likewise very complete.

The business was established in 1895, under the name of "Librairie et Papeterie des Habitants," and in 1903 it was taken over by Mr. Noël Couve, who changed its title to "Retail and Wholesale Stores." In 1910 it came into the possession of Messrs. R. de Spéville and Co., when its present designation was assumed. It is under the able direction of Mr. Raoul de Spéville, the sleeping partners being his brothers, Messrs. Adrien and Edouard de Spéville.

NOUVELLE SOCIÉTÉ HUILIERE DE DIEGO ET PEROS.

THIS Society was established in 1893 and renewed in 1912 for a further period of twenty years. It has a capital of Rs. 660,000 divided into 1,320 shares of Rs. 500 each, and has paid a dividend which has averaged 14·10 per cent. for the last ten years, or 17·83 per cent. for the last six years.

MAGASIN GENERAL DES HUILES DE COCO, IMMIGRATION SQUARE.

The Directors of the Society are the Hon. Henri Leclézio, C.M.G., Chairman; Messrs. Lewis Rogers, Edouard Desbleds, Henri G. Ducray, Ivanoff Desvaux, Joseph Mallac, Paul Rougier Legane, Edgar de Robillard, and André de Chazal. The manager of the business in Mauritius is Mr. Richard Lionnet.

The Society owns the islands of Deigo Garcia and Peros Banhos in the Chagos Archipelago. Diego Garcia is administered by Mr. Walter Cummins, and Peros Banhos by Mr. Bussy de Saint Romin.

The Society is devoted to the manufacture of coco-nut oil and the exploitation of copra. The average production of Diego Garcia Island for the last ten years has been 57,071 velts of oil, and that of Peros Banhos 29,034 velts (the velt being equivalent to 7·45 litres). From both islands about 135,000 coco-nuts are annually imported into the Mauritius market. The products of the islands are conveyed to Mauritius by the barque *Ste. Marthe*, also the property of the Society, and the oil is stored and sold in Port Louis at the Magasin General des Huiles de Coco, of which the Society is co-owner with its contemporary, the Société Huiliere d'Agalega. The oil not required for local demands is exported, chiefly to South Africa for the soap factories there. Although the Society has hitherto not done much trade in copra, it is now making arrangements for extending its operations very considerably in that direction.

SOCIÉTÉ HUILIERE d'AGALEGA.

THE Société Huiliere d'Agalega, which is engaged in the manufacture of oil and the preparation of copra, was established in 1892, and renewed in 1912 for another period of twenty years. It has a capital of Rs. 595,000, and since 1903 has paid an average dividend of about 13 per cent. The Directors are the Hon. Henri Leclézio, C.M.G., Messrs. R. Lionnet, J. Mallac, G. Labat, E. de Chazal, G. Lincoln, and O. V. Garreau; the manager of the business in Mauritius being Mr. A. de la Roche.

SECTION OF MAGASIN GENERAL DES HUILES DE COCO, IMMIGRATION SQUARE.

Agalega is composed of two islands, the chief of which, the South Island, is about 5,000 acres in extent, and is administered by Mr. Louis Frichot. On it is the Society's factory, which has just been equipped with a new Rhyder plant of machinery. The North Island, the other part of Agalega, is also about 5,oco acres in extent, and is administered by Mr J. Scott under the control of Mr. L. Frichot.

The average production of oil from Agalega during the ten years preceding the cyclone of December, 1911, was 66,000 velts—a velt being equal to 7·45 litres. Coco-nuts are also exported from Agalega to Mauritius.

The Society's products are conveyed to Mauritius by the schooner *Brazil* of 240 tons, H. Montigny, master, and the oil is stored and sold at the Magasin General des Huiles de Coco, Port Louis.

ORIENTAL TELEPHONE AND ELECTRIC COMPANY, Ltd., Rempart Street.

FROM the time when Sir Benjamin Franklin astonished the world by harnessing the lightning and making it subservient to human requirements, the utilisation of electricity in every direction has undergone amazing development, which, nevertheless, may be regarded as insignificant in comparison with its infinite possibilities. The telephone was unknown in Mauritius until 1882, when it was introduced here by the Oriental Telephone Co., Ltd., which was incorporated in London on February 4th, 1881, and assumed its present title of the Oriental Telephone and Electric Co., Ltd., in 1892. It was reconstructed under that name in 1894, and has now branches at Madras, Moulmein, Singapore, and Rangoon, as well as in Mauritius. Connected with it are the subsidiary companies, the Telephone Company of Egypt, Ltd.; the Bengal Telephone Company, Ltd., the Bombay Telephone Company, Ltd., and the China and Japan Telephone and Electric Company, Ltd.

E. L. LALONDE.

The capital of the Oriental Telephone and Electric Co., Ltd., is £500,000, divided into £200,000 in Ordinary shares, on which an average dividend of 8 per cent. has been paid during the last few years, £100,000 in 6 per cent. Preference shares, and £200,000 in 4 per cent. Debentures.

The Company's business in Mauritius has undergone great development, which is still continuing. In Rempart Street, Port Louis, the Company is erecting large and handsome new premises, which are expected to be completed by the end of 1913. There is a branch establishment at Curepipe. Another has recently been opened at Rose Hill, and arrangements are being made for the extension of the telephone system to Moka and Flacq. The Company is the only concern in Mauritius paying a tax on its revenue, in consideration of which it has from the Government the monopoly of the telephone system in the island.

NEW PREMISES OF THE ORIENTAL TELEPHONE AND ELECTRIC CO., LTD.,
in course of construction in Rempart Street by Mr. Ivanoff Manuel.

The Company performs electrical engineering of all kinds, and supplies all materials pertaining thereto. It also supplies motor cars, cycles and accessories of every description, and the excellent facilities and resources of its machine shop are admirably adapted for speedy and skilful repairs of every kind.

The progress which the business has made and is making here is due to the indefatigable efforts and ability of Mr. E. L. Lalonde, who has had its management since 1889. Mr. Lalonde is a native of London, and what he does not know about telephones and electrical engineering may be regarded as in the category of the negligible.

SAVERYMOOTOO FRÈRES and Co., Merchants, 10, Bourbon Street.

SAVERYMOOTOO FRÈRES AND CO.'S PREMISES.

SEWING GUNNY BAGS IN SAVERYMOOTOO FRÈRES AND CO.'S PREMISES.

From left to right:—
(Standing) G. ANTONEEMOOTOO, A. VADAMOOTOO;
(Seated) A. PYNEEANDEE, A. SAVERYMOOTOO.

THE Indians play a very prominent and important part in the commerce and industry of Mauritius, and amongst the most noteworthy of them is the firm of Messrs. Saverymootoo Frères and Co., whose business was established in 1880 by Mr. A. Saverymootoo and carried on by him until 1906, when he was joined in partnership by Messrs. M. Antoneemootoo, G. Antoneemootoo, A. Vadamootoo, and A. Pyneeandee, all of the Vellalas caste, India. With the exception of Mr. Pyneeandee, they are Roman Catholics.

Although Messrs. Saverymootoo Frères and Co. deal in oil, rice-dahl, ghee, etc., their chief trade is in gunny and vacoas bags, and the average stock in their extensive range of warehouses in Port Louis represents a value of about Rs. 400,000.

One of the accompanying illustrations shows some of their employees sewing gunny bags in the courtyard at the back of their offices in Bourbon Street.

COO-MOOTOOSAMY and Co., Merchants, 14, Little Mountain Street.

COO-MOOTOOSAMY AND CO.'S PREMISES.

From left to right:—SANDRAGASSEN MOOTOOSAMY, GOVINDASAMY MOOTOOSAMY, COO-MOOTOOSAMY; (Boy) NAGAMOOTOO MOOTOOSAMY.

THIS prominent and important Hindoo business was established in 1855 by Mr. Coo-Mootoosamy, a native of Tranquebar, India, and of the Vellalas caste. In 1909 he admitted into partnership with him his two sons, Messrs. Sandragassen Mootoosamy and Govindasamy Mootoosamy, these three gentlemen being now the sole partners in the concern.

The firm deal chiefly in guano and vacoas bags, chemical manures, casia seeds, oils, rattans, etc., etc., which they import from India and England. They own considerable property in Port Louis and Grand Port, and have a branch establishment at New Grove Village. They are owners of an estate at New Grove, where they have 200 acres under cultivation. They also buy canes from the small Indian planters and send them to the factories for crushing. They are the chief lessees of lands at La Rosa Sugar Estate.

Their agents in London are Messrs. Kempton, Wood and Co., 9, Gracechurch Street, E.C.

P. FURCY ADÉLE, Fish Contractor, 67, Church Street.

MR. P. FURCY ADÉLE is the leading representative of the fishing industry of Mauritius. He began his career as a salesman in the market about a quarter of a century ago, and from that humble position has risen by his own ability and enterprise to the place of distinction and influence which he now occupies amongst the local toilers of the sea, whom he supplies with boats and gear, and between whom and the public he acts as agent. The fishing industry of Mauritius is carried on by eighteen different companies, each composed of about twelve men with three or four boats, and Mr. Adéle has practically a monopoly of the sale of their catches. The surplus stock is deposited by him in the cold storage chambers of the local ice factory, so that he has always in hand an adequate supply for the public in the event of bad weather preventing the fishing boats from going out to sea. He employs twelve salesmen in the market, and has been contractor to the Government for the supply of fish for twelve years. Mr. Adéle acts also as financial agent for many of the fishermen, and thoroughly well merits the confidence which they repose in him.

GROUP AT MELROSE SUGAR ESTATE, MOKA.
From left to right:—(3) CHIEF OVERSEER, (4) V. AYASSAMY, (5) MANAGER DE LA TOUR, (6) MOOTOOSAMY, (7) NARAYANEN.

DWELLING ON MELROSE SUGAR ESTATE, MOKA.

V. AYASSAMY, Merchant, 7, Little Mountain Street.

MR. V. AYASSAMY is one of the leading Hindoos of Mauritius, where he was born in 1871, his family hailing from Tranquebar, India. In 1888 he became a partner in the firm of Valaydon and Co., and in 1907, when that business was wound up, he became identified with another partnership concern. In 1909 he started in business for himself as a merchant, and has made excellent progress. Although dealing in general merchandise, his commodities are gunny and vacoa bags, and other commodities from India. He has three warehouses in Port Louis, which are supplemented in crop time by other premises in Grand Port, Savanne, Flacq, and other parts of the island. Mr. Ayassamy also exports rum, sugar, and other local products. He is the largest shareholder of Melrose Sugar Estate, Moka, and is President of the Sokalingum Meenatchee Ammen Temple, a very ancient one, and the greatest of the Hindoo Temples in Mauritius.

H. C. FAGET, Ladies' and Gentlemen's Outfitter, Hairdresser, etc., Port Louis and Curepipe.

AMONGST the few men in Mauritius who were born in France is Mr. H. C. Faget, who came from Bordeaux to the island in 1906, and started business in Church Street in premises which soon became inadequate for his increasing trade. He then removed into his present establishment in the same thoroughfare, which establishment he has since enlarged and improved to meet the busy demands made upon it. It is the chief tonsorial emporium in Port Louis, and its antiseptic service and expert operators meet all requirements. It is well stocked with a large variety of high-class perfumery, ties, shirts, collars, umbrellas, boots and shoes, and gentlemen's outfitting goods of all kinds.

In 1910 Mr. Faget opened his well-known premises in Curepipe, adjoining the entrance to the grounds of the Family Hotel. These premises are divided into two sections: one is for hair-cutting and shaving, and is patronised by the officers of the Army and the leading gentlemen residents of the garden town. The other is an extremely popular shopping resort for general fancy goods and everything pertaining to ladies' and gentlemen's outfitting.

At the beginning of this year, 1913, Mr. Faget opened the establishment at No. 39, Church Street, under the name of "High Life Tailors," where skilled workmen exemplify the sartorial trade in all its branches. Mr. Faget's latest enterprise is seen in the store at the end of Rempart Street. close to the Railway Station, Port Louis, under the name of "The Misses Roubin," where fashionable clothing for both sexes is supplied.

Three-quarters of the goods sold by Mr. Faget come from England, and the remainder are imported by him from France.

IBRAHIM BAHEMIA and Co., General Hardware Merchants, etc., Royal Street.

ISMAEL IBRAHIM BAHEMIA.

ONE cannot tell with certainty the character which a child may develop when its full physical and mental growth is attained, and the same may be said of many business ventures. Started in one specialised department of activity, many a concern has eventually evolved into an undertaking as different from its inceptive nature as night is from day. The history of the business of Messrs. Ibrahim Bahemia and Co. is an excellent illustration of this fact. This well-known house was inaugurated in 1845 by a Mahommedan gentleman, Mr. Bahemia, who laid its sound financial foundation by starting operations as a money changer. Afterwards he launched out as a dealer in cocoa-nut oil, and finally he turned his attention to the general hardware trade, of which business he is now one of the principal representatives in Mauritius. In 1886 Mr. Bahemia made his son Ibrahim a partner in the concern, which was then carried on in their joint names until 1894, when it was given its present designation. The founder died about 1890, and the partners now are Messrs. Ibrahim and his sons, Cassim, Ismael, Amode, and Mamode.

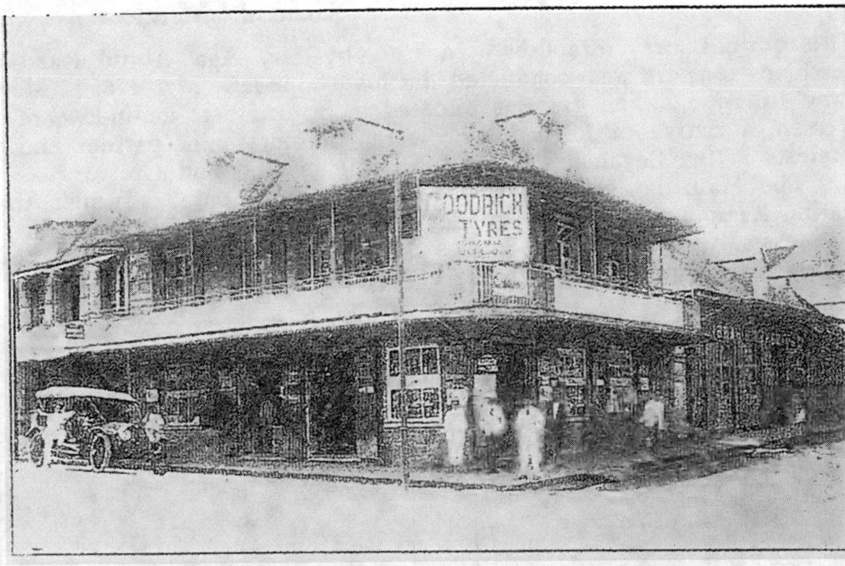

IBRAHIM BAHEMIA AND CO.'S PREMISES.

The goods in which the firm deal are bewildering in their great variety. Not only do they include tools, lamps, stoves, enamelled-ware, scales, lawn-mowers, plumbers' and carpenters' requirements, but also glassware and crockery, rubber articles, building materials, corks, cycles, and motor-car requisites, etc. They are agents for the Goodrich motor tyres, I. P. Clark's thread—of which they sell one thousand gross of reels monthly—Halidger's ink, and "Haley's Comet" matches.

IBRAHIM BAHEMIA AND CO.'S SIX-CYLINDER MITCHELL MOTOR-CAR.

Messrs. Ibrahim Bahemia and Co. have five or six warehouses in Corderie and Royal Streets, the resources of which are taxed to the utmost with the extensive stock which the firm find necessary to keep always in hand to meet the demands of their large trade. Their telegraphic address is "Bahemia, Mauritius," and they use the fifth edition of the A B C code.

I. I. TOORAWA and Co., General Merchants, 11 and 13, Farquhar Street.

Mr. IBRAHIM ISMAEL TOORAWA, the founder and principal of this firm, is a native of Surat, Bombay Presidency, and came to Mauritius in 1862, in which year he started business as a retail merchant in Flacq, where he still has a branch devoted to the sale of grain, provisions, hardware, textiles, and general merchandise of all kinds. He also at the same time commenced operations as a wholesale dealer in

Port Louis in Corderie Street, whence he removed, after some years, to premises in Hospital Street; and in 1885 became established at his present headquarters—his own property—in Farquhar Street, where he has by his enterprise and ability built up a concern that is of no small influence and importance in local commercial circles.

Mr. Toorawa has also stores in Rémy Ollier Street, and is an extensive importer from England and India. In partnership with him are his sons, Messrs. Ismael and Abdulla Toorawa. Mr. Toorawa, Senior, is one of the wealthiest of the Mahommedan merchants in Mauritius, and is President of the Soonee-Surtee Mussulman Society. He is Chairman of the India Boat Company, and is also a shareholder in the Dock Companies, the Mauritius Commercial Bank, Les Forges et Fonderies de Maurice, and other local concerns.

HAJEE AGA ABDUL RASSOOL and Co, Mauritius; and SAID and Co., Seychelles, General Merchants.

THIS business was established in 1861 by Mr. Aga Abdul Rassool, a Persian gentleman. After his death in 1897 it was conducted by his son-in-law, Mr. Hajee Mahomed Medee, until he, too, passed away in 1909, when he was succeeded by another son-in-law of the founder, Mr. Hajee Mahomed Hossen, a native of Bagdad, who is the present senior partner and personally supervises the firm's large interests in the Seychelles under the name of Said and Co.

The Mauritius concern, which is the parent house, is under the direction of Mr. Hajee Mahomed Carim Rassool, son of the founder and a native of the island. In his absence the firm are represented by Messrs. C. Mapara and Sandos Seeraman. Their premises in Royal Street, Port Louis, are excellently equipped with iron tanks capable of holding 1,000 tons of the oil in which they operate very extensively.

ALLY MAHOMED CARIM RASSOOL (Son of Hajee Mahomed Carim Rassool).

HAJEE MAHOMED CARIM RASSOOL.

AYOOB EBRAHIM.

Messrs. Hajee Aga Abdul Rassool and Co.'s chief business is in the Seychelles, where they trade as importers of grain, provisions, textiles, hardware, and merchandise of all kinds, the operations connected therewith having been since 1910 under the management of Mr. Ayoob Ebrahim, a native of Bombay. The firm own several islands in the Seychelles group, as well as portions of La Digue, Denis, Cows, Des Roches, Daros and Poivre Islands, where they have extensive estates for the cultivation of cocoa-nut, or copra, and vanilla, which they export to London, Marseilles, and Mauritius. They are also shippers of turtle-shell, and have three schooners for carrying their cargoes between the Seychelles and Marseilles.

Mr. Hajee Mahomed Hossen is, we may add, President of the Seychelles Co-operative Lighterage Co., Ltd., which acts for all the steamship companies whose vessels call at the islands.

HAJEE ABOO BAKUR MAHOMED TAHER.

HAJEE ABOO BAKUR MAHOMED TAHER.

Mr. Hajee Aboo Bakur Mahomed Taher was born in 1847 at Ahmedabad, Gujerat, India, and came to Mauritius in 1878 as accountant to the then prominent firm of H. E. M. Sulliman. In 1885 he became manager of that business, and since the death of its principal in 1902 and consequent winding-up of the concern, he has acted as Mr. H. E. M. Sulliman's testamentary executor.

Mr. Taher is one of the most influential and respected leaders of the Mahommedan community, and is President of the Soonee-Surtee Mussulman Society. He is owner of much real estate in the island, including Roche Bois Aloe Fibre Factory.

RUSTOMJI MERWANJI MEHTA, Merchant, etc.

RUSTOMJI MERWANJI MEHTA.

TEMUSASP RUSTOMJI MEHTA (Son of Rustomji Merwanji Mehta).

The variety of races forming the population of Mauritius is extremely interesting to the student of ethnology; and while the people from India are in the great majority, it is noteworthy that there is in the island only one Parsee business, viz., that of Mr. Rustomji Merwanji Mehta.

The Parsees are the remnants of the followers of the ancient Persian religion established or reformed by Zoroaster, and which flourished exceedingly throughout the East up to the time of Alexander the Great. Its ethical code is summed up by purity of thought, word and deed—a religion that is for all and not for any particular nation, as the Parsees themselves say. Ahura-Mazdâo, being the origin of light, is symbolised by the sun, moon, and stars, and by fire. Parsee temples and altars must ever be fed with the holy fire brought down, according to tradition, from Heaven; but however great the awe felt by Parsees with respect to fire and light they never consider these as anything but emblems of divinity. In 1901 there were 94,190 Parsees in British India, two-thirds of them being in Bombay, the headquarters of the race, where they form the most prosperous section of the community. These greatly respected people, who are almost the only Eastern race abstaining from smoking, bear the highest character for honesty, industry, and peacefulness; while their intelligence, benevolence, and magnanimity outvie that of most of their European fellow-subjects.

Mr. Rustomji Merwanji Mehta comes from Bombay, where he was engaged for many years in commercial pursuits. and started business in Port Louis in 1910. He is an extensive importer of food-stuffs from Great Britain and India, and exports sugar and rum. He is likewise a general commission agent. and money-lender, and has stores in various parts of the city.

Mr. Mehta was a member of the special committee appointed in 1911 to arrange the celebration in Mauritius of the Coronation of His Majesty King George V.

MOOSAJEE ISMAELJEE HARIFF.

MOOSAJEE ISMAELJEE HARIFF, General Merchant, Hospital Street.

THE Mahommedans, erroneously termed Arabs, are undoubtedly the most picturesque section of the business community of Port Louis, and the influence they are exerting in local commerce is very considerable and continually increasing. Prominent amongst them is Mr. Moosajee Ismaeljee Hariff, who, like his contemporaries, is a general merchant, dealing in grain, provisions, textiles, hardware, etc., and has various stores in Port Louis as well as a large amount of house property. He is a native of Kathor, near Surat, India, and has been in business in Mauritius for nearly forty years. Mr. Moosajee Ismaeljec Hariff is a member of the Soonee-Surtee Society, and is a director of the India Boats Co. At the time of our visit, his son, Ismael Moosajee Hariff, was studying at the Royal College for the Senior Cambridge Examination.

N. M. OSMAN and Co., General Merchants, 8, Hospital Street.

MESSRS. N. M. OSMAN AND CO. are one of the noteworthy Mahommedan firms in Mauritius. Their business was established in 1905 by Mr. Noor Mahomed Osman, who has now in partnership with him his brothers, Messrs. Jonas and Adam Osman. The last two gentlemen attend to the interests of the concern at its establishment at 10, Amratolla Lane, Calcutta, under the name of Adam Osman. The firm are general merchants, and, like their contemporaries, deal principally in grain.

Mr. Noor Mahomed Osman, who controls the business in Mauritius, was born at Calcutta in 1874. He is a member of the Cutchee Maiman Society and the Committee of Direction of the Mosque in Port Louis.

NOOR MAHOMED OSMAN.

GOOLAM MOHAMED ISSAC, Wholesale Dry Goods Merchant, etc., 11, Corderie Street.

THE vast range in the production of textile fabrics is nowhere in Mauritius better seen than in the premises of Mr. Goolam Mohamed Issac, wholesale merchant, who imports his supplies chiefly from the manufacturers in Great Britain. In the Homeland clothing, especially in the winter, is reduced to a dull, drab monotony that is in striking comparison with the bright hues and light garments worn throughout the year by the inhabitants of this charming isle. Besides its large white population, whose tastes in dress materials are as choice as those of any European community, are the hundreds of thousands of Asiatics, whose love for the most gorgeous apparel, in the most vivid of colours, necessitates for the local representation of the wholesale dry goods trade an assortment of fabrics that embraces the entire versatility of textile output. Consequently Mr. Issac's stock exemplifies a variety of design and colour impossible of realisation except by actual inspection.

Mr. Issac, who is a native of Mauritius and one of its best-known men, started his dry-goods business in 1905, previous to which he was a partner in various local concerns. The fact that his turnover now is about Rs. 1,000,000 per annum is an illustration of the extent to which, through his enterprise and ability, his business has developed.

Amongst Mr. Issac's other activities is the exportation of sulphate of ammonia; and he is proprietor of Union Park Sugar Estate, of 935 acres, which he purchased for Rs. 300,000, and which yields on an average 800 tons of sugar per annum. He is also principal partner in the Union Society, which has at Mabon an aloe estate and factory producing about twenty tons of fibre per month. Mr. Issac is the chief lessee of the evening newspaper *Le Petit Journal* and owner of the morning newspaper *Le Journal de Maurice*.

In 1911 and 1912 Mr. Issac was Deputy-Mayor of Port Louis, and represents Ward No. 2 in the Municipal Council. He is President of the Soonee-Surtee Mussulman Madrassa Society, which maintains several schools in Mauritius and controls the Mahommedan cemetery.

A portrait of Mr. Issac appears on page 301.

C. GELLE, Tailor and Outfitter, 21, Church Street.

TRISTAN GELLE.

How to be well dressed at the lowest possible outlay is the problem that always confronts the man of moderate means. The problem is excellently solved by Mr. Gelle, whose skilful workmanship and reasonable charges entitle him to the consideration of everyone residing in or visiting Mauritius desirous of obtaining a suit cut and finished in the latest style and of the best and most suitable material. Mr. Gelle knows the sartorial trade in all its phases, and is thoroughly well qualified to execute the most difficult or most important work that may be entrusted to him. Clothes are an index to character; consequently the character which Mr. Gelle endeavours to give his customers is one of neatness, good taste, and refinement. He has twelve expert workmen employed on his clean, airy and well-appointed premises. The front portion comprises a store filled with a fine assortment of gentlemen's outfitting goods of all kinds—underclothing, hosiery, ties, shirts, collars, boots and shoes, travelling requisites, umbrellas, walking-sticks, and a specially good assortment of hats, including those made by the celebrated firms of Lincoln and Bennet, Henry Heath, and Christy, London, all of which provide a selection to meet the most particular requirements.

C. GELLE'S STORE.

The business was established in 1904 by Mr. C. Gelle, who retired from it in 1912, and his son, Mr. Tristan Gelle, who had been identified with it since its inception, then became its proprietor.

THE ELECTRIC AND MOTOR CAR CO., LTD.,

Church and Rémy Ollier Streets.

A VERY noteworthy indication of the wealth and prosperity of the Mauritian community is afforded by the hundreds of private motor cars in the island and the rapidity with which their number is continually increasing. The demand in this direction is ably met by The Electric and Motor Car Co., Ltd., who, in September, 1912, took over the business that had been established since 1898 under the name of The Engineering and Cycle Works, and which, under the new Company's régime, has already undergone great development. Forty skilled men are employed in the concern; and the commodious machine shop with its up-to-date equipment of powerful lathes, drilling machines, and everything necessary for the avocation represented, is certainly an establishment which local motor-car owners are fortunate in having at their disposal. The Company execute repairs of every description with the utmost efficiency and promptitude at thoroughly moderate charges. At the time of our visit to the premises there were no fewer than eleven motor cars being repaired there. The excellent facilities and resources which the Company possess enable them also to manufacture component parts equal to anything of a similar nature imported. Besides its utility for the work already mentioned, the fine plant, operated by Hornsby-Ackroyd and Crossley oil engines of nine and five nominal horse power respectively, is also used for general mechanics.

MACHINE SHOP OF
THE ELECTRIC AND MOTOR CAR CO., LTD.

Amongst the most popular of the numerous motor cars imported by the Company are the celebrated Darracq, De Dion, Flanders and Ford makes, the Phelon and Moore and "F.N." motor cycles, and the Raleigh cycles. Their stock of Dunlop, Clincher, and Michelin tyres, and all accessories, is large and comprehensive, and they sell also photographic materials.

SALES DEPARTMENT OF
THE ELECTRIC AND MOTOR CAR CO., LTD.

The Directors are Messrs. Evanor Tostée (Chairman), Léon Maurel, Jules Morau, Louis Vigier de Latour, and Aristide Maurel. The Manager is Mr. George Renaud, and the Chief of the Clerical Department Mr. Maurice Planel.

ARISTIDE COLIN PIAT,

Civil and Mechanical Engineer and Importer of Motor Cars and Accessories, 11, Place d'Armes.

ARISTIDE COLIN PIAT.

MR. ARISTIDE COLIN PIAT, eldest son of Mr. Aristide Piat, was born in Mauritius in 1884. He left the island in 1904 to complete his education at the Central Technical College, London, where he gained his diploma of Civil and Mechanical Engineer. In 1908 he returned to Mauritius, and in the following year proceeded to Paris, where he acted as agent for the celebrated Renault motor cars until the end of 1912, when he once more came back to his native island, and is now busying himself in the representation of the cars mentioned, of which he has sold quite a number locally. He is also agent for the Renault oils, and for Messrs. Mestre and Blatge, Manufacturers of Motor-Car Accessories, Paris.

The Renault factory at Billancourt, near Paris, has an area of 12,000 square metres, gives employment to about 4,000 men, and turns out daily between thirty and forty cars. These cars are more popular in Great Britain than anywhere else, and their simplicity, reliability, and general excellence, together with their moderate price, which ranges from Frs. 4,000 to Frs. 20,000, according to size and capacity, well merit the consideration of everyone desirous of purchasing the best automobile.

CHARLES LAVERDANT.

CHARLES LAVERDANT, Commission Merchant, 13, Royal Street.

GENERAL commission agency business, which is so characteristic of the trade of Mauritius, is well adapted to local conditions, and offers opportunities for commercial enterprise that are well taken advantage of by Mr. Charles Laverdant, who, since he began business here on his own account in 1905 has made excellent progress, and introduced many specialities in different lines of supplies. Mr. Laverdant imports goods of all kinds on commission, and amongst the firms for whom he is sole agent here are the following:—

Vincent Percy & Co., Commission Merchants and Exporters, Paris.
Scheitlin and Co., Commission Merchants, Paris.
R. Renouard d'Adrien, Commission Merchants, Paris.
Fernando Esser and Co., Manufacturers and Exporters, Elberfeld, Hamburg, and Paris.
A. Sachse and Co., Manufacturers and Exporters, Bohemia, and Venice.
Société Française d'Aerophone, Gramophones and Records, Paris. (Sole agent and consignee in Mauritius.)
Lunau and Co, Manufacturers and Exporters, Bordeaux.
Eugène Vincent and Co., Manufacturers of Liquors, Lyons.
André David, Manufacturer of Corks, Lavardac, France.
F. Weil, Chemical and Pharmaceutical Products, Paris.
P. Laroche, ,, ,, ,,
H. Lacroix, ,, ,, ,,
Delage et Pottier, ,, ,, ,, ,,
Alphonse Jouve, Commission Merchant, Marseilles.

Mr. Laverdant was born in Mauritius, and before starting his present business travelled in India as representative of the Crédit Foncier of Mauritius, Ltd., in connection with the Indian grain and sugar markets. He has also travelled extensively in Europe and Australia, and his knowledge and experience of general commercial affairs are demonstrated by the able methods controlling his business activities.

Mr. Laverdant has taken an active part in the local race meetings. He was co-owner of *Majestic*, one of the best race-horses ever seen in Mauritius, and which won five of the principal races in the island in 1910. He was also co-owner of *Sir Frank*, which won the Léopold Cup in July, 1909, and the Draper Cup in August of the same year.

GENEVE and HALL, Civil and Mechanical Engineers, Chaussee.

MESSRS. GENÈVE AND HALL have been established since 1911, and operate in everything pertaining to general, civil and mechanical engineering. The partners are Mr. C. H. Genève, graduate of the Central Technical College, London, and Associate of the City and Guilds Institute; and Mr. F. V. Hall, sworn land surveyor, who was previously in the Government Public Works and Survey Department.

The firm are contributing greatly to the potentialities of the aloe fibre industry by means of their patent aloe fibre machine, which, invented by Mr. D. J. McGregor, proved unsuccessful until taken up and improved by Mr. C. H. Genève. It is in use at the following factories:—Albion, Cazoté, Providence, Balaclava, Choisy, and at the firm's own factory, Riche Terre. The capacity of the apparatus is double that of the ordinary scraper, and the superiority of the fibre produced by it was demonstrated at the Exposition Horticole, Curepipe, in 1912, where the firm were awarded a silver medal for their fibre, which was not specially selected but taken at random from one of their bales ready for shipment.

The machine does away with the necessity of skilled labour, thus reducing the working expenses of a factory to a minimum. On page 245 is an illustration of one of the machines in use at the Albion Factory, belonging to Mr. Evanor Tostée.

DRY DOCKS AND SLIPS COMPANY.

THIS business was established in 1856, and its dry docks and other resources are admirably adapted for the repair of steam and sailing ships. The docks belonging to the Company are as follows:—

	Extreme length.	Extreme breadth.	Depth of water.
Stevenson Dock	429 Eng. feet. ...	60 Eng. feet. ...	20 Eng. feet.
Hay Dock	$318\frac{3}{4}$ „ ...	$49\frac{1}{2}$ „ ...	$15\frac{3}{4}$ „

These docks are excavated in solid basalt with sloping sides, and are situated in a large basin known as Trou Fanfaron, the entrance to which is protected by a long breakwater. There are moorings for seven vessels at the head of the basin, which has an average depth of water of from nineteen to twenty-four feet, and which is sufficiently large to allow a vessel of 350 feet in length to be turned.

S.S. "SECUNDER" IN THE STEVENSON DOCK.

By reducing the height of the keel blocks to the level of the inverted arch or sill at the entrance, a vessel fifty-two feet broad, drawing twenty-two feet aft and seventeen feet four inches forward, with a 412 feet keel, can be taken into the Stevenson Dock. This dock can be easily lengthened to 510 feet when two vessels could be taken in at the same time. On the 30th March, 1872, it was lengthened by eight feet to enable the French Mail steamer "Pei-Ho," 3,325 tons, to be repaired. In December, 1898, this dock was again lengthened to its present dimensions—429 feet. The water can be pumped from it in three or four hours, the motive force of the three centrifugal pumps being supplied by two steam engines of 100 horse power each.

The Company have a patent slip, 112 feet long and twenty-four feet broad, capable of hauling up vessels of from 100 to 120 tons.

Six acres of land are occupied by the concern, and the various buildings include a machine shop.

The Company's charges are as follows:—

Fifty cents per gross tonnage for the first twenty-four hours in one dry dock.

For the first day, for vessels of from 1,000 to 2,000 tons, fifty cents per ton. Above 2,000 tons, forty cents per supplementary ton.

For the following days, for vessels of from 1,000 to 2,000 tons, ten cents per day. Above 2,000, five cents per supplementary ton per day.

A lump sum for vessels not 1,000 tons to be determined according to tonnage and length of stay in the dock.

The capital of the Company is Rs. 480,000, and the Directors are the Hon. G. A. Ritter, C.M.G., Chairman; A. Piat, J. Mallac, G. Labat, and E. Piat. The Manager is Mr. Henry Vitry.

H. DU BREUIL, Civil, Military, and Ladies' Tailor, 25, Church Street.

H. DU BREUIL.

STYLE in clothes is the general effect which everybody notices produced by careful exactness in many details that pass unobserved. One person may spend a great deal of money on dress and yet not have that dressy distinction which is so much desired, while another individual may, at a fraction of the same outlay, exemplify sartorial perfection in his apparel. It all depends on the way clothes are made. The effort and purpose of Mr. H. Du Breuil is to make, out of the best and most suitable materials, clothes that are models of skilful workmanship, and his success therein is expressed by the encomiums of his numerous customers, who have the gratifying assurance that their orders are executed on his clean and sanitary premises, and not, as is so often the case in the tailoring trade, amidst surroundings that entail the gravest risk to health and life.

Accuracy in measurements is a cardinal essential, without which the most skilful workmanship will not turn out clothes that will please and impress. Mr. Du Breuil, who makes a speciality of sporting suits, devotes exceptional care to measurements and cutting, and gives employment to a staff of skilled workmen.

Previous to starting business in Port Louis in 1909, Mr. Du Breuil was established in Pretoria, Transvaal, from 1900 to 1906, and was tailor by appointment to the officers of the British Army, receiving the patronage of General and Lady Lyttleton, Lord Henry Seymour, Lord Basil Blackwood, and other notabilities. In his establishment is always to be found a large and comprehensive assortment of English, Irish, and Scotch tweeds, serges, worsteds, and general outfitting goods.

H. DU BREUIL'S PREMISES.

HENRI de BRUGADA VILA, Commission Agent.

THE potentiality of effective advertising is difficult to adequately appraise. In every branch of trade so many excellencies now contend for popular favour, where formerly a select few held the field, that it has become impossible for the purchasing public to discriminate between and compare their respective merits. At this impasse advertising steps in and forges a weapon wherewith the producer may effectually combat the modern dragon of competition, and, in an age when survival is only to the fittest, prove his own title to rank amongst the limited elect. Publicity must obviously be the initial step in converting a new commodity from an unknown quantity into a household word known and used of all men. Printers' ink has never been used with such an understanding of its possibilities or with such telling effect as it is at the present day. But side by side with the era of printed publicity has been a corresponding development in the recognition of the personal equation; and no method can ever be evolved to supplant the efficacy of the personal factor in commercial undertakings in a small place like Mauritius. Practical recognition of that principle is the foundation of the flourishing business which Mr. Henri de Brugada Vila has built up for himself in the island. If we may be allowed to perpetuate a paradox, he is a resident commercial traveller; at any rate, that term, if not distinguished by logic, conveys an adequately accurate idea of the nature and scope of his activity. He is a representative of leading English and French manufacturers of textile fabrics, and at his offices can be seen a large assortment of the numerous patterns of dress materials in which he operates. He is also agent for Les Administrateurs de la Compagnie Générale d'Outre-Mere, Paris; Société Anonyme des Verreries du Nord—the well-known glass manufacturers of Antwerp; Zwanunburg and Co., Commission Merchants, Amsterdam; J. Prom and Co., Wine Merchants, Bordeaux; A. Domange et Fils, Belt Manufacturers, Paris; and La Mutuelle Life Assurance Co., of Lyons. Since Mr. de Brugada Vila took up the latter agency in 1906 he has secured for the Company 560 clients in Mauritius, with policies representing a total of Frs. 1,200,000.

Mr. de Brugada Vila is also agent for the *Didot Bottin*—the great French directory of the world's commerce and industry, the information in which is kept up-to-date by inspectors travelling all over the globe.

Mr. de Brugada Vila is a native of Mauritius, and started his business career in 1889 as a clerk in the offices of the New Mauritius Dock Co., where he remained until 1894, when he joined the Mauritius Commercial Bank, Ltd. While in the service of these concerns he devoted his spare time as agent for Messrs. Boggio and Co., Paris, and met with such success in that direction that in 1906 he resigned his appointment with the Bank and began his present business, which has undergone great development.

LA COMPAGNIE GÉNÉRALE DE QUINCAILLERIE,

corner of Royal and Church Streets.

EDOUARD DESBLEDS.

THE ironmongery and hardware trade is one of the best represented departments of activity in Port Louis, and in the business of La Compagnie Générale de Quincaillerie has a noteworthy exponent. In this Company's premises are held in large variety estate supplies, household requirements, paints and oils, tools, fittings, bar and sheet iron, and all the numerous goods associated with the vocation.

The Company was formed in 1883 with a capital of Rs. 130,000, and its record has been one of uninterrupted prosperity. The business is under the able management of Mr. Edouard Desbleds, assisted by Messrs. George Antelme and Lucien Conacaud. The Board of Directors comprises the following gentlemen:—the Hon. G. A. Ritter, C.M.G., Chairman; Messrs. Emile Sauzier, Senr., Maurice Montocchio, André de Chazal, F. B. de la Giroday, and Léopold Antelme.

"SINGER'S STORE," Rempart Street.

THERE are many excellent sewing machines, but none more extensively used than the Singer, which is to be found in every part of the world where civilisation has penetrated. In homes everywhere the Singer machine helps in the solution of economic problems, and by it countless dressmakers and tailors earn their livelihood. The history of its production is one of the most interesting chapters in the records of inventive genius, and the great establishment at Clydebank, near Glasgow, where many thousands of skilled men are employed in its manufacture, illustrates the vast dimensions of its demand and supply.

Since 1880 a business has been established in Port Louis for the sale of the Singer machines, and is known as the "Singer's Store." This concern was started and carried on in premises which were destroyed by the great fire in the Chaussée district of the town in 1893. The business was then transferred to its present quarters in Rempart Street. But the stock in that attractive emporium is by no means confined to the Singer sewing machines. The goods obtainable there are of the most varied description and include glass, china, and crockery ware, pictures, mirrors, lamps, furniture, boots and shoes and clothing for ladies and gentlemen, perambulators, travelling requisites, clocks, and, in fact, everything pertaining to the outfitting of the home or the person.

The business is distinguished by the fact that it is owned and managed entirely by ladies, the principal being Miss Laura Shaw. Women are demonstrating their equality with men in every sphere of activity, and the future is great with potentiality in that direction. Feminine fitness and ability in the strenuous arena of commerce is shown by the able manner in which Miss Laura Shaw and her colleagues cater for the public in their many departments of trade. It is noteworthy that in certain lines of supplies feminine knowledge and judgment can be far more relied upon than men's for the most suitable and meritorious goods. Not only is the fair sex pre-eminent in the creation of fashion in apparel but also in the equipment and adornment of the home, and in the latter direction what man can equal a woman in the harmonious combination of elegance and utility at the smallest expenditure of money? It is not to be wondered at, therefore, that the "Singer's Store" is an extremely popular source of supply, and that it is a household term in Mauritius.

NG CHENG HIN, General Retailer of Haberdashery, Tobacco, Perfumery and Fancy Goods, Wholesale Wine, Spirit and Provision Merchant, and Boot and Shoe Manufacturer, 19, Royal Street.

THE popularity of Mr. Ng Cheng Hin's Store at 19, Royal Street is evidenced by the continual ingress and egress of its customers and the busy activity of its twenty-five employees. Mr. Ng Cheng Hin knows exactly the articles best calculated to please the public, and certainly the variety of things he sells makes his establishment well worth a visit by those unversed in the Chinese genius for securing goods of novelty and utility and selling them at prices that are a powerful inducement to purchase, although the need for such things may not always be the pressing requirement of the moment. What touches the pocket touches the most delicate nerve, and a buyer's first consideration is how much that same

PORTION OF NG CHENG HIN'S PREMISES.

nerve is to be touched in the transaction. Mr. Ng Cheng Hin is an able exponent of the wise policy of quick sales and small profits and the augmentation of his stock by new goods. These include gentlemen's hats, boots and shoes for both ladies and gentlemen, haberdashery, perfumery, pictures, lamps, chinaware, domestic utensils, tobacco, toys, and fancy goods of every description.

He is also a wholesale wine, spirit and provision merchant, and has premises in Corderie Street for his trade in these directions. The manufacture of shoes has in him a very capable and enterprising representative, and the footwear which his workmen produce is excellent in every respect, both as regards style and comfort.

Mr. Ng Cheng Hin hails from Canton, and has been thirty-seven years in Mauritius, thirty-two of which he has been in business here on his own account.

VVE. NG CHEONG, General Merchant, 16, Royal Street.

No people have a better reputation for commercial integrity than the Chinese. Their word is as good as their bond, and to them the greatest shame and disaster is inability to meet obligations. The writer has been in every quarter of the globe, and amongst his varied experiences of different races, there are none which he recalls with greater pleasure than those of China and its inhabitants. Amongst the most notable of the Chinese concerns in Port Louis is that of Vve. Ng Cheong, whose establishment at No. 16, Royal Street is very popular because of the many classes of goods obtained there at prices that please. At the time of our visit it was crowded with customers, who were being waited upon by a staff of about twelve assistants. The supplies include haberdashery, perfumery, boots and shoes, cutlery, lamps, crockery, glass and chinaware, ornaments and general fancy goods, provisions, etc. The firm have also storage premises in Corderie Street.

PREMISES OF VVE. NG CHEONG.

The business was established in 1898 by Mr. Ng Cheong, and carried on by him until his death in 1909. It is managed for his widow by Mr. Ng Ah Kim, who has been in it from boyhood, and who hails from Kiang Chin, having been brought to Mauritius as a child by his parents. All the members of the staff, with one exception, are also natives of China.

C. LARCHE and Co General Hardware Merchants, Royal and Bourbon Streets.

THE numerous departments of manufacture include many that are sustained entirely by the vagaries of fashion and fancy, and by the demand for articles that have no intrinsic utilitarian merit whatsoever. But of all the countless branches of activity where brains and machinery are unceasingly employed for the production of goods of the most useful character, there are none more indispensable than those contributing to the general hardware trade, of which the comprehensive stock in the premises of Messrs. C. Larche and Co. is an admirable demonstration. Everywhere the demand is for the best in ways and means, for the saving of time and labour, and for the perfection of process and result; and anyone able to differentiate in such matters will find many tangible and interesting illustrations thereof amongst Messrs. C. Larche and Co.'s numerous supplies. The man who operates with tools must have tools of the best quality, if his ambition is to make his work, whatever it may be, an example of the superlative. The tools which Messrs. C. Larche and Co. provide are obtained from manufacturers of world-wide reputation. The woman who desires kitchen utensils—not the unsatisfactory kind which spoil meals and tempers and are a waste of money, but those that prevent culinary disasters and reduce domestic economy to delightful simplicity—is catered for by this enterprising firm with intelligence that concentrates on details—the little things, and it is the little things that count. Indeed, anyone needing almost anything in iron, brass, copper or tin will find that the entire resources of the hardware trade are made subservient to the firm's importations, even coal briquets, coke, tar, glass, leather being amongst the goods they stock.

The business has contributed to local facilities in the foregoing directions for many decades. About thirty-six years ago it was taken over by its present partners, and in 1897 removed from its former premises at the opposite corner of Royal and Bourbon Streets to the stores where it is now conducted. Messrs. C. Larche and Co. transact a large trade with the sugar estates, and are contractors to the Government of Mauritius and the Municipality of Port Louis. The active partner is Mr. G. L. Larche.

J. A. R. NALLETAMBY, Importer and Manufacturer of Furniture, 34, Church Street.

THE problem of house-furnishing so as to attain maximum results in utility and ornamentation at minimum outlay finds solution in the business of Mr. J. A. R. Nalletamby, who during the past eleven years has manufactured and supplied furniture of all kinds for the people of Mauritius. In no department of trade is the combination of utilitarian and artistic effect more in requisition, and, therefore, more greatly exemplified, than in the production of house equipments; nor is there any direction where individual tastes find fuller expression than in the various materials that go to make up the modern home. The subtle influence exerted by the things so constantly seen and used in the home is an interesting subject for reflection; and there are few persons who cannot recall the impressions received in childhood from ordinary and prosaic articles. Who is there, too, who does not remember or cherish some specimen of woodwork or other material of a value not reckoned in cash—sacred because of association with persons and times vanished for ever? Amongst the assortment of goods supplied by Mr. Nalletamby there are surely some such things that will in future years be numbered amongst highly-prized possessions.

J. A. R. NALLETAMBY'S PREMISES.

Mr. Nalletamby gives employment to a staff of skilled workmen, and there is no article of cabinet or upholstery work which he is not prepared to make to order. In his two-storey establishment is a comprehensive stock that embraces many examples of European production. Mr. Nalletamby makes a speciality of iron and brass bedsteads, which he imports from leading manufacturers in England and France. He devotes also particular attention to bentwood furniture, which he receives from America and Vienna, and his chairs and couches of that kind, eminently suitable for local conditions, are well worth inspection.

Mr. Nalletamby is a native of Mauritius, and has been engaged in business in the island since 1867.

EDOUARD PIAT,
Manager of the Colonial Dock Co.

THE COLONIAL DOCK COMPANY,

Offices, Dumat Street.

THE Dock Companies in Port Louis have a scale of charges common to them all, and, while being distinct and separate concerns, their operations are like those of one great, complete business. The Colonial Dock Company has twenty stores with accommodation for about 100,000 bags of sugar, and gives employment to about one hundred men. It has what its contemporaries do not possess—traction engines and wagons, which are of great utility in the handling of the extensive consignments entrusted to the Company's care.

The Colonial Dock Company was formed between 1850 and 1860, and its capital of Rs. 160,000 yields an average dividend of about six per cent. The Board of Directors comprises Messrs. V. Huteau, Gustave Antelme, and Gustave Labat. The Manager is Mr. Edouard Piat, who has occupied that position since 1885.

RAOUL NOËL, Commission Agent, Auctioneer, etc., Church Street.

MR. RAOUL NOËL commenced his business career in 1894 as a clerk with Mr. Durand Deslongrais, notary, with whom he remained until 1897, when he became a partner in the firm of H. Vitry and Co. After the liquidation of the latter concern in 1901 he commenced operations as a house, land, and cattle agent, and continued as such until 1903, when he became sub-manager of the Mauritius Tramway Co., Port Louis. That undertaking also came to disaster through lack of financial support by the Government, and so Mr. Noël, who has had his share of ill-luck, resumed his former agency business, and became a sworn auctioneer in 1910.

Mr. Noël is agent for Messrs. Walter Spencer and Co., Crescent Steel Works, Sheffield, and the Export Metal Company of Mauritius. In 1912 he was elected to the Municipal Council of Port Louis as representative of Ward No. 3, and is proving a very capable and energetic Councillor, zealous in every direction for the welfare of the community. His portrait appears on page 301.

CH. CURÉ, The Colonial Pharmacy, Corner of Royal and Corderie Streets.

FEW people realise the inestimable blessing of good health and freedom from pain until it is emphasised by natural law in sorrow and repentance. Most physical ailments are the results of sins of omission or commission, either by the sufferers themselves or their ancestors; and because humanity, either through ignorance or wilfulness, disregards Nature's warnings and indulges in acts without care or forethought, a great portion of the world's industrial and commercial activity is sustained; a portion that is illustrated in any modern pharmacy, of which there are quite a number in Mauritius. Amongst these is the Colonial Pharmacy belonging to Mr. Ch. Curé, who started it in 1902; and his comprehensive stock is eloquent of the great range of remedies which knowledge and experience have evolved for the amelioration of disordered physical conditions from acquired or inherited causes. As one inspects the bottles and jars, with their differently coloured drugs and chemicals of many kinds, the numerous daintily put-up patent medicines, and all the paraphernalia for the enhancement of physical well-being, one cannot help thinking of the long history of painful experiences, searchings, and experiments through which such potential goods have been evolved. On such things a bulky volume could be written, without anything like a depletion of the many subjects which they offer for reflection. But the assortment of remedial agents in the Colonial Pharmacy would be useless without the knowledge and skill necessary for their formation into prescriptions, and to this important work Mr. Curé and his son Eugène devote their personal attention. Both gentlemen are Pharmaceutical Chemists of London.

T. FOURMOND, Importer of General Fancy Goods, etc., 40, Church Street.

WERE a poll taken of the opinions of the people of Mauritius regarding the store most popular in Port Louis for general haberdashery and fancy goods, it is safe to say that the vote of a very large number would be in favour of the one belonging to Mr. T. Fourmond. His establishment comprises two sections, with separate entrances from Church Street, and certainly cannot be described as palatial. But what it lacks in size is made up for by its supplies; and the continual ingress and egress of its customers throughout the day indicate how well these multifarious supplies are taken advantage of. Mr. Fourmond is agent for the great French firm of universal providers, Manufacture Française d'Armes et Cycles de St. Etienne, whose large illustrated catalogue of 1,200 pages includes almost everything pertaining to human requirements, from living birds and animals to the latest Parisian fashions in dress materials, so that the range of Mr. Fourmond's importations from them and other leading manufacturers throughout the world is of the most comprehensive character.

Mr. Fourmond has been established in business in the city for twenty-six years, twenty-two of which he has been in his present premises. During that long time the stocking of his immense variety of goods has been evolved into a clever exemplification of the old adage, "A place for everything and everything in its place." Haberdashery, perfumery, household furnishings, jewellery, stationery, and fancy goods of every description at the lowest possible prices provide in his emporium allurements to all in need of such things. Mr. Fourmond supplies something for everybody in all stations of life, from the cheapest trinkets for the unsophisticated Indian to choice samples of textile production for the lady to whom artistic and fashionable apparel is a subject of constant study and importance. Nor are the children neglected, and for them Mr. Fourmond has toys, dolls, masks, games, picture-books, and everything else that childhood holds dear.

Mr. Fourmond is a successful exponent of the wise policy of quick sales and small profits; and although most of the purchases made in his establishment are small individually, they are large collectively. Thousands of people visit his premises for Christmas presents, and at that season of every year his stock is exceptionally attractive.

CURepipe.

C. GUILLEMIN and Co., Ladies' and Gentlemen's Outfitters, Importers of Jewellery and General Fancy Goods, etc., Port Louis and Curepipe.

THE handsome and palatial store into which Messrs. C. Guillemin and Co. transferred their Curepipe branch on November 1st, 1912, is the largest and finest shopping resort in Mauritius. Situated in the best and most central position in the charming garden town, its impressive *ensemble* is in striking contrast to the unpretentious appearance of the other local stores. It has twenty-five large plate-glass windows, and provides a very noteworthy and commendable combination of elegance and utility in appointments and supplies. The section on the right of the imposing entrance is filled with a magnificent assortment of articles that manifests the triumphs of artistic manufacture in nearly every material amenable to human manipulation. Here are seen gold and silver cunningly fashioned into plate of choicest designs, jewellery of every description, watches ranging from inexpensive samples, and including the celebrated "Omega" make, for which the firm are agents, to those representing superlative achievements of the watch-making craft; exquisite bronze and other statues and ornaments, illustrating many beautiful conceptions; optical goods, mirrors, pictures, musical instruments, clocks, dainty stationery, photograph frames, handbags, cut glass and china ware, bonbons, and innumerable things that play havoc with economic resolutions, and tempt the beholder to more extensive purchases than are intended before entering this splendid store.

DEPARTMENT FOR JEWELLERY AND FANCY GOODS, ETC., IN C. GUILLEMIN AND CO.'S PREMISES, CUREPIPE.

DEPARTMENT FOR CLOTHING AND OUTFITTING IN C. GUILLEMIN AND CO.'S PREMISES, CUREPIPE.

The section on the left is devoted chiefly to dress materials for both ladies and gentlemen, and reflects continually the latest novelties and fashions throughout all the multiplicity of pattern and texture in textile fabrics. To describe the stock here would occupy more pages than there are inches at our disposal.

Facing the entrance is a broad staircase that leads to the upper floor, on which, in the form of a gallery overlooking the staircase from both sides, are attractive tables and chairs, where tea and other light refreshments

EMMANUEL GUILLEMIN. CLAUDIUS GUILLEMIN, Senior. CLAUDIUS GUILLEMIN, Junior.

of the best quality are obtainable at moderate cost. The rest of the upper floor is taken up by eight residential flats, each containing ten airy rooms.

The building covers about 20,000 square feet of ground, and the basaltic stones of Levieux Castle, not far from Curepipe, were used for its construction.

STAIRCASE IN C. GUILLEMIN AND CO.'S PREMISES, CUREPIPE.

Messrs. C. Guillemin and Co.'s two-storied establishment in Pope Hennessy Street, Port Louis, is also the largest shopping resort in the capital, and is heavily stocked, not only with all the classes of goods in the one at Curepipe, but also with chronometers, barometers, and numerous requirements for sailors and passengers. It has likewise excellently equipped departments where repairs to watches, clocks, jewellery, nautical instruments, optical goods, etc., are executed by expert workmen.

The business was started in 1860 by Mr. Claudius Guillemin, who carried it on in his own name until 1872, when its present title was assumed. In 1892 Messrs. Claudius and Emmanuel Guillemin, sons of the founder, were made partners in the concern, and in 1904, on the retirement of their father, they became its sole proprietors.

C. GUILLEMIN et Cie., Horlogerie, Bijouterie, Articles pour Hommes et Dames, Articles de Fantaisie, etc., Port Louis et Curepipe.

Les splendides magasins où MM. Guillemin et Cie., ont transféré leur branche de Curepipe depuis le ler. Novembre, 1912, sont les plus beaux du pays. Situés au milieu de la position la plus centrale et la meilleure à tous les points de vue de la charmante ville, leur aspect imposant offre un contraste frappant avec les dehors modestes des autres magasins du pays. Dans leurs vingt-cinq vastes vitrines sont exposés, avec beaucoup de goût et de méthode, les principaux articles en vente, et celles-ci offrent à la vu une harmonieuse réunion de l'élégant et de l'utile en des choses qui seraient certainement à leur place dans l'étalage d'un des magasins les plus réputés du monde. Le rayon de droite comprend un magnifique assortiment d'objets qui sont comme la manifestation du triomphe de la manufacture artistique touchant presque tous les éléments accessibles à la manipulation humaine. Ici l'on peut voir des objets d'art en or et en argent finement travaillés d'après les modèles les plus délicats, des bijoux de tous genres, des montres, depuis les moins coûteuses telles les fameuses "Oméga," dont la Maison est seule consignataire, jusqu'à celles réalisant les derniers perfectionnements de l'industrie horlogère ; d'exquises statuettes et des bibelots de bronze ou d'autre métal, illustrant quantité de belles conceptions de l'idéale forme humaine, des articles d'optique, des miroirs, des tableaux, des pendules, de la fine papéterie, des cadres de photographie, des sacoches, de la verrerie et de la porcelaine, des bonbons, et mille autres choses qui ébranlent les résolutions d'économie les plus fermes et poussent le visiteur à faire des acquisitions beaucoup plus étendues qu'il n'en avait l'intention en entrant.

Le rayon de gauche est surtout consacré aux articles d'habillement pour hommes et dames, et là se reflètent, à travers la multiplicité des produits et des modèles de l'industrie textile, les dernières nouveautés de la mode. Décrire en détail l'assortiment de ce rayon nous entraînerait bien au delà de la place que nous avons à notre disposition.

C. GUILLEMIN AND CO.'S PREMISES, CUREPIPE, NEARING COMPLETION.

Face à l'entrée, à l'intérieur du bâtiment, un large escalier conduit à l'étage ; là, dans une galerie immense dont les deux parties dominent l'escalier, sont placées d'attirantes petites tables entourées de chaises ou l'on peut se faire servir du thé et d'autres rafraîchissements légers d'excellente qualité à des prix modérés. Le reste de l'étage forme huit appartements possédant chacun dix pièces aérées.

L'emplacement couvre une superficie de terrain d'environ 20,000 pieds carrés, et le bâtiment a été construit principalement avec les pierres basaltiques qui composaient "Chateau-Levieux," situé non loin de Curepipe. Les plans en furent élaborés et la construction dirigée, pour le compte de MM. C. Guillemin et Cie, par M. Maurice Loumeau, le talentueux Mauricien dont nous parlons ailleurs.

Le Magasin à étage de MM. C. Guillemin et Cie à Port Louis, Rue Pope Hennessy, est le plus grand de la capitale et est abondamment assorti, non seulement des mêmes marchandises qui se trouvent au magasin de Curepipe, mais encore de chronomètres et des autres objets utiles aux marins et aux voyageurs. Il possède aussi des ateliers fort bien outillés où des réparations aux montres, aux pendules, aux bijoux et aux instruments nautiques et d'optique sont habilement exécutées par des ouvriers compétents.

La Maison fût fondée en 1860 par M. C. Guillemin, qui la dirigea sous son propre nom jusqu'en 1872, où elle prit son titre actuel. En 1892, MM. Claudius et Emmanuel Guillemin, fils du fondateur, y devinrent intéressés, et en 1904, lorsque leur père se retira des affaires, ils en restèrent les seuls propriétaires.

THE GENERAL ELECTRIC SUPPLY COMPANY OF MAURITIUS, LTD.,

Curepipe.

THE first plant for generating electricity in Mauritius was installed by Messrs. Louis and Adrien Mallac in 1888, at Curepipe, and was driven by steam; but it proved a failure as the working expenses were too high. In 1892 the plant was taken over by the firm of Goudin, Coutanceau and Co., who endeavoured to operate it more economically by the use of gas, but with no better result. In 1902 the concern was bought by Messrs. Fanucci, Adam and Co., who also purchased from the Hon. George Robinson the Tamarin Falls and about 350 acres of land in their vicinity, and formed at the end of December, 1903, the General Electric Supply Company of Mauritius, Ltd., which has successfully made the beautiful falls subservient to an electric supply that is undergoing great development.

POWER-HOUSE, TAMARIN FALLS.

Although the Company at present provides electricity for lighting purposes only to Curepipe, Vacoas (including the Military Camp there), and Phœnix, it has been authorised by the Government to extend its operations for motive as well as illuminating power to Port Louis, and is accordingly making arrangements to convey 500 B.H.P. to the city, after which it intends to extend its service to sugar and aloe factories and workshops along the line of its connections. The Company is also studying the question of introducing electric tramways to connect Curepipe, Mangalkhan, and Vacoas.

The fall of water at Tamarin is about 960 feet—the highest in Mauritius, and the power available is 1,500 kilowatts, of which only 250 kilowatts are used during the night. In connection with the falls the Company has built two dams, one on the Aigrettes River and the other on the Tamarin River. The latter river is diverted by a trench, 1,000 feet long, into the Aigrettes River, whence the water runs in an open canal, 3,000 feet long, to the pipe-line, which has a length of 2,800 feet and is composed of lap-welded steel pipes, 24 by 22 by 20½ inches, supplied by Messrs. Stewarts, Lloyd and Co., of Glasgow, and fitted with air-valves. The pressure of the water at the end of the pipe-line driving the electric machinery in the power-house at the bottom of the magnificent glen is 450 pounds to the square inch.

The electric machinery in the power-house comprises one "Voith" high-pressure turbine, 500 revolutions per minute, direct coupled, with a three-phase 250-kilowatt "A.E.G." generator—6,600 volts, 50 periods; one Escher Wyss high-pressure turbine, 750 revolutions per minute, direct coupled, with a three-phase 300-kilowatt Westinghouse generator—6,600 volts, 50 periods; one Westinghouse switchboard with the necessary instruments;

PIPE LINE, 2,800 FEET LONG, FROM THE AIGRETTES RIVER TO THE POWER-HOUSE, TAMARIN FALLS.

one set of Westinghouse arrestors; one set of liquid lightning arrestors; and there is spare room for two more turbo-generators.

In view of the extension of its electric supply to Port Louis, the Company is increasing the plant in the power-house, first by a 500, and, subsequently, by a 750-kilowatt turbo-generator.

The electric current is conveyed from the power-house by aerial wires to Curepipe, about five miles distant, and thence to Vacoas and Phœnix, a further distance of about four miles. A direct line of aerial wires will be erected from the power-house to Port Louis, a distance of about twenty miles.

The Company's transformer stations are as follows:—

Curepipe—	3 of 50 kilowatts
	1 of 10 "
	2 of 20 "
	1 of 2-10 "
Vacoas —	1 of 75 "
	1 of 2-20 "
Phœnix —	1 of 10 "

The Company has a nominal capital of Rs. 500,000 (which can be increased to Rs. 1,000,000), and a paid-up capital of Rs. 179,400. No dividend has been paid to the shareholders as all the profits have been, so far, devoted to the extension of the business.

The following figures show the Company's revenue from 1904 to 1912 inclusive:—

Year.	Total Candle Power.	Rs.
1904	23,796	24,050·81
1905	30,480	31,394·35
1906	41,676	45,300·60
1907	48,048	54,091·88
1908	52,321	62,133·23
1909	57,870	67,641·69
1910	67,452	76,849·27
1911	70,856	93,023·19
1912	79,399	102,914·56

The Board of Directors comprises Messrs. Maurice P. Pitot, Chairman; Pierre Adam, Ivanoff Desvaux, H. Fraise, Tristan Mallac, and Aristide Rey. The Secretary is Mr. Adrien de Spéville.

In closing this sketch due recognition must be made of the ability shown by Mr. J. E. Tarby, A.M.I.E.E., who was Manager of the Company from its inception until May, 1913, and on whom devolved all the materialisation of the Company's achievements up till that time. Mr. Tarby left Mauritius in the month mentioned to reside in England. His successor is Mr. Dermine, one of the chief engineers of the Gramme Société, Paris.

THE FAMILY HOTEL, Curepipe.

THE FAMILY HOTEL, CUREPIPE.

THE only hotel worthy of the name in Mauritius is the Family Hotel, Curepipe. It has accommodation for about twenty-five people, and, besides the main building shown in the accompanying illustration, it has three excellent bungalows, two of which are utilised for guests. The bedrooms of the hotel are airy and comfortable, some of them being very large, and those on the upper floor of the main building have spacious verandahs. The grounds of the hotel are about an acre in extent and include a fine tennis-court. The establishment is under the direction of Miss A. Wiehé, who took it over in 1908, and who is a member of an old and respected French-Mauritian family.

PALAIS DES SPORTS, Curepipe.

PALAIS DES SPORTS, FROM THE STAGE.

Since the inauguration of the Palais des Sports in February, 1912, Curepipe has been provided with a means of entertainment and recreation that has proved, and is proving, extremely popular with the residents of the garden town. The Palais des Sports is a well-built structure, admirably arranged to serve as a skating rink, picture-palace (where excellent films are shown), theatre, ball-room, etc., and on one of its galleries is a cafe for refreshments of all kinds. The establishment, which has also grounds for tennis and other games, is owned and managed by Mr. Antoine Guerin, a Mauritian gentleman, who is worthy of every commendation for the enterprise he has displayed in establishing an institution that is exerting no small influence in fusing more closely the French and the English sections of the community, and that has met a long-felt want in Mauritius, where, with the exception of amateur concerts, the only public entertainments previously provided were in the Theatre, Port Louis, on the rare visits of theatrical companies to the island.

MAHÉBOURG.

EDOUARD DE CHAZAL, General Engineer, Mahébourg.

It has long been difficult for any individual to give adequate expression to the fulness of the combination of contemporary science, art, knowledge and practice recognised in engineering. The ordinary vague idea of an engineer is of a man who does a great and constantly increasing number of things falling within a wide category. To people careless of etymology, *ingineering* instead of engineering would give

EDOUARD DE CHAZAL'S PREMISES, MAHÉBOURG.

a better idea of his versatility. The suggestion in the name would be removed from association with the word engine, and would be placed where it rightly belongs with the root idea which gives us the words ingenious, ingenuity and others. Such might well be applied to the work performed by Mr. Edouard de Chazal, whose establishment at Mahébourg, excellently equipped with machinery, and giving employment to about one hundred men, affords admirable facilities for general engineering repairs and metal working of all kinds. The premises occupy about one acre and a half of land, and have a branch line running into them from the railway.

Mr. de Chazal is a contractor to the railway for castings, of which he has supplied hundreds of tons to that department, and has also built waggons for it. He is also a contractor to the Public Works Department, the Woods and Forests Board, and the sugar factories. He has repaired boilers tested at 200 lbs. hydraulic pressure to the square inch, and undertakes everything to which his resources can be made subservient.

Mr. de Chazal is a native of Mauritius and was for three years and a half in charge of the drawings, patterns, and foundry of the Natal Government Railways. Afterwards he was for thirteen years assistant engineer at the Forges et Fonderies de Maurice, and resigned his position there to start another business, which he continued until 1910, when he established his present undertaking at Mahébourg.

VACOAS.

N. ROSE, General Merchant, "THE ENGLISH STORES," Vacoas.

FROM Vacoas, Port Louis is about sixteen miles distant and Curepipe about four, so that prior to the early part of 1909 the residents of Vacoas experienced great inconvenience through being so far away from shops. Moreover, when they did go to town considerable time was lost in searching amongst the various establishments for the particular articles required, as the modern departmental store was at that time *non est* in the island. This state of affairs was communicated to Mr. N. Rose, who had been in business in South Africa and London, and, in order to study the matter for himself, this gentleman came to Mauritius and at once realised the great potentialities which Vacoas afforded for a business that would supply the entire shopping requirements of the district. There was no small rejoicing, especially amongst the military, when it was known that he had started to meet the long-felt want; and on April 1st, 1909, when he opened the premises which he had specially built for his enterprise, the event was hailed with great approbation, for it marked the introduction of facilities and resources previously unknown in any centre of population in the island.

SECTION OF "THE ENGLISH STORES."

GROCERY DEPARTMENT, "THE ENGLISH STORES."

"The English Stores" is a miniature "Whiteley's," where requirements of the most dissimilar character are met with commendable thoroughness and ability. Careful organisation and up-to-date methods are observable throughout all the departments, which include groceries and provisions, wines and spirits, complete house-furnishing, paints and oils, hardware and ironmongery, stationery, sporting goods, patent medicines, perfumery, toys and general fancy articles, boots and shoes, ladies' and gentlemen's outfitting, tailoring, etc., etc. A speciality of its sartorial department is made-to-measure clothing, cut and fashioned by experts in England, and the extensive range of patterns provide a selection that cannot fail to please the most exacting tastes.

FANCY GOODS DEPARTMENT, "THE ENGLISH STORES."

Amongst the improvements which have been effected to the premises is an ærated water factory—started in November, 1911—lighted by electricity from its own dynamo, and equipped with Barnet and Foster machinery of the latest type, having a capacity of producing daily about five hundred dozen bottles of ærated waters of the finest and purest quality. The factory has its own department for mechanical repairs, and the scrupulous cleanliness and care with which the manufacturing operations are conducted are certainly worthy of encomium.

Mr. Rose is sole agent here for the Van Ryn Wine and Spirit Co., Ltd., of Capetown, and his bottling department is a noteworthy indication of the trade which he transacts in that direction.

Mr. Rose makes a speciality also of catering for the military in every department, and the business is very popular amongst both officers and men.

Briefly, "The English Stores" solves many an economic problem to the people of Vacoas, and its service and supplies are an undoubted attraction towards residence in the district.

Mr. Rose is ably assisted in the management by Mr. Julius Koenigsfest, who has been identified with the concern since its inception.

ROSE HILL.

ATCHIA BROS., Mauritius Hydro Electric Co., Rose Hill.

THIS business was established in 1900 by four brothers, Messrs. Mamode Ibrahim Atchia, Amode Ibrahim Atchia, Hossen Ibrahim Atchia, and Sulliman Ibrahim Atchia. The firm supply electricity of about 5,000 candle-power to Rose Hill, Beau Bassin, Quatre Bornes, and Moka. Their power-house is situated near the Réduit Falls, and is in charge of Mr. Hossen Ibrahim Atchia. They also do all kinds of electrical work and supply electric fittings, etc., using the metallic filament instead of the carbon filament.

Messrs. Atchia Bros. are proprietors of New Mill Aloe Fibre Factory, Pamplemousses, which is capable of producing twenty tons of fibre monthly. An illustration of that factory appears on page 241. They also own l'Industrie Sugar Estate of 450 acres in Pamplemousses.

GROUNDS OF "KINGSTON," QUATRE BORNES,
RESIDENCE OF MR. ARTHUR J. BROAD.

LAKE IN ROYAL BOTANIC GARDENS, PAMPLEMOUSSES.

DAIRY, LABOURDONNAIS ESTATE, RIVIERE DU REMPART.

PIGGERY, LABOURDONNAIS ESTATE, RIVIÈRE DU REMPART.

THE PRESS.

AT the time of the French Revolution, when Mauritius still belonged to France, Port Louis had three newspapers, which, however, disappeared immediately after the island passed into the possession of the British. During the first twenty or thirty years of the nineteenth century the only newspaper of any importance here was *The Mauritius Gazette*, an official publication in which no articles attacking the Government were allowed to appear.

At the time of his first mission to London, in 1831, Mr. Adrien d'Epinay obtained for Mauritius from the Home Government the liberty of the Press and a Legislative Council which, although composed of only the Governor and the chief officials, was a step in the path of progress. Thenceforth the laws framed by the local administrators, and approved by the Secretary of State, rendered less frequent the necessity for Orders in Council drafted or inspired by ministers 9,000 miles from the island; whilst the Proclamations formerly issued by the Governor were replaced by local Ordinances.

LE CERNÉEN.

When the liberty of the Press had been secured, and the acts of the Government could be submitted to regular public examination and criticism, there appeared on the 14th February, 1832, *Le Cernéen*, Mr. Adrien d'Epinay's journal, with four pages, each a little larger than foolscap size; its name being derived from *cerne* (swan), the designation given to the island when discovered by the Portuguese. In 1835, when *Le Cernéen* was enlarged, an illustration of a swan figured at the head of the second page over the leading article.

The motto adopted by the journal at its foundation was *Libertas sine Licentia*, and the part played by *Le Cernéen* in the public life of the colony has been considerable. Originally its policy was one of firm and dignified opposition to the Government, but when other journals, representing the various sections of the community, appeared, *Le Cernéen* became the special organ of the white population of French origin, although for a long time its columns contained English translations of its leading articles. Founded as a Liberal organ, and admirably conducted as such while it was inspired by Mr. Adrien d'Epinay, as well as for forty years afterwards, *Le Cernéen* became eventually, by the force of circumstances, a Conservative paper. Its mission was then no longer to uphold the white population, towards whom the Government was more and more disposed to give a large share in the direction of the affairs of the colony. So much was this the case that when Mr. (now Sir) William Newton and several of his friends amongst the governing classes took steps to ask the Home Government to grant to the colony the election of members to the Council of Government, they had an energetic opponent in *Le Cernéen*, which was at that period under the inspiration of the late Sir Célicourt Antelme, K.C.M.G., one of the richest and most influential planters in the island. The administrators of the journal were at that time blind to the fact that its founder, Mr. Adrien d'Epinay, had made the most heroic efforts during the greater part of his life to bring about the restoration to Mauritius of the elected Colonial Assembly, which had been granted to the people in 1791 by the French Revolutionary Government. It must, however, be said that when the necessity of reform was at last recognised by the Home Government, and later when the election of members to the Council of Government was an established fact, *Le Cernéen* openly allied itself to the policy of Sir John Pope Hennessy, who had assisted Sir William Newton and his coadjutors in the fulfilment of their aims.

During the last fifty years the four pages of *Le Cernéen*, which is the oldest of the local newspapers, have been the size of those of *The Times*. Although a few years ago its policy appeared to be one of vacillation, owing to the manœuvres of certain political agitators, it has re established its reputation as the organ of advanced Conservative principles, and has great influence in the island.

THE PLANTERS' AND COMMERCIAL GAZETTE.

The daily newspaper, *The Planters' and Commercial Gazette*, is the result of the amalgamation of the *Commercial Gazette*, founded in June, 1850, with *The Merchants' and Planters' Gazette*, founded by Mr. G. Houet in January, 1882.

EUGÈNE HENRY.

The Commercial Gazette, conducted by Mr. J. Wilson, was first produced at the printing establishment of Mr. A. J. Tennant, in the Place d'Armes, and was half the size of *The Planters' and Commercial Gazette* of to-day. The amalgamation in question was effected by Mr. G. Bouic in 1894, and the journal under the title of *The Planters' and Commercial Gazette* was taken over in 1903 by Mr. Eugène Henry, who also started at the same time the Standard Printing Establishment, which is one of the largest concerns of the kind in the island.

LE MAURICIEN.

In 1908 Mr. Henry founded the daily newspaper *Le Mauricien*, and amalgamated with it *The Daily Publisher*, founded in 1889, and *Le Vrai Mauricien*, founded in 1886. *Le Mauricien* has for its political advisers the Hon. Henri Leclézio, C.M.G., and Sir William Newton, K.C., and is controlled by a Board of Directors, with the Hon. Emile Sauzier, K.C., as President. It has thereby a great political influence amongst the white French population, and its circulation is claimed to be the largest of the daily morning papers.

The machinery of *The Planters' and Commercial Gazette* and *Le Mauricien* was wrecked by rioters of the black population during the Government election of 1911, but, much to the surprise of many, both newspapers managed to appear three days after, being the first of the destroyed journals to do so, although for a few days in a reduced form.

Mr. Eugène Henry, born in Mauritius in 1872, is an Officier d'Académie and Agent for the Equitable Life Assurance Society, Atlas Assurance Co., and the Federal Marine Insurance Co.

LA CROIX.

La Croix was started on July 7th, 1891, as a daily morning newspaper by some Mauritian gentlemen at the instigation of the Right Rev. Dr. Meurin, Bishop of Port Louis. Unsuccessful attempts had already been made to run a political paper professedly Roman Catholic. Prior also to the formation of *La Croix* the Roman Catholic community had as their organ the *Annales de l'Union Catholique*, which was founded as a monthly periodical in October, 1882, but was issued every fortnight from October, 1884, and every week from January, 1891.

Shortly after the death of Bishop Meurin at the end of 1895 the publication of *La Croix* was suspended. It was, however, resumed at the beginning of 1896, with the amalgamation of *Annales de l'Union Catholique*, and under the title of *Croix du Demanche* was published weekly until February 1st, 1911, when it became again a daily morning newspaper, and assumed its former title.

La Croix is Liberal and Democratic in politics, Catholic in religion, but unsectarian and friendly to all men of good will.

LA PATRIE.

The evening newspaper, *La Patrie*, was started on August 1st, 1912, by Mr. Edouard Laurent, its proprietor, who had just relinquished the editorship of *Le Petit Journal*. It professes to be an organ of the Democratic or Liberal party, but is, nevertheless, open to the expression of all opinions couched in moderate and proper terms. Its policy on general lines is ruled by the motto: "Mauritius for the Mauritians," and logically the object aimed at by that policy is self-government. Politics are banished from the Saturday issue, which is entirely devoted to interesting literary subjects. *La Patrie* has an excellent circulation and is well supported.

LE RADICAL

F. L. MOREL

5

Quelques réflexions

The Navy
The Mediterranean

Notes et Impressions

FRONT PAGE OF *LE RADICAL*.

LE RADICAL.

Le Radical was founded in 1898 by Mr. F. L. Morel, who is its proprietor and chief editor. It was the first afternoon paper to be issued at one o'clock—two hours before the others; and since 1909 it has had a second edition published at two o'clock, and containing three columns of the latest news.

As its name indicates, it is essentially a political newspaper, and is represented by some of the ablest and most prominent men of Mauritius; the greatest freedom being accorded to its various contributors. English as well as French articles on politics, literature, sport, and social matters, etc., are published in *Le Radical*, and its news service is particularly good. A lively journal, full of varied reading, *Le Radical* soon proved a success and became popular amongst all classes of the population. It has a circulation of about 2,000 copies, a large number of which are sold at the Central Station, Port Louis, at the departure of the afternoon trains.

Mr. F. L. Morel was born in Mauritius in 1865, and belongs to a well-known French family long established in the island. He started his journalistic career in 1890, and was for many years a Municipal Councillor. He is, we may add, a member of the Curepipe Club.

LA DÉPÊCHE.

The evening newspaper *La Dépêche* was founded about fifteen years ago by its present owner and editor, Mr. G. V. Hart de Keating, who was in 1901 the delegate of the Mauritian Press to their Royal Highnesses the Duke and Duchess of Cornwall and York (now their Majesties the King and Queen) on their visit to the island. Although sometimes publishing political articles it is specially a literary and social paper.

OTHER NEWSPAPERS.

The other local daily newspapers are as follows:—

Le Journal de Maurice, a morning paper, founded about twenty-five years ago by Mr. Charles Newton; Chief Editor, Mr. Henri Béchet. *Le Petit Journal*, an evening paper, founded in 1899 by Mr. Charles Newton; Chief Editor, Mr. J. Montarby. The morning dailies *Le Vrai Progrès Colonial*, and *Hindustani*, of which information has not been obtainable.

DEPENDENCIES OF MAURITIUS.

ALL the Dependencies are situated in the Indian Ocean to the north of Mauritius, the most northerly being about 6° south latitude, and between the meridians 51° and 72° 50′ east of Greenwich. With the exception of Rodrigues they are of coral formation. Bird guano is now extracted from many of the islands, and probably exists in more or less rich deposits on them all. The labourers on the islands are generally recruited from Mauritius, and a magistrate visits each, as a rule, every year, or more frequently if there has been any unusual trouble with the *personnel*.

RODRIGUES.—The last survey of Rodrigues, the largest of the Dependencies, was made by Commander Wharton, R.N., in 1874, when in command of H.M.S. *Shearwater*. The length of the island is, from east to west, about nine miles and three-sevenths, and its greatest breadth somewhat less than four miles and a half. It is elliptical in form, the major axis lying about east-north-east and west-south-west, and mainly consists of a single mountain of basaltic origin rising almost immediately from the beach—except towards the western and south-western ends where the land is less lofty—gradually terminating at the south-west end in an undulating plain of ancient compact coral, very cavernous. The area of Rodrigues is about forty-two square miles.

The island is surrounded by coral reefs, except for a few hundred yards at the south-eastern corner. These reefs run on the eastern side of the island for more than two miles and a half close in with the shore. Turning to the north-east corner of the island they continue close to the shore for four miles and a half up to a large and shallow bay called Grand Bay; the western point of this bay is the most northern land of Rodrigues. From there the reefs continue nearly due west, whilst the shore trends south-west. The reefs, therefore, gradually recede from the shore, and in some places are more than four miles from the mainland. On the western side the reefs run nearly north and south about two miles and a half from shore. On the southern side, beginning from the west, the reef runs eastward for six miles at a distance of about four miles from the shore. After this they follow a sinuous course in a north-easterly direction until they disappear at the south-eastern corner of the island.

S.S. "SECUNDER," PLYING BETWEEN MADAGASCAR, RÉUNION, MAURITIUS, AND RODRIGUES.

The capital of Rodrigues is called Port Mathurin and is situated on the northern shore. This is the only point at which vessels communicate, and it contains the only shops in the island. It is here also that the magistrate and the police are stationed. There is no harbour proper, but there is a large and commodious roadstead with good anchorage—sheltered from the south-east trades during the greater part of the year—between the reefs close inshore and a large shoal called "the middle ground." It was here that the British Indian fleet anchored in 1810 previous to the capture of Mauritius. The troops on that occasion were chiefly encamped on the site of the present village, while the headquarters were about half a mile to the eastward at the entrance of a gorge traversed by an abundant stream. A little beyond was a small battery about forty feet above the water, on the site of which was erected, in 1874, the house from which the transit of Venus was observed by Lieutenant Neate, R.N., and his assistants. The latitude of this point is 19° 40′ 23″ south, and the longitude 63° 25′ east.

In the tableland of the interior are many small agriculturists who cultivate beans for exportation, and sweet potatoes, manioc, and maize, for home consumption. A number of the fishermen also reside here, rejoining their families on the Saturday night and returning to work on Monday morning. There is a great exportation of goats and bullocks, tobacco, and fruits, such as oranges, citrons, alligator pears, custard apples, limes, pine-apples, etc.

At the time when the British fleet lay off Rodrigues in 1810, there was no other place to windward of Mauritius where it could have assembled; indeed, with the exception of the Cargados Bank to the north-east, there is practically no anchorage to windward nearer than Australia or the Island of Diego Garcia in the Chagos Archipelago. At that time Rodrigues was tolerably well wooded and abounded in giant tortoises. There is now scarcely a tree standing and the tortoises are extinct. The only refreshments that ships can get are water, beef, and goat's flesh.

The island was formerly frequented by American whalers resorting to the Indian Ocean in pursuit of the sperm whale, but since they have been prevented from cutting down the scrub in the ravines, they have altogether deserted Rodrigues and resorted to Seychelles.

According to the last census on 31st March, 1911, the population of Rodrigues was 4,829; of these 2,523 were males and 2,306 females. There are several villages on the hills, the Nassola, St. Gabriel, Pavillon, Cascade, Trefles. At Mare Lubine is a hospital, close to which the Government Medical Officer resides. The temperature up the hills is delightful. At St. Gabriel is the principal Roman Catholic church of the island.

Since November, 1901, the submarine cable connecting South Africa with Australia passes through Mauritius, Rodrigues, and Cocos Island. This cable places Rodrigues in daily telegraphic communication with the rest of the world, and adds considerably to the importance of the Dependency. The Eastern Telegraph Extension Company keeps a large staff in Rodrigues as it is a transmitting station.

DIEGO GARCIA.—This is the most important of the Oil Islands and lies between 7° 13′ and 7° 27′ south latitude and 72° 25′—72° 34′ east longitude. It is formed by a narrow strip of land—in some places very narrow and others one mile and a half broad—enclosing a lagoon twelve miles in length and from four to six miles in breadth. The island is low and is covered with cocoa-nut plantations. There are six villages or camps and several isolated houses. The population in 1911 consisted of 517 persons, 315 males, and 202 females. There are two hospitals on the island. In July, 1911, according to the magistrate's report, there were eighty-one asses, three horses, three bullocks, and one mule. The population is employed in fishing, in the cultivation of cocoa-nut, and the manufacture of oil. The mills for extracting oil are all very primitive, and animal traction is the only power employed for driving them. The exports consist of poonac and copra, oil, salt fish, and tortoise-shell, and in 1911 amounted to Rs. 54,517.

AGALÉGA.—This is the most important of the Oil Islands after Diego Garcia, and in 1911 exported 519,740 litres of cocoa-nut oil valued at Rs. 76,739, and 115,500 cocoa-nuts valued at Rs. 2,280. It consists of two islands separated by a narrow strip of sand which dries in patches at low water The extreme northerly point is 10° 20′ south latitude and extends to 10° 30′ south latitude. It lies between east longitude 56° 32′ and 56° 42′. Agaléga has a large establishment which in 1911 employed 415 persons (228 males and 187 females) In addition to the cultivation of cocoa-nuts, another industry has recently been started in the form of horse-breeding. The animals are fed on poonac—the residue of the cocoa-nut—and are said to be thriving. In 1912 there were on the island 102 donkeys, twenty mules, eight horses, eighteen colts and fillies, three stallions. The rats constitute a very serious plague at the present time, and it is estimated that nearly twenty-five per cent. of the nuts are destroyed by them, in spite of the fact that about 125 rats are caught daily. The labourers appear to live under more favourable conditions at Agaléga than on any of the other smaller Dependencies. A large kitchen garden is cultivated on the estate.

FARQUHAR consists of a shallow lagoon eleven and a half by six miles, surrounded by coral reef. The two principal islands are situated at the extreme east of the lagoon, which lies between south latitude 10° 5′ and 10° 15′ and east longitude 51° 2′ and 51° 12′. These islands produce cocoa-nuts, charcoal from filao wood, tortoise-shell, salt fish, and manufacture cocoa-nut oil and turtle oil for export. In 1911 the total exports amounted to Rs. 43,242, and the population consisted of ninety-nine persons—fifty-six males and forty-three females.

ST. BRANDON—Cargados Carayos Group.—This group lies between south latitude 16° 18′ and 16° 57′ and east longitude 59° 30′ and 57° 44′. All the islands are small and low, many being liable to be submerged in heavy weather. The eastern side of the reef is about thirty-four miles long in a curved line. The population of this group at the census of 1911 consisted of ninety-seven males and thirteen females, in all 110 persons. The exports consist of salt fish, guano, and tortoise-shell. The total value amounted to Rs. 56,597 in 1901. A ship from Mauritius calls about once a month.

EAGLE ISLAND, TROIS FRÈRES, and DANGER ISLAND on the Chagos Bank lie between 6° 7′ and 6° 24′ south latitude and 71° 10′ and 71° 32′ east longitude. The main island (Eagle Island) is two miles and a half long and half a mile broad. In 1911 the population of the group consisted of 104 persons—fifty-eight males and forty-six females. The exports consist principally of cocoa-nut and its bye products, and salt fish. The total exports amounted to Rs. 6,053 in 1911. There are five primitive mills for the extraction of the oil.

OIL ESTABLISHMENT, AGALÉGA.

SIX ISLANDS.—Lie between south latitude 6° 37′ and 6° 41′ and east longitude 71° 16′ and 71° 22′. The reef forms an oval five miles and a half long and two miles broad enclosing a lagoon. The establishment is on South East Island. In 1911 the population consisted of 156 persons—eighty-eight males and sixty-eight females. The principal product is cocoa-nut oil. The total exports amounted to Rs. 9,313 in 1911. In August, 1911, there were six mills in good working order. Fifty-three asses and fifteen horses were then employed. It is reported that rats do an immense amount of damage to the crop.

PEROS BANHOS.—The twenty-seven islands and reefs of this group form a rough square; the interior is a large lagoon. They lie between 5° 13′ and 5° 28′ south latitude and 71° 40′ and 71° 56′ east longitude. The population in 1911 consisted of 165 males and 135 females, making a total of 300 persons. The industries consist of fishing, the cultivation of cocoa-nuts, and manufacture of oil. The total exports amounted to Rs. 28,833 in 1911. There are eight mills on the islands.

SALOMON.—Also known as Onze Iles; lies between 5° 17′ and 5° 22′ south latitude and 72° 13′ and 72° 17′ east longitude, and are distant from Mauritius about 1,250 nautical miles. The establishment is on Boddam Island. In 1911 the population amounted to 160 persons—ninety males and seventy females. The products consist of cocoa-nuts and tortoise-shell. There are seven mills for the manufacture of oil, all of which are worked by horses and asses. In 1911 there were twenty-eight horses and forty-nine asses. The total products amounted to Rs. 20,850 in 1911.

[The foregoing information regarding the Dependencies of Mauritius has been taken from *The Mauritius Almanac.*]

NOTES ON SOME OF THE GOVERNMENT OFFICIALS AND PROFESSIONAL MEN OF MAURITIUS.

Antelme Family.

THE Antelme family, one of the oldest in Mauritius, was established here by Mr. Jerome Valentin Antelme, a native of Provence, who was amongst the defenders of the island in 1810. One of his sons, Sir Célicourt Antelme, K.C.M.G., and Knight of the Legion of Honour, whose portrait appears on page 200, once a French barrister, was one of the most remarkable men of the colony, and the founder of the Crédit Foncier of Mauritius, Ltd., the Agricultural Company, and the Mauritius Sugar Estates Co. He was also connected with many other local Boards, and was one of the ablest members of the Council of Government.

Mr. Léopold Antelme, brother of Sir Célicourt, was a broker, and owned extensive forests, where he organised hunting parties with great hospitality. In 1901 he was preparing a hunting party in honour of H.R.H. the Duke of Cornwall and York (now His Majesty King George V.), when he died, after a short illness. In accordance with his express desire, his sons did not alter in any way the preparations, and received in a fitting manner the future sovereign, who, on his departure, presented a souvenir of his visit to each of Messrs. Léopold and Ernest Antelme. The Antelmes are the most notable hunters in the island, and have shot amongst them upwards of 5,000 deer.

Antelme, The Hon. Gaston,

Manager of Stanley Sugar Estate.

Born in Mauritius in March, 1867, and after being educated at the Royal College, became chief overseer on Stanley Sugar Estate, owned at that time by his celebrated uncle, Sir Célicourt Antelme, K.C.M.G. Mr. Antelme was thereafter manager of The Mount and Plessis Sugar Estates for seven years, and was a shareholder in the Deep River Sugar Estate, owned by his family. In 1894 he was appointed inspector to the Mauritius Agricultural Co., and the Crédit Foncier of Mauritius, Ltd. After the death in 1899 of Sir Célicourt Antelme, he went to Europe, and returned in 1901, when he resigned his connection with the afore-mentioned companies. His uncle's estates had now been formed into a limited liability company, of which Mr. Antelme was one of the principal shareholders, especially of Stanley Estate, of which he became manager. He afterwards bought the Black River Sugar Estate, and sold it at a good profit some three years later. Thereupon he resumed the management of Stanley Sugar Estate, now the property of the Anglo-Ceylon and General Estates Co., Ltd.

In 1901 Mr. Antelme was elected member for Black River in the Council of Government, and has remained as such until the present time. He is a member of the Committee of the Woods and Forests Board, Station Agronomique, Chairman of the District Board of Black River, and member of the Board of Commissioners for the Town of Curepipe.

Avice, Tristan,

Assistant Registrar-General.

Born in Mauritius in 1871, and educated at the Royal College; passed matriculation examination, and entered the Government service in 1893 as clerk in the Procureur-General's Department; transferred in 1894 to the Registration and Mortgage Department; and appointed Assistant Registrar-General in 1905.

Baissac, Paul,

Notary.

Mr. Paul Baissac was born in Mauritius in 1874, and in 1891 became assistant to his uncle, Mr. Gustave Baissac. He was appointed a notary on November 2nd, 1904, and succeeded to Mr. Gustave Baissac's business on the death of that gentleman in 1906.

Mr. Baissac possesses the minutes of—

L. E. Baissac	1873 to 1885
G. M. F. Sevene	1836 to 1868
Theodore Sauzier	1868 to 1873
Gustave Baissac	1886 to 1904

He is owner of Esperance Sugar Estate at Poudre d'Or, financial agent of the Sena Sugar Co. of the Zambesi, Chairman of the Ile d'Ambre Sugar Estate Co., Ltd.; Director of the Gentlemen's Store Co., Ltd.; President of the Mauritius Jockey Club, and a Steward of the Mauritius Turf Club.

Bertin, Henri,

Attorney-at-Law.

Born in Mauritius, Mr. Henri Bertin became an attorney-at-law in 1864, being now the senior attorney in the island. He spent many years in England and France, and recently attended successfully to two big appeals in London before the Privy Council; Mr. H. H. Asquith, now Prime Minister, and Sir Robert Finlay acting as his counsel.

Mr. Bertin represented Mauritius at the Franco-British Exhibition in London in 1909, and was elected President of one of the sections of the Jury for the awards. He is a keen sportsman, and in 1902 was the owner of "Micawber," which won several races in that year. He is one of the oldest members of the Athenæum Club, having been a member of it since 1871.

Biden, A. G.,

Auditor.

Born 1878; educated at Radley College and Trinity College, Oxford; B.A., 1902; Colonial Audit Department, London; Assistant Auditor, Gold Coast, 1904; Local Auditor, Gambia, 1905; Assistant Auditor, East Africa Protectorate, 1908; Auditor, Mauritius, 1912.

Bilsborrow, Right Rev. J. R., O.S.B.,

Bishop of Port Louis.

Born in 1862 near Preston, Lancashire; ordained priest, June 23rd, 1889; arrived in Mauritius in 1896 as Secretary to the late Bishop O'Neil; Vicar-General, 1899; named Bishop of Port Louis, September 15th, 1910; consecrated at St. Edmund's Monastery, Wolverhampton, February 24th, 1911.

Brebner, Captain C. W., F.R.G.S., F.R.S.A.

Born at Lucia, Parish of Hanover, Jamaica, West Indies, in 1856, Captain C. W. Brebner has been at sea since he was sixteen years of age, and became a captain at the age of twenty-four. After serving in the Loch Line of Glasgow from 1874 until 1881, he came from Melbourne to Mauritius in the latter year, and joined what was then known as the Old Country Service, or the Old East India Service, and four years later gave up his command of the "Canada" (late of the Cunard Line) for that of the famous China tea-clipper "Sir Lancelot," photo and particulars of which appear on page 342. After leaving the "Sir Lancelot" in 1894 he was master of the "Grosvenor" until 1901, when all the Old Country Service ships were replaced by steamers. Captain Brebner then went to England and purchased the steamer "Secunder," of which he is captain and proprietor. The "Secunder," of which there are illustrations on pages 410 and 429, plies every fortnight between Madagascar, Réunion, and Mauritius, chiefly in the cattle trade, and has been during the last five years under contract with the Mauritius Government for the carrying of the mails every two months between Mauritius and the Dependency of Rodrigues from March until December.

Captain Brebner is a Fellow of the Royal Geographical Society and the Royal Society of Arts and Sciences. He is the author of "The New Handbook for the Indian Ocean, Arabian Sea, and Bay of Bengal," dealing with miscellaneous subjects for sailing ships and steamers, Mauritius cyclones and currents, moon observations, sail-making, etc. It is from that excellent and valuable work that our particulars of the "Sir Lancelot" have been taken. He is also the author of another admirable book, "South Indian Ocean Cyclones."

Buswell, Venerable Archdeacon H. H.

Born in 1839 at Cambridge, and educated at the C.M. College, Islington, London; ordained, 1862; C.M.S. Missionary, Jaffna, Ceylon, 1862-65; Incumbent of St. Thomas's, Beau Bassin, 1866-85; Chaplain of St. Clement's, Curepipe, and Acting Chaplain to the Forces, Mauritius, 1885-94; special mission to Réunion and Rodrigues, 1874; Seychelles, 1879, 1885, 1888, and 1900; Chaplain to Bishops Royston and Walsh; Canon and Sub-Dean, St. James's Cathedral, Port Louis, 1894; Archdeacon, Seychelles, since 1895; Secretary, C.M.S.

Cauvin, N.,

Pilot.

Born in the Seychelles Islands in 1872; was master-mariner of sailing ships and steamers for many years, and appointed pilot on April 7th, 1902; is a member of the Merchant Service Guild.

Celestin, L. A.,

Superintendent of Inland Revenue and Distilleries.

Born in Mauritius in 1857, and is the oldest Government servant in the Treasury Department; entered the Government service in 1875 as Assistant Schoolmaster of Beau Bassin Government School; appointed Headmaster in 1880; Inspector of Schools, 1883; District Cashier, 1886; Chief Inspector of Distilleries, 1893; Superintendent of Distilleries, 1900; Senior Audit Examiner, 1901; Chief Clerk, Treasury Department, 1903; Pay Clerk, Treasury Department, 1909; Superintendent of Inland Revenue and Distilleries, 1913.

Chancellor, H.E. Major Sir John Robert, R.E., C.M.G., D.S.O.,

Governor and Commander-in-Chief.

Served with expedition to Dongola in 1896, with force at Suakin (medal and Egyptian medal); in operations on the N.W. frontier of India, 1897-8, with Tirah expeditionary force, action of Dargai (mentioned in despatches); Secretary to the Colonial Defence Committee, October, 1906; Assistant Secretary to the Imperial Conference on Naval and Military Defence, 1909; created C.M.G., 1909; appointed Governor and Commander-in-Chief, Mauritius, 1911; knighted in 1913.

Couve, Octave,

Sworn and Exchange Broker.

Born in Mauritius in 1875, educated at the Royal College, and started his business career in the office of his father, Mr. Léopold Couve, sworn and exchange broker, who died in 1900, in which year Mr. Octave Couve also became a sworn and exchange broker. Mr. Octave Couve is an enthusiastic sportsman, and has figured prominently in connection with the local race meetings.

Davson, Charles S., B.A., LL.B.,

Puisne Judge.

Mr. Justice Davson, eldest son of Mr. G. I. Davson, for many years manager of the British Guiana Bank, was born in 1857 at Georgetown, British Guiana, and educated at Westminster School (Queen's Scholar) and Trinity Hall, Cambridge (honours in law). He was called to the Bar, Middle Temple, in 1881; admitted to the Bar of British Guiana, 1882; Stipendiary Magistrate, 1888; acted as Solicitor-General on many occasions; appointed Solicitor-General, 1898; acted as Attorney-General on several occasions, and also as Puisne Judge; appointed Puisne Judge, Mauritius, 1905.

Dawson, John Wilding, Assoc.M.Inst.C.E., F.I.S.E.,

Assistant Director of Public Works and Surveys.

Mr. John Wilding Dawson, Associate Member of the Institute of Civil Engineers, Fellow of the Institute of Sanitary Engineers, was born at Barrow-in-Furness in 1866, and educated at the Independent College, Taunton, and the Science and Art School, Barrow-in-Furness.

After serving six years with Messrs. Gradwells' Exors., at that time the largest contractors in North Lancashire, he went in 1888 to British Columbia, and was engaged in the construction of important buildings for the Canadian Pacific Railway Co., and in the construction of the Electric Railway between Vancouver City and New Westminster until 1892, when he returned to England.

In November, 1894, he was appointed Assistant Engineer on Drainage Works, Mauritius, and in August, 1898, Drainage Authority.

In December, 1904, he was promoted to Assistant Director of Public Works and Surveys, and in 1907 and 1910 acted altogether for thirteen months as Director of Public Works and Surveys.

de Chazal, Andre.

Mr. André de Chazal was born in Mauritius in 1874, and when eighteen years of age became assistant to his father, Mr. P. E. de Chazal, C.M.G., who had been established as an attorney-at-law since 1860, and whose business he now manages. Mr. André de Chazal is a director of the Central Rum Warehouse Co., Diego and Peros Oil Co., Colonial Fire Insurance Co., Compagnie Générale de Quincaillerie, and director and co-proprietor of Beau Vallon Sugar Estate and Rivière des Anguilles Sugar Estate.

de Froberville, Leon Huet,

Acting Chief Clerk, Supreme Court.

Like many other Mauritians of French descent, Mr. Léon Huet de Froberville belongs to an ancient noble family of Normandy that settled in Mauritius before the island passed into the possession of the British. From his youth he has taken great interest in historical researches, and is the author of several valuable works and many historical notices. His most interesting production is "Le Combat du Grand Port et la fin de l'Occupation Française," published in 1910, for which the decoration of "Officier de l'Instruction Publique" was conferred upon him by the Government of the French Republic. Mr. de Froberville joined the Mauritius Government service in 1878, and was appointed Acting Chief Clerk of the Supreme Court in October, 1910.

Delafaye, K.C., Sir Victor.

Born in 1842; called to the Bar at the Middle Temple, 1863; Municipal Councillor, Port Louis, 1870; member of the Prison Board, 1884; member of the Civil Service Commission, 1884-95; Acting Puisne Judge, 1884-85 and 1890-92; Q.C., 1892; Puisne Judge, 1894; Acting Chief Justice, 1898; Chief Justice, 1898; retired in December, 1912.

de Maroussem, A.,

Sworn and Exchange Broker.

Mr. A. de Maroussem was born in Mauritius in 1872, and started business in 1892 in the office of his uncle, Mr. A. Boule, broker. When the latter gentleman died in 1906 Mr. de Maroussem succeeded him. He is a director of the Central Dock Co.

d'Emmerez de Charmoy, D.,

Curator of Museum and Government Entomologist.

Born in Mauritius in 1873; entered Government service as Assistant-Superintendent of the Museum, 1891; appointed Curator in 1895; assistant to Professor Ross in 1897; officer in charge of the anti-malaria campaign in 1898; Government Entomologist, and author of "Report on the Smithi (Arrow) and other Beetles injurious to the Sugar-Cane"; Hon. Secretary of the Royal Society of Arts and Sciences of Mauritius.

de Robillard, Edgar,

Notary.

Mr. Edgar de Robillard was born in Mauritius in 1857, and in 1882 began his professional career as an assistant to Mr. Victor Barry. In 1895 he became a notary and started in business for himself. He possesses the minutes of—

Audibert	1789 to 1792
Barry	1838 to 1842
Bonnefin	1825 to 1833
Bouic	1833 to 1839
Chateau de Baylon pere	1772
Chateau de Baylon fils	1791 to 1806 (An X)
Ducray, Pamplemousses	1829 to 1834
Ducray, Grand Port	1831 to 1842
Ducray, J. M. R. G.	1833 to 1857
Ducray, J. M. R. G	1872 to 1874
Ducray, M. F. G.	1874 to 1878
Durant, père	1791 to 1796—An V.
Durant, fils	1805—An IV. to 1819
Leroy	1819 to 1825
Maingard, C. G. A.	1857 to 1872
Pépin	An VIII. to 1808—An IX.
Pilot, C. J. C.	1878 to 1884
Toussaint, Grand Port	1791 to 1820
Vigoreux de K/Morvan	1885 to 1888
Maingard, J. M.	1888 to 1895

Mr. de Robillard is co-owner of Argy Sugar Estate of 2,500 acres, which is capable of producing 3,000 tons of sugar annually, including the canes supplied by small planters. He is President of the Notaries' Chamber, Secretary of the Curepipe Club, Vice-President of the Union Catholique de l'Ile Maurice, and a Director of the Nouvelle Société Huiliere de Diego et Peros.

Desplaces, W. E.,

Manager of Beau Champ Sugar Estate and Annexes.

Born in Mauritius, and when twenty years of age was manager of Beau Champ Sugar Estate, Savanne. After two years in that position he left for Australia, and managed successfully for twenty-five years sugar factories in Queensland; in 1904 was appointed Government Inspector of the Government Central Sugar Factories, Queensland; selected in 1910 by the Liberal

Federal Government of Australia as technical member of a Royal Commission to inquire into the sugar industry; returned to Mauritius in 1912 as manager of Beau Champ Estate, Factory and Annexes, Flacq.

Ducray, Henri G.,

Sworn and Exchange Broker.

Born in Mauritius in 1860, Mr. Henri G. Ducray commenced his business career in 1878 as a clerk in a notary's office in Port Louis, where he remained for one year, and then acted as assistant to his uncle, Mr. J. Deglos, general broker, and became partner with him in 1885. In 1887 Mr. Deglos left the island for Paris, where he still lives, and continued in partnership with Mr. Ducray until 1902, since when Mr. Ducray has been operating on his own account.

Mr. Ducray is a member of the Chamber of Commerce and the Chamber of Agriculture, a Director of the New Mauritius Dock Co., Colonial Fire Insurance Co., Ltd., Nouvelle Société Huiliere de Diego et Peros, and Mauritius Pharmacy Co., Ltd., and town manager of Trianon Sugar Estate and Rich Fund Sugar Estate. Mr. Ducray was for several years President of the Mauritius Commercial Bank, and is a Director of it when the regulations permit. He is also a member of the Committee of the Club de Curepipe.

Duncan, C. W.,

Deputy Inspector-General of Police.

Mr. C. W. Duncan was born in British Guiana in 1881, and in 1899 became a clerk in the Colonial Secretary's Office in Georgetown, where he remained until 1901, when he joined the British Guiana Police Force as Sub-Inspector. In 1905 he became District-Inspector, and in 1910 was selected to command the first police party sent to suppress the disorder and outlawry in the Wenamu gold district on the Venezuelan border. The journey from Georgetown to the affected area occupied a month, and on a subsequent trip Mr. Duncan established the Wenamu Police Station. In 1911 he was appointed Deputy Inspector-General of Police, Mauritius.

d'Unienville, Baron,

Planter.

Mr. Albert Marrier, Baron D'Unienville, owner of La Lucie Sugar Estate, Flacq., is a descendant of a very old French family, many members of which occupy prominent positions in the agriculture of the island. His great-grandfather settled here at the time of the French Revolution, and was a member of the Colonial Assembly. After the conquest of the island by the British he filled several important administrative positions under the governorship of Sir Robert Farquhar, and accompanied that gentleman when he went to England for the purpose of improving the affairs of the colony. On his return to Mauritius Baron D'Unienville compiled, at the request of the Government, "The Statistics of Mauritius," which is still consulted as a reference book.

Mr. Albert Marrier, the present holder of the family title, by which he is chiefly known, is, like his relatives, held in much esteem for his hospitality, kindness of heart, and other sterling qualities.

Duvivier, L. A. Aime,

Custodian of the Archives.

Born in Mauritius in 1858; joined the Civil Service on Nov. 1st, 1879, as clerk in the Archives Office; appointed Custodian of the Archives, Jan. 1st, 1891. He is Officier de l'Instruction Publique, Churchwarden of Port Louis Cathedral, member of the Committee of Superior Instruction, Hon. Treasurer of the Mauritius Institute, and member of the Historical Records Committee.

Dykes, A. J.,

Railway Locomotive, Carriage, and Wagon Superintendent.

Mr. A. J. Dykes was born at Crewe, Cheshire, and served his apprenticeship in the large locomotive works of that town, after which he was employed by the Great Northern Railway Co. from 1897 until 1904, when he was appointed to his present position.

Edwards, W. T. A., M.D. Paris, C.M.G.,

Chairman of the Board of Directors of the Mauritius Institute.

Dr. W. T. A. Edwards, C.M.G., was born in Mauritius in 1837, and is the son of the late Hon. Arthur Edwards, who was a sugar planter, merchant, and member of the Council of Government. An M.D. of the Faculty of Paris, Dr. Edwards has taken an active part in everything pertaining to the improvement of the sanitary conditions of the colony since 1872. He was elected member for Pamplemousses and Savanne respectively in the Council of Government from 1891 to 1906, and was a member of the Executive Council from 1897 to 1909. He was created a Companion of the Order of St. Michael and St. George by King George V. when His Majesty, as Duke of Cornwall and York, visited the island in August, 1901, accompanied by Her Majesty, then Duchess of Cornwall and York.

Dr. Edwards is President of the Board of Commissioners for the Town of Curepipe, where he has been in practice for the last forty years. He is also Chairman of the Board of Directors of the Mauritius Institute, and has been President of the Chamber of Agriculture.

Esnouf, Edouard Amand,

District and Stipendiary Magistrate, PORT LOUIS.

Born in Mauritius in 1842, and called to the Bar at the Middle Temple in 1865; was appointed District Magistrate, Seychelles, in 1870; Grand Port, Mauritius, May, 1878; District Magistrate, Moka, 1883; Junior District Magistrate, Port Louis, August, 1884; acted as Master of the Supreme Court, May, 1886, and from December, 1887, to January, 1888; Senior District Magistrate, Port Louis, March, 1890, to March, 1892; December, 1892, to February, 1893; May to August, 1896; District Magistrate, Port Louis, 3rd division,

February, 1898; District and Stipendiary Magistrate, Rivière du Rempart, March, 1898; District Magistrate, Port Louis, 3rd division, March, 1899; Substitute Master of the Supreme Court, August, 1901.

Esnouf, The Hon. V. Amand,

Barrister-at-Law.

Born in Mauritus in 1871, and was called to the Bar at the Middle Temple at the end of 1893, returning in the following year to practise in Mauritius. In 1899 he became a member of the Municipal Council of Port Louis, and, with the exception of a few months, was identified with that body until 1912. He was Mayor in 1906 and 1910, and in 1911 was elected member for Plaines Wilhems in the Council of Government.

Mr. Esnouf has taken a prominent part in local racing, and his horse "Orion" won the Maiden Plate in 1903, and the cup presented by Sir Cavendish Boyle in 1904. He is a son of Mr. Edouard Amand Esnouf, District and Stipendiary Magistrate for Port Louis.

Ferriere, Dr. Joseph Anthony.

Born in Mauritius in 1880; Laureate of the Royal College in 1898; M.B., B.S., L.R.C.P. London, M.R.C.S. England, 1904; Obstetric Assistant and Resident Surgeon, University College Hospital, London; Resident Medical Officer, Hospital for Women, Soho; Assistant Resident Medical Officer, London Fever Hospital, Islington, from 1904 to 1907; since when he has been in practice in Mauritius.

Francis, The Hon. B. A., B.A.,

Protector of Immigrants and Poor Law Commissioner.

Born in 1878 in Devonshire, and educated at St. Edmund's School, Canterbury, and St. Catherine's College, Cambridge, B.A. (Classical Tripos), 1900; Lieutenant, Royal Artillery, 1900 to 1908; appointed Inspector of Immigrants, Mauritius, 1908; Protector of Immigrants and Poor Law Commissioner, July, 1912.

Galea, Maurice,

Journalist.

This clever young Mauritian was born in 1888, and educated at the Royal College. After spending five years in the office of the Hon. G. A. Ritter, C.M.G., attorney-at-law, he relinquished his post there, and became employed by Mr. Eugene Henry, proprietor of the Standard Printing Establishment and founder and chief editor of the newspapers "The Planters' and Commercial Gazette" and "Le Mauricien." Mr. Galea has given ample evidence of his journalistic ability, and his leading articles in "Le Mauricien" are very noteworthy for so young a man. He is the leading writer on local racing, and is the author of "Le Livre du Centaire du Mauritius Turf Club." Mr. Galea rendered able assistance in the compilation of "Mauritius Illustrated," acting as assistant to the editor during the five months the latter was in the island.

Ganachaud, Jacques,

Attorney-at-Law.

Born in Mauritius in 1874, and educated at the Royal College; started business in 1896 in the office of his father, Mr. Evanor Ganachaud, who died in 1905; became an attorney-at-law in 1902; elected member of the Municipal Council of Port Louis in 1902, and remained so for three years; Treasurer of the Vacoas Tennis Club; member of the Curepipe Club, and owner of race-horses.

Gebert, The Hon. Gaston,

Land Surveyor and Land Owner.

Born in Mauritius in 1856; elected in 1898 member for Grand Port in the Council of Government, and returned unopposed at the last election of 1911.

Gentil, Dr. J. C. H.

Born in Mauritius in 1862; L.R.C.P. and L.R.C.S., Edinburgh; L.F.P.S. Glasgow, 1899; Special Diploma in tropical medicine, University of Edinburgh, 1902; 1st prizeman in anatomy, Minto House; silver medallist, materia medica and therapeutics, practical anatomy and practical chemistry, Minto House, and R.C.S., Edinburgh; practised at Stockton-on-Tees from 1886 to 1904; also practised near Sunderland, and at Shotton Bridge, near Haswell; has been in practice in Mauritius since 1904.

Goupille, Pierre,

Sworn and Exchange Broker.

Mr. Pierre Goupille was born in Mauritius in 1878, and was elected to the Muncipal Council of Port Louis as Councillor for Ward 3 in December, 1912. A very enthusiastic sportsman, he has been connected with the local turf since 1901, and was prominent in the formation of the Mauritius Jockey Club. He has been the owner of about twenty race-horses, which contested nearly 200 races, and won many prizes.

Grannum, The Hon. Edward Allan,

Receiver-General.

Born in Barbados in 1869, and passed the Civil Service Examination there in 1886; was third clerk in the Registrar's office from January to October, 1885; second clerk, October, 1885, to November, 1887; clerk in the Master-in-Chancery's office, November, 1887, to June, 1888; Honours Graduate, Diploma, Ontario Commercial College, Canada, and Affiliated Institute of Chartered Accountants, Canada, December, 1889; practised as public accountant, Barbados, to August, 1897; acted as Assistant Auditor, Sierra Leone and Gambia, from September 25th, 1897 to January 15th, 1900; Auditor from May to November, 1898; Assistant Auditor, Gold Coast and Lagos, January to March, 1900; Auditor, March, 1900; introduced the system of double entry accounts into the Gold Coast Post Office, July, 1901; and prepared a scheme for the introduction of double entry system of accounts for the Accra Town Council, 1901; became local Auditor, Cyprus, in

1902; Auditor-General, Mauritius, May, 1909; Receiver-General, 1912.

Mr. Grannum is an ex-officio member of the Executive Council and the Council of Government, and is also a member of the West India Committee and the Royal Colonial Institute, London.

Guibert, G. J. M., K.C.

Mr. G. J. M. Guibert was born in Mauritius in 1843, and was Laureate of the Royal College in 1859. He was called to the Bar at the Middle Temple in 1864, and, returning in that year to Mauritius to practise, became Queen's Counsel in 1891. Mr. Guibert took an active part in the reform movement which led in 1886 to the introduction of elected members in the Council of Government. In the same year, after unsuccessfully contesting one of the seats for Port Louis, he became a nominated member of the Council of Government, and continued as such until 1889, when he resigned, and was elected member for Port Louis, representing that constituency until 1891. He was then returned as member for Plaines Wilhems, remaining so until 1901, when he lost his seat by a few votes. He was, however, elected again in 1906 as member for Plaines Wilhems; but in 1911 was compelled to relinquish his public life on account of failing sight. He is now totally blind, but still practises as K.C.

Mr. Guibert was Chairman of the Committee of Education from 1888 to 1900. He is a director of Savannah Sugar Estate Co., Ltd., and is legal adviser to the Crédit Foncier of Mauritius, Ltd., and other local concerns.

Haycraft, Thomas Wagstaffe, B.A.,

Puisne Judge.

B.A., St. John's College, Oxon.; called to the Bar, Inner Temple, 1885; practised in S.E. circuits, Sussex sessions; Examiner of the Court, 1889 to 1899; appointed Arbitrator on the Board of the London Chamber of Arbitration, 1897; President of the District Court of Larnaca, Cyprus, 1899; Police Magistrate, Coroner, and Inspector of Schools, Gibraltar, July, 1911; Puisne Judge, Mauritius, February, 1913; author of "Executive Powers in Relation to Crime and Disorder," and "Bills of Sale Acts" (second edition, 1911).

Hein, Jules,

Sworn and Exchange Broker.

Born in Mauritius in 1870, Mr. Jules Hein became a sworn and exchange broker in 1898, and is a director of the Mauritius Commercial Bank, Colonial Engrais Chimiques Co., Albion Dock Co., and the Mauritius Fire Insurance Co.

Herchenroder, Furcy Alfred,

Chief Justice.

Born in Mauritius in March, 1865, and is great-grandson of Captain J. J. H. Herchenroder, of the French Army, who settled in the island about the end of the eighteenth century. His Honour was Laureate of the Royal College in 1885, and was called to the Bar at the Middle Temple in 1888; appointed Acting Crown Prosecutor, Mauritius, 1893; Legal Adviser, Police Magistrate, Crown Prosecutor, Conservator of Mortgages and Curator of Vacant Estates, Seychelles, May, 1898; Judge, Seychelles, 1900; Chief Justice, Seychelles, 1903; Procureur and Advocate-General, Mauritius, April, 1905; King's Counsel 1905; Chief Justice, Mauritius, January 1st, 1913.

Hugues, L. A.,

Acting Puisne Judge.

Born in Mauritius in 1854, and called to the Bar at the Inner Temple in 1877; appointed District Magistrate of Grand Port in 1893; District Magistrate, 1st division, Port Louis, 1903; District Magistrate, 2nd division, Port Louis, 1907; Master and Registrar of the Supreme Court, 1911; and Acting Puisne Judge of the Supreme Court, 1913; published in 1905, "Digest of the Reported Decisions of the Supreme Court," a volume highly prized by the legal profession in Mauritius.

Innes, T. W.,

Planter.

Mr. T. W. Innes spent ten years in Demerara as a sugar planter, and left that colony to take charge of a central sugar factory in Porto Rico. While there he received from the Anglo-Ceylon and General Estates Co., Ltd., the offer of his present position as manager of Britannia Sugar Estate and Factory, which he has held since 1902.

Jollivet, Arthur B. Y., L.R.C.P. Edin., L.F.P.S. Glasgow,

Medical Superintendent, Barkly Asylum.

Born in Mauritius, Dr. Jollivet entered the Government service as Health Officer for Port Louis in 1885, and was appointed Medical Superintendent of the Barkly Asylum on November 15th, 1895.

Kerr, Louis Lyndon,

Inspector-General of Police.

Mr. Louis Lyndon Kerr was born in 1863 in British Guiana, and became a clerk in the Immigration Department of that colony in 1887. In 1888 he was transferred to the Clerical Department of the Police, and in 1891-1892 was Acting Inspector of Police. In 1892 he was also Acting Paymaster, and in the following year he was a District Inspector and a Justice of the Peace. From June to October, 1895, he was in charge of the Uruan frontier station. In 1897 he was promoted to County Inspector of Police; in September, 1899, to Acting Deputy-Inspector of Police; in May, 1900, to Chief County Inspector; and in March, 1905, became an Official Visitor of the Onderneeming School. In October, 1908, he was made Chief County Inspector of Police; and in February, 1909, he became Superintendent of the Georgetown Fire Brigade. In March, 1909, he was promoted to Acting Inspector-General of Police and Inspector of Prisons, which was followed in July, 1909, by the appointment of Inspector-General of Police of Mauritius. He took up his present post at the end of 1911.

Koenig, The Hon. Etienne,

Procureur and Advocate-General.

The Hon. Etienne Koenig is a member of a well-known Mauritian family, which was established in the island about the end of the eighteenth centry. He was born in the island in 1862, and was Laureate of the Royal College in 1881. Called to the Bar at the Middle Temple in 1884, he practised in Mauritius until 1900, when he became Crown Prosecutor. He was appointed Assistant Colonial Secretary in 1903; Substitute Procureur and Advocate-General, 1904; Acting Puisne Judge in 1906, 1907, 1908, and 1910; Procureur and Advocate-General, January 1st, 1913.

Koenig, H.,

Acting Chief Clerk, Railway Department.

Born in Mauritius and educated at the Royal College; was appointed writer in the Colonial Secretary's Office, November, 1894; 6th class clerk, Audit Department, March, 1897; 5th class clerk, April, 1900; 4th class clerk, July, 1902; 3rd class clerk, Storekeeper-General's Department, July, 1903; Chief Railway Storekeeper, April, 1911; Acting Chief Clerk, Railway Department, March, 1913.

Koenig, Paul, I.N.A.,

Director of the Department of Forests and Gardens.

Born in Mauritius in 1870 and left the island in 1890 to complete his education in Europe. He studied first at the Agronomique Institute of Paris, then at Cooper's Hill College, England, and thereafter went through a special course of training in forestry at Havoner (Germany). Returning in 1894 to Mauritius, he was appointed in 1896 to the Department of Forests and Gardens, and was promoted to his present position in 1904.

Labat, Gustave,

Sworn and Exchange Broker.

Born in Mauritius in 1857, Mr. Gustave Labat commenced his commercial career in 1876, in the office of Messrs. Ireland, Fraser and Co., with whom he remained two years, and then became assistant to Mr. Frederick Tennant, broker, and a member of the well-known family of that name in Glasgow and South Africa. Mr. Frederick Tennant (Mr. Labat's father-in-law) died in 1903, and was succeeded in his business by Mr. Labat, who is Director and Secretary of the Union Chamouny Sugar Estate Co. and the Belle Vue Sugar Estate Co., also a Director of the Colonial Fire Insurance Co., Colonial Dock Co., Agalega Oil Co., Magasin General des Huiles de Coco, Dry Docks and Slips Co., Mauritius Public Stores Co., Ltd., and the Magasin General de Cuirs et Harnais.

Latter, George,

Superintendent of Permanent Ways, Railway Dept.

Born in 1856 at Tunbridge Wells, Mr. George Latter became a storekeeper on the Mauritius Government Railways in 1871, and in 1875 was made a training plate-layer. In 1878 he was promoted to full plate-layer, and in 1881 to Superintendent of Permanent Ways.

Laurent, The Hon. Eugène A. O., B.S. and B.M. London, M.R.C.S. England.

Born in Mauritius in 1859, and was Laureate of the Royal College in 1876; medallist in medical jurisprudence, clinical medicine, pathology, materia medica, and therapeutics, and M.B., London University, 1881; B.S., 1883; Assistant to Dr. Holland, Soho Square Hospital, 1880; Clinical Assistant to Sir Douglas Powell, Brompton Hospital, 1881-1883; Senior Resident, Bedford Hospital, 1884-1885.

Returning to Mauritius in 1885, Dr. Laurent has been in practice here since that year. Notable articles from his pen have appeared in "The London Medical Journal" and "The Lancet," one of these articles being reprinted in Sir Morel McKenzie's book on diseases of the throat. In that volume mention is also made of Dr. Laurent's invention for the removal of fish bones from the throat. He also sent contributions to the "British Medical Journal" on abscesses of the liver, and took an active part in combating the smallpox epidemics of 1890, 1905, and 1913, in Mauritius.

In 1892 Dr. Laurent was elected a member of the Municipal Council of Port Louis, and while he was Mayor of the city in 1905, 1907, 1908, 1909, 1911, and 1912, the following occurred:—

Subscription for erection of Rémy Ollier's statue in the Company's Gardens started in 1905; statue finally erected in November, 1909. Inauguration of the electric lighting of the city in August, 1907. Fire Brigade Station greatly improved and connected electrically with Fort Adelaide and the Police Stations. Kiosques constructed in the Company's Gardens, Plaine Verte, Boulevard Edward VII. Inauguration of Sir John Pope Hennessy's statue in Theatre Square in November, 1909. Statue of Edward VII. (by Prosper D'Epinay) unveiled, June 24th, 1912, on the Champ de Mars, on the site formerly occupied by the fountain erected by Lavoquer. Municipal Laboratory instituted. Municipal Poor Law Doctor nominated. Codification of the Municipal regulations. Construction of several ferro-concrete bridges in Port Louis.

In January, 1906, Dr. Laurent was elected member for Port Louis in the Council of Government, and was re-elected in 1911 for the same constituency. He was the first to speak in Council of the antimalaria campaign, which resulted in the Secretary of State sending Sir Ronald Ross to Mauritius in connection with that matter in November, 1907.

Dr. Laurent was one of the leaders of the agitation regarding the local Government finances, which resulted in the visit to the island in June, 1908, of the Commission of Inquiry, composed of Sir Frank Swettenham, Sir Edward O'Malley, and Mr. Woodcock, K.C. He was likewise the first to introduce a progressive tax in Mauritius, and to instal it at the Municipality of Port Louis in the form of a tenant's tax.

Dr. Laurent is the leader of the Liberal Democratic Party. He is a Director of the Mauritius Institute, and has been a member of the Board of Education since 1895. He took a very active interest for some years in local racing, and was the owner of the well-known horses "Vice," "Lightning," "Grand Roi," "Stag," and "Gyp," which won many prizes, including the Labourdonnais Cup.

Leclézio, Ernest,

Barrister-at-Law.

Mr. Ernest Leclézio is a son of the Hon. Henri Leclézio, C.M.G., and was born in Mauritius in 1865, educated at the Royal College, and in 1889 called to the Bar, Middle Temple, after which he returned to the island to practise, and is now one of the foremost of the local barristers.

Leclézio, The Hon. Henri, C.M.G.,

Attorney-at-Law.

The Hon. Henri Leclézio, C.M.G., was born in Mauritius in 1840, and was Laureate of the Royal College in 1878. He did not, however, avail himself of the privileges pertaining to that honour; and the table at which he now sits in his office in Tribunal Street is the same which he used when, at the age of eighteen years, he commenced business with his father, Mr. Eugène Leclézio, attorney-at-law. Mr. Henri Leclézio's brother, Eugène, was Laureate of the Royal College in 1850, and was Chief Justice of the colony prior to his departure in 1897, when eighty years of age, for Paris, where he still lives.

Mr. Eugène Leclézio, Senior, died in 1893, and was succeeded in his business by his son Henri, who had in 1880 qualified as an attorney-at-law, and in 1886 was elected member for Moka in the Council of Government, which he has continued up to the present time. He is one of the ablest leaders of the Conservative Party, and from 1891 till 1911 was a member of the Executive Council. In 1897 he was made a Companion of the Order of St. Michael and St. George.

The Hon. Henri Leclézio is President of the Chamber of Agriculture, and is proprietor of Alma Sugar Estate (upwards of 3,000 acres) and Factory, capable of producing between 6,000 and 7,000 tons of sugar in 110 days. He is Chairman of the Albion Dock Co., and is a Director of the Mauritius Commercial Bank, Colonial Fire Insurance Co., Mon Désert Sugar Estate Co., Sans Souci and Bel Etang Sugar Estate Co., Beau Séjour Sugar Estate Co., Valetta Sugar Estate Co., Diego and Peros Oil Co., and Agaléga Oil Co. He is also a member of the Woods and Forests Board, and a Commissioner of the Hurricane Loan Board.

Leconte, L.,

Acting District Magistrate for PORT LOUIS.

Born in 1881 in Mauritius, and was Laureate of the Royal College in 1899; called to the Bar, Middle Temple, 1903; appointed Acting Crown Prosecutor, Mauritius, 1906; Magistrate for Dependencies of Mauritius, 1909; Acting District Magistrate for Port Louis; acted in 1912 as Master and Registrar of the Supreme Court.

Lesur, Dr. F. M. Aimé.

Born in Mauritius in 1863; M.R.C.S. and L.R.C.P. London, 1893, since when he has been in practice in Flacq, Mauritius.

L'Homme, Leoville,

Litterateur and Municipal Librarian.

Mr. Leoville L'Homme was born in Port Louis. Son of a printer, he also in his youth followed the typographical profession, which he relinquished in order to devote himself to journalism and literature. At the age of twenty-three he was contributing articles to the "Argus," a newspaper started by Sir (then Mr.) William Newton, with a view to the reform of the constitution of the local Government. Towards the end of 1883 Mr. L'Homme became the editor of "La Sentinelle de Maurice," then one of the chief newspapers in the island. By this time he had published a small collection of poems, and staged with success in the Port Louis Theatre a little one-act drama in verse, entitled "Le Dernier Tribut" (The Last Tribute), inspired by the famous naval battle of Grand Port.

In 1886 he gave up the editorship of "La Sentinelle," and founded "Le Droit," a newspaper which played a most active part at the time of the new political régime, and the first legislative elections of that year. He also became a contributor to various other newspapers; but soon withdrew from politics, and in 1902 was appointed Librarian of the Municipal Library, Port Louis. He writes weekly articles for "Le Radical," and poems by him appear from time to time in various publications of the colony.

Amongst the most noteworthy of Mr. L'Homme's works is his volume entitled "Poemes, Paiens et Bibliques," published in 1887, regarding which Mr. Maurice Bouchor, the French poet, wrote in the Parisian review "Le Passant," of October, 1887, as follows: "I admire a poet who, in a country which no longer forms part of our dominions, writes so finely in the French language, at a distance of four thousand leagues from France." Referring to another of his books, "Pages en Vers" (of which a revised and enlarged edition appeared in 1905), the brilliant French critic, Mr. Augustin Filon, in the issue of April 25th,

1906, of "Le Journal des Débats," said of Mr. L'Homme: "He moves evenly and without effort in the field of Greek antiquity, as if he were the exclusive *alumnus* of Keats and André Chénier. Witness the exquisite piece entitled 'The Centaurs and the Nymphs'; this poem could well be reinstated with the Ionic dialect without altering a single touch."

In response to the request of Prince T. de Bouffremont, member of the Congress of Mons, Belgium, Mr. L'Homme wrote an interesting treatise on the French language and literature in Mauritius. The preface to it was written by the Prince, who, after reviewing the life and work of the talented Mauritian, said: "Mr. L'Homme's verse is at once sonorous and powerful, full of grace and force, with something luminous, which makes one think of the tropical Nature in the midst of which the poet lives. . . . Undoubtedly Mauritius has left its trace upon the genius of this poet; and the poems which he has devoted to his native land are not the least splendid of his productions."

It is regrettable that there is not sufficient space in "Mauritius Illustrated" for more than the one of Mr. L'Homme's poems, which appears on page 158. His article on the scenery of the island has lost greatly by translation from the French, in which, although he is proficient in English, all his works are produced. The idioms and imagery in the original were beyond the capacity of the local translator to render with equal beauty into English; and as the editor received the translation too late to go over it with Mr. L'Homme, and as the original manuscript was left in the island, some of the finest parts had most unfortunately to be deleted owing to the ambiguity of names and certain matters which the translator had not made clear. Nevertheless, the article reveals much of the elegance of diction, and the subtlety and beauty of thought characteristic of Mr. L'Homme's writings.

Lejeunne, R.,

Deputy Collector of Customs.

Mr. R. Lejeunne was born in Mauritius in 1865, and joined the Government service in 1883 as a clerk in the Colonial Secretary's office, where he remained until 1902, when he was promoted to Assistant Storekeeper-General. In 1910 he was made Deputy-Collector of Customs.

le Juge de Segrais, The Hon. Paul, M.I.C.E.

Born in Mauritius in 1868; Laureate of the Royal College in 1887; studied also at Cooper's Hill from 1887 to 1890; appointed Government Surveyor and Superintendent of Public Works, Seychelles, June, 1891; Government Engineer and Architect, Mauritius, September 14th, 1896; acted as Surveyor-General, 1896-97; Director of Public Works and Surveys, Mauritius, November 1st, 1904.

Lincoln, G.,

Assistant Protector of Immigrants and Poor Law Commissioner.

Mr. G. Lincoln was born in Mauritius in 1864, joined the Government service in 1884, and was appointed to his present position on July 1st, 1912.

Louis, Léon Jean, M.B., Ch.B. Edin.

Born in Mauritius in 1873, educated at the Royal College, and studied medicine at the Edinburgh University; M.B. and Ch.B., 1899; practised for various periods at Epchester (County Durham), Wakefield, Bradford, Birmingham, Leeds, and nine years at Sunderland; returned to Mauritius in 1912.

Macdonald, Captain Murdo Stewart.

Born at Bernera, Island of Lewis, Scotland, in 1849, Captain Murdo Stewart Macdonald was at sea for twenty years, and commanded from 1882 to 1887 the famous China tea-clipper, "Sir Lancelot," of which we give an illustration and particulars on page 342. He came to Mauritius in 1887, and was appointed in 1890 Examiner for Masters' and Mates' Certificates. In 1892 he became Surveyor to the Vice-Admiralty Court, and in 1895 Surveyor to "Lloyd's Register." He is a member of the Chamber of Commerce, Chairman of the Presbyterial Committee of the Church of Scotland, and Honorary Treasurer of the Mauritius Auxiliary of the British and Foreign Bible Society.

Martin, The Hon. J. A. Maurice,

Analytical Chemist, Planter, etc.

Born in Mauritius in 1872, and educated at the Royal College. When he was twenty years of age he left the island to continue his studies in chemistry at the Agricultural College of Grignon, where he remained from 1893 to 1896, and gained his diploma. He then spent six months in analytical work at the Paris Museum, after which he specialised in sugar analyses in the laboratories of Gallois et Dupon, now known as Gallois et Fils Successeur.

On his return to Mauritius, Mr. Martin became chemist to the Co-operative Engrais Chimiques Co., Ltd., and when that concern amalgamated with the Colonial Engrais Chimiques Co. in 1902, he was appointed chemist to the latter company.

In 1912 Mr. Martin was elected unopposed member for Rivière du Rempart in the Council of Government. He is proprietor of Melville Estate, about 800 acres, at Poudre d'Or, on which he has an aloe fibre factory. He is administrator of the Antoinette Sugar Estate, of about 2,000 acres, belonging to the heirs of his father, Mr. G. Martin, who was the oldest planter in the island, and who died in August, 1912, at the age of ninety years. Mr. Martin has eighty acres of land at Moka devoted to experiments in the cultivation of tea, and is attaining excellent results in that direction. He is Vice-President of the Chamber of Agriculture,

President of the Yemen Hunting Club of Mauritius, and one of the leading members of the Mauritius Turf Club and the Mauritius Jockey Club. He is also one of the Commissioners of the Mare aux Vacoas Water Supply, and a member of the Woods and Forests Board and the Financial Committee.

Masson, A. F. G., M.B., Ch.B. Edin.,

Health Officer and Assistant Government Medical Officer, PORT LOUIS.

Dr. A. F. G. Masson was born in Mauritius in 1875, and was Laureate of the Royal College in 1895; qualified as M.B. and Ch.B. Edinburgh, in 1901; appointed Assistant Government Medical Officer, Port Louis, in 1904; seconded for duty with the Military—Camp Hospital, Curepipe—in 1904 and 1905; and appointed Health Officer in 1912.

Merandon, René.

Mr. René Merandon was born in 1882 of an old family of planters. Educated at the Royal College, he studied engineering in France and England, read for the English Bar at Gray's Inn, and was called in 1906. His long stay in England, part of which he spent in the country, has made him thoroughly acquainted with English ways and ideas.

On his return to Mauritius he felt the call of the land, and proved himself very successful as the owner of an aloe estate. He and his brother are owners of upwards of 2,000 acres of pasture land in Black River District, and take the deepest interest in the local breed of cattle. which they are trying to improve, as well as in country life generally.

Concerning politics, Mr. René Merandon's name will remain associated with the series of public meetings which, in the face of bitter opposition, he originated for the approval of the appointment of the Royal Commission proposed by the Home Government, and which visited the island in 1909. Upheld by a large number of the inhabitants of the colony, he asked for the reform of the laws dealing with companies, the establishment of an agricultural bank, and the study of the irrigation problem, all of which matters have already been, or are being, dealt with. Only thirty-one years of age, strongly opposed to some of the financial circles, whom he accuses of taking too large a share of the planters' profits, and being a popular and brilliant French orator, Mr. René Merandon seems destined in the near future to become one of the foremost leaders of his dearly-loved country.

Montocchio, Maurice,

Sworn and Exchange Broker.

Mr. Maurice Montocchio was born in Mauritius in 1868, and started his business career in 1888 as assistant to his father, Mr. Edward Montocchio, who had been established as a broker in Port Louis since 1864, and who died in 1899. After the latter event, Mr. Maurice took over the control of the business, and is one of the leading brokers in Mauritius. He is a Director of the Forges et Fonderies de Maurice, Albion Dock Co., Mauritius Commercial Bank, Compagnie Générale de Quincaillerie, Colonial Engrais Chimiques Co., Sans Souci and Bel Etang Sugar Estate Co., Ltd., Savannah Sugar Estate Co., Ltd., Queen Victoria Sugar Estate Co., Ltd., Bonne Mère Sugar Estate Co., Ltd., Mauritius Sugar Estates Co., Ltd., Belle Vue (Allendy) Sugar Estate Co., Ltd., Valetta Sugar Estate Co., Ltd., and is broker for Sans Souci and Bel Etang, Belle Vue (Allendy), and Cote d'Or Sugar Estate Companies. Mr. Montocchio is also a member of the Chamber of Commerce and the Chamber of Agriculture.

Morrison, John Smith,

Head Accountant and Chief Storekeeper, Railway Department.

Mr. John Smith Morrison was born at Carluke, Scotland, in 1872, and educated at Doune, Perthshire, and at Dalkeith, Midlothian. In 1885 he became a clerk in the Engineer's Department of the North British Railway at Edinburgh, and was Assistant Book-keeper there in 1912, when he came to Mauritius to fill his present position as Head Accountant and Chief Storekeeper of the Railway Department.

Nairac, The Hon. G. Edouard,

Barrister-at-Law and Mayor of PORT LOUIS.

Born in Mauritius in 1876, and was Laureate of the Royal College in 1895; called to the Bar, Middle Temple, 1898; elected member for Ward 2 in the Municipal Council of Port Louis, 1908; returned at every succeeding election, and became Mayor in 1913; elected member for Port Louis in the Council of Government, 1911; is a member of the Committee of Superior Education, and editor of the Supreme Court Law Reports.

Naz, Joseph Lois, A.C.G.I., M.I.C.E., F.I.S.E.,

Government Sanitary Engineer.

Born in Mauritius in 1872, and is nephew of the late Sir Virgile Naz, K.C.M.G.· educated at the Royal College, Mauritius. Central Technical College, and University College, London; pupilage under W. J. Harrison, A.M.I.C.E., Westminster, and Osbert Chadwick, M.I.C.E., C.M.G., Consulting Engineer to the Colonial Office; practical experience under C. H. Cooper. M.I.C.E., Engineer and Surveyor of Wimbledon, and F. W. Pearce, Engineer and Surveyor to the District Council of Twickenham; returned to Mauritius in May, 1901, and was appointed to the Public Works and Surveys Department; is now Sanitary Engineer to the Medical and Health Department, in charge of the antimalaria campaign.

Newton, Sir William, K.C.

Sir William Newton was born in Mauritius in 1842, and was Laureate of the Royal College in 1860. He was called to the Bar at the Middle Temple in 1864, after which he returned to Mauritus to practise, and was appointed Queen's Counsel in 1891.

His treatise published in 1884, in "Le Journal de Droit International Prive," then edited by Clunet, ably demonstrated that French people suffer no loss of their nationality outside of Mauritius through naturalisation in the island; and the principles he elaborated so cleverly in that notable composition were adopted as conclusive authority by the French Court of Cassation in a case that arose soon afterwards for its decision. For the service he rendered to French law in this direction Sir William Newton was made in 1889 a Knight of the Legion of Honour. In 1885, whilst he was Chairman of the Chamber of Agriculture, he published a paper on the sugar crisis, which attracted the attention of the Board of Trade, and which was printed in a Blue Book and presented to Parliament.

In 1884 he became a nominated member of the Council of Government of Mauritius, and took a leading part in the reform movement, which led in 1886 to the introduction of elected members in the local legislature. In 1888 he was elected member for Port Louis, and continued as such until the election of 1911, when he lost his seat. He refused the offer of another constituency, and then retired from active public life.

In 1886 Sir John Pope Hennessy, Governor of Mauritius at that time, was recalled to England for an explanation of certain charges made against his administration by the so-called Democratic Party. Sir William Newton also proceeded to England, and so well did he champion there the cause of Sir John Pope Hennessy that the allegations made against the latter were entirely refuted, with the result that Sir John Pope Hennessy was reinstated as Governor, and arrived back in the island amidst the acclamations of the people.

Sir William Newton was an unofficial member of the Executive Council of Government from 1906 to 1911, and received his knighthood in 1909, in recognition of the services he had rendered to the colony.

He is Chairman of the local board of the Crédit Foncier of Mauritius, Ltd., President of the Royal Society of Arts and Sciences, President of the Board of Commissioners for the Town of Quatre Bornes, a Director of the Mauritius Institute, and Honorary Member of the Mauritius Jockey Club.

Newton, W. H.,

Crown Prosecutor.

Born in Mauritius in 1870 and called to the Bar at the Middle Temple in 1896, after which he practised in Mauritius until October, 1901, when he became Crown Prosecutor, and is now Acting Additional Substitute Procureur and Advocate-General.

Noël, The Hon. Martial,

Registrar-General, Receiver of Registration Dues, and Conservator of Mortgages.

Born in Mauritius in 1860, and educated in Paris and London; B.A. and Licencie en Droit de la Faculté de Paris; called to the Bar at the Middle Temple in 1885; was appointed Crown Prosecutor, Mauritius, in 1892; District Magistrate for Port Louis, 1900; Registrar-General, Receiver of Registration Dues, and Conservator of Mortgages, 1907.

Oldershaw, W. G., Lieut., R.N.R.,

Assistant Harbour Master.

Born in 1877, Mr. W. G. Oldershaw was a sailing-ship apprentice for four years. From 1898 he served in various companies until 1901, when he joined the White Star Steamship Co. as fourth officer. After four years in various grades with that concern, he underwent twelve months' training in H.M. Navy as a lieutenant in the Royal Naval Reserve. Rejoining the White Star Co. in 1907, he had reached the position of first officer of the "Teutonic," when he was appointed Assistant Harbour Master, Mauritius, and began his duties as such in August, 1912.

Paddle, James Isaac, F.R.C.S. Eng. and M.D. London,

Medical Superintendent of the Lunatic Asylum and Government Analyst.

Born in Mauritius, and was Laureate of the Royal College in 1873, passing the B.A. London University Examination; studied medicine at the University College, London, and passed B.Sc. Examination in 1876; L.R.C.P. London, 1880; F.R.C.S. England, 1880; M.B. London University, 1880; gold medallist in midwifery and in medical jurisprudence; M.D. London University, 1881; entered Mauritius Government service September 8th, 1890, as Acting Government Medical Officer for the district of Plaines Wilhems; appointed Medical Superintendent of the Lunatic Asylum, June 15th, 1898.

Pezzani, E. Roger,

Barrister-at-Law.

Born in Mauritius in 1885, and was Laureate of the Royal College in 1904, winning previously the smaller scholarships in the lower forms; read for the Bar, and was called in Hilary, in 1908, at the Middle Temple; left Mauritius in 1910 to argue various cases in the sister colony of Seychelles; read international law (public and private) with Sir Thomas Barclay, whose Private Secretary he also was in 1911; returned to Seychelles in December, 1911, at the instance of London companies interested in Seychelles; Officiating Legal Adviser to the Seychelles Government, from April to November, 1911; received thanks of Government, and declined offer of grant in recognition of his services; has been practising at his native Bar since December, 1911.

Piat, Aristide.

Mr. Aristide Piat, belonging to one of the largest French-Mauritian families, of which an illustration appears on page 139, started his business career in 1866 in the office of Mr. Stanislas Pelte, notary, whose business he took over in 1893. In 1909 he retired from his notarial activity, and his time is now occupied by attention to his numerous investments. He is Chairman of the Terracine Sugar Estate Co. and the Combo Sugar Estate Co., and a Director of the Mauritius Commercial Bank, the New Mauritius Dock Co., Dry Docks and Slips Co., and the Salomon Oil Island Co.

Pilot, Joseph H.,

Assistant Receiver-General.

Born in Mauritius in 1863, and educated at the Royal College. In 1881 he entered the Auditor-General's office as clerk, and in 1903 was appointed Head Accountant, Railway Department. He was promoted to his present position in 1912.

Pitot, Albert.

Mr. Albert Pitot, whose able writings form so large a part of this volume, is one of the most learned natives of Mauritius. He is an authority on the history of the island, and is the author of "T'Eylandt Mauritius Esquisses Historiques, 1598-1710." He is an advocate of Edinburgh, and Licencie en Droit of Paris; but unfortunately his legal career was ruined by deafness, the result of a chill, and he is now employed in clerical work in the offices of Messrs. Rogers and Co., Port Louis. Mr. Pitot is a highly-esteemed member of one of the oldest and most numerous families in Mauritius.

Pitot, The Hon. L. E.,

General Manager of Railways.

Born in Mauritius in 1866, and was educated at the Royal College and Cooper's Hill College, Surrey, England. On April 11th, 1889, he was appointed Government Surveyor and Superintendent of Public Works, Seychelles; and in April, 1891, he became Government Engineer and Architect, Mauritius. On September 14th, 1896, he was promoted to his present post of General Manager of Railways, and became a nominated member of the Council of Government on May 15th, 1911.

Pougnet, D. E., A.C.G.I., A.M.I.C.E.,

Government Surveyor.

Mr. D. E. Pougnet was born in Mauritius in 1867, and is a graduate of the Central Technical College, London. In 1887 he was appointed a clerk in the Procureur-General's Department. Transferred in 1888 to the Public Works and Surveys Department, he was promoted to Government Surveyor in March, 1912.

Mr. Pougnet is the inventor of two excellent agricultural machines—one for throwing water in a sprayed form over comparatively large areas, and the other for gathering, compressing, cutting, and burying trash, leaves, etc.

Rae, Albert,

Chief Clerk, Procureur-General's Department.

Born in Mauritius in 1857, Mr. Albert Rae was educated at the Royal College, and joined the Government service in 1877, being now Chief Clerk in the Procureur-General's Department. Mr. Rae is a good musician, and plays equally well on the violin and viola. He devotes his leisure hours to the study of stamps, and is an expert in the stamps of Mauritius. He possesses a valuable collection of books and documents relating to the history of the island, in which direction he is an authority, and he is a member of the Historical Records Committee.

Rae, William Charles,

Colonial Postmaster.

Mr. William Charles Rae was born in Mauritius in 1859, and by competitive examination entered the public service in November, 1876, as a clerk in the Colonial Secretary's office, becoming in March, 1894, Clerk of the Executive Council and the Council of Government. In 1896 he compiled a "Handbook on the Constitution Practice, and Proceedings of the Council of Government"; and in August, 1900, he became Chief Clerk in the Colonial Secretary's office. On November 9th, 1903, he was promoted to Second Assistant-Colonial Secretary, and was appointed Colonial Postmaster on July 1st, 1905.

Raffray, Rene,

Sworn and Exchange Broker.

Mr. Rene Raffray was born in Mauritius in 1878, and began his commercial career in 1898 as a clerk with the Planters' Chemical Manure Co., Ltd., with whom he remained for about eighteen months, and then went to fill a similar position with Messrs. Chevreau and Co. A year later he was appointed to a clerical position in connection with the Bureau Syndical of Brokers, which he held until 1899, when he joined the Bank of Mauritius, Ltd., and left that concern in 1904 to take up his present occupation as a sworn and exchange broker. Mr. Raffray is a Director of the Mauritius Pharmacy Co., Ltd.

Regnard, Gabriel,

Sworn and Exchange Broker.

Born in Mauritius in 1863, Mr. Gabriel Regnard started business in 1881 as a clerk in the office of his father, Mr. Aristide Regnard, and became a sworn and exchange broker in 1898. Mr. Regnard, Senior, died in 1903, and he was succeeded in the business by his son, Mr. Gabriel

Regnard, who is Treasurer of the Chamber of Commerce, Vice-President of the Royal Society of Arts and Sciences, member of the Chamber of Agriculture, and a Director of the Albion Dock Co., Mauritius Pharmacy Co., Ltd., and Union Beau Bois Sugar Estate Co. His brother, Mr. J. Gustave Regnard, is the Secretary of the last-mentioned company, which owns the third largest sugar factory in the island, and turns out in the crushing season about 7,000 tons.

The Union Beau Bois Sugar Estate Co. was formed in 1911, and took over the estates formerly owned by the Regnard family, which still possesses half of the shares. The dividend paid bv the company in 1912 was 10 per cent.

Regnard, Jules,

Sworn and Exchange Broker.

Mr. Jules Regnard was born in Mauritius in 1845, and became a sworn and exchange broker in 1879. He is Syndic of the Bureau Syndical of the Corporation of Sworn and Exchange Brokers, and is Secretary to the Mon Désert Sugar Estate Co., Ltd.

Ritter, The Hon. G. A., C.M.G.,

Attorney-at-Law.

The Hon. G. A. Ritter, C.M.G., was born in Mauritius in 1840, and was educated at the Royal College. He commenced his business career in 1858 as a clerk with Mr. Antony J. Colin, Senr. attorney-at-law. In 1859 he became secretary to Mr. Justice Dupont, and was appointed secretary to Sir Charles Farquhar Shand on that gentleman's arrival in the colony as Chief Justice, on August 20th, 1860. In 1864 Mr. Ritter qualified as an attorney-at-law, and then began practising on his own account. In 1872 he succeeded Mr. James Henry Sladge as Registrar of the Vice-Admiralty Court, which he continued until 1890, when legal changes necessitated that position being filled by the Registrar of the Supreme Court. In 1892 Mr. Ritter became a nominated member of the Council of Government, and in 1902 was made a Companion of the Order of St. Michael and St. George.

The prominent and influential position which he occupies in the colony is also demonstrated by the following:—

He is Vice-President of the Mauritius Institute, Chairman of the Board of Commissioners of Port Louis, member of the Board of Commissioners of Curepipe, member of the Chamber of Agriculture, and is one of the Commissioners of the Mare aux Vacoas Water Supply and the Hurricane Loan Board, and is also one of the Trustees of the Morris Legacy. He is Chairman of the Central Rum Warehouse Co., Mauritius Pharmacy Co., Ltd., Dry Docks and Slips Co., Ltd., Compagnie Générale de Quincaillerie; and a Director of the Terracine Sugar Estate Co., Ltd., Combo Sugar Estate, Mon Loisir Sugar Estate Co., Ltd., Mauritius Sugar Estates Co., Ltd., Constance La Gaieté Sugar Estate Co., Ltd., New Mauritius Dock Co., Mauritius Engrais Chimiques Co., Colonial Fire Insurance Co., and the Mauritius Commercial Bank (when the regulations permit).

Rouget, François Auguste, M.D.,

Medical Superintendent of the Civil Hospital.

Born in Mauritius, and was Laureate of the Royal College in 1885; studied medicine at Edinburgh University; graduated M.B. and C.M. in 1887, and M.D. in 1906; joined Government service in 1890 as Acting Police and Prison Surgeon, and was confirmed as such in 1895; appointed in 1902 Medical Superintendent of the Civil Hospital.

Rouillard, Edouard,

Sworn and Exchange Broker.

Mr. Edouard Rouillard was born in February, 1867, in Mauritius, and started business in 1885 as a clerk with Messrs. Elias, Mallac and Co., with whom he remained until April, 1890, when he became a sworn and exchange broker. He is co-owner of Mon Loisir (Rouillard) Estate, and is a Director of the Bel Ombre Sugar Estate Co., Ltd., Constance Sugar Estate Co., Ltd., Central Dock Co., Mauritius Pharmacy Co., Ltd., Central Rum Warehouse Co., Forges et Fonderies de Maurice, and the "Flore Mauricienne." He is broker for Messrs. Elias, Mallac and Co., and the following sugar estates: Belle Vue Mauricia (Nemours Harel), Bel Ombre, Constance, The Mount, Bel Air (A. J. Wilson), and St. Felix (A. J. Wilson).

Mr. Rouillard is Deputy-Chairman of the Bureau Syndical of Brokers, a member of the Committee of the Club de Curepipe, and the Société Horticole de l'Ile Maurice, and a director of "Le Mauricien" newspaper. He is also a member of the Chamber of Commerce, the Union Catholique de l'Ile Maurice, the District Board of Rivière du Rempart, and is a steward of the Mauritius Turf Club.

Rouillard, The Hon. F. M. Louis,

Barrister-at-Law.

Born in March, 1886, and was Laureate of the Royal College in 1885. Called to the Bar at the Middle Temple, in 1889, he became a Licencie en Droit de la Faculté de Paris in 1891, in which year he returned to his native island to practise. On January 26th, 1913, he was elected member for Savanne in the Council of Government. Mr. Rouillard is one of the directors of the Mauritius Commercial Bank.

Sauzier, Emile, Senior,

Attorney-at-Law (retired).

Mr. Emile Sauzier, Senior, is one of the oldest attorneys in Mauritius. He was born in the island in 1843, and educated at the Royal College and the College of Réunion. In 1860 he became a clerk with Messrs. J. Guibert and F. Roberts, attorneys-at-law, and remained with them until he became an attorney-at-law in 1866, when he started practising on his own account. He has now practically retired from his legal activity, and devotes his time to his numerous investments and public business of various kinds. Mr. Sauzier was largely instrumental in the formation of the Colonial Engrais Chimiques Co. and the Central Dock Company (of both of which he is Chairman), Compagnie Génerale de Quincaillerie and Forges Coloniales, and is a Director of the last two concerns. He is also Chairman of Beau Plan Sugar Estate Co., a Director of the Savannah Sugar Estate Co., and was formerly proprietor of St. Joan of Nova Oil Island, which he sold. He is father of the Hon. Emile Sauzier, K.C.

Sauzier, The Hon. Emile, K.C.

The Hon. Emile Sauzier, K.C., was born in Mauritius in 1867, and, when eighteen years of age, left the island for London, where he completed his education. He was admitted to the Honourable Society of the Middle Temple in 1886, and called to the Bar in 1889. He then returned to Mauritius to practise, and was appointed King's Counsel in 1903. He is an expert debater, and is one of the leading members of the Council of Government, where he has sat as elected member for Pamplemousses since 1896.

Mr. Sauzier was instrumental in securing the following reforms in local law :—

Ordinance No. 36 of 1899, repealing Articles Nos. 253, 254, 255, and 256 of the Penal Code, wherein adultery, which still remains a ground of divorce, was punishable by imprisonment as a misdemeanour.

Ordinance No. 37 of 1902, relative to natural filiation, whereby legitimate and illegitimate children were placed on an equality as regards their right to prove their filiation, for instance, by *possession d'etat.*

Ordinance No. 23 of 1907, amending the provisions of the Civil Code respecting the right of the surviving spouse in the succession of the deceased spouse. When the deceased spouse leaves no legitimate descendants or ascendants nor any heir in the legitimate collateral line within the third degree inclusively of relationship, nor any descendants of nephews or nieces, the *whole* succession shall, according to the Ordinance in question, devolve upon the surviving spouse, if that individual is not, at the opening of the succession, divorced or judicially separated *a mensa et thoro.*

Ordinance No. 35 of 1909, providing for the protection of the personal property of minors and interdicted persons. By this Ordinance a guardian cannot any more dispose of the incorporeal chattels of a minor or interdicted person without the consent of the family council. In certain cases the consent of the Ministère Publique is also required.

Ordinance No. 3 of 1911, giving certain powers to District and Stipendiary Magistrates regarding the taking down of evidence.

Mr. Sauzier has also brought before the Council of Government a draft Ordinance for the creation of a Criminal Court of Appeal, which, at the time of writing, has not yet been dealt with

Mr. Sauzier is President of the Club de Curepipe, the Mauritius Turf Club, and Board of Directors of the newspaper "Le Mauricien." He is a Director of the Mauritius Commercial Bank, Mauritius Sugar Estate Co., Ltd., Bel Ombre Sugar Estate Co., Ltd., Mauritius Pharmacy Co., Ltd., and the "Flore Mauricienne." He is also a member of the Board of Commissioners for Curepipe, and is President of the Société Horticole de l'Ile Maurice.

Scroggs, The Hon. Harold Charles, Lieut. R.N. (retired),

Collector of Customs and Harbour Master.

Lieutenant Harold Charles Scroggs was born at Bishop Teignton, Devonshire, in 1865, and educated in the "Britannia" naval training ship, Dartmouth. In 1880 he joined H.M.S. "Agincourt," in the Channel Fleet, as Midshipman, and in 1882 went to the Pacific Station in the "Swiftsure," flagship of Sir Algernon McLennan Lyons, K.C.B., afterwards serving in the "Constance," on the same station. After passing his examination for Sub-lieutenant, he returned in 1885 to England as an Acting Lieutenant in H.M.S. "Matine," and joined in 1886 the Naval College, Greenwich, where he qualified as Sub-lieutenant, and proceeded as such in the gunboat "Bullfrog" to the North American Station. Promoted to Lieutenant in 1888, he was appointed to the "Rover" and then the "Ruby" in the Training Squadron. In 1889 he became Navigating Officer of H.M.S. "Swallow," and was in her, on the Cape Station, until 1893. He was next appointed, in 1894, Navigating Officer of H.M.S. "Spartan," on the Mediterranean Station, and in the same year was invalided home, when he resigned his commission, which was afterwards restored to him under the Order in Council for Emergency Officers.

In June 1893, he married the second daughter of the late Captain Hand, R.N., and has one son and one daughter, his son being now a Midshipman in the Royal Navy.

On June 23rd, 1903, Lieutenant Scroggs became Harbour Master of Mauritius, and on November 1st, 1910, was also appointed Collector of Customs, thereby becoming an ex-officio member of the Council of Government.

Serret, A.,

Additional Substitute Procureur and Advocate-General.

Born in Mauritius in 1864, and called to the Bar at the Middle Temple in 1887, after which he practised in Mauritius until 1892, when he became Crown Prosecutor; appointed in 1901 Additional Substitute Procureur and Advocate-General; from 1904 to 1905 Acting Puisne Judge of the Supreme Court; from

December, 1911, to September, 1912, Acting Chief Justice, Seychelles.

Shand, C. F.,

Sworn and Exchange Broker.

Mr. C. F. Shand is the second son of the late Sir Charles Farquhar Shand, LL.D., Chief Justice of Mauritius from 1860 to 1879. He was born in Edinburgh, and was educated at the Royal College, as well as for six years at Trinity College, Glenalmond, Perthshire, during the wardenship of Dr. Hannah, D.C.L., who was afterwards Vicar of Brighton.

Returning to Mauritius in 1872, Mr. Shand served for some years as a clerk with Messrs. Ireland, Fraser and Co., and afterwards with Mr. E. Thévenau, one of the leading sugar brokers of his time.

He started business for himself as a sworn and exchange broker on December 26th, 1878, and has been since in his present office on the Place d'Armes.

Mr. Shand is correspondent for Reuter's Telegraph Co., London, and is a member of the Meteorological Society and the Royal Colonial Institute, London.

Simpson, Major-General Charles Rudyerd, C.B.,

General Officer in Command of the Troops.

Major-General Charles Rudyerd Simpson, C.B., son of Mr. Charles Turner Simpson, formerly of 14, Cornwall Gardens, London, S.W., and Millmead House, Guildford, was born in 1856; entered Lincolnshire Regiment, 1874; became Captain, 1882; Major, 1893; Brevet Lieutenant-Colonel, 1898; Brevet Colonel, 1904; Colonel, 1905; Major-General, 1911; served in the Nile Expedition, 1898; was present at the battles of Atbara and Khartoum (twice mentioned in despatches, medal with two clasps, Brevet Lieutenant-Colonel); was A.D.C. to Governor and Commander-in-Chief, Malta, 1881-84; Staff Captain at Headquarters, 1888-90; D.A.A.G. there, 1890-93; Professor at Staff College, 1894-96; A.A.G., W. Command, 1905-8; Brigadier-General-Commanding 5th Imperial Brigade, Aldershot, 1908-11; appointed General Officer in Command of the Troops, Mauritius, 1911. Married in 1884 Leonora, daughter of Mr. Charles F. Devas, of Pickhurst Manor, Hayes, Kent; and was created a Companion of the Bath in 1911.

Standley, C. A.,

Audit Examiner in Audit Charge of the Railway Department.

Born in Mauritius, and educated at the Royal College; matriculated at the London University in 1883; joined the Colonial Secretary's Office in 1884; appointed financial clerk, Woods and Forests Department, 1886; clerical branch of the Customs, 1887; Audit Department, 1897; Acting Chief Clerk, Audit Department, and Senior Audit Examiner in Charge of the Railway Department, 1913.

Stockdale, R. H.,

Government Electrical Engineer and Telegraph Inspector.

Born at Preston, Lancashire, 1880, and educated at the Preston Grammar School; joined in 1896 the Electrical Department of the London and North Western Railway Co., where he remained until 1906, when he was appointed Government Electrical Engineer and Telegraph Inspector, being, as such, equivalent to the Board of Trade in England, part of his duty being to keep the electrical companies up to the mark, and to see that the laws and regulations for the public safety are duly observed. He is in charge of the electrical installations belonging to the Government as well as those of the Post Office and Railway Telegraphs. Particulars of his invention for the railway will be found on page 278.

Thompson, A.S.,

Pilot.

Born in the Shetland Isles in 1873, and went to sea when fifteen years of age; passed examination for master mariners in 1900, and served as second and first officer on various large vessels until 1902, when he joined the Mauritius pilot service.

Ulcoq, Louis,

District Magistrate for Flacq.

Mr. Louis Ulcoq was born in Mauritius in 1883, and was called to the Bar at the Middle Temple in 1907, after which he returned to the island to practise. In 1910 he was appointed District Magistrate for Pamplemousses, and in 1911 became District Magistrate for Flacq.

Walter, A., F.R.A.S.,

Director of the Royal Alfred Observatory.

Born in 1877; joined the Royal Observatory, Greenwich, in 1891; appointed Assistant-Director of the Royal Alfred Observatory, Mauritius, 1897; elected Fellow of the Royal Astronomical Society, 1901; seconded in 1909 to act as Statistical Adviser to the Mauritius Royal Commission; appointed Census Commissioner for Mauritius, 1910-11; Director of the Royal Alfred Observatory, 1911; is Hon. Secretary of the Meteorological Society and the Board of Directors of the Mauritius Institute; member of the Primary Instruction Committee; ex-officio member of the Board of Examiners for Masters and Mates; author of "The Sugar Industry of Mauritius, and a Scheme of Insurance of the Crops against Cyclones"; "Effect of Forests on Rainfall"; "Agricultural Labour"; "Errors of Thermometers"; compiler and editor of "The Mauritius Almanac" since 1912.

The following biographical notes were received too late for insertion with the others in alphabetical order:

Barbeau, Louis Gabriel, M.B., C.M. (Edin.), D.P.H. (Lond.),

Assistant Director of the Medical and Health Department, etc.

Born at Port Louis, 1866; Laureate of the Royal College in 1887; studied medicine at Edinburgh and in London, also at Paris, where he worked at the Pasteur Institute; Fellow of the Royal Institute of Public Health of England; entered the Government Medical Service of Mauritius in 1895; acted as Temporary Director of the Medical and Health Department from May, 1908, to July, 1911, and is now Assistant Director and Chief Sanitary Officer; also Director of the Bacteriological Laboratory.

Denman, The Hon. Dr. Robert,

Director of the Medical and Health Department.

Born 1860; educated Marlborough College and Guy's Hospital; M.R.C.S., England, 1886; L.S.A., London, 1886; D.Ph., Cantab, 1905; Government Medical Officer, Seychelles, 1896; Chief Medical Officer, 1900; Health Officer, Perak, 1908; Director of the Medical and Health Department, Mauritius, 1911.

Emtage, The Hon. Thomas Allen, M.A.,

Director of Public Instruction.

Born in 1862; educated at Harrison College, Barbados; scholar, Pembroke College, Oxford, 1880; 1st class. mathematical mods., 1881; 1st class, final mathematics, 1883; 1st class, natural science, 1885; University College, Nottingham, Mathematical Lecturer, 1885; Assistant Professor of Mathematics and Physics, 1889; Professor of Mathematics and Physics, 1891; Principal, Technical Institute, Wandsworth (L.C.C.), 1895; Examiner, Oxford Locals, Mathematics, 1888, 1889; Examiner, final honours, School of Natural Science, Oxford, 1890, 1891; Director of Public Instruction, Mauritius, 1900; Nominated Member of the Council of Government, 1911; Fellow of the Physiological Society, London; Author of "Mathematics of Electricity" (Oxford Press), and other works.

MEANS OF COMMUNICATION.

MAURITIUS is reached by three principal steamship lines, all of which carry the English mails.

Messageries Maritimes de France.

The steamers of the Messageries Maritimes de France leave Marseilles every fourteen days direct for Mauritius. The mails call at Port Said, Suez, Dijibouti, and thence proceed either to Mombasa, Zanzibar, and the ports of Madagascar—Mayotte, Majunga, Nossi-Bé, Diégo Suarez, and Tamatave - the voyage occupying thirty days, or to Aden and Seychelles and thence to Madagascar (Diégo Suarez, St. Marie and Tamatave), Réunion, and Mauritius; the voyage by this route occupying only twenty-five days.

The journey from London to Marseilles may be made either from Charing Cross *viâ* Dover-Calais or Folkestone-Boulogne, or from Victoria *viâ* Newhaven-Dieppe or Dover-Calais. The route followed—skirting the East Coast of Africa and Madagascar—presents some features of special interest to English travellers.

The Company's London offices are at 75, Fenchurch Street, E.C., and 62, Pall Mall, S.W., and their agents in Mauritius are Messrs. Blyth Bros. and Co. The fares are:—To or from London, 1st class single, £69 15s. 2d.; return, £107 10s. 4d. Second class single, £46 12s. 11d.; return, £72 5s. 10d.

The Union Castle Line.

Mauritius may also be reached from London by the Union Castle Line *viâ* the Suez Canal or the Cape of Good Hope. The Mauritius service of this line outwards and homewards is a monthly one.

Passengers by the West Coast route, *viâ* Cape Town, proceed from Southampton by either the Royal Mail or intermediate steamers, and tranship at one of the South African ports, usually Durban, by the connecting Mauritius steamer. The ports of call on this route are Madeira, Teneriffe, Las Palmas, Ascension, St. Helena, Cape Town, Mossel Bay, Port Elizabeth, East London, Durban, Delagoa Bay, and Beira.

Passengers by the East Coast route, *viâ* Suez Canal, can embark at Southampton or travel overland (at their own expense) to Marseilles or Naples, joining the steamer at either of these places, a reduction in the fare being allowed in that case. The ports of call on this route are Gibraltar, Marseilles, Naples, Port Said, Suez, Port Sudan, Aden, Mombasa, Zanzibar, Port Amelia, Chinde, Beira, Delagoa Bay, and Durban, and passengers for Mauritius tranship to the connecting steamer at either Beira or Durban.

The outward or homeward voyage by either route occupies thirty-five to forty days, according to connections.

The homeward Royal Mail steamers sail from Durban on Sundays, and an intermediate steamer every week.

The fares to and from England are as follows:—

By Royal Mail Steamer *viâ* the West Coast—

1st Class	42 to 54 guineas, according to cabin.	
2nd „	32 „ 36 „ „ „	
3rd „	20 „ 22 „ „ „	

By intermediate steamer *viâ* the West Coast—

1st Class	33 to 41 guineas, according to cabin.
2nd „	28 „ 32 „ „ „
3rd „	14 „ 19 „ „ „

By intermediate steamer *viâ* the East Coast—

1st Class	45 guineas (inner cabins 10 per cent. less). A supplement is charged for deck cabins and also for single berthed cabins.
2nd „	30 to 32 guineas according to cabin.
3rd „	18 guineas.

All fares *viâ* the East Coast, including supplement, are subject to a surtax of 10 per cent.

The fares between Mauritius and South Afrcan Ports are as follows:—

	1st Class.	2nd Class.	3rd Class.
To Cape Town	£21 0 0	£14 0 0	£10 10 0
„ Algoa Bay	17 17 0	11 18 0	8 18 6
„ East London ...	15 15 0	10 10 0	7 17 6
„ Durban	13 13 0	9 2 0	6 16 6
„ Delagoa Bay... ...	12 12 0	8 8 0	6 6 0
„ Beira	12 12 0	8 8 0	6 6 0

A reduction of 10 per cent. on the two single fares is allowed on ocean return tickets, available for twelve months, and should a single ticket be booked, a re-booking concession of 10 per cent. is granted on the amount of the single journey back if the passage is taken within a year. This latter concession does not apply to passages between Mauritius and South and East Africa Ports, and return tickets, available for six months, are issued at the rate of a fare and a half.

Military Officers are granted a reduction of 15 per cent., and their families 10 per cent. Civil Servants and their families are granted 10 per cent.

The Union Castle Line Offices in London are at 3 and 4, Fenchurch Street, E.C., and theii agents in Mauritius are Messrs. Blyth Bros. and Co., and Ireland, Fraser and Co.

The British India Steam Navigation Co.

The British India Steam Navigation Co. is not a direct line between London and Mauritius, but runs between Colombo and Mauritius. Passengers may proceed to Colombo and thence either by the B. I. home steamer, the P. and O. Mail steamer, or any of the steamship lines plying between London and Colombo, but they will have to run the risk of hotel expenses in Colombo, as vessels leave Mauritius only once a month at irregular dates, and generally at an interval of about four weeks. The steamers may, however, be ordered to Bombay direct on the return voyage should inducement offer. The Company is not subsidised by Government for carrying the mails between India and Mauritius, and the service is in consequence more. or less irregular, but it offers a very pleasant and interesting alternative route.

The Company's London offices are at 9, Throgmorton Avenue, E.C., and the agents in Mauritius are Messrs. Scott and Co.

The fares by this line are:—

	1st Class.	2nd Class.
To or from London *viâ* Colombo by sea ...	Rs. 632.50 ..	Rs. 484.00
„ „ Marseilles	605.00 ...	451.00
„ „ Colombo	220.00 ...	137.50
„ „ Calcutta or Bombay	30.000 ...	187.50

INDEX

INDEX